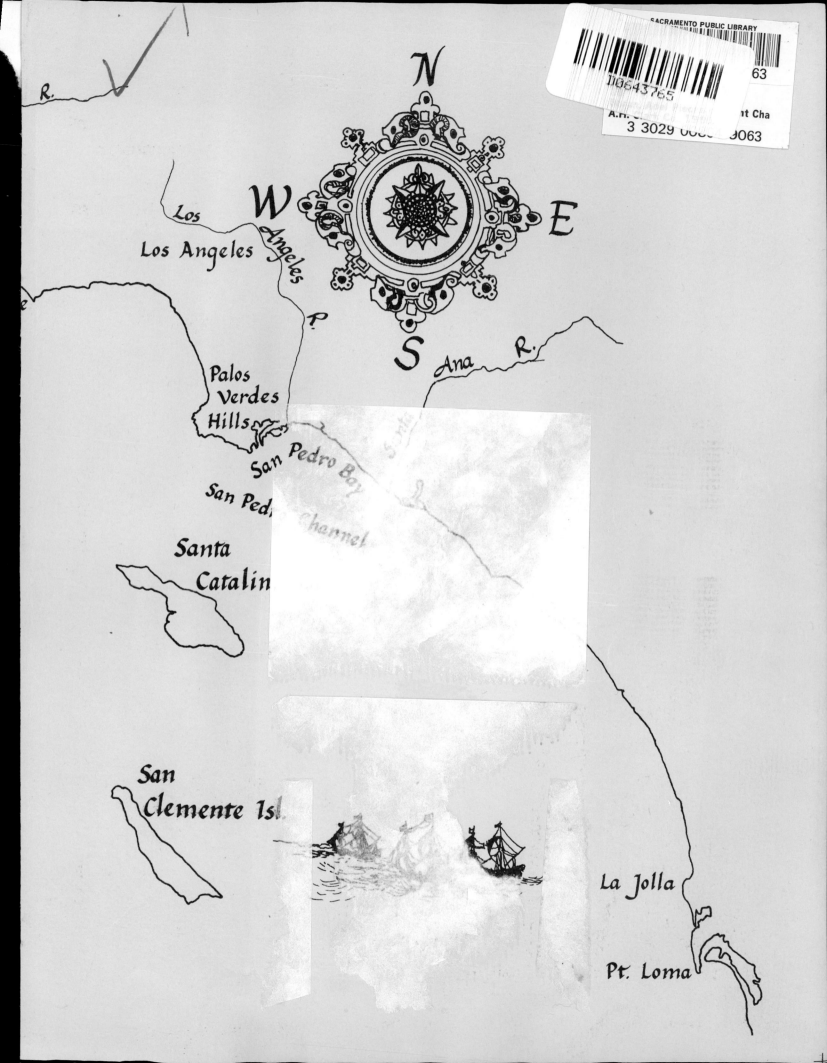

N

W   E

S

R.

Los

Los Angeles

Angeles

P.

S Ana R.

Palos
Verdes
Hills

San Pedro Bay

San Pedro Channel

Santa

Catalina

San
Clemente Isl.

La Jolla

Pt. Loma

Pieces of Eight Channel Islands

Pieces of Eight
Channel Islands

A Bibliographical Guide and Source Book

by Adelaide LeMert Doran

Privately Printed for the Author

The Arthur H. Clark Company
Glendale, California, 1980

LIBRARY OF CONGRESS CATALOG CARD NUMBER 80-66447
ISBN 0-87062-132-7

Acknowledgements

It would not be difficult to detail the various ways in which my husband, Charles Fremont Doran, has put his shoulder to the wheel for the successful production of this project. Under the heading of HEW comes a great deal—Homemaking, Errands, and What-have-you.

Another individual participating in my appreciation is Mr. Bruce Bolinger. While in the Armed Services, Washington, D.C., he took personal time to investigate and to xerox some of the archival material about Santa Catalina. This has added greatly to the expansion, the quaintness, and the humor of the story on the island's transfer of title.

My thanks go to Mr. Robert A. Clark of the Arthur H. Clark Co., publishers and booksellers of rare and choice books. Through his supervision this publication is given a distinction of enduring quality.

The beautiful line drawings, sketches, and cover design are the work of Patrice Sena of Pasadena. The calligraphy on the maps is by Atara Clark.

With a publication of this type, so full of detail, other persons with superb workmanship are to be recognized. These individuals are Mrs. Anna Marie Hager and her husband, Mr. Everett G. Hager, professional bibliographers and indexers. Through their efforts much of the clumsiness of locating or relocating details in the book have been avoided. They prepared the index for this book.

Appreciation is recognized for cooperative assistance from the various libraries and museums which it was my opportunity to use. Such service included the personnel at the Huntington Library, the California State Library, the Los Angeles Public Library, the Santa Barbara Museum of Natural History Library, the Los Angeles County Museum Library, and the Southwest Museum Library. In some instances, being allowed in the stacks and files resulted in 'finds' that were not possible otherwise.

To my many friends and relatives, who must have begun to believe the singleness of my love and affection, go my heart-felt acknowledgement for their patience in this, my final literary indulgence.

Adelaide L. Doran
Glendale, California

Contents

Introduction 9

Island of San Nicolas **13**
   Descriptive Material 13
   Geography, Topography, Water, Geology & Place Names 17
   Anecdotes—Snatches of History 21
   Natural History 24
   Archaeology 26
   Chart: Photos of San Nicolas 31
   The Lone Woman of San Nicolas 32
   Chart: Bibliography connected with "The Lone Woman" 41
   Chart: Lone Woman Story—Characters 42

Island of San Clemente **45**
   Description—People—Place Names 45
   Transfer of Lessee Title to San Clemente 53
   Snatches of Geology and Geography 54
   Natural History 56
   Indians and Archaeology 60
   Chart: Photos of San Clemente Island 62

Island of Santa Catalina **65**
   Anecdotes—Topography—Place Names 65
   Geology 77
   Natural History 81
   Indians and Archaeology 87
   The Ranch that was Robbins and Early Mining Interests 90
   Environment—Education—Conservancy 97
   The Bannings 98
   Chart: Island Development under the Bannings 99
   The Wrigleys 100
   Chart: Island Development under the Wrigleys 100
   Chart: Poems about Santa Catalina Island 102
   Chart: Photos of Santa Catalina 103
   Chart: *Catalina Islander* 106

Island of Santa Barbara **111**
   Description—Place Names 111
   Natural History 115
   Archaeology 119
   National Park Status 119
   Chart: Photos of Santa Barbara Island 120

Poems: Santa Barbara Islands **121**
      The Channel of Santa Barbara

PIECES OF EIGHT

Island of Anacapa **123**
Geology 123
Anacapa's Uses 124
Natural History 126
Archaeology 129
East Anacapa 130
Middle Anacapa 131
West Anacapa 133
Caves and Marine Gardens 134
Chart: Photos of the Anacapas 137

Island of Santa Cruz **141**
Description—Place Names 141
Geology 153
The Main Ranch 154
Archaeology 156
Transfer of Island Title 159
Chart: Island Ownership 164
Natural History 165
Chart: Photos of Santa Cruz Island 174

Island of Santa Rosa **179**
Geology and Allied Subjects 179
Description—Geography—Topography 182
Transfer of Title 191
Chart: Transfer of Title 197
Chart: More Family Holdings 199
Natural History 200
Indians and Archaeology 204
Chart: Photos of Santa Rosa Island 209

Island of San Miguel **211**
Environment—Physical Features—Bits of History 211
Geology 219
Transfer of Lessee–Title 220
Natural History 223
Ethnology 231
Chart: Photos of San Miguel Island 235

Appendices
A. Island Statistics 239
B. Early Voyages with Bibliographical Notations 240
C. Channel Island Names 245
D. Chart of Alta California Governors 247
E. Geologic Time Chart 248
F. Chronological List of Island Botanical Collections
   and/or Authorities 250
G. Botanical Queries 254
H. Indian Linguistics 255
   Part I: Place Names
   Part II: General Linguistic Information
I. Museums with Channel Island Indian Artifacts 256

J.   "Precis Indus Californicus" 257
     Part I: Alexander S. Taylor
     Part II: Other Sources, Authorities
     Part III: Diagnostic Pointers
K.   Residents of the Town of Santa Barbara at the same
     Time as the Carlos Carrillo Family 261
L.   Bald Eagle View, Land in Early California 265

Bibliography **271**

Author Index **327**

General Index **331**

Introduction

This is a bibliographical guide. But it is not a guide in the ordinary sense of the word, for it also has a story-format to which the reader can adjust with comparative ease. On the one hand the format uses the historical, natural history, and archaeological, as a prime choice for its organization; on the other hand, some of the material is bibliographical, even biographical, in nature.

When deemed advisable some of the material becomes analytical and informative about authors and publications. However, the printed page does offer a continuity for the reader, whether he or she be a developing student, an historian, a scientist, a collector of Americana, or a specialist on the Channel Islands.

Although the author had initially desired to write such a story about each island, such prospects diminished as the number of references multiplied. At the same time, prospects also dimmed for finding some likely organization to handle such a miscellany of references.

Yet, an over-all interest in the islands and their subject matter matured more rapidly than did substitute thoughts of producing just a bibliography—full of many words, but stripped of all life.

Somehow, T. D. A. Cockerell's "Recollections of a Naturalist" came to mind. Cockerell had stated that he hoped there might be someone who would attempt a study of the natural history and related disciplines, that "it may contribute to general culture, and come to be a not inconsiderable factor in education . . . which may be carried on with or without academic control."

The author was on just such a threshold—to attempt such a challenge even with the snowballing of references. Snowballs, at times, have produced an avalanche-effect. But, "A step at a time, at a time" echoed and reechoed in a third ear, and *Pieces of Eight* painstakingly began to materialize.

Another decision was necessary. As a part of our historical and social heritage, place names for the various islands needed to be highlighted. This important topographical contribution in *Pieces of Eight* is offered by the use of larger type-face for the first mention of each place name, found mainly under descriptive material.

San Nicolas Island is a "first" to be discussed. Not only is San Nicolas the most distant island from the mainland, but equally important is its position in "Believe it or Nots." This, because a human being was left in isolation for eighteen years, surviving the rigors of her existence, only to succumb to the dietary refinements of a civilized world.

San Clemente Island is the most southern island

of all, and *Pieces of Eight* tells its story next, then moves northward in its discussion, ending with San Miguel Island. This arrangement also allows the two islands selected as a National Monument in 1938, Santa Barbara and Anacapa, to take a central position. The arrangement is advantageous for charts, with Santa Barbara considered one of the more southern islands and Anacapa considered one of the more northern four.

Charts are included in both the text and the appendices. For the sake of brevity, initials only for the islands have been used: S. N. is used for San Nicolas, S. Cl. for San Clemente, S. C. for Santa Catalina, S. B. for Santa Barbara, Ana. for Anacapa, S. Cz. for Santa Cruz, S. R. for Santa Rosa, and S. M. for San Miguel.

In regard to the bibliography, it might be noted that it was organized in 1974. This means that some newer works could not be added to it without displacing the devised coding system. However, these additional references are fully recognized by having been inserted within the text itself, and as addenda to the Bibliography.

Since the bibliography is so extensive, a system of code numbers for the references has been contrived. Each individual reference has its own number, while each section of the bibliography has its own letter reference: J refers to Journals, P for Periodicals, B for Books, N for National publications, C for those belonging to the State of California, U for University publications, and M for Miscellany, which includes ephemera, manuscripts, pamphlets and booklets, and newspapers, beginning with those from San Francisco and moving southward.

The book section of the bibliography is organized in two parts, the first part relating to the earlier, 19th century authors and publications, and the second related to later 20th century publications. About eight publications for the 19th century have been listed with the original author, rather than the translator or editor, in mind. These may be recognized through the use of parenthesis marks around the dates. However, in the Authors Index the recent translator, editor, sponsor, or author is included in the alphabetized list.

Perhaps there can never be a definitive bibliography. Even with this extensive one for *Pieces of Eight*, it is not all inclusive—for a variety of reasons. It is suggested to every reader, however, that additionally-known-references be sent to the author, % The Clark Publishing Co., P.O. Box 230, Glendale, California 91209. Perhaps, as the list grows, new material may come to light.

The author is warmed by the fact that many have been aware of the near impossibility of completing such a work as *Pieces of Eight*. However, once successfully completed, may all readers find a degree of satisfaction in its pages, regardless of the publication's frailties and inequities.

San Nicolas

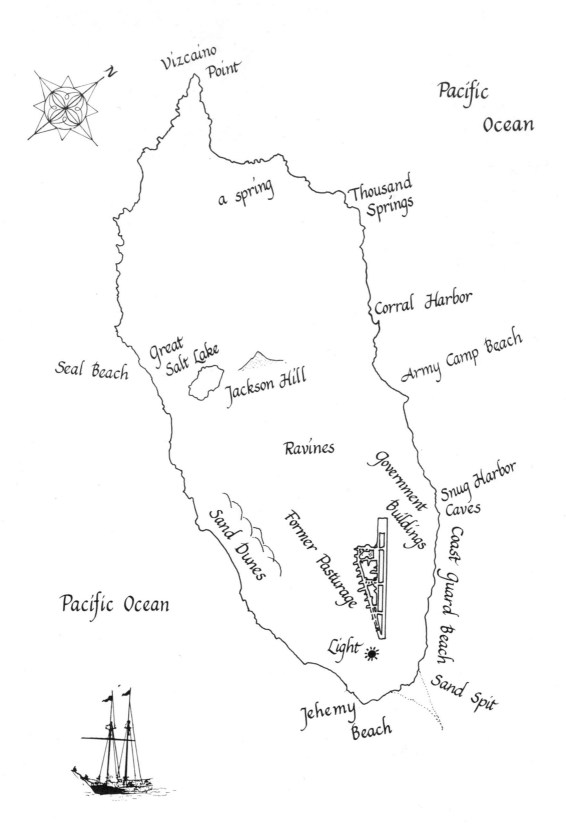

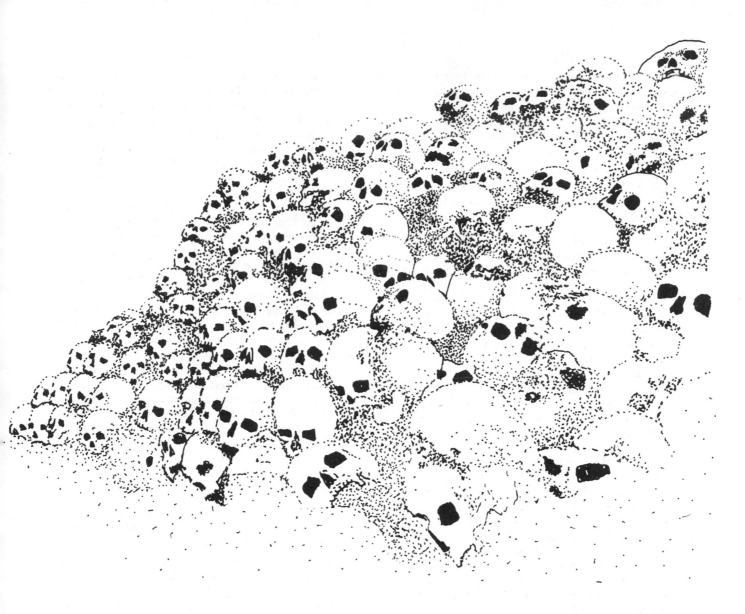

San Nicolas

Descriptive Material

In the *Coast Pilot of California* [N34, 1889], Davidson said that San Nicolas Island

is the driest and most sterile. Like San Clemente, it is comparatively flat-topped, with a moderate slope towards the northward . . . with very bold, precipitous sides of coarse sandstone on the southern and eastern faces and on part of the northeastern face . . . Two-thirds of the surface of the island is covered with sand, and the remaining . . . with coarse grass. Small patches of scrub oak are found in a few places, but no trees show on the island as made from seaward.

One of the earlier accounts with descriptive matter comes from Dr. Stephen Bowers in the 9th Annual Report of the State Mineralogist [C17, 1899]. It was for purposes of collecting Indian artifacts for Major J. W. Powell of the Wheeler Survey in 1875 that Bowers began his visits to San Nicolas.

One of the comments made by Dr. Bowers is that he thought two-thirds of the island could be cultivated, but in 1897 Mrs. Trask found tons of pebbles on the uplands, and no soil. What a difference a few years can make in the compositon of the surface!

John L. Kelly [M19], wrote a "Description of a trip to San Nicolas Island in the Year 1897." In it he comments, "Mr. Bowers told us afterwards when we

13

met him in Los Angeles that in the four weeks they spent upon St. Nicolas they made a collection of relics which sold for $1200.00."

Parts of Mr. Earle's article, "The Santa Barbara Islands," for the *Land of Sunshine* [P44, 1896], appear in another section of this bibliographical guide. Quite descriptive in nature, it is excellent but limited in scope for San Nicolas. But this is what Britton [P47, 1897], had to say in "Our Summer Isles," about San Nicolas,

> . . . This island is about nine miles long, east and west, and four miles north and south. It is the farthest out of the group, being about sixty miles from the nearest mainland. Landing here is safer than at Santa Barbara because San Nicolás is well provided with beaches. Our party landed on the east coast where are shanties and corrals inhabited by sheep-men and horses during shearing time. Troughs on the roofs conduct water to a stone cistern.
>
> Along the shore are innumerable shell heaps, some of them half an acre in extent. Among the abalone, limpet, mussel and other shells are stone mortars, pestles and sinkers, bone and asphaltum whistles, portions of the skeletons of whales and the like—the debris of living of an extinct people. These people were found in full prosperity by Cabrillo in 1542. Seal-skins stretched over whalebone sheltered them, and canoes or rafts of rushes carried them between other islands and the mainland. Early in this century Russian traders placed Innuits with the San Nicolás Indians for the purpose of barter, the Russians coming from Alaska at intervals to remove the seal and other furs secured by their subordinates. . .
>
> There were trees on the island at the time of its occupancy, but fire, sheep, changes of winds and currents have since made of San Nicolás a waste of sand, cactus, buckthorn and ice plants, with only here and there patches of fertile soil. Back from the sea miniature mountains and cañons and slabby amphitheatres rise tier on tier to the bluffs and plateau where a small flock of sheep finds fairly good pasturage. One circular cañon, hundreds of feet deep, and a half mile across, contains a thousand symmetrical little peaks of sky-blue slate set off exquisitely by a scattered growth of green, red and golden grasses, and silhouetted against a clear snowy background of smooth sand, blown over by biting winds from the west coast.
>
> Over the bluff, acres of red pebble-rock are swept clear of dirt and sand. A short distance farther the surface for miles is as smooth and white as snow. The one time "Corral Harbor" on the northwest coast has been literally filled in by this shifting whiteness. A Chinese abalone-hunter's cabin is buried to the eaves. As we floundered along we came upon a strange spectacle. Upon the side of the knoll two miles from the coast a score of whitened human skulls and skeletons lay in the sand, uncovered by the ghoulish wind. A little scraping about revealed other remains, for this was a burial ground. In each case the skeletons had been disarranged by the elements, but in nearly every case all the bones could be found in fairly good condition, owing to the dryness of the soil. Often the skeleton was perfect, though as often there was a hole through the temporal bone, made perhaps by an Innuit weapon. No relics were found with the remains to indicate that the slightest ceremony accompanied their interment. Indeed the bones may never have been covered at all save when the sand sifted over them. Doubtless for years to come these human remains will be at intervals revealed by the wind until relic-hunters have removed the last yellowing knee-cap and tooth. In the meantime seals bark, sea-birds scream, and nomadic abalone-hunters and shepherds come and go, leaving traces of their camps along the sea-shore.

Also good, but limited, is the Mathis article in the Los Angeles *Times*. Mr. Mathis spent three weeks on the island and as a consequence knew first hand what San Nicolas offered by way of climate, archaeological remains, the old Chinese hut and the sheep-herder's shack, etc. [M122, 1899].

When we speak of Charles Frederick Holder we speak of a man who may be considered among the top for those who knew the islands well. Dr. Holder didn't resist [J311, 1899], the temptation to capsulize Juana María's story, which is included in this two-page article.

Although tending to emphasize archaeological aspects, this is a first hand, early account of a yachting party's experiences in getting to and being on the island. Interesting besides, are his few sentences about the single inhabitant, the French herder, with his two half-breed shepherd dogs crouched near him.

William M. McCoy's article published by *Outing* is the longest one of its type [P68, 1917]. The party sailed on the *Dreamer*, Arthur Sanger's schooner. Absorbing in content, it is also a first-hand account and contains many photos of geologic nature.

Much of human interest is presented, including

McCoy's reactions to a Basque shepherd-hermit or "Robinson Crusoe," who didn't even have a dog for company. With a little history, it has a bit about caves, the sand spit, and much about the weather and the trouble it causes.

By 1897 Mrs. Trask was collecting plants on San Nicolas. Tireless in her efforts on most of the islands, much of her collected material went to the California Academy of Science, some to Stanford University; the U. S. National Herbarium had also been a recipient of her vast botanical and ethnological specimens.

Mrs. Trask has earned an enviable reputation for her ability to put into words what so many can but feel. The following article expresses some of these reactions [P54, 1900].

Dying San Nicolas
by Blanche Trask.

It is but an isle, nine miles long, about seventy-five miles out from Port Los Angeles; the tops, it would seem, of submerged peaks. Narrow and lean, it yet stands firmly in the sea; reef-bound and without a harbor.

Day after day and week after week the battle endures. The snows of the sea chill yet deeper the heart of the black lava reefs; a hopeless battle witnessed only by the shags, the gulls, the otters and the seals.

Briny are the waters which steal silently through the sand-carved and wind-swept and sand-filled arroyos; now and then the little stream sinks quite away, and great cañons hundreds of feet deep are really "snowed in" by the sand.

All day long and all night long the wind and the sand are working away, building great castles, while gnomes and giants and dragons start up on every side. Even on the comparatively "level-top" of the island one must pass through gorge after gorge fantastically wind-and-sand carved. It is not unusual to be stopped by an erosion from 10 to 100 feet in depth, when following the main ridge, and have to go far out of your way to reach its head.

Three miles from and extending to the west end, the "Indian mounds" are found—vast numbers, covered by thousands of red abalone shells, besides small shells innumerable; snails, key-hole limpets, owl limpets, sea-urchins, frog-shells, spiral shells, sea cradles, the bones of the whale, otter, seal, and probably those of a dog and various other small animals and sea birds, besides human bones.

How thickly inhabited the place must have been! Human skulls are everywhere about, and at camp we used the upper parts as baskets oftentimes, when we were short of tin cans.

After a day of blinding storm—not of rain or of snow, but one of fog and sand and small pebbles and wind—a storm so fierce (although so strange) that one cannot face it, but gladly stays in his tent and "fixes" his "finds"—after such a day, how good to see sunshine in the early morning, even a touch, through the grey fog which is in truth the mantle chosen by San Nicolás, and which he rarely allows the wild wind to blow from over his shoulder.

This morning new (old) bones are found exposed and delicate relics which the wind has uncovered. Everywhere the sand is piled fresh and the wind has given to the banks the exquisite markings which in colder lands he gives to the snow-drifts.

At the west end, only the long, long stretches of endless mounds and the black rim of the reefs below, with the great sea rushing in, so sure of its victory. Seven breakers, twenty feet high, one after another, with the wind bearing away more and more and yet more new particles to the spit; the spit which stretches lazily to eastward with its stolen life; out of the fog and into the arms of the spray which the sunlight turns into rainbows. In all this somber isle this one spot alone is joyous, this spit where the great rainbows play hour after hour, though there are none to see them.

In March, after the rains, here and there about the central summit are gay sparkles of little flowers. About one hundred species were collected by the writer: several before unknown to botanists. San Nicolás is indeed a dying land. In all his length was found but one shrub seven feet high, and in three or four localities Leptosynes grow from four to six feet high, their gold stars beaming gladly in this solemn land. One tiny lake, too, was found begemmed with bullrush.

In the weird and briny streams you walk with cautious step, in the shifting sand-bed of these narrow arroyos, hastening onward, lest your feet sink deeper, gazing up at the trembling crags—crags which often shut out the blue of the sky. Sad places, enlivened only by the green of the iceplants which grow on the drifted sands. No whirr of wing, no sound of bird, no trickle from those briny waters which glide but do not flow, and gliding sink!

Rarely a raven, like those of Santa Catalina, flies past, and two or three foxes are seen; these too, like those on Santa Catalina, a species

15

which is said to be found only on the coast islands. One of these foxes (lame) afterward identified as one the mate had shot a year previous.

Nearly all the mounds are, as has been said, to westward. They lessen suddenly as you go towards the east. The cause is apparent upon thought. At the west end fresh water drips from the rocks just above the reefs; it diminishes suddenly as you go toward the east, until none is found.

The east end, though it has not fresh water, has that for which the west end can never hope, for beyond the long sand-spit, beyond the billow-lulled and rainbow-encircled spit, rise the ridges and rest the cañons in which wind and sand have spent the greater part of their strength and time. There you may walk through defiles hung with stone lacework, and climb stairways strangely carved. You may rest in old ruins and lean against a Corinthian column which holds within it still the heart of a Greek; and the dragon which starts out here and there—do not forget that he too is but stone!

You may wander from terrace to terrace and hear no sound save the far-off murmur of the sea which breaks a thousand feet below; and below, just above the sea, in a riven flat, you behold that which is too strange to fathom: for leagues away is the city, yet the park seems to be before you. There are dashes of scarlet amongst emerald green; there are stripes of gold against banks of silver; there are mounds of "apple green" stained with bright lavender and rose red. The park! The dust of the city soils your soul at thought of it. Strange assemblage! In which the ice plants (Mesembryanthemums) and the Hosackia argophylla, the suaedas, and the sea verbenas (abronias) thrive in mingled glory; while close to the breakers the happy cream-cups (Platystemon Californicus) toss, no whit alarmed by dragons or winds or sands.

"You'll find no flowers on San Nicolás," the wise captain said; "it's a barren land." And yet—who would change the place if it lost even the few flowers it now has? "A land without ruins is a land without memories."

Far down the southern coast are the pyramids, dark peaks, grim and heavy with age; rising out of the sand, shaking it from their shoulders as the black shag shakes aside the white foam.

Great fires could be built of the wreckage on San Nicolás, but, happily, there is no one to build such fires, and the waiting and listening pyramidal peaks learn much of the world as the wreckage is tossed to and fro.

There is only one break in the reefs where a skiff may enter in safety (and that but in a calm); inside this "break" there is a sort of basin, fifty feet in width, which the water fills at high tide. This tiny shelter is dignified by the name of "Corral Harbor," named from obvious reasons. But Corral Harbor is distant from drift-wood at least an hour, and packing it to camp over the reefs or through the sand is a bit out of the idea of our present age, to say nothing about our muscles.

Another harbor is marked on the sea-charts, but it is not to be depended upon in certain winds, and the landing must be made through breakers; while at Corral Harbor you stand the chance of a good landing—pull at the right minute and run with the swell. Of course, at times, you stay inside Corral Harbor on the high sands, if you are there; if you are in ship among the reefs, you weigh anchor and run to Catalina Harbor. There is no rest for white wings at San Nicolás in "a blow"; it comes from all four corners at once.

There is an old house built of stones yet standing, half "snowed in" by sand, at Corral Harbor. At the "East end" there are a cabin, a barn, shearing sheds, a cistern and a platform which drains its rain water into a reservoir. All these improvements are due to the once ambitious ranchmen who seem now to have abandoned the sheep; about 500 are occasionally seen, with long and beautiful white wool, almost as lovely as that of the Angora. They doubtless subsist largely upon the ice-plant which here, owing to the briny streamlets, thrives upon the summits, growing to the height of three and four feet, and wetting through both boot and leggin as the plant is crushed; becoming slippery on the broken gorges; indeed in this land of erosions the ice-plant is to be avoided as extremely dangerous. The cactus which on Santa Catalina or San Clemente one goes many a mile to avoid in the course of a day, in San Nicolás is met but rarely.

Here and there, in the dull, dead stretches, you come upon yet duller and more dead skeletons of boards. They become a wonder to you, lying so silently there in the great silence round about, worn into strange shapes by wind and sand; here and there given an eye or a hand or a face; large nails projecting, singularly staunch and strong, while the wood in which they were once imbedded has been worn away; and all this so finely done by the wind and the sand that the old boards no longer resemble themselves. The shredded boards are like satin to the touch. There yet were a few posts standing (but worn almost to the ground), while by the fallen boards could be traced the boundaries of a fence; at another place the boards were on each side and had fallen into the bed of a briny stream, suggesting that a house had once been there before the water had worn its way through, below; and this I learn to be the fact, from conversing with my old friend Captain Parsons who is spending his last days on his beloved island of Santa Catalina. The Captain visited San Nicolás some forty years ago, when a man and his wife lived in this house, the man making his living by shooting otters at night; for at night the otters would come up on the rocks and munch the abalones. Being interested in their work they were easily shot.

It is possible to walk entirely around the island on the reefs; with seal and otter, gull and osprey, to forget the human creature and all his ills, to watch the black shag build her nest of bright and happy seaweeds, the osprey hers of driftwood. At last, to see the sun sink like a ship on fire, far, far beyond the west and beyond the reef which runs out to Begg's Rock; yes, far, far beyond Begg's Rock itself.

Yet even here, all is not peace. For wild winds never cease to roam day and night, and cold fogs mantle the isle and sharp sands smite the face. In this old and dying island you must shiver in the cold and be lost in the fog, and suffer in the sandstorm. When you hunt for the little implements of bone and ornaments of abalone on the mounds, your hands are benumbed and your eyes are tearful, while the thought of warm blankets sends you early each night to find them. Blessed it is to lie snug in the tent and listen to the beat of the sand against the canvas, while it is not uncommon to find a coverlet of sand all over your bed in the morning, despite the last tying of "flaps" and pinning of gaps. Camp life here is serious. The tents must be buried a foot to keep them down, and large stakes (brought for the purpose, not one to be found on San Nicolás) driven into the rocky soil beneath the sand. After a drift, the sands must be shoveled away from the tents to prevent bedding in; again, it must be dampened to keep it from blowing off and completely unsanding the tent. No bonfires lend their cheer to the evening, nor lunches 'neath the trees gladden the heart at noontide.

For aye there is silence in the briny heights; on the reefs, the solemn roll of the breakers and the cries of the sea-birds; and ever dainty shells of rainbow tints are tossed on the sands by the thousands.

A dying land, and yet there are no words for the charm, as there are no words for the silence.

Geography, Topography, Water, Geology and Place Names

Josiah D. Whitney (1819-1896) was the first State Geologist and served from 1860 to 1874. He was recognized as one of the best geologists of the country and later held a professorship at Harvard University. However, Whitney was eventually removed from his State responsibility due to disagreements with the Legislature, perhaps over finances [J59, 1868-72].

This particular survey [C13, 1865], was fairly unproductive for the archipelago and included only the four southern islands of the group.

The eminent Dr. J. G. Cooper worked with Professor Whitney as a zoologist, as well as serving in other capacities. Through Whitney, Dr. Cooper commented on San Nicolas,

> . . . The island is distinctly terraced along the northeastern side, having three raised beaches at 30, 80, and 300 feet, the last being near the summit. On these terraces are shells of existing species, few in number on the highest, but more numerous on each succeeding one below, and most of all on the present beach, all being of a rather northern type. The summit appears to have been raised from very deep water containing no shells; but its surface is now strewn with shells and bones left there by the Indians. This island is occupied as a sheep-ranch, and the animals appear to thrive remarkably well, although the vegetation consists wholly of cacti, and other plants apparently unfit for pasturage.

Later, in 1894, Cooper made a short list of mollusks.

By 1874 the geological work for California was placed with the University of California and through them we find some excellent island workmanship, especially for Santa Catalina and San Clemente. In 1880 a State Mining Bureau was created.

Fairbanks [in 1897, U53], offered a long paragraph on San Nicolas geology in which he mentioned that Dr. Yates "gives a long list of Pliocene fossils from San Nicolas island." This thought of the fossils being Pliocene is questioned, however.

As an abstract, "Geological list of the San Nicolas Island Region" [J169, 1953], it is nonetheless instructive, for Norris said that Pliocene rocks do not occur in the region and that at the close of the Pliocene period there was submergence of the island. How-

17

ever, some authorities refute this idea of submergence on a zoological basis.

Dr. Jones has told us that two geologists, Messrs. Homer Hamlin of the U. S. Geological Survey, H. O. Woods of Los Angeles, and five others took a trip to San Nicolas in 1901 because they were "interested in the exploitation of the island as an oil field, should the reports of the geologists prove favorable" [J207, 1901].

From the *Los Angeles Times*, Mr. Windle, of Santa Catalina Island, obtained the information that six local men were interested in San Nicolas in order "to prospect for oil, and in furtherance of that plan they have filed applications with the local land office for oil and gas permits" [M187, 1924].

Although published in 1963, a geologic investigation was begun in 1955 by Vedder and Norris. The investigation was for the purpose of making available geologic information on the petroleum potential of the island [N46].

Perhaps one of their better comments on this point is that an understanding and correct interpretation of the exposed rocks and the surrounding sea floor could aid in an evaluation of petroleum possibilities for all the continental borderland off southern California.

Conclusions did not lead to anything positive concerning petroleum deposits around San Nicolas, but the report was well-written and is a "must" for geologically inclined readers. Maps are included.

As early as 1902 a Mr. Lowe spent three weeks in scientific research during the month of February. However, his findings were of a different nature. From Lowe we gain a list of over thirty-five marine shells found on the Indian mounds [J227, 1903]. Reed [B118, 1933], believed that some Eocene fossil mollusks were to be found.

At an annual meeting held in Los Angeles a Luis E. Kemnitzer delivered a paper, "The Geology of San Nicolas Island, California" [J22, 1936]. He, and others, have said that the rocks of San Nicolas are almost wholly of Eocene age.

He further indicated the submarine contours as reflecting a trend in an uplift toward Santa Rosa Island. It was Cockerell, in *Scientific Monthly* [J319, 1938], who remarked that a shallow bank no deeper than ninety-six fathoms runs from San Nicolas to Santa Rosa Island.

Mr. Harry Allen of U.C.L.A. found terrace deposits of marine origin near the top of the island. Shells from these deposits have been identified by

Dr. U. S. Grant as Pleistocene shells. According to Norris, the terraces developed on the island during the Pleistocene age. To him, such topography was the result of stream and wind erosion; wind velocity being between thirty-five and fifty-five miles per hour in all seasons.

Dr. Shepard of Scripps Institute and Dr. Cockerell of the University of Colorado also found shell deposits in 1939 [J54, U36, B87].

Though only thirteen lines, Israelsky is still informative [J323, 1956], and one of his statements was, "Except along the sea cliffs the Eocene strata are generally mantled by marine deposits of Pleistocene age, sand dunes, and Indian kitchen mounds." Israelsky made faunal collections from several sections of the island for the purpose of establishing correlations and zoning.

In this same regard, Vedder and Norris [N46, 1956], referred to their collection of over 250 species of marine mollusks and other invertebrates which they had collected. They seemed to feel that their listing is the most complete for southern California, as little had been published on such fossils since Dr. Cooper's short list of 1894.

Another aspect of the topography of the island are the land snails. With photos to illustrate, Mr. Walker spoke of them and thought that they might be mainly responsible for the denuding of the island and the forming of the hard casing on the trees [J225, 1948].

Walker continued with a discussion of three stages of Indian culture on the island; one of his theories: "The trees grew upon the debris of the first island people but under the campgrounds of the second . . . [the sand trees being] formed just prior to the time of Columbus."

The area in which numerous calcareous casts of the roots of shrubs and trees are located is that of the dunes. The dunes occupy most of the western third of the island, but the more active dunes are located between SEAL LION BEACH, VIZCAINO POINT, and THOUSAND SPRINGS.

Calcareous casts probably resulted from a combination of land snails, their shells, fog and rain. Woodward [J5, 1940], said that the snails are the only indication that the area was once covered with vegetation. This type of calcification may also be found on San Miguel Island and San Clemente.

A much later article on sandstone tree casts has been done by Max Miller, which he illustrated with photos [P161, 1956].

Another basic point of discussion for the island of

San Nicolas is its sand spit. Norris [J322, 1952], who was with the Scripps Institution of Oceanography at the time, concluded that the sand for the spit comes from the northern coast, with the form of the spit being influenced by the west-flowing current south of the spit. Both wind and wave create and recreate the spit.

Emery [B88, 1960], has an excellent aerial view of the spit. Bryan [B6, 1970], also took considerable interest in the sand spit. He first saw it in 1926 and it appeared to be at least a mile long; later, by only a few weeks, a storm had cut down three-fourths of it.

Bryan indicated that the shores on all sides of the spit go down very suddenly, so that there is little beach. Yet it appeared to have been the favorite landing place, until the pier in front of Captain Nelson's shack was built.

According to Vedder/Norris, the spit has shifted southward; in part this could be due to a 1951-52 breakwater constructed at COAST GUARD BEACH. Charles F. Holder had named the spit, "Ferrelo's Point," but no one has followed that suggestion.

On the southwest central shore there is a partially hidden petroglyph cave. Named, "Cave of the Killer Whales," it has been visited by many who were able to locate it.

The Southwest Museum has been the recipient of one portion of that cave, a fallen wall containing some of the markings made by the Indians. One description of the cave indicated that there were drawings on all faces of the cave.

Vedder and Norris [N46, 1956], with the cooperation of the U. S. Department of the Navy, produced several maps of San Nicolas. Each with a different purpose, there are at least a dozen place names of which we can be assured.

DUTCH HARBOR, on the south side, is where Arthur Woodward found eel grass twisted weaving [J6, 1941]. Mrs. R. E. Agee, wife of the caretaker of San Nicolas, had unearthed in 1932 some rare pieces of grass skirts from the island. This information comes from the School of American Research, New Mexico, in *El Palacio*.

Vedder and Norris said that there are relatively wide sand beaches, up to one mile in length, thus breaking the continuity of the shorter sandy beaches. The wider beaches are: Dutch Harbor, one mile east of the Harbor, along the spit, ARMY CAMP BEACH, DAYTONA BEACH, and at two other places between Thousand Springs and Vizcaino Point.

The U. S. government buildings are shown on the Vedder/Norris maps; these buildings are on the plateau, former grazing pasture for the sheep.

Seal Lion Beach and Vizcaino Point are named, which are the areas for sea lion rookeries. The western seal rookery area is extensively dissected with channels, pools, deep coves, and some caves. There is also a SEA ELEPHANT BEACH about the south-center of the island.

CORRAL HARBOR is a reef area and entrance can be made, should the weather permit. On this subject Davidson [N34, 1889], spoke,

> Corral Harbor.—On the north side of the island, three and one-fourth miles in a straight line from the extreme western point, is a very small boat harbor, where a whaleboat may be carried to, but the passage is only twenty feet in width, so narrow that the oars must be trailed for a distance of forty feet to pass through. [It] has a smooth sand beach, and is protected from all swell . . . A shearing shed and a sheep corral on a little rise near the shore can be seen from the outside and mark the place.

To the west of Corral Harbor is the Chinese hut, which by 1899 was all but covered by sand. To the east of the 'harbor' is the shack used by Captain Nelson.

By the descriptions in the literature, the names of CHINESE HARBOR and NORTHWEST HARBOR, names used by early writers, might be one and the same spot as Corral Harbor. The old RANCH HOUSE LANDING, now in disrepair, is close by.

SNUG HARBOR is mentioned. This name was first applied by Bruce Bryan in 1926; he said there are caves at the location.

Two heights for San Nicolas are indicated. The higher is 907 feet, called JACKSON HILL. It was named for a Navy man who had lived on San Nicolas in U. S. employ for some time. CENTRAL PEAK, 850 feet, has been called a volcanic crater by Alice Eastwood.

TULE CREEK has not been outlined by Vedder and Norris. Perhaps it, too, is near the northwest coast.

Is Vizcaino Point another name for LANDS END, a name formerly used for a location good for lobster and abalone catching?

Vedder and Norris tell us that there are small springs of brackish water occurring along several faults on the south side of the island between Seal Lion Beach and Dutch Harbor [N46, 1956]. Burnham, *et al*, say there is a lack of such springs along the south edge of the island [N49, 1963].

Vedder and Norris tell us that fresh water flows from several springs along the sandy beach on Vizcaino Point. Burnham, *et al*, extends the line of these springs from Vizcaino Point to Corral Harbor.

Vedder and Norris say that there is a potable water spring flowing from between an Eocene siltstone bed and Pleistocene dune deposits high in the western dune area. Other springs are in the deeper canyons where the stream bed intersects large faults, and some appear between the bedrock and Quaternary deposits in a few drainage systems.

Vedder and Norris say that a deep water well was drilled at 560 feet on the terrace between CELERY CREEK and the main road intersection. This was done between 1950 and 1954. There are three shallow wells, drilled in 1952, in the upper basin of Tule Creek. Burnham, *et al*, say that little is known of the water properties of such wells.

Vedder and Norris tell us that these wells, together with catchment basins beneath a line of springs in the deep canyon cut by Tule Creek, provided the fresh water supply during their field work on the island. These catchment basins and wells supplied about 60,000 gallons of water per day in 1956.

They suggest that more water could be obtained if other catchment basins were constructed in the large drainage systems. A diversion of additional gullies into the upper Tule Creek basin would also serve to recharge the wells now in operation.

Hillinger [M154, 1956], stated that the U. S. base on San Nicolas was the only one on any of the islands where water does not have to be barged.

Burnham, *et al*, wondered about the large amount of storage that would be needed for any practical water system to be developed. They believe that the wells and Tule Creek water have more dissolved salts in their water than do the north shore spring waters.

Vedder and Norris remark that before 1956 the fresh water was collected from small springs along the contact between Eocene rocks and dune deposits in the sea cliff at Thousand Springs, which is to the northwest in the general region of Corral Harbor. Burnham, *et al*, add that practically all of the water moves northwestward toward that water-bearing area. In an archaeological report from U.C.L.A. [U43, 1962], Reinman remarked that

All along this northern end of the island are several of these sandstone exposures, most of which bring fresh water to the surface. The water apparently percolates down through the

rock from underground springs and comes to the surface along these exposed edges.

"An ancient water system . . . has been discovered," writes *Science News Letter* [J308, 1963],

The water system was constructed to take advantage of the meager flow of a spring that percolates through a sandstone bluff. Two main channels are carved in a sandstone shelf at the foot of the bluff. One channel is 38 feet long, and the other five feet. Eight smaller feeder channels occur along the main channel to collect seepage over the shelf.

The layer of rock containing the channels is soft enough to be worked with stone tools. Peck marks along the ledge indicate such tools were used by the Indians.

A tidal flat adjacent to the site is rich in shellfish—abalone, limpets, crabs and the like. Such an abundant food supply and the rather elaborate water system indicate that this was an important dwelling site of an ancient Indian population.

We are not told the site's exact location [U43, 1962; M157, 1963].

These references may be considered illustrative for the briefer references to water on San Nicolas:

Dittmann told Murray that, "Upon reaching the beach we stopped at a spring that forms a little pool of water under a sort of mound of rocks and situated but a few yards from the beach. One of the peculiarities of this spring was its surface which seems to be continually playing over the pool. I noticed it on this occasion and at several times afterwards. The water was invariably clear and cool. Its source I should judge must have been high up in the ridge" [U13, 1853].

Greenwell wrote to Guthrie, ". . . good water can be found near the northwest point . . ." [N28, 1856-57].

Schumacher said that there was "another spring of good water at Chinese Harbor" [P82, 1875]; and on its northeast side [N41, 1877].

Grinnell said that they camped at the east end near the old ranch house, "where there is a cistern of water" [J249, 1897].

Britton said of the east coast shanties, "There are troughs on the roof to collect the water" [P47, 1897].

Trask referred to the 'East End,' "where there are a cabin, a barn, shearing sheds, a cistern, and a platform which drains its rain water into a reservoir." She mentioned the west end where "fresh water drips just above the reefs" [P54, 1900].

Lowe also mentioned the west end where "there is a spring of fresh water," where the Japanese hunt lobsters and abalone [J227, 1903].

From Reinman, "At present, the only other source of fresh water on this [northern] end of the island known to the writer is a spring some 2 miles inland and some 600 feet up on the plateau" [U43, 1962].

Bryan was told by Captain Nelson of a spring in the ravine where the hills slope to the sand spit, but Bryan could not find it [B6, 1970].

There are other place names and points of interest, but they lie a little distance from the island.

CORTES SHOAL or BANK came under considerable discussion about 1853; this discussion the U. S. Coast and Geodetic Survey found necessary to continue for several years. The part of the shoal lying nearest San Nicolas is about three and three-fourths miles northeast of Army Camp Beach on the north coast of San Nicolas, and is about two miles long and three and a half miles wide. On this part of the shoal lies BEGG ROCK, situated on the prolongation of the longer axis, seven and three-fourth miles from the extreme western point of the island.

Begg Rock was so named after the ship *John Begg,* which was nearly lost when it struck upon the ground around it on September 20, 1834. The Rock is a volcanic cone rising about 40 feet above the sea, bold and well-defined, and can easily be seen at a distance of ten miles. The soundings close to the Rock are fifty fathoms. The bottom is gravel and shells, without an extensive kelp-patch.

Another part of the Cortes Bank lies south and to the west of San Nicolas, and is about seventeen miles long, with an average width of three and a half miles. Upon this bank lies BISHOP ROCK, fifteen feet above the surface of CORTES BANK. It is now known to be the shoalest and most dangerous part of the Bank.

Captain Cropper of the *Cortes* reported his experience of witnessing some form of volcanic activity on Cortes Shoal in 1853 and this was readily investigated. James Alden of the U. S. Surveying Steamer *Active,* called the phenomena a heavy rip tide, after T. H. Stevens, Lieutenant Commanding, U. S. Surveying Schooner *Ewing,* anchored upon the shoal for several days for observation purposes.

William P. Blake gave Captain Cropper a little

more credit for having witnessed something of an unusual nature than did some of the other Survey personnel. Although Blake felt that the apparent spouting of the water might be merely the breaking of the waves on a reef, the Captain was confident that the commotion was of a different kind and of a volcanic nature, for he witnessed steam and an explosion. The peculiar spouting up of the water in columns at regular intervals, together with his observation of the change in the form of the bottom, are the evidences of the possible volcanic character of the disturbance [N26, 1854-55].

Lieutenant MacRae later discovered a ledge of rocks on the shoal that remained unnoticed up to the time of the eruption—or the breaking of the waves. If an eruption did take place, Blake reminded us, the depth of the shoal here was very probably lessened, with the sea then removing all the accumulation, or evidence [N28, 1956-57].

A subsequent report in 1857-58 negated the Cropper report and focused on the fact that Bishop Rocks is the locale on the shoal where the depth is but ten fathom, as compared to forty-two fathom for the rest of it. The clipper ship *S. S. Bishop,* did strike upon one of its rocks and so, in 1856, the bank was completely sounded out [N29, 1857-58].

By 1857 James Alden concluded that since the discovery of the dangerous rock, large vessels should avoid that passage; he furthermore recommended that a lantern be elevated by about fifty feet above the sea, so that the fog could not so easily obscure it.

Anecdotes—
Snatches of History

The biography of William Heath Davis, 1822-1909, is interesting at this point because of his smuggling activities, with San Nicolas being an important locale in the crime [B16, 1956].

Dr. Rolle says that Eliab Grimes, partner with Davis, wrote to Davis on April 7, 1846 and warned the young man, "I wish to impress deeply upon your mind, not to smuggle my goods on the coast of California."

Then Rolle continued [B16, 1956]

Ignoring these instructions Davis, prior to his landing at Monterey, had made a side trip to San Nicholas [sic] Island. In caching there part of the *Euphemia's* most dutiable goods, he had followed the practice of Abel Stearns and of many others, who used southern California's channel islands, for hiding supplies from Monterey's custom authorities. Davis, incidentally, omitted all mention in his printed writings of his excursion southward; yet this detour had made his first trip to California a resounding success.

Hittell [B35], tells us that Davis was a trader, and that he had married into the Estudillo family. In the Publisher's Preface of *Seventy-five Years in California* by John Howell, 1929, it is said that

Davis first visited California as a small boy in 1831. He came a second time in 1833, and at length, in 1838, he arrived aboard the "Don Quixote" to enter the service of his uncle Nathan Spear as a clerk in the latter's store in Monterey.

Davis was a "Junior," but was raised by John Coffin Jones in Hawaii as a 'stepson,' after Davis' own father's death. [William G. Dana was a nephew of Davis, Sr.]

Dawson, about three years younger than W. H. Davis, also went to San Nicolas, but as an otter hunter [B17, 1841].

His *Memoirs* is a first-hand account, has about sixty-five pages concerning Dawson's experiences in California and Texas, and is earthy. Such experiences were lived during a period from which little written historical material has been made available. This tiny book is one of the nicer finds of the author's research, thanks to the California State Library in Sacramento.

Dawson's Chapter IV, "Otter Hunting on the Santa Barbaras," mentions Dye, Sparks, Nydever [sic], and A. B. Thompson, M. Thompson's license for otter hunting permitted Dawson, Sparks, Nydever [sic], Dye, and others to hunt through it.

The subject of the abandoned woman, so famous in San Nicolas history, is also in the *Memoirs*; Dawson said, "[we] failed to find her, although we found her tracks."

Avoiding the Lone Woman of San Nicolas story at this time, 1835-1853, we turn momentarily to sheep herders on the island, not otter hunters. Information concerning them is so fragmentary that fill-ins must come from many sources.

From the archives, Deed Book I [C42], we learn that on September 15, 1870 Mr. M. M. Kimberly "hath resided himself or his employees, and kept sheep, cattle, and horses for fourteen years past, . . . [sells] all houses, buildings, corrals, wells, and improvements thereon situate."

In Deed Book J for the year 1872, January 22, we find that Abraham Halsey sold to Agnes M. Hamilton, *et al* for $2,000, two tracts of 160 acres each, both tracts had been "taken up and located by Capt. M. M. Kimberly, and James Crab . . ."

This would place Kimberly on San Nicolas about 1856, not 1853, as stated by Jones [J207].

We do not seem to know where Kimberly's wells were, but Jones said that "the house and buildings erected by Mr. Kimberly are covered [1901] many feet deep with drifting sand which has almost obliterated the cañon just west of Corral Harbor" [J207, 1969]. This would mean that "Chinese Camp," with the stone house, a name offered by many writers, was a part of Kimberly's holdings. The shack east of Corral Harbor might also have been a part of Kimberly's holdings. Captain Nelson was living in it in 1926, still tending sheep for a Captain Brooks. [The San Miguel story has more on Robert Brooks.]

Mrs. Kimberly [B56, 1927] had something to say on the life of her husband; more of it may be found under the Anacapa story. M. J. Phillips', *History of Santa Barbara County*, contains this unusual biographical sketch from an interview with Mrs. Kimberly.

It was Jane Kimberly who has said that her father had a store in Santa Barbara until 1874. Perhaps with the wish for more adventure, he sailed to Japan as an otter hunter; on his second trip in 1878 he lost his life.

On the 23rd day of September, 1872 the heirs of William Hamilton conveyed their interest to the Pacific Wool Growing Co., a corporation, for the sum of $6,000.

All of this is very interesting due to the fact that San Nicolas was never privately owned, but had always been part of the public domain.

It is said [M147] that Captain William Howland, of Santa Catalina Island, leased the island in 1875 and put sheep on it. And one source [B25, 1917], states that Mr. Howland was still running sheep on San Nicolas in 1917, with a Basque hermit doing the tending [P68]. By 1919 he had sold his interest to the Vail Bros., who were also sheep grazing on Santa Rosa Island.

Mr. Brooks was running sheep on San Nicolas much before 1926, with Captain Nelson tending. It was this old sheepherder who told Bruce Bryan about a wild red stallion running loose and free upon the island. Rather than kill the animal, its owner had it shipped to the island. Bryan had seen the creature from a distance, only [B6, Preface].

There is some type of change, with an unexplained

factor, by the 19th day of April, 1902, for L. M. Shaw, Secretary of the Treasury of the United States, enters the picture with W. J. McGimpsey, owner of a fishing company, obtaining some form of lease on the island through him [C43].

Headline: "Marooned Men likely to Starve—Three Fishermen left on San Nicolas with Little Food" [M61]
These fishermen in the employ of McGimpsey had been left on the island November 1, 1902. "The fishing company employing the men were refusing to pay the owner of the schooner," so that the men were abandoned and had to live on coffee and salt [M62].

Finally, on November 17th, Captain Hyder of *Western* and E. S. Stout of San Pedro rescued the three men, who had been forced to eat sea gulls—when they could be caught.

Captain Hyder said that the men would have died had they been left a week longer; they were just about ready to sacrifice their pet cat as a means of staving off starvation.

It seems as though the W. J. McGimpsey Fish Company of Los Angeles was having difficulties with Captain Frank Manna and the problem was pending in court. The abandoned men said they would demand damages from the McGimpsey Company for the sufferings they had endured [M62].

But, returning to the lease arrangements, on February 23, 1904, McGimpsey leased the island to the San Nicholas Development Company, a corporation, for the sum of $362.50 per annum [C43]. It is also stated that by April 15, 1907 the lease from the government would expire, at which time an extension of such lease through the United States would be necessary.

The *Los Angeles Times* [M147, 1949], reported that early in the 1930's the San Nicolas lease had changed hands with L. P. Elliot, formerly of Anacapa [1891], and Roy Agee taking over the grazing rights of the island [C43]. From whom this lease was obtained is not stated.

In 1936 Judge Windle of the *Catalina Islander*, #22, stated that a Miss Alma MacClain was sent to San Nicolas Island to teach two pupils [M187].

In 1939 Agee purchased Elliot's share of the lease, and remained on the island until 1941, when the lease was revoked. It was Woodward who said that in 1939 a Reggie H. Lambert went to San Nicolas with his wife and two children to work for Roy Agee with his sheep [B62, 1957]. The Lamberts housed and fed Dr. T. D. A. Cockerell for ten days, while he studied on the island.

The story told by Clarence M. Martin [M140, 1930], brings a grim note into the San Nicolas story. It appears that on February 23, 1930, eighteen-year-old Milton Prentice shot and killed a fisherman, Steve Semerenko, who was thought to be stealing sheep from the island.

Prentice was tried in Ventura County; the outcome of the trial is unknown to this author. Robert Brooks of San Miguel Island testified at the trial.

At the time of this incident, Mr. and Mrs. Roy Agee and daughter, Frances, were living on the island, guarding the 1,200 sheep pastured there.

In speaking of housing and buildings, as well as leases, Mrs. Trask told us [P54, 1900], that an otter hunter and his wife lived in a shack about the year 1860. Mrs. Trask also said that some house was at the head of Snow Cañon, and that the couple who lived there raised vegetables [M130, 1906].

C. F. Holder had remarked that some couple had lived in a wooden house on the island for about a year. Mrs. Trask's information came from Captain Parsons of Santa Catalina Island, and Mrs. Trask partly described the remains of some of the fence and the house in her article.

From Bruce Bryan's home-made map we can see that there was yet another shack at Dutch Harbor, and one on Vizcaíno Point.

Mr. Jones added [J207] that in 1901 with Mr. Hamlin they explored the eastern end of the island from the place he called Anchorage, where they had landed. On that shore they located a hut for the sheep herder, used by Jones and his party for their camp.

Norris referred to the date of 1886 as the time when "an unusually optimistic real estate promoter divided the entire island into lots." Norris [J84, 1960], had obtained his information from Dr. C. F. Holder's book [B38].

An anecdote, only four paragraphs long, is about C. B. Linton and his cook. It is amusing—at least a part of it is. The cook, without permission, had killed a *Laysan* Albatross. At the time it was thought to be *Diomedea albatrus*; it served as the Mexican cook's meal, while Mr. Linton got the head for his collection. This happened on April 5, 1909. Later, Linton sold his collection to Thayer, now in the Museum of Comparative Zoölogy [J150, 1938].

The next year another party left Long Beach early in July and enjoyed three days on the islands of Santa Barbara and San Nicolas. C. B. Linton was again in the group. From the report it seems that they but observed birds, taking no specimens on this particular trip.

In part, Mr. Robertson said of the trip [J121, 1910],

Leaving Santa Barbara Island about 3 p.m. the trip was made to San Nicolas Island, reaching the sand spit at the southeast end of the island about 8 p.m. . . . On returning to the landing it was found that the sea was so rough that it would be impossible to land a skiff, so all hands turned to and collected firewood, and were soon comfortable with a roaring fire, in one of the caves above the tide line. A hearty repast was made from one five-cent package of chewing gum, and while a more substantial meal would have been appreciated by the eleven left on shore, no one complained of the lack of food; but all were unanimous in their desire for drinking water . . . Monday morning, the wind having gone down, the skiff was landed easily and we reached the launch with little trouble. After a hearty breakfast, much enjoyed by all, Mr. Linton and O. W. Howard returned to shore to find Linton's father [who] was camping at Northwest Harbor. We expected this would take but a short time, but, as it developed, it took all day, and as the wind again blew as strong as the day before, they were compelled to stay all night on shore.

On Tuesday, July 6, after picking up Linton and Howard we started for Northwest Harbor and there found Linton, Sr., and, after taking him aboard, started for Long Beach, . . .

About twenty-one years later, 1931 [P146], when Sheldon visited San Nicolas, another almost-grim note was injected onto the scene,

. . . I was finally beached with my outfit for a three weeks stay. I learned much about San Nicolas in the three weeks, but still more when my captain failed to return for me on schedule. I've been in the desert sans water, in mountains without food, but to be on a wilderness island and run out of cigarettes . . . How I got back is another story, but to be brief I hailed a fisherman, with a dish towel, and my frantic signals were answered.

. . . A picture more desolate I had never seen unless it was the Dakota "badlands" . . .

O'Neill remarked that in 1939 San Nicolas had a naval radio operator, maintaining the weather station [B53]. By 1946 the Navy occupied San Nicolas and had established a missile testing range [M154, 1956]. Mr. Hillinger also said, "In the past 10 years a

$5,000,000 labyrinth of electronic networks had been scattered about the sand-encrusted island hills here."

Hillinger tells of the San Nicolas missile men driving to Lands End to obtain a catch of lobster with their bare hands. At night and at low tide they would gather pink, blue, and black abalone.

Through his own experience Hillinger relates how the "playful pinnipeds [sea lions] . . . stirred up a storm . . . howling, barking, sneezing, yawning, squealing as they wriggled to the edge of the rocks and flipped into the water," while the sea elephants hardly moved.

San Nicolas, once known to some as SEA OTTER ISLAND [N34], has also been dubbed MISSILE ISLAND by Monroe, Hillinger, and others [B109, 1963]. This is "because test rockets and other missiles streak toward it every day from Point Mugu across seventy miles of open sea.

"The Navy placed a giant Air Missile Test Center on the coast in 1945 to watch the 'birds' go by. This 27-square-mile heap of sand is now populated by 250 navy and civilian technicians."

While California and the rest of the nation have grown and developed phenomenally in two hundred years, little San Nicolas has ironically seen the opposite trend. Gone are the otter, gone is most of the plant life, gone are the Indians. White men, sheep, wind and snails have inflicted multitudinous wounds. Now, only the Navy, maybe the little fox, the white-footed mouse, the sand lizard, and our winged friends can give a future accounting of "Dying San Nicolas."

Natural History

Flora

Alice Eastwood and Blanche Luella Trask were friends, as well as associates. Miss Eastwood was also curator for the Department of Botany, California Academy of Sciences, so that we can expect some published material through Miss Eastwood of Mrs. Trask's findings [J64, 1898].

Miss Eastwood's contribution through, "Studies in the Herbarium and the Field," offers a distribution of botanical species. These had been obtained for the Academy by Mrs. Trask, who had been on San Nicolas in 1897. Among the eighty or more species, nine are described as new, three as new varieties.

In speaking of Mrs. Trask, Millspaugh and Nuttall [B105, 1923], said,

Mrs. Trask lived on [Santa Catalina Island] from

1895-1907, spending the winter months at Avalon and the summer at Fisherman's Cove near the Isthmus. She was an indefatigable pedestrian and thought little of walking over the ridge trail from Avalon to the Isthmus and back in a day, or even making the trip one way in the night.

According to another author, Mrs. Trask also had an interest in archaeology, and did some collecting in that area. Miss Eastwood took many excursions with her friend.

In 1932 the California Academy sponsored another Templeton Crocker Expedition; John Thomas Howell, then Assistant Curator of the Botany Department, was a member of the expedition [J69, 1935].

With some amount of descriptive material on their experiences while on San Nicolas, Mr. Howell concluded that "the present collection of vascular plants from San Nicolas consists of 34 members representing 32 species and varieties, 7 of which were not reported in [Mrs. Trask's] Miss Eastwood's list." His total number of plants known from San Nicolas Island is eighty-nine.

Cockerell [J54, 1939], in *Bios*, has a statement or two about the mosses of the island, and those of San Miguel. One, in particular, he mentioned, *Ceratodon purpureaus*. Millspaugh had also listed and discussed mosses in 1923.

Raven [B120, 1967], gives listings of the Channel Island endemic vascular plants. Two single-island endemics are mentioned for San Nicolas, six, which the island shares with other southern islands, and five, shared with some northern and southern islands.

Alice Eastwood mentioned that Blanche Trask found the California Holly, *Heteromeles arbutifolia*, on San Nicolas Island; *Artemisia californica* var. *insularis*; the sunflower, *Baccharis* var. *consanguinea*; *Coreopsis gigantea*; the box thorn, *Lycium californicum*; and two *Opunta* species, the Prickly Pear and the Cholla [J74].

See Appendix G for other possibilities. There may be a complete listing of flora for San Nicolas, somewhere.

Fauna

In 1868 [J59], Dr. Cooper noted the presence of a Saurian type lizard, No. 989, on the island. Apparently it was also seen on San Clemente and Santa Barbara Islands.

Dr. Bowers [B69, 1891], remarked about a "sand lizard"; Dr. Grinnell was on San Nicolas in 1897 [J66], where he found the night lizard, *Zantusi riversiana*. Slevin, in 1911, obtained 112 specimens of some lizard.

Of the salamanders, not much is said. It is difficult to determine whether *Batrachoseps pacificus* or *Batrachoseps attenuatus* is the salamander referred to in the literature.

Helix Facta and *Helix Tryoni* [N45, 1875], land snails, were found on the island. Schumacher referred to *Olivella biplicata* and *Helix strigosa* [N41]. Apparently San Nicolas has a few species of bats. Both Grinnell and Bowers mentioned the white-footed deer mouse living on the island [C17; U37]. Bowers [B69, 1891], referred to the island's field mouse.

At least at one time, there was a little fox on San Nicolas, mentioned by Bowers [B69] and Cooper [J59]. Dr. Cooper thought them to be very wild, which is a different characteristic from the foxes found on Santa Cruz Island. According to Raven [J156], and Remington [J251], introduced feral goats once lived on the island.

In 1938 Dr. Cockerell visited San Nicolas Island and camped for ten days at the Agee Ranch, with Mr. and Mrs. R. H. Lambert as host and hostess [J54; J248, 1938].

Dr. Cockerell was born in the British Isles and grew up there. At one time curator of the Kingston, Jamaica Museum, he later came to the United States. While connected with the University of Colorado as a zoologist, he took an interest in California's Channel Islands; his friendship with Francis Darwin, son of Charles Darwin, indicates their common interest in all islands.

While on San Nicolas he discovered a new Bemecine Wasp, although Cockerell remarked that it was quite common. Cockerell was also on San Miguel, Santa Catalina, San Clemente and Santa Cruz Islands for research purposes.

His comments [J54, *Bios*, 1939], are worth noting,

The transportation of snails by birds has not been well understood . . . There is a remarkable genus of slugs called *Binneya*, discovered on the small Santa Barbara Island long years ago. Last year I found a couple of *Binneya* shells in a superficial deposit on San Nicolas Island.

From about 1956 Mr. Charles Hillinger of the *Los Angeles Times* took more than an ordinary interest in the Channel Islands. One might term it one of his specialties. This interest, coupled with an ability to express himself, has often furnished unusual comments. This time,

> saucerlike pockets of clear water nestled in rocks at Lands End were filled with gorgeous ocean life . . . deep purple sea grass, sea urchins, brown sea moss, hermit crabs and sea anemones were found [M154, 1956].

Approximately ten years later, R. I Caplan and Boolottian made a report of the Intertidal Ecology of San Nicolas Island for the biological *Symposium* [B120, 1967]. A comparison of tidal pools of Anacapa and San Nicolas might be quite rewarding.

Dr. George A. Bartholomew, Jr. is an authority on seals and sea lions of southern California, and taught zoology at U.C.L.A. From him we learn that the extreme west end of San Nicolas is the coast on which the rookeries are located. With but a few Stellar Sea Lions, one Guadalupe Fur Seal, it is the Harbor Seal that still breeds on the island. The Northern elephant seal is a conspicuous member of the seal population, with the North Fur Seal being conspicuous for its absence.

Before the sealers began their program of extermination, the Guadalupe Seal was common from the Farallones, south and into Lower California. The survivor seen on San Nicolas, 1928, could be the last survivor, according to Bartholomew [J183, 1950; J184, 1951].

Avifauna

Dr. Grinnell collected four specimens of the uncommon House Finch while on San Nicolas. They are also to be found on San Clemente and Santa Barbara [J41, 1898].

Grinnell found the rock wrens to be quite numerous on most parts of San Nicolas in the spring of 1897. However, he considered them indistinguishable from other southern California specimens, but thought they could be a subspecies [J40, 1898]. Grinnell also collected foxes, as no doubt did many of the visiting ornithologists.

Grinnell had found, on another occasion, a rock wren nest with one egg; and he again stated that he was unable to discern any appreciable difference between these wrens and those of the mainland [B112, 1912].

In a short writeup, Linton of Long Beach described what the nest of the San Nicolas Rock Wren was composed of and where it could be found, which was under the eaves of a storehouse within fifty feet of the ranch house. The nest contained four young

birds [J124, 1911]. On one trip in 1911 he secured a set of four incubated eggs of the Wren [J45]. Linton, it will be observed, collected abalone pearls, as well as birds and their eggs [J150, 1938].

George Willett's name appears in avifaunal literature as early as 1910 [J122]. In 1941 he was Senior Curator of Ornithology for the Southern California Academy of Sciences. He, too, questioned the wren as being a subspecies.

Mr. H. S. Swarth reviewed the San Nicolas Rock Wren specimens and was unable to distinguish any differences in color or pattern. He concluded that two handfuls of bird-skins at random selection could contain some differences [J131, 1914].

Dr. Grinnell finally said that he was compelled to accede to the justness of Dawson's lack of acceptance concerning the rock wren of San Nicolas as being a subspecies [J138, 1927].

Regardless of this somewhat futile discussion about the rock wren, it is known not to leave the island. Mr. Rett did some work on San Nicolas Island in the spring and fall of 1945 [J151, 1947]. And Mr. Linderman [M94, 1945], is the one who remarked, "Among the 25 or 30 birds obtained by Rett for mounting, three species never leave the island. These are the raven, horned lark, and rock wren." Mr. Phil C. Orr was on this trip with Mr. Rett in 1945.

Archaeology

Our earliest names of those who dug on the islands are Gustav Eisen, León de Céssac, and Paul Schumacher. Dr. Eisen, a noted zoologist, states that he was on the islands in 1873 and 1897. He merely referred to de Céssac, who was on at least four of the islands between 1872 and 1879.

Paul Schumacher was on four islands for the Smithsonian Institution in 1875. He reacted strongly to de Céssac's coming to the United States and boxing tons of artifacts for a Paris museum. Schumacher's collecting spree lasted about three months and was based on the fact that the Institution wanted as large and as complete a display as possible for the Centennial Exposition, 1876, to be held in Philadelphia.

The French visitor, de Céssac, made his entry to one island, and then to others, through a friend, Justinian Caire, owner of Santa Cruz Island. His rivalry and jealousy with Schumacher is evident in the printed page, with de Céssac getting just about what he came for, perhaps more.

Dr. Heizer of the University of California, Berkeley, helps the reader by his editorship of source material printed through the Archaeological Research Facility:

1951, Report #12, Paper #13, 1 [U6]. de Céssac, Leon. "Observations on Sculptured Stone Fetishes in Animal Form Discovered on San Nicolas Island." Reports of the Archaeological Survey.

1957, Report #38, Paper #53, 10 [U9]. de Céssac, Leon. "A Steatite Whale Figurine from San Nicolas Island." Reports of the Archaeological Survey.

1960, Report #50, Paper #76, 1 [U10]. "A San Nicolas Island Twined Basketry Water Bottle." Reports of the Archaeological Survey. [First reported by G. Eisen in 1904; this could be the artifact given to C. J. W. Russell by George Nidever, 1856.]

At a later date, a Cyrus Barnard collected in 1883 a wooden dipper from San Nicolas. Mr. R. F. Heizer gives a few lines to discussing this artifact.

1960, Report #50, Paper #77, 4 [U11]. "Some Prehistoric Wooden Objects from San Nicolas Island."

Dr. Schumacher told of his trip to San Nicolas through the *Overland Monthly* of 1875 [P82], and again in 1877 [N41].

. . . We reached that island on a dark night, with the wind blowing lively, which compelled the captain to select the south end of the island as an anchorage. We fancied a campaign worse, if possible, than that at San Miguel, as the island appeared to be a faint lump in a thick fog-like cloud of sand which was whirled densely over our neat craft, although we were a half-mile off shore. The captain, with a shrill-sounding voice, recited his usual spicy prayers with much vehemence; on the sand-spit, not far off, the breakers, which form a half-mile in length, rise to a great height, and cause a roaring like thunder; at intervals we heard the howling sea-lions in the kelpy water, if not at their rookery on the near shore; which, with the darkness, the annoying sand, and the furious wind rattling the anchor-chain in madness, gave the impression that we had left rather than landed. With good prospects to lose our anchor and find ourselves the next morning probably at Santa Catalina, we awaited the coming dawn, trusting ourselves to the captain's care. The next morning was beautifully clear and almost calm; the sea was still rough, and as the swells, caused by a strong current that passes the south end, swept the shore in an angle, care had to be taken to pre-vent the boat going broadside on, which is equivalent to capsizing.

The island is a lump of soft coarse yellowish-gray sandstone, about 500 feet in height. The broad backbone, which seems almost level on its top, falls off on both sides in steep gulches and ravines, where the eye is met by innumerable cave-like carvings done by the grinding sand. The eastern end is sandy; dunes stretching there across the island, beginning with the depression at the end of which the house is located. The vegetation of the island is like that of San Miguel, ruined by overstocking it with sheep, which are here found in like starving condition. On the eastern end, near the house, we found some malva-bushes cleaned of their foliage to the reach of a sheep, which gave them the appearance of scrub oak-trees when seen from a distance. There are a few trees near the house, where a strong never-ceasing spring supplies the necessary water, which has a somewhat sweetish taste. The shifting sand has almost buried the adobe house, and its old inmate, the superintendent of the Stock-raising Company. Farther on to the north-eastward, at the so-called Chinese Harbor, is another spring with good water. It is at the eastern end, on the dunes, where we found the shell-mounds abundantly, although some are found at intervals all along the shore from the house toward the sand-spit on the south and, beyond which but few small ones exist; also a few on the western shores. The mode of burial on this island is different from that previously investigated. The bodies rest in distinct graves by themselves, lying on their backs, feet drawn up, and arms folded over the chest; the head either resting on the occiput, the side, or sunk to the breast. The skeletons, as a rule, were facing the east, although other directions were observed. Some show signs of having been buried in matting coated with asphaltum. Most of the skeletons and implements are laid bare by the winds. Our *modus operandi* was here changed; spade and pick were dispensed with, and in the first days our party went over the shell-mounds and piled the findings in heaps, which afterward were conveyed to the boat by horses procured of the "governor" of the island (as the old man styles himself), and thence taken by water to our camping-ground for a careful packing in boxes brought with us from San Francisco. We obtained 127 mortars—a heavy collection by itself—about 200 pestles, cups, trinkets, a small lot of quite unique sculptures, and some articles new to science.

PIECES OF EIGHT

The money deposits on this island are remarkable. In some places on the shell-mounds we noticed, apart from the skeletons, and not buried with them, numerous small heaps of shells of the *Olivella bipicata*, and some of the land shell *Helix strigosa*; also, a uniform size of pebbles, seemingly blackened by fire, averaging in quantity from a half to one cubic foot, which were evidently stored there, and afterward exposed to the drifts of sand, forming conspicuous diminutive hillocks. We found as many as sixty of these deposits on one shell-mound. This, with the position of some of the implements we observed, seems to point to the fact that the last inhabitants were taken off suddenly. We found, for instance, instead of being buried with the dead, many mortars set in the ground to the rim, the pestle either resting in its opening or lying longside, as if it had done its duty only some days before.

De Céssac went to San Nicolas in 1877 and from there collected fetishes, stone vases, mortars and pestles, molluscs, abalone shell fish hooks, flutes, whistles and bone implements.

These artifacts from San Nicolas, and the other islands of the group, were then displayed on the waterfront at the town of Santa Barbara. With the help of old Indians, de Céssac learned the use of various artifacts.

Before leaving for France in 1879 he felt that he had obtained enough information to reconstruct the ethnography of the Chumash Indians [U7, 1951].

Rev. Stephen Bowers had begun his collecting from the islands about 1875 while working for the Smithsonian Institution. He was on San Nicolas Island about 1889, but his gathering of specimens and artifacts came mainly from Santa Rosa, Santa Cruz, and San Miguel islands.

Bowers turned collector in his own right, but his career has been a controversial one, having been criticized by some for being more of a pot-hunter than an archaeologist. There are also some who felt that Bowers was inclined to assume credit for others' work and discoveries.

P. M. Jones stated in 1897 that Mr. De Moss Bowers, son of Rev. Stephen Bowers, made a collection of some 1203 pieces while on San Nicolas.

In 1897 a printed catalogue [M28], was issued, listing the collections from this island; it was probably published by a Mr. Rust. This list may be seen through the California State Library. In 1902 William Henry Holmes, of the Smithsonian Institution, reported that Mr. H. N. Rust of Pasadena had some of Rev. Stephen Bowers' collection.

Dr. Philip Mills Jones, M.D., wrote a letter to Mr. Charles F. Lummis on the 13th of November, 1901. A copy of the letter is presented at this time. The letter carries a critical tone, coupled with a degree of arrogance, as Dr. Jones expressed himself [M20].

Philip Mills Jones, M.D.
Mills Building, Room 32, 9th Floor,
San Francisco, California

> 1820 Grover Street,
> Los Angeles, Nov. 13th, 1901.

My Dear Mr. Lummis:

The Los Angeles "Herald" of November 3rd published an article on San Nicolas island, in many respects like other articles on poor San Nicolas which have appeared in various press from time to time;—it is made up of equal parts of ignorance and lie. In February last I examined the island very carefully, in company with Mr. Homer Hamlin, of the U. S. Geo. Survey, and intend to "nail" a few of these misstatements. Would you care for an article from me on this subject for the "Land of Sunshine"? I think I can furnish you with a few photographs, if you desire. If you do not care for the copy, please let me know and I shall give it to the "Times."

The above address will reach me for the next two weeks, after which I shall return to San Francisco. I hope to have the pleasure of calling on you, however, before I leave for the north.

Trusting that you are well and that everything is going nicely so far as the "Land of Sunshine" is concerned, I beg to remain,

> Very sincerely yours,
> Philip Mills Jones

Mr. Chas. F. Lummis,
1100 Avenue 43, Los Angeles.

The present author is endebted to the Southwest Museum for the privilege of seeing this manuscript. More recently, 1969, the *Masterkey* carried an account of Jones' 1901 trip to San Nicolas. The article is highly valuable and, fortunately, within easy access of any reader.

It is ironic that while Dr. Jones was critical of F. W. Putnam and others, he also came under criticism by some authorities, concerning his methods of exploration and excavation on Santa Rosa Island.

The Chicago *Record* furnished the information for *Current Literature* [P19, 1901]. Contained in their four or five paragraphs is one of the earliest statements about interest in the islands by Stanford University, and "several denominational colleges in southern California." The young scientists visited the Chinese camp at Corral Harbor.

Dr. Hector Alliot was the first director of the Southwest Museum, serving from 1909 to 1919. He was also president of the Southern California Academy of Sciences at one time, and a professor of art at the University of Southern California. Born in France in 1862, he died in 1919 when but fifty-six years of age.

It is from Dr. Alliot that we receive a 1916 account of the burial methods of the Indians who lived on San Nicolas [J341; M138, 1916; see also J208, 1969, as a reprint]. Along with Alliot on this 1914 expedition was William Herman Golisch, who was in charge of the expedition from the Southwest Museum. In their six-week stay on the island, Golisch also secured geological and conchological collections for himself and the Museum.

Alliot [J341], said, "The success of the Golisch party's mission was largely due to the length of time spent on the island, a period of six weeks, rendering possible systematic and reliable observations . . ."

Five years later, the *Catalina Islander* gave a report on Glidden's activities [M187, 1921],

> With provisions to last the party four months, Ralph Glidden left Thursday evening for San Nicholas Island . . . representing the Museum of the American Indian . . . it will take them about two days to unload their equipment at Corral Harbor . . . This is the third trip that [Glidden] has made to this desolate island . . . With Professor Glidden is Arthur Taschenberger, who has had several years experience in the work of unearthing Indian relics on the Channel Islands.

On San Nicolas Island, in particular, Dr. Kroeber [N16, 1925], had little to say,

> There was enough brush for huts, but most dwellings were reared on a frame of whale ribs and jaws, either covered with sea-lion hides or wattled with brush or rushes . . . The island may have afforded sufficient timber for plank canoes.

Bruce Bryan's book, *Archaeological Explorations on San Nicolas Island*, was published by the Southwest Museum in 1970 [B6]. It took dedication and hard work, with many personal experiences, to have been able to produce such an interesting edition.

Mr. Bryan began his work in 1926 on this island for the Los Angeles County Museum. The expedition remained on San Nicolas for about two and a half months; Arthur Sanger was with them as a private collector, writer, and field archaeologist.

Four shorter publications by B. Bryan probably helped to direct his willingness into being "coaxed" back to the world of archaeology [J179, 1926; J32, J33, 1930; P143, 1957]. Many of us may now share those experiences.

Bruno Oetteking [J19, 1930], wrote about an arthritic skeleton found on San Nicolas, a four-page article.

No one's name ranks higher than Arthur Sanger's as an Indian artifact hunter and collector. In Mr. Clark's article [P157, 1944], he said, "It all began when Sanger acquired *The Dreamer*, a 76-foot schooner (1911)."

After having spent the summers for the next thirty years on the islands [M98, M151], one can imagine the size of Sanger's collection! He sold artifacts to the Heye Foundation of New York, to the Los Angeles County Museum, to the Southwest Museum, and to the State of California.

Even by 1944 Sanger's Indian collection from southern California was considered to be the finest in the world [P157]. *Masterkey* reported his death in 1971 [J209].

The Coast Guard now protects the island from intruders, but Mr. Woodward was allowed on the island, where he worked off and on for several years. He was helped with his transportation by the Allan Hancock Foundation of the University of Southern California.

Mr. Woodward has been on the staff of the Museum of the American Indian, Heye Foundation, New York City. Also a director of history and anthropology for the Los Angeles County Museum, he was on San Nicolas Island in 1940 for both biological and archaeological purposes.

Several articles have been written by Mr. Woodward, one published by the American Indian Museum, one by the Southern California Historical Society, one by *American Antiquity* [J5, 1940], and one by *The Pacific Northwesterner*, under the editorship of W. W. Robinson [B62, 1957].

San Nicolas appears to have been one of Woodward's specialities. He took a particular interest in Juana María's solitary life on the island. The reader is referred to his research on the Indian woman, who lived for eighteen years alone on the island of San Nicolas, while white men on the mainland were making up their minds whether to rescue her or not. [B62].

Phil C. Orr did most of his archaeological work on Santa Rosa Island, but he also went to other islands. In 1938 he became Curator of Anthropology and Geology for the Santa Barbara Museum of Natural History. He remained in that capacity for thirty years, and through that organization someone has visited Santa Rosa annually since 1947.

However, in 1945 Mr. Orr made two trips to San Nicolas Island through the courtesy of Lt. Commander D. O. Parker, Commanding Officer, San Nicolas Island. Mr. Rett of the Museum joined Mr. Orr on those trips. [Minor references about this island may be found in J284, J285, 1945; J286, 1946.]

M. C. Irwin, Librarian of the Museum, stated that in 1945 Mr. Orr found on San Nicolas a steatite bowl filled with fishhooks in all stages of completion, and parts of the tools used in making them. [See also, P143, Bryan].

By 1951 University men from U.C.L.A. began to find their way to four islands, three islands being of the southern group. Dr. McKusick focused on Anacapa and San Clemente, while Dr. Meighan studied Santa Catalina and San Nicolas.

In 1954 we were given a zoning of the middens and a listing of the artifacts to be found on San Nicolas. The artifacts included steatite bowls, mortars and pestles, tubes and pipes, beads and pendants, tools, whistles and flutes. The middens in the areas northwest and southwest of Seal Beach and near the coast between Dutch Harbor and JEHEMY BEACH were not zoned.

Evidently, the U.S. Navy personnel were cooperative with Orr, Bryan and Rozaire, and Eberhart and Meighan. At various times these men were taken to San Nicolas, housed, fed, and transported by jeep around the island. [See M148, 1951; M190, 1953; M150, 1953; J11, 1953; J78, 1954; U42, 1960; U43, 1962; U44, 1964.]

The Southwest Museum, in Highland Park, California, has always been interested in Indian artifacts and enjoys practically the best collections in the United States. It is a non-profit organization and the institution does much to encourage and forward the work of the many who have a similar interest. From *Masterkey*, their own publication, come many references to San Nicolas. [See J186, 1936; J197, 1959; J199, 1960; M156, 1961; J200, 1962; J211, 1973, and a 1974 *Masterkey* article, "An Unusual Stone Effigy from Southern California."]

In the *Los Angeles Times* of 1970 was a lengthy writeup for the Museum, including a fair-sized photo of the Museum's director, Dr. Dentzel, and the curator, Bruce Bryan. Dr. Dentzel's remarks in William S. Murphy's article are appropriate to "Dying San Nicolas." "The Indian had respect for nature, beauty and his environment . . . Now almost when it is too late we realize that they in their primitive wisdom and experience held the key to unlocking much of value in their environment without destroying it."

Photos of San Nicolas Island

Date	Code #	Author	Photos	Reference
1896	P90	Yates	The Cave Dwellings	*Overland Monthly*
1896	P44	Earle	Sand erosion on San Nicolas	*Land of Sunshine*
1899	J311	Holder	[contains five photos]	*Scientific American*
1899	M122	Mathis	The Lone Sheepherder	*Los Angeles Times*
			Curios in . . . Graves	*Los Angeles Times*
1900	P54	Trask	East End Cliffs	*Land of Sunshine*
			Reefs at Low Tide	*Land of Sunshine*
			A Dragon [rock formation]	*Land of Sunshine*
			A Monster [rock formation]	*Land of Sunshine*
1907	P112	Tenney	Corral Harbor	*Pacific Monthly*
1917	P68	McCoy	A typical crevasse in the rock rim	*Outing*
			The ghost of a wrecked forest—sand	*Outing*
			The petrified remains of a large tree— sand	*Outing*
			Below . . . repose the bones of San Nicholans	*Outing*
			The . . . forgotten battlefield	*Outing*
1922	M187	_____	Glidden Camp, on Wind-swept Island	*Catalina Islander*
1944	N51	Wheeler	Photo of the island	*U.S. Naval Instit. Proceedings*
1948	J225	Walker	Trees of Sand	*Natural History*
1956	P161	Max Miller	Casts of trees	*Westways*
1956	M154	Hillinger	Lands End	*Los Angeles Times*
			Sea Lion Center	*Los Angeles Times*
			Sea Elephant close-up	*Los Angeles Times*
1957	B62	Woodward	Ranch House area [1939-40]	*Pacific Northwesterner*
1960	J84	Norris	Abalone on Northwest Coast of San Nicolas	*Discovery*
1960	B88	Emery	Aerial View of Sand Spit	*The Sea off Southern California*
1962	M47	Thorne Hall	A baby sea elephant	*Odyssey of the Calif. Islands*
			Waves splash at Lands End	*Odyssey of the Calif. Islands*
			Scrawlings on walls of Cave of Killer Whale	*Odyssey of the Calif. Islands*
			One of the jolly St. Nicks	*Odyssey of the Calif. Islands*
1967	B120	Bartholomew	Northern elephant seal, San Nicolas	*Symposium* [biological]
			Cows and pups, elephant seal	*Symposium* [biological]
1968	B54	Orr	Sand cast of tree trunk from San Nicolas	*Prehistory of Santa Rosa Island*
1970	B6	Bryan	U. S. Navy aerial view of island	*Archaeological Explorations*
			Lorenzo G. Yates and skeletons [from Overland Monthly]	*Archaeological Explorations*
			Pencil-drawn map of San Nicolas, [drawn by Wm. H. Golisch, 1914]	*Archaeological Explorations*
			A typical kitchen midden	*Archaeological Explorations*
			Camp at Corral Harbor; Captain Nelson included	*Archaeological Explorations*
			Buried small house on north shore, as of 1901	*Archaeological Explorations*
			U. S. Navy barracks	*Archaeological Explorations*
			Southeast coast of San Nicolas	*Archaeological Explorations*
			Cave of the Whales petroglyphs	*Archaeological Explorations*

THE LONE WOMAN OF SAN NICOLAS
AN EVALUATION OF THE BIBLIOGRAPHY
WITH DISCUSSION OF THE
HISTORICAL EVENTS

Juana María, an Indian woman, was "accidentally" left to her fate for eighteen years on the island of San Nicolas in 1835. The other remaining native inhabitants were removed to the mainland in 1835 on the *Peor es Nada*, Better-than-Nothing. No one seems to know exactly who instigated the removal.

Isaac Sparks had chartered the boat at Monterey, and with his group had gone otter-hunting in Lower California just prior to the tragedy. The accidental incident was apparently common knowledge, but not much attention was paid to this mother's plight by those responsible or capable of helping her.

The reason given for the hunters leaving the island so abruptly was that the day was increasing in storminess and there was fear of total disaster at sea. Perhaps the otter-hunters had intended to return for this poor soul, who had swum to shore in order to pick up her baby left in the hills. And besides, what was one or two Indian lives, as compared to the quest for quick profit.

No one will ever know exactly what happened on that fateful day or for the next eighteen years of the woman's life. In 1853 Nidever and Dittmann accomplished the mission of finding her and taking her to Santa Barbara, where she lived with the Nidever family until her death. By 1853, however, the Lone Woman was unable to communicate, and died shortly thereafter, probably from her inability to tolerate a change of diet.

We are left with any number of accounts, some quite fragmentary. The first complete reference did not find its way into print until three years after the Lone Woman was finally 'rescued' in 1853. This story came through Russell, "Narrative of a Woman who was Eighteen Years Alone upon the Island of San Nicolas, Coast of California," published by *Hutchings' California Magazine* [P27, 1856].

Russell's account was obtained from Nidever while they were both on the island of San Miguel, each pursuing his own business. It was even twenty-five years after the woman's rescue by Nidever and Dittmann that their separate interviews were recorded by Murray in 1878.

The following information presented to the reader is not a repetition of the story, but rather a discussion of the literature on the subject. Such literature is sometimes contradictory in detail; but throughout the material the main threads of the incident remain intact. There will probably never be a completely accurate rendition of the Lone Woman story.

The reader is left to seek recommended references for a fuller accounting than given within these pages, or choose to glean from these evaluated references what was under discussion during that period of time. A chart at the end of the discussion is included; it should be helpful to the reader in identifying the various personalities involved.

Readers will do well to obtain the manuscripts of Nidever and Dittmann for their basics on the Juana María tale. These may be obtained through the Bancroft Library. Excerpts from such, as well as a compilation of the literature through Heizer and Elsasser [U13, 1961], are within comparatively easy access. Ellison [B51, 1937], contains the story of Nidever's life, and is another fine source for the Lone Woman.

Only one other recommended-for-reading account of the Lone Woman is Hardacre's "Eighteen Years Alone," published by *Scribner's Monthly* [P123, 1880]. The rest of the literature, although possibly furnishing some insights, are fragmentary or emersed in fanciful remarks that obscure the real story, and are therefore more questionable. However, they should be considered in the literature on the Lone Woman.

The author begins with the older references starting with the year 1893, which are basically the least acceptable, and moves toward the two manuscripts on Nidever and Dittmann, taken by E. F. Murray in 1878, the only first person accounts available.

Beginning with Gibbons' account, "The Wild Woman of San Nicolas Island" [P15, 1893], we find some unreliability, thus creating skepticism of his article. Gibbons said that the reason the story

> can be so given now is due to the zeal and the thoughtfulness of Mr. D. W. Thompson, one of the fathers of the City of Flowers, and to him we are indebted for a decidedly curious page of history. In 1882 Mr. D. W. Thompson, accompanied by a shorthand reporter [unnamed], sought out those principal actors—the venerable pioneers George Nidever and Charlie Brown—and by elaborate questioning obtained full particulars connected with the unfortunate woman's career.

Gibbons' article was in no-less-than C. F. Holder's *Californian Illustrated*, 1893. Usually Holder can be relied upon for quality, with a little flair, but this

32

article is less than satisfactory; a mixture of fanciful quotes and statements; it ended with,

> not until her very nature was so changed that she had become contented with her lot and had ceased her cry of "Manequauna" to the passing ships, were any measures taken to remove her from her rocky isle. Then they carried her off, unfortunate Juana María Better-than-Nothing! White men made her suffer. She lost her babe or babies; she lost her family; she lost the knowledge of her language; and at last, poisoned by the luxuries of a more civilized race, she lost her life.

This quotation alone gives Gibbons' article value in the literature on that poor soul, a human being, left by otter-hunters and others to her fate.

Herein follows a discussion of some of the little known local history for that period, which includes the name of D. W. Thompson, and others.

We are faced with the fact that we know nothing about Gibbons' source information, D. W. Thompson and the shorthand reporter, 1882. Was Thompson, for instance, Dixie [Dixey] Wildes Thompson, the nephew of Alpheus B. Thompson? This appears conceivable. Alpheus had been assured half-ownership of Santa Rosa Island through his father-in-law, Carlos Carrillo.

A Captain Dixey Wildes owned the *Paragon*, built in Massachusetts in 1815, with the *Paragon* doing business in sandalwood in the Sandwich Islands—as did the Winship brothers and Captain William Heath Davis, Sr. [See Gast, *Contentious Consul, A Biography of John Coffin Jones*, 1976.]

It was the *Paragon* of Marshall and Wildes that took John Coffin Jones to the Sandwich Islands in 1821, where Jones served as the business representative for the maritime merchantile merchants of that company. Jones also 'informally,' but directly, served as the representative for the United States as Consul.

It was Marshall and Wildes who made Alpheus B. Thompson a subordinate to John Coffin Jones, to serve as supercargo on several of the firm's vessels. Alpheus was being sponsored by his uncle, Captain Dixey Wildes [Gast].

In the meantime Alpheus moved to Santa Barbara and in the year 1834 Dixie Wildes Thompson began his career in Santa Barbara by working for his uncle, Alpheus B. Thompson, on the island of Santa Rosa [B53]. For such purposes Dixie Thompson had purchased the steamship, *Sophia*.

This Thompson, D. W., was one of those who later laid a claim against J. C. Jones in the A. B. Thompson/J. C. Jones litigation suit, as did Luis Burton—only to find that such financial obligation for the care of livestock on the island was the obligation of A. B. Thompson, not that of J. C. Jones. Such are the ramifications of this period of history [Gast].

To keep the topic of D. W. Thompson completely unclear, we are given the information by Woodward [J367, 1938], that in his Southwest Museum researches he discovered an unpublished interview of George Nidever, made by a J. Terry in 1882. F. W. Hodge was Director of the Southwest Museum at the time that Woodward was doing some of his research on the Lone Woman.

Although this interview reference does not appear to have been used, could this J. Terry be the unnamed reporter connected with D. W. Thompson in 1882, and from whom Gibbons obtained his information?

Another article of questionable value is Stephen Bowers' 1892 account of "The Lone Woman of San Nicolas" [M27]. It was DeMoss Bowers, son of Stephen, who wrote to Dr. Alliot of the Southwest Museum in 1916, to remind Dr. Alliot that his father, Stephen, had sent his personal material on the Lone Woman to the museum.

Bowers' pamphlet is a reprint from the Ventura *Weekly Observer* under the dates of December 9, 16, and 20 of 1892 [M95]. Dr. Bowers was the editor of the *Weekly Observer*, having come West in 1869, living in the Santa Barbara/Ventura area between 1894 and 1906; deceased, 1907.

What is really important is a statement made by Rev. Bowers that

> The account may also be found in the archives of the Santa Barbara Mission preserved by the Mission fathers. We secured a translation of their record of the event by a competent Spanish Scholar some fifteen years ago.

Although this mission record has not come to light, should we use Bowers' date of 1878, it would place this particular translation obtained from the Mission at about the same time as the E. F. Murray manuscripts on Nidever and Dittmann. In fact, the Mission story, if it does exist or were ever to be found, might contain many statements of fact on material that we do not presently possess.

We can short-circuit the Thompson and West account [B70, 1883], found in Chapter 17 of the book. According to the compilers of the book on the history of Santa Barbara and Ventura Counties, it was Dr. Dimmick, who came to Santa Barbara as a physician in 1872, who furnished the notes for their "The Lost Woman" story. The result is a combination of first and third person accounting.

Interestingly enough, Mrs. Emma Chamberlin Hardacre arrived in Santa Barbara in 1876, four years after Dr. Dimmick's arrival. In her account of the Lone Woman, as well as in Dimmick's, there are four Indian words given—"hide," "man," "sky," and "body." This could mean that one of their sources may have been the same, or that one could have used the material of the other.

Even though Mrs. Hardacre's "Eighteen Years Alone" is completely third person, her story is insightful. For comprehensive reading, no secondary account comes close to hers [P123, 1880]. With some drama, and perhaps a few misstatements, the account has real merit; she had interviewed Jeffries, Nidever, Dittmann, and others.

Nothing new is added through the *Pioneer*, "Left Alone on a Desert Island for Eighteen Years; California's Feminine Crusoe" [M84]. Furthermore, the date of publication, 1879, for this newspaper account, is too far removed from the actual occurrences to be of much value.

But both the title and the ending of Russell's account [P27, 1856], to be discussed later, leads one to feel that his material had been read by the *San Francisco Chronicle*—the *Pioneer* having obtained its writeup from the *Chronicle*, according to the *Pioneer*, 1879. Hardacre's title also carries some of the same words and might reflect that she, too, had read Russell.

We have been moving backward from 1893 to 1878, at which time the E. F. Murray reporting of interviews of Carl Dittmann and George Nidever surrounding the Lone Woman took place.

Ellison [B51, 1937], gives credit to the Bancroft Library for use of these two documents. He also states that his footnote material came from the *Pacific Historical Review*, and that his source for other material came from Dr. George Hammond and Vol. II of *New Spain and the Anglo-American West*. Thus we have some of the best thinking of this period.

At this point we reach a second detour in order to see the relationship of the various pieces of literature on the Lone Woman story and the historical events of that period. This refers specifically to Ellison [B51, 1937], Richard Henry Dana [B15, 1835],

H. H. Bancroft [B1, 1885], T. H. Hittell [B35, 1898], and others.

It was Ellison who stated that E. F. Murray was an assistant to H. H. Bancroft. Murray had been recommended by Judge Benjamin Hayes, friend of J. J. Warner [M96], to take the dictation from Dittmann and Nidever about the Lone Woman. Murray had taken such a type of dictation from many of the old residents of the area.

Three footnotes in Ellison are of interest. In footnote #1, readers are reminded that "John" Nidever was an uncle to young Nidever. But readers, at the same time, must be wary of the use of three given names for George Nidever. Both Dr. Stephen Bowers and Dr. Dimmick called George Nidever by the name of "John."

In *Masterkey*, Vol. 53, #4, we learn that Harrington referred to Nidever as "Jacob." Elsewhere, we are given the impression that the younger Captain George Nidever was a "Junior," which is apparently true [B56]. The other son's name, however, was "Jacob," or "Jake" [J282, 1930].

Footnote #87 states that A. B. Thompson was supercargo between 1831-1834 and up to 1838. He was also a shipbuilder. This brings up Nidever's statement that "For many years after the loss of the 'Peor es Nada,' the only craft on the coast were small boats to which the long distance and rough sea of the outer rim of the Channel would render a trip extremely dangerous." Yet statements of the known craft plying between the Sandwich Islands and our west coast, and the amount of otter hunting in the region of the Channel Islands gives lie to Nidever's statement. Even Wm. G. Dana owned the schooner *Santa Barbara*, said Bancroft, Vol. II. Indeed, Nidever was being generous, if not evasive.

Take, for instance, Richard Henry Dana's comments on this subject [B15], for the year 1835,

> The second day after our arrival, a full-rigged brig came round the point from the northward, sailed leisurely through the bay, and stood off again for the south-east, in the direction of the large island of Catalina. The next day the *Avon* got under weigh, and stood in the same direction, bound for San Pedro. This might do for marines and Californians, but we knew the ropes too well. The brig was never again seen on the coast, and the *Avon* arrived at San Pedro in about a week, with a full cargo of Canton and American goods.
>
> This was one of the means of escaping the heavy duties the Mexican lay upon all imports.

A vessel comes on the coast, enters a moderate cargo at Monterey, which is the only custom-house, and commences trading. In a month or more, having sold a large part of her cargo, she stretches over to Catalina, or other of the large uninhabited islands which lie off the coast, in a trip from port to port, and supplies herself with choice goods from a vessel from Oahu, which has been lying off and on the islands, waiting for her. Two days after the sailing of the *Avon*, the lorriott [sic] came in from the leeward, and without doubt had also a snatch at the brig's cargo . . .

John Coffin Jones owned both the *Avon* and the *Loriot*, perhaps even the unnamed Hawaiian brig, using Santa Catalina and "other of the large uninhabited islands which lie off the coast."

These statements lead to another footnote, #97, on the subject of *Peor es Nada*. It is said that the craft was twenty-ton, built in Monterey by Joaquin Gomez, and was launched on August 30, 1834 with Captain Hubbard in charge [B51].

Charlie Hubbard was German and a naturalized Mexican, who had come to California in the early '30s. In charge of the *Peor es Nada*, Sparks and Burton and others chartered it through Hubbard, going to Lower California in October of 1834.

Contained in the same footnote is the statement that John C. Jones chartered *Peor es Nada* during March of 1835 for the return trip from Lower California. Storke [B69, 1891], also remarked that the *Peor es Nada* "returned in March under John Coffin." This can only mean that Jones was involved with this first round trip—and could have been throughout this period of time.

The other sailing date for the ill-fated *Peor es Nada* was when "someone" took it back to Lower California in the "Autumn." And as Mrs. Storke put it, the *Peor es Nada* "returned in March under John Coffin, and made a second trip in the autumn."

This makes for an interval of time, between March and August, that is unaccounted for, in terms of what the men, Jones, Sparks, Isaac Williams, Burton, Francis D. Dye, Captain Marcus Harlow, *et al*, were doing with the *Peor es Nada*. Just otter hunting?

If the Indians on San Nicolas were picked up, and the Lone Woman left behind in August of 1835, this was done between the two trips to Lower California, not on one of them; March is in Spring and Autumn does not include August.

It was during September of 1835, after returning from Lower California and after Nidever and the

Black Steward had been picked up at Santa Barbara for their trip to Santa Rosa Island, that Sparks told Nidever of the Indian woman's abandonment.

With a load of lumber on board, the *Peor es Nada* continued its trip but capsized in San Francisco Bay, and nothing more was heard of her, but the Lone Woman story lingers on and on.

Nidever and Dittmann gave their interviews to Murray in 1878, long after Isaac Williams of Los Angeles had died, 1856; Robbins, likewise, in 1857, Wm. G. Dana in 1858, Isaac Sparks in 1867, J. C. Jones in 1861, and A. B. Thompson in 1869. This left only Burton, Nidever, and Dittmann as the living characters in Santa Barbara for this drama. Burton passed away in 1880 and Nidever in 1883.

Hubert Bancroft [B1, Vol. II], spells out some of the rudiments of Dittmann's life:

Dittmann (Carl), came to California in 1844, German sailor, known in Cal. as Charley Brown, who came on the *Euphemia*, engaged in otter-hunting with Nidever and others, an occupation interrupted by mining in '48-50. Sta. B. was his home town to '78, when he dictated for me his *Narrative of a Seafaring Life*, an interesting record of many adventures . . .

According to Hittell [B35], another historian of early California, Carl Dittmann was born in Prussia in 1822 and came to California in 1844. He was thirty-one years of age, as compared to Nidever's fifty-one years, when they went to San Nicolas to search for the Lone Woman. Dittmann used an alias (Charlie Brown), had been a deserter from an American whaler, and from Santa Barbara pursued the trade of an otter hunter.

It is hard to resist repeating some of the first hand, vivid material that comes to us. From Mrs. Brown, sister of Carl Dittmann, is this heart-string-pulling tale of a baby otter,

I have an otter skin which is fifty-seven years old. It was one of the last taken by my only brother, Charley Dittmann, who was hunting with Capt. George Nidever and his son, young George, in the waters of Lower California in 1865. He shot the mother otter and she had this baby in her arms.

She dropped it and as it was drowning my brother killed it. "See," said Mrs. Brown, displaying the skin, "how fine and glossy the fur still is. I have kept it wrapped up for a long time" [B56].

We refer again to H. H. Bancroft for another capsulated briefing, this time on Nidever:

> Nidever (Geo.) came to California in 1833 . . . In '41 he married Sinforosa Sanchez, . . . piloted the U. S. coast survey craft in a survey of the Sta. B. islands '50; in '53 rescued the famous old Ind. woman of S. Nicolas Isl.; and about the same time bought an interest in S. Miguel Isl., where he raised stock for 17 years, and though wellnigh ruined by the drought of '63-64, sold out in '70 for $10,000. In '78 . . . at the age of 76 . . . gave me a long and most valuable narrative of his *Life and Adventures* . . . He died in '83. A brother John, who died at Sta. B. in '73 is sometimes said to have come with Geo. but I think he came after '48. Another brother, Mark, was killed by the Ind. before reaching Cal.

The Santa Barbara Deed Book H tells us that Nidever and his two sons sold their interest on San Miguel to Hiram W. Mills for $5,000.00. This transaction carried the date of May 8, 1867.

Nidever hunted otter, beginning his career in California with George Yount around San Francisco Bay. In 1835, and for about two years after, he was hunting otter under the Wm. G. Dana license, "Capt. Denny's." On other occasions he worked for A. B. Thompson.

It is stated in Ellison that Nidever purchased a schooner in San Francisco in 1850; Nidever uses the date of 1852 for that purchase. Nonetheless, by 1850 Nidever had an adobe hut on San Miguel Island and had stocked the island with sheep. It was probably on one of his trips to San Miguel to care for his business that he and Capt. Russell met, camped together, and discussed the Woman and how she had been abandoned on San Nicolas.

As we move away from 1878 toward the earlier period, we find in *Overland Monthly*, 1872 [P79], Josephine Walcott's "Hona María." Without too much to recommend "Hona María" Walcott is, nevertheless, imaginative and understanding when she says,

> The effect of long seclusion upon her mind so crude and undeveloped, can not be conjectured. In her solitary abode she knew the ways of the birds of the air and fishes of the sea, and fashioned nets to capture them, which, with seals and roots, furnished her sustenance.

Now we turn to the earliest of records, 1841, and move toward the date of 1856 and C. J. W. Russell who wrote the first complete story about the Lone Woman which was after her death in 1853.

We find for 1841, Phelps' "Logbook of the Alert," [U13]. It may be recalled that Richard Henry Dana returned to the East on the *Alert*, a sailing vessel belonging to Bryant and Sturgis, mercantile businessmen.

In the one paragraph that comes out of the Logbook bearing on the San Nicolas Island drama, we are told that Capt. Thomas Robbins called at the island with his 'vessel' in order to pick up the remaining inhabitants of the island.

This is the only mention of Robbins in any of the literature pertaining to the Lone Woman. A direct command from Robbins seems unlikely, for Sparks was supposedly working under the Dana license, not a Robbins license.

Actually, all five of Carlos Carrillo's sons-in-law or to-be-sons-in-law, were in the otter hunting business, some with licenses, with others doing illicit hunting and contraband trading. Since in business, "profit" was the name of the game, and the Indians on San Nicolas Island were seemingly the only Indian inhabitants left on the Channel Islands, could their presence have been an impediment to the smuggling business, for instance?

Dawson's *Memoirs* [B17, 1841], is well worth the reading, if for no other reason than to learn of Dawson's concern for his horse near starvation. It was James Alexander Forbes, English Consul from Mexico, who saved the day for the horse and Dawson's feelings about it, by caring for the creature.

In the little book Dawson speaks of his, Sparks, Nydever [sic], Dye, and Simmons having gone into partnership with A. B. Thompson for otter hunting. If Thompson was conducting business on a legal basis or not, it is not mentioned.

But through Gast's *Contentious Consul*, we have learned that Jones and Thompson were denied hunting licenses in 1831. They decided, therefore, to do illegal business and continued such into the middle '40s, at least. Dawson said, "We . . . killed several otter . . . We searched on shore for a lone woman . . . but failed to find her, although we found her tracks."

The third early reference to the Lone Woman comes from the *Overland Monthly* under the title of "A Woman's Log of 1849." The reference is given by A. Woodward [J367], and is taken from Vol. 16, 2nd series, July-Dec., 1890, pp. 273-280. A Mrs. McDougall was one of few women passengers in 1849 on the *California*'s first trip to San Francisco. She kept a diary, and on page 275 of this article Mrs. McDougall is quoted as saying,

> In coming to Santa Barbara we passed an island about sixty miles from the coast, on which there is a lone woman living . . . Some three years ago they caught her, but she was perfectly wild and had lost her speech, so they left her.

Actually, when the Indian woman was taken off the island she was found to be of mild disposition and quite verbal.

Such material verifies the fact that knowledge concerning the abandonment was common. But some remained skeptical of her continued existence, Nidever being one. In Dittman's 1878 interview with Murray he said, "Nidever . . . was not very sanguine about finding her as he had come to the conclusion that the dogs had eaten her and was very doubtful if even her bones could be found . . ."

From the *Daily Democratic State Journal* of Oct. 13, 1853 we find these words,

> The wild Indian woman who was found on the Island of San Nicolas, about seventy miles from the coast, west of Santa Barbara, is now at the latter place, and is looked upon as a curiosity. It is stated that she has been some eighteen to twenty years alone on the Island. She existed on shell fish and the fat of the seal, and dressed in the skins and feathers of wild ducks, which she sewed together with the sinews of the seal. She cannot speak any known language—is good-looking, and about a middle age. She seems to be contented in her new home among the good people of Santa Barbara.

This publication came out six days before the Lone Woman died of dysentery, from eating fruits and vegetables to which she was unaccustomed. Dr. Brinkerhoff attended her [P123].

Through Woodward [J367, 1938] we are told that the *Daily Alta California* in 1853 carried the story in November, concerning the Lone Woman's death, by making the announcement that on the evening of Tuesday the 15th of November there would be a Ladies' Fair and Raffle in the Musical Hall on Bush Street, San Francisco.

> . . . a great variety of curiosities will be on exhibition, some of which, from their rarity and peculiarity, will be well worth the attention of the scientific and the curious. Some of the most singular objects will be disposed of by lot or raffle or as may at the time be thought proper and advisable. One of the most singular things

on exhibition will be the dress of an old Indian woman who for seventeen years lived:

> Alone, alone, all, all alone
> Alone in the wide, wide sea—
> And ne'er a soul took pity on,
> *Her* soul in agony.

This stanza is a fitting paraphrase from Coleridge's "The Rime of the Ancient Mariner."

Hutchings' California Magazine ran the first 'complete' story of the Lone Woman after she was found. Called, "Narrative of a Woman who was Eighteen Years Alone upon the Island of San Nicolas, Coast of California," it was published in November of 1856 [P27].

It was C. J. W. Russell who wrote the article, and he said that Nidever related it to him while they were on San Miguel Island. Nidever was otter hunting and tending his sheep there; Russell was doing tidal observations for the United States. The article is published in the third person, not the first person.

Immediately, various newspapers and others published the contents of the article. Questions relating to possible errors and omissions were promptly raised. Answers were categorically offered, and it was not until June of 1860 that the initial strength of human reaction tapered. In reality, Russell had but started further investigation, for in five ways his tale appears to be fiction and fact.

The San Francisco *Evening Bulletin* of November 25, 1856 [M69], recalled Capt. C. J. W. Russell's article in *Hutchings' Magazine*. Then the Los Angeles *Star* of December 13, 1856 carried the story through J. J. Warner of San Diego [M96].

The Honorable J. J. Warner had evidently written to the Los Angeles *Star* in 1856, presenting his version of the removal of the Indians from San Nicolas [M96]. But even though the newspaper used the words, "facts herein contained," for Warner's presentation, other newspapers and persons continued to question some of the 'facts.'

Albeit, Warner's version brings us somewhat closer to the shape of the story, even though the dates, the numbers exterminated on the island in previous years, and by whom, remained in question.

One statement can be categorically denied; the Lone Woman when found was not "old, infirm, and decriped" and not suffering from hunger; malnutrition, no doubt. In the same vein, Putnam [N45], had called the Woman "an old hag."

Warner initiated the thought to the public that the decision for taking the remaining Indians from the island rested with two Los Angeles residents, not with the Mission fathers. Nidever added to this thought when he said, "I am sure Williams had an interest in the matter, as he afterwards took one of the Indian women to live with."

Hugo Reid wrote for the Los Angeles *Star*. In fact he had written a series of twenty-four letters about the southern Indians before his death in 1853. According to Alexander S. Taylor [M51], by 1860 Reid's material had already become scarce. It is entirely possible that J. J. Warner of San Diego kept in touch with many Indian events in and around Los Angeles through Hugo Reid's material.

We learn from *Pacific Discovery* [J83, 1960], that Reid was a Scot who settled in California in 1835. In 1837 he married a mission-trained Indian woman named Victoria, and Reid acquired a family by adopting her children from a previous marriage.

A few details may be mentioned about J. J. Warner. Six-foot-three inches tall, Don Juan José Warner appeared to be an educated man. He came from Connecticut in 1831, having been born in 1807 [B58, 1939]. By 1843 Warner had asked for a license so that he could hunt otter; he had hunted the poor creatures in 1831 with George Yount. By 1844, after having become a Mexican citizen, he was granted the Rancho Agua Caliente [B29, 1960]. In those early times his place was the first settlement to be reached by travelers coming over the desert from the Colorado River [B35, 1898]. By 1853, according to the *Daily Democratic Journal*, J. J. Warner had been elected to a San Diego judgeship.

Both Taylor's [U13] and the Sacramento *Union*'s [M81] rehearsal of the Santa Barbara *Gazette* and the Los Angeles *Star* are substantially identical. The following came from the *Union*, as previously told by the *Gazette*,

In the year 1811, a ship owned by Boardman & Pope, of Boston, commanded by Capt. Whittemore, trading on this coast, took from the port of Sitka, Russian America, about thirty Kodiak Indians, a part of a hardy tribe inhabiting the Island of Kodiak, to the islands in the Santa Barbara channel, for the purpose of killing sea otter, which were then very numerous in the neighborhood of these islands. Capt. Whittemore, after landing the Kodiaks on the island, and placing in their hands fire arms and the necessary implements of the chase, sailed away to the coast of Lower California and South America.

In the absence of the ship, a dispute arose between the Kodiaks and the natives of the islands, originating in the seizure of the females by the Kodiaks. The Kodiaks, possessing more activity, endurance and knowledge of war, and possessing superior weapons, slaughtered the males without mercy, old and young. On the Island of San Nicolas, not a male was spared. At the end of a year, Capt. Whittemore returned to the islands, took the Kodiaks on board, and carried them back to Sitka.

This killing off of all males is in line with what the Logbook reported: two females and Black Hawk surviving. It also approximates Warner's statement of two females and two males having escaped the massacres. Neither statement is necessarily so; certainly they do not conform to Nidever's statement about Sparks and others having taken 17 or 18 Indians off the island in 1835.

And speaking of 'killing off,' Orr [B54], reminds us that there were more than 450 Northwest Indians and eighty Hawaiian hunters on the California coast between 1803 and 1811. And Adele Ogden [J93], said that the Russians were on San Nicolas Island for seven months in 1815. Perhaps the Pope and Boardman incident of 1811 was but one of many massacres.

Referring again to a later issue of *Hutchings'*, we note that the February 1857 article [P29], gives the *Gazette* credit for its addition to the 1856 *Gazette* story.

Hutchings' said that Captain Russell, who was from a family of whalers on the east coast [P28], went to Santa Barbara for a second meeting with Nidever. It was then that George Nidever gave to Russell a waterbottle made of grass and covered with asphaltum, a stone mortar, a necklace, and other things that had been made by the Lone Woman during her solidary stay on the island. The bottle and other articles were subsequently given to the California Academy of Sciences, March 30, 1857.

It is also through *Hutchings'* that the story is first mentioned about a good-sized cave which the Lone Woman had used for shelter. It is stated, also, that on the walls of the cave she had kept a rude record of passing vessels. Nidever corroborates that in the "rainy season she lived in a cave nearby." There *is* a nearby cave.

The March 30th, 1857, California Academy of Sciences tells about the disposition of Juana María's effects [J367]. Nidever verified the statement when he said, "Her dresses, bone needles and other curiosities were taken possession of by Father González, with my consent, and sent to Rome."

Woodward [J367], contributes with the *Golden Era* reference of 1857. It relates the fact that Capt. Russell's financial offer to Nidever to display the Lone Woman in San Francisco and other towns was rejected. Capt. Trussil of Santa Barbara had also made a similar offer of $1,000, according to Nidever in his report to Murray.

Tenney prefaces "Hermit of San Nicolas" [P112, 1907], by saying, "What little has been published about San Nicholas has long been out of print, and is now inaccessible to the reading public."

His writeup is fairly accurate, if not thorough. He used Thompson and West and the Boston paper's 1811 account of Boardman and Pope's trip to San Nicolas. But should there be a need to choose what is to be read, it would not be this 1907 version of the story.

O. M. Paul in 1911 used the same title as the 1853 *Daily Alta California*, "Female Robinson Crusoe." He told us that Jeffries went to San Nicolas a second time with Nidever to find the woman, but this cannot be substantiated.

It is interesting, however, that Paul began his article in a most unusual fashion,

It was at this time that the event occurred which the writer gives verbatim as told him by an old English sailor on the water front of New York City, at the time reporter on a daily journal of the great metropolis. The story was substantiated by an old log-book in the possession of the sailorman . . .

Since but one logbook reference exists, Phelps' of 1841, one wonders about this second reference some seventy years later. In some ways the account follows the salient facts rather carefully. Yet, one does wonder. Perhaps these words were but a journalistic beginning to an article, and should be dismissed as such.

There is a Stephen Bowers' file [M22] in the Southwest Museum. And in it is found a manuscript:

In November, 1915, I met at Alamos Harbor, Santa Cruz Island, George Nidever, 70 or more years of age. He was there (with his wife) engaged in crawfishing. His father, Capt. George Nidever, brought the lone Indian woman from San Nicolas Island to Santa Barbara in 1854. The son, though then a small boy, remembers

having seen the woman. Nidever told me that when he was about 10 years old he went to San Nicolas with Capt. who went there to kill the dogs on the island and that all were shot that could be found. I presume this was done so that the island might be safely stocked with sheep. He told me that the dogs were of the *Alaskan breed!*

This reference seems to be important for the Lone Woman story from but one standpoint: the name of one of the games being played by the actors in this drama could have been thoughts of "sheep raising on San Nicolas," not otter hunting, which instigated the removal of the Indians in 1835. The amazing thing about this above first-person comment is that the dates would place George Nidever and his son George on San Nicolas in 1857 for the dog-shooting—the same year that Kimberly probably left Santa Cruz Island for San Nicolas, which he stocked with sheep.

Dr. Jones had gone to both San Nicolas and Santa Rosa Island in 1901 for archaeological work. Seemingly, he felt that his knowledge of San Nicolas was above average for accuracy and quantity, and that it should be contributed in some manner. It was for that reason that he wrote to Lummis, editor of *Land of Sunshine*, to see if he would like to publish the material.

But we hear about Jones' contributions through the Southwest Museum's *Masterkey*, Vol. 43, 1969 [J207], and Heizer. It was Jones who furnished much of the material for the University of California's Archaeological Report #55.

In a footnote on page 87 of the Jones journal, Dr. Heizer said, "Deleted here is a lengthy account with long quotations from published sources of the Lone Woman of San Nicolas. All of these have been cited and reproduced [elsewhere]."

In this same *Masterkey* article, it was said that a Mr. Charles Merritt of Santa Barbara was the brother-in-law of M. M. Kimberly, and

In 1866 Mr. Merritt found a cave in which the lone woman had lived, and in it were a number of her former possessions, still in a fairly good state of preservation. He mentioned a garment of some sort, made of a kind of netting fashioned from sinew and covered with feathers fastened on with sinew, some arrow-points, stone knives, and a few abalone pearls. There were no pictographs or markings on the walls of the cave, at that time, though the walls were smoke-blackened.

PIECES OF EIGHT

We can but wonder about two things: 1. When did Kimberly stock San Nicolas Island with sheep (Jones said about 1853), and 2. Why did the above quoted information not come sooner to the attention of others. There is a long stretch of time between 1866 and 1901.

The *Santa Barbara News Press* was the bearer of good news on February 20, 1944 [M93]. Research students at the Mission Santa Barbara discovered Juana María's burial record in the Mission archives. Where previously Father Engelhardt [B24, 1965], had said this record did not exist, it was finally located:

> On the 19 of October of 1853 I gave ecclesiastical burial in this cemetery to the mortal remains of Juana María an Indian brought from the Island of San Nicolas, and since there was no one who understood her language she was baptised conditionally by Father Sánchez; and that this may stand as true I sign it. Father José María de Jesús González.

The entry is the 1,183rd in the record book and appears opposite page 114. Later [B24], Father Geiger made the remark, "When she died, González Rubio conducted her funeral services and buried her in the Mission cemetery. The location of her grave is unknown . . ."

Arthur Woodward [B62], said that in 1939-40 he went to San Nicolas Island. While there, he followed Ellison's account of the route taken in 1853 by Carl Dittmann and George Nidever while seeking the Lone Woman. They finally located her in the Corral Harbor area.

Woodward gave about fifteen pages to Juana María, sometimes using quotes from her discoverers, sometimes using third person. His bibliography is excellent, as well as his understanding of the subject matter.

Too many early Californians had found the islands to be lucrative. "Pieces of Eight," "Pieces of Eight," said the green parrot, the smuggler, the poacher, the fishermen, the otter hunters, and the stock raisers. And Juana María's life was caught in the cross current of it all. God rest your soul, Juana María!

LONE WOMAN
Abandoned, August, 1835
Found, August, 1853
Taken to Santa Barbara, end of August, 1853

JUANA MARÍA
Baptised by Father Sánchez, mid-October, 1853
Burial by Father González, October 19, 1853
Nidever plot, Mission cemetery

Bibliography Connected with
"The Lone Woman of San Nicolas," 1835-1853

1841		Phelps, Logbook of the *Alert* [See U13]
1841	B17	N. Dawson, *California in '41, Texas in '51, Memoirs of N. Dawson*, pvtly. pntd.
1849		"A Woman's Log of 1849," *Overland Monthly*, 1890 [See J367]
1853		*Daily Democratic State Journal*, Oct. 13, 1853 [See U13]
1853		*Daily Alta California*, Nov. 13, 1853 [See U13]
1856	*P27**	C. J. W. Russell, "Narrative of a Woman who was Eighteen Years Alone upon the Island of San Nicolas, Coast of California," *Hutchings' Calif. Mag.*
1856	M69	"A California Crusoe," *San Francisco Evening Bulletin*
1856	M96	J. J. Warner, "Interesting Narrative," *Los Angeles Star*
1856		*Santa Barbara Gazette* [See U13]
1856	M70	"Further Particulars of the California Crusoe," *San Francisco Evening Bulletin*
1856	M81	"Further Particulars of the California Crusoe," *Sacramento Union*
1856		Alexander S. Taylor, *California Farmer* [See U13]
1857		*California Academy of Science* [See J367]
1857	M51	*Golden Era* [See J367]
1857	P29	Anonymous, "The Indian Woman of San Nicolas," *Hutchings' Calif. Mag.*
1872	P79	Josephine Walcott, "Hona María," *Overland Monthly*
1878	*Ms*	*The Life and Adventures of George Nidever, 1802-1883*, E. F. Murray, reporting [Bancroft Lby.; See also B51 and U13]
1878	*Ms*	Carl Dittmann's *Narrative of a Seafaring Life on the Coast of California*, E. F. Murray, reporting
1879	M84	"Left Alone on a Desert Island for Eighteen Years; California's Feminine Crusoe," *Pioneer*, San Jose, Calif.
1880	*P123*	Emma Hardacre, "Eighteen Years Alone," *Scribner's Monthly*
1883	B70	Thompson and West, Pub., *History of Santa Barbara and Ventura Counties*, Ch. 17
1892	M95	Stephen Bowers, "Lone Woman of San Nicolas Island," *Ventura Weekly Observer*
1892	M27	Stephen Bowers, "The Lone Woman of San Nicolas"
1893	P15	James M. Gibbons, "The Wild Woman of San Nicolas Island," *Calif. Illus. Mag.*, C. F. Holder, Ed.
(1901)	J207	Philip Mills Jones, "San Nicolas Island Archaeology in 1901," *Masterkey* (ed. by R. F. Heizer)
1907	P112	W. A. Tenney, "Hermit of San Nicolas," *Pacific Monthly*
1911	P99	O. M. Paul, "Female Robinson Crusoe," *Overland Monthly*
1915	M22	Stephen Bowers File, Southwest Museum
1937	*B51*	*The Life and Adventures of George Nidever, 1802-1883*, Ed. by William H. Ellison, U. of C., Berkeley
1944	M93	*Santa Barbara News Press*
(1949)	B24	O. F. M. Maynard Geiger, *Mission Santa Barbara, 1782-1965*
1957	B62	Arthur Woodward, "Juana María; sidelights on the Indian occupation of San Nicolas Island," in *The Pacific Northwesterner*
1961	*U13*	"Original Accounts of the Lone Woman of San Nicolas Island," *Arch. Survey*, U. of C., Berkeley

*Note: Code number and date in italic indicates a work of superior importance.

Lone Woman Story, Characters

NAME: From	Married to	Trade, Remarks	Comments
DR. S. B. BRINKERHOFF, (1823-1880): New York, 1852 at age 29	Lucy A. Noyes, 1877 at age 54	Medical doctor; Tended Lone Woman until her death at Nidever home	"the silent benefactor of the poor . . . was threatened with financial ruin at the hands of those whose benefactor he had been. He never recovered from the shock; . . . We miss the enterprising citizen, the good doctor, the general companion, the true friend" [B70]
LUIS T. BURTON, (? -1880): Tennessee, 1831 w/Wolfskill party, settled in Santa Barbara	María Antonia, 1839 (2nd wife) niece of Carlos Carrillo	Mercantile business for 30 years, otter hunter, farmer	Nearly killed by robbers; nursed to health by Carrillos; with Sparks, 1835, removed Indians from San Nicolas; 1835, hunted on Wm. G. Dana license; 1860, bought "Burton Mound" from A. F. Hinchman (on beach); acquired wealth
WILLIAM GOODWIN DANA, (1797-1858): Originally from Boston, then Hawaii, 1826	María Josefa, 1828, daughter of Carlos Carrillo	Merchant, otter hunter, farmer, stock raiser	Cousin, Richard Henry Dana; Alcalde, 1836; held other offices; owned *Waverly*, 1827-28; built 33-ton schooner *Santa Barbara*, 1829, for trade and otter hunting; co-owner, *La Fama*, with Carlos Carrillo; grantee, Nipomo Rancho, 1837, 38,887.71 acres
DR. L. N. DIMMICK, (? -1884): Arrived California, 1872		Medical doctor	Thompson and West [B70], used Dimmick's notes about Nidever and the Lone Woman
CARL DITTMANN, (1822- ?): Prussia, 1844; alias "Charlie Brown"		Whaler-sailor, deserter, otter hunter	Instrumental in locating Lone Woman on San Nicolas Island. Interviewed by Hardacre
EMMA HARDACRE: Arrived California, 1876			Interviewed Nidever, Dittmann, Jeffries, *et al*; wrote story of Lone Woman for *Scribner's Mo.*, 1880
JOHN COFFIN JONES, (1796-1861): Originally from Boston, commuted, 1830-1838, settled from Hawaii, 1844-46	Manuela, 1838 (1820-1900) daughter of Carlos Carrillo	Consul—Hawaii, merchant, otter hunter, ship owner	1821-30, representative, Marshall & Wildes, in Hawaii; wife was owner of ½ Santa Rosa Island and claimant for La Calera Rancho; chartered *Crusader*, 1832; chartered *Convoy*, 1832, 1834; on coast, 1830-40; co-owner, *Bolivar* (renamed *Oajaca*), 1843; owned brigs *Loriot*, *Volunteer*, *Louisa*, & schooners *Harriet Blanchard*, *Avon*, *Griffon*, *Rasselas*; chartered cutter *Margarita*

42

NAME: From	Married to	Trade, Remarks	Comments
GEORGE NIDEVER, (1802-1883): Tennessee, Arkansas, 1834 w/Capt. Walker	Sinforosa Sanchez, 1841 (? -1892)	Trapper, bear hunter, Indian fighter, otter hunter, stock raiser, sheep grazer	Hunted on Wm. G. Dana license, 1835; promised land by Alvarado, 1836; promised ½ Huasma Rancho by Sparks; 1840, purchased "Burton Mound" from Joseph Chapman, sold to Hinchman, Santa Barbara attorney, 1850; 1850-70, w/ 2 sons, cattle and sheep on San Miguel Island; Thomas Robbins, his tenant; 1878, he and wife lived with youngest daughter just outside Santa Barbara; interviewed by Hardacre
THOMAS ROBBINS, (? -1857): Nantucket Island, 1827	Encarnación, 1834, daughter of Carlos Carrillo	Owned a store, 1830, 1st Mate, *Waverly*	Commanded *California*, 1837-39; grantee, Santa Catalina Island, 1846; grantee, Rancho Las Positas y Calera, adjoining Santa Barbara
DR. JAMES BARRON SHAW: England, 1853	Helen A. Green, 1861, Londoner	Supt., Santa Cruz Island Co., 1853-69, for Barron, Forbes & Co.	Had most stylish residence in Santa Barbara. Was seen by Lone Woman on arrival. He was on a horse
ISAAC J. SPARKS, (1804-1867): Maine, 1832 w/Ewing Young's 2nd trapping group; to Santa Barbara, 1833	Mary Ayers, Scottish	1836, owned trading store, otter hunter; see Santa Rosa Is., helped to remove Indians from San Nicolas	Built first brick house in Santa Barbara; was 1st Postmaster of Santa Barbara, 1836; purchased Julien Foxen home, 1843; grantee Huasmo Rancho though not married to a Californian; grantee, Pismo Rancho and 5 others
ALPHEUS B. THOMPSON, (1797-1869): Originally from Maine, commuted, 1825-34 from Hawaii to California	Francisca, 1834, (1815-1841) daughter of Carlos Carrillo	Merchant, otter hunter, farmer, stock raiser, supercargo, shipbuilder	Nephew of Capt. Dixie Wildes, uncle of Dixie Wildes Thompson; wife was owner of ½ Santa Rosa Island; supercargo, *Washington*, 1825-30; co-owner & supercargo, brig *Bolivar*, 1832-40; owner of *Famer* (*La Fama*?), 1842; supercargo, *Loriot*, 1833-34
CAPT. ISAAC WILLIAMS, (? -1856): New York; from New Mexico with E. Young, 1832, to Los Angeles; called "Julian"	Antonia María de Jesús, daughter of Antonio Lugo	Farmer, trader, trapper, stock raiser	Collector for port of San Pedro; inherited Chino Rancho, San Bernardino County, granted to Lugo, 1841; took an Indian from San Nicolas, 1835, to live with him

San Clemente

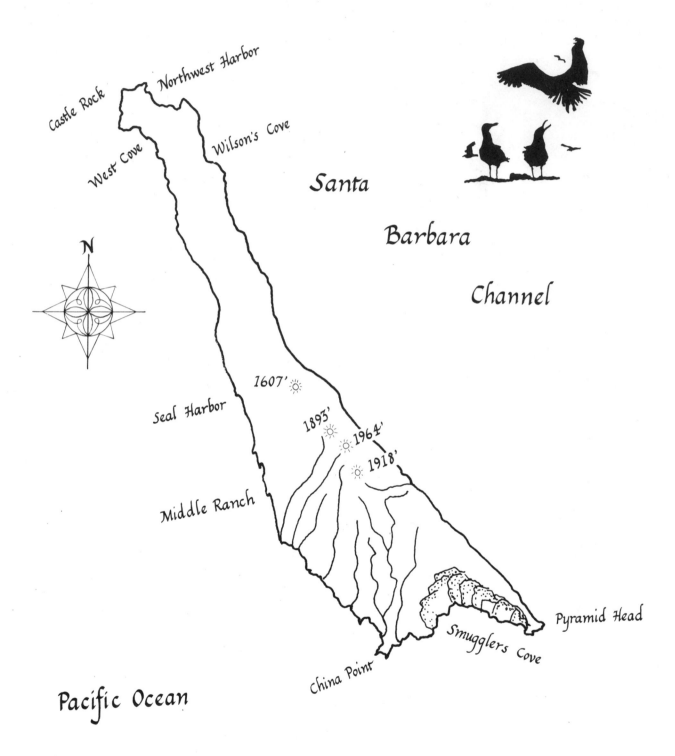

Castle Rock

Northwest Harbor

West Cove

Wilson's Cove

Santa

Barbara

Channel

N

1607'

Seal Harbor

1893'

1964'

1918'

Middle Ranch

Pyramid Head

Smugglers Cove

China Point

Pacific Ocean

San Clemente

Description—People—Place Names

Each of the islands is unique, and has deservedly received unique attention by writers, scientists and other scholars. However, for its size San Clemente has some of the most excellent descriptive material available.

The earliest description is Cheetham's 1888 account of his trip to San Clemente Island when he served as a cabin boy for Captain Peterson of yacht *San Diego*, not published until 1940 [J368].

They landed at GALLAGHER'S COVE and as the story proceeds, we hear of the hermit Gallagher, something about the fauna of the island, and the types of Indian artifacts to be found. He mentions a petrified forest to the north; Smith [N40], said there were petrifications opposite WILSON COVE, some of the former trees being six inches in diameter.

Heading for Avalon, Santa Catalina, the excursion terminated with an air of conviviality, for there was a dance in progress at the Metropole [Hotel], and there was "Hardware on Ice" to be found on a barge anchored in the cove between Sugar Loaf and the hotel. Shatto, who owned the island, did not allow liquor to be sold on Santa Catalina.

Britton's article in *Land of Sunshine*, just a few pages long [P47, 1897], has San Clemente sharing descriptive material with the other islands. He referred to smuggling at "Smugglers' Cove," to shallow tide pools in the mouths of wooded cañons, to caves and their Indian artifacts, which included "dried bits of hair and flesh of dogs . . . buried in bags of woven eel-grass." He does not overlook the Irish sheepman, Aleck O'Leary, the osprey screaming overhead, and the booms of the sea, as it enters and leaves the ocean caves.

Ruth Tangier Smith's "One of California's Desert Islands," is also a *Land of Sunshine* prize; she furnished a tiny map and several worthy photos, one of them, "The Resting Herds" [P51, 1899].

Ms. Smith made her acquaintance with the island while on a geological trip with William Tangier Smith. After an uncomfortable crossing, they landed at Wilson's Cove to the northeast, where Gallagher had his cabin.

Some of her description included the level crest of the ridge, the flora of the desert areas, and some on the island fauna, lizards, and such. Information about the terraces, and the cañons which cut across them, comes to a conclusion as she said "Good-bye," to Gallagher and San Clemente Island. This trip to the island had been in 1896.

We sailed out of the cove in the sunset, and this was our last view of San Clemente; the water was silver blue, the rugged cliffs rising above them, black against the saffron sky, and nestled in the shadow of those beetling hills, the little cabin, pathetic in its loneliness, with the sturdy old man sitting on the porch, his dogs and fowls around him, watching the vessel out of sight.

Flynn of the U. S. Navy, has the longest of these descriptive accounts [N50]. He brings in slightly more history than do the other authors; actually he had more opportunity to know more history; but he did dwell on the descriptive.

We have tried skiing down these steep, slippery banks and it is great sport . . . At low tide you will find large amounts of asphalt oozing out from beneath the rocks, . . . in one small area no larger than a house, we picked fourteen different varieties of wild flowers . . . Seal Rock, one of the biggest seal rookeries on the coast, . . . is protected from man and well protected from the sea . . . On the east side of the island the only point of interest is Mosquito Harbor. Here is the most picturesque spot on the island; the little harbor is snuggled at the foot of towering cliffs that rise 1,800 feet . . . The Marine

Gardens at Mosquito Harbor are very beautiful . . .

The ravens, the meadow lark, the bald eagle, the quail, and many other species come in for their share of comments. Flynn ended his nine pages of concentrated discourse by giving the names of various lessees of the island, then concluded with,

While standing on Mount Thirst, the highest point on the island, one can survey it from end to end and it is hard to imagine how the Indian came out here and chiseled out an existence for himself while the white man has to rely on help from the mainland to subsist. One wonders which race was really civilized.

Outstanding features such as caves, canyons, cliffs and water appear to take precedence in the writings of Smith [N40], Davidson [N34], even Holder [B38], thus they furnish the base of information for such areas.

Pieces of Eight, as this book's title, comes to mind when dealing with material on San Clemente—with emphasis on "pieces." Faced with fragmentaries of thirty or more articles, it is only by fitting such fragmentaries together that the writer can come up with anything resembling a whole; such is this jigsaw puzzle section.

After some geological overview, Smith remarked that Mt. Cortez [N40, 1896; M40, 1925], now known as Mt. Thirst, is the highest point on the island, being 1964 feet high. A little to the east of center,

the descent to either extremity of the island is so gradual that a horse and wagon could easily travel the greater part of the entire length . . . the main water-shed lies very near the northern coast, and is continuous from one end of the island to the other. From this watershed, for most of its length, the descent on the northern side is very abrupt—in one case amounting to 1,800 feet in half a mile. Along the higher parts of the northern coast there are only two or three places where the shore may be reached from above; and although one may descend some of the larger canyons on this side for several hundred feet, the descent is sooner or later checked by waterfalls of considerable height.

Some of San Clemente's canyons resemble miniatures of the Colorado [J249, 1897]. This was Grinnell's thought. Trask [M135, 1906], mentioned Grand Cañon with its caves and goats, as it stands in tiers for a thousand feet.

Everyone who has visited San Clemente has remarked about the number of caves on the island. In fact, Holder called the caves the most prominent feature of the island [B38]. Trask said that there were caves between Gallagher's and the isthmus at NORTHWEST ANCHORAGE [M187].

Holder referred to the tiny caves in the center of the island where he saw little lambs lying. The caves were just their size and Holder suggested this rift, home for the lambs, be named CAÑON OF THE CAVES. Perhaps this is Trask's GRAND CAÑON. It is not until CAPE PINCHOT [Cape Horn?] is rounded from the northwest, near the northeast tip of the island, that he says the coastal region of caves is found,

> Here is a series of six or seven very large caverns, just at the water's edge and running in some forty or fifty feet, literally cut out by the sea. One of these is a two-storied cave; that is, the cave has a cellar down through which one can pass and reach the ocean . . . One large cave, which must have been fifty feet across the opening, stood out half-way up the mountain . . . One afternoon, while lying off a picturesque cañon near the "spring" on the east end, one of the party began to fire at a mark, when out from a cave half-way up the mountain began to stream sheep in pairs, single, and in companies of a dozen or more, . . . There are from ten to fifteen thousand sheep on the island, and they have seized upon these caves as homes . . .

Davidson said that there were more canyons on the north slopes than on the south side, but that on the southeast the canyons were deeper. The sides of the canyons and mesas are covered with cactus of several varieties, and a low growing thorny bush.

The canyon bottoms and the ravine beds contain clumps of bushes and trees. One author mentions a clump of wild plum trees growing around a spring at the north in an altitude of about 1500 feet [J384, 1906]. Another refers to thickets of wild cherry bushes in the ravines, which in a few places reach a height of fifteen feet or more. Some tree varieties are endemic to the islands.

It was Davidson who has somewhat unclearly stated that

> The only spring of water on the island is at the head of a small gulch on the northeastern face, about midway between the northwest and southeast ends and just at the foot of the southern end of the highest plateau [N34].

Some have remarked differently—for other than three successful wells on San Clemente [N40] (one at NORTHWEST HARBOR with a windmill [N50], one at the south end with a windmill [P47; N50], and an artesian well at the east end [J334-5]), two springs to the north and two to the south, the island is "without" water.

There are water holes or "tanks" at the foot of waterfalls in the recesses and beds of the deepest gorges. Sheep and goats have worn paths to the water contained in these natural cavities, sharing it with the birds and other natural creatures, including man.

LORENZO TANK on the west was made of cement and held 200,000 gallons of water. This tank was connected with a sluice from the middle of the island, and was used for catching rain. There was another tank at EAGLE RANCH, with a barn, house and corrals [N50]. West side dams were also built by the herders in order to catch water for their flocks. There is a natural tank near the center of the island [N34].

Although there are relatively few beaches on the island, some may be found on both sides of the isthmus near the northwest end [N34]. Flynn was more specific and mentioned Northwest Harbor as having one of the finest swimming beaches on the coast [N50]. There are sandy beaches about CHINA POINT, SMUGGLERS' COVE [N40], and a smaller one at HORSE BEACH [B73].

San Clemente Island is about eighteen miles long in a northwest and southeast direction, and has an average width of two and a half miles. The bolder, more rocky and higher part is near the southeast end [B114, 1917], with the slope toward the northwest, which end is covered extensively with high sand dunes [N41, 1877].

Holder spoke of a forty-foot deep crater at the extreme northwest, the remains of an extinct volcano. Rider also mentioned this phenomena; both remark that the crater looked like a chimney. It is believed, however, that Rider obtained some of his material from Holder. (Rider is coded "M40," but should have been "B" code.)

The NORTHWEST POINT of the island is the "very low and sharp extremity of a single terraced head," the head being nearly one and one-half miles long and rising 192 feet above the sea [N34]. One-sixth of a mile from the point the land is but twenty-one feet above the sea.

The northwest end does not receive the amount of rain that the southeast does. Even then there are two fresh water ponds, but they dry up in the summer [B114, 1917].

It is said that the storms frequently advance toward the island from the south and settle over the higher parts. The western advance of clouds changes its course and swings around, giving most of the moisture back to the southeast [N34].

No doubt this helps to account for the sand dune area of the northwest and the depth of the stream canyons on the southeast of the island. Mrs. Trask had also noted this differentiation in the amounts of rainfall for the two parts of the island.

On the northern edge of these dunes overlooking Northwest Harbor and the cape is where Griesbach found a very large accumulation of what he termed "fulgurites." Also near Northwest Harbor lies an area of scrubland and sand dunes [J254], where hundreds of acres of shell mounds once existed.

As many as twenty skeletons have been taken from the cave by archaeologists [J254, 1947]. Woodward gave us the name BIG DOG CAVE, and described it as being about seventy feet across the mouth, thirty-four feet in depth, with a ceiling of perhaps seventeen feet [J6, 1941; U41, 1959; B73, 1959]. Two ceremonially-wrapped chickens were found [B128, 1941], and "the desiccated body of a large dog with tawny yellow hair. The animal had been lovingly wrapped in a sea otter fur robe . . . we dubbed the place Big Dog Cave."

Holder referred to a vast cave eaten out of the rock as being so large that it formed a small harbor [B38]. It was here, Smuggler's Cove, that some Chinese abalone-hunters had made their headquarters about 1890. Holder continued on page 356,

> Twenty years ago I landed at San Clemente Island and found that a clever old Chinese genius was carrying on a twofold business, making it pay both going and coming. The old Chinaman was a smuggler, but on the surface he was an abalone fisherman. He made his headquarters on San Clemente Island, a place rarely visited in winter. Some one who owned a little schooner brought Chinamen up the coast from Mexico and landed them at San Clemente—an easy thing to do when the Government had only one revenue cutter on the coast, and that up north all the time. As soon as the men landed they began to collect abalones, and the day I stumbled on their camp they had hundreds piled up in heaps—shells and meat. Upon seeing me a number of men ran for a big tent. I ran after them, and when I reached the tent I threw open

the fly. They were a demoralized lot of smugglers. I laughed, and that raised their spirits; they had taken me for a revenue officer.

> The abalone shells were shipped to Germany, the meat went to China. Every week, I fancy, a few Chinamen were sent over to the mainland in an old junk that was always drifting up and down the channel. . . . The old junk would run into San Pedro in the morning, and her Chinese crew, *with certificates*, would land the crop of abalones, after which they would set sail again for San Clemente.

There are a couple of noteworthy comments about the dune area. Back in 1877 Schumacher [N41], said that he

> was informed by a gentleman of the United States Coast Survey of the existence of large shell-mounds on the island, especially of one located on the high dune, of great circumference.

Phil C. Orr had something to say about the dunes in "Island Hopping" [J270, 1949],

> Crossing the high ridge on the east side, the island slopes away to an entirely new vista of windswept desert. High sand dunes that only need a camel and an Arab to complete the calendar picture effect of the Sahara, are interspersed with the greyish ancient Indian mounds, where shells, bones, broken bowls and occasionally the skeleton of a long dead Indian are weathering out.

According to Davidson, eastward of the head's northern termination lies CLEMENTE ANCHORAGE, three-fourths of a mile wide and one-half mile deep. There, he said, the Coast and Geodetic Survey had their secondary astronomical station of 1852, on a grassy rise. Clemente Anchorage sounds as though it could be Trask's Nor'west Anchorage mentioned earlier, or Northwest Harbor.

S. E. Flynn was a Lieutenant Commander in the U. S. Navy and served on San Clemente; what is more important, he wrote "The History of San Clemente Island," published in the *Proceedings of the U. S. Naval Institute* [N50, 1942]. Here is one of the things that he said about Northwest Harbor,

> At Northwest Harbor lived George Holland [Howland] for 25 years; he had several hundred acres under cultivation, raising beans and small grain, and had a windmill and well that pumped fresh water, these are still in use by the Navy in 1936.

And according to Flynn, Trask, and Holder, the "Banyan," *Lycium richii,* related to the currant family, was found at Northwest Harbor. The only other Banyan known to the islands lives on Santa Catalina Island.

DRIGG'S COVE is eastward of the head's [cape's] southern point and lies directly across from Clemente Anchorage, with a small connecting valley between the two coves. This second cove on the west side afforded "a partial lee from the westerly swell. A line of sand sweeps over the point into the beach at the cove" [N34]. Drigg's Cove must be WEST COVE.

In 1909 [J120], Mr. Linton mentioned a HOWLAND'S RANCH on HOWLAND'S BAY [probably less than] four miles from the west end [J118], thus giving this cove a third name. Holder visited Mr. Charles Howland there in 1907; Howland had a long lease on the island.

Another WEST END "rancho" was where Johnny Robearts lived [M135, 1906]. "Johnny brought a few goats to the West End but they wandered into the caves between Gallagher's and the isthmus at the Nor'west Anchorage, eating cactus for much of their sustenance" [J335, 1904].

Mrs. Trask also said that "there is but one man who knows San Clemente Island. That is John Robearts, and he has lived on the island over twenty years." This means that John, sheepherder, went to San Clemente about 1884. At the time Mrs. Trask mentioned this, there were two sheepherders on the island [J334, 1904].

Mrs. Trask named one gorge ROBEARTS' GORGE, "in commemoration of his heroic explorations for the love of nature in its sternest forms . . . [the gorge's] pinnacles uplifted for a thousand feet, it lies a half hour's row westward from Mosquito Harbor" [J335].

Before Robearts, Don Alonzo, a picturesque old Spaniard, held forth on the west side ranch. According to Holder, Don Alonzo had one of the best conducted sheep ranches in the country [B38].

According to Mrs. Trask, Tom Gallagher was really the first herder on the island; she uses the date of 1868 for his coming. Homer Earle said that Gallagher arrived in 1865 [P44]. Smith referred to one permanent inhabitant of thirty years [N40, 1897]. [See also Santa Catalina's Isthmus report for more on Gallagher.] It was also Homer Earle who said that a Peter Jensen lived with Gallagher in 1896, both of them tending sheep.

It is noted that the Santa Barbara Deed Book F, in mentioning the sale of Santa Cruz Island by Wm. E. Barron, *et al,* to Justinian Caire, *et al,* says that Thomas J. Gallagher was involved in the 1869 purchase. Can this really be the same Gallagher, a former resident of Santa Catalina, and so well known as a San Clemente character?

The Historical Society of Southern California gives us our earliest account of Gallagher. This was information of 1888 by Cheetham and reads,

> We saw a man standing in front of the cabin. We learned afterwards that his name was Gallagher . . . As to the cause of his being a hermit, they were not able to ascertain anything. He was a man of intelligence. The first thing he asked for was for books and magazines. But he was very reticent concerning his own life. In fact he refused to give any information touching his part.
>
> We soon learned that the island contained about twenty thousand head of sheep, which belonged to a firm in Los Angeles. That it was their custom to send a ship over once a year with men to corral and shear the sheep. That no other vessel had ever visited the island up to that time. In fact, Gallagher said that we were the first pleasure party that he had ever seen visiting San Clemente [J368, 1940].

Mrs. Trask, in her article for the *Los Angeles Times,* remarked that Gallagher took a pair of goats to San Clemente, "and today goats are common there at the East End; and in all the caves of the Grand Cañon . . . their little heads are to be seen as though looking down at you from the windows of their homes" [M135, 1906]. Of course, de Mofras reported goats in 1844, twenty-five years earlier [B48].

Dr. Holder added his bit about this old-timer when he said [B38],

> The San Clemente Channel is a rough place at times, yet Gallagher crossed it with a skiff with a flour-sack sail, and the last time I saw him he came sailing into Avalon Bay with his poor skiff, a goat, four or five hens and a dog. These he boarded out until he made up his mind to return, which he did at night, rowing the skiff the [twenty] miles.

A reminiscent anecdote comes from the *Catalina Islander* in 1920. Part of the yarn went,

> After dinner [we] sat around the fire again, listening to the yarns of the men, and old Gal-

lagher, a herder, who had lived on the island many years . . . Few people visited the island in those days, and Gallagher's life must have been a Crusoe-like existence. Sometimes he remained on the island a year or two, accumulating wages and merit; then he would be seized with a desire to leave, and would row across the twenty-mile channel to Santa Catalina in a skiff, take the steamer from Avalon, and in Los Angeles distribute his wealth; a week or so later he would again be king of San Clemente.

GALLAGHER'S COVE is about four miles south of the north end or two and one-half miles east-southeast from Clemente Anchorage [N34]. According to Ruth T. Smith, Tom Gallagher's place was just above the shore at WILSON'S COVE [Gallagher's] and "near it are the few rough buildings used by the sheepmen" [P51, 1899].

At Wilson's Cove rain water was collected in tanks of considerable size, furnishing the only supply of water at this point [N40].

From Davidson [N34],

The anchorage may be recognized by a long, low ranch-house on the western side of the valley facing the water, and a few yards from high water mark. To the eastward of this ranch-house about one hundred yards are the corrals and shearing sheds of the company which own the sheep on the island. A wooden water-tank adjoining the house has fallen into disuse, and water, as well as wood, is brought from the mainland during the shearing season.

Should we follow the windward side of the island on a southerly course, we would return to West Cove. The land back of it is level, something of a plateau, and had been under cultivation for many years by the white inhabitants of the island [N50]. Further down are sand dunes, some of them forty to fifty feet in height. More dunes are at Seal Harbor.

The next place names mentioned in the literature are EEL POINT and EEL COVE, where McKusick and Warren located middens and skeletons [U41, 1959]. These two locations appear to be somewhat above midway on the west side of the island, with WALL ROCK CANYON about one and eight-tenth miles southeast of Eel Point [J156, 1963].

But in 1889 Davidson used the names SEAL HARBOR POINT [MIDDLE POINT and SOUTHERN POINT], not Eel Point or Eel Cove [N34]. According to him, Middle Point is half way between SEAL HARBOR and Southern Point, with five miles north to Seal Harbor

and five miles south to Southern Point.

Seal Harbor, he said, is about midway on the west side between the two ends of the island. The southern point is an irregular rocky cliff that is three and two-third miles from the nearest part of PYRAMID HEAD, which is on the southeastern point of the narrow island [N34].

Just a few years later, Smith's map for the United States Geological Survey, 1897, used the place names of Seal Harbor, MIDDLE RANCH, and China Point at the southern extremity. No doubt these names are interchangeable with Davidson's.

Middle Ranch, also known as EAGLE RANCH [B38], HALF WAY HOUSE, or HAY RANCH, is in the middle and western portion of San Clemente. Through Middle Ranch Canyon the stream comes down, and according to Smith, there is a fault in the canyon that has a throw of some thirty feet over which the water drops. Through this same canyon one finds excellent horseback riding [N50]; on reaching Seal Harbor to the north, Indian artifacts were to be found [U31, 1893; N50].

Wall Rock Canyon is the second canyon south of Seal Cove, with BOX CANYON the next main canyon south of MIDDLE RANCH CANYON, and HORSE CANYON the next one south from Box Canyon. Olmstead mentioned a major fault on the west side of HORSE COVE, near the south side of the island [N47, 1958].

From Seal Harbor to China Point there are seals, a few otter, and sea elephants [N50]. In 1928 Paul Bonnot wrote an article about the Sea Lions of California [C2].

The article offers some historical background for the need of protecting the sea lion population. There is a short anecdote about a half-drowned Steller sea lion at Seal Harbor, with the photos and much of the remaining material dealing with San Miguel Island and the 1927 mass slaughtering there.

Between Horse Canyon to the east and CHINA CANYON to the west, there is a road southward to CHINA POINT. Murbarger spoke of sand dunes at CHINA COVE where Indian artifacts have been found. Grinnell said there were wild cherry bushes at China Point [J249, 1897]. Since the area is also abalone-covered [B73], China Point appears to offer much of interest.

Bonnot placed CASTLE ROCK at the southwest end of San Clemente [C2]; Trask mentioned a SOU'WEST'S ARROWHEAD POINT.

Smith remarked that the cliffs on the southern side

of the island are comparatively low, with but an average of twenty-six feet in height [N40]. Water holes, found at the edge of the plateaus where the cliffs begin, are made by whirling rocks in the holes during heavy rainfalls [N34]. Since many of these holes are inaccessible, they held the carcasses of sheep having unsuccessfully tried to reach the water.

The second canyon beyond China Canyon carries the name of RED CANYON. It is here that a narrow sheet of volcanic ash may be found [N40]. It is also at Red Canyon that the best example exists for a stream that has cut down to sea level. It was in Red Canyon, too, that Chinetti was found dead—the old-timer who hid his wages, paid in gold.

Beyond China Point at the south, and somewhat nearer Smugglers' Cove eastward, is HORSE BEACH. Inland a short distance is a large deposit of "soft diatomaceous earth . . . In this material are imbedded large fossil marine mammals which have in places eroded out" [B73]. There is also an Indian cave [N50], which is large enough to furnish shelter for about fifty people [N40, 1896].

PYRAMID COVE lies about midway between China Point and Pyramid Head. There are two large gulches or ravines at the shoreline opening onto the beach, forming long stretches of sand.

> The eastern [gulch] has a pond of brackish water at its mouth near the beach . . . The "water-holes," or tanks of fresh water, up this gulch are about a quarter of a mile from the beach and contain from one to three thousand gallons of fresh, cold water. Barrels may be conveniently filled here and rolled to the beach [N34].

Others have remarked about SMUGGLERS' COVE [Pyramid Cove], one of them having been Max Miller [B108, 1959], in which he gave about three paragraphs to the *Itata* Affair of 1891. Chilean insurgents then used Pyramid Cove to transfer smuggled arms from the *Robert* and the *Minnie* to the *Itata* before the U. S. S. cruiser *Charleston* could do anything about the situation. Smugglers' Cove has been known by pirates, bootleggers, and others desiring to keep out of view of the authorities [N50].

Various ways have been used to describe the southern entrance to the ranch where Salvador Ramirez [Chinetti] lived. One said Chinetti's ranch was about midway of the southern shore [P51, 1899]. Another, the port of Chinetti's station was Smugglers' Cove near CAPE PAEZ [B38, 1910]. CHINETTI CANYON is the main canyon on the south and is in the middle of Pyramid Cove [J156, 1963]. And from another, "the mouth of Chinetti Canyon is at Pyramid Cove" [J350, 1946]. CAVE CANYON, south from Mt. Thirst, could be another name for Chinetti Canyon.

Ms. Smith described the setting for Chinetti's cabin [P51, 1899],

> About midway of the southern shore is a tiny cabin, in the lee of a great cliff, which hides it from the water on one side. The sea makes around it on the adjoining side, and even reaches almost under it in a large cave. In the house one can hear the water, as it roars and rushes through the cave, and feel the vibration as it beats, apparently directly underneath. Near the house is a well with a windmill (usually run by horse power) which supplies most of the sheep and cattle with water in the dry season. The water is so brackish that it seems at first impossible to drink it, but the cattle make half a day's journey to get it.

Chinetti worked for George Howland, as did others. His ranch

> includes about ten miles of the most God-forsaken country I have ever seen. This man did not see a human being perhaps once a month. He did not leave the island but once or twice a year. I remember Chinetti, at San Clemente, told me that the foxes would eat from his hand, and even come into his house [B38].

Mr. Flynn added something to the Chinetti story when he said [N50],

> Mr. Chennetti [*sic*] received $40 per month in gold and buried his wages somewhere in the vicinity of Pyramid Cove; he worked for Mr. Holland [*sic*] for many years and never went to town. He could neither read nor write and had no relatives. Mr. Chennetti was found dead at Red Canyon by Mr. Holland and he took the secret hiding place where he had buried his savings with him . . .

In the April 18, 1923, *Catalina Islander* there was a little writeup of Chinetti's death at about age seventy-four. He had worked on Santa Catalina Island for many years before leaving Avalon for Smugglers' Cove on San Clemente Island. Quoting the writer about Chinetti,

> on board of his little sailing boat he had three goats and a number of foxes. He said he was going to start a goat farm, and the foxes were going to be his pets.

Many island visitors, including Grinnell, 1897, used Smugglers' Cove and Chinetti's Ranch as their headquarters. Britton remarked [P47, 1897], that there was a windmill, tanks, troughs, and an automatic pump to supply water for the sheep and cattle scattered over most of the island. Trask said that the pumping plant was used in connection with a "brackish spring." Flynn used the term "Southside Well," where there was about twenty-five feet of water in 1936.

By moving eastward we come upon the south-easternmost point of the island known as Pyramid Head, so-called because from the distance this vast sandstone height reminds one of a pyramid [N34].

Trask described Pyramid Head as being at the EAST END [J334, 1904]. A little more interesting way of stating its location came from Woodward when he said, "the counterpart of China Point is Pyramid Head" [B73, 1959].

The northern shore of Pyramid Head is precipitous for about three miles [N34]. Caves are numerous as the conglomerate of this area breaks up, and under the effects of weather, thousands of caves of all sizes and shapes are produced [B38]. In many places the caves are so numerous that in the distance the cliffs appear to be honeycombed [N40, 1896].

At this east end there are stretches of sandy beaches with low outlying points. There is also an artesian well [J335]. In speaking of artesian wells, it is noteworthy enough to refer to a statement made by George C. Yount as early as 1833, "Clementina is destitute of water except as stands in basins of the Rocks—but when watered by artesian wells it will become immensely valuable" [J85].

He further remarked,

On the east side of the Island of Clemente, at very low tide, . . . a little more than half way down the Island, was found a ledge of rock projecting out into the sea, which was full of Gold— Doubtless the Island has since much washed away & the ledge must be quite under water except in extremely low tides.

On the east coast, Flynn found MOSQUITO HAR-BOR to be the most picturesque spot on the whole island [N50]. Holder must have had some same thoughts for he referred to the rain coming down at Mosquito Harbor, "displaying countless falls and cascades . . . seen only by the few fishermen caught here during the gale."

Mosquito Harbor is about four miles from the east end, 350 yards in circumference, and is protected by kelp of the ocean. In relation to Smugglers' Cove, it is almost directly opposite.

At the harbor the cliffs are extremely abrupt and precipitous. The cañon is called "Mosquito" because of water in the solid rock basins tending to serve as breeding ponds for mosquitoes [B38]. Another author said there were no mosquitoes on the island. Of course, the birds are there, too.

There is a tongue of land on the north side of the harbor and it is here that O'Leary's cabin was located. It was made of boards and shingles with a dry floor of pulverized stone [P47]. There is the house, comfortably-fitted, smaller buildings, two fig trees, a nice spring, and a marine garden—all of this at the foot of towering cliffs.

The hermit, Aleck O'Leary, had lived at Mosquito Harbor about four years by 1897. He was "a tall, polite, middle-aged Irishman" whose only companions were a "sky-terrier, two goats and a kitten" [P47, 1897].

In 1913, as a boy, Wheeler had visited Mosquito Harbor soon after Al Shade had established a small fish camp there. Shade had planted two fig trees just about that time, and the trees have lived there ever since. Probably there was enough water from the neary-by spring to keep the trees alive [N51, 1944].

The next one to have the camp was Snyder and he operated "Snyder Camp" from about 1916 to 1921. Then the camp became "Michaelis Camp," for Michaelis operated the camp for yachtsmen interested in the 'resort.' Zane Grey camped there in 1921.

Michaelis was also marshall of San Clemente, in order to keep peace between the Wool Co. and visiting fishermen. Michaelis had a marine specimen collection at the camp worth $20,000—before it burned in 1924 [M187].

Before concluding the general topic of locations and place names, the reader might profit by a listing of some of the lesser-known names: BEN WESTON COVE, CAPE HORN, POT'S VALLEY, a Japanese Camp for abalone drying, a board fence that crossed the island, SOUTH BAY, Grand Cañon, CHALK CLIFF CAÑON.

Cape Horn is "a great lava cape" [B38]. Is this cape at the north end? The board fence might have closed this north end from the sheep. Trask said that a tree daisy was to be found in Chalk Cliff Cañon; Flynn mentioned Chalk Canyon as the location of prehistoric animals [N50]. Holder referred to a gigantic sandspit on San Clemente [P115, 1896], and used Figure 1 to illustrate.

A newspaper article of 1926 spoke of South Bay being used as a base for hunting blue whales [M187], and Ben Weston Cove is referred to as having silver-mining shafts [N50].

Transfer of Lessee Title to San Clemente Island

It probably all began with papa, Captain William S. Howland, and his neighbor, Frank Whittley of Santa Catalina.

Whittley had gone to Santa Catalina about 1850 and had made some improvements on 'his property.' Howland went to that island around 1858. Both men had established squatters' rights, but James Lick did not like the idea. Many of the squatters were evicted through a lawsuit, 1868-72, but Howland, Harris, and Whittley were allowed to remain; by 1887 the Lick Trustees had granted them grazing rights.

Howland was a business man. According to the *Los Angeles Times* [M147], Captain William Howland had leased San Nicolas Island in 1875, and had 16,000 sheep on that island's fertile grazing land. By 1919 he had sold his lease to the Vail Bros., at which time there were about 11,000 sheep on the island.

Although exact dates are hard to come by for San Clemente Island, some approximations can be made. For more definite information as to when the San Clemente Sheep and Wool Company was formed, for instance, old Lease Books at the Los Angeles County Recorders Office could probably be consulted with success.

It is not difficult to accept Flynn's comment [N50], that Mr. Whitney [Whittley] and the Howlands raised sheep and/or horses on San Clemente, leasing the island for five years for the fee of $15,000. Although no date is given, this could have been as early as 1868 when Gallagher went to the island; he was still there in 1896. According to the *Morning Call*, 1883, there were 10,000 sheep on the island then.

The name is "Whitney" to Flynn, but a Frank Whittley and William Howland were friends, sheep or horse raisers, and squatters at the Isthmus, Santa Catalina Island. Gallagher was there, too. Flynn is the only person spelling the names "Whitney" and "Holland," perhaps enunciation errors.

By 1895 the Howland children were adults. By using a backward count on dates, and expecting Flynn to have obtained correct information from

Mrs. Pauline Blair, the Murphys, and George Willett of the Los Angeles County Museum, these earlier years would be within the time that Whittley and/or the Howlands were on San Clemente Island as lessees, or squatters, in their own right.

To include Flynn's information for other than the Howlands—the Vail Bros., the Smiths, then the younger Vail Brothers all had five year leases to graze sheep, before Mr. E. G. Blair and Penwell of Montana leased the island for twenty-five years in 1916 [B125, 1945].

Mr. and Mrs. Theo Murphy went to San Clemente with Blair, Mr. Murphy still riding the range in 1942, although sheep grazing had been discontinued in 1934.

Additional dates from the past might be helpful for the reader in gaining more of a time-sense about those living on the island.

In 1893 [P14], through *Californian Illustrated*, Walter Mayhew said that San Clemente was deserted "save by a single herder who gives welcome to the yachtsman."

Mr. Flynn has said that Mr. George Howland had lived on this island for twenty-five years, but we have no date as to when he arrived.

In 1903 Mrs. Trask was on the island. In her report she used the title, "San Clemente Wool Company," and said that there were two herders on the island. Also in 1903, Breninger [J43], said that there was a man and his wife living on the island, in charge of the sheep.

Breninger noted that his host had spent most of fifteen years on the island. One can but speculate as to whether Breninger's host was Mr. Charles Howland of West Cove, or another.

Mr. Linton [J120, 1909], was on San Clemente as an ornithologist in 1908. He really helped by saying,

I wish to tender my sincere thanks to Mr. Charles T. Howland, lessee of San Clemente Island; and to Mr. Robert Howland and the "boys" of Mr. Howland's various ranches, for the many favors extended to myself and party while working this island.

This could mean that Mr. Robert Howland, another son of William S. Howland, might have lived on the remaining ranch of the island, Middle Ranch.

According to Howell [B114, 1917], Mr. Howland had lived almost continuously on the island for fifteen years. Linton's date and that of Howell's, 1909 and 1917, is a difference of eight years, but contain the same information. Perhaps some leeway for literature interpretation might be necessary.

At least one of the Howlands, Charles, was on San Clemente in 1912-13 [J147]. There seem to be no more dates available on this subject until 1932. From *Condor* and Mr. Huey, we learn that Mr. E. G. Blair, President of the San Clemente Sheep Company, referred a Mr. Clinton G. Abbott to Mr. Charles T. Howland, "who had earlier been interested in the live stock on the island." Mr. Howland replied to Mr. Abbott, in answer to his question about quail having been taken to the island some time in the past.

The following year two events took place: "We have made an inspection of all the Channel Islands with a view to including them in the National Park Service," said Captain Rhodes, Superintendent of Lighthouse Service for the Pacific Coast [M187].

But the next month a new Navy air field had been constructed. It was below the isthmus and south of Northwest Harbor [M187]. Diagonally it went, "30,000 feet from the north end of the island, between two ranch houses . . . Two 1600-foot runways have been completed, and the entire field marked with crushed shell and stone . . . " In 1934 sheep grazing was discontinued.

In 1956 [M175], Hillinger said that GALLAGHER'S LANDING, with its beautiful emerald bay, had a 500-foot steel pier, as well as a landing field, built by the 11th Naval District. And at Wilson Cove there were radar towers where the Air Force could check on all coastal craft. In 1956 the Navy had fifty personnel on the island [M154]. By 1971 there were 240 permanent male residents living in a small village above Wilson Cove.

By 1979 San Clemente does not seem any closer to becoming a part of a National Park system than it did in 1933.

Snatches of
Geology and Geography

The Geological Survey of California had been preceded in 1853 by the newly organized Geological Survey of the State of California, with Mr. John B. Trask in charge [J256].

The second attempt at achieving information on the geology of the State was none too successful, even though field work was begun in 1860. By 1865 the islands had not been visited by their geologists and the scant information presented in the survey on the islands was obtained by Dr. Cooper in 1863 while making some zoological collections [C13, 1865].

Some of Dr. Cooper's more important findings about San Clemente are herein expressed by Whitney,

> . . . there is sufficient evidence that each one of the terraces, of which there are about seven, has been at one time the beach of the island. This evidence consists of the fact, that the bluffs forming the steps from one terrace to another are all hollowed out by numerous caves, like those existing in the cliffs along the present shore. Some of the latest upheavals have greatly lengthened the island at the northwest end, from which a reef now extends out about a mile, while along the middle of the eastern side, a depth of 600 feet was sounded by Dr. Cooper within a quarter of a mile of the shore, and no bottom found with a line of 840 feet at a mile distance.

Dr. Cooper was a zoologist but with an eye for geologic processes, as well.

Dr. LeConte also had an interest in both of these disciplines. He was busy on our islands as early as 1876, when he did some work for the George M. Wheeler Geological Survey West of the 100th Meridian in the area of species identifications.

Born in Georgia in 1823, LeConte was writing for the *American Journal of Science* and the California Academy of Sciences in 1887. From 1869 to 1901 Dr. LeConte was a professor of geology at the University of California.

Dr. LeConte had his own theories about the terraces and their geologic history, as did W. S. T. Smith and A. C. Lawson of that University, and George Davidson of the U. S. Coast and Geodetic Survey.

By the time Lawson and Smith were working on the island, the responsibility for the study of California's geology had been transferred to the University of California.

Dr. Lawson succeeded LeConte at the University, and both he and Dr. Smith had much to say about San Clemente. In 1897 Dr. Andrew C. Lawson mapped in detail the island, with the aid of his field assistant, Dr. Smith.

Dr. Davidson

In 1873 Davidson expressed some of his views in "The Abrasions of the Continental Shores of Northwest America" [J60].

Dr. George Davidson came from England, having been born there in 1823. He joined the Coast and Geodetic Survey at Dr. Bache's request, and by 1849 his astronomy professor, Dr. Bache, selected Davidson to chart the waters of the Pacific Coast.

By 1885 his title was Professor George Davidson, A. M., Ph. D., Assistant, U. S. Coast and Geodetic Survey. And he had already done a great deal of writing for Survey publications, which included the historical aspects for the very early voyages of discovery.

In 1891 LeConte mentioned the fact that Davidson was the one who had discovered the deserted channels of the coast, such channels having geological significance [J162].

Dr. Lawson in 1893 said that although Dr. Davidson was not a professional geologist, science is indebted to him for his live interest in the terraces and topographic forms of the islands, his maps, and his theories [U31].

In 1914 the California Academy of Sciences mentioned Davidson as having been largely responsible for the existence of that Academy; he had secured an endowment from James Lick for the purpose [J67].

Dr. Wagner said in 1932 that Dr. Davidson tried very hard to determine the proper names of the localities for the Survey [J91].

By 1897 three distinct views had been presented on the origin of San Clemente's caves. Cooper thought they had been formed by wave action [C13]. Lawson stated that the caves and cavernous recesses were the original characteristic of the lava flows, only exposed by erosive agencies [U31, 1893]. Smith said that at least a majority of the caves were formed by a sort of undermining process through the agency of percolating waters [N40, 1896].

Dr. Lorenzo Gordin Yates expressed his own thought in 1902 when he said, "however well his [Lawson's] theory may fit to San Clemente, it will not apply to any of the other islands . . ." [J127].

Of these northern islands Yates was referring to, he stated that the "beating of the waves has worn these caves and tunnels . . . some of these caves or tunnels are cut through the islands, . . . and later the roof falls." Anacapa is the best example.

Turning to the San Clemente terraces, by 1863 Dr. Cooper had expressed his wave-action-view on the subject; Davidson considered their origin as being due to that of ice action.

Neither Lawson nor Smith accepted Davidson's opinion, using the uplift theory, elevated ocean strands, for numerous terraces on San Clemente Island. Both of their articles are long and worthy of

detailed study. At later dates Smith spoke again about these terraces [U32; J30].

Griesbach, on the island for four months, made a few comments about streams, fauna, flora, benches, and caves of the island [J254, 1947], but this article remains the only one discussing the possibility of "fulgurites," as he called them. He said,

> The reasons for this large accumulation of fulgurites in one area of about roughly three hundred by five hundred yards—wherein lie actually thousands of fine specimens and hundreds of thousands of passable specimen fragments— is highly conjectural. It may quite well be that there is a massive body of iron-rich rock or ore underlying the area and which acts as a definite attraction to lightning, . . .

De Mofras [B48], reported, "A few Indians, . . . go to San Clemente, and bring back bits of kaolin or sulphate of iron."

Griesbach concluded the subject by asking the question, "Why?" should one small area of about three hundred by five hundred yards have them. The answer, of course, may be in others' hands.

Both field work and rock collection for analysis were done for Olmsted's 1955 geologic report [N47, 1958]. Olmsted's reference to previous study of the geologic features of San Clemente gave Dr. W. S. T. Smith the honor for being particularly helpful.

Another fine aspect of Olmsted's report is the indicating of an alignment of the surface faults with those continuing beneath the sea floor. The two outstanding faults are the one on the west side of Pyramid Cove and the one on the west side of Horse Cove; both are on the southern side of the island. Reed [B118, 1933], suggested a fault along San Clemente's north side with its Miocene volcanic and associated rocks.

Smith [N40, 1896], described "Miocene" beds on the island as, "beginning as sandstones and passing into yellowish to grayish white shales, the bulk of which consists of diatoms, associated with radiolaria and foraminifera, and showing abundant impressions of *Pecten peckhami Gabb.*"

Both Smith and Olmsted suggest that the rhyolite, dacite and andesite of the island are petrologically related.

In 1922 Dr. George F. McEwen, special investigator for Scripps Institution, took soundings and temperatures about the Channel Islands. It revealed that a southward flow of water exists at the southeast of San Clemente Island [M187].

PIECES OF EIGHT

In 1936, Waldo Drake of the *Los Angeles Times* was quoted in the *Catalina Islander* [M187], saying that the Coast and Geodetic Survey personnel were conducting a wire-drag survey of the waters surrounding the island. The reason given for such a survey was that "dangerous pinnacles on the sea floor . . . will be vital to submarines." The Navy was evidently attaching new importance to its base on San Clemente Island.

The following year F. P. Shepard reported a steep escarpment northeast of San Clemente Island leading down to the broad Catalina Basin [J161; J167, 1941].

In 1941 Shepard and Emery said there is also a V-shaped valley southeast of San Clemente Island to be found at a depth of 5,000 feet below the surrounding levels; it is thought to be a fault valley. A bank nearby had a depth of but 250 feet.

Natural History

A representative list of visiting authorities on San Clemente Island during the nineteenth and early twentieth centuries, is presented below.

1863	J. G. Cooper [C13]	zoologist
1875, '77	Paul Schumacher [J250; N41]	archaeologist
1884	Wm. S. Lyon [J72]	botanist
1885	Lyon & J. C. Nevin [B105]	botanists
1887, '90	Chas. F. Holder [B38]	naturalist
1888	C. H. Townsend;	zoologist
	J. Van Denburgh [N7; J42]	herpetologist
1893	A. C. Lawson [U31]	geologist
1894	A. W. Anthony;	zoologist
	E. A. Mearns;	zoologist
	Brandegee [N7]	botanist
1896	W. S. T. Smith [N40]	geologist
1897	B. L. Trask [U27]	botanist
	J. Grinnell [J238]	ornithologist
1899	H. C. Oberholser [N5]	ornithologist
1902	B. L. Trask [J334; J335]	botanist
1903	Trask, H. Hasse [J340; J328]	botanists
1904	O. W. Howard [J384]	ornithologist
1904	G. F. Breninger [J43]	ornithologist
1905	J. Van Denburgh [J66]	herpetologist
1907	C. B. Linton;	ornithologist
	A. W. Anthony;	ornithologist
	T. S. Brandegee [J116]	botanist
1909	C. B. Linton [J118]	ornithologist
1911	E. A. Mearns [J46]	zoologist
1912	J. R. Slevin;	herpetologist
	J. Van Denburgh [J68]	herpetologist
1913	C. L. Edwards [P116]	M.D., U.S.C.
1917	A. B. Howell [B114]	ornithologist

Flora

Dr. Greene [J72], said that Mr. William S. Lyon spent three days in September, 1884 studying botanical life on San Clemente. The following year he spent three weeks of June and July continuing his researches; and in April, 1885 he was accompanied by Rev. J. C. Nevin to San Clemente; they botanized for four days.

Asa Gray, who had been on San Clemente, named the eighty-one species that Lyon had collected. According to Alice Eastwood [J74], Gray reported six of the species as new. The *Botanical Gazette* of 1886 listed Lyon's collections.

In 1903 Mrs. Trask spent three months on the island of San Clemente. Her words on the trip may be found in the *Southern California Academy of Sciences, Bulletin*, Vol. III. Nos. 5 and 6 [J334 and J335].

In Hasse's article of 1903 he listed twenty-two species of lichen-flora from San Clemente, and gave Mrs. Blanche Trask credit for having been the one to make the collection [J328].

As Brandegee, in *Zoe*, had published material in 1890 on the flora of the California islands, Mrs. Trask quite naturally queried, "It seems strange that *(Lyonothamnus floribundus)* has not been reported before. It is not included in Brandegee's list, which, I believe, covers all previous lists." She made these comments through *Erythea* [U27, 1897], which publication was being printed in England and Germany, as well as in the United States.

According to Trask, she found groves upon groves of the tree in bloom up the canyons on San Clemente [U27], and stunted groves on the island's coastal heights [J335].

Alice Eastwood [J74, 1941], tells of Mrs. Trask's collecting on San Clemente,

she described the appearance and habitat of some important species that Lyon did not list. Among these were the two oaks, *Quercus chrysolepis* and *Q. tomentella, Crossosoma californicum* . . . and *Lavatera assurgentiflora*, the tree or bush mallow, restricted apparently, to San

Miguel, San Clemente, and Anacapa islands.

The Trask list and collection of specimens were both lost in the 1906 San Francisco fire. But Trask listed about seventy specimens from San Clemente Island [J334-335], some that Lyon had not mentioned in 1886; about fifteen of the list is referred to by Raven [B120], as being in endemic categories.

Perhaps a few of her most interesting species should be mentioned. To Trask, *Convolvulus macrostegius* was "the light of the caves." *Cereus Emory,* along the entire south coast, swung from many caves. She found the ordinary magenta *Mirabilis California* on the island, and also a variety with white flowers, sometimes with magenta veins; this is the "four o'clock."

Trask mentioned a "new" *Astragalus,* a silver-leaved bladder pod on the West End dunes. She wanted to call it *Astragalus Robeartsii Eastwood.* She said the *Prunus* on San Clemente should not be confused with *Ilicifolia,* but should have a specific rank. A *Lycium richii* was found by her at Northwest Harbor; Raven listed endemic *Lycium hassei* for San Clemente and Santa Catalina.

Trask referred to a lavender-flowered "new" *Malacothrix,* which overhung the gorges, and a climbing *Galium Catalinense,* also to be found on Santa Catalina. To her, there was a shrubby "strange" *Castilleia,* two to four feet tall, with rich canary-colored bracts. And a "peculiar form" of *Oenothera,* also on Santa Catalina, common near the sea, should also receive recognition.

Here is C. F. Holder's description of *Cereus Emory,* at home on San Clemente [B38],

If one wishes to see cacti, San Clemente is the place; in the east end the finest and most exasperating growth of the real choya I know of on the California coast is to be found. Here are great patches of various species. But the most spectacular growth of cactus I have ever seen, Mr. Gifford Pinchot, Mr. Charles Howland, and I discovered one day in a knife-like cañon on San Clemente.

Out of these (caves), hanging down ten, twenty, or more feet, were swinging in the draft, myraids of snakes of vivid green. The resemblance was so perfect that it was more than startling. The snakes were cacti about the diameter of a large python, and they descended from the caves in a most suggestive manner . . . [B38].

Refer to Appendix F for any other details [J156, J157, J158, B120].

Fauna

Cooper has a limited section, "Island Faunas," in C13, 1863. This aspect of his work is interesting only because of its early date. He listed four pages of charts for mammals, land birds, swimming birds, and reptiles found on the four southern islands. However, LeConte wrote for the Wheeler Survey on the subject of insects from species given him by Dr. Cooper and Dr. Bache.

John Van Denburgh had gone to San Nicolas and San Clemente as early as 1905 and had written a paper on his findings, but the paper was destroyed in the 1906 San Francisco fire. When he returned to the islands in 1912, Joseph R. Slevin was with him; this time they also went to Santa Catalina Island [J66].

They collected for three days on San Clemente in October, 1911 and secured the only two kinds of lizards previously known from there. Mearns and Anthony had found *Uta stansburiana* while there in 1894 [J66], Grinnell had found it in 1897; in 1889 Charles H. Townsend had found two species, the other being *Zantusia riversiana.* This species is also on San Nicolas, Santa Barbara, and Santa Catalina Islands.

Still another collector has mentioned a salamander from San Clemente Island, seemingly of the *Batrachoseps* group.

There are some bats, deer mice, field mice, and foxes on the island. [*See* U37, N50, B38, and B120 for some few short statements.] The Navy retired about ten horses to the island about 1946.

When Flynn was on the island [N50], he found it free of insects, flies, ants, and mosquitoes; but there was a wild bee, "holicitus calaliensis."

Fortunately, C. L. Edwards' article, "The Abalones of California," offers more specifics for San Clemente [P116, 1913], even though it is in another area of thought.

Four photos of a Japanese camp and its activity on the island are included. Edwards' contributions lay in his discussion of the catching of abalone, processing the meat, usages of the shell, and the finding of pearls in abalone—how they grow, or how they can be grown. One photo in particular shows free pearls from the abalone, the center pearl being unusually large.

This collection of pearls belonged to C. B. Linton. Edwards' remark on Linton's activities in pearl culture—"Mr. C. B. Linton has succeeded in producing . . . culture pearls by drilling a hole through the shell center, pushing in a round ball, made from shell, and filling the outside end of the hole with beeswax and cement." Yes, Linton was interested in more than ornithology.

After his discussion on methods for growing abalones, Edwards remarked that "abalones may be raised in the sea as easily as chickens upon the land."

Edwards ended the article with strong verbalization for the conservation of our natural resources,

> The inherent tendency of man to rob the earth and sea in order to promote his own selfish interests must be restrained for the larger benefit of his fellows and the salvation of his descendants from want. The sea is the last great field for human exploration and exploitation. We know so little of its vast resources that we can scarcely dream of the possible future industries which will arise under a wisely administered system of aquaculture.

In 1962 Cox mentioned the catch of abalone for the year 1952. He said that approximately 2.4 million pounds of it came from two of the Channel Islands—Santa Barbara and San Clemente. Santa Cruz and Anacapa appear to be good hunting grounds, too.

From Max Miller [B108, 1959], we receive a little more insight of the numbers of abalone and how they grow. Referring to San Clemente Island, he said, "I saw hundreds of abalones living in the open air, hundreds and hundreds of them when the tide was out, many of them piled on top of one another so that they almost resembled heaps of empty abalone shells which had been thrown away."

Avifauna

Mr. Charles Townsend, a resident naturalist of the steamer *Albatross* for the United States Bureau of Fisheries, collected as he went. He was on San Clemente Island in 1888 and 1889, where he collected the House Finch [J41].

When A. W. Anthony and Dr. Edgar A. Mearns of the National Museum were on the island in 1894, they collected a "good series of [House Finches] on San Clemente" [J41]. As Mearns continued, he said that Dr. Grinnell had collected them on Santa Barbara, San Nicolas, and San Clemente Islands in 1897. Grinnell had remarked about the Finch, "[It is] the most abundant bird on San Clemente Island . . . Forty-seven specimens of the House Finch were obtained on this island."

In 1904 Breninger found House Finches in the sheep-sheds at the ranch, the nests lining the build-ings. However some built in the prickly pear, others in the rocky wall of the sea, and one pair built their nest in the sticks of an eagle's nest [J43].

Evidently there had been some discussion of eliminating the San Clemente House Finch from a species list. But Van Rossem said that specimens from five of the islands and those of the mainland had been studied. He concluded that the proposed elimination could not have been made from a first-hand study of the case [J136, 1925].

Anthony and Mearns had also collected a series of wrens from San Clemente that were different from Vigors' Wren, and were thought to be a new species. Anthony, in *Auk,* offered a description of them and said, "The species is quite common in the thick cactus and low brush . . . but owing to its habits is quite difficult to secure" [J36, 1895].

When Breninger was there he noted that the wren nested in holes and crevices of the rock, and some in holes of trees, besides being in the prickly pear [J43].

Evidently a professional debate ensued, and in 1899 H. C. Oberholser, Assistant Biologist for the Department of Agriculture, Smithsonian Institution, wrote an article, "A Revision of the Wrens of the Genus Sclater." He had made quite a study of the wren, and had used Dr. Grinnell's collection of these California birds, in order to better understand the various western forms [N5].

He concluded that there was a new subspecies for Santa Catalina, one for Santa Rosa and Santa Cruz, and one for San Clemente, *Thryomanes Bewickii Leucophrys;* he had examined thirty-one specimens from San Clemente.

Grinnell had been on San Clemente on two separate occasions in 1897 for about fifteen days in all. In his notes for that period he enumerated thirty-one species of land birds and twenty-four species of water birds. He had observed these birds at San Nicolas, Santa Barbara, and San Clemente [J249].

Breninger went to San Clemente in 1903 at the request of the curator of the ornithological department of the Field Columbian Museum. His elucidating report lists about twenty-five water and land species, which included the Burrowing Owl. It is five pages long, and one of the more interesting articles of its type.

Linton was on the island for part of the first four months of 1907 and October, 1907 [J118]. He submitted a list of fifty-eight species to Dr. Grinnell, who "has carefully examined the specimens secured and pronounces the . . . identifications correct."

As Mearns continued his report [J41], he said that Dr. Grinnell had remarked about the San Clemente Linnets,

> In such places, especially in the vicinity of the water 'tanks', the linnets fairly swarmed, and their full, rollicking songs reverberated incessantly. Their food appeared to be mainly composed of the fleshy cactus fruits, of which there was certainly an abundant supply . . . The nesting season begins early, . . . On June 5, incubated eggs were taken . . .

And about the Shrike on San Clemente, Dr. Grinnell made this observation [J41], "This bird was without question the shyest and hardest to be secured of any on the island. Indeed it was as shy as any hawk I ever saw."

Oberholser, once again, made comments in an attempt to settle a discussion [J49, 1922]. In "Notes on North American Birds," he indicated that the Shrike, *Lanius ludovicianus anthonyi*, would be found on Santa Cruz, Santa Barbara, Anacapa, Santa Catalina, and probably Santa Rosa Islands. But the *Lanius ludovicianus mearnsi*, described by Mr. Ridgway [J42, 1898], should be recognized as different. "Examination of a good series of both island forms from San Clemente and Santa Cruz islands shows that there are, however, excellent characters to distinguish *Lanius ludovicianus mearnsi*."

Grinnell collected six new Towhee specimens of the twelve that he saw while camping at Smugglers' Cove. Of them he said, "They were shy, and usually remained closely hidden in the clumps of wild cherry bushes which lined the beds of the ravines" [J37].

The *Osprey* of 1897 furnished two photos of an osprey nesting on San Clemente. Grinnell spoke of them, too, saying that ospreys nest on rocky cliffs, and one of the nests was so large that the average museum would be unable to display it [J238]. Holder found numbers of nests of the American Osprey at Mosquito Harbor.

One of Breninger's observations was about the Auklets [J43]. This is his rather disturbing comment,

> I am at a loss to account for the mortality among the Auklets (Ptychoramphus aleuticus) frequenting the water about the island. Along the shores and on the water dead Auklets were seen everywhere. Eagles and Duck Hawks fed on those that were not yet dead, while ravens and gulls fed by day on the dead that were thrown up among the rocks, and the foxes for-

aged over the same ground at night.

Another rather disturbing anecdote through Breninger concerns the Bald Eagle.

> . . . One season, at sheep-shearing time, one of the employees of the Wool Company, fresh from a land where there were no eagles, essayed to ride to the edge of the barranca and have a look at the young eagles. From above the old eagle swooped with unerring aim, and it was fortunate the grasp was not deeper, as with angry screams she flew away with his hat, dropping it into the sea. It was with this same eagle I was dealing. My man had gone down after the eggs, and while I was giving some minor directions, in an unguarded moment, a little dog that had followed from the house ran with a pitiful whine under my legs and curled up there in mortal terror. I had sat down on the ground, perhaps on account of proximity to the edge of the abyss and at the same time to have 'full swing' at rapid shooting. A moment after the dog had taken refuge an eagle came within a foot of striking me in the face with its wing. My gun came to my shoulder instantly. Bang! and a fine white-headed bird lay dying at the bottom of the barranca. The female, too, was secured.

Where once the Bald Eagle had been among the most plentiful of winged creatures on San Clemente, it has disappeared. Perhaps man has been its worst enemy.

O. H. Howard made three trips in this period of time to San Clemente in order to pursue his general interest in ornithology, and Dusky Warblers in particular. In a narrow canyon at about 1500 feet, he found a spring of water. The continued moisture around the spring,

> was the cause of these [probably cherry, not plum] trees being of unusual size, and the dense foliage formed an unusually good retreat for birds . . . in the very top of the tallest trees, about thirty feet above the ground . . .

He found the nests of the Dusky Warbler [J384, 1906]. The nest is usually three to ten feet above ground.

Mearns referred to a pallid western form of the Mourning Dove on the island. C. F. Holder saw it around Chinetti's and at Howland's near the tanks. Holder had quite a bit to say about birds.

Another Ridgway contribution [J42], is his discussion of a San Clemente Sparrow, which had been obtained in 1889 by C. H. Townsend. Apparently a new species, Van Rossem [J135, 1924], referred to it as *Melospiza melodia clementae*.

Another bird, the Flycatcher, has come under scrutiny. Oberholser gave a "Description of a new *Empidonax,* with notes on *Empidonax Difficilis,*" in 1897 through *Auk*. By 1905 Grinnell [J108], wrote an article through the *Condor*, "The Flycatcher from the Santa Barbara Islands." In the article he disagrees with Oberholser that *E. insulicola* and *E. difficilis* are distinct. One wonders if this question has been finally resolved.

In mentioning the Quail on San Clemente, Grinnell [J249, 1897; J41, 1898], referred to Gallagher as a real possibility for having placed the quail on the island, but "on account of the poor cover, and the abundance of foxes which killed the sitting birds in the Spring, they have scarcely been able to hold their own." Another person mentioned Robearts as the one responsible for bringing the quail to the island. Sometimes called the Valley Partridge, Holder had found them on the upper part of the island.

Huey [J147, 1931], brought up the subject of quail having been liberated on San Clemente Island. Through written communication with Mr. Charles Howland, it appears that Howland had sent for, and had received about twenty dozen quail from the Banning-Coachella district.

Obviously, there had been an earlier import, even though the Valley Quail and the Gambel Quail had been introduced in 1912-13 by Howland.

Indians and Archaeology

While on San Clemente, Schumacher found boulders of basalt near 'Chinese Point' that were suitable for the manufacture of mortars [J250], and from one grave on the island he secured some whistles made from the tibiae of deer [U14].

Additional comments were about the extinct race of dogs that were once on the island [N41, 1877],

Tradition speaks of an extinct race of dogs that inhabited these islands. Even in 1857 a reliable gentleman thought he had seen some of these same dogs on San Clemente, which he described to me as large, slender, coarse, and hairy canines, resembling rather a coyote or wolf than our better-natured domestic species.

Scant information came from Eisen; he said that there were Indians yet living on San Clemente as late as 1838 [M30].

California Farmer [M51, 1860], quoted from the *San Francisco Herald,* which paper quoted Reid that,

about from the year 1818 to the year 1834, Santa Catalina, San Clemente, and the other islands of the Santa Barbara Channel, were often invaded by the Indians of the northwest coast, who came down and killed great numbers of those of the islands . . . The remains of those of San Clemente, which were collected in caves on the island about 1833, showed in their heads, "*the whole of them* to have been possessed of double teeth all round, both in the upper and lower jaw!"

C. F. Holder remarked [P115, 1896], that musical instruments had been taken from San Clemente,

The flutes which are now in Mr. Plumb's collection at Islip, Long Island, were about eight inches in length, perforated with four or five finger holes, while the largest end was covered with asphaltum, into which was set the square or oblong piece of pearl, evidently selected for its beauty and luster . . .

Of Britton's trip in 1897, he said that there were signs of former aboriginal inhabitation of the caves and he enumerates the kinds of Indian artifacts that could be found in them [P47].

Glidden of Santa Catalina went to San Clemente in 1922 and made his main camp at Northwest Harbor. This was his fourth expedition there, having been sent out by Mr. George E. Heye of the American Indian Museum, to search for Indian remains of one type or another [M187].

Glidden's comment in 1923 was that the Indian burial places were hard to locate among the ever-shifting sands as he went the full length and breadth of the island [M187].

Bernice Eastman Johnston remarked that refugees from the fierce Aleuts in those earlier days were assigned to Mission San Luis Rey, San Diego County [J192, 1955].

McKusick and Warren spent a week on San Clemente [U41, 1958]. Their presentation had best be made by reading their seventy-seven-page report. One of their projects was that of reviewing the contents of Big Dog Cave, which Woodward had checked out in April, 1939. [J6 gives a listing of its contents.]

The McKusick-Warren report contains six appendices. McKusick had gone to U.C.L.A. from Yale University, and it was about this time that the Los Angeles office of the University took over the archaeological work of the ten southern counties of California.

From *Masterkey* [J202, 1962], it is said that Bruce Bryan and Charles Rozaire of the Southwest Museum recovered an Indian skeleton in May of that year, about one and a half miles north of 'Eel Point.'

In 1963 the same source said that the actual excavations on San Clemente were being carried out by the Archaeological Survey Association, but under the direction of Bruce Bryan of the Museum.

Meighan [U45, 1959], reported 196 Indian sites located by U.C.L.A. on San Clemente, as compared with six that had been located by U.C., Berkeley. Naturally, permission and cooperation of the Navy had first to be obtained [J203].

Nell Murbarger said that her first trip to San Clemente was made with her father about 1922. Later, she spent five months with an exploring party on the island, while the members collected many artifacts for the Bowers Memorial Museum of Santa Ana. Mr. Wilbur B. Murbarger obtained about 800 artifacts, later displayed in the Orange County exhibit.

Nell Murbarger's article, "California's Vanished Islanders" [P22a] was published in the *Grizzly Bear Magazine* in 1947 and can be cited as a worthy account. It contains information indicating her intimate acquaintance with the island.

In speaking of artifacts and caves, Mrs. Murbarger remarked that there are fewer caves on the north half of the island than elsewhere. Regardless of this fact, near Northwest Harbor and West Cove there are hundreds of acres of shell mounds representing the debris after Indian consumption of the shell's contents. Others, too, have referred to this sand dune area as being former sites for Indian villages.

Of all Murbarger's material, the most fascinating and dramatic is her description of what her father found while exploring on San Clemente,

Nearly a quarter of a century ago, on a grassy promotory on the Island's lee side, my father found a sizeable area paved with abalone shells laid in the shape of a perfect arrowhead. It measured 30 feet from tip to shank and 15 feet across its greatest breadth. The shells were laid as closely as flagstones, each set flush against its neighbor and neatly placed in one-two order, the smaller end toward the point of the arrowhead.

Further examination revealed that a four-foot circle in the pattern's center was laid with shells three deep, each layer nested closely over its predecessor. Although abalone pearl is well-nigh indestructible, the top layer of shells crushed to powder at the touch. The second and third layers (doubtless because of the protection afforded by the surface layer) were still stout and pearly.

Whether the result of coincidence or design, the tip of the arrow form pointed directly toward the rising sun of midwinter. It is further interesting to note that the eastern, or lee side, of San Clemente, is frequented by practically no abalones, all members of the genus preferring the pounding surf of the south and west sides. Therefore, the hundreds of shells forming this pattern were necessarily carried not less than six miles over extremely rugged terrain, indicating that the strange installation had been of considerable importance to its makers.

As Schumacher was unable to locate the remains of the Temple to the Sun on Santa Catalina Island, so, too, are nil the chances for anyone rediscovering this 'arrowhead' to the rising sun on San Clemente Island.

Photos of San Clemente Island

Date	Code #	Author	Photo	Reference
1896	P44	Earle	Gallagher's Landing	*Land of Sunshine*
1896 -97	J40	Smith	Maps	*U. S. Geological Survey*
1899	P51	Smith	The Resting Herds	*Land of Sunshine*
			At the Watering Trough	*Land of Sunshine*
			A Tiny Cabin	*Land of Sunshine*
1910	B38	Holder	Great Cave of San Clemente	*Channel Islands*
1913	P116	Edwards	The Japanese Camp at San Clemente	*Popular Science Monthly*
			Drying Frames at the Camp	*Popular Science Monthly*
			From the Boiling Tank	*Popular Science Monthly*
			Abalones drying in the sun	*Popular Science Monthly*
			Free Pearls from the abalone (C. B. Linton collection)	*Popular Science Monthly*
1928	J139	Pemberton	Nest of Osprey	*Condor*
1944	N51	Wheeler	Mosquito Harbor	*U. S. Naval Instit. Proceedings*
1956	M154	Hillinger	Jeep beside Indian burial mound	*Los Angeles Times,* Mar. 18
			Clemente Freeway, sand-skiing	*Los Angeles Times*
			Baby goat (black), bottle-fed	*Los Angeles Times*
1959	U41	McKusick & Warren	Indian Sites	*An. Rpt., U.C.L.A. Archae. Survey*
1962	M47	Thorne Hall	Fantastic dunes of sand	*Odyssey of Santa Barbara Kingdoms*

Santa Catalina

West End Light
Eagle Rock
Black Point
Parson Landing
Arrow Point
Johnson's Landing
Emerald Cove
Howland Landing
Bousheys
Ship Rock
Lion Head
Bird Rock
Mt. Torquemada
Isthmus Cove
Whale Rock
Perdition Caves
Lobster Bay
Catalina Harbor
Ballast Point
Empire Landing
Little Spgs. Cyn.
Vally of Ollas
Cabrillo Harbor
Goat Harbor
Little Harbor
Big Springs Cyn.
Italian Gardens
Sentinel Rock
Catalina Airport
Ben Weston Beach
Long Point Light
Mt. Orizaba
Black Jack Mtn.
White Landing
Eagle's Nest
Willow Cove
China Point
Gallagher Beach
Middle Ranch
Frog Rock
Hamilton Beach
Avalon
Casino Pt.
Salte Verde Pt.
Palisades
Avalon Bay
Pebbly Beach
Jewish Point
Church Rock
Light
Seal Rocks

San Pedro Channel

Pacific Ocean

N

Santa Catalina

Anecdotes—Topography—Place Names

Beginning at the ISTHMUS near CATALINA HARBOR and circling the northern end of the island to ISTHMUS COVE, there are seven large rocks, Pin Rock, Whale Rock, Ribbon Rock, Eagle Rock; then Indian Rock, Ship Rock, and Bird Rock.

On the beach near EAGLE ROCK, the *Catalina Islander* [M187], stated that in 1923 there had been one thousand cases of whiskey cached. Federal authorities were investigating the situation.

Judge Windle made it known in his comments that none of the local boatmen would go near Eagle Rock while its immediate use was under investigation. Eagle Rock has had its name since about 1892.

Another rock, BIRD ROCK, was in 1891 called WHITE ROCK [P12]. It was after Wrigley's ownership of Santa Catalina Island that a Mrs. Helen K. Motor of San Francisco claimed ownership to White Rock Island.

It seemed that in some supposed legal way some relatives had made an 1848 arrangement with Guadalupe Hidalgo for the rock. But it was not until 1925 that Mrs. Motor became aware that her "script" could be used to obtain the White Rock Island property [M187]. Her stated claim expired with time.

In a *Fish and Game Department Bulletin* [C3, 1962], Cox said that experiments were being conducted with some abalone of that region. They had moved black abalone from Bird Rock to WHITE POINT, in an attempt to determine the effect of environmental changes on growth. Since the abalone at White Point had not gained much weight, it was suggested that water pollution could have been a factor. The abalone transplanted from White Point to Catalina Harbor had done much better.

Continuing south and around the island to the point of beginning may be listed TWIN ROCKS, once called PINNACLE ROCKS in 1892; HEN ROCK, SUGAR LOAF ROCK, FROG ROCK, SEAL ROCKS, CHURCH ROCK, BINNACLE ROCKS, and SENTINEL ROCK, which is off of a projection several miles south of LITTLE HARBOR. But two of these rocks come in for comments. One is Sugar Loaf.

The headland on the north side of AVALON BAY, called CASINO POINT, at one time culminated in Sugar Loaf Rock, a former favorite spot by many for picture-taking. It was also a temporary home of the Santa Catalina's Wireless Office [J313, 1903].

A Frank H. Sellers tried to climb Sugar Loaf Mountain in 1886, but he gave it up, as the gulls by the thousands were in possession and resented intruders [M187].

A trip to Seal Rocks, three miles south of Avalon, has been rewarding to those interested in a close view of the seals living there, as they bark raucously at the passengers, who in turn keep a safe distance from the rookery. Big Ben, the pet seal of Avalon, lived at Seal Rock. Poor Ben—drowned in a fisherman's net!

The interior north of the Isthmus contains at least three place names of interest, MT. TORQUEMADA, SILVER PEAK, and BOUSHEY'S.

Mt. Torquemada, as a place name, has existed since at least 1892 and is no doubt named in commemoration of Father Torquemada, a chronicler for Vizcaíno in 1602. Mt. Torquemada is opposite LOBSTER BAY.

Silver Peak, also known as SILVER HILL is probably so-called due to the discovery of galena containing silver north of the Isthmus. It is midway of PARSON'S LANDING and IRON BOUND COVE.

Boushey's is inland from JOHNSON'S LANDING and today it is known as the SMALL HILL MINING CLAIM. Around it has developed considerable lore and fact,

thus making it one of the more interesting and oldest anecdotes for this island. More on that later.

PARSON'S COVE on the north side "is unfit for landing in a skiff. Here, upon the rocky beach, just at the very edge of the boulders, there is yet to be seen the old camp of the captain . . . Up the broken arroyo above the beach a tiny spring still trickles away seaward" [M130, 1906].

The cove lies about a half hour beyond Johnson's Landing under the lee of RAM POINT, now termed STONY POINT, or ARROW POINT. Back of Arrow Point and between it and Johnson's Landing to the south is a region containing soapstone.

> old [Capt. Parsons] thought nothing of rowing around Catalina, or over to San Clemente, or up to Santa Barbara Island . . .
>
> It was over fifty years ago that "Uncle Thof," . . . used to take relic hunters to both San Nicolas and San Clemente Islands, so that it is no wonder that these grounds are now but poor fields for the seeker of curios.

Mrs. Trask had more to say on the quaint character of Captain Parsons [M130].

At Johnson's Landing was a RANCH. Here there is both a good landing on a pebbly beach and close by was to be found a house, corrals, and a well of good water [N34]. There was a John L. Johnson and a James Charles Johnson who had come to the island in 1854.

In 1928 the *Catalina Islander* included a long column written by Percy H. Howland,

> At the time my grandfather raised sheep on the Island, Jim Johnson was living at Johnson's Landing and using the west end of the Island for his range. Howland used the center portion of the Island, and Frank Whittley, with headquarters at White's Landing, used the east end of the Island. There were quite a number of men raising sheep on the Island at the time, but the three last mentioned acquired the interests of the others by purchase, and remained there for a number of years . . . The shearing corrals were about three hundred feet back of the main street circling the bay, and about on Sumner Avenue.

Perhaps it should be noted that the name "Whittley" is, on equally good authority, spelled with one letter "t."

This northwest end of Santa Catalina is the locale, the arrowhead, which created some of the island's earliest history. George Yount, Samuel Prentiss

[Prentice], and Louis Bouchette [Boushey, Bouchet], were some of the leading characters. At least two of them were also of greater California, as well as of the island.

George Yount was an 1830 pioneer to California, born in 1794, he died at the age of seventy-one in 1865 [J85, 1923]. He had come overland to California with Wolfskill, Pryor, Laughlin, and Prentiss. First a trapper, he tried his hand at otter hunting through the Dana license. He, with the others mentioned, built themselves a schooner at San Pedro with sea-otter hunting in mind.

It was on one of these trips that he found some rich outcroppings on Santa Catalina [J361, 1912]. He returned to the island three times in an attempt to locate his lost lode, but without success. His last trip, made in 1854, was the year of Prentiss' death.

Samuel Prentiss, also a friend of a Bouchette, was a native of Rhode Island. An otter hunter, and a stone mason [J360, 1906], he still took much time to hunt for buried treasure. In 1823 at the age of thirty-two he rowed alone from San Pedro to Santa Catalina to hunt for a treasure, with "Bouchey's" assistance; such treasure was known about and its location mapped by Indian Chief Turei of the Pumubi Ranchero [M187].

Prentiss remained much of the time on the island hunting the treasure; he had made himself a cabin at Johnson's Landing and there in 1854, at the age of sixty-three, he died. His crude headstone remains at the landing [J361, 1912]. Another has said that the grave is at WILSON'S VALLEY [M57, 1864].

A Louis Bouchette [B48, 1844; B76, 1876], was born in 1779 in France. In 1828, at the age of forty-nine, he went to Monterey with a Mexican passport. At a not much later date he went southward to Los Angeles, becoming naturalized in 1831. Bancroft has said that he owned a large vineyard there, along with W. L. Hill.

But this is about all we know of Louis Bouchette, other than also being called "William" Bauchet and/or Bonchot. Louis died in October of 1847 at the age of sixty-eight, having previously married in the early '30s.

According to the Catalina records, particularly that of Lick vs. Howland, *et al*, 1868, the first name of a Frenchman, Bouchette [Bouchey] was Stephen. It is not inconceivable that he was the son of Louis. Stephen Boushey [Bouchette, J317] was still working the Small Hill Mining Claim in the '80s.

Some of the other familiar persons named in Lick's suit against the squatters were Diltz, Swain, Howland, Gallagher, Guerrera, Johnson [Johnston], and Wilson, all of whom had been in pursuit of their affairs much before the Union troops arrived [N20].

Litigation finally ended in 1872 but without total success for Lick, for during the proceedings it had been determined that in 1867 Dr. Hitchcock had sold his mine to Bouchey for the sum of $7,000.

The miners disappeared after the Union troops arrived—by official order. Bouchette was left with title to his mine; the years during which Captain Parsons continued to supply Bouchette's transportation needs for the ore have not been made clear.

In one 1906 account, through Mrs. Trask, we find Bouchette having had his difficulties [M130],

[There is a] slope of green ascent which leads from Jim Johnson's at the beach up to "Bushey's". The old house erected in these regions as the home of the man who was conducting the mining interests here has now been blown down to the ground . . . Lively times were those of the old mining days . . . The men who then kept sheep on the island did not like to see Bouchey's long line of burros; not, however, because it blurred the landscape, but because they ate so much . . . Bushey's burros died suddenly; one by one, . . .

From the *Catalina Islander* and editor Judge Windle, we learn that Bouchette disappeared in the eighties, "after having built a fine home on the island" [M187]. The *Scientific American* [J317, 1926], said, "Bouchet, a Frenchman, drifted a tunnel and built wooden rails and dump carts nearly half a century ago . . ."

A third account indicated that a John Sullivan was living at Isthmus Cove in 1886. Mrs. Trask [M128, 1906], said that he was the only one living at the Isthmus at that time. "Then the Portuguese came and went, and afterward three fishermen settled . . ." John Sullivan's cabin and a "Big Corral" were on the south coast at the Isthmus, where rattlesnakes abound [M133, 1906].

Another tale from the *Catalina Islander*, told by Frank H. Sellers of Pasadena, was reminiscent of his 1886 trip to the island. In part, it went,

On the whole island at that time, I believe there was but one permanent resident—an escaped convict. He lived on the northern end of the island and when we came to call, he met us with a rifle, with a fresh skin of sheep over his shoulder. He presented a picturesque sight and we went away from there.

PIECES OF EIGHT

There is likelihood that this Sullivan was not the Sullivan who in 1858 paid Albert Packard $500 for one-fourth of the island. This was before Hitchcock had purchased from Packard and before Bouchey paid Hitchcock $7,000 in 1867, probably for the mineral rights. Yet it is provocative to find the same name for two separate incidents in the history of the island, with two given names, John, and Eugene.

Johann Beghn and his Spanish wife had settled at the Johnson Place following Johnson. Beghn [or Behn] was a brother-in-law to Thomas Whittley. Tom Whittley, and "Mexican Joe" had been boys together. Beghn's farm was well laid and was sometimes known as BEHN'S PLACE [B44, 1906].

Southward along the coast is EMERALD BAY or WILSON'S COVE. Both Johnson's Landing and Emerald Bay are closer to the Bouchette mine than was Captain Parsons' old cabin.

The selected site for a miner's town was at Wilson's—Emerald Bay—and was to be known as QUEEN CITY, in the eyes of R. I. Shipley, William Hazeltine, "and Company" [C34].

> [On May 24, 1864 the little valley and the adjoining hillsides were staked out,] forty acres of land . . . situated one-half mile from Wilson's Harbor and running Southerly covering Wood or Beach Valley, running Southerly towards the Main Ridge and lying West of Silver Hill and East of Bouchey's new Road to the Mines,

After Wilson's Cove [Spencer H. Wilson] comes HOWLAND'S LANDING [William S. Howland]. Here, lived Mr. Howland and his wife and family and servants, having purchased squatter rights from Harvey Rhoads. Here, Howland had a well from which water was drawn and taken for the use of the Union troops stationed at the Isthmus, 1864 [N27].

CHERRY COVE and FOURTH OF JULY COVE are about two miles below Howland's. They are slight indentations serving as anchorages and are about a mile apart.

The first mine discoveries were made in Fourth of July Cove, Cherry Cove, and MINERAL HILL, known as SMALL HILL. The first location of a claim was made in April 1863 by Martin M. Kimberly and Daniel E. Way. "It was supposed at the time that it was Yount's lost mine" [J361, 1912].

At Fourth of July Harbor there once were thirty to seventy miners living. Some water was available at CHERRY VALLEY but it was of an inferior quality, so the miners, too, went to Howland's for their water, even though there was a spring at ISTHMUS COVE,

a well at Catalina Harbor, and another well just south of FISHERMAN'S BAY or COVE, all of them closer to Wilson's Cove than Howland's Landing.

The Isthmus is the small neck at the northern end of Santa Catalina Island, and was a burying ground for the Indians [P75, 1914]. Its west side is known as Catalina Harbor, with CATALINA HEAD to its immediate north and BALLAST POINT to its south. The east side is now known as Isthmus Cove, with some still visualizing Fisherman's Cove as a part of Isthmus Cove.

Of "The Great Depression," Duflot de Mofras [B48, 1844], had this to say about the Isthmus,

> The majority [of the islands] have good anchorages, with wood and water. Of these the best are at Santa Catalina, especially on the west side near the center of the depression where ships from Boston frequently come to salt down their hides, . . .

Before being killed off, the sea elephant had used this shore for basking purposes.

D. B. Diltz, Esq. occupied land adjoining the two bays. He lived at Catalina Harbor, had a fresh well and a house there, as well as a storehouse at the end of Ballast Point.

It was a part of Captain West's plan to have a road cut from the Diltz well to the other side of the Isthmus, in order to help supply the needs of the army retained there. Mrs. Trask has reminded us that "there was a well on one of the beaches at Catalina Harbor from which water was drawn by bucket for many long years—indeed, until about five years ago . . ." [M128, 1906].

In the Bulletin of the U. S. Geological and Geographical Survey [N41, 1877], Paul Schumacher has a map of Catalina Harbor. On it is indicated the Diltz house, well, and government road to the barracks. It also indicates where once were the Indian graves at the Isthmus Cove, and the location of a spring, not too far away.

H. R. Wagner, well-known cartographer [B75, 1937], said that Puerto de Santa Catalina was the original name for Isthmus Cove,

> The present name was given to the island by Vizcaíno November 25, 1602, in honor of Santa Catalina whose day it is. Palacios made a small plan of it from which it would seem that the anchorage at the isthmus on the east side had been named Puerto de Santa Catalina and I think this is probably correct.

A topographical survey of Santa Catalina Island

had been made by the U. S. Coast and Geodetic Survey and in 1889 [N34], it was stated that anchorage in Isthmus Cove was "in seven or eight fathoms of water over dark-grey sand, with the large white house on the isthmus . . . three hundred yards back from the beach was the United States barracks, built in 1863 . . ."

Whittley had lived at the Isthmus after 1850 and the Records [N20, 1864], have a map of his improvements there. [See also B84.] Whittley brought his sheep here from Mexico when the later Captain Whittley was but a child of four [M128, 1906]. With them came "Mexican Joe" [Presciado] [M43, 1941], an endearing nickname for a boy who was "wild and climbing and always after goats."

From Marco R. Newmark [J373, 1953], we learn more about this wild and climbing boy,

Because I knew him well before the gasoline launch had entirely supplanted the row-boat for trolling, I am tempted to say a word about a picturesque character known as Mexican Joe.

An article in the *Los Angeles Morning Herald* of October 30, 1903, contains a sketch about him. He was born in 1843 and baptized Jose Presciado. He came to the island as a child in 1850, and lived there the rest of his life. He never went to school; he never was in an elevator; he never used a telephone but he did know Catalina. As he himself expressed it, "If there is a tree on the island I do not know, it must have grown last night.

Occasionally, he served as a guide for huntsmen who sought the wild goats of the island; but he spent most of his time rowing his angling clients intent on capturing the denizens of the surrounding waters. He took pride in his trade and was a master of it; and even though it was a humble one, he played a part in life; and perhaps he deserves a tiny niche in a hall of fame.

The corrals at the Isthmus belonged to Whittley and the army decided to leave them there, to be used to store forage for the animals. The fence between the two bays belonged to William Howland and were to be removed. However, Howland persuaded the Captain to allow him to move the fence to the hillside. In this way the sheep were kept away from the Isthmus and Howland could continue to have some method of restraining his flock.

From San Francisco's *Daily Alta California* have come four articles, valuable from the standpoint of the 1853 and 1864 dates, if for no other reason.

Monday, June 13, 1853 [M52],

Dr. Creal of Los Angeles [who lived on the island since 1850] . . . took possession of the island and was at once monarch of all he surveyed . . . he has lately transferred his interest in the goats on the island to a wealthy firm at the rate of four dollars per head, . . . Messrs. Pierce & Reed, of California Street, are now fitting out a schooner to take the goats from the island to the mainland.

July 15, 1853 [M54],
A vessel now plies regularly between Catalina and San Pedro, bringing over from the Island large numbers of goats, which are landed at the beach and herded preparatory to being driven to San Francisco and the mines. There are said to be 25,000 goats at Catalina, and the gentlemen engaged in the speculation propose taking 15,000 to the northern markets. Dr. Creal, who has been living upon the Island for three years past, and who is regarded as the proprietor of this description of stock has built large corrals and made other improvements and at present is employing a number of men in the transportation of the goats . . . Under the name of *mutton*, they will feed many hungry miner and merchant. The skin of some of the most valuable bucks bear a strong resemblance to that of a grizzly bear.

June 12, 1864 [M57],
EDITORS ALTA—A rugged island is the Santa Catalina. Its bold and rocky shores, its deep gorge, called the Isthmus, almost dividing it into two islands, with its elevated mountain ranges, give it an air of grandeur well suited to its position so far out from the main in the ocean. There are numerous small valleys on the island, but none of them extend entirely across it except the Isthmus. The other valleys are narrow and short, running from the coast shore of the island, and terminating in ravines up the mountains.

The Isthmus
Is a beautiful location, although treeless and uncultivated. It does not exceed a furlong in width, and in length scarcely exceeds half a mile. Its course is north and south, and it has a harbor at each extremity. The north, or landward harbor is well suited for the small craft now engaged in trade from San Pedro. But a weird and bold scenery surrounds the south harbor, called, by way of pre-eminence, "Catalina Harbor." Though small, it is deep and almost landlocked, affording safe anchorage for vessels of large tonnage at almost all seasons of the year. The Isthmus is almost exclusively occupied by the military

now stationed there. Captain West, the officer in command on the island, is a quiet, estimable gentleman, and a genial companion. His mild but firm discipline has endeared him to his men. Barracks are in process of erection, and it would be wisdom in the Government to be liberal in its appropriations for military improvements on the island of Santa Catalina.

The Fourth of July Valley,

Or, rather, Glen Haven, as it has been recently named, in honor of that excellent lady, Mrs. Floyd Johnson, now a resident of the Isthmus, is half a mile westerly from the Isthmus. It is not more than two hundred feet wide, and terminating in a mountain ravine in less than half a mile from its pleasant little harbor. It contains eight dwelling houses, two tents, two workshops and several out-door forges for sharpening picks. Its inhabitants number three ladies, thirty miners, no children. There is neither horse, cart, cow nor grog-shop in Glen Haven, but its mineral wealth can scarcely be estimated.

Cherry Valley,

Half a mile westerly from Glen Haven, is larger and pleasanter, and rivals it in mineral wealth. It numbers about forty men, without a woman or a child among them. It, however, boasts one store, kept by Mr. Freid, lately of San Francisco, and one grog-shop, where thirsty souls may drink and yet be ever dry. Here soldiers, when off duty at the Isthmus, most do congregate, to turn their greenbacks into *current* liquidation, notwithstanding such brokerage is contraband.

Howland's Valley

Nearly two miles farther westerly, is broader than the other, and occupied only by himself, family and servants as a sheep ranch. He has been located here about ten years. He sends his wool to San Pedro for shipment to San Francisco. In the upper part of the valley, where it shrinks into the vile dimensions of a rocky ravine, there are a few miners, but many rich mining claims—in the estimation of their hopeful locators. The fine roadstead in front of this valley affords safe anchorage for small craft during the greater part of the year.

Wilson's Valley,

A mile further westward, is the largest and most pleasant of the three last named. It has a fine beach in front, and equals Howland's in its water privileges. Its proprietor, after whom it is named, is a man of some wealth, and has been located here with his family for quite a number of years. His sheep and goats range the mountains undisturbed, and at the proper season of the year

return to yield him their golden fleece. The only grave I saw upon the island was at this place. Opposite his residence, scarcely a furlong distant, on a pleasant slope near the seashore, is a solitary grave, surrounded by pickets painted dark-brown. The lonely occupant [probably Samuel Prentiss] of that small enclosure doubtless sleeps well. I looked upon it, and sighed, wondering if his days had been spent in toiling—mining—or busy trade; envied the lot of the sleeper, and passed on to the shore, to hold communion with the deep, dark, rolling, restless sea.

These Valleys

Are all within five miles of the Isthmus, either by land or by water. The land communication is by a mere trail over mountains and gulches, and is sometimes so narrow and precipitous, especially where it passes around the bluffs overhanging the sea, between Glen Haven and the Isthmus and the same place at Cherry Valley, that it would really be dangerous for a nervous or inebriated person to attempt the passage after nightfall. The water communication is made in small row-boats. This is much more safe and pleasant. The sea along this shore is very clear, exceedingly rank in its marine vegetation and affords to the lover of the beautiful the most attractive ocean scenery. You can see the fish, large and small, pass in and out of the bowers where they seek refuge from the bright rays of the sun. The gold fish, so much prized in San Francisco, is here seen in all its beauty in its native element. The white fish and the red fish are abundant and afford many a hearty meal for the weary miner. The abalone, with its fine single shell, is found on the rocks along the shore.

The Mining Region,

So far as yet developed, is chiefly confined to the part of the island above described. The claims laid out are almost innumerable. Scarcely any regard has been paid to original locators. Litigation will be abundant, provided the mines prove rich, to settle conflicting interests. Many tunnels have been run from twenty-five to fifty feet and abandoned. Galena is the prevailing mineral, and will doubtless be found in rich and permanent abundance—but probably not to exceed in the proportion of one to forty of the claims already made. There are many indications of gold, and no doubt copper and silver will be found in paying quantities. The Argentine, situated in Cherry Valley, is yielding silver rock which looks as if it would pay well. Opposite to the Argentine, in the same valley, commences the little Gem of the Ocean. This claim has yielded more and richer galena than any other mine on the Island, but it has not yet struck the lead in its water-level tunnel, and its upper tunnel has every appearance of being run out. It was probably only what is called by lead miners, a chimney; besides, it is claimed to be a part of the Albion lode of the Monster Company, and the Gem may have to resort to expensive law suits in order to keep the claim.

On each side of the Fourth of July Valley, beginning at the beach and running to the very summit of the mountain, overlooking the ocean southward and westward, are to be seen holes and tunnels without number. The old Santa Catalina, the San Francisco, the New England, the Monster Consolidated, and several other Companies, have done much work on their claims, and bid fair to have a rich reward for their labors. The latter Companies have run tunnels into three of their leads, adjacent to each other, and have found well defined veins. They are now sinking a shaft at the mouth of the Albion, intending to go one hundred and fifty feet deep, and then drift across the three leads and test them all at once. The shaft is already seventy feet deep, following the vein, which has increased from two inches at the top to twenty-four inches in width at that depth, with galena and quartz.

One Word
To all who visit the Island on business or pleasure. There is not a hotel or restaurant on the Island. Take blankets with you, and strong underclothing; fine calf skins are of no account; and if you intend to travel over the mountains—hills, the miners call them—don't wear fine broadcloth. A broad brimmed hat, old stogies, and coarse over-alls, are not to be sneezed at by the pilgrim who traverses the mining region of Santa Catalina.

Johnson's Harbor,
On the eastern part of the Island, is about fifteen miles from the Isthmus. It is a large harbor, and more convenient for shipping than any of those above named, except the Catalina Harbor. Some ten or twelve years ago, Mr. Johnson located here, and established a ranch, which is now so well stocked with sheep and cattle, that he furnishes the Government and citizens, from his shop on the Isthmus, with beef and mutton, at from eight to ten cents per pound. There is but little timber on the Island. The South sides of the mountains have far less of the loose rough shrubbery which grows on the Island than there

is on their northern descent. At Queen City, a new town, lately laid out at the head of Wilson's Valley, by Col. Shipley, about a mile from the shore, it is said there are cottonwood trees, which have assumed quite tree-like proportions. This city is on an elevated table land above the valley, level and commanding, in the midst of a good mineral region, and really looks well—on paper, and is, in fact, a desirable location. It is the pioneer city of the Santa Catalina.

G.R.P.

According to the military record, John [L.] Johnson and [James] Charles Johnson went to the island in 1854, Francisco Guerrero in 1856, William Howland in 1858, and Spencer H. Wilson in 1859. Swain Lawson, owner of a vessel, was also one of the earliest settlers and has two place names on the island in his 'honor.'

The Isthmus had been laid off in town lots by some squatter, just as Queen City had been laid off by Colonel Shipley. Three shanties had been built, but they were ordered removed. The bay was given the name of UNION BAY by the military, which included Fourth of July Cove on the north and Fisherman's Harbor to the south. Then came the letter of September 25, 1864 [M58],

Letter from Santa Catalina
. . . September 20, 1864 . . . military has been removed . . . barracks empty . . . mining population has seemingly passed away . . . there were 1,001 claims . . . located last fall and winter . . . Agents, with full powers, have been sent to New York to flood that market with worthless Catalina Island stock . . . the Monster Company takes the lead [in activity].

[Signed John Johnston]

On leaving the "Arrowhead" of Santa Catalina Island and sailing southward from Union Bay, the next points of interest are caves. Once called BLAKES' CAVES, as late as 1892, the three caves now have their own names and are known as BLUE CAVERN, PERDITION CAVE, and SPOUTING CAVE. Saunders [B122, 1923], referred to them as "the lava caves about the Isthmus. . ."

World's Work, 1902 [P178], said,

At the bay known as the Isthmus on Santa Catalina, the verdure creeps down to the edge of a precipice in which is found a singular though not large cave. The entrance is wide and high, but the cave is shallow, terminating in a little beach. Once in, a long tunnel is seen, just about the width of the boat, through which the careful

PIECES OF EIGHT

voyager may pass, coming out around a point. The entrance of this ocean cavern is filled with kelp, and in shallow water many varieties of seaweed grow flashing tints of red, yellow, green and gold.

Charles F. Holder offers the longest description of Blue Cavern in his *Scientific American* article of 1897 [J309]:

The islands off the coast of Los Angeles and Santa Barbara Counties, Southern California, abound in some remarkable caves. An interesting one is situated on the island of Santa Catalina, which is a trip of about three hours and a half from Los Angeles. The cave lies on the eastern side near what is known as the isthmus, and from the sea presents the appearance of a large, shallow room, the entrance being, at low tide, thirty or forty feet in height. The writer's attention was attracted to it by the strange play of light on the front walls and roof, giving the impression that it was covered with the webs of spiders, moving in a tremulous manner. At the entrance the water is so deep that the largest ship could thrust the tip of her bowsprit into the cavern, and of a rich blue, telling of great depth. This blue tint directly in the entrance of the cave has given the name Blue Cavern to the great opening in the rock.

Pushing a boat in, one is surprised to find a small tunnel branching off to the right—the real cave. The writer entered this in a small boat one day when the tide and sea were low, and penetrated it without difficulty. The water was about six feet deep, over a perfectly level floor covered with pebbles and seaweeds, while here and there could be seen the sparkle of the pearl of the abalone. The sides were too narrow to use oars, and the wall so low that every wave that came rolling in through the tunnel lifted the boat unpleasantly near the roof, showing that at very high tide, when the wind was fresh, the attempt to enter the Blue Cavern might be accompanied with some danger. By standing up and pushing the boat by hand, using the sides and roof, the passage was easily made for about one hundred and fifty feet, the boat suddenly coming out around a point some distance from the main entrance. For unknown centuries the waves have been working at this cave, gradually eating it out, with the result given. At night, when the waves roll in, the spectacle here is a grand one. The seas passing through the long tunnel burst into the larger cave, sweeping up against the sides and bathing them in a rich phosphorescent

light that falls in gleaming rivulets down the black walls, producing a weird and spectral effect.

Then he concluded his article by remarking, "not far from here are several smaller caves below the water, which emit strange noises as the waves are forced in, while one sends out, apparently from the very rock itself, a mass of spray, appearing like a geyser." Obviously, these are Perdition and Spouting Caves.

About half way between the caves and EMPIRE LANDING is to be found a rock quarry, once known as "Government Quarries." The rock was barged by the Wrigleys to San Pedro for their breakwater [M187]. There is also another quarry to the north of Empire Landing, but it is for marble. Knopf [J241, 1938], mentions garnet and green serpentine as being in the area just south of Empire Landing.

In a depression about a mile from Empire Landing, and once known as POT HOLE HARBOR, is POTS VALLEY, or VALLEY OF OLLAS. According to Hamilton, by following the Big Springs Cañon to the north, Pots Valley may be found [C25, 1915].

According to Schumacher [J250, 1878], by following Little Springs northward one may find it as "a wide hollow cañon . . . several hundred yards below the spring at the ravine to the right . . ." Davidson states [N34] that Pots Valley opens on the north shore "about 4 miles east of the isthmus."

Schumacher was on Santa Catalina Island at least twice, and W. H. Holmes visited the Catalina quarries in 1898—after Shatto had lost the island, but prior to Banning obtaining it through James Lick. Holmes wrote an excellent account of these quarries in 1902 [N15].

Charles Francis Saunders [B122, 1923], who once held a financial interest in the island, said that the Empire Landing area had prehistoric quarries "where the Indians once chipped out their steatite ollas and cooking pots, leaving behind them, to this day [1923], the marks of severance and even some half-fashioned jars still joined to the mother rock . . ."

Even as late as 1923 San Pedro commercial fishermen were carrying off quite a lot of sheep from Empire Landing, leaving three skins on the beach after the sheep had been slaughtered [M187].

Following the coast southward, other place names for various locations come to our attention: RIPPERS COVE, LITTLE GIBRALTAR POINT, CABRILLO HARBOR, GOAT HARBOR, and ITALIAN GARDENS. Other than place names, there appears to be no

72

further information for this area, which is immediately north of LONG POINT. Long Point has had its name since before 1891.

Just south of Long Point and about four miles from Avalon is BUTTON SHELL BEACH. Formerly known as MOONSTONE BEACH, many picnickers and those interested in pretty rocks or shells have boated there with pleasing results for their efforts.

Southward is WHITTLEY'S COVE or PLACE, where some of Whittley's buildings once were. Today it is known as WHITE'S COVE or LANDING and some of the oldest Indian burying grounds were found here. White's Cove was also the former home of the island hermit, "Swayne Larsen," about 1862. He lived alone with only a few tame goats as his companions [M187]. About 1902 White's Cove became the new site for a wireless telegraph station.

There is a WILLOW COVE further south, known as SWAIN'S LANDING in 1893. And just back of it is SWAIN'S CANYON, having received this name even earlier.

TOYON BAY, then GALLAGHER BEACH, next come into sight. Back of Gallagher Beach is GALLAGHER CANYON, probably named for Thomas Gallagher, one of the evicted squatters.

Avalon

The story of the square mile incorporated city of AVALON is better known than any other area on the Island of Santa Catalina. The townspeople, the island owners, and the development of the town and island resources evolved into a highly interwoven and sometimes complicated picture of interaction. Only Avalon's earliest history is discussed here.

The earliest known written records of Avalon Bay deal with the nineteenth century Spanish ownership of Alta California. Spain was not proving to be successful in controlling the waters along the coast from American and others' contraband trade. It was in this type of setting that Captain William Shaler's experiences with authorities took place. R. J. Cleveland and Shaler had purchased the *Lelia Byrd* in 1801 and were using it for profit along the coast.

One of the more complete and better secondary accounts of the Spanish problem comes in Millard F. Hudson's article, "The Battle of San Diego," to be found in a Historical Society of Southern California's *Annual Publication* [J359, 1906].

Captain William Shaler's initial trouble in 1803 was at San Diego where a bloodless battle took place between the officers and crew of the Boston brig, *Lelia Byrd,* and the military establishment at San Diego. All of it had to do with some otter skins. The *Lelia Byrd,* although considerably damaged, got on her way and circumnavigated the globe. At some point during the San Diego affair the ship stopped at Avalon. Shaler and Cleveland named it Port Roussillon, after Conte de Roussillon, a friend and passenger [B65].

The finest of references for an account of Shaler is to be found in *Journal of a Voyage between China and the North-Western Coast of America made in 1804 by William Shaler.* It was first published in the *American Register* in Philadelphia in 1808. In 1935 the Saunders Studio Press of Claremont printed it and this publication contains a fine introduction written by Lindley Bynum of San Marino [B65, 1935].

In 1804 Shaler, now without R. J. Cleveland as a partner, sailed again for the west coast of America, arriving in February of that year. On this second visit to Santa Catalina in March of 1804, Shaler had this to say:

> The 14th of March, I paid a visit to the island of Santa Catalina, where I had been informed, by the Indians, that there was a good harbour. We remained there a few days only, to ascertain that point. We found the harbour everything that could be desired, and I determined that, after collecting all the skins on the coast, I would return to it and careen the ship, which she was by this time greatly in want of. After completing our business on the coast, we returned to Santa Catalina, and anchored in the harbor on the 1st of May.

Dr. R. G. Cleland's *History of California* has Shaler's first-hand story of his visit to the island [B10, 1922]. It has also been quoted in Adelaide Doran's *Ranch that was Robbins'* Appendices [B84, 1963]. Readers are referred to these sources for the rest of the Shaler story.

Shaler was born in 1778, was well-educated for those days, and lived a full life. He left Santa Catalina on June 12, 1804 for Canton, was Consul at Havana, Cuba, dying of cholera in 1833 at the age of 55.

Resentment to American trappers and traders who were penetrating California in search of furs was growing in the government of California in the early 1800s. When Jedediah S. Smith arrived on the coast in 1826, having made the first overland trek into California from the Rockies by an American, he had difficulty in convincing the authorities that he was in a harmless and peaceful pursuit of his trade. It took the signatures of three well-known otter hunters before Smith was allowed to go on his way [B14, 1868],

> In testimony whereof we have hereunto set our hands and seals, this 20th day of December, 1826.
>> William G. Dana,
>>> Captain of schooner *Waverly*
>> William H. Cunningham,
>>> Captain of ship *Courier*
>> Thomas M. Robbins,
>>> Mate of schooner, *Waverly*

An interesting sidelight in this affair is the fact that Smith made a brief stopover at Santa Catalina during his stay in California. He had been held in San Diego by government authorities for several months. He was finally released and gladly accepted Captain Cunningham's offer of transport to San Pedro near the Mission San Gabriel where his men were staying. Quoting from his recently published (and heretofore unknown) journal, Smith relates his brief stopover [Brooks, Geo. M., ed., *The Southwest Expedition of Jedediah S. Smith* (Glendale, 1977), p. 125]:

> Every thing being ready, we sailed and on the third day came to anchor on the East side of the Island of St Catalina. The Island of Santa Catalina is about 20 WSW from St Pedro. It is about 18 miles long and 8 broad having high hills covered with grass wild onions and small timber. Capt. Cunningham had a house on the Island for the purpose of salting hides. He was about to take some Cows Hogs and fowls for the use of men there employed. After remaining at the Island 2 nights, we sailed for St Pedro which is merely a good anchorage . . .

Of this particular period of history, Theodore H. Hittell, in his *History of California* [B35, 1897], says,

> The general feeling of distrust against Americans was . . . exhibited in 1827 in reference to a house or hut which had been erected in 1826 by Captain Cunningham of the American ship *Courier* on Santa Catalina Island. It is not unlikely that the maintenance of this establishment, though claimed to be for hunting purposes, may have had something to do with illicit trade. Whatever may have been the case, the government, as soon as it heard of it, issued a preemptory order to Cunningham for its immediate destruction; and the tone of the mandate showed that there was a much more violent and bitter feeling in regard to the subject than would have

74

been evoked by a mere smuggling rendezvous. Cunningham recognized this feeling and promptly replied that he would hasten to obey the order he had received.

The same tone of suspicion again cropped forth. In the *California Historical Society Quarterly* of 1944, "Alfred Robinson, New England Merchant in Mexican California" [J97], we find a footnote #46 taken from the Bancroft Library transcripts,

> Governor José Maria Echeandía in June 1828, accused Bradshaw of a number of illegal acts, including smuggling at Santa Catalina Island, and he ordered him to deposit his cargo in order that it might be examined. On July 16 the *Franklin* cut her cable and, while the captain and crew openly defied the Mexican authorities, ran out of port followed by gunfire from the fort.

Bradshaw was an associate of Cunningham. And it is supposed that they continued to use the building, known at that time as Bradshaw's Fort. As late as 1886 the building was still standing.

This is the period of the island's history when the smuggling trade continued to flourish. Of it, Sir George Simpson [J15, 1841], said,

> The revenues consist of exhorbitant duties and dues amounting to about 125 percent on prime cost, . . . These prohibitory exactions defeat their object, by the encouragment they afford to smuggling, three-fourths of the goods introduced into the country being run ashore, and the remaining one fourth only passing through the customs.

Richard Henry Dana's *Two Years before the Mast* [B15, 1840], refers to the smuggling activities of the *Avon* at Santa Catalina Island; the *Avon* being owned by John Coffin Jones.

Abel Stearns

Abel Stearns, who came to California from New England, became a naturalized citizen of California after his arrival in 1828 or 1829 [B35, 1898; J371, 1953].

José Figueroa, Governor of California, was a friend of Abel Stearns in 1835 and was in office when Abel was accused of smuggling and maintaining a large warehouse in San Pedro [B58, 1939].

According to the Southern California Historical Society [J353, 1900], "Historic Seaports of Los Angeles," by J. M. Guinn, Stearns had purchased the only building in San Pedro from the San Gabriel Mission Fathers and continued to use it as a storehouse for hides. Since the Captain of the Port protested to a continued 'development,' Stearns did not build more, but did maintain what he already had.

On September 22, 1831 Stearns and Alpheus B. Thompson had drawn up an agreement for the use of this warehouse. Alpheus B. Thompson, it may be recalled, had married into the Carrillo family, as did Robbins, Covarrubias, Jones, *et al.* Thompson, later, was possessor of half of the island of Santa Rosa, was a trader, an otter hunter, and a smuggler.

Rolle, *An American in California* [B16, 1956], has said that Abel Stearns, and many others, used southern California's channel islands for the hiding of supplies from Monterey's custom authorities. And there is not much doubt that Captain Cunningham's building on Santa Catalina at Avalon was used in conjunction with Abel Stearns' warehouse at San Pedro. It is this very warehouse at San Pedro that was later acquired by Phineas Banning for his transportation and storage businesses [J353].

By 1842 Abel Stearns had already acquired Rancho Los Alamitos [J380, 1974]. According to Mawn, Stearns had built up the "largest land and cattle empire in southern California." Part of today's Long Beach, Los Alamitos contained 28,027 acres when patented; Fremont wanted to purchase the acreage from Stearns, but Stearns did not want to sell.

Stearns did more than collect land and hides and run a store [J371, 1953]. He was one of the three who sent written objections, May 1, 1830, to Mexico for sending convicts to Santa Cruz Island, using the island as a penal colony [B1; B51]. Santa Rosa Island was being considered for the same purpose.

It was Abel Stearns, then sub-prefect of Los Angeles, who was given an order by Pío Pico to save the Mexican archives when it was seen that the United States would soon annex Alta California.

Mawn's article [J380, 1974], reminds us, however,

that men of integrity such as Fremont, Larkin and Stearns, of whom the last two were well versed in Mexican land law, should have become involved in claims that were later rejected for fraud or very questionable documentation suggests the degree to which people were swept away by the speculative fever of the times.

In 1864 J. H. Ray purchased Santa Catalina Island from Packard/Covarrubias. It was even before 1864 that present day Avalon became known as TIMM'S LANDING. However, both Davidson [N34], and Lawson [U31], used the name, DAKIN'S COVE.

Captain Augustus W. Timms was virtual owner of the town of San Pedro, having started in the transportation and storage business there as early as 1856, as indicated by Frank Lecouvreur, *From East Prussia to the Golden Gate* [B44, 1906]. Timms also had several boats at his command at Santa Catalina—*Pioneer, Ned Beale,* and *Rossita;* he also raised sheep on the island [M137, 1914].

At the same time that Timms was in the staging and freighting business, Phineas Banning was operating the same type of business between San Pedro and Los Angeles.

While Lecouvreur was out of a job, he visited Santa Catalina. This was the year 1856. It was John Behn of the island who urged A. W. Timms to hire Lecouvreur as a clerk in his commission and forwarding house; this was accomplished, 1857. But about a year later Timms sustained financial reverses and Lecouvreur had to leave his employ. Timms later sold to a creditor, Goller, by name.

There is a Lecouvreur story [B44], of the April 27, 1863 explosion of the *S. S. Ada Hancock* at Wilmington, resulting in the loss of twenty-nine lives and a totally wrecked ship,

Mr. Banning himself was on board of the vessel at the time of the explosion and was thought to have been dangerously wounded. He sent me word by express to come to his aid at once, . . . My first duty was, of course, to put order into the interrupted course of business. With a number of good men I started the routine work of assorting a few tons of freight in the warehouse . . .

Mr. Banning survived, but only three or four of the fifty on board escaped injury or death, among them the engineer, Clark, and the fireman.

From T. D. Allin, President of the Pasadena Historical Society, comes some related news, portending future events. As Judge Windle quoted [M187, 1934],

In June, 1886 . . . I made my first trip to Santa Catalina Island [in Hancock Banning's sailboat] . . . about 11 o'clock two men in a small sail boat, rowing, passed us, and Hancock Banning told them to have the sheepmen come for us in rowboats . . . early next morning [they set up] the first camper's tent that summer . . . The only building at Timm's Landing at that time was a shack about 12 by 16 feet about 150 yards back in the brush from shore, used to store wool when shearing sheep.

Percy H. Howland, grandson to William Howland,

confirms the relative location of the shearing corrals [M187, 1928].

Early in Shatto's ownership of the island, 1887-1891, another change took place. Timm's Landing, now the town of "Shatto," received its new name—Avalon. According to Mrs. Etta M. Whitney, wife of Edwin J. Whitney, and sister of George R. Shatto, she chose the name of "Avalon" for the town.

In Webster's dictionary the name "Avalon" means "Beautiful Isle of the Blest," and "Bright Gem of the Ocean" [J355, 1903]. A 1979 Webster dictionary says that Avalon is an island in the western seas held, especially in Arthurian legend, to be an earthly paradise.

Lick had owned the island before selling to Shatto. Shatto's failure in 1891 to pay the Lick Trustees his mortgage of $26,666.66 resulted in the trustees selling the island to William Banning. The Bannings were not unacquainted with Timm's Landing and the island's resources.

John Brinkley lived at Avalon. He is one of the old-timers who went to Santa Catalina at an early date; for him, 1885. He was forty-one years old when he arrived and lived on the island for forty-six years before he died in 1931. Johnny had gone to the island during Lick's ownership; endeared by all, he was affectionately known as "Chicken John." His farm was in a canyon back of Avalon and Johnny supplied the many wants of the townspeople and visitors [M187].

South of Avalon and north of PEBBLE BEACH, jasper is found; also silver with lead. Somewhat farther on is a rock quarry.

JEWFISH POINT might have been so named because of the supply of jewfish, black sea bass, found in the waters off this point. This fish has been one of the largest taken from the waters around Santa Catalina Island, some having attained a weight of 400 pounds—a real challenge for those enjoying the sport.

Above Seal Rocks on the southern end of the island is the Renton Vein for silver and lead. Church Rock is five miles south of Avalon.

There is a SALTE VERDE POINT on the southwest side of the island and above it are the Salte Verde lava beds, about two miles wide and five miles long. Of this Salte Verde Country, ["The Green Leap"], Mrs. Trask [P46, 1897], said,

Volcanic and sun-burnt, the edge of old and splintered rocks, of river cañons, of glaring li-

chen and of the rainbow cliffs . . . On the rainbow cliffs the eagles build their great nests of drift-wood. There is the bark of the seals, for they have a home below; and now and then the plaintive cry of a kid. This is one of the homes of the goats; here they come up to you, and after regarding you with undisguised interest, turn back to their grazing or their play. Their trails are the best of trails in the wild Salte Verde . . . Treacherous indeed are the cliffs of Santa Catalina; . . .

The cliffs are Nature's hazard for the goats, but the hunters are a worse hazard.

There is CHINA POINT before reaching BEN WESTON POINT and BEN WESTON BEACH. Ben Weston was another early squatter. What is now MILLS LANDING went by the name of CRAIG BEACH in 1893. Sentinel Rock is reached; but a mile or so farther is LITTLE HARBOR, five miles beyond EAGLE NEST.

Little Harbor is recognized by authorities as a submarine canyon; at this location a kitchen midden may be seen. Green talc schist is found in the area. Of Little Harbor and the heyday of hunting, the *Catalina Islander* in 1936 remarked [M187],

. . . goat country [was] at Eagle's Nest, Cottonwood and Cape Canyons . . . The late George Greeley, master of the old Eagle's Nest hunting lodge, and the Sportsmen's Hotel at Little Harbor, was the 'ace' driver . . . Little Harbor [was] where the old government barracks had been converted into a hotel used as headquarters during the [goat] hunt . . .

The Interior

There are about eight reservoirs and a large dam scattered about the interior of Santa Catalina: Wrigley Reservoir, north of the SUMMIT; Haypress Reservoir and Patrick Reservoir in the GRAND CANYON area; Cape Canyon Reservoir; Buffalo Springs Reservoir in COTTONWOOD CANYON near the Airport; Lower Buffalo Corral and Upper Buffalo Corral Reservoirs in LITTLE SPRINGS and BIG SPRINGS CANYONS; a Deep Tank Reservoir just off of the road north of the Valley of Ollas; and Thompson Dam near Middle Ranch.

Thompson Dam, constructed in 1924, stores water for domestic use in Avalon, with the Southern California Edison Company in charge. This body of water at full capacity is about half a mile long and close to seventy-five yards wide.

A small spring existed below the airport; a kitchen

midden and Indian artifacts were once found there. SILVER CREEK is in SILVER CANYON, where a never-ending stream supplies water for the thirsty cottonwood trees. There is also running water in most of the canyons through the year [J348, 1936].

ECHO LAKE [CRATER LAKE] is full of water in the rainy season; it is about a mile northeast of Black Jack Peak at an elevation of 1300 feet. This lake is believed to have been shut in by faulting in geologic times. Black Jack is at about a 2000-foot altitude; once called MT. BANNING, and again, CATALINA PEAK.

El Escondido Ranch was an Arabian horse farm, built in Cottonwood Canyon. Middle Ranch has been used for producing stock, fresh fruits and vegetables, and is located in MIDDLE CANYON.

MT. ORIZABA, almost in the center of the island, is the island's divide; it is the highest peak, and attains an altitude of 2109 feet.

Somewhat to Mt. Orizaba's east is BLACK JACK PEAK. Whereas the original weather station was for years at Pebble Beach, it is now at Black Jack. It is believed that this Weather Search Radar installation will improve the forecasting of weather for the area south to the Panama Canal and west to Hawaii. The Catalina Weather Bureau Office is located at the Catalina Airport in the Sky.

Older maps gave Black Jack Peak the name of MT. BANNING, but today a Mt. Banning is between CAPE and Cottonwood Canyons. There is a WHITTLEY PEAK and a TORQUA SPRINGS between WHITE COVE and SWAIN'S CANYON.

Other peaks have been named. A MT. MARTHA, MT. WASHINGTON, MT. SHATTO, and MT. WILSON are in the area south and west of Avalon. The name of one of these peaks was changed to MT. ADA, site of the William Wrigley, Jr. mansion. What today is called CACTUS PEAK was once known as MT. VIZCAÍNO.

There are camps for various organizational groups located as follows—

Banning Beach	Camp Toyon
White's Landing	Y. M. C. A.
Gallagher's Landing	Camp Whittier
Isthmus	Camp Cabrillo
Cherry Valley	Pasadena Boy Scouts
Howland's Landing	Catalina Island Boy Scouts
Fourth of July Cove	Long Beach Boy Scouts

Geology

Before Smith, there was Lawson, and before Lawson there was Cooper. In 1893 it was Lawson of the University of California who made geologic comparisons between San Pedro Hill, San Clemente Island and Santa Catalina Island.

Through his logic and with the evidence obtained, Lawson came to the conclusion that both San Pedro Hill and San Clemente Island emerged from the sea in Post-Pliocene times. In contrast to this, he stated that "Santa Catalina was a land-mass, subject to the forces of subaerial degradation, at the time when San Pedro Hill and San Clemente began to emerge from the waters of the Pacific, in Post-Pliocene time" [U31]. Lawson explained this sentence about the differences between the other two land masses by saying that while they are emerging from the sea, Catalina has been submerging.

In 1863, Dr. Cooper had been the first to surmise that Santa Catalina was possibly sinking, not rising [C13]. In relation to this theory, he found "many new and interesting species of shells about the island by dredging to a depth of 120 fathoms."

The ideas presented by Lawson have resulted in a train of statements by other authorities on the geologic time of submergence for the island of Santa Catalina. Some authorities appear to have agreed with Lawson and some with Smith, who felt the island was in conformity with the general coastal area—rising, not sinking.

Smith's initial detailed study of the island in 1897 was made while preparing for his doctorate. He [J63], also presented a geologic map indicating the various rock formations and discussed the subject in a seventy-page report.

The further study and hypotheses of Santa Catalina's geologic features, rock formations, possible connections to the mainland, supposed related facts about its subsidence and/or uplift, have been continuing.

Fairbanks got into the discussion and the *American Geologist* presented his views [U53, 1897]:

The conditions at Santa Catalina Island bear out exceedingly well the view of a former elevation. The submarine contours around the island have a curve very similar to that of the shore, indicating an extension of the main features of the topography to a depth of over 300 fathoms. The island is very steep, and rugged and the absence of terraces is no proof, as Lawson seems to think it is, that the island was never submerged. Mr. W. S. T. Smith has recently shown that the land was submerged during the Miocene as much as 1400 feet below the present level and that in the recovery from the depression, at least one terrace was formed. He also expresses the opinion that in pre-Miocene times the island was elevated 2000 to 3000 feet above the present level. A recent subsidence is shown to have taken place amounting to about 350 feet. Thus many facts go to show that the history of the island in a general way corresponds to that of the mainland. The same thing is probably true of the Santa Barbara islands.

At a later date [J30, 1933], Smith reviewed his former ideas [U32]; this was previous to Ritter's [J300, 1901] thoughts on the subject. Smith's was a thirteen-page article, in which he considered the various factors concerned in the development of wave-cut features, and the conditions determining the presence or absence of drowned valleys on a submerged coast line.

The evidence Ritter used for agreeing with Lawson was that "while dredging in forty-five fathoms about three-quarters of a mile off Long Point, on the north side of Santa Catalina Island, the dredge brought up large numbers of cobble stones . . . most of them were very smooth and round, . . ."

To Ritter, not a geologist, there could be no other conclusion but that the stones and pebbles testified that Santa Catalina had been sinking in recent geologic times.

While Lawson in 1924 declared that Santa Catalina had no elevated wave-cut terraces, Smith declared that "the apparent absence of terraces on the rugged Santa Catalina Island," should not bring one to the conclusion that the more recent general movements of the islands and the coast have not been the same [J30, 1933]. Further, he stated that Lawson made but rapid reconnaissance of Santa Catalina; such is not suitable to understand the island's intricate topography.

Apparently Alfred Oswald Woodford joined with Smith in the discussion [U33, 1924], by saying,

My few observations on Catalina confirm yours concerning marine terraces. On the southwest side there are a number of well defined terraces which notch the ridges between the canyons. At least one of these terraces—at 700′ approximately—bears marine shells, rounded pebbles, and worn shell fragments. I think it probable that Catalina had a mature topography before the submergence and re-emergence which has left its record in the Clemente and Catalina terraces.

Smith mentioned rolled pebbles on two benches at 1000-foot and 1060-foot levels at the southwestern end of the island, the direction of the open sea and the side of the island most subject to the vigorous wave action. According to Smith this suggested not subaerial [surface] erosion but rather marine abrasion, a more direct answer to Ritter's logic.

Smith found additional worn pebbles on the main ridge of Santa Catalina south of Avalon, and on the main ridge a short distance southeast of the head of Middle Ranch Canyon.

Shell deposits and worn pebbles were found by him, "in an erosion saddle in the late-Miocene andesite near the middle of the island, about three-fourth of a mile southwesterly from the island's highest point, at an elevation between 1400 and 1500 feet . . ." He continued [J30]:

If, . . . this deposit is limited to the saddle . . . it can scarcely be other than Pleistocene . . . [then] the deposit clearly indicates a Pleistocene submergence of the island of more than 1400 feet, followed by a re-emergence,— . . .
All of which confirms the view that the leveled summits of Santa Catalina are the result of marine abrasion.

In true-Trask-style, Blanche Luella hit upon the controversial subject almost before it became controversial. This is indicated in her words from "Fossil Peak, Santa Catalina Island" [J336, 1904].

The *Bulletin* of the *Southern California Academy of Sciences* [J336], published this information,

The fossil *Pecten estrellanus* Con. was found three years ago on one of our greatest elevations. It appears like a powder along the trail, while below, the eroded cliff-edge is thick-set with the shells from one to six inches in diameter.
Most of them are cracked and packed in the limestone as though by heavy pressure.
An adjacent peak is topped with rolled pebbles, while the great dikes of volcanic rock are visible here and there. In these, erosion rainbows seem to be imprisoned, and when the winter rains set the emerald grasses aglow the effect is dazzling.
In the thousands of miles I have tramped here no other trace of fossils have been found. The elevation is about 1,500 feet above the sea.

Smith concluded his 1933 article [J30], by saying,

. . . other evidence tends to show that the recent depression of Santa Catalina was contemporaneous with and not appreciably greater than a corresponding depression definitely indicated for the neighboring islands and mainland. In short, from all facts now available [Kew, J164; Rand, C27] it would seem that instead of differentiation there has been a remarkable uniformity in the general later Pleistocene movements of all the southern California islands and the neighboring mainland coast as well.

At least by 1937, F. P. Shepard was studying the marine sediments around Santa Catalina. By 1939 he and two other authors came to the conclusion that there should be a reexamination of the evidence for a recent uplift of Santa Catalina Island [J31].

Evidently, having studied Smith's line of reasoning rather carefully, they stated that shells from a high point had proven to be Miocene, not Pleistocene, as Smith had reasoned. They then proceeded to guess that the presence of rounded cobbles at various levels could have been the work of Indians, and that the flat summits may be representative of the remnants of a pre-Pleistocene epoch. Obviously, they could not agree with Smith. Therefore, they said that "unless [new] information is found it would seem more likely that Lawson's opinion that the island had undergone a different history from that of its neighbors is correct."

A later follow-up of the Trask 'find' is that made by T. D. A. Cockerell some thirty-five years later. He reported on the marine invertebrate fauna of the California Islands through the Sixth Pacific Science Congress at the University of California, Berkeley [U36, 1939].

Cockerell had been to Santa Catalina, as had Dr. F. P. Shepard. Cockerell found no marine Pleistocene beds on Santa Catalina, nor did Dr. Shepard. Dr. Shepard in 1938 had climbed to the top of Mount Orizaba, 2109 feet, following a report of some shells there. Perhaps he looked at too high an altitude. But Dr. Shepard did say that he had found some shells to be *Pecten* of Miocene, not Pleistocene Age [J31, 1939].

Clements and Dana [U49, 1944], on the subject of marine sediment near Catalina Island, have seemingly accepted Shepard's suggestion that a previous rise of sea-level had been as much as three hundred feet since the last glacial period. This, of course, could account for some of the rounded pebbles off the shore of the island found by Ritter in 1901.

By 1955 T. Clements, "The Pleistocene History of the Channel Island Region, southern California,"

Essays in Natural Sciences, had this to say on the subject of terraces:

> A study of aerial photographs of the island corroborated the presence of the terraces. However, the terraces appear to be more highly dissected than those on the other islands, suggesting their having been cut at an earlier date . . . [or] because of the presence of more resistant rock, as suggested by Smith . . . Recent seismic activity in the area indicates certainly that it is by no means quiescent. Whether or not the region is rising faster than sea level can be answered only in the future.

Bailey drew some conclusions from his study of the island [M24, 1941]. He thought several observations to be important for analytical purposes:

1. At approximately 1500 feet above sea level there is an older, practically level surface.
2. "Orizaba" and "Black Jack" rise abruptly above the surface.
3. Small terraces are found at one hundred feet, twenty-five feet, and ten feet at various points.
4. There are no other undoubted terraces on the island.
5. Numerous landslides with nearly horizontal slopes along the ocean superficially resemble terraces.

James W. Valentine and Jere H. Lipps, in their 1967 Symposium report [B120], stated that marine terraces, probably all of post-Pliocene age, have but a relatively thin veneer on parts of most islands. Another remark, the sediments above 1000 feet are not well-documented, but that marine fossils in sediments may be found on surf-cut terraces to 2000 feet. But on Santa Catalina, the fossiliferous marine sediments are a problem, due to the island's highly eroded terraces.

The controversial discussion of similarity of geologic history of Santa Catalina with the other islands seems to remain inconclusive. However, Santa Catalina had a mature topography in Miocene days, with the topographic highs emerging after that period. Viewed from this standpoint, Smith's conviction of the general uniformity in the Pleistocene movements of the islands and the neighboring mainland still contains merit.

Dr. Cockerell, in his "Natural History of Santa Catalina Island" [J320, 1939], stated that he doubted that Santa Catalina ever had mainland connections. This view is shared by Peter H. Raven and others, and thus has become another subject of controversy,

79

appearing at intervals in the literature.

Rocks and Minerals

Dr. Cooper was one of the first, if not the first, to mention Santa Catalina's rock composition [C13, 1865]. He described the formations as being almost exclusively metamorphic, "with frequent volcanic outbursts and lava streams of vesicular basalt. Near the great break [the Isthmus] in the island is a vein of ferruginous [rust-looking] matter, about a foot thick, containing masses of galena, which may be traced for some distance . . . and the galena is said to contain silver." Knopf [J241, 1938], said this region contained gold outcroppings, as well.

Dr. Smith's geologic work [J63, 1898], on Santa Catalina is well recognized by many and it appears that he gave the island more study than any other geologist. In summarizing his findings of the rock formations in a 1933 *American Journal of Science* article [J30], he said,

> The northwestern two-thirds of the island is underlain by a group of metamorphic rocks which are believed to be a facies of the Franciscan series, of Jurassic (?) age. They consist chiefly of various quartz, albite and amphibole schists, talc schist, serpentine, and garnet amphibolite, and are exposed over an area of about thirty-seven square miles, or approximately half the island. These rocks have a variable, although generally considerable, angle of dip.

> The southeastern third of the island consists chiefly of massive quartz hornblende diorite porphyry which has been intruded into the metamorphic rocks. This is exposed over an area of about twenty square miles.

> Overlying a part of both the metamorphic rocks and the porphyry is a series of volcanic flows, chiefly andesites, in part if not wholly of late-Miocene age. The principal occurrence of these rocks, having an area of about thirteen square miles, is found near the center of the island. In addition there are a number of small, scattered areas, totaling about four square miles. The largest and most northerly of these, just southeast of Isthmus Cove, contains an intercalated group of beds of tuff and diatomaceous earth, between one and two hundred feet in thickness.

Woodford remarked [U33, 1924], that the rocks of Santa Catalina are unusual metamorphics, in large part derived from sedimentary material; so unusual that the resulting facies are "sufficiently extensive and texturally qualified to be considered regionally metamorphic."

Somewhat more simply stated than Smith's summarization of the rock formations, Bailey [M24, 1941], remarked that more than one half of the rock is Basement Complex [Woodford's Metamorphic Facies of the Franciscan series]. Smith had suggested two-thirds.

Bailey said that about one quarter of the rock is intrusive; Smith had suggested one third. Bailey had surmised that slightly less than one quarter of the rock is volcanic. Smith suggested that this principal area was about thirteen square miles.

Crawford [C24, 1893], said that there are beds of diatomaceous earth [silicified skeletons of minute algae] over seventy feet in thickness occurring on the island. This earth is beyond Empire Landing. Smith [J30], indicated there were beds of tuff and diatomaceous earth between one and two hundred feet in thickness occurring southeast of Isthmus Cove.

Crawford also stated that there is much green steatite on Santa Catalina, the best known body being in the Valley of the Pots, and in that same general region.

Hamilton [C25, 1915], reported steatite "about a mile from Empire Landing on the north shore of the island, and in a depression known as Potts' Valley . . . near the south of the Isthmus . . . there is also a large body of steatite."

Knopf [J241, 1938], reported on Empire Landing and "its long abandoned quarry of green serpentine or steatite . . . The quarry lies about a mile back from the beach [and south], where skiffs can land in any but stormy weather." A "very fine variety of soapstone is found about a mile back from the beach to the west of Howland's Cove. It can be visited by landing at Johnson's, but that landing is more exposed and rough."

Several authors feel that the interesting geology is confined to the central area, lying roughly between Empire Landing and ORIZABA PEAK. It appears to be "the outstanding mineralized district of the interior" and is embraced by and adjacent to Black Jack Peak and Mt. Orizaba.

Tucker [C26, 1927], remarked that in the vicinity of Black Jack and RUBY PEAKS there is considerable garnetiferous hornblende; however, the peaks are of volcanic tuff and lava.

One Black Jack vein is made up of garnetiferous hornblende, quartz, calcite, barite, and muscovite and some of the veins are from four to fifteen feet wide.

Bailey remarked that silver-bearing galena is the the principle ore of the Black Jack Mine.

GARNET PEAK [Ruby Peak] is between Mt. Black Jack and the Isthmus [J241], accessible only by foot trail. Garnets are said to also be in the Empire Landing region, north of Orizaba Peak, at BUFFALO SPRINGS [M24]; and Judge Windle [M187], said, "a fine quality of garnet is to be found on the western end of the island beyond the Isthmus, but no effort has been made to find them."

At the Catalina Airport there is on display a boulder about twenty-four inches in diameter completely studded with garnets; it had been unearthed from the island.

Randolph [J213, 1935], credited some of Santa Catalina's hidden resources as being found in the form of jasper, onyx, agate, crystals, and moonstones. Other resources in lesser quantity and value appear to be fuchsite, opal, zircon, and actinolite [M24]. The jasper, called "Catalinaite," is in a silica base and is to be found in the Pebble Beach area.

Of the 'moonstones' that Kinsell [P87, 1891], referred to as "glistening pebbles of which I am so fortunate as to possess a garden walk," Hamilton said that these beach stones were "pebbles of nodules of quartz weathered out of a rhyolite rock—composed of sanidine feldspar on quartz." Kinsell's moonstones were probably obtained at Button Shell Beach.

Holder [B38], while he discussed a large cave near the Isthmus, said that close by is an outcropping of "red paint" from which the Indians made their color; Mexican Joe had pointed out this outcropping many years before 1910.

Natural History
Flora

Although Dr. William Gambel, ornithologist, was from Philadelphia, Pennsylvania, he is the first recorded collector of flora on the island of Santa Catalina [J72, 1887; B105, 1923]. His was a small California collection from the year 1843, but he mentioned several new generic types. He found *Crossosoma californicum* on the island, then it was described by Thomas Nuttall in 1898. Frank H. Vaslit had also discussed *Crossosoma* in a half-page note in *Zoe* [J392, 1890].

Thomas Nuttall had been to California seven years earlier than had Gambel, 1836, using the overland route [P83]. On his return voyage to Harvard University at Cambridge, Massachusetts, he was on a Bryant and Sturgis sailing vessel. Dana's account of Dr. Nuttall is highly interesting. Here are but a few of his comments [B15]:

> I had left him quietly seated in the chair of Botany and Ornithology, in Harvard University; and the next I saw of him, was strolling about San Diego beach, in a sailor's pea-jacket, with a wide straw hat, and barefooted, with his trousers rolled up to his knees, picking up stones and shells . . . Sometimes, when I was at the wheel of a calm night, and the steering required no attention, . . . he would come aft and hold a short yarn with me; . . . I was often amused to see the sailors puzzled to know what to make of him . . . The *Pilgrim's* crew christened Mr. N. "Old Curious," from his zeal for curiosities, . . .

Dana had come to this Coast on the *Pilgrim* and had returned to the East Coast on the *Alert*, both of Bryant and Sturgis.

Of the *Crossosoma*, Sherwin Carlquist in *Island Life* [B82, 1965], has also offered comments,

> Flowering plants offer many examples of how islands are instrumental in preserving relicts . . . *Crossosoma*, with two species, constitutes a family related to the rose family . . . *C. Californicum* occupies the islands Santa Catalina, San Clemente, and Guadalupe . . .

In 1884 and 1885 W. S. Lyon and Rev. J. C. Nevin visited the island. Lyon's list of 151 species for Santa Catalina included *Lyonothamnus;* the list was published in a 1886 *Botanical Gazette*, said Greene [J72]. Fifteen of Lyon's 151 Santa Catalina species were reported as insular. The one making identifications for Lyon's Catalina and San Clemente species was Asa Gray. He named both *Lyonothamnus* and *Prunus Lyoni* [cherry] for Lyon. Gray was successor to Nuttall as a botany professor at Harvard when Nuttall returned to England [P83].

San Bernardino's Mr. S. B. Parish, *Zoe* [J397, 1890], spoke of a Pacific *Lavatera*, the "malva rosa," possibly having originally come from Anacapa, thought Parish. Parish indicated that there was no European type to which this *Lavatera* could be compared. Dr. Greene had thought the species to be an island endemic.

The *Botanical Gazette* of 1903 included Mr. Parish's, "A Sketch of the Flora of Southern California," [U50]. His comments about Santa Catalina and San

Clemente, as parts of the general coast-island flora, are not exactly in line with Greene's,

> Emergent peaks they certainly are, but a more reasonable theory regards them as belonging, not to another continent, but to a chain of mountains paralleling the present Coast Range, now, save for them, sunk beneath the waters of the ocean, whose waves roll over what was once a broad valley separating the two ranges. Under this theory the peculiar insular plants, such as *Lyonothamnus* and the species of *Lavatera,* are to be regarded as the remnants of a flora, antedating the period of subsidence, once common to the whole coast region. . . The islands are . . . to be considered as a subarea of the Cismontane area, and but slightly differentiated from the Coastal subarea.

Both Parish and Brandegee were collecting on the island in 1916; Alice Eastwood was there in 1917.

To the California Academy of Sciences Mr. Townshend S. Brandegee gave an interesting account of his recent botanizing trip to Santa Catalina Island. He briefly described the island's climate and topographical features, and its most striking and interesting plants [J394, 1980].

In another article on the island by Brandegee, he remarked that the "flora, as a whole, very much resembles that of Santa Cruz Island, and at first sight appears to differ from it only in the abundance of *Crossosoma* and *Rhus laurina*" [J395]. If *Crossosoma* is not to be found on Santa Cruz, this remark is somewhat confusing.

As editor of *Zoe,* Brandegee published several articles, after having been on the island many times. He added about fifty-six species, some few not found on the mainland. Brandegee had been to Santa Catalina in 1884, 1889, 1890, 1899, and 1916 [B105].

Anstruther Davidson and A. J. McClatchie visited Santa Catalina Island between 1892 and 1895. According to Millspaugh [B105], the full extent of McClatchie's collection is not known.

In 1894 [U25; U26], McClatchie reported on the fact that he had collected about twenty-five plants that had not previously been reported from the island, "five of these have since been reported by Dr. Davidson, . . ." McClatchie, in his five-page *Erythea* report, credited Professor E. L. Greene and Mr. S. B. Parish for their assistance in identifying many of the plants.

Davidson's catalogue for Los Angeles County was published in 1896 [J325]. Of the thirty-six pages,

there is but an occasional reference to Santa Catalina and San Clemente.

Mrs. Trask, who had been collecting since about 1895, also reported through *Erythea* in 1897 [U27]. She said that the "groves of this oak [Quercus tomentella] are in deep and sheltered cañons . . . they are comparatively tall, over fifty feet in height, straight of limb, and majestic."

C. F. Holder had much to say about the flora of Santa Catalina Island in his *Channel Islands of California* [B38, 1910]. Here are a few important remarks:

> I became entangled in the greasewood and led and pulled my weary horse down the side of a steep ravine leading to Swain's Cañon on the north coast, where I came upon a grove of dark green trees which I knew to be *Lyonothamnus,* one of the rarest of trees, confined to Santa Catalina, San Clemente, and Santa Cruz. Mr. Harry Polley, another devoted botanist of the island, had written me about it long before, as follows:

"Dear Mr. Holder:

"Am sorry I was delayed in answering yours in regard to the *Lyonothamnus floribundus*. The nearest grove to Avalon, and one of the best on the island, is up Swain's Cañon about half a mile and can be seen from the beach. Is a thick dark green clump of straight trees about thirty feet high, covering space of one hundred by one hundred feet on side of steep hill one hundred feet above cañon to the left; and just across a small cañon above to the southwest is another small clump.

"Next nearest clump is away up on Black Jack, perhaps fifty yards below the ridge trail to the Isthmus, about on a line between the peak and White's Landing.

"Another clump is a little way up the left cañon from Goat Harbor."

There are several groves in the little-visited north or west part of the island beyond the Isthmus . . . Lyon's ironwood is one of the most interesting trees in the country . . . It loves conspicuous and high places, where it can look out on the world.

One of the unique plants on Santa Catalina is a dogwood, discovered by Mr. Polley, which bears his name (*Cornus polleyii*). He also discovered here the five-leaved oak (*Rhus diversiloba*), and the California holly (*Heteromeles arbutifolia*), from which is made the tanned bark of the fishermen. Its berries are yellow instead of red.

The species of currant, incorrectly called a banyan tree, at Avalon, is the only one not found on the mainland or the neighboring islands . . . The cottonwood and willow are the conspicuous trees of the cañons; and here Mr. Polley has found the rare oak, *Quercus MacDonaldii,* known only here and at Santa Cruz . . .

The island oak [*Quercus tomentella*] is another rare tree. It attains a height of nearly sixty feet, and is found only at Santa Catalina and Guadalupe far to the south . . .

Of *Lyonothamnus,* Carlquist [B82, 1965], had this to say, ". . . this large tree, with unique and easily recognized leaves, is today known only as a single species *L. floribundus,* from Santa Cruz, Santa Catalina, and San Clemente Islands." Munz has placed *Quercus MacDonaldii* on Santa Rosa, also, and the *Quercus tomentella* on Santa Rosa, San Clemente, and Santa Cruz Islands.

One of the more important sections of *Flora of Santa Catalina Island* [B105, 1923], is Millspaugh and Nuttall's annotated list of collectors and bibliography. The book is sizeable; a "must" for botanists.

Charles F. Millspaugh collected on the island in 1919 and L. W. Nuttall in 1920. In 1921 E. C. Knopf, who lived on the island for nine years, a professional lapidarius and jeweler, "made a complete collection of the island's flora for the Field Museum of Chicago." The book [B105], is a result of the efforts of all three men—collecting, identifying, and compiling.

Millspaugh was a professor of the Field Columbian Museum of Chicago, an M. D., and wrote on American medicinal plants. By his efforts, and that of others, 1923 produced over thirty new species for the island, many of them endemic to Santa Catalina.

Another 'must,' other than the Lyon list and the Millspaugh list is that effort made by Alice Eastwood, and published in 1941 by the California Academy of Sciences [J74]. Of her work she stated, "The list of species has been compiled from scattered publications of scientific societies, floras, revisions, monographs, lists, and general descriptions . . . A bibliography at the end of the list will give the chief sources of my information, especially those concerning the insular species."

From the *Masterkey* [J187, 1937], came some comments by Ralph D. Cornell:

One of these plants, that occurs naturally on Santa Catalina, San Clemente, and Santa Cruz islands, is found in the happy family on Museum Hill . . . It is the Catalina cherry that carries the botanic name *Prunus lyoni* [an arboreous plant] . . . In April or May it covers itself with a snowy blanket of white flowers . . . these flowers are followed, later in the season, by large purple to black fruit that are chiefly seed and skin, with a thin layer of sweet pulp between.

The Catalina cherry grows to a height of 35 or more feet, with a trunk diameter up to 18 inches . . . The fruit of this Catalina cherry . . . used to form one of the fresh-fruit foods of the island Indians. . .

This island form grows naturally in dry, rocky or gravelly soils, . . . The plant has been grown by nurserymen for years . . . evergreen and distinctive . . .

Dr. R. F. Thorne [J157, 1967], in "A Flora of Santa Catalina Island, California" remarked that "the heavy collecting on the island since the Millspaugh-Nuttall survey, . . . has turned up 145 species unlisted for the island flora by Millspaugh and Nuttall." This L. W. Nuttall is not to be confused with the earlier Thomas Nuttall.

A few paragraphs on Dr. Thorne's efforts on Santa Catalina Island were published in the August 17, 1967 issue of the *Catalina Islander.* Dr. Thorne had evidently been collecting and classifying data and plants from the island for about three years. Dr. Thorne is a taxonomist of the Rancho Santa Ana Botanic Garden.

El Aliso published Dr. Thorne's "A Supplement to the Floras of Santa Catalina and San Clemente Islands, Los Angeles County, California" in 1969 [J158]. Worthy of note, due to additions and/or changes, the article is recommended for review by some, and for study by others.

Also in *El Aliso* [J156, 1963], is Raven's comment, "Of the approximately 200 species found on Santa Catalina that do not extend to San Clemente, only 12 are not present on the adjacent mainland."

Dr. P. H. Raven [B120, 1967], said of Santa Catalina that there are one species, one subspecies, and two varieties endemic to this particular island. Of the twenty-one species, subspecies, and varieties endemic to more than one island of the four southern islands, twelve of them are on Santa Catalina. And of the seventy-six endemics for all eight islands, twenty-six of them may be found on Santa Catalina.

Dr. Thorne's somewhat later summary allowed four species and three subspecies for the island.

Obviously, further discoveries and discussions make the flora subject matter anything but definitive.

Fauna

Appendix JJ of the U. S. Geographical Survey [N45, 1879], listed two snails for Santa Catalina. It is said that the snail *Helix facta* is peculiar to three of the islands, San Nicolas, Santa Barbara, and Santa Catalina. The snail *Helix Gabbii* is found only on San Clemente and Santa Catalina.

Without mentioning a technical name, Mrs. Trask [M134], said that "the largest of all snails is the one most common on Santa Catalina [and] are said to rival in delicacy of taste the famous snail so relished by the Frenchmen."

Alice Eastwood and Mr. F. A. Seavey collected insects on Santa Catalina during the month of August 1892. The short collection list was published under six major headings [J400, 1892]. H. C. Fall collected insects in 1892 and 1894 and added over one hundred species to the previous record [J98, 1897].

In a review of the collections of reptiles and amphibians taken from Santa Catalina, Van Denburgh said that a Mr. A. M. Drake took the salamander *Batrachoseps attenuatus* [J66, 1905]. They seemed to be common and look like lizards [M134].

Both Mr. J. I. Carlson and Professor Cope recorded *Uta stansburiana* from the island [J66], and a Mr. J. J. Rivers was sent several *Zantusi riversiana* that had been taken from the island. Dr. Yarrow and Paul Schumacher each obtained a specimen of rattlesnake in 1876.

In a later article by Van Denburgh and Slevin [J68, 1914], it was said that "with the exception of two rattlesnakes taken on Catalina, these are the only snakes that have ever been collected on any of the California islands." But Cooper in 1868 had reported a *Lampropeltis Boylei* taken on the island [J59, 1868]. The addition of a *Hyla* from Santa Catalina made six herpetofaunal species in all [J68].

By 1967 J. H. Savage [B120], stated that the island had a herpetofauna of eleven species, which included one other salamander type, two species of lizard, and three more snakes. He did not include *Zantusi riversiana*. He remarked that "it appears likely that the ingredients of the present insular herpetofauna invaded the islands during the late Pleistocene times . . ."

Don Meadows prefaced his article [J348, 1936], on moths and butterflies with these remarks, "until the material for this paper was assembled no extensive collection of island butterflies and moths was made . . . Excluding the micro-lepidoptera . . . 167 species of lepidoptera were taken."

From the *Symposium* [B120], came the following information from Jack C. von Bloeker, Jr.: Of the land mammals, those existing on Santa Catalina are the Shrew, Mouse-eared Bat, Lump-nosed Bat, California Myotis, and Pallid Bat; ground squirrels are found only on this island; there are the Harvest Mouse, the Deer Mouse, and the Channel Island Fox.

Mrs. Trask [M134, 1906], said that the large field mouse, common on all the Channel Islands, is called the "Kangaroo." Of the fox, she explained that they "make and maintain tiny trails all their own which no other animal seems to use . . . John Brinkley finds it necessary to keep fox traps set at his chicken ranch, near Avalon . . ."

Although the listing of fauna is not large, it should be noted that the attempt to discover new species has been going on since 1879.

Avifauna

Of the ravens on Santa Catalina Island, Otto J. Zahn remarked [J50, 1895], about their tameness—unless you have a gun along. He found their nests—one nearly hidden in the thick lining of sheep's wool. Another nest was made of coarse sticks, measured twenty-two inches across, with the cavity about five inches deep and a foot wide.

A first mention of the ravens on the island was made by Vizcaíno when he described the Temple to the Sun at the Isthmus, and spoke of how the ravens were considered sacred by the Indians.

In Gustav Eisen's account of the Indians on the Santa Barbara Islands [M30, 1904], he remarked that at that time the islands were overrun with ravens similar to those seen by Vizcaíno. They are "equally impudent and will approach with little fear."

Mr. David P. Fleming, in writing about the island for *Arrowhead* [P4, 1908], reiterated this observation by saying, "the peculiar ravens of the island have long been famous for their boldness."

Mr. Childs spoke of Mr. O. W. Howard's visit to Santa Catalina in May of 1905. He had gone there in the hope of finding the Santa Barbara Flycatcher breeding [J385, 1906]. The following quotation is quite typical of the explanations made by ornithologists, bent on being more concrete than merely making observations of the birds in their natural habitat:

on May 4th he took two sets of four eggs each; also the nests and the parent birds. The nests were found in a canyon, six to seven hundred feet altitude, one being in the fork of a limb of a large shrub some eight feet from the ground; the other in a like situation ten feet from the ground. Both nests are well built, the material used being bark fiber, vegetable down, grasses, moss, etc. The eggs are exceedingly handsome, and our colored plate represents one set exactly as to size and color. Both sets with nests and skins are in our collection.

Joseph Grinnell enjoyed going to the island, a trip which he made on numerous occasions. He was there for eight days in December 1897 and as a result gave a briefly annotated list of the birds detected on the island during that visit. His three-page list evolved from Dove to Eagle to Flicker, Owl, Phoebe, Raven, Shrike, Thrush, and finally to Wren [J39, 1898].

In 1908 Mr. Charles H. Richardson, Jr. went to the island on two different occasions for a total of about thirteen days. As a result, he was able to compile a list of twenty-nine species, published in *Condor* [J110].

Quite briefly G. K. Snyder mentioned Dusky Warbler nests in a canyon in 1909, and referred to Bald Eagles' nests [J235]. When he returned to the island in 1914 he examined eleven nests of the Allen Hummingbird [J130]. P. I. Osburn spoke of the Frazer Oystercatcher and the Ancient Murrelet in his notes of 1911 [J123].

Mr. Meadows also took notes in 1929 on the island's avifauna [J143]:

In checking over my notes . . . I find several records that are additions to the known avifauna of the island . . . Including the following [17], thirty birds have been added to the island list since the publication of Howell's "Birds of the Islands off the Coast of Southern California." The list now numbers 124 species.

The following year Meadows mentioned seeing the Pileolated Warbler, the Brewer Blackbird, and the Thurber Junco, all having been reported at a much earlier date [J144].

Alden H. Miller of the Museum of Vertebrate Zoology, Berkeley, California [J155, 1955], stated that the Acorn Woodpecker had been seen on Santa Cruz and Santa Rosa and even Santa Catalina, and that this is the first formal record of the extension of their range. He also "noted small groups of this species in the oaks in Avalon and in the oaks of the bottoms of the two canyons northwest of Avalon," and seemed to feel that such reflects a definite colonization of the woodpecker.

In 1900 Mr. H. C. Oberholser commented on one male and one female quail being taken from the island [N6]. In 1906 Grinnell made a somewhat more detailed study of the Catalina Island Quail [J44]. "In view of the differences characterizing the Catalina Island Quail it seems to me most probably that they belonged to the original fauna." When James C. Johnston, resident of the island, was interviewed by Mr. Grinnell, he affirmed that the quail were already on the island when he arrived. This was in the 1850s.

Professor Charles F. Holder, an authority on the natural history and ethnology of the California coast islands, had the same opinion. But Dr. Cooper in 1870 thought the quail, "was probably carried there originally, as a flight of eighteen miles at once would probably be too far for a bird with so short wings." However, Cooper might not have considered all possible factors involved with their flight.

Marine Gardens
and Sea Serpents

H. P. Earle remarked [P44, 1896], that all of the Channel Islands plunge abruptly into the ocean and the water surrounding the islands becomes suddenly deep. But he enjoyed the glass-bottom boat cruise close to shore where he could watch the movements of the fish as they swam or rested in their natural environment.

Marine life was a chief interest of Charles Frederick Holder, and it was he who persuaded the Bannings to build an Aquarium at Avalon for the educational benefit of visitors. It was also Dr. Holder who encouraged the creation of the glass-bottom boat to further augment the visitor's liberal education in marine zoology. Any area concerning fish or fishing was his lively interest—from catching to conserving to publicizing [J314, 1904; J315, 1906].

Of the glass-bottomed boat he said,

. . . The first glass-bottom boat was a large yawl or barge capable of holding twelve people, . . . The first glass-bottom boat was propelled by a man who sat forward and rowed, also acting as a guide, pointing out the wonders of the deep with no sluggish imagination . . . The evolution of the glass-bottom boat continued, . . . a large power boat with a commodious well . . . being very flat, so that she could pass over the floating kelp and run in the shallowest water . . .

PIECES OF EIGHT

In M. O. Bolser's "Souvenir of Santa Catalina's Submarine Gardens," may be found many photos—of moss, sponge, kelp, star fish, devil fish, and many more. Bolser included a list of the most common of the seventy different growths to be found in the gardens—another partial education in itself [M4, 1908].

Review of Reviews [J253, 1909], tells of Dr. Charles Frederick Holder's September 1909 *National Geographic Magazine* article on submarine life and the glass-bottom boat. Dr. Holder is quoted from that article, as he told about the growing interest of the public and the increasing business value of investing in the glass-bottom boat. The article ended by allowing Dr. Holder to say, "Surely here is a new and valuable ally to education."

As Edwin Markham [B106, 1914], described the wonders of California, he did not exclude Santa Catalina Island. He especially referred to the submarine gardens,

Tiny blue fishes dart into the weedy tangles, just as the bluebirds dart into seclusion of the thickets. Gold fishes, black perches, gaping sheepsheads all are found here in their busy idleness.

Then Markham quoted from George Sterling's *House of Orchids* [B124, 1911]. Sterling's five stanza poem is on any garden of the sea. For better or worse as a bit of poetry, the poem reflects another's ecstasy as he momentarily experiences sharing the life of underwater creatures and plants.

The *Catalina Islander,* 1921, referred to the *Empress,* one of the glass-bottom boats, stating its superiority over the row boat era, "The sixteen thousand candle power lights are . . . in water tight pontoons, and throw sufficient light to illuminate a 200-foot radius at a depth of 75 to 100 feet."

From Charles Francis Saunders [B122, 1923]:

The preeminent matter, however, is the marine gardens of the bay. The waters are transparent . . . There are forests of long-fronded, swaying kelp, and shrubberies of seaweeds of many forms and hues, rooted in the rocky clefts and gravelly slopes of the submerged mountain . . . Brilliantly colored fish in red, orange, blue and motley, . . . dart hither and yon. Starfish, sea cucumbers and sea anemones loll about the . . . caverns; palpitating jelly fishes, trailing liquescent wings and veils, float under the boat . . .

It is time to move from the sublime and soothing experiences of viewing submarine gardens to the hair-raising and jolting thoughts of other forms of marine life—SEA SERPENTS!

It is not that we need believe in sea serpents in the Age of Mammals. But they do appeal to the imagination—just as does the Loch Ness monster, "Yeti" of Asia, "the Abominable Snowman," "Big Foot" of our northwestern coast, or the UFO, thought to have been experienced on a world-wide basis.

From the *Catalina Islander*, Aug. 10, 1920, located in the files of the Huntington Library, comes this tale of the deep,

"It had eyes as big as saucers, and it gave me the woolies every time it moved," said Harry Hubbard . . . the sea monster he had seen in the channel . . . "we were about eight miles from Avalon when I first saw it" . . . continued Mr. Hubbard, after he had drawn a rough sketch of the head of the monster. "There it is, and I want to tell you it was the most peculiar sea animal or fish I have ever seen in all my years at Catalina. It stayed on the surface looking at us for quite awhile, and then slowly moved off in the opposite direction. The face of the monster was about six feet across, and its head was shaped like that of an elephant.

From *Veiled Horizons* [M41, 1939], also found in the Rare Book Room file of the Huntington Library, comes this story,

. . . So, what I saw I saw from about a quarter of a mile away and through the lenses of field glasses.

Such an experience as I had comes only to a fortunate few. Coming face to face with an impossible creature, something unknown, something that cannot be, rocks one's powers of judgment and observation . . . Then a series of breaking seas hid it and I saw it no more. But it was enough to tell me that the tales which had been brought in about something strange and large out in that channel had a foundation in fact.

I have said that others have seen the Thing . . . I am a moderately good judge of distance, horizontal and vertical, and I am of the firm belief that the Thing, when I saw it, lifted up a good twenty feet.

There was nothing serpentine about it, except, perhaps, the head. The impression I gathered was of a huge neck which must have led to an unbelievably huge body . . .

The Thing has been reported all along the Pacific Coast from Monterey to Ensenada, although it has been seen most often in the San Clemente Channel and fairly close to the island. I am satisfied there is more than one . . . I feel certain that it is a mammal and must come up to breathe . . .

So fas as I know there have been three other men closer to the Thing than I was . . .

Suddenly the Thing came out within two hundred feet of them . . .

I don't think there is a shadow of a doubt but that, here in our Southern California channels, and to northward, there exists an unknown species of a great sea creature—perhaps come down to us out of the pre-historic past. I have further corroborative evidence, other than that of those who have seen the Thing, to support me in this. About seven years ago a Los Angeles man, . . . was at anchor in Acapulco Bay . . . In walking down the beach he came to great, three-toed tracks leading up out of the sea and across the *wet* sand. There was a mark between, like a furrow, that might have been caused by the drag of a tail. He found where the creature had rolled and wallowed in the warm sand, the barrel like depression make by its body, and its track back to the sea . . . He measured the tracks as best he could and estimated that they were fully *three feet long and over two feet across* . . .

I can't help it if the men of science do say there can be no such thing. I know better, for I have seen it . . .

In any event I did see something strange and terrible. I can only wish that any skeptics might have been with me that September morning off Clemente and seen that Thing lifting above the surface, and looked into those great eyes!

In a somewhat popular vein, Chester Stock [P154, 1941], briefly referred to reptiles of the sea. And then he said that newly uncovered remains in California makes us conclude that the mosasaurs, marine lizards, once lived in our coastal waters—but that they disappeared by the end of the Age of Reptiles. Dr. Stock's description of this extinct creature included a skull nearly a yard long, and a body which must have been twenty feet or more. Their necks were short and their bodies long and somewhat eel-like.

From the *National Geographic*, 1945 [J217], came a few summaries apropos of this subject:

It is more than likely that there is a real 'sea serpent', [says Dr. J. L. B. Smith of Rhodes University College, South Africa] . . . a book has been written to prove there *is* a sea serpent; it describes many reports of a huge-bodied, long-necked creature, somewhat resembling the supposedly extinct plesiosaurus . . . Most nightmarish of known sea monsters is the giant squid, whose body may be up to 20 feet long, with eyes as big as dinner plates . . .

Once again, one wonders about the Wonders of Nature.

Indians and Archaeology

Translated by Lesley Byrd Simpson of the Huntington Library and printed by the University of California [B47, 1938], we have a limited, but extremely valuable picture of our coastal Indians of 1792 in "The Expedition of José Longinos Mártinez."

Of Santa Catalina, Mártinez made the following observations,

The nations in the vicinity of San Gabriel are accustomed to carry small stones, which they acquire at a great price from the Indians who bring them from the Island of Los Angeles. These stones are of lead in galena *ferulate,* with silver. It is to be noted that these stones are not esteemed because they contain either of these metals as no use is made of them, but the value of the stone lies in the current belief that he who carries a bit of it with him will acquire more valor and bravery and that he will be immune from being harmed by others. This belief enables the gentiles (Indians) of that island to sell these stones at a good price.

I sent an Indian of mine, accompanied by another from Mission San Gabriel to act as interpreter, to gather for me all the products of that island. The interpreter did very well with the chief, assuring him that I was sent by the Great Chief . . . The chief, with his native intelligence, sent me everything which to his way of thinking was valuable in the domains of his island. This came to two sealskins, two sea-otter skins, several strings of abalones and limpets, one of the small stones of silver and lead that I have already described and several others of quartz, sardonyx, and jasper.

. . . I was assured on the coast that the chief of the island made many fine expressions of thanks [for gifts] toward our Great Chief . . .

About seventy years after the Mártinez expedition, several records surface [N20; B84]. In Lamont's *War of the Rebellion* is Brigadier-General Wright's letter to the Adjutant-General of the Army in Washington, D. C.,

". . . From a special report which I have just received from the officer commanding on the island I am well satisfied that it is better adapted for an Indian reservation than I at first supposed."

The subject at hand was continued by James F. Curtis in his report of January 2, 1864 when he stated, "No more fitting place could be found for a general hospital or depot for Indian prisoners."

Pursuing the matter, E. D. Townsend of Washington, D. C., told Wright that the "Interior Department has been requested to make Catalina an Indian reservation."

Then, Wright replied to F. F. Lowe, Governor of California, that he had changed his mind and that he now did not agree "with the petitioners as to the value of the island for the purposes of an Indian reservation."

This could have been a tongue-in-cheek remark, for Wright then wrote to Townsend and said, "I would recommend still that the whole island be held as an Indian reservation in order that improper persons can be removed without any difficulty." Or could it have been that he was suggesting a circuitous route be taken in order to remove "improper persons," meaning some of the miners on the island.

At any rate, the thought of using Santa Catalina Island as an Indian reservation was kept alive by some, Senator James G. Fair being one. Senator Fair had been a mining executive in Nevada and went to California during the gold rush; he became a multimillionaire from the discovery of gold in the Comstock lode.

It was he who wrote to Lucius Cincinnatus Lamar, Sec'y of the Interior under President Cleveland. A 1936 *Catalina Islander* gave an Anaheim newspaper credit for producing the story,

Washington, Apr. 10, 1886

The Hon. I. C. Lamar,
Dear Sir:
    I beg to enclose the pamphlet of which I spoke to you yesterday. By examining the map you will see the exact position of Santa Catalina Island. It is isolated and too far from shore for any ordinary boat to reach it. My idea is that if the Apaches were put on this island, they would require no guards, and all that would be required would be a small tender and crew to run between the island and Wilmington for the purpose of communication and supplies. This would, in my opinion set the Apache question

at rest forever, would save the country many valuable lives, and the government millions in money. The title to the island is perfect. As near as I can remember the price asked by the owners is either $3 or $4 per acre. Owing to the location of the island the climate is as mild and salubrious as can be found anywhere in the world. If you should look with favor upon my suggestion as to the value of this island for the purpose named I shall be glad to go more into detail with you upon the subject.

Very truly,
James G. Fair

The *Los Angeles Herald,* 1886, remarked that the use of the island for the untamable Apaches "is represented as being a natural prison, [but is] too good for the proposed occupants" [M187].

It was not much later than nine years after the Civil War incidents that the archaeologists began to stir. One of the earlier 20th century accounts of the Indians of the Santa Barbara Islands was that of Gustav Eisen, whose material was published in Prag [M30, 1904].

A very much-discussed topic about the Indians was their Temple to the Sun at the Isthmus. Eisen said that he was on Santa Catalina in 1873 and "found no remains of such a place." Such information preceded Paul Schumacher's visit to the island.

Schumacher was on the island in 1875. In his *Overland Monthly* article [P82, 1875], he complained,

The archaeology of this island is said to have been ransacked by a scientific gentleman of merit, who lingered formerly around the picturesque isthmus. He told me himself, some time ago, that he had even spotted the "fat boy"—meaning the image of the temple to the sun . . . To my deep regret I found that there was but little left for our party to gather, and nothing new to science. Even the thick singularly-shaped cranium, much of a *dolichocephalic* pattern, has already been described by Bret Harte as the prehistoric skull of the Stanislaus.

Who was this "scientific gentleman of merit"? W. G. W. Harford had been to Santa Catalina in 1873, Wm. H. Dall and G. Eisen in 1873 and 1874 [B105].

Schumacher wrote more about the Isthmus Cove in a later article [M41, 1877],

At the Isthmus Cove, we found quite extensive remains of a *rancheria*, but all our efforts to find the graves of its former people were of no avail. Back of the marshy bottom at this cove several marks of houses are still noticeable, and there we found some graves. In front of the barracks still can be traced, on the highest ground of the isthmus, some slight depressions in the earth, where formerly houses of the aborigines stood, . . .

The village site has been utterly destroyed, what with former fishermen's huts, government barracks, and a "Camp Cabrillo" of Banning days, which included a restaurant, a bakery, a dancing pavilion, and houses.

Blanche Trask [M128, 1906] gives some insight about the artifacts which have been collected from the Isthmus,

> Here the most beautiful work was found; engraved pots and many also inlaid with abalone and other shells; . . . Knives and weapons of whalebone had beautiful handles of shell with carved and inlaid work, and all manner of ornaments and implements were wrought from stone with spear heads of obsidian and knives of the same stone with shell handles, as also were the arrowheads fastened to the shaft . . .

Much has been said about the potstone to be found on the island. This is important because the rock was used extensively by the Indians, both for domestic and export purposes.

In 1878 Schumacher reported on the subject [J250],

> . . . I gained the assurance, during my short stay on Santa Catalina, that the stone [potstone] exists in certain places on that island, but did not then succeed in finding the quarries. But during my last expedition to that locality, in behalf of the Peabody Museum, . . . I made the discovery, found pits and quarries, the tools used and unfinished articles. I noticed that the softer stone, usually obtained in pits, which is of a more micaceous character, was used for pots, while the close-grained rock of darker color, serpentine was mainly used for the weights of digging sticks, cups, pipes, ornaments, etc.
>
> While in camp at Little Springs, my attention was first arrested [to the potstone] . . . entirely covered with marks where pot-forms had been worked out or left in various stages; . . . At the foot of the bluff . . . many tools of hard slate in shape of chisels, and scrapers of quartz.
>
> From the Little Springs we followed the cañon to the northward, . . . into Pots Valley. It is a

wide hollow cañon . . . Several hundred yards below the spring at the ravine to the right, . . . is found a pit . . . Between this place and the second ravine about fifty yards to the northwestward, is another pit . . . Besides these places there are many more pits in the valley, . . . and a quarry . . . to the eastward from Pots Valley boat landing, close to the steep ocean shore . . .

> The scrapers, usually made of milky quartz, found in abundance all over the island, . . . [with] distinct signs of metallic tools having been used. These were probably of iron and like those which we frequently found in the burying-ground on the Isthmus.

Following this information Schumacher gave a one paragraph description on how the pot was formed from the living rock, and finally broken off.

In another article through *The American Naturalist* [J20, 1878], Schumacher enlarged on his topic,

> Not only were cooking vessels extensively manufactured on this island, but also flat dishes, cups, pipes, stone rings . . . and all kinds of trinkets . . . The quarries are more abundant in number towards the southeastern end of Santa Catalina where for about two miles square not less than three hundred quarries and pits were discovered on my last visit, . . .

H. C. Yarrow in Appendix JJ [N45, 1879], gave his directions to some of the quarries on the island,

> The main quarries were ten miles northeast of Avalon at Pots Valley and Little Springs. A third quarry lies about 50 yards to the northwest between Pots Valley and the second ravine. A fourth quarry is about 400 yards east of Pots Valley boat landing close to the steep cliff. Some of the quarry pits, where the Indian followed a good "vein" are up to fifteen feet in diameter and five feet deep.

Wm. Henry Holmes, "Anthropological Studies in California" [N15, 1899], offered plates and views of aboriginal work at Soapstone Quarry and of soapstone artifacts that came from it. He mentioned two noted archaeological sites on Santa Catalina, one of them being at the Isthmus. Holmes was aided in his work by C. F. Holder and E. L. Doran of Avalon.

Sunset of 1898, Vol. II, No. 2, described the uses of potstone, called soapstone, and the uses of serpentine. Soapstones can be used as a "filler" for soap and paper.

Included in this article is a report from the U. S.

Geological Survey of 1897 in which it is said that Catalina's serpentine is highly prized because it can take a polish and can be lathe-turned to a porcelain-thin dimension. Serpentine can also be used as a substitute for marble and is well adapted for monument-making, fire bricks, and wall finish. It is both non-absorbent and a non-conductor of electricity.

Finding a *Los Angeles Times* publication [M129, 1906], which included Mrs. Trask's "Indian Workshop," is one of the nicer things that can happen to one interested in archaeology. Mrs. Trask has much by way of first-hand, insightful information on this subject:

> . . . the middens are small; in not one instance is there what could be called "a large mound," those at the Isthmus, Johnson's, White's, Little Harbor and Pot's Valley being the largest . . .

> Steatite is the massive variety of talc, and it is of this that the Indians used to make their pots. There is a quarry of this at Johnson's, where it was taken out first by the Indians and later by the Bannings. Old John Sullivan here found a whale carved from this rock . . .

> Near the wharf at Pot's Valley is the sheep corral where the old midden used to be—one of the largest on the island, while the rock from which the pots were cut is an easy half-hour's tramp . . . up the valley . . .

> [From whence the Indians obtained their serpentine to carve their precious ornaments is not known.] Two years ago, a pipe about four inches long was found lying upon a rock at Catalina, with the mouthpiece of this real serpentine in the form of an oblong tube most exquisitely engraved and with the asphaltum which had been used to fasten it into the pipe still intact and the piece in place. The pipe itself was of a red volcanic . . .

> The largest workshop of the Indians lies far in the heart of Catalina and has never been disturbed. Here the goats roam over trails which their little feet have worn as smooth as satin, and kick out of their way many a precious thing that the Indians chiseled. It is very strange, this magic drop in under the crest where the "serpentine" thrusts up its head. You pass from one projecting bit of ledge to another and see the same tell-tale incisions upon the soft rock. Oftentimes it has been cut clear down to the ground itself and even below, so that now a shallow basin exists where once the aborigines were busily working.

> There are tiny pots small enough to have been used as a child's bowl and others too heavy for a white man to lift! . . . you come across them in all stages, from the largest one not yet loosened from its base and still standing firmly two feet high, to the chiseled ones rounded and modeled so that a mere touch of hand or foot will set them rolling; . . .

Mrs. Burton Williamson offered a four-page catalogue of Indian relics that were found on Santa Catalina Island [J333, 1904]. Many of the artifacts came from graves at the Isthmus, Pots Valley, Johnson's Place, and Whittley's Place.

When Ralph Glidden was digging in 1916, he found "abalone pearls, some of which weigh from four to eight ounces," beside a buried skeleton [M187]. It was reported in 1920 that Mr. Glidden excavated at Empire Landing, Howland's, Little Harbor, and White Cove.

Judge Windle thought that the oldest Indian townsite on the island was at White's Landing. When in 1925 Mr. William Wrigley had engaged a John Duncan Dunn to lay out a new golf course at the Landing, Dunn uncovered 267 skeletons. These were shipped to the Museum of the Heye Foundation of New York.

C. F. Holder had said that he located at least twenty town sites on the island by 1896 [P115]. It was with this background of knowledge that he was able to assist W. H. Holmes.

In 1953 the University of California at Los Angeles began survey and excavation efforts on the island. According to Clement W. Meighan [J82, 1957], it is only in the airport area that soapstone is found. Though this information is not exactly correct, it is possible that a portion of Mrs. Trask's description of soapstone locations fits that general area.

In a later report through *Masterkey* [J196, 1957], Dr. Meighan amended his former statement by saying that the mining activity was concentrated in the middle of the island, with more than a hundred such locations to be found within a two-mile radius. This information, Schumacher had also given to us.

In 1973 and 1974, #1, *Masterkey* presented two more articles; these were on stone artifacts. One, "An incised steatite tablet from the Catalina Museum" [J211]; another, "An unusual stone effigy from southern California." Robert L. Hoover is the author of both articles; each contains a photo of the artifact discussed.

The Ranch That Was Robbins' and Early Mining Interests

Some of the information used in the following report has been taken from long-hand copies filed in Washington, D.C. [N38, dockett #351]. It constitutes a real addition to other sources.

In Robbins' 1839 petition to Governor Alvarado, and in his second petition to Governor Pío Pico, he had stated that he wished to use the island of Santa Catalina for his home, for agricultural purposes, and for the breeding of cattle.

The second petition was made July 4, 1846, seemingly written by José María Covarrubias, friend and neighbor to Robbins, and signed by Governor Pío Pico and Robbins, allowing Robbins to seek or solicit judicial possession.

It is said that Covarrubias mistakenly took the petition to Monterey, where it was accepted on February 4, 1850, by H. W. Halleck of Halleck Peachy and Billings. It was not until April 12, 1850 that a note to the petition, with a corrected latitude, had been signed by Robbins. This time it was again taken to Monterey by Covarrubias, but was deposited through Don Pablo de la Guerra. On August 31, 1850 Robbins conveyed the island to Covarrubias for $10,000.

By March 14, 1854 the above legal representatives withdrew their services and Mr. Albert Packard became counsel for the claimants. He appeared for them beginning September 2, 1854.

The records indicate that October 13, 1853 was the date on which Covarrubias deeded the island to Packard for $1,000. There must have been some oral arrangement. Mr. Packard was a Santa Barbara attorney who had arrived from New England via Mazatlan about 1845. He was still living in 1891. More information may be found on Packard in Thompson and West [B70].

To substantiate Robbins' 1846 petition, an Edward A. King testified before Commissioner S. B. Farnell on October 25, 1854 [N38],

About the first of March 1847 I lived at the port of Santa Barbara on the Brig *Elizabeth* bound for San Pedro, after discharging some freight, and some for Capt. Robbins, Capt. was a passenger, arriving in San Pedro on the 2nd of March, and about the 6th I visited the Island of Catalina for a depot for salting hides, . . . Capt. Robbins . . . told me he owned the Island and told me to go and look, he told me anything I wanted on the Island I could have and that I would find some of his men there and they would give me anything I would ask for. I selected a spot, killed a calf, and went to his house built of adoubias and wood. The house was on the north part of the Island, there were two men there taking care of Capt. Robbins cattle, saw a corral near the house. Saw some land broken up evidently for cultivation, I returned that same evening to San Pedro, a few days afterward I went to the Island again in company with Capt. Robbins, saw the same men and carried some stores for Capt. Robbins, was on the Island several times and saw the same men there, saw a patch of land under cultivation . . .

Additional information coming from the Washington, D.C. archives is that reported by J. Tyler, Jr. on Feb. 17, 1857. Sent to the Honorable C. Cushing, Attorney General of the United States, here is a summarization of his report,

1. Thomas Robbins petitioned in 1846 for the island because he wished to "dedicate himself to agriculture and the raising of stock."

2. "There was no approval of the grant by the Departmental Junta; nor was there any Judicial possession given."

3. J. J. Warner had testified for José María Covarrubias and "establishes the fact that the signature of the said Robbins to the Petition is genuine; but he does not testify as to its presentation at any time."

4. "Warner, testifies that the chirography of the note, as well as that of the body of the Petition, is that of José María Covarrubias, . . ."

5. ". . . scarce three days before the American flag covered the Californias, the said Robbins presented a petition for . . . the island . . . in 43° 20' of north latitude."

6. "By a note to this Petition, added and signed, apparently by 'Robbins', the situation is said to be 34° 40' . . ." This latitude is correct, according to George Davidson.

7. ". . . the Petition, concession, and Patent of Title . . . are hurried through in *one* day."

Tyler nevertheless concluded that he does not "see how the appeal can be sustained . . . It is . . . with extreme reluctance I recommend its dismissal. The whole evidence in its entirety and parts I take to be meagre and incomplete to say nothing concerning the question of fraud arising out of the documents and Testimony in the case."

The U. S. District Court decided to discontinue the case on December 4, 1865 and on December 21, 1865 this information was recorded in Monterey.

PIECES OF EIGHT

José María Covarrubias

José María Covarrubias was born in France and went to Mexico at the age of twenty. He came to Alta California with the Hijar-Padre Colony in 1834, became naturalized in 1837, during Juan B. Alvarado's governorship, and married María Carrillo in 1838.

His mother-in-law was Concepción Pico and his father-in-law was Domingo Carrillo, son of Don Raymundo Carrillo. Domingo was a brother to Carlos Antonio and José Carrillo. Thus two of his kinsmen-by-marriage were José and Carlos, the two gentlemen who finally had obtained the island of Santa Rosa as a grant from Governor Micheltorena [1843] before Covarrubias came into possession of Santa Catalina Island through Robbins.

Tomás Robbins, who sold Santa Catalina to Covarrubias in 1850, was married to Encarnación, daughter of Carlos Antonio Carrillo. Thus, the two principals concerning Santa Catalina were married to cousins, María and Encarnación.

In 1843, during Manuel Micheltorena's term of office, José M. Covarrubias was granted Castaic Rancho, lying in Ventura and Santa Barbara Counties. This was seven years prior to obtaining Santa Catalina from Robbins. In February of 1846 Governor Pío Pico sent Don José María of Santa Barbara to Mexico, for aid in the impending war with the United States. Shortly after, Covarrubias obtained Santa Catalina from Robbins.

Covarrubias had sons and daughters; one of them was Nicolás. When on April 1, 1870 J. M. Covarrubias died at the age of 61, his son, Nicolás, inherited the family adobe; this he maintained until it was sold in 1907. It was Nicolás, U. S. Marshall in 1896, who went to San Miguel Island to oust Captain Waters, the first "King of San Miguel." This was because Captain Waters would not allow the Coast Survey personnel to land on the island.

The older Covarrubias, José, was in the State Assembly when California was admitted to the Union, Pío Pico having earlier appointed him as Secretary to the Department of California.

From Volume II of Bancroft we glean these few particulars,

Covarrubias, (José María), 1834, nat. of France, naturalized citizen of Mex., . . . intending to be a teacher . . . a partizan of Carrillo in the contest of '38 . . . grantee of Castaic rancho in '43 . . . sec. of the assembly and alcalde of Sta. B. . . . succeeded Bandini as sec. of Gov. Pico,

justice of the sup. court . . . In '49 he was a member of the constit. convention, and of the 1st Legislature, being 4 times reelected, and county judge of Sta. B. in '61. Covarrubias died in '70 at the age of 69 . . . his eldest son, Nicolás, was for a long time sheriff of Sta. B. County.

Additional information on his life comes through *Noticias* [J290]. In the Southern California Historical Society publication [J377, 1973], several references on his activities may be found.

On June 9, 1858, Packard had sold one fourth of the island to a Eugene Sullivan for $500. Sullivan, in turn, sold to a Dr. Hitchcock for $1,864. No doubt there were unrecorded conditions in the transaction, for by 1864 José Covarrubias and Albert Packard had sold the whole island to J. H. Ray of New York for $12,500.

The initial petition for the island's use as a ranch moved rapidly into the mining arena. By 1860 James H. Ray, 106 Wall St., New York, had taken an active interest in the island. He wrote to D. W. Middleton, attorney in Washington, D.C., inquiring about its final title, and if such title also carried title to the minerals. As he continued his letter, he said [N38],

As I may be requested to use the answers in London, I would take as much "Red Tape" about the document as is compatible.

If you think there is any other questions, that John Bull would naturally ask, please supply them—I am desirous of getting the answers at the earliest possible moment, when I will at once remit your charge.

If I have asked anything out of the usual way, place it to the account of *ignorance*.

Middleton told Ray to refer his questions to Mr. Carlisle, Ray's counsel.

Book A of the Santa Catalina Mining District has not been available for reference. But some information may be obtained from the *Deeds* and *Miscellaneous Records* of the Los Angeles County Recorder's Office.

A paragraph found in the June 12, 1864 *Daily Alta California*, "Mining on Santa Catalina Island" [M57], mentioned the "Argentine" mine in Cherry Valley, "Little Gem of the Ocean," "Albion" lode of the Monster Company, old "Santa Catalina," "San Francisco," "New England," and several other companies, as well as the type of mineral to be found at the Isthmus.

From the *Overland Monthly* [P86, 1890], and its

92

reprint in the Historical Society of Southern California publication [J361, 1912], comes J. M. Guinn's account, "The Lost Mines of Santa Catalina."

In a little more than a year after the first [mineral] discovery the camp was abandoned . . . [to] a howling waste. The wild goats came down from the mountains and ate up the mining notices, dips, spurs, angles, and all. The jewfish and the shark gamboled in the placid waters of Wilson Harbor, unvexed by rudder or keel. Quiet reigned on Catalina [P86].

Nine days after Ray's purchase of the island he had sold one-half of it to James Lick for $4,150. And exactly one year later, Hitchcock sold his one-fourth interest to Lick for $15,000, May 23, 1865. But Hitchcock must have retained title to the mineral rights; Ray still held his one-fourth of the island.

Final decree to the title of Santa Catalina was obtained on December 4, 1865, but the patent was not issued until October 10, 1866. By 1867 both a W. H. Lowry of New York and James H. Ray were applying separately for the patent. Apparently, James Lick, Esq. was communicating with Lowry, requesting the Honorable Joseph S. Wilson, Commissioner of the General Land Office, to send the patent to the Surveyor General's Office in California.

In Ray's May 17, 1867 communication to Commissioner Wilson, he said [N38],

The patent is *not* wanted in California but here, to be used by me in England, as will fully appear to you by the authentication of the Title papers by the British Counsul of San Francisco, now in your Department. I think I may be pardoned when I say that the evidence is in your Department; showing the Transfer of José María Covarrubias' interest to be in me, and I having made no other conveyance than that to Mr. Lick, that any interference is simply impertinent, and I deem you must consider it so also. Any change in your decision of the 10th of April would be seriously prejudicial to me, and I most respectfully extract your adherence to it.

Ray then changed his mind and decided to go to San Francisco instead of to London.

Another deed reference gives us fragmentary but vital facts: Benjamin Wood of San Francisco filed suit against Ray for the sum of five hundred thirty-three dollars and thirty-two cents ($533.32). This was in December of 1865. By June 26, 1866, T. A. Sanchez, sheriff of Los Angeles County "did sell to the undersigned (Crockett) all the right title and interest of the said defendant James H. Ray in and to the island of Santa Catalina"; he was the highest bidder—$1,363.87.

There is need for amplification of the written record, for it appears that Crockett paid $1,526.56 for "said premises"; then, "therefore in consideration of the sum of $1,526.56 paid to me by James Ray of New York I do hereby assign and transfer . . . said premises to said James Ray of New York his heirs or assigns."

This transaction was short-lived for Sheriff Sanchez found it necessary to deal with a Walter Hawxhurst, County of Contra Costa, against James Ray whose "last day to recover" (his part of the Island) was January 6, 1866. On November 9, 1866 Hawxhurst paid $4,000 for part of the Island, through auction.

James Lick must have been following Ray's legal involvements for almost immediately, December 22, 1866, Hawxhurst received $4,140 from James Lick; the final date for business transaction concerning right to Island title is given as September 16, 1867 [B84, 1963]. Lick now owned the whole of Santa Catalina Island and had paid $23,790 for it.

It became Lick's turn to try and interest Londoners in the minerals of the island. On June 19, 1872 Lick gave to John G. Downey, John Forster, and Max Strobel an option to buy the island for $1,250,000 [B50, 1930].

There was a John Foster, age thirty-eight, who had testified on September 5, 1859 that he and James Johnson, who was living on the island in the '50s, had petitioned Governor Alvarado in 1839 or 1840 for the island.

The spelling of Foster [Forster] stands between reality and query as to whether he was the same person to whom Lick had given option for the island. It was stated [J361] that Forster was a landowner. It also was stated in the Washington, D.C. archives that Foster was interested in the island for mining and agricultural purposes [N38].

Finally, in 1873 Major Max Strobel of Anaheim was commissioned by Lick to go to England in an attempt to sell the island. "Liberally supplied with rich mineral specimens, he negotiated a sale to a syndicate of London capitalists for one million dollars" [J361].

Harris Newmark [B50, 1930], had the following story to tell,

Major von Strobel . . . was a German [winemaker, real estate promoter, journalist] . . . The last grand effort of this adventurous spirit was the attempt to sell Santa Catalina Island. Backed by the owners, Strobel sailed for Europe and opened headquarters near Threadneedle Street in London. In a few weeks he had almost effected the sale, the contract having been drawn and the time actually set for the following day when the money—a cool two hundred thousand pounds—was to be paid; but no Strobel kept tryst to carry out his part of the transaction. Only the evening before, alone and unattended, the old man died in his room at the very moment when Fortune, for the first time, was to smile upon him! . . .

Lick's ownership of Santa Catalina was stormy. In 1868 he began litigation against the squatters and the Boushey mine owners. In 1872, when the litigation was over, Lick had lost to Stephen Boushey, for in 1867 Dr. Hitchcock had sold to Boushey the Small Hill Mine for $7,000. Obviously, Boushey could prove his case, but the squatters did not protest.

There is a 1903 Newman's Tract Directory of the Los Angeles County showing the location of the Small Hill Mine [M29]. And in the Miscellaneous Records of the County it is possible to obtain a

> map of a portion of the island of Santa Catalina showing the location of the Small Hill Mine, the property of Stephen Boushey and F. P. F. Temple surveyed in accordance with a decree of the District Court of the 17th Judicial District in the case of Lick vs Howland *Et Al.* By E. J. Weston, U. S. Dep. Min. Surveyor, October, 1874. [Book 2, pp. 608 and 609, MR.]

Thomas Robbins ended his days in 1857, having previously received a grant of the Las Positas y Calera Ranch [B25, 1917]. Lick ended his days in 1876, with his Will and Estate becoming the responsibility of the Lick Trustees.

To the California Academy of Sciences went a seven-story building on Market Street in San Francisco [P13, 1893; J67, 1914]. The Lick Observatory was also a result of Lick's Will. Santa Catalina was in a state of limbo, but Charles Crocker was Director of the Lick Estate, and a friend of Captain William Banning [J369].

By the time the Lick Trustees had granted grazing rights to William Howland, Harris, and Whittley in 1887, they were also ready to sell Santa Catalina. This they did, to Shatto.

Lick's Trustees sold Santa Catalina Island to George R. Shatto for the sum of $200,000 on August 11, 1887, having received a down payment of $133,333.30. Reservations in the exchange were: the Small Hill Mining Claim, rights of the United States for a lighthouse, and the lease of the island (except Avalon) for grazing ground, to Mr. Whittley, Mr. Harris, and Mr. Howland.

Shatto had also made a deal on April 26, 1889 with the International Mining Syndicate, Ltd. of England, to convey to them his rights to the Island. The balance was to be paid in sums during three years, but the payments defaulted. So Shatto, himself, was unable to make payment on August 11, 1892. For the sum of $1.00 on December 30, 1891, George and Clara Shatto conveyed the "Island, wharf and water works, boats, boathouses to J. B. Banning" [B84].

From the *Sacramento Daily Record-Union* of April 16, 1889 [M74], we find a now familiar theme of the story,

> Colonel Smith and a party of English capitalists Saturday visited Catalina Island and made a thorough inspection of the property and mines. This evening to a *Chronicle* reporter Colonel Smith, who is the head of the company, said: "We have about decided to purchase the island. The price I cannot tell yet, but it is not set far from $300,000. We expect to improve the island as a resort and to develop the silver mines. The ore is low grade, but we can ship it to England as ballast very cheaply, and it can be reduced at Swansea so as to pay. We shall develop the other resources of the island to the fullest extent."

The English Syndicate did buy for $400,000, making a substantial down payment to Shatto and the Englishman.

Even before Shatto had developed the town of Avalon, it was considered an ideal location for camp-outings. Here is C. A. Gardner's description of the accommodations there [P108]

> A beautiful tent furnished the main building, and bough mattresses the extra sleeping apartments, . . . Amusements were not lacking . . . They are not without their social life, either, those campers at Catalina . . . lots are already two thousand dollars apiece . . .

Charles A. Sumner must have been a partner with George R. Shatto. He was publisher of *Catalina Jewfish* in 1888, and for the *Los Angeles Times*, May 12,

1918, "Early Days in California" [M139], he wrote,

> At San Pedro the Evening Express gave the whole racket away. 'Catalina Island sold to George R. Shatto and C. A. Sumner for $200,000 . . .'
>
> The next thing to be done was surveying the townsite, building a wharf, the hotel, laying water pipes and so on . . . Carpenters kicked because they could not get beef every day; plumbers objected to fresh fish and eggs . . . and the roustabouts swore all the mutton was goat . . .
>
> At last the hotel was finished, the wharf completed, and the opening day for the town of Shatto arrived, . . . The date, Thursday, October 13, 1887, will be a memorable day in the annals of Avalon as the opening day of its great popularity, . . .
>
> Next day the work of selling lots began . . . The "Hardware" store was demolished but the proprietor moved to a scow in the bay, and for a time supplied tonic to the needy . . .
>
> The ground on which the hotel was built turned out to be an old Indian burial place and when the foundations for the building were dug, hundreds of Indian relics were discovered, bowls and pipes and beads and arrow points . . . everyone that happened along took what he wanted . . .
>
> I was able to persuade Mr. Charles F. Holder and his wife to come over and spend the summer with us and incidentally do some writing . . .
>
> . . . an unfortunate railway accident took place. Mr. Shatto was riding in a caboose, . . . was violently thrown down . . . so that his neck was broken . . .
>
> Mr. Lowe of the Banning Company went over to London to finally close out the syndicate interest and all was cleaned up.

The article also contained a close-up of the new Metropole Hotel, taken in 1887.

Let Carol Green Wilson [J369, 1945], tell another version of the story,

> . . . But [Billy Staats'] greater relaxation always came when, as second mate, he would sail out of San Pedro Harbor with Hancock Banning on *La Paloma* . . .
>
> Several years of hectic post-boom financing had intervened since that December day in 1887 when Hancock had first pointed across the Channel to the Island as a source of rock for the Wilmington breakwater. The Banning ownership had come about quite unexpectedly. Shatto,

a visionary with the confidence of the old boom days, had made a new attempt to attract European investors. Through a Pasadenan with English connections he had negotiated with the representative of a syndicate to sell the Island for $400,000. The promotion schemes of the Santa Catalina Island Development Company had been the signal for launching the luxurious *Hermosa* and undertaking enlargement of the business program of the Wilmington Transportation Company.

In the meantime Shatto, flushed with his dreams of wealth, had spent the entire $40,000 received from the Englishmen on a showy Los Angeles residence, counting on future installments to meet his own remaining indebtedness to the Lick Estate. The English promoter, too, had his ideas of grandeur. With the $60,000 left out of the $100,000 he had brought from London—hard-earned savings of staid Birmingham investors in a scheme headed by the Queen's own Secretary, Lord Ponsonby—he ordered elaborate maps and surveys. His propaganda once ready for a gullible public, he chartered Banning boats and ordered champagne for his prospective victims.

At this point Charles Crocker, Director of the Lick Estate, sought out his friend, Captain William Banning. The boom was over; the public was getting wary. Shatto was stone broke. No more funds were forthcoming from London. Why shouldn't the Bannings themselves take over the Island? They could have it by assuming Shatto's obligations to the estate, plus whatever he had paid for town lots and improvements in the city of Avalon. They could develop the resort as an adjunct to their transportation business. Crocker knew his fellow-directors would welcome the integrity of the Banning word as surety for future payments. But Captain William hesitated. He recognized great potential opportunities, but at the same time sensed serious risks. Crocker countered with the rumor that the bankrupt Londoner was about to sail for home.

The son of General Phineas was not long indecisive. He whipped up his mule-team and drove splashing through the mud to his office at 222 West Second Street, Los Angeles. Here he gave quick orders to his secretary, Frank H. Lowe, "Draw a thousand dollars from the bank and catch the first boat out of New York. Get to London ahead of Smith." Lowe was to get all the facts about the English Syndicate and then use his own judgment. If he could not do more, perhaps he could at least sell the *Hermosa*.

That was in November, 1889. The day before Christmas, Captain Banning had a cable from Lowe, "The Island is yours." The strange process by which this was achieved was not revealed until Lowe's return early in the new year. His first step, it seemed, had been to consult an acquaintance, the financial editor of a London paper. Between them they had ferreted out the names of all subscribers. These men were then circularized with an ad: "For sale; for $126,000, the Island of Santa Catalina, twenty-one miles off the coast of Southern California." In a few days Lowe had a summons to appear before the Queen's Bench with all his facts and papers. The judge then called a meeting of the stockholders in the Santa Catalina Island Company. Lowe was invited, but did not go, sending instead the English surveyor, still unpaid for his maps and work—a man who had been won at once to help Lowe get a new set-up for the Island. According to English law, if a corporation fails to meet its obligations, it is automatically dissolved. The disillusioned speculators saw no sense in trying to raise $360,000 to pay for an island now available for $126,000. Accordingly, the $400,000 contract of sale with Shatto was declared null and void, and the company ceased to exist. The surveyor telephoned to Lowe, who cabled to Banning, and then departed for home via Paris before any *bona fide* purchaser could upset his plans.

It was 1892 before the deed actually passed from the Lick Estate to the Bannings. In the meantime, Shatto died in a train wreck. The new owners paid his widow $25,000 for town lots in Avalon, assumed the mortgage on the remainder of the island, and proceeded to make this tiny green speck, first discovered by Cabrillo, into a "Paradise of the Pacific," known and loved by sportsmen the world over.

On September 20, 1892 William Banning paid to the Trustees of the Lick estate the sum of $128,740, thus Lick had made a gross profit of $238,283.30 from the two sales of the island.

Shatto reserved large blocks of lots which he had sold, about two hundred in all. He also reserved anything still due from the International Mining Syndicate. The other exception was:

Hotel Metropole and its site . . . and waterfront lying east of the westerly line of Crescent Avenue between the southerly line of Metropole Avenue and the northerly line of Whittley Avenue, both said lines extended to the Pacific

Ocean . . . thus including the wharf erected partly thereupon and partly in the sea [B84].

For a short period of time the Bannings had indicated some interest in the minerals and mining possibilities of the island; this gave way to concentrating more on the island becoming a resort, a project that succeeded quite well.

By 1890 the State mineralogist, E. B. Preston [C22], made a few brief statements to the effect that very little, if anything, was being done to mine the quarries of steatite and rock on the island. This state of affairs held true for many years.

On May 7, 1896, William Banning deeded the island to the Santa Catalina Island Company, which had been formed. The first owners of the stock were the Banning brothers, William, J.B., Hancock, and the sisters, Katherine S. and Anna O. Banning [B84]. The father, Phineas, had died in 1885.

In February of 1919 William Wrigley, Jr. became the chief stockholder in the Company by purchasing the Banning interests for three million dollars. Included in their multi-faceted activities has been that of mining. Through the *Catalina Islander* many tidbits of such information come to us:

1923   "Pebble Beach is to become the site of a large rock crushing plant . . . A pier is to be built . . . A tramway will connect the quarry in the canyon with the pier . . . Graham Bros. of Long Beach have taken a fifteen-year lease of the quarry site."

1924   "The 'Black Jack Mine' is now one of the six mining claims that are being developed under the supervision of Mr. Renton . . . The other lead, silver, and gold mines are located at Cherry Valley, Howlands, and Johnson's Landing, near the Isthmus."

1926   "Three hundred and fifty tons of zinc concentrates were shipped directly to Belgium from the flotation mill at White's Landing last week . . . Some 600 tons of silver and lead concentrates await shipment at the mill to the smelter in Selby." [The zinc to Dunkirk, France] "will net approximately $14,000 in revenue, according to M. Patrick."

1933   "between 500 and 1000 tons of Catalina rock is now being placed daily on the finishing courses of the breakwater at Santa Monica."

1934 "The Newport Harbor program calls for 526,740 tons of rock to be brought from Santa Catalina Island by barge."

1936 "Now the barge will take clean white sand dredged from the bottom of Newport Bay to build a fine new bathing beach at Catalina."

From another source, *Scientific American,* in 1926 comes more information about "A Treasure Island in the Pacific" [J317]. Briefly, Herbert O. Warren said,

> There are 20 veins being worked at Catalina, [at] Seal Rocks . . . Catalina's famous seals flop around on rocks of silver. East of Mt. Black Jack has been found a copper deposit running 156 dollars a ton . . . at White's Landing . . . is the flotation mill . . . [zinc concentrates] shipped directly to Belgium . . . Pebble Beach [they ran] into a silver and lead vein so rich in minerals as to be unsuitable for the contractors . . . the Renton Vein . . . this mine alone will keep another flotation plant in full operation . . . even Mr. Wrigley's palatial home atop Mt. Ada has been discovered . . . over a silver vein . . .

He also referred to the older Isthmus area as being the sites for other silver and lead mines.

In Gay and Hoffman's report on the "Mines and Mineral Deposits of Los Angeles County, California" [C29, 1954], they have indicated that "almost all of the lead-silver-zinc ore that has been produced in Los Angeles County has come from deposits on Santa Catalina Island." The island's resources are mentioned on about nine other pages of their report.

Perhaps the most reliable source for information concerning mining activities on the island since 1919 would come through the Santa Catalina Island Company itself.

Environment—Education—Conservancy

Highly important as this section is, there appear to be more gaps than substance in the literature. Without apology, the reader would do well to extend his reading and research.

It is worthy of comment that as early as 1898 [M121], the *Los Angeles Times* carried an article, "The Interior Catalina Island." Harry Brook's statement that "Within a few years, the interior of Catalina will be as widely celebrated and visited as the seacoast now is" comes close to being a prophetic statement. But it was a seventy-seven-year span of time before Santa Catalina even became a Conservancy.

Going back those seventy-seven years, we have found Charles F. Holder successful in his efforts to give the island an aquarium and zoological station—practically seventy-five years before U.S.C.'s Marine Science Laboratory at Fisherman's Cove was constructed.

Through Holder the Banning Company built a twenty by sixty foot building on the water front, equipping it with about fifty tanks for fish and other sea life. "As an educational feature it is one of the most important movements yet made in southern California [to] give a fresh impetus to scientific investigation . . ." [P52, 1899]. In 1906 the Banning Aquarium continued to create active interest [M132, 1906], and remained in existence through the early '20s [M187].

While C. F. Holder maintained his interest in the aquarium [N22, 1908], he also sought, through letters and articles, other means of education and conservation. A referral to Appendix H of *The Ranch that was Robbins'* [B84], will repay the reader by finding four letters written to Dr. Holder on the subject of the need for conservation of the island's resources.

A law making Santa Catalina a fish reservation was passed in 1913. A one paragraph quotation from the California statutes may also be found in B84. The effect in 1914 seemed magical, according to Dr. Holder [C4; M34].

A later report in 1920 [M187], appeared to indicate that there had been some lapse in enforcement against the use of purse seine nets. As a consequence the Middle Ranch and Isthmus sheepmen noted increased depredations of their animals: "Early one morning one of the sheep herders missed a band of 30 sheep. He traced them to Button Shell Beach near Long Point, and found evidence where a row boat had been used to carry the animals off the island to a waiting fishing launch."

Leaving the sordid, *Arrowhead* [P4], of 1908 gives a description of Ben, the tame seal, and his antics:

> Who could study a bone of the Stone Age at Avalon, or even a big collection of all the relics found here, which a citizen has, while a boatman is giving a practical demonstration on the beach not fifty feet away of the tameness of giant sea lions. The man stands at the water's edge holding an albacore in his hand shouting, "Ben". Presently out of the sea pops a big black head which utters a blood curdling roar, and then up

the beach slowly and with a caterpillar-like movement comes a bull sea lion who answers to the name of "Ben". He certainly weighs a ton and would be guessed at two or three, and is followed by others. Up he comes, a ferocious looking fellow, and takes the albacore from the man's hand, then gallops back into the water, and there the fish is torn up, tossed into the air by the school of half a dozen not ten feet from you. These interesting creatures live at the rookery about two miles down the island, which is reached in a short and attractive sail.

Felix J. Koch [P100, 1912], gave us a photo of Big Ben—"Ben . . . the leader of the great herd of seals inhabiting these waters, . . ."

Old Ben was still alive in 1923 [B122]: ". . . Ben the sea lion who barks about the incoming fishing craft, polling his wet nose and whiskers even into the boat itself in quest of his toll of fish." Ben was drowned by a fisherman's net at a not much later date.

Then there was "Bill," the sedate pelican, who loved to lounge on the wharf and have his ridiculous head stroked, . . ." [B122].

By 1940 information came to the newspaper that the United States Bureau of Marine Fisheries of the California Division of Fish and Game had been successful in their efforts to artificially spawn the abalone, "The scarcity of small abalone in districts where commercial taking of these mollusks is permitted has concerned the Division since an exhaustive investigation of these areas was made last Fall" [M187].

A *Catalina Islander* report twenty years earlier remarked that Japanese fishermen sent abalone shells to Japan for the purpose of having them made into ornaments. A need for conservation was already developing.

From a 1922 *Catalina Islander* comes a brief statement that the University of Southern California was making an effort to establish an experimental station for the purpose of growing plants. As far as is known, this effort did not materialize.

Another tidbit from a 1923 *Catalina Islander* is that "Camp Wrigley," about a quarter of a mile this side of the Summit, was the locale for an astronomers' meeting. More particulars must be obtained elsewhere.

Phil C. Orr's article, "Island Hopping" [J270,

1949], informed us that the *Orca*, a one hundred foot former Coast Guard ice-breaker, was converted into a floating marine laboratory. The *Orca* may still circulate; it did have a crew of fourteen, with only the skipper and the engineer as non-scientific personnel. A more detailed study of their activity is another's province.

By 1967 the Marine Science Center for research and teaching was under construction by U. S. C. By late 1973 [M118], U. S. C. was given a marine study grant by the U. S. Commerce Department. And by 1974 the University of California, and others, were using Santa Catalina Island for field study trips, both plant and animal. The Marine Science campus covers forty-five acres.

The Trojan Family of March 1977 contains a photo of Big Fisherman's Cove and the Catalina Marine Science Center. The Center now has a hyperbaric chamber, a life-saving device, used on diving victims.

In early 1974 the Santa Catalina Island Co. was granted a fifty-year easement, thus opening the way for more public use of the island's interior [M182]. This was quickly followed in 1975 by a donation to the County of Los Angeles from the Island Company of almost fifty miles of the interior and shore land.

It is called the "Los Angeles County Santa Catalina Nature Conservancy." Deeds have been recorded. The purpose of the Conservancy is preserving native plants, animals, geological and geographical formations, and open space. This Conservancy amounts to about eighty-five percent of the island—outside of Avalon.

According to a May 1975 issue of *Westways*, with slight exaggeration, "Goats, hogs and people are [the] major problems to be faced by the Santa Catalina Nature Conservancy, a new attempt at joining environmental preservation with public recreation on the island."

The Bannings

General Phineas Banning came to California in 1851; he served as commander of the First Brigade of the California State Militia and was appointed Brigadier-General, 1889 [B45].

From the Southern California Historical Society of 1900 we learn,

Banning, the man of expedients, did business on the bluff at the old warehouse [San Pedro, a port of one house purchased by Abel Stearns in 1834 or '35]. Banning and Tomlinson were rivals in staging, freighting, lightering, warehousing and indeed in everything that pertained to shipping and transportation . . . In 1858 he abandoned old San Pedro on the bluff, and built a wharf and warehouse at the head of the San Pedro slough, . . . J. Ross Browne visited Wilmington in 1864 . . . he said a "small boat of a similar kind [propelled by steam for the purpose of carrying passengers from steamer to Wilmington] burst its boiler a couple of years ago, and killed and scalded a number of people, including Captain Seely, . . ."

To Santa Catalina went the Concord Coach owned by Captain William Banning, son of Phineas. This six-horse coach was used on the road from Avalon to the Isthmus, serving as an added thrill for the visitors of the island who took the ride to Wishbone Loop, to the Summit, and back down. Eagles Nest Lodge was part of the stage coach route, the coach serving as transportation to sportsmen for goat-hunting, also.

Another son, Hancock, had the *La Paloma* built. Its home anchorage became Santa Catalina Island with the formation of the Catalina Yacht Club at Avalon in 1892 [J375]. Hancock also built a home, "Descanso," near Avalon.

Joe Banning, son of Phineas Banning, built at the Isthmus and did some development there, his preference being at the north end of the island, not at Avalon. Judge J. B. Banning's old home and the old windmill were still there in 1941.

W. W. Robinson [M43, 1941], has said that the Bannings encouraged southern California to ride the steamers to Santa Catalina, to ride the fishing boats, to go sight-seeing on glass-bottom boats, and to ride the stage coaches.

SOURCES FOR DEVELOPMENT UNDER THE BANNINGS

Code	Date	Author, Title, Publication, Notation
P124	1887	T. J. McCarty, "Mineral Springs of Santa Catalina Island," *So. Calif. Practioner.* Dr. McCarty of U.S.C. thought the mineral springs of the island were quite healthful.
J369	1892	C. Wilson, "A Business Pioneer in So. California," *So. Calif. Hist. Soc. Qtly.* She made use of some details about the Banning brothers usually not found elsewhere. Well edited.
J375	1893	H. W. Splitter, "Los Angeles Recreation, 1846-1900," *So. Calif. Hist. Soc. Qtly.* For those attracted to yachting toward Santa Catalina, the article holds interest.
P172	*1894* *	Irvin Ashkenazy, "Pigeon Express," *Westways.* The Zahn brothers brought carrier pigeon service to the island in July, 1894.
M3	n.d.	Pamphlet, "California, Brief Glimpses of her . . . ," *Burlington Route.* Written for visitors, the virtues of Santa Catalina are told. At that time, Avalon was looked upon as an orderly, large camping-ground.
M2	1895	Pamphlet, "Summer in Southern California," *Santa Fe Route.* Written to attract visitors to the island. From submarine gardens, to bath-house, to coach road are discussed.
M6	1896	Pamphlet, "California Game 'Marked Down,' " *Southern Pac. Co.* Advertising for the island; they note especially the excellent fishing.
J373	1900	Marco R. Newmark, "Early California Resorts," *So. Calif. Hist. Soc. Qtly.* He mentions the oldest existing hotel as the Glenmore of 1900. The first wireless station on the Pacific Coast exchanged messages through White's Point on Aug. 2, 1902.
P128	1901	C. F. Holder, "Rod, Reel and Gaff in Southern California," *Sunset Magazine.* It is 10 pages long; best appreciated by fishermen.
J313	1903	C. F. Holder, "Santa Catalina's Wireless Newspaper," *Scientific American.* The short article tells of the pigeon route to Avalon.
M79	1903	_____ , "Catalina Landing," *The Record Union,* Feb. 3, 1903. Senator Savage objects to Senator Hubbel's bill as Invasion of Banning's Vested Rights. After huge Banning investments, including a dance pavilion, yachting clubs wanted to land free of charge to enjoy the island's attractions.
M65	1904	_____ , "Will Organize Exclusive Club," *San Francisco Daily Chronicle,* Dec. 12, 1904. A. S. Levy of New York, promoter, plans to organize for memberships into the Pilgrim's Club for sportsmen of means. A $50,000 Clubhouse!

Code	Date	Author, Title, Publication, Notation
M31	1905	Michael Rieder, "Santa Catalina Island." The chief contribution are the photos for places in and around Avalon. References are made to the Stage-coach drive, trip to Seal Rocks, and to Moonstone Beach. Johnson's Landing for a picnic is not omitted.
M11	1906	"The Hotels and Resorts . . . ," *Norman Pierce Co.*, Southern California. Hotels and Resorts organizations of southern California advertise the island.
M7	1906	John Sebastian, "California, the Golden State," *Rock Island Lines*. The Rock Island Lines also plug the virtues of the island. Special mention is about the submarine gardens, tent city, with special space to the available hotels to be found—also their 1907 prices.
P2	*1906*	David P. Fleming, "The Magic Isle," *The Arrowhead*. His business interest in the island does not keep this write-up from being any less interesting. Excellent.
P111	1907	C. F. Holder, "The Rod on the Pacific Coast," *The Pacific Monthly*. Fishing.
B121	1913	C. F. Saunders, "Winter on the Isle of Summer," *Under the Sky in California*.
C5	1914	Dwight G. French, "Fishing at Santa Catalina Island," *California Fish & Game Commission*. He briefly describes kite-fishing at Avalon, originated by Captain George Farnsworth in 1909.
M35	1915	J. B. Scofield, "The Land of Living Color," from *Sunset Magazine*.

*Note: Code number and date in italic indicate superior information.

The Wrigleys

William Wrigley, Jr., the chewing gum magnate, began his regime on Santa Catalina Island in 1919. For a period of time the honeymoon between the new owners and the City of Avalon kept pace with the new owner's abundant spending on improvements. About this time Mr. Wrigley was hailed as being a generous person, for he was selling forty to fifty lots on easy terms of $300 apiece.

In 1920 the Wrigley mansion was built above Buena Vista Park atop Mt. Ada. Sketches and details of the terrace mansion were published [M187]. Mr. Wrigley entertained in his new island home, one of the guests was to have been Warren G. Harding— on the day of Harding's death in San Francisco, 1923.

By 1924 Mr. Wrigley was able to announce his eight-part program for Catalina. In the same year he commented, "Why, I have spent two and a half million since we arrived on the Pacific Coast last month" [M187].

It is recalled that in 1927 the Fleming-Weber Company of Wilmington held an active interest in the island. This included David P. Fleming, Charles H. Weber, Mr. and Mrs. William Wrigley, Jr., and J. H. Patrick.

Mr. Wrigley died of acute indigestion in 1933 and was buried in a specially constructed mausoleum in Buena Vista Park overlooking Avalon. Today, instead of the mausoleum there is a Wrigley Memorial and Botanical Garden in the canyon back of Avalon.

By 1933 P. K. Wrigley was thirty-eight years old and took over where his father left off. During 1934 "P. K." explained his Early California plan for development of Avalon. His own home, built in 1927, was on Sunshine Terrace, called Casa del Monte.

In 1970 [P21], "P. K." stated that he expected his son, William, age thirty-seven, to succeed him. Shortly after "P. K." passed away in 1977 most of the island of Santa Catalina was in the hands of Los Angeles County Conservancy.

SOURCES FOR DEVELOPMENT UNDER THE WRIGLEYS

Code	Date	Author, Title, Publication, Notation
J99	*1921**	P. Roualeyn Gordon, "The Magic Isle," *Chamber's Journal*. Published in London! A good write-up of what Santa Catalina has to offer.
B81	1928	M. Breeden, "The Magic Island . . . ," *The Romantic Southland of California*.
P156	1944	Nancy Langley, "Maritime Catalina," *Westways*. Gives a brief glimpse of what the Maritime Service Training Station is doing on the island.
	1962	"Flying across to Catalina," *Sunset*. A one column description of the Catalina Airport which is open to the public.

Code	Date	Author, Title, Publication, Notation
P133	1962	"Catalina Holiday," *Sunset.* An up-dated version of what to do while in Avalon. Good photos accompany.
P141	1964	"Catalina," *Travel.* Contains 5 excellent photos, a little History, some present activity.
M162	1965	"Conversion Plant Assures Santa Catalina Water," *Los Angeles Times.* The plant is at Pebble Beach to supply half of the island's water needs.
P66	1965	"Long Island West?" *Newsweek.* Speaks of P. K. Wrigley's Master Plans for the future through Pereira.
M161	1965	"Santa Catalina Island: Major Transformation Due," *Los Angeles Times.* A review of planned major transformations for the island.
M48	1965	"Catalina—the Beguiling Isle," Southern California *Auto Club News* Pictorial. With colorful photos the 'Beguiling Isle' is described, including reference to El Rancho Escondido, Arabian horse farm.
M166	1966	"Catalina Face-Lifting to Raze Old Landmarks," *Los Angeles Times.* Discusses Edison's sea water conversion plant, beginning of Marine Biology plant, razing of St. Catherine Hotel, closing the Aviary, etc.
	1967	"Finish of SC Marine Lab Points to New Catalina Era," *Los Angeles Times.* Discusses finishing of Fisherman's Cove Marine Lab of U.S.C., includes a map and picture, and a sketch of Pereira plans.
P170	1968	W. S. Cass, "A Catalina Safari," *Westways.* A 3-page pictorial account of the island and discusses big game hunting.
P61	1969	Robert P. Kingett, "Avalon Looks Up," *Motor Boating.* Plans for steamer and pier development is the major thrust of the article.
	1969	"Keel has been Laid for Catalina Vessel," *Hi-Desert Star.* A 500-passenger turbo liner for travel to the island is being built.
P21	1970	"Island Kingdom of P. K. Wrigley," *Forbes.* The Company plans for a year round place to live. Improvements are noted.
P22	*1971*	M. J. Renton, "Development of Santa Catalina Island," *Forbes.*
	1971	"Avalon's Problem: How to End Its Stagnation," *Los Angeles Times.* Wrigley and merchants differ on how to end Avalon's stagnation. Wrigley owns 70% of Avalon.
	1972	"A New Way to Reach Catalina," *Los Angeles Herald-Examiner.* Tells of new transportation ways to reach Catalina.
	1973	"Wrigley Fights Huge Catalina Tax Boost," *Los Angeles Herald-Examiner.*
	1976	"Frankly, Avalon?" *Westways.* Avalon remains the same even though some want it to become more modern.

*Note: Codes and dates in italic indicate excellent material.

Poems About Santa Catalina Island

Date	Code #	Author	Poems	Reference
1870	P76	C. W. Stoddard	"Avalon"	*Overland Monthly*
1889	P110	D. Morley	"The Hermit of Santa Catalina"	*Pacific Monthly*
1890	B46	H. L. Lunt	*Catalina, the Bride of the Pacific*	
1890	P85	N. Eames	"Mystery of Catalina"	*Overland Monthly**
1890	P108	C. Gardner	"The Island of the Blest"	*Pacific Monthly*
1890	P109	C. Gardner	"The Belle of Avalon"	*Pacific Monthly*
1893	B84	H. L. Hunt	"Catalina"	*Avalon Crusoe**
1896	P43	A. W. Wayne	"Catalina"	*Land of Sunshine*
1896	B43	S. Lauer	"A Paradise of the Pacific"	*Life and Light from Above**
1897	P1	J. G. Clark	"Santa Catalina"	*Arena**
1897	P92	M. Pruyn	"Santa Catalina"	*Overland Monthly*
1897	P93	S. L. Covey	"A Catalina Island Cañon"	*Overland Monthly*
1897	P94	N. W. Driscoll	"The Idol Cup" (fiction)	*Overland Monthly*
1898	P50	B. Trask	"Avalon, Santa Catalina Island"	*Land of Sunshine*
1898	P95	L. Macnab	"The Birth of Catalina"	*Overland Monthly*
1901	P96	R. F. Field	"The Banyan Tree at Avalon, Catalina Island"	*Overland Monthly*
1904	P70	B. Trask	"Catalina Fog"	*Out West*
1904	P71	E. F. Lewis	"At Catalina"	*Out West*
[1908]	B84	B. Trask	"Moonlight at Catalina Island"	*History of Santa Catalina Island**
1910	P98	N. C. Wilson	"Santa Catalina"	*Overland Monthly*
1914	P75	M. White	"Ode to Catalina"	*Out West*
1915	P102	O. Shepard	"Avalon, Catalina Island"	*Overland Monthly*
1921	B92	C. Herr	"A Romance of Santa Catalina"	*Their Mariposa Legend**
1924	M37	N. E. Dashiell	"Catalina" (fiction)	Excerpt from *Catalina**
1931	P106	M. W. Phillips	"Moonlight at Avalon"	*Overland Monthly*
1941	M187	B. Coates	"Sunny Catalina"	*Catalina Islander*

* The references with the asterisk have been reproduced in B84, *The Ranch that was Robbins'*—Santa Catalina Island. Other references are only listed.

Photos of Santa Catalina Island

Date	Code #	Author	Photos	Reference
			Transportation	
1952	P160	N. F. Swenson	"The Falcon," Bannings'	*Westways*
1968	J180	R. A. Weinstein	"Ferndale," in the background, Shatto's	*Museum Alliance Quarterly*
			Isthmus	
1877	N41	P. Schumacher	Map of Catalina Harbor; Indian sites	*U.S. Geol. & Geog. Survey,* Vol. III
1944	N51	S. Wheeler	Emerald Bay	*U.S. Instit., Naval, Proceedings*
1952	P160	N. F. Swenson	There was a Tent City at Isthmus	*Westways*
1962	M47	Thorne Hall	Isthmus Cove	*Odyssey of the California Islands*
			Coves, Harbors, Beaches	
1891	B39	A. T. Johnsson	Banning's Beach	*California, an Englishman's Impression*
1905	M31	M. Rieder	"Descanso," Residence of Hancock Banning	*A Pamphlet*
1905	M31	M. Rieder	Pebble Beach	*A Pamphlet*
1913	P116	C. Edwards	Japanese Abalone Camp at White Point	*Popular Science Monthly*
1921	M187	_____	Wireless Telephone Sta., Pebble Beach	*Catalina Islander*
1931	M187	_____	A Glimpse, Grounds, Hotel St. Catherine	*Catalina Islander*
			Rocks and Islands	
1894	P40	C. F. Holder	Sugar Loaf and 11 people	*Land of Sunshine*
1901	P128	C. F. Holder	Arch Rock	*Sunset*
1905	M31	M. Rieder	Sugar Loaf, Avalon Bay	*A Pamphlet*
1905	M31	M. Rieder	Seal Rocks	*A Pamphlet*
1909	P73	C. L. Edholm	Arch Rock	*Out West*
1909	P73	C. L. Edholm	Sugar Loaf Peak	*Out West*
1909	P73	C. L. Edholm	On Catalina Island [Peter Gano's home, built about 1891; still exists as a landmark]	*Out West*
1968	J180	R. A. Weinstein	Sugar Loaf Rock	*Museum Alliance Quarterly*
1968	J180	R. A. Weinstein	Sugar Loaf Rock with 84 steps	*Museum Alliance Quarterly*
			Fauna	
1902	J312	C. F. Holder	Tame Sea Lions at Santa Catalina	*Scientific American*
1902	J312	C. F. Holder	Tame Sea Gulls at Avalon	*Scientific American*
1909	P73	C. L. Edholm	"Old Ben," the Pet of Avalon	*Out West*
1912	P100	F. J. Koch	Photo of Ben	*Overland Monthly*
1935	M187	_____	Mountain Goats on a Mountain Side	*Catalina Islander*
1956	M156	C. Hillinger	Land of Buffalo	*Los Angeles Times*
1962	M47	Thorne Hall	A Buffalo herd including calf	*Odyssey of the California Islands*
			Flora	
1891	B39	A. T. Johnsson	Cactus and Cañon	*California, An Englishman's Impression*

Date	Code #	Author	Photos	Reference
1895	P41	_____	An Elderberry "Bush" [a tree]	*Land of Sunshine*
1921	M187	_____	Catalina Cottonwoods	*Catalina Islander*
1921	M187	_____	Catalina Ironwood Trees in Blossom	*Catalina Islander*

Fish and Fishing

Date	Code #	Author	Photos	Reference
1894	P40	C. F. Holder	A 351½-pound Jew Fish	*Land of Sunshine*
1900	P128	C. F. Holder	World's Record Black Sea Bass, 384#	*Sunset*
1900	P128	C. F. Holder	Yellow Tail caught with Reel, 41#	*Sunset*
1905	M31	M. Rieder	Black Bass	*A Pamphlet*
1905	M31	M. Rieder	Fishing Scene, Avalon Bay, ½ page Fishing Pier	*A Pamphlet*

Glass-Bottomed Boats

Date	Code #	Author	Photos	Reference
1891	B39	A. T. Johnsson	Glass-Bottomed Row Boats	*California, An Englishman's Impression*
1901	P128	C. F. Holder	Submarine Garden Life	*Sunset*
1905	M31	M. Rieder	At Moonstone Beach in a Boat	*A Pamphlet*
1906	P2	D. P. Fleming	"Empress," at Moonstone Beach	*Arrowhead*

The Interior

Date	Code #	Author	Photos	Reference
1905	M31	M. Rieder	Eagle's Nest	*A Pamphlet*
1905	M31	M. Rieder	Stage Road, from Summit	*A Pamphlet*
1915	M35	_____	Stage Coach and Four Horses	*Sunset*
1921	M187	_____	Wishbone Loop on Stage Route	*Catalina Islander*
1924	M187	_____	Dam under Construction, Middle Ranch	*Catalina Islander*
1926	M187	_____	Catalina Chimes Tower, View of Avalon	*Catalina Islander*
1933	M187	_____	Catalina Airport	*Catalina Islander*
1963	P165	_____	Eagle's Nest Lodge	*Westways*
1968	J180	R. A. Weinstein	The Banning Six-horse Stage	*Museum Alliance Quarterly*

Clubs

Date	Code #	Author	Photos	Reference
1901	P128	C. F. Holder	Headquarters of the Tuna Club, 1899	*Sunset*
1905	M31	M. Rieder	Clubhouse and Golf Course	*A Pamphlet*
1906	P2	D. P. Fleming	Golf Links and Club House	*Arrowhead*
1906	P2	D. P. Fleming	Home of the Pilgrim Club [excellent]	*Arrowhead*
1952	P160	N. F. Swenson	Founding Members of the Tuna Club, 1898	*Westways*

In and About Avalon

Date	Code #	Author	Photos	Reference
1889	B45	_____	Avalon Harbor and Hotel	*Lewis Publishing Co.*
1891	B39	A. T. Johnsson	The Bay of Moons, Avalon	*California, An Englishman's Impression*
1894	P40	C. F. Holder	Avalon; white tents, pier, Sugar Loaf	*Land of Sunshine*
1895	J50	O. J. Zahn	Avalon; pier, Dance Pavilion, tents	*Avifauna*
1901	P128	C. F. Holder	Avalon, 1899	*Sunset*

Avalon

Date	Code #	Author	Photos	Reference
1895	M2	_____	Pier, Boathouse, Tents	*A Pamphlet*
1905	M31	M. Rieder	Aquarium!!!!	*A Pamphlet*
1905	M31	M. Rieder	Angels' Flight	*A Pamphlet*
1905	M31	M. Rieder	Metropole Hotel	*A Pamphlet*

Date	Code #	Author	Photos	Reference
1905	M31	M. Rieder	Bathhouse, Avalon Bay	A Pamphlet
1905	M31	M. Rieder	Avalon, Main View	A Pamphlet
1905	M31	M. Rieder	Pavilion	A Pamphlet
1905	M3	_____	Six-in-hand Stage Coach	A Pamphlet
1906	P2	D. P. Fleming	Hotel Metropole [excellent] Chas. Ironmonger, photographer	*Arrowhead*
1906	P2	D. P. Fleming	Glenmore Hotel	*Arrowhead*
1906	P2	D. P. Fleming	Harbor and Town of Avalon	*Arrowhead*
1909	P73	C. L. Edholm	The Island Villa Annex	*Out West*
1914	M33	F. W. Benton	Avalon Bay, Metropole	*Semi-Tropic California*, Pamphlet
1915	M35	_____	Four-horse Stage Coach, Steamer	*Sunset*
1919	M36	Zane Grey	Avalon Bay with Sugar Loaf and 1891 home to the right	*Tales of Fishes*
1921	M187	_____	Sugar Loaf Casino, dancing palace	*Catalina Islander*
1923	M187	_____	Looking down on the Wrigley Home	*Catalina Islander*
1925	M187	_____	H. Bannings Greek Amphitheatre	*Catalina Islander*
1927	M187	_____	P. K. Wrigley Home	*Catalina Islander*
1928	M187	_____	Mount Ada, Home of Wm. Wrigley, Jr.	*Catalina Islander*
1932	M187	_____	Villa Park, 1920	*Catalina Islander*
1935	M187	_____	Avalon Bay, 1892	*Catalina Islander*
1935	M187	_____	The First Casino, Sugar Loaf Point, 1916 [framework now encloses Aviary]	*Catalina Islander*
1952	P160	N. F. Swenson	Metropole Hotel, center of activity [from J. C. Davis collection]	*Westways*
1962	M47	Thorne Hall	1½ page spread, Avalon	*Odyssey of California Islands*
1968	J180	R. A. Weinstein	Shatto's elegant Catalina Hostelry	*Museum Alliance Quarterly*
1968	J180	R. A. Weinstein	Tent City	*Museum Alliance Quarterly*
1968	J180	R. A. Weinstein	Pier, Wharf, Sugar Loaf, Cog wheel tramway	*Museum Alliance Quarterly*
1968	J180	R. A. Weinstein	Piers, Avalon Ballroom, moorings	*Museum Alliance Quarterly*
1968	J180	R. A. Weinstein	Hotels on the Water Front	*Museum Alliance Quarterly*
1968	J180	R. A. Weinstein	Tent City	*Museum Alliance Quarterly*

Maps

Date	Code #	Author	Photos	Reference
1892	P12	C. F. Holder	Map of Santa Catalina Island	*Californian Illustrated Magazine*
1898	J63	W. S. T. Smith	Geological Map of Island	*Calif. Acad. Sci. Proceed.*, Vol. I
1923	B105	C. Millspaugh	Map of Santa Catalina Island	*Flora of Santa Catalina Island*
1962	M47	Thorne Hall	Map of Southern Calif. Islands [indicates 16 altitudes on S.C.]	*Odyssey of California Islands*
1963	B84	A. L. Doran	Map of Santa Catalina Island	*Ranch that was Robbins'*

Miscellaneous

Date	Code #	Author	Photos	Reference
1905	M32	I. Williams	Map; Photos	A Pamphlet
1909	P73	C. Edholm	Photos	*Out West*

Note: All photos listed in this Bibliography have not been listed in B84. See B84 for additional listings. Neither list is definitive.

Catalina Islander

Date and Volume	Reference

UNDER THE BANNINGS

Vol. VII, #30, Aug. 10, 1920	J. S. Mathes, editor of *The Wireless,* published during Summer, 1903
Vol. VII, #32, Aug. 24, 1920	First wireless telephone equipment now on display at Pebble Beach
Vol. VII, #42, Nov. 2, 1920	Alma Overholt tells of old pirate ship, "Ning Po"
Vol. VIII, #25, July 5, 1921	" " " " " " " " "
Vol. VIII, #29, Aug. 2, 1921	" " " " " " " " "
Vol. IX, #52, Jan. 10, 1923	" " " " " " " " "
Vol. IX, #51, Jan. 3, 1923	Original Bathhouse formerly on present Tuna Club site
Vol. X, #1, Jan. 17, 1923	Catalina Three-Six Club founded; "More sport, less fish," 1908
Vol. X, #22, June 13, 1923	Incline Railway built, 1914; from Greek Theatre to Buena Vista Park; abandoned 1923
Vol. X, #30, Aug. 8, 1923	In 1904, *Los Angeles Examiner* used 20 homing pigeons to Santa Catalina
Vol. XXII, #10, Mar. 7, 1935	In 1915, Pilgrim Club back of Metropole now owned by Roy Carruthers of San Francisco
Vol. XXII, #17, Apr. 25, 1935	In 1915, 134 parcels owned by 118 people in Avalon
Vol. XXII, #48, Nov. 28, 1935	A listing of properties destroyed by 1915 fire
Vol. XXIII, #32, Aug. 6, 1936	Chinese pirate junk "Ning Po" still on exhibition in Avalon Bay, 1916
Vol. XXIII, #33, Aug. 13, 1936	In 1916 Old Sugar Loaf Casino turned into a skating rink
Vol. XXVIII, # , Nov. 28, 1941	Cause of 1915 fire remains mystery; plans to rebuild Tuna Club and Sophia Yacht Club

UNDER THE WRIGLEYS

Roads

Vol. X, #10, Mar. 21, 1923	Widening of road to Pebble Beach begun
Vol. XIII, #19, May 19, 1926	Sky-line Road completed from Renton mine to Howland's Landing; Island ½ encircled
Vol. XXII, #4, Jan. 24, 1935	Stage Line now passes Avalon, Farnsworth Loop [Wishbone Loop], Summit, Mt. Orizaba, Government Quarry, Isthmus, Little Harbor, Middle Ranch, Eagle's Nest on round trip of the island
Vol. XXVII, #49, Dec. 5, 1940	In 1920 Metropole Street needed paving

Water

Vol. VII, #15, Apr. 27, 1920	Good well located in Descanso Canyon; 1,000 gallons per hour
Vol. VIII, #34, Sept. 6, 1921	Abundance of water on west side of island, Middle Ranch, and Cottonwood Canyon
Vol. VIII, #39, Oct. 11, 1921	The Jail Canyon well is still at its original level
Vol. VIII, #51, Jan. 3, 1922	Howland's has a well from which water is pumped to the Isthmus
Vol. VIII, #52, Jan. 10, 1922	Tunneling is active for water at Pebble Beach, Golf Links, Chicken John Canyon, and Falls Canyon
Vol. XXVII, #33, Aug. 15, 1940	Two water tanks demolished; water is brought over the ridge at west and is good

Construction

Vol. VII, #5, Feb. 17, 1920	Construction camp in Falls Canyon where gas plant will be located
Vol. VIII, #10, Mar. 22, 1921	Wrigley gives $25,000 for school house after $125,000 public utilities indebtedness paid by Avalon
Vol. VIII, #30, Aug. 9, 1921	Gas and electric plants are now in Falls Canyon
Vol. X, #16, May 2, 1923	War Department has permitted new Bathhouse to be completed
Vol. XI, #4, Feb. 6, 1924	Wrigley spent $2,500,000 since January on boats, bungalows, water

Date and Volume	Reference
Vol. XI, #14, Apr. 16, 1924	Wrigley explains 8-part program of development including a railroad, complete lighting system, playground, complete water piping system
Vol. XIII, #18, May 12, 1926	Catalina Hospital has future plans
Vol. XIV, #19, May 18, 1927	Wrigley holdings spelled out: hotels, steamers, etc.
Vol. XV, #4, Feb. 1, 1928	Stables moved; a new jail; Aviary under construction; Social Hall
Vol. XV, #10, Mar. 14, 1928	Brick and tile factory built at Pebble Beach
Vol. XV, #21, May 30, 1928	Santa Catalina Island Co. has a new laundry in Falls Canyon
Vol. XVI, #16, Apr. 24, 1929	Santa Catalina Island Co. hopes for sea plane landing near Sugar Loaf pier
Vol. XX, #32, Aug. 9, 1933	Wrigley has interests in the Island Co., Wilmington Transportation Co., Angels Baseball; Santa Catalina Airline; Fleming-Weber Co.
Vol. XXIII, #22, May 28, 1936	There is Christian Hut, Hoover Groceries, Seven Seas Trading Post at Isthmus
Vol. XXVII, #21, May 23, 1940	There will be an Airport at Buffalo Springs
Vol. XXVIII, #7, Feb. 13, 1941	The mountain top for Airport has been leveled

Real Estate

Vol. IX, #19, May 24, 1922	Wrigley selling lots for $300 and up on easy terms. See map at Co. office
Vol. X, #52, Jan. 9, 1924	Santa Catalina Island Co. now owns full block from Strand Theatre to Beacon St.
Vol. XIV, #32, Aug. 17, 1927	Fleming-Weber Co. is developing over 100 lots
Vol. XXIII, #25, June 18, 1936	In 1926 the Island Co. had established a real estate department of their own
Vol. XXVIII, #8, Feb. 20, 1941	Los Angeles County Board of Supervisors gives Avalon town the right to purchase delinquent property

Hotels and Housing

Vol. VII, #8, Mar. 9, 1920	Hotel Atwater has 160 rooms, European plan
Vol. VII, #24, June 29, 1920	Wrigley, Jr.'s home sketched with description of terrace mansion house plans
Vol. VIII, #34, Sept. 6, 1921	Opposite Atwater Hotel are 40 acres of Island Villa
Vol. VIII, #45, Nov. 22, 1921	Kitchenettes for Independent Forresters Inn under construction
Vol. XIV, #9, Mar. 9, 1927	Hotel St. Catherine serves 1,000 at luncheons; Hotel is American plan
Vol. XV, #48, Dec. 5, 1928	Santa Catalina Island Co. has built 17 houses at Pebble Beach for employees
Vol. XVI, #19, May 15, 1929	There is a Spanish Village back of Avalon for Mexican-American labor
Vol. XXIII, #26, May 25, 1936	Hotel St. Catherine has a remodeled beach with tons of imported sand

Cafeterias

Vol. VII, #25, July 6, 1920	Hotel Atwater has a new cafeteria
Vol. IX, #17, May 10, 1922	Boos Bros., formerly on the main street, has leased Atwater Hotel cafeteria
Vol. XIV, #30, Aug. 3, 1927	Atwater Hotel cafeteria has been deserted for several years
Vol. XVIII, #37, Aug. 26, 1931	Childs Cafeteria has purchased their lease from Boos Bros.

Ranching and Farming

Vol. VIII, #10, Mar. 22, 1921	Over 10,000 sheep have been sheared at the Isthmus camp
Vol. VIII, #30, Aug. 9, 1921	Middle Ranch is 10 miles into the interior of the island
Vol. VIII, #52, Jan. 10, 1922	John E. Maurer and Co. runs thousands of sheep on Santa Catalina Island
Vol. IX, #51, Jan 3, 1923	Middle Ranch has the only cultivated land on the island

Date and Volume	Reference
Vol. X, #43, Nov. 7, 1923	Middle Ranch will receive electricity from Avalon; Avalon to receive water from Middle Ranch
Vol. XXII, #18, May 2, 1935	141 head of Hereford steer were shipped to mainland from Buffalo Springs, Black Jack, Echo Lake, and Empire Landing. They were loaded at White's Landing; others held in Cape Canyon

Movie Making

Vol. VII, #23, June 22, 1920	Fox film being produced at Middle Ranch
Vol. VIII, #14, Apr. 19, 1921	Metro producing "Off Shore Pirate"
Vol. VIII, #16, May 3, 1921	Metro producing "Best of Luck"
Vol. VIII, #39, Oct. 11, 1921	Goldwyn producing "Yellow-Men and Gold"
Vol. VIII, #51, Jan. 3, 1922	Paramount producing "Beyond the Rocks"
Vol. IX, #34, Sept. 6, 1922	Lasky experimenting with submarine pictures
Vol X, #12, Apr. 4, 1923	Lasky producing a South Sea story at White's Landing
Vol. XXII, #21, May 23, 1935	M.G.M. producing "Mutiny on the Bounty" [Began production on San Miguel, B103, P62]
Vol. XXIII, #2, Jan. 9, 1936	Lasky Film Co., in 1916, arranging to produce "To Have and To Hold" Other pictures or shots taken on the island are "Rain," "Bird of Paradise," "You Said a Mouthful," "Isle of Lost Souls," "Fast Life," "King of Kings," "Old Ironsides," and "Treasure Island"
Vol. XXIII, #10, Mar. 5, 1936	World Film, in 1916, producing "A Pearl of Paradise"
Vol. XXIII, #30, July 23, 1936	Natural Film Color Studios photographing the Island of Santa Catalina for the Co.
Vol. XXIII, #47, Nov. 19, 1936	Paramount producing "Souls of the Sea" at the Isthmus

Santa Barbara

Arch Point

Shag Rock

Cliff Canyon

Webster Pt.

North Peak

Landing Cove

West

Cave Canyon

Slope

Middle Canyon

Graveyard
Canyon

East

Signal Peak

Slope

Cat Canyon

Sutil Island

Pacific Ocean

Santa Barbara

Description—Place Names

Throughout the years, professional men and others, have visited Santa Barbara Island. Either imbued with their own discipline or hastily surveying this 'rock,' at least ten gave us a description, but all in minutiae. We are left, therefore, with but three early descriptions.

Dr. Cooper made an investigation of the island, and Dr. Whitney in 1865 wrote some results of Cooper's survey. Below is the subject matter of that report [C13].

Dr. Cooper encamped on the island of Santa Barbara for twenty days, with a party engaged in hunting sea-lions. He describes it as composed entirely of vesicular basalt, with very little tendency to a columnar structure, and nothing like a volcanic crater or lava streams. There is an imperfect terraced arrangement due to the action of water in the intervals of successive upheavals, of which three or four seem to have occurred since the island was raised from the sea. The whole surface is covered with a deep and apparently good soil, containing much lime, very light and ashy, and averaging four or five feet deep; it seems difficult to account for its uniformity of composition and depth, except on the supposition that it was, to a great degree, formed from the decomposition of animal remains. The island is about 500 feet high, and has two miles of shore line, everywhere rocky and abrupt, and presenting on the northeast and south sides, perpendicular cliffs exposed to the full force of the ocean-swell. The area of the summit of the island is about thirty acres, and near the highest point there is a bed of shells of living species and very fresh appearance, which have been brought there by the Indians, who formerly resorted to this place for eggs and seals. There is also a raised beach, about thirty feet above the sea, on the southeastern face of the island, in which are found shells, one species of which has not been discovered elsewhere on the coast of California. This bed may probably be the same age as the Post-Pliocene strata at Santa Barbara.

In regard to the animal life of this island Dr. Cooper remarks, that it is now the resort of great numbers of sea-lions, and was also formerly frequented by the sea-elephant, a much larger species of seal, now nearly exterminated along this coast. Myriads of birds, of several species, come to it to lay their eggs, and from these animals the large proportion of lime in the soil is derived; some of this is also washed into the water, thus affording the necessary calcareous material for the shells of great numbers of mollusca, which are found here in an abundance quite unusual on volcanic islands. The land is perfectly alive with snails, of which three new species were obtained, one of which belonged to a new genus *(Binneya notabilis)*. These landshells appear to have inhabited the island from a very early period, and fossil forms of the two larger species are found, differing considerably from those now living. . .

It is a curious fact that sheep thrive on Santa Barbara, although there is no water there during the summer, or for more than half the year; they appear to get moisture enough from the fogs and the succulent plants on which they feed. Even a cat has succeeded in sustaining life there for four years, living on birds and mice, of which there is an abundance.

In Dr. Bache's 1855-56 report to Guthrie [N27], he tells of Assistant Greenwell's erection of a signal on Santa Barbara Island. Then he mentions what Greenwell had said,

> Since then, I visited the island again, for the purpose of leaving a heliotroper, but, after two days spent in fruitless efforts to land, was at length forced to abandon the attempt. The extent of this little island in shore-line would not exceed two miles. Its elevation in the highest part is about five hundred feet, and the surface contains some twenty or thirty acres covered with soil, but no water occurs, and not a vestige of wood. The shores are rocky and abrupt, presenting on the northeast and on the southern side perpendicular surfaces, exposed to the full force of the ocean swell.

George Davidson of the Coast and Geodetic Survey is the one who gives us more detailed description of the coast line of the island in his 1889 report [N34; N28]. No doubt he used the material and information from those making the survey of the islands, as well as having made his own personal visits along the coast.

SANTA BARBARA ISLAND

This is one of the only two small islands of the Santa Barbara group. It lies on the line, and very nearly half way, between the north end of San Clemente Island and the east end of Santa Cruz Island. It is visible at a distance of twenty-seven miles.

The general direction of the island is north and south, and its extreme length is one and a half miles. The width east and west is one mile. When seen from the east or west the island rises as two islets, the southern one appearing the higher. Steamers crossing the Santa Monica Bay make it out in good weather as two small flat islets on the horizon, the apparent eastern being the larger. They appear joined for a short time. There are two points half a mile westward of the eastern face of the island, which lie two-thirds of a mile from each other on a north two-thirds east and south two-thirds west (N. 2/3 E. and S. 2/3 W.) course. The southern one is five hundred and forty-seven feet above the sea, and the northern one five hundred and seventeen feet, the latter reaching that elevation in less than one hundred feet from the sea. The depression between them is four hundred and twenty feet above the sea.

The island is very bold and high on every side, and presents precipitous cliffs to the full force of the ocean swells. The bluffs are honeycombed with great caverns into which the sea breaks with a loud noise. The base of the island is a variety of basalt, while above lies a yellowish coarse sandstone covered with alluvium.

Kelp surrounds the island out to ten fathoms of water, . . .

Dangers.—Off the southwest point of the island, one-third of a mile distant, is a rocky islet two hundred and fifty-seven feet high, with kelp around and beyond it. . . Off the western point of the island the kelp makes out over one mile, . . .

Landings and Anchorage.—Landing is at all times difficult, and can be effected at only two points. The better landing place is on the east face half a mile from the south point, and was marked by a sealer's hut on the rocks just at the landing. The anchorage off this landing is in eight fathoms of water, clean sandy bottom, not good holding ground, in a clear space just inside the outer edge of the kelp, with the sealer's hut bearing south sixty degrees west (S. 60° W), . . . The landing is very rough and rocky, and the proper course is between the two outermost rocks awash and then between others of the same character into a small opening on the north side of the rocky ledge upon which the sealer's hut is situated.

The other landing is on the north side of the western point of the island, about six hundred yards from the extreme western point, and is marked by a small shanty on the west side of a small break in the bluff. This landing is bad at times, but in April, 1871, was as good as that on the east side.

There is not a drop of water on the island; no grass, but plenty of prickly pear and shrubs. . .

J. R. Britton in *Land of Sunshine* [P47, 1897], offers us the less technical but more vividly descriptive account of the island. After having stayed there for a week, his appraisal and comments are worthy.

SANTA BARBARA ISLAND

Santa Barbara Island measures, north and south, some two miles. It is scarcely half the distance across. A few miles off it resembles the tip of a camel's back. Upon the higher hump stands the decaying beacon of the U. S. Coast Survey.

Anchoring a few hundred yards off the east coast, we landed on a narrow shelf on the rocks where a crayfisherman has built a hut of lath and canvas.

On another shelf across a deep chasm are a wooden trough and trying-pot of cemented stone about which hangs an odor of seal oil, for within a decade Santa Barbara Island has been a favorite sealing place. The cows and pups lived here and the bulls came down from the north in the autumn to remain until spring. The sealers shot the bulls in the water with rifles. At low tides the pups were clubbed in the ocean caves. Finally the hunters began killing the cows; and as a result the animals are now so nearly exterminated that the industry is practically abandoned.

North of our camp a stone's throw the tireless breakers have gnawed a hole in the rock the size of a house. Farther back is a smaller chamber whose mouth is visible as the swell recedes. Into it the water gurgles, to be cast out with a gasp and explosion that discharges spray, smoke-fine, with terrific force.

As we rowed just outside scores of "woolies," eddies and whirlpools along a bit of the most rugged of coast, other wonders unfolded. An arch large enough for a fishing schooner to pass through is tunneled under the extreme northeast point and the water moans and splashes through it. Here just off the rocks and within a circle of kelp that breaks the swell, fathoms down the blue-gray cement-like bottom gleams through luxuriant shells and corallines of all colors of the rainbow. A yellow-crimson "garibaldi's" every movement can be minutely observed, so crystal clear is the water. There are hundreds of these fish and larger ones, seemingly floating in a vacuum above which the skiff is suspended.

Around a bend the water pours into a cavern thirty feet from arch to base. It has two distinct chambers. Well above the ocean a shelf extends inward, evidently designating the one-time course of the ocean, whence the waters have long ago receded. Scores of long-necked cormorants have built their nests of mud on high.

Farther in, red-footed guillemots whiz out. Lighted matches discover their eggs carelessly laid under huge boulders which from time to time have crumbled from the sides of the cave. Fresh water drips from the roof—the only fresh water on the island.

Westward along the coast, vistaed through arches side by side like the barrels of a gun, gleam bits of ocean. The northwest point is honey-combed. There are wells, caverns and windows in fantastic confusion, some opening to the sky, others to the water. They are blow-holes formed by high seas.

Inland, hundreds of screaming gulls poise overhead. Along the bluff, in the wet ice-plant, their nests, scooped out of the ground, contain big green spotted eggs, as edible as hens' eggs. Scattered about are skulls and hoofs of sheep put on the island as a business venture some years ago. For a time they throve; but a dry year came, the grass withered, and visiting fishermen found the poor brutes too weak from starvation to stand. Many died and the remainder were removed.

In a field of malva weed hundreds of burrows contain auklets sitting upon their single white eggs. Numerous little cañons over the hill to the east are luxuriant with cactus and a peculiar inverted umbrella-shaped plant of unknown identity. It grows in some cases to a height of ten feet with a stock four inches through, having an odor and taste like parsnip.

After a week's stay on Santa Barbara we left for San Nicolas.

113

PIECES OF EIGHT

From Bartholomew [C12, 1951], and especially Philbrick [U29, 1972], we receive the two most informative, and practically the only maps of Santa Barbara Island. The reader's cross-reference of the maps with George Davidson's and Britton's description of the island could make both types of information more vivid.

WEBSTER POINT is the extreme western end of the island at the north. Davidson told us that here there is a landing "marked by a small shanty on the west side of a small break in the bluff." Evidently it has not been used as much as the landing on the east side of the island. Britton furthered our understanding of Webster Point by his comments on its honey-combed condition.

Davidson had already reminded us of another landing spot other than the north side of Webster Point,

> The better landing place is on the east face half a mile from the south point, and was marked by a sealer's hut on the rocks just at the landing . . . The landing is very rough and rocky, and the proper course is between the two outermost rocks awash and then between others of the same character into a small opening on the north side of the rocky ledge upon which the sealer's hut is situated.

By following the coast from Webster Point in a northeasterly direction, one may see the homes of sea lions, elephant seals, and cormorants. At the same time, this route moves between SHAG ROCK, 125 feet high [B114, 1917], and the island. Then one arrives at the northernmost point, given the name of ARCH POINT.

At this corner Indian midden debris may be found. Here, according to Holder, "there are arches through the rocks, double-barreled ones high above the sea" [B38]. There is a small battery-powered lighthouse atop Arch Point that is maintained by the U. S. Coast Guard as a navigational aid, we are told.

The top of the island has been called a mesa, smooth, and cut on the east side by several short ravines—called canyons. It is through Grinnell [J249, 1897], that we read,

> This mesa supports a rather abundant growth of grass, weeds, and in the eastern part, scattered low bushes. There is considerable cactus among the ravines. On many parts of the island a kind of ice plant [*mesembryanthemum*] forms a thick carpet very disagreeable to walk through.

114

Holder contributed by saying that "gulls lay their eggs in the brilliant ice plant masses." Even the auklets and murrelets build their nests right on the ground. In 1973 [P136], an environmentalist suggested, "Be careful to go around the nesting area so you won't endanger the birds."

Howell [B114, 1917], substantially gave the same description as Grinnell, after an intervening lapse of some twenty years between these two visiting ornithologists.

Greenwell, 1855, Cooper, 1865, and Bowers, 1889, said that the mesa had deep rich soil; in 1865 it was four or five feet deep. C. H. Townsend [N4, 1891], reported "long coarse grass that grows thick and tangled everywhere, making walking difficult." Philbrick said the soil "on the terraces . . . is deep, fine, friable, and fertile" [U29, 1972].

As one sails southerly along the eastern coast, there is a CLIFF CANYON. Next comes LANDING COVE, where there is a small Indian midden. A little farther south is what is known as CAVE CANYON, then MIDDLE CANYON, and after that, GRAVEYARD CANYON. It has not been specified as to what type of graveyard this canyon is—animal, Indian, or merely a place name.

At the most southern end of Santa Barbara a place name of CAT CANYON is given; perhaps such a name has something to do with the numerous cats having once lived on the island. It is a wonder that there is not a rabbit or a hare canyon—for the same reason. PRIMERO CANYON has been mentioned, but its location has not been described [J350]. Supposedly, a shack existed here, too.

Tacking a westerly course, SUTIL ISLAND is one-third of a mile out at sea from the southwest end of the island. Heald [J81, 1957], called this small island, GULL ISLAND. E. G. Gudde [B29, 1949], stated that it "was named Sutil Island by the Geographic Board. The *Sutil* was a ship of the Galiano expedition of 1792."

Davidson called the island a danger point as "it is a rocky islet two hundred and fifty-seven feet high, with kelp around and beyond it." Pelicans and gulls have made their home on this island.

SIGNAL PEAK is on the West Slope of the mesa. Five hundred forty-seven feet high, it was the location for the Geodetic Survey beacon in the 50s. NORTH PEAK is a short distance inland, opposite Shag Rock, it's height, some five hundred seventeen feet. The mesa between these two peaks is about four hundred twenty feet.

If Thorne Hall [M47, 1962], is correct, there is a light on both Signal Peak and North Peak; this for navigational aid. It is just northeast of North Peak where remnants of the Giant Coreopsis may be seen; Darwin Lambert, in writing for the National Park Service, has even said that this spectacular plant is more abundant on Santa Barbara Island than on Anacapa [N52, 1969].

Phil C. Orr does a nice descriptive job of the Coreopsis in "Island Hopping" [J270, 1949],

> On land, there grows a veritable forest of *Coreopsis gigantea*, the giant sea dahlia. Tufts of large yellow flowers and foliage at the top of a bare tree-like trunk gives the appearance of a weird forest, for although the "trees" are only three feet high, there is nothing else on the island for comparison.

There appears to be no disagreement among those visiting the island when it is said [M50, 1970], "Numerous caves, rock bridges, offshore pillars, and spray-spouting stacks create beautiful and dramatic sea-scapes."

Another area of agreement is Grinnell's statement [J249], that "There are [practically] no beaches and the sides of the island are extremely precipitous."

The subject of water on the island is but a partial topic, but has drawn forth two-points-of-view. As far back in time as Davidson's report, 1889, the island was said to be without water. In 1910 C. F. Holder slightly changed this thought when he mentioned that fresh-water dripped from a two-chambered cave at the northeast end of the island. The question is, does the drip dry-up during the summer months? Probably so. Sumner has reported two cement cisterns where water had been collected.

A discussion of the island's plant life is considerably more complex.

Natural History

Flora

Ralph N. Philbrick produced a 24-page article for *Madroño* in 1972 [U29], entitled, "The Plants of Santa Barbara Island, California." But there is much more in the account than a discussion of the island's flora. Philbrick moves from one relatively short paragraph to another, he explains something about Santa Barbara Island's physical features, soil, climate, rainfall, fauna, avifauna, and geology, even before discussing plant life.

The article contains about thirteen photos of plants, maps or charts, and Philbrick animates island life by referring to the Alvin Hyder family, who lived on the island from 1915 to 1926.

Mr. Philbrick took a particular interest in the rabbits, their rise and decline in population, and the population's effect on the plants of the island.

No person appears to have any more intimate knowledge of the island, what with Philbrick's numerous visits to the island, his personal interviews, and his research. His findings, therefore, serve as a pivotal point for comparisons with those of others. Hopefully, this will lead to an eventual resolvement of numbers and species of plants.

Lowell Sumner of the Park Service had done some collecting on Santa Barbara Island. And Peter H. Raven of Stanford University has done an in-depth study through the use of outstanding literature on the flora of the islands. Both are helpful for purposes of comparisons.

Raven named and listed one single-island endemic for Santa Barbara Island, eleven endemics in common with another island or islands, and forty native California species not endemic to the islands. Philbrick named and listed three single-island endemics, eleven endemics in common with another island or islands, and sixty-eight native California species, not endemic to the islands. Of the mixed endemics, three of Raven's list are not on Philbrick's Table I, and two of Philbrick's are not on Raven's list.

Raven thought that eight island endemics were shared between San Clemente and Santa Barbara; Philbrick gave us ten. Raven gave us six endemics shared by Santa Catalina and Santa Barbara; Philbrick offered eight. For San Nicolas and Santa Barbara, Raven considered four endemics to be in common; Philbrick said there were six.

There are other differences:

1. Philbrick listed *Trifolium palmeri* for Santa Barbara; Raven listed it for only San Nicolas, Santa Catalina, and San Clemente.

2. Philbrick found *Galvezia speciosa* on Santa Barbara; it is listed for only San Clemente and Santa Catalina by another.

3. *Artemisia californica insularis* has been listed by Munz for San Nicolas and San Clemente. Philbrick added Santa Barbara Island.

4. Raven listed *Malacothrix foliosa* for San Clemente and Santa Barbara. Sumner listed it for San Miguel, and Philbrick for Anacapa; this would make it a mixed north and south island endemic.

5. Raven listed *Malacothrix insularis* var. *squalida* for Santa Barbara, Anacapa, Santa Cruz, and Santa Rosa. Philbrick does not list it, nor does Munz describe it.

6. *Lavatera assurgentiflora* is listed by Raven for Santa Barbara along with the other islands, with San Nicolas being the exception. Philbrick has not listed it; Munz says, "On the Santa Barbara Islands."

7. Raven listed *Phacelia floribunda* for Santa Barbara and San Clemente. Philbrick says of the Santa Barbara *Phacelia* that it has some characteristics of *floribunda*.

Sea Otter and Seal Hunting
Aftermath

In Adele Ogden's article, "Russian Sea-Otter and Seal Hunting on the California Coast, 1803-1841" [J93, 1933], she has furnished information based upon the journal of the *Albatross.* From that journal it is said that the *Mercury,* the *Isabella,* and the *O'Cain* were actively hunting on Santa Barbara Island in 1810 and 1811.

A party of hunters, with their canoes and women were left at the Island of Santa Barbara to take otter. During the three days they were left here the hunters took about sixty prime sea otter skins . . . It seems that the two captains Winship pursued their business of hunting and trading on joint account, in different directions, and with gangs on various islands, the ships moving between the points of observation, supplying their wants and collecting the proceeds of the parties.

At a not very much later date, Charles M. Scammon was on the California coast. He lived from 1825 to 1911, was a sea captain, and began his career in 1842. His command of a sailing ship for the California gold fields determined his future career.

Traveling south, he entered the bay at Avalon, waiting for a small schooner, the *Marin,* then sailed toward a new whaling ground, only to find himself hunting seal instead [B64, 1969].

They went to Santa Barbara Island and his account, though well-written, is not a pretty picture. And although Scammon characterized the sealers as being barbarous, nonetheless it was he who was in charge of the schooner.

To give a more extended and detailed account of the Sea Lions, we will relate a brief sketch

of a sealing season on Santa Barbara Island. It was near the end of May, 1852, when we arrived; and, soon after, the rookeries of "clapmatches," which were scattered around the island, began to augment, and large numbers of huge males made their appearance, belching forth sharp, ugly howls, and leaping out of or darting through the water with surprising velocity; frequently diving outside the rollers, the next moment emerging from the crest of the foaming breakers, and waddling up the beach with head erect, or, with seeming effort, climbing some kelp-fringed rock, to doze in the scorching sunbeams, while others would lie sleeping or playing among the beds of sea-weed, with their heads and outstretched limbs above the surface. But a few days elapsed before a general contention, with the adult males, began for the mastery of the different rookeries, and the victims of the bloody encounters were to be seen on all sides of the island, with torn lips, or mutilated limbs and gashed sides; while, now and then, an unfortunate creature would be met with, minus an eye, or with the orb forced from its socket, and, together with other wounds, presenting a ghastly appearance. As the time of "hauling up" drew near, the island became one mass of animation; every beach, rock, and cliff, where a seal could find foot-hold, became its resting-place; while a countless herd of old males capped the summit, and the united clamorings of the vast assemblage could be heard, on a calm day, for miles at sea. The south side of the island is high and precipitous, with a projecting ledge hardly perceptible from the beach below, upon which one immense Sea Lion managed to climb, and there remained for several weeks—until the season was over. How he ascended, or in what manner he retired to the water, was a mystery to our numerous ship's-crew, as he came and went in the night; for "Old Gray"—as named by the sailors—was closely watched in his elevated position during the time the men were engaged at their work on shore.

None but the adult males were captured, which was usually done by shooting them in the ear or near it; for a ball in any other part of the body had no more effect than it would in a grizzly bear. Occasionally, however, they are taken with the club and lance, only shooting a few of the masters of the herd. This is easily accomplished with an experienced crew, if there is sufficient ground back from the beach for the animals to retreat. During our stay, an instance occurred, which not only displayed the sagacity of the animals, but also their yielding disposition, when hard pressed in certain situations, as if naturally designed to be slain in numbers equal to the demands of their human pursuers. On the south of Santa Barbara Island was a plateau, elevated less than a hundred feet above the sea, stretching to the brink of a cliff that overhung the shore, and a narrow gorge leading up from the beach, through which the animals crawled to their favorite resting-place. As the sun dipped behind the hills, fifty to a hundred males would congregate upon the spot, and there remain until the boats were lowered in the morning, when immediately the whole herd would quietly slip off into the sea and gambol about during the day, returning as they saw the boats again leave the island for the ship. Several unsuccessful attempts had been made to take them; but, at last, a fresh breeze commenced blowing directly from the shore, and prevented their scenting the hunters, who landed some distance from the rookery, then cautiously advanced, and suddenly, yelling, and flourishing muskets, clubs, and lances, rushed up within a few yards of them, while the pleading creatures, with lolling tongues and glaring eyes, were quite overcome with dismay, and remained nearly motionless. At last, two overgrown males broke through the line formed by the men, but they paid the penalty with their lives before reaching the water. A few moments passed, when all hands moved slowly toward the rookery, which as slowly retreated. This maneuvre is called "turning them," and, when once accomplished, the disheartened creatures appear to abandon all hope of escape, and resign themselves to their fate. The herd at this time numbered seventy-five, which were soon dispatched, by shooting the largest ones, and clubbing and lancing the others, save one young Sea Lion, which was spared to ascertain whether it would make any resistance by being driven over the hills beyond. The poor creature only moved along through the prickly pears that covered the ground, when compelled by his cruel pursuers; and, at last, with an imploring look and writhing in pain, it held out its fin-like arms, which were pierced with thorns, in such a manner as to touch the sympathy of the barbarous sealers, who instantly put the sufferer out of its misery by the stroke of a heavy club. As soon as the animal is killed, the longest spires of its whiskers are pulled out, then it is skinned, and its coating of fat cut in sections from its body and transported to the vessel, where, after being "minced," the oil is extracted by boiling. The testes are taken out, and with the selected spires of the whiskers,

find a market in China—the former being used medicinally, and the latter for personal ornaments.

At the close of the season—which lasts about three months, on the California coast—a large majority of the great herds, both males and females, return to the sea, and roam in all directions in quest of food, as but few of them could find sustenance about the waters contiguous to the islands, or points on the mainland, which are their annual resorting-places. They live upon fish, mollusks, crustaceans, and sea-fowls; always with the addition of a few pebbles or smooth stones, some of which are a pound in weight.

About 1826 George C. Yount reported that on the island of Santa Barbara he took ten sea elephants and otter in great abundance [J85, 1923].

Coxe, 1780, gave a graphic description of how and why the Aleuts killed the sea otter [B64],

Of all these furs, the skins of the Sea Otters are the richest and most valuable. These animals resort in great numbers to the Aleutian and Fox islands; they are called by the Russians *Boobry Morfki,* or sea beavers, on account of the resemblance of their fur to that of the common beaver. They are taken four ways: struck with darts as they are sleeping upon their backs in the sea; followed by boats and hunted down until they are tired; surprised in caverns, and taken in nets.

Such preceding information is highly important for its concreteness, allowing all concerned to be aware of how and why the depopulation of all the sea mammals became so grave. Such utter-otter cruelty and seal-suffering speaks for itself!

The *California Fish and Game Bulletins* from Bonnot to Bartholomew are worthy of note. Even by 1940 the Department of the Interior only counted approximately 1,000 sea lions on Santa Barbara, some 500 of them thought to be breeding there regularly. The mammals were making a come-back.

By 1950 Bartholomew [C12], remarked that while in 1928 the sea lions

were confined to a small area on the northwest part of the island, [now] . . . the suitable beaches on all sides of the island were occupied by at least a few animals. This more general distribution of the sea lions on the island is undoubtedly associated with the greatly increased size of the population.

Bartholomew referred to the Elephant Seal, Steller Sea Lion, and the California Sea Lion on Santa Barbara [B120; J270].

Fauna

T. D. A. Cockerell [J257, 1938], is the first to offer a record for bees from Santa Barbara, Santa Catalina, and San Miguel.

In H. C. Fall's accounting of the Coleoptera of the southern California islands [J98, 1897], he said, "As far as I can learn from the literature at hand, the following fifteen species of Coleoptera are all that were described or reported from the islands up to 1875." Then he mentioned five from Santa Cruz, [three] from Santa Catalina, four from San Clemente, and three from Santa Barbara Island. According to him, these were nearly all taken, either by C. M. Bache or Dr. J. G. Cooper, and given to Dr. LeConte, by whom they were described. Fall added about twenty-three for the islands of Santa Barbara, San Nicolas, or San Clemente.

Oscar Loew [N45, 1879], remarked that the snail *Binneya notabilis* was to be found only on Santa Barbara Island. He reported *Helix Tryoni* as being on both Santa Barbara and San Nicolas islands, and *Helix Facta* on Santa Barbara, San Nicolas, and Santa Catalina.

J. G. Cooper, who had visited the four southern islands, made a chart of what he saw. But he thought there was nothing unusual about the island fauna, other than the reptile of *Saurian* type [J57, 1868]. This is presumably the lizard, *Gerrhonotus coeruleus*, called "Alligator" by Holder.

The lizard, *Zantusia riversiana*, is mentioned by John Van Denburgh [J66, 1905]. It is a night-lizard, endemic to the California islands, or at least to most of them. Mr. C. H. Townsend and later Grinnell, had found it on Santa Barbara Island. Nine years later, twenty-one specimen of the species were taken from the island by Van Denburgh and Slevin, 1914.

L. Sumner referred to the White-footed Mouse *(Peromyscus maniculatus elusus)* as being nowhere else in the world but on Santa Barbara Island, 1939. Other authors do not entirely agree with this statement; it is a subject of discussion.

Imported to the island of Santa Barbara were the rabbits. And rabbits multiply very rapidly. They became such a problem that by 1955 methods of control were necessary. From a couple of thousand rabbits living off the island's vegetation, mainly *Mesembryanthemum, Calystegia,* and *Coreopsis,* the rabbit population was reduced to less than half; further

control appeared necessary, however.

But with an accidental fire in 1959, destroying both rabbit and vegetation, the thirty remaining rabbits were easily done away with. It was Lowell Sumner who reported this information to Mr. Philbrick.

Before the problem with rabbits, it was the house cat. The Department of Interior reported in 1940 that Santa Barbara Island lost much of its native bird population because of the multiplying of domestic cats brought to the island prior to 1908. Seemingly, they have also been eliminated.

Strange, other islands have experienced felines, but on Santa Barbara Island, Mother Nature has needed more than an average amount of outside assistance to protect her own, as her struggle for survival continues its slow pace with the passage of time.

Avifauna

In the spring of 1897 Dr. Grinnell and his "scientific exploring party" camped on the east side of Santa Barbara Island during four different months. Their camp was on a shelf at the landing.

While there, they observed eight species of birds: Mourning Dove, Bald Eagle, Streaked Horned Lark, Western Wood Pewee, American Raven, Rock Wren, and House Finch. Their collection amounted to 450 bird skins and many eggs [J249]. The collection included two sets of fresh eggs of the Farallon Cormorant and thirty sets of eggs of the Brandt Cormorant in all stages of incubation, including the newly-hatched young [B115, 1933].

In 1898 Mearns mentioned the Linnet and described a new bird from the island, the House Finch. Mr. Charles Townsend had obtained the Finch in 1888 and 1889 on San Clemente and Santa Barbara. Mearns also mentioned that Grinnell had collected fourteen of the Finch from Santa Barbara [J41, 1898].

A. B. Howell [B114, 1917], referred to the Finch, saying that it fed on the fruit of the opunta cactus "until their whole fronts are stained by the red juice . . ." They nested in the pockets of the cliffs and the cactus.

H. Robertson in 1903 wrote five paragraphs on the Cassin Auklet from a visit he had made to Santa Barbara Island on June 8, 1899 [J106]. He said that their party was on a two-week cruising trip "to extend . . . ornithological investigation and add a few more specimens of birds and eggs . . ." They were anchored in a large cove on a large rock and pulled their skiff onto the rock. They scrambled, with the best of [their] ability, and by the aid of an old rusty chain, to the top of the island. [They] threaded [their] way among the gulls' nests and, after examining a few, proceeded to the southern end, where the higher land slopes gradually toward the cove. Here [they] found a number of auklet burrows and at once went to work.

Most of the article is a description of the burrows since there was no particular rule to follow in the auklets' methods of home-building. They took numerous specimens back to Santa Monica.

In 1904 L. Miller took an adult female Ashy Petrel and reported that he saw the California Brown Pelican [B115, 1933]. In 1905 O. W. Howard visited the island and photographed the nests and eggs of the Western Gull, formerly quite plentiful [M124, 1904; J383, 1905].

By 1909 Robertson was back on Santa Barbara Island with O. W. Howard, C. B. Linton, Otto J. Zahn, H. A. Gaylord, and others [J121]. More specimens, including a nest and four eggs of the Island Horned Lark, were taken before leaving for San Nicolas Island the following day. While they were on the island they observed eighteen species of birds, and visited several nesting colonies of Cassin Auklet and Western Gull.

In July of 1912 Wright and Snyder made a trip to Santa Barbara, Anacapa, Santa Cruz, Santa Rosa, and Prince islands. There is more bird-talk in the article, also the naming of the species seen and taken from the islands [J127]. They found between 300 and 400 birds nesting, with all the nests containing young [J122].

In 1924 A. J. Van Rossem reported in *Condor* that there were three races of song sparrows on the island, but that *Melospiza melodia graminea* is confined to Santa Barbara Island. According to Sumner, the sparrows appeared to be holding their own as late as 1958.

By 1927 Pemberton visited the island, listing in 1928 seven birds from there. He noted a Black-and-White Warbler on Santa Barbara, new to any of the islands [J139].

Back to the island in 1929 he saw eight more species not "heretofore recorded for that island." And as an aside, he said, "some recently imported sheep . . . are rapidly dying because of the absence of fresh water . . . there will be plenty of wool for their [Ravens] nests next spring."

Pemberton's new list included the Eared Grebe,

Pacific Loon, Heermann Gull, Bonaparte Gull, Caspian Tern, California Great Blue Heron, Belted Kingfisher, and Raven [J142].

In speaking of birds, and gulls in particular, H. J. Snow [B67, 1910] remarked in 1768 that

> The chase of the otter is not the only thing which makes sea-otter hunting so attractive. If the season is right, seabirds' eggs are gathered in thousands, and stored in barrels in sand, as in that position they will keep for a long time.

Egg-gatherers were still collecting in 1850, some having come to the island from the town of Santa Barbara to obtain these gull-goodies; George Nidever was actively interested.

One cannot but wonder if the collecting instinct of collective ornithologists might not also have had something to do with the avifaunal population depletion!—not to mention otter-men-egg-gatherers.

Archaeology

Although G. Eisen was more inclined to think that a sizeable Indian population was once on Santa Barbara Island, most archaeologists do not share that view-point [M30, 1904].

Schumacher [N41, 1877], called the island a "way-station" for the Indians, for he found but a small midden with fragments of pestles and mortars.

In 1958 Swartz and Sutton found no house pits or burial grounds on the island [U39]. But they did find an abalone pry, chips of quartzite, basalt, chert, bone, and shell. They were on the island for a week during August 1958.

While there, they investigated a number of caves but found nothing of value, but they did discover "one rather extensive workshop site . . . on a bluff overlooking the landing"; much of it had been disturbed.

In 1959 a Paul J. Schumacher of the National Park Service located four additional sites and recovered a mano from the island [U48].

The following year Meighan, Director of U.C.L.A. archaeological investigations, remarked that five sites had been found on Santa Barbara Island, whereas the Berkeley archaeologists had found none previously [U45].

National Park Status

In 1938 President Roosevelt proclaimed Santa Barbara Island and The Anacapas to be a National

Monument. However, the public was not allowed on the islands until about 1961.

The two islands are now under the administration of the Department of the Interior, National Park Service. The Service is hopefully attempting to preserve the geological and biological values of the islands for the more serious-minded visitor. At present only primitive conditions for visitors prevail on these islands. A 1967 bill to make the four northern islands a National Park died [P173].

ADDENDA, 1980. Fortunately, the status of these islands has changed once again, and as recently as March, 1980. President Carter has just signed such a bill, giving Santa Barbara, Anacapa, Santa Cruz, Santa Rosa, and San Miguel the status of a national park—Southern California's first.

Although it may be anticipated that several years may pass before some of the island's acreage could be open to the public, other portions will no doubt be available for use as early as this coming summer. With so many more anticipated visitors and tourists to these islands, it is to be hoped that both the Park Service and the visitors will cooperate in maintaining a fairly protected environment for the scenic, biological, and botanical features of this new national park.

Photos of Santa Barbara

Date	Code #	Author	Photos	Reference
1939	J349	Comstock, J. A.	Santa Barbara Island from east [shows camel humps]	*So. Calif. Acad. Sci. Bulletin,* Vol. 38
1944	N51	Wheeler	Santa Barbara Island	*U.S. Naval Instit. Proceedings*
1951	C12	Bartholomew	Map of Santa Barbara w/ 2 rocks	*California Fish and Game Quarterly*
1956	P162	Thornburgh	Sea Elephants and Sea Lions	*Westways*
1972	U29	Philbrick	Map of Santa Barbara w/ 2 rocks	*Madroño*

Santa Barbara Islands

I.

Majestic mountains of the sea,
Marvelous you seem to me,
Across the waves of sparkling blue
A silhouette of darker hue.
In changing light are clearly seen
Arch, peak, broad upland and ravine—
Marvelous you seem to me,
Majestic mountains of the sea.

II.

Magic mountains of the sea,
Mysterious you seem to me,
Invisible though bright the day
As if a thousand miles away.
Beneath a Hermes cap of waves,
Hide crags and peaks and Indian graves—
Mysterious you seem to me.
Magic mountains of the sea.

III.

Matchless mountains of the sea,
Miraculous you seem to me,
For when the Sunset Artist pours
His gold unstinted 'round your shores
You float in glory, turquoise blue,
Then amethyst, and darker, too—
Miraculous you seem to me
Matchless mountains of the sea.

Carrie W. Egan
1928, P145

The Channel of Santa Barbara

It lies a liquid opal on the breast
  Of soft Pacific seas; heaves when they breathe
  With every swinging sigh. The thin mists wreathe
Those fair encircling isles that guard with zest
This jewel of the wooing waves' bequest,
  From out the depths where tempests rave and seethe,
To happy dwellers on its shores of rest,
  Soft smiling skies their benisons bequeathe;
For Peace herself builds here her brooding nest:
  Where way-worn pilgrims can at any time
  Of their wan woefulness themselves divest,
  Escape the summer scorch, the winter rime,
In slumber dream at their own will's behest,
  Nor ask of God another perfect clime.

Juliette Estelle Mathis
P10, 1891-92

121

Anacapa

N

Caves;
Marine Gardens

Santa Barbara Channel

Vela
Peak (930')

(600')
Plateau   Diving Location

Cat Rock

Indian-Water Cave

Frenchy's Cove; Cave

Tide Pools

Arched Passage

Bat Ray Cove

Winfield Scott
Shipwreck

East Fish Camp

Cathedral Cove

Cathedral Cave

Pacific Ocean

Lighthouse   Arch Rock

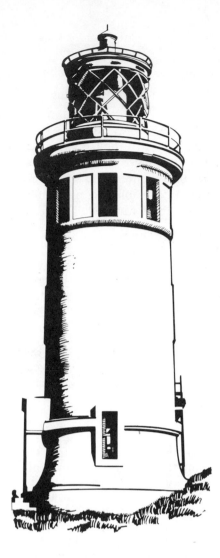

The Anacapas

Geology

In George Davidson's, "The Abrasions of the Continental Shores of Northwest America, and the supposed Ancient Sea Levels" [J60, 1873], he remarked that Anacapa's ridge is composed of dark gray sandstone. However, one doubts that he meant to imply the island was composed of sandstone.

Yates [J262], stated that the Anacapas "are more exclusively of volcanic origin than any other of the Channel Islands." Others contribute by saying that the island is a mass of black vesicular basalt, covered later by other formations of volcanic rock, then topped or mixed with a coarse and very-much decomposed sandstone, or in places, with a light, sandy soil [M126, U38]. The black sand on a few beaches are actually tiny particles of black lava, indicative of the island's Miocene origin.

Davidson noticed that "two-thirds of the length, [of the three segments] reckoned from the eastern extremity, has been planed off. . . [and] the line of the level of the summit of the eastern parts is marked around the flanks of the western, notwithstanding the deep gulches, with almost vertical sides, which cut from the summit to the top of the bluff" [J60].

Nearly all articles referring to The Anacapas mention the almost perpendicular characteristic of the islets, with numerous wave-cut caves eroded from their sides.

John Southworth [B123, 1920], expressed himself by saying that Anacapa

rises out of deep water and is surrounded by kelp, . . . the coast [being] a maze of strange caves . . . Many of the caves are beneath or just on the surface, and are constantly hissing like living things, spouting water in great jets with tremendous force of compressed air.

His remarks are reminiscent of C. F. Holder's overall description of Anacapa's caves.

Dr. Yates discussed the geology in bits, about as frequently as he wrote articles. He wrote for *West*

American Scientist, American Geologist, and others. Code numbers for four other articles are J262, 1889; C19, 1890; U52, 1890; and J163, 1892.

Of the caves about the island(s) Yates said,

> soft places in the lava rock have allowed the waters of the ocean to form the numerous caves, ocean-floored caverns, columns, arches and fantastic outlying rocks, for which the islands are noted. . . The beating of the waves has worn these caves and tunnels into the vesicular basalt, carving out chambers whose roofs are supported by grand pillars; or into low, cavernous, arched tunnels which extend to unknown distances under the island. In some instances the openings are high, gradually decreasing in height until the roof becomes so low that the crests of the waves touch the roof and fill the caves, the confined air causing reverberations similar to the discharge of artillery.

Yates took quite an interest in caves in general, and the most outstanding ones in particular. His more generalized remarks are these [J327, 1902],

> . . . of the large number of caves visited by me, I know of two only which, in ordinary times, have any portion of their floors exposed above the ocean level, and one of those is covered at high tide, and the other is dry by reason of its lying back of a mass of rocks which have fallen from the bluff.

More recent articles on the geology of this tiny group of islets may be found in J25, 1959; J324, 1960; J245, 1963; and J175, 1964. Their emphasis, however, is not on caves.

Another unusual characteristic of The Anacapas is the mirage-effect that at times it creates. It was witnessed as a mirage on October 31, 1890 [P87, 1891],

> The Anacapa first became a balloon, then a dragon, as became the Island of Demons; next a turreted fortress, then a medusa, and lastly a devil-fish, with antennae writhing, and crouching like a great sea tarantula for a spring.

Anacapa Island is a Three-in-one, "born of the mystic laws of refraction in a mist-laden air" [B25].

More realistic than even a mirage, an air-view gives the island the appearance of a narrow backbone, like a curving, five-mile long, east-northeast, segmented reptile with a wide head and a tapering snoot.

124

Anacapa's Uses

Seal Hunting

Our earliest record for the users of Anacapa dates to 1855. Where previously the Indians had made Anacapa at least a home, others came for profit, including seal hunters, abalone, lobster and crayfish hunters, bird hunters, and sheep raisers.

It was W. M. Johnson, in writing to Bache on October 1, 1855, who gave us our first cue,

> During the time we were surveying at Anacapa there was a small vessel engaged in seal hunting. The party employed consisted of five men; they had erected try-works on the north side of the middle island, at the boat landing, and up to the time of landing had tried out eighty-five barrels of oil . . . [N26].

A much later report [B70, 1883], from Thompson and West's *History of Santa Barbara and Ventura Counties,* came the following descriptive account,

> Sealing on Anacapa Island is usually carried on in December, because they congregate in great numbers at the beginning of the winter, and for another reason that they then are fattest, yielding the largest quantity of oil, being ten to forty gallons to the seal. There is no wood or water on the island; the cracklings or scraps of the *tried* blubber is used for fuel, and water has to be carried in barrels to sustain the party through the hunt, which may last two or three months. In early days the islands, or the different portions of the Anacapa which are separated by channels, was so covered with seals that it was impossible to converse in their vicinity from their noise, which is something between the barking of a dog and the noise of hogs. The seal hunters generally shoot the seals on the shore from boats, and tow the bodies to the landing where the blubber is stripped off and boiled in the kettles provided for the purpose . . . The handling of the oil, whether in the shape of blubber or cutting it up and boiling it, or handling it in barrels, is a disagreeable business, but like everything else that offers a remuneration, finds willing hands. Thirty or forty barrels of oil is the usual catch of the crews hunting seal on Anacapa.

Sea Otter, thought to be entirely extinct, due to being hunted, have been seen more recently in the waters by the California Division of Fish and Game. They are now being doubly protected through a patrol of the area [P159, 1947].

Sheep Raising

By 1869, at least, the sheepmen were on Anacapa. The California Archives furnish such information as is available [C42; C43]. From July 29, 1869 through April 3, 1873 Uncle Sam appeared to have taken no part in the transactions.

On July 29, 1869, William Dover sold all of his interest in Anacapa to Louis Burgert and W. H. Mills for $1500, furnishing a quitclaim to "certain pieces or parcels of land possessed and owned by me . . ." In 1872 W. H. Mills and H. W. Mills sold to the Pacific Wool Growing Co. for $1,000 ". . . three certain small islands . . . known as the Anacapa Islands." Their business transaction ended in 1873 when Warren H. Mills of San Francisco made final arrangements with the wool company. The Mills brothers were also involved with sheep on San Miguel Island.

In 1890 Captain Elliot was running sheep on the Anacapas. Later, Louis le Mesnager rented the Anacapas, and he did so for a term of five years. Beginning in April 1902, he leased, after having agreed to "not erect any permanent buildings upon any part of the said Island." His $25 yearly fee carried him to April 1, 1907.

In September of 1904 Walker of the *Los Angeles Times* had this to say,

It may sound like exaggeration when I tell you that there are now, and have been for a number of years, several hundred sheep on this island who subsist entirely on the scant vegetation and with only such water as congeals from the fogs and mists and from the winter rains . . . The title to this rock pile is vested in Uncle Sam and is leased for a term of years to a French resident of Los Angeles named Mesnager, who owns the sheep now on it.

"Old Charlie" watched the sheep for Mesanger.

Gidney [B25, 1917], brings us a little closer to knowing when Captain Webster took charge of the sheep on the island, ". . . several hundred head of sheep are kept there the year through by the lessee, Cap't Ray Webster, who has had charge of the island for nine years."

When Burt [J125, 1911], and Rosamond [P74, 1912], were on the Anacapas, they each referred to a Mr. Webster and/or a WEBSTER BAY on the lee side of the island. This Bay was probably renamed FRENCHY'S COVE with a change of tenancy.

Homer C. Burt and party had the use of a "little shanty up under the cliffs" during their stay on West Anacapa. Before arriving, they had launched to the island with Mr. Webster,

. . . [we left] Ventura harbor . . . on the launch "Ana Capa", owned by Mr. Ray Webster of Ventura . . . Mr. Webster was unable to bring the launch up from San Pedro [before] where it had been in anchorage for the winter.

. . . we afterward enjoyed more than one fish and mutton dinner fixed up by [George] and Mrs. Webster, who came over two days later to stay until the sheep shearing was over.

. . . Mr. Webster agreed to take us aboard the launch and land us down on the east end the following morning. We found Mr. Webster very willing to assist us in any way he could during our stay on the island, . . .

Sidney B. Peyton, who wrote for *Oölogist,* "A Collecting Trip to Anacapa Island" [J236, 1913], was a member of Burt's party in 1911.

Webster might have been one of the sheepmen of San Buenaventura about whom C. F. Holder referred, in his *Channel Islands of California,* as running sheep on the island.

Le Dreau, as "Frenchy," went to Anacapa in 1928 and remained until some time in 1958. Dr. Ellison [B128, 1941], said there were four shacks on the island, "one of which is occupied by an old [lobster] fisherman," who likes to oversee the national monument.

E. Lowell Sumner, Regional Wildlife Technician for the National Park Service had many discussions with Frenchy, and McKusick was informed of much through Sumner.

McKusick [U40, 1959], concludes this section by saying, "Until the late 1930's sheep were grazed on all three island segments . . . At the present time there are a few sheep on East Anacapa and remnants of a barbed wire fence can be seen on Middle Anacapa."

Abalone and Lobster Fishing

In referring to The Anacapas, Homer P. Earle [P44, 1896], remarked,

Anacapa is uninhabited unless one counts campers and the Chinamen who spend a part of the year there in a tent amid piles of iridescent abalone shells and square yards of the evicted tenants, drying in the sun, to be shipped to Chinatown.

Of the lobster fishing, Harry H. Dunn of the *Los*

PIECES OF EIGHT

> There are extensive lobster fisheries on Anacapa, . . . so that the island is populated during the lobster season, with a cosmopolitan crew of Japs, Greeks and other foreigners engaged in the preparation of these crustaceans.

On crawfishing, Rosamond had 1912 comments [P74],

> . . . The law on crawfish has been in force for two years and is just out. The fishermen are busy with their traps! We found a cove where large crawfish abound, and went to get one, with no other weapon than the oars. The water was clear and shallow, and there they were hugging the grass-grown walls of the cove only three feet beneath us . . .

According to Sumner in 1939, Raymond LeDreau was allowed to remain on West Anacapa, his sole means of livelihood, seemingly, consisted in selling lobsters to passing fishing boats. He was about sixty years old at that time.

The only other inhabitant was another fisherman by the name of Cal Vellim, who lived on the south side of Middle Anacapa. He, too, had lived on the island for many years, probably lobster fishing.

Natural History

Flora

Material available on the subject of the island's plant life offers no sense of security in terms of accuracy for the statistics involved.

Hoffmann, or Hoffmann and Sumner, through Sumner, listed seven island endemics not found on other lists. *Castilleia hololeuca,* for instance, is not in Jepson, but is in Munz as an endemic. Hoffmann and Sumner found it on Anacapa; by some it is considered to be a northern island endemic.

There are six mixed north and south island endemics listed by Sumner which do not find a like place on other lists: *Convolvulus macrostegius, Malacothrix saxatilis* var. *implicata, Prunus lyoni, Lupinus* bicolor var. *umbellatus, Lotus scoparius* var. *dendroideus,* and *Quercus tomentella.*

There are, however, four mixed northern and southern island endemics which have seemingly found acceptance with at least one other author: *Astragalus miguelensis, Lavatera assurgentiflora, Hemizonia clementina,* and *Mimulus Flemingii.*

Munz agrees with Hoffmann that *Eriogonum nu-*

dum var. *grande* is on Anacapa; its place appears to be that of a mixed north, south endemic. Raven listed *Eriogonum arborescens* in the same category, but did not include Anacapa.

To summarize, one author gave Anacapa eight mixed island endemics; Hoffmann and/or Sumner credited her with twelve. Of native plants, the count among Hoffmann, Sumner, and Bond appears to be 125, or fifty-five more than given by others. The count of about twenty for introduced plants is not a part of other totals.

Fauna

Van Denburgh and Slevin [J68], gave Dr. Grinnell credit for having collected in 1903 seven specimens of one lizard found there. Grinnell gave himself credit for locating *Utas* on Anacapa [J115, 1908].

A lizard identified as *Gerrhonotus coeruleus,* is supposed to have been found by a Dr. Bond in 1939, said Sumner.

Savage [B120], placed a salamander, *Batrachoseps Pacificus,* on the island, and two species of lizard, the *Uta Stansburiana* and the *Gerrhonotus Multicarinatus.*

The little island fox is thought to now be extinct. But the white-footed little mouse, *Peromyscus maniculatus sp.,* is very present. However, J. H. Lipp [J175, 1964], felt that the present race, *P. maniculatus anacapae,* is "markedly smaller in size and . . . distinct from the new species, and clearly not closely allied to it."

Rats, Cats, and Rabbits

It is said that there are rats on West Anacapa. Writers' Project [B128, 1941], conjectured them to be descendants of rats surviving the *Winfield Scott* submergence.

Seemingly, there were also descendants of the once-domestic, turned ferocious, feral cats on the islets. However, none have been seen recently.

As late as 1935 the Los Angeles County Museum introduced rabbits to East Anacapa, and with the second world war, someone brought more to the island. "In 1940 a total progeny of more than one thousand" rabbits existed [B128]. The extent of their thriving has not been recently determined.

Avifauna

H. S. Swarth of Los Angeles was one of the first collectors on the island of Anacapa [J104, 1899]. His hunting and collecting experiences are given in detail; quoted perhaps, because it seems inconceivable that such a type of activity ever took place. It could be that eighty years later the collective consciousness has achieved a higher level; or, has it?

Black Oystercatchers

On June 4, 1899, we dropped anchor near the southern end of Anacapa Island and prepared to go ashore and collect, although it was already late in the day. While we were getting ready, a shrill whistle was heard, followed by a loud clattering noise, and as we looked up, two large, dark-colored birds flew past and lit on a rock near by, still keeping up their noisy clamor. Their bright red bills and shrill notes easily established their identity as Black Oystercatchers, though we had hardly expected to see any on the islands. We got into the skiff and started to row around the island in search of a landing place, from which we could reach the top of the island, no easy job anywhere, and appearing from the boat almost impossible. We had not gone very far when two Oystercatchers were seen on some rocks. They allowed us to come within shooting range and I dropped one with each barrel, one falling dead on the rocks, while the other, only wounded, fluttered into the water.

Although there was a strong current and a heavy swell running, the wounded bird swam easily and swiftly to another clump of rocks fifty or sixty feet away, upon which it clambered and then fell exhausted. It was a matter of no little difficulty to retrieve either of the birds, and without a strong, experienced boatman it would have been impossible to have brought the boat close enough to the rocks for a person to jump out and in, without having the boat dashed to pieces. Both birds were retrieved without accident, however, and we went on in our search for a landing. Before long we saw another Oystercatcher in a similar place to the others, which was also secured. This bird was so un-suspicious that we were within thirty feet of it before we saw it, and were obliged to row further away before it could be shot.

These were all that we saw for the day, but on June 6, when we rowed along the other two islands of the group, six or eight of the birds were seen; all, however, in places where it would have been unsafe to have taken the skiff. All the birds were in pairs, except one that I shot, but on dissecting the three that I secured (a male and two females) it was evident that they were not breeding. All the birds that were seen were very tame and un-suspicious and paid very little attention to us. The crops of the three birds

secured were filled with small mussels and they were all extremely fat.

In 1903 Dr. Grinnell was on Anacapa Island. With but an hour at his disposal, he still was able to list eight birds which he observed: Rock Wrens, Belted Kingfisher, Black Turnstones, Sandpipers, Bald Eagle, Mexican Raven, Wandering Tattlers, and the Black Oystercatcher. It was on this same trip that he obtained seven specimens of the lizard, *Uta Stansburiana* [J115].

By 1910 Dr. Willett, with others, made a trip to the four northern islands on the *Niedra*, a 32 foot launch [J122]. His list for Anacapa exceeded Dr. Grinnell's, besides adding the Pigeon Guillemot, the California Brown Pelican, and the Xantus Murrelet.

It was during early spring of 1911 that Burt, Peyton, and party stayed for several days on Anacapa, Mr. and Mrs. Webster, host and hostess [J125]. They added the Marsh Hawk and the Sparrow Hawk, killing both for their collection. They collected Western Gulls and Pelicans. It was on CAT ROCK where they found the Xantus Murrelet, and took some eggs, "prized very highly as they are the only ones to my knowledge that have been taken in the United States in recent years . . ." [J236].

When H. Wright and G. K. Snyder arrived on Anacapa [J127, 1913], of the Xantus Murrelet, they found "three dried-up remains, one whole egg and numerous shells testif[ying] to the breeding of this bird on the island during this or some previous season."

It was Burt who told in quite some detail their photographing of and egg-collecting from the Bald Eagle, fortunately without too much success. Here is the account [J125, 1911]:

Eagle Egg Eagerness

The other party arrived soon afterwards with good news which put us all in high spirits. They had located an eagle's nest on one of the high cliffs of the north side of the west island, with the old bird on the nest, so things certainly looked promising for the morrow [West Anacapa].

We were up bright and early the next morning, Wednesday, and loading ourselves with camera, shot-gun, lunch, and 130 feet of rope, we started up over the rough trail for the nesting site. Traveling was comparatively easy after reaching the top of the island, where there was a surprising heavy growth of clover and fox-tail grass, making a delightful home for the Island Horned Larks and Meadow-larks which were common on all sides. No time was lost in reaching the top of the cliff above the nest, which turned out to be on one of the highest cliffs of the island.

It would have been impossible to pick out a wilder or more commanding site than the one selected by this pair of birds. One hundred and forty feet down from the top of the cliff a pinnacle twenty-five feet high had been formed by the years of crumbling away of the rocks, and it was on the very top of this that the mass of sticks had been shaped into a nest. And there reaching from the base to about half way to the top of the pinnacle was another great pile of sticks which had no doubt been used for years as a home by the eagles, but had been deserted for the new site.

The rope, which was in two pieces, was tied together and one end dropped over the edge of the cliff, but it lacked about ten feet of reaching to the base of the pinnacle. Luckily for us though, there was a ledge on the face of the cliff down about 100 feet, which was wide enough to give a safe footing, and also giving the opportunity to get some photos of the nest at close range, as the top of the pinnacle stood out within thirty-five feet of the ledge.

Peyton went down first on the rope, taking the collecting pail and the shot-gun in case things got too warm for us. I followed next with the camera, and was soon on the ledge beside him. A photo was taken of the nest and the two eggs, which could be plainly seen in the cup-shaped place in the center of the nest. A section of the rope was next lowered down to us by Mr. Harrison, and with the assistance of this, Peyton got on down to the base of the pinnacle. By climbing up over the old nest he was soon on top of the pinnacle and reaching over after the two dirty white treasures, which were carefully packed away in the collecting pail.

The nest, which was about five feet across, was built up of sticks and limbs of all sizes up to the size of a man's wrist, the top being a soft bed of dead fox-tail grass. As there are very few trees on Anacapa, the sticks used in making the two nests must have been carried over from Santa Cruz Island, which lies about five miles to the west. From the size and amount of material used it must have been the accumulation of years, and required a great deal of labor and perseverance on the part of the old birds.

We had expected trouble from the old birds while getting the eggs, but they kept well out over the water while flying back and forth, never coming closer than seventy-five yards while we were down at the nest.

The following day, Thursday, was spent in canvassing the middle island . . . With the field glass the cliffs were carefully scanned on the south side of the east end, and a second nest of the Bald Eagle was soon located by Peyton. This nest was built in a similar location to the first one found, being on top of a sharp pinnacle well down from the top of the cliff. Looking through the glass a white head could be seen rising up above the edge of the nest, and the old male was located sitting on the top of a cliff near by.

Our time was limited on the island, so we made directly for the eagle's nest located the day previous [East Anacapa]. The old male sighted us as we neared the cliff, and flew out over the water giving an alarm note repeated several times, but the female did not leave the nest until we peered down over the top of the cliff. As she sailed out over the water we gazed eagerly to see if there was a set of two or three eggs in the nest. Instead of eggs we spied two moving objects that looked like balls of downy cotton in the center of the mass of sticks and grasses. The young eagles looked to be about two or three days old. A half-eaten fish was lying on the edge of the nest, while several backbones of good sized fish could be seen scattered around. Not wishing to keep the old bird away from the nest too long we passed on around the island, leaving them in their glory.

. . . While passing up the island, near the cliffs [West Anacapa], a third nest of the eagles was located on the ledge of a cliff, and the old bird could be seen on it. It was a great temptation to stay another day on the island, but everything was packed and loaded on board, so we had to pass it up, and say good-by to Anacapa and the eagles.

Today, there are four pair of nesting eagles on Anacapa. The nests have been, from time to time, raided for their eggs; they are presently under the protective custody of the National Park Service.

A Burrowing Owl was unofficially reported by Mr. Webster in 1911. In 1939 E. L. Sumner mentioned thirty-two birds as having been seen. Among them, he referred to a nest belonging to an American Bald Eagle in an island oak tree, *Quercus tomentella,* and to a Golden Warbler nest in a large cherry tree, *Prunus lyoni* [U40]. This count of thirty-two is four or five higher than the sum total of the previous references.

"A Great Pelican Rookery"

It was through *Museum* [Vol. v, March, pp. 71-72 of the year 1899], that Charles F. Holder mentioned a colony of California Brown Pelicans said to nest on Anacapa. But J. Grinnell, in referring to it, remarked that "exact data apparently [is] missing," and the Brown Pelican was not given an official listing.

This is unfortunate because Holder appears to have been the first to mention such a rookery. In fact, the east end of Anacapa, where many of the pelicans are, is one of the major features of the island's wildlife activity! Instead, Willett [J122, 1910], twenty-one years later, is given credit for the official listing of the Pelican's breeding north of Mexico.

In 1940 the National Park Information Service noted that approximately 2,000 pair of the pelicans nested on the island. When officially visited, there were newly hatched chicks to one-fourth grown pelicans.

West Anacapa is closed to protect other pelican nesting areas. Even that is apparently not enough, for the pelicans have been running out of food since 1978, according to a most recent *Los Angeles Times* article.

Anchovies commercially harvested by thousands of tons supply some of the ingredients for chicken feed, thus depriving the pelicans. As a result, the pelicans are said to walk away from their chicks "because of their apparent inability to find food for them."

The issue appears to be between the California Fish and Game Department for the protection of the pelican, and the National Marine Fisheries Service, responsible for managing the anchovy harvest. It could be just a matter of time before the Great Pelican Rookery shrinks even further, perhaps to the point of extinction.

Archaeology

Yates', "The Deserted Homes of a Lost People" [P90, 1896], brings up another subject,

> a short distance from the only [group of] buildings upon the island, we found a rock-shelter or cave facing toward the main land, which would afford shelter from the storms of the winter, . . . We found an extensive deposit of refuse at this point, and also at other places . . . ; although Mr. Schumacher informs us that he found no shell deposits, . . .

Schumacher [N41, 1877], had had this to say about Anacapa, "I passed this island from all sides, but could not discover any shell-deposits. It seems quite probable that there are none, as there exists no water on this island."

De Céssac, Schumacher's contemporary, had a different point-of-view,

> I then went to the neighboring islets known by the name of Ana Capa. The explorers who preceded me there believed this spot never to have been inhabited. I was immediately convinced that not only had this little group served as a gathering place for indigenous fishers from Santa Cruz, but that several families had even lived there. I discovered traces of a little village where I collected two skulls and a basin, as well as a small number of collection objects [U7].

Yates [U52, 1890], had reported a superficial

> deposit of water-worn pebbles and fragments of quartzose and metamorphic rocks extending diagonally across the top of the middle island near its southeasterly corner, and from which the aborigines selected material for the manufacture of their weapons, . . .

which probably meant arrows and spear points. According to him, many of these "fragments show[ed] evidence of having been broken and flaked off by the hand of man."

Rosamond [P74, 1912], said that they

> climbed the middle island and visited the ancient burial ground. Judging from the dimensions of their camping ground, which is strewn with decomposed sea shells, there must have been a large tribe here at one time.

Although East Anacapa is the most inaccessible of the group, it appears to have been most intensively occupied. This is evidenced by the substantial accumulation of shell midden debris on this eastern segment of the islets. It has been reported that there are four fair-sized middens present here [U40].

Mr. Orr reportedly found two Indian sites above EAST FISH CAMP, which is at the windward landing [U40], and McKusick and Clune [U38, 1958], reported the possibilities of seven sites on Middle Anacapa.

So far, the most extensively occupied of the three islets is West Anacapa, with its ten Indian sites. There are two sites between the two highest peaks, one is in FRESHWATER CAVE, and several others back of LeDreau Cove, located by Van Valkenburg in 1939-40, while working for Arthur Woodward of the

Los Angeles County Museum [U38].

According to Meighan [U45, 1959], twenty-one sites in all have been located on the Anacapas. According to Lipp [J175, 1964], in some of the middens were found the bones of a diving duck *(Chondytes)*, indicating that Anacapa once represented a roosting area for these birds.

East Anacapa

A current runs southeasterly along the inside shore of East Anacapa and comes out against a stiff west wind, thus making for a very rough sea. And abreast of Arch Rock there are tricky tidal currents, deterring many a skipper from venturing too close [N34; M126; P135].

Little Anacapa, or East Anacapa, is the most inaccessible of the three island segments. The top, however, is flat and contains approximately one hundred acres, terraced, with a height of from one hundred to about 225 feet [U40]. Indian middens, perhaps four, have been reported, and near the lighthouse about four [water] seepages have been detected [U38].

When Kinsell spoke of the east end of Anacapa she referred to a GULL ROCK, "one and one half miles from shore, [it] is a fortress-like column, accessible only to water-fowl, seals, and expert climbers." On the top of it may be found a vast guano deposit [P87, 1891].

The eastern end of the Anacapa chain is known as the ARCH ROCK, forty feet high; Yates called it the GRAND ARCH. It is a high, broad and very regular arch from north to south through which a small yacht might sail. Yates [J327, 1902]:

> the passages which separate the three Anacapas from each other are, in one, less than a quarter of a mile, the other only sufficiently wide to permit the passage of a row boat.
> This manner of division of the islands is plainly shown at the eastern end of the Anacapas, where an individual arch is left standing at some little distance from the extremity of the Eastern Island, and between it and the island a column which formerly supported two other arches which connected the present arch with the island.

In 1925 [M40], the arch still united its parts by a land bridge. The arch disappeared in a severe storm about 1936, and was replaced by a wooden bridge [B128, 1941].

According to Homer P. Earle in 1896 [P44],

The east end is brilliantly white with the deposits of sea birds; otherwise the coloring is unusually dark. The bold, black contour, the savage attack of the breakers on the misshapen rocks give an impression of grim solitude; but at a rifle-shot, the air is suddenly darkened by an outstanding swarm of pelicans, gulls, and shags, and filled with thousands of harsh cries.

Weldon F. Heald [J81, 1957], has reminded us of the same spectacle by saying,

> cliffs roundabout the arch are streaked white with bird droppings, for here is the nesting colony of 2,000 pairs of California Brown Pelicans, considered to be the island's chief wildlife exhibit . . .

On the north side of Little Anacapa there is a seal rookery [U52], a CATHEDRAL CAVE and COVE, which is used as a boat landing [N34; P135].

> The east island has a few landings—but it does have a spectacular cave, navigable by dinghy in calm water, through its north-westerly point. The cave has a small entrance on the west side, an underwater window that casts an eerie, acqueous light in one of its rooms, and a dramatic double arch entrance on the east side; from this opening you can go through another arch to a secluded cobblestone-beach cove . . .

This cave, as well as one on West Anacapa, has been called "Cathedral." Very confusing!

One of the longer and more dramatic stories concerning The Anacapas developed after the *Winfield Scott* went ashore, and was wrecked. [See Middle Anacapa.] This happened December 2, 1853. And because of this wreck, the U. S. Coast and Geodetic Survey Report of 1853-54, reported on the subject of establishing a lighthouse on the island.

From San Francisco, T. H. Stevens, Lieut. Comdr., U. S. A. Schooner *Ewing*, had written to Prof. A. D. Bache, Superintendent of the U. S. Coast Survey, on the 21st of September, 1854,

> Sir: I have to report that, in compliance with instructions, I have made an examination of the island of Anacapa, with a view to the selection of a site for a light-house, and find that the part of the island suitable for this purpose, being the eastern portion, is a mass of rock of volcanic formation, about ninety feet in height, perpendicular on every face, and with an ascent inaccessible by any natural means.
> . . . The best anchorage is off the east end of

the middle part, near the wreck of the *Winfield Scott,* in eleven fathoms water, an eighth of a mile from the shore . . .

Considering the location of a light-house at this point as impracticable without very great expense, which the interests of commerce do not now demand, . . . I would respectfully report against the establishment of a light at this point, which could not be erected without a great outlay of means . . .

The loss of the "Scott," which first seems to have attracted attention to this point as a necessary one for the establishment of a light, was one of those unaccountable accidents which sometimes befall the most capable officers; but as the line of steamers to which she belonged now use a different route, and as they are the only ones that could be benefited, the necessity for its erection no longer exists.

I enclose, herewith, a sketch of the island, drawn by Mr. McMurtrie.

Respectfully, yours,

However, Bache had recommended a light be placed on Anacapa, Appendix #76 [N26].

Fifty-eight years later, in 1912, an automatic beacon was placed on East Anacapa. Nonetheless, on September 8, 1923 a tragedy of the sea occurred when seven United States Naval vessels piled up while blindly following their leader through the area near Point Concepcion. With twenty-three officers and men having been lost in the catastrophe, the present LIGHTHOUSE was finally erected in 1932.

The structure is cylindrical, was built on the easternmost tip of East Anacapa, and stands 277 feet above the ocean. The light from the station is 600,000 candle power and is operated under the jurisdiction of the Coast Guard. There is a fog signal, a radio beacon, a distance finder, a landing place, and a wharf [J81].

James Whistler

Stevens' "sketch of the island, drawn by Mr. McMurtrie" brings out another part of the story, as do Wm. P. Blake's remarks [N26, 1854-55],

The great value of accurate sketches of coast scenery, when the topography is given in detail, could scarcely be more clearly shown than in this instance. Aside from the importance of such sketches in enabling the navigator, who may have never visited the coast, to recognise his position at once, the sketch [in this instance, harbor of Santa Catalina by Mr. McMurtrie] . . . not only authorizes valuable deductions re-

specting the rocks, their sedimentary character, and geological age, but we are enabled to recognize a grand dynamical result, hitherto unobserved west of the Rocky mountains.

It seems that James Abbot McNeil Whistler worked as an engraver for the U. S. Coast and Geodetic Survey in 1854. After McMurtrie had drawn the view of Anacapa's eastern extremity from the south, the drawing got into the hands of the engravers, Whistler being one of them. To him we are endebted for the embellishment of the sea gulls flying around that end of the island—which is so characteristic of the scene.

The story of Whistler's change of occupation through others' accountings may or may not be true. What is true is that Whistler left the Coast Guard in 1855, which might have been on his own volition, not that of others. What is also true is that shortly after that, Whistler left for Paris and London. By 1872 his art work was acclaimed by Europeans, for the portrait of his mother appeared in the Louvre, Paris. [B53 appears to be the better reference but contains but one paragraph on Whistler, 1939.]

Whistler's temperament could have been at stake; or perhaps the temperaments of those in charge of the solemn process of the work of the Coast Survey. But out of it all we are left with Whistler's etching on Plate No. 414A of the U. S. Coast and Geodetic Survey.

And as has been said in *Westways,* June 1940, "Fame and appreciation came slowly but nevertheless surely. When in the summer of 1903, he died, in London, he was recognized as one of the greatest artists of all time, and honored by the governments of practically every nation."

Middle Anacapa

When referring to Davidson [N34, 1889], we are reminded that Middle Anacapa rises to

three hundred and twenty feet elevation, is nearly two miles long by five hundred yards wide . . . the gap separating the middle and eastern islands is over two hundred yards wide, but so completely filled with rocks as to be impassable for boats . . .

Rosamond [P74, 1912], added to this description when he said of the wide gap, "the waves of the south meet the channel waves, making a great roar as they come together."

Yates reported on the eastern end of Middle Anacapa in the *Ninth Annual Report of the State Mineralogist* [C19, 1890], with the comment that "We learned of [an] 'Indian Cave' at the eastern extremity . . . but did not visit it . . ."

On the southern coast near the eastern end of the island are the remains of the *Winfield Scott*, viewable by divers.

The Pacific Mail Steamship Company owned the *Winfield Scott* and was carrying passengers from San Francisco to Panama when she ran ashore

> during a dense fog at midnight, December 2, 1853, in calm weather. The vessel was steaming at full speed, and ran between and upon the rocks with such force that she remained fast by the bow until heavy weather broke her up. The course of the steamer had been taken from Point Concepcion, but without a knowledge of the currents. Two hundred and fifty people were on the island eight days, and were rescued by the steamship *California* [N34].

Of about seven other references to the wreck of the *Winfield Scott*, not one is primary, and each version embellishes the story, but without a bibliography to substantiate its statements. Walker [M126], refers to a man by the name of Crane, who revisited the island fifty-one years later. Max Miller [B108, 1959], beginning with page 175, gives even more intimate details through a Richard Keen.

M. J. Phillips [B56, 1927], *History of Santa Barbara County, California*, interviewed Mrs. Jane Merritt Kimberly on the story of the *Winfield Scott*. Although the date given for the accident seems incorrect, it is probably correct to say that Captain Martin Kimberly, later her husband, was living on Santa Cruz Island at the time of the incident. This is partially what she told Mr. Phillips,

> The *Winfield Scott* was a large vessel en route from San Francisco to Panama, with many miners returning home, and much gold dust aboard. When she went on the rocks she was abandoned. Passengers and crew—and gold dust—took to the open boats, sacrificing everything else.
>
> Captain Kimberly and the old sailor saw the ship on the point of Anacapa, and went over to investigate. They found it filled with the choicest sort of food and wines, and a great many other things.
>
> They made several trips in an open boat, appropriating what they wanted. My husband told me that one of the things he took off for his Santa Cruz Island home was a large mirror.

Within a few days the wreck broke up and sank. One of the ornaments which was saved, and which afterwards hung for many years in the old Lobero Theater, was a great eagle.

Mrs. Kimberly had more to say on other subjects, in terms of her husband, in this interview with Phillips.

According to T. H. Stevens [N25, 1853], "the best anchorage is off the east end of the middle part, near the wreck of the *Winfield Scott*, . . . an eighth of a mile from the shore." Davidson [N34], reported another good anchorage on Middle Anacapa, which he said was located one-quarter of a mile north of its middle and lying in eleven or twelve fathoms of water. From here a boat-landing is possible.

There is another bay or cove about the same distance south of its middle, but it is not a good landing place. Rosamond [P74], called it STINGAREE BAY, "a narrow beach, the entrance of which is lined with jagged rock-points." This is probably the same location as BAT RAY COVE, a name given at a later date, where stingarees are found in large numbers on the sandy bottom.

On the windward side of the middle island, and just about opposite Bat Ray Cove, is EAST FISH CAMP. McKusick [U40, 1959], stated his preference of three available coves as being here.

We are indebted to Martinette Kinsell's descriptive article in *Overland Monthly* about West Anacapa [P87, 1891], in which she speaks of both Santa Cruz Island and Anacapa.

In her visiting party, 1887, were "two amateur artists, three newspaper reporters, the landscape painter, Mr. H. C. Ford, and his wife, and Mr. E. P. Roe and sister, son and daughter of the novelist."

They used Middle Anacapa's facilities through Mr. Elliot, as did Yates and his party in July, 1890, who had sailed to the island in the sloop, *Brisk*, also owned by Elliot. Yates found some good buildings on the middle island toward the northern end, Elliot's property. The members of this exploring party, for both fun and gain, were Mr. I. B. Hardy, Prof. H. C. Ford, Mr. Wm. Nobel and son, Mr. Wm. Ford, Mr. I. N. Cook, Mr. Harry Jenkins, and Dr. Yates.

In the *American Geologist* [U52, 1890], Dr. Yates offered some descriptive paragraphs about a visitor's walking-tour on Middle Anacapa,

> . . . point Lookout; which point may be reached by following a well made trail starting at the settlement and following an easterly direction, skirting the northerly line of the uplands, grad-

ually tending downward until a point is reached from which an excellent view of the west island may be had, also of the natural arches and entrances to the caves, . . .

Following the trail a short distance farther we round the point where the north side of the eastern island comes into view, presenting with the eastern portion of the middle island an entire change of color and outline . . . The barking sea-lions and seals impress us with a beauty and grandeur impossible to describe or imagine, and well worth the trouble it costs to reach the locality . . .

. . . Retracing our steps we regain the higher ground and reach a point . . . From this point we see the entire length of the eastern island, and the sinuosities of its southern side; the whole length of the southern exposure shows perpendicular cliffs from the shore to the top of the island some three or four hundred feet high, with the eastern end of middle island . . . in the foreground, and over which . . . we see the shore line of the eastern island, the peculiar form of which resembles the rim of an immense crater, . . .

For a sailing-walking-tour, from the northern end of the island, *Sunset* [P135, 1967], has given a second description,

Sailing east along the north shore, you can see Anacapa's only grove of trees—blue gum eucalyptus, their upper branches stripped bare by the wind—high in a draw on the western third of the middle island. If you trace the draw down to the shore, you will see a tiny inlet in the rock where a skilled boatman can put people ashore. From the inlet's left side, a path leads uphill past a concrete cistern and through the eucalyptus grove (site of a vanished shepherd's camp), and on up to the gently rolling plateau atop the island . . .

Of this cistern, Walker [M126, 1904], said,

Mesnager owned the sheep on the island and Old Charlie had been looking after them for about five years. Charlie looked after the sheep, fishes, gathers abalones, and traps crayfish for market . . . [and] has a small cement cistern supplied by the water which falls on the roof of his shack during the rainy season.

Today, the cistern is crumbling its way into nothingness.

West Anacapa

West Anacapa is separated from Middle Anacapa by a gap ten feet wide, through which boats can pass [N25]. Yates [C19], spoke of West Anacapa's arched passage,

the ocean has encroached on the land from both sides, leaving a narrow strip, only a few rods in width, through which the wind and waves have formed a beautiful arched passage, by which one may pass on foot from the channel to the ocean side of the larger or Western Anacapa . . .

In another article [U52], Yates spoke further of this "natural bridge" near the east end of the west island. Rosamond [P74], said that they

passed through an arch in the ridge of the island and explored a portion of the south side afoot, the beaches where the moonstones abound and the shells of many pattern lure one into searching for them.

Walker, of the *Los Angeles Times* [M126, 1904], had something to say about the anchorages,

There are two good anchorages on the southeast side of the island where a vessel can ride out the wolly northwesters which blow here a large portion of the time.

The best anchorage is on the northeast side, Frenchie's or LeDreau's. It has been said that there are three Indian sites above FRENCHIE'S BEACH [U38]. Also pointed out, is the existence of an intermittent spring fairly close to LEDREAU COVE.

West Anacapa has a high ridge that broadens out into a small plateau between the two highest peaks [U40]. In the saddle near the eastern end is where the Conejo Volcanics are [J175; J324; U38]. On the western side of the saddle there is no thick soil, but there are kitchen middens, perhaps two; in the middens, bones of the white-footed mouse may be found.

On the southern side of the island there is a spur leading to the channel, where a good beach may be found [U38].

The northern slope away from the ridge is bisected by seven ravines, five of which open out as a cliff upon a terrace 200 feet above the sea [U40]. Here, at the ravine heads, several small clumps of trees, Toyon, Island Cherry, and Island Oak may be found [J81, 1957]. The highest terrace is 600 feet with a 930 foot peak, "VELA," on its western side. The widest part of the island is two miles.

From an historical standpoint it should be noted

that in 1891 Captain Elliot, who was then running sheep on the island, had planted a small acreage to grains, fruits and alfalfa on its highest part [P87].

In 1940 there existed a WEST FISH CAMP, with cabins. Here Dr. Comstock and the Los Angeles Museum expedition party made their headquarters, even though they had landed on the east side. McKusick preferred this camp, too, because it had a less steep slope to the interior of the island [U40]. The J. W. Sefton Foundation Expedition also stayed at West Fish Camp [U58, 1965].

On the southwest coast there are some natural asphalt seepages, and there is a CAT ROCK. The story goes that Frenchy's house cats got on the rock and couldn't get off, thereby the name. Around Cat Rock, and south, there are tidal pools.

David Bank Rogers [B73, 1929], remarked that the western section of the Anacapa group had more of interest for the naturalist than the other two sections. One of those interests was that of exploring the tidal pools.

According to John Southworth [B123, 1920], although to the naked eye "the island is arid, . . . all the pools and crevices are filled with animal life, and beautiful anemones line the rocks." From Heald [J81, 1957], "Here are sea anemones, limpets, abalones, crabs, crayfish, lobsters, and scores of other animals and plants." Holder, 1910, had said that the abalones were piled high on one another, despite the ravages of the Chinese and Japanese hunters.

Davidson [N34], spoke of a boat landing on the north side of West Anacapa. And according to Heald [J81, 1957], the best place from which to explore the west island is from a "small protected cove on the north side of the west end. The coast here is a maze of caves eaten into the rock and one could probably cross the island through underground passages." Walker [M126, 1904], was quite in agreement,

> There is . . . a fine anchorage on the north side, more exposed, but where there is a fine pebbly beach and where most visitors to the island stop on account of better facilities for making camp.
>
> Here there is a natural tunnel running through the solid formation from one side of the island to the other, and a half-mile west is the show cave of the island; a boat can be rowed right into it, and there are small beaches inside where one can go ashore and explore the semi-dark corners of the cavern.

C. F. Holder had this to say about the same location [B38, 1910],

> . . . With a sixty-ton yacht we found the most comfortable landing behind a little neck on the north side of the west end of the western island. Here are a little cove, good anchorage except in a southeastern, a fisherman's hut, and a sandy beach . . .

Caves and Marine Gardens

Before 1965 the number of caves reported found on The Anacapas was four. But although many more caves since then have been seen through field glasses or binoculars, these additional caves have not been investigated.

"The Largest Cave"

There is one cave on the north and western end of West Anacapa, probably Walker's "show cave of the island," that, due to its impressiveness, has been described many times.

At first called "the largest cave," it has been termed "CATHEDRAL" CAVE, then "PAINTED" CAVE; it received its latest name, "YATES" CAVE in the 1950s. The following accounts trace this change of names; from Yates [U52, 1890],

> The largest cave on the Anacapas into which we rowed our boat consists of a chamber of about 400 feet in width, running back about 150 feet from the arched entrance, with a dome-shaped roof perhaps 100 feet high, rising from the circumference in a regular curve to the center. The floor of this cave is covered by water, and edged by a pebbly beach which extends around the interior, upon which we landed.

Of the cave Martinette Kinsell [P87, 1891], remarked,

> Passing many outlying rocks and reef islands, we sailed into the Cathedral Cave. An arched roof one hundred feet high sloped down to the floor of four hundred by one hundred and fifty feet at the bottom. This floor was white sand, rimming a bay of clear water, through which marine plants, shells, and darting fishes, could be clearly seen at the pebbly bottom.

Reuben Rosamond [P74, 1912], gave even more detail concerning this cave,

> They secured one of the Captain's skiffs—and started toward the marine gardens and the Painted Cave, which are only a short distance west of the harbor.
>
> Soon they were looking over the edge of the skiff at the wonders beneath them. Mysterious,

busy life swarmed everywhere. The marine gardens extend to the very entrance of the Painted Cave. Golden kelp swings back and forth as the violet waves go slowly in and out; but beyond the narrow entrance the water widens into a miniature lake, and the receding walls and roof are plainly visible.

Within the great dome-like cavity a narrow beach makes a half circle, and here they left the skiff, climbing up the sloping back-wall as if passing up the aisle of some great theater. Water lashing against the stony beach sent up a sound to be pitched back and forth against the walls until it became a hollow, awesome sound, filling the cave with a roar.

The cave is about three hundred feet in diameter and over a hundred high. It is color rather than dimension that makes it attractive. It looks as if a painter had mixed, in turn, the brightest colors with green, throwing the result promiscuously against the walls and roof. The fact that the colors are always fresh and vivid is a mystery to many.

The Painted Cave is the most beautiful wonder-spot about Anacapa. The nature lover will travel as far to see it as the art lover to view a masterpiece in painting.

West of the Painted Cave perpendicular walls of rock come down to meet the sea. A bald-headed eagle was perched on a high pinnacle like a guardian of the isles.

Then Mr. Orr came along and renamed the cave [M100, 1951],

The most interesting cave is on West Island and we named it YATES CAVE in honor of the explorer who first reported it. This huge room, hollowed out by wave action along a fault plane measures 200 feet across with an arched ceiling 100 feet high. Water occupies most of this cave and a 40-foot boat could ride at anchor in it . . . The remarkable coloring on the roof and walls is a blending of the yellows, greens and browns of algae and minute crystals of aragonite.

Marine Gardens

Walker [M126], said that the "smaller caves farther west are worth one's time to visit, and the beautiful marine gardens along the route are equal to any that I have ever seen at Catalina or elsewhere." Yates [U52, 1890], must have felt the same way,

In passing along the bluffs in which the caves are situated, they present a panorama of unique and beautiful scenery, where the richness of color and peculiarity of outline are unequaled at any other point, the water for a great portion of the distance being perfectly calm, and so transparent that the flora and fauna of its depths may be as easily studied as upon the surface; bright orange-colored fishes darting in and out among the dark green sea-weeds, the shells, corallines and other inhabitants of the deep can there be studied in their native element.

Freshwater or Indian Cave

Yates mentioned this cave in at least two different articles [C19, 1890; U52, 1890]. Here is his *American Geologist* article report,

Many of the caves on these islands are interesting, one of them which we called Freshwater or Indian cave, shows evidence of having been inhabited by the aborigines for a long period. At the mouth of this cave is a spring of good water seeping from the rocks into basin-shaped cavities which are evidently artificial. One of these fills up at the rate of 70 gallons every 24 hours. Among the refuse matter deposited in this cave by the Indians we found but little except some fragments of ropes made of sea-grass. Some of these ropes were braided with three strands, the others twisted like ordinary rope used at the present day. We found also bones of a variety of animals which had been used as food.

The only addition from the *State Mineralogist* was that "a large number of bones of various fish and cetaceans, mixed with marine shells and other refuse of an Indian rancheria," were found in the cave. Yates thought the artificially carved "basins" for collecting water in INDIAN CAVE to be of Indian manufacture [U38].

Three other quotable reports of this cave come to us through the literature from primary sources. Kinsell [P87], speaks again,

Another spacious cave, high above tide water, is a veritable mine of aboriginal relics. A clear fountain of good water—the only spring on the island—gushes from a cleft in the rock into several artificial rock basins. For several feet in depth this cave is floored with all sorts of bones, shells, and other debris of an Indian rancheria.

Rosamond [P74], visited the cave, too,

The Water Cave was the next place to be visited. Here the only fresh water, excepting that caught in a cistern below the houses [Middle Anacapa] trickles down the walls, watering the wild flowers growing in natural jardeniers, being finally caught in a cement basin some thoughtful fisherman had made some time before.

Rogers [B63, 1929], remarked that the spring issued from the floor of the rock shelter, and was submerged at high tide. However, he failed to remark that Yates had found the cave as early as 1890.

"The Dark Cave"

Although there is sparse information leading to recognition on the locality of caves, still some clues remain. Apparently, Yates has offered two versions of the same cave,

> . . . the *Dark Cave,* is in the shape of a long gallery just about large enough to admit a small rowboat, but extends for some distance. It is divided into three distinct chambers, the openings between being so small that we had to bend over in order to pass through. The interior was so dark that, although we had two candles burning we could only tell where the walls were by alternately bumping our heads and elbows against them.

In another reference he said,

> Others are only large enough to admit a small rowboat, but extend to some distance under the island, alternately widening and narrowing, forming a succession of chambers into which we carried lights, but the darkness was too intense to allow the lights to penetrate to any distance,

and we all gave a sigh of relief as we passed back to the light of day.

Kinsell referred briefly to "still another cave, or series of caves [reaching] far into the mountain, and is inaccessible at high water" [P87]. And Thompson and West [B70, 1883], said, "There is a large cavern on the island of unknown depth, which can be entered by a boat, though it is considered dangerous."

In "The Orca goes Underground" [J276, 1951], Orr refers to a SEA LION CAVE on West Island,

> [it] must be entered by its six-foot tunnel at low tide or during periods of no surge, for the ceiling is too low to risk being smashed against it by a heavy wave. The tunnel goes back a hundred feet, then turns to the left.
>
> The heavy resonance of sea lions barking within the cave is depressing to the ear and makes one wonder if one of these five hundred-pounders will land in the boat. However, they gathered on the little beach at one end of the cave and posed for flashlight pictures and, while some made frantic efforts to escape, none landed in the skiff.

Other caves

A KEYHOLE CAVE has been named by Phil C. Orr, which he mentioned had received its name due to the outline of a keyhole as the entrance. We are not told where this cave is located. On Middle Anacapa, Orr also named an ABALONE CAVE; though we do not know of its location, either.

Photos of the Anacapas

Date	Code #	Author	Photos	Reference
1889	C19	Yates	Arched Passage; east end, West Anacapa	*State Mineralogist*
1891	P87	Kinsell	The Great Cave	*Overland Monthly*
			A Natural Bridge	*Overland Monthly*
1896	P44	Earle	Chinese Gathering Abalone	*Land of Sunshine*
1911	J125	Burt	Arch Rock [excellent]	*Condor*
1912	P74	Rosamond	Painted Cave	*Outwest*
			Fishermen's hut, Middle Anacapa	*Outwest*
			Birdseye view of Anacapas	*Outwest*
			The Arch	*Outwest*
			Landing at Webster Harbor	*Outwest*
			From Interior of Painted Cave	*Outwest*
1917	B25	Gidney	Anacapa Arches	*History of S. B., S. L. O., V. Counties*
1939	J349	Cockerell	Anacapa from West Anacapa	*So. Calif. Acad. Sci. Bulletin*
1944	N51	Wheeler	Coast Guard Lighthouse	*U. S. Naval Instit. Proceedings*
			Giant Coreopsis, 8 feet high	*U. S. Naval Instit. Proceedings*
			Anacapa Island	*U. S. Naval Instit. Proceedings*
1951	J276	Orr	In Yates Cave	*Museum Talk*, S. B. Museum
1954	J79	Lange	Yates Cave; Fault in ceiling can be traced	*Pacific Discovery*
1956	M154	Hillinger	Close-up of stairs and crane, E. Ana.	*Los Angeles Times*
1956	P162	Thornburgh	U. S. Coast Guard Light Station	*Westways*
1957	J81	Heald	California Brown Pelicans	*Pacific Discovery*
			Cabrillo Arches, home of pelicans	*Pacific Discovery*
1958	U38	McKusick & Clune	Map of Anacapas, 18 Indian sites	*U. C. L. A. Reconnaissance*
1958	J218	Warren, Jr.	Map, Anacapa Light & Arch Rock	*National Geographic Magazine*
1959	U40	McKusick	Map, Anacapa Island Indian sites	*U. C. L. A. Archaeological Survey*
1959	J291	Spaulding	Map, relationship of 4 northern islands to coast locations	*Noticias*, S. B. Museum
1960	B88	Emery	Sketch, made by McMurtrie and Whistler, with Gulls	*The Sea Off Southern California*
1962	B119	Rockwell	Airview, Lighthouse & Living Quarters	*California's Sea Frontier*
			Airview, Cliff side w/ hoist	*California's Sea Frontier*
1962	M47	Thorne Hall	Arch Rock	*Odyssey of S. B. Kingdoms*
			Hoist; First Landing	*Odyssey of S. B. Kingdoms*
			Lighthouse Tower	*Odyssey of S. B. Kingdoms*
			Spanish-tiled houses	*Odyssey of S. B. Kingdoms*
1963	P166	Hillinger	Coast Guard Lighthouse; Arch Rock	*Westways*
1963	P180	Bugay	Coast Guard Photo, Lighthouse	*Yachting*
1967	P135	————	Landmark Arch	*Sunset*
			Anacapa Light	*Sunset*
			Map, Anacapas and Santa Cruz w/ Place names	*Sunset*
			Cat Rock; Tidal pools, West Anacapa	*Sunset*

Date	Code #	Author	Photos	Reference
			Skiff in cave, arch to cove on northwest point of E. Anacapa	*Sunset*
			Freshwater Cave, west of Frenchy's Cove on W. Anacapa	*Sunset*
1969	P173	Ashkenazy	Picnicking, Frenchy's Cove	*Westways*
			Other photos	*Westways*
1973	N53	Scott	In color, Island chain, fish, sea plants, etc.	*National Wildlife*

Santa Cruz

N

Santa

Barbara

Channel

San Pedro Pt.

Scorpion Harbor

Smugglers Cove

Montañon

Potatoe Harbor

Shaw Anchorage

Coche Point

1770'

Chinese Harbor

Aquaje Escondido

Prisoners Harbor

La Playa

Valley Anchorage

Pelican Bay

Tinkers Harbor

Orizaba Flats

Main Ranch

Platts Harbor

Center Mountain 1374'

Diablo Point

Red Hill

Coches Prietos

1800'

Boat Landing

Picacho Diablo 2407'

Cañada Valdez

Painted Cave

Forney's Flats

Laguna Harbor

Cañon Cervada

West Point

Indian Mounds

Punta Arena

Forney's Cove

Johnston Lee

Fraser Point

Kinton Point

Pacific Ocean

Santa Cruz

Description—Place Names

Dr. Greene was one of the first, if not the first, to visit and study Santa Cruz Island. There for several weeks, he became familiar with the island's physical aspects. His four-page article in *West American Scientist* [J258, 1886], is concentrated and the reader feels a specialist has done a remarkable task of initiating the neophyte into some of the island's more interesting features. This includes comments on history, flora, fauna, and Indian life.

Kinsell's "The Santa Barbara Islands" [P87, 1891], published five years later, is also a gem. This author was on Santa Cruz during the same season in which Dr. Greene was botanizing there,

Our botanists filled their portfolios, though only

203 specimens of plants were found. But Professor Greene, who did the Island flora very thoroughly the same season, found and enumerated 341 species, according to his article in the Bulletin of the Academy of Sciences on collection of "Classified Ferns and Plants of Santa Cruz Island."

Fourteen pages in length, Kinsell's article leads us to see how much the author and her party enjoyed sailing the waters of the Channel and investigating Anacapa, Santa Rosa, and Santa Cruz.

Filled with the concrete, Kinsell nevertheless captured something so many adventurers have been unable to put into words:

On these expeditions we hardly spoke. Often

our artists, professionals though they were, sat in a sort of daze, watching the lights and streamers and prismatic tones that each sunrise and sunset hung, a glorified aurora borealis, over the universe, with the Channel for its mirror . . .

Bits of history, natural history, and cave explorations come alive with Kinsell's rendition.

Kirk's "Another Treasure Island" [P129, 1905], written some fourteen years later, is all too brief, but is still another masterpiece of description. He furnished excellent photos of coastline scenery and carries the reader with him on and around Santa Cruz. His article contains just enough history to make one feel comfortable. And he imaginatively remarked, "Santa Cruz Island has a great and prosperous future before it . . . But this will only come to pass after suitable hotels have been built upon it and the transit of the channel between Santa Barbara and the island has been improved."

Charles Frederick Holder had an intimate touch with Santa Cruz Island, as he had with most of the other islands of California's archipelago [B38, 1910]. However, much of the strength of Holder's description about Santa Cruz is in the direction of life on the Caire ranch, such as sheep-shearing, fishing, and wine-making.

Of the former inhabitants he mused,

I could readily see this charming isle of summer with its mountain-environed cañons and valleys peopled by a race that attained happiness at least; men and women to whom imaginative values had some significance, and who fought a good fight in the field of human endeavor.

H. H. Sheldon's "Saints in the Sea," published in 1931 [P196], was to be one of the better descriptions for Santa Cruz and San Nicolas Islands. Though brief, Sheldon managed to weave his account around the island's flora, avifauna, and fauna in a most enlightened fashion.

Mrs. Jane Kimberly evidently related to Sheldon some of her memories of Captain Kimberly on Santa Cruz, making his account more personalized. Sheldon also discussed the lot of the little fox; evidently Sheldon's scientific interest extended over and beyond his interest in the picturesque beauty of the islands.

Written in 1958, Earl Warren, Jr. succeeded in getting a report of his trip to Santa Cruz, Santa Rosa, and San Miguel published in the *National Geographic* [J218], "California's Ranches in the Sea." Warren described his experiences in PAINTED CAVE, and spoke of PRISONERS' HARBOR and how it received its name. He briefed the reader on Caire's endeavors, mentioned Edwin Stanton, his activities and friendship with the Warren family. This all-around article moves swiftly and informatively; reading it results in a decided plus for the time involved, twenty-nine pages, including photos.

The geology, the topography, the life on Santa Cruz all focused around CENTRAL VALLEY. This valley divides the island longitudinally, bordered on the north by the higher range. On the south it is bordered by a lower, narrow and rounded ridge with the nearly 1500 foot SIERRA BLANCA PEAK as the range's highest point.

Sierra Blanca is a volcanic formation that is similar to the greater part of the northern coast of Santa Cruz [B70]. The greater height of the northern ridge has the name of PICACHO DEL DIABLO, 2434 feet. It is situated about the center of the western half of the northern ridge, with a considerable portion of the north ridge being over 2000 feet in height. Mt. Diablo is occasionally covered with snow for a few days at a time in the winter months [B107].

RED HILL, north of the MAIN RANCH and in from TINKER'S COVE, is 1796 feet high; here is a U. S. Coast and Geodetic Survey Station [C18]. PICACHO DE LOS ENCINOS, in the north range, is west of Mt. Diablo and is the next highest peak of the range, rising "like a citadel, above a forest of live oaks" [P129]. From Hillinger [M154], we gain the information that "atop one of [the] . . . highest hills is a network of radar, radio, telephone, theodolite and timing towers."

More exact location of other hills are unknown to the author but Davidson [N34], indicated RAGGED MOUNTAIN as being 1331 feet high. It is north of PUNTA ARENA. CENTER MOUNTAIN, 1376 feet, is in the WILLOW HARBOR area. Both are in the southern range of the island and both are U. S. monuments.

Central Valley is in reality a series of valleys containing three distinct drainage systems. CHRISTY CAÑON toward the west, about four and one-half miles long, drains toward CHRISTY RANCH near the southwest coast.

CAÑADA POMONA, the old CAÑADA DEL MEDIO, drains slightly southeast from Main Ranch. SUR RANCH was about one and one-fourth miles from Main Ranch, where there used to be a good adobe house. The stream from the canyon used to supply Sur Ranch with its water before emptying into BLUE BANK, about one and three-quarter miles farther on. Formerly Blue Bank was known as PUERTO DE LA CAÑADA DEL SUR [C18].

The middle valley, Cañada del Medio, forms a juncture with CAÑON DEL PUERTO, at which junction the RANCHO MAJOR is situated, about two hundred feet above sea level [C18]. From this AR-ROYO PRINCIPAL the waters of Cañada del Medio, Portezuelo Creek, are discharged by CAÑADA DEL PUERTO, having cut a gorge for about four miles through the northern volcanic range to enter the sea at Prisoners' Harbor [J297]. Thompson and West [B70], called this stream, CAÑADA DEL AGUA.

The lower, more central part of the valley has been given the name Cañada del Medio. Westward, on the way to Christy Ranch, there is a steep grade carrying the name of CAÑADA DEL PORTEZUELO. It is an upland valley and on it, at Portezuelo, there is an old half-adobe, half-log cabin. It was once a headquarters, has been used as a cook house, and semi-wild sheep for shearing have been corraled there.

Somewhat westward is BUENA VISTA, part of the plateau separating the central valley from the lower, CUESTA VALLEY, or Christy Cañon, through which CUESTA CREEK flows [B63].

At Christy Ranch, formerly known as WESTERN RANCH, there was a two-story adobe for the foreman and his family. Other buildings included a dining room for the men, horse barn, shearing shed, corrals, an adobe bunk house with a telephone connection to the main ranch [B38]. One of the buildings at Christy Ranch is used for gun hunters [M171, 1969]. Weather at the ranch is often windy, cold, and foggy [B107].

Goodyear [C18, 1890], described the course of the largest stream,

> . . . the Cañada del Medio, heads a mile or so to the west of the Picacho del Diablo, and after going southerly for a short distance bends to the east, and follows the latter course for five or six miles through the central portion of the island to the Main or Middle Ranch (Rancho del Medio), where it turns to the north and enters the Cañada del Puerto . . .

At some seasons of the year there may be fifteen or twenty running streams; three are perennial. The streams, rising in the high hills, run for short distances before sinking underground, McElrath ex-

plained. They are sufficiently fresh, however, for the livestock, or even a thirsty human.

There are any number of springs, some with very good water. One is just below the yard at Main Ranch [B107]. Below the ridge from the crest of Mt. Diablo, Rogers [B63, 1929], reported such a spring in a gorge leading from its southern slope:

> Here, beside a spring of fresh water, surrounded by a forest and perfectly sheltered from the winds, was one of the few well-developed, interior village [Indian] sites. This is about one mile northeast of the well-known site on the crest of Buena Vista plateau, . . .

However, from the AQUAJE [ESCONDIDO], a former Indian village site on the north coast, to the Sur Ranch on the south coast, no water may be found, not even a spring. And in the central area, without water, sheep have subsisted on ice plant, called Siempre Viva [B107].

Santa Cruz Island has a second high volcanic ridge that crosses the island at the east end, being nearly at right angles to the main ridge. Woodbridge [J77], said that by looking across from China Bay toward the east, one could see this ridge crossing the main axis of the island.

Bremner tells us to look to the east of Cañada del Puerto for the MONTAÑON, this brush-covered ridge running oblique to the trend of the northern range [J297, 1932]. Its highest point is 1770 feet. In front of it, between the Cañada del Puerto and the Montañon, there is a steep, rolling grass-covered area attaining over 1,400 feet at the divide.

Davidson [N34], remarked that

> the summit of the eastern head is a cross ridge running northwest by west and lying three miles from the eastern point. The elevation of the highest part . . . is visible from a distance of forty miles.

According to McElrath [B107, 1967], the MINAS DE LOS INDIOS is located on the northwest shoulder of the Montañon, for here may be found holes that are four by six feet deep and ten to twenty feet wide. The Indians had extracted white flint from the volcanic rock for the making of arrowheads.

It is at this eastern end, beyond the Montañon, that some members of the Caire family have the remaining acreage, the rest of the island having been sold to Edwin L. Stanton in 1937. SMUGGLERS' COVE, COCHES PRIETOS, POTATOE HARBOR (or TYLER HARBOR), SCORPION RANCH, are of the

Caire family; the ranch having been maintained for sheep-raising. Scorpion Ranch is approximately fourteen miles from the main ranch.

Around the Island—Caves

There is a low projecting point of land on the southwest end of Santa Cruz Island, known as FRAZER POINT. The rock is volcanic, jagged, and has been known as BLACK ROCK [J376], no doubt called 'black' because of its volcanic composition. The little islet just off this point is 'white'; hundreds of pelicans roost there [C18, 1890]. There is a STELLER LION ROOKERY at Frazer Point [C2, 1928]. And Mr. R. H. Beck of the California Academy of Sciences worked at this end of the island in 1899 [J102].

About a mile and a half northward of Frazer Point is WEST POINT. Here, Linton and party, ornithologists, made their second camp. They termed it NORTHWEST HARBOR or ANCHORAGE, the island's northwestern extremity [J113]. Linton said,

> This is the desert portion of the island and is bordered by a rocky, precipitous coast. Ten days were spent here before we could round the north end of the island, owing to severe storms.

Beginning at West Point, and for a distance of about six miles eastward, there are steep cliffs that sheer off into deep water. There is a stretch of about nine miles where no less than eleven V-shaped stream canyons break through the volcanic cliffs, thus affording some sandy beach landing facilities [B63, J297].

By the time voyagers reach Prisoners' Harbor, where Cañada del Puerto empties, these beaching conveniences end abruptly. Although Santa Cruz Island has about as many other landing facilities, they are distributed more or less unevenly around the rest of the island.

To Kirk [P129], this northern stretch is the most picturesque part of the shore line; the sea has cut archways through the volcanic reefs and projecting headlands, and

> for many miles, westward from Valdez, the cliffs and headlands rise abruptly and plant their feet firmly on the reefs or in the deep sea. All along their bases are beautiful marine gardens brilliant with the color of mineral rocks, sea weeds, fan corals, anemones, abalone, and other shells.

To Walker [M126, 1904], it is from FORNEY'S COVE on the southwesterly end to Smugglers' Cove on the easterly end that the island's rugged beauty exists, where

144

beautiful little harbors backed by picturesque cañons with brooks of clear, fresh water down to within a few hundred feet of the ocean, are scattered at short intervals along its entire coast.

Heald [J222], intrigues the reader by saying that the north coast is honeycombed with caves; Orr [J276], remarked that from West Point to SAN PEDRO POINT on the east there are about one hundred of these caves. Some have names; others do not.

Of caves in general, Holder [B38], said:

> If I should attempt to designate the most striking feature of Santa Cruz I should name its caves, as the entire coast on the water line appears to be cut and perforated by the gnawing sea. Some are large and open; others spout water and air with undisguised ferocity; some merely hiss, growl, and moan as the sea rushes into them; while others again appear so far beneath that the impact merely shakes the rock with a dull heavy reverberation.

Phil C. Orr spoke about specific caves in "The *Orca* goes Underground" [J276, 1951]. He referred to caves off COCHE POINT without going into detail, he mentioned ALGAE CAVE, BABY'S CAVE, and SPONGE CAVE, and gave his readers a map of Sponge Cave, 350 feet long with an entrance height of seventy feet. Evidently it is more accessible than some of the other caves.

Without naming the cave, Kirk [P129], remarked,

> Turning sharply around the first point west of the Painted Cave into a narrow rock-walled bight, two more cave entrances appear on the left—very low, but sending out the same loud thunder of waters and bark of sea-lions. Westward still, there are many more cave openings; and one of the caves is a worthy rival of the Painted Cave itself. It is entered in the same way, by boat from the open sea.

This "one of the caves" must have a name; but what is it? Could it be Drury's CATHEDRAL CAVE [B86, 1935], or is it one which the *Orca* visited, under another name?

Kinsell [P87], also increases our understanding of some close-by cave,

> There is another sea-lions' den near [the Painted Cave]. It is a hole or natural tunnel leading to unknown caves under the mountain. The sailors say that it must be miles long, and contain high and dry chambers, for when full tide covers the entrance and shuts off the hideous roarings and bellowings always heard at other times, the sea-

lions do not come out, as they must from a cave filled with water. Thousands of them breed here.

But we are moving eastward and the next place name, about one and one-half miles east of West Point, is CHASE ANCHORAGE. Then after passing a PROFILE POINT, there is PAINTED CAVE, approximately another one and one-half miles farther away from West Point. All along this area, from West Point past Painted Cave, there appear to be marine terraces, known as FORNEY'S FLATS.

Descriptive material on Painted Cave may be found in:

P87   1891   M. Kinsell, "The Santa Barbara Islands," *Overland Monthly*

P45   1897   R. C. Owens, "Caves of Santa Cruz Island," *Land of Sunshine*

J309   1897   C. F. Holder, "Some Pacific Caves," *Scientific American*

P129   1905   H. Kirk, "Another Treasure Island," *Sunset*

M136   1909   J. E. Reynolds, "Cruising in a Sailboat," *Los Angeles Times*

B38   1910   C. F. Holder, *Channel Islands of California*

M40   1925   A. F. Rider, *A Guide Book for Travelers*

P146   1931   H. H. Sheldon, "Saints in the Sea," *Westways*

P179   1954   S. Robertson, "California Cruise," *Yachting*

J222   1956   W. F. Heald, "Cave of the Sea Lions," *Nature Magazine*

B108   1959   M. Miller, *And Bring All Your Folks*

P173   1969   I. Ashkenazy, "Island Voyage aboard the 'Swift'," *Westways*

To select articles for varying degrees of descriptive excellence can hardly be accomplished; each article has something to commend it. However, should there be a reader time-element, Rob C. Owens' *Land of Sunshine* article in 1897 and W. F. Heald's *Nature Magazine* article in 1956, each about two pages in length, offer the most.

Kirk said that Painted Cave opens "like the nave of a great Norman cathedral, its lofty, wide-sprung arches resting on massive pillars to left and right" [P129]. Heald remarked that its entrance rises "to a pointed Gothic arch, sixty to seventy feet high,

flanked by two massive buttresses" [J222]. From Owens we read that the "first arch is lofty enough for a merchant vessel to enter" [P45].

Torches seem to be the better way to light the inner recesses of the cave, although this method has its drawbacks; the seals are more easily frightened and the fumes of the torches make breathing more difficult as one penetrates farther into the cave. However, the ordinary flashlight is no match for the intense darkness within the cave.

Depth of penetration of the cave has been varied and with as many explanations. For example:

the cave turned abruptly to the right, and we went cautiously along, with boat hooks feeling for the walls, the torch, except for a small circle around us, making only deeper the darkness [M136].

for 300 feet [the height] gradually lowers . . . ending in a throatlike constriction about five feet high, and six feet wide. Inside is a vast cavern extending a quarter of a mile under the island [P179].

After the fifth [arch] is passed, the chambers gradually get smaller, till on looking back, the great entrance seems but a mere knothole [P45].

C. F. Holder felt that the full length of Painted Cave had never been reached and that it penetrated to a much greater depth than is generally supposed. Woodbridge [J77, 1954], thought the cave to be navigable for about one-fourth of a mile.

Every author has been aware of the colors exhibited in Painted Cave, and each has extended his imagination in describing them. [From Heald:]

We saw . . . why Painted Cave is a fitting name. The limestone wall and ceiling have been dyed by the salts through the centuries into fantastic patterns of brilliant yellows, soft browns, reds, greens and vivid white [J222].

[From Kirk:] The arches and groin-like ceilings are bright with many colors that contrast with the reds and blacks of the volcanic rocks. Gradually, the side walls approach each other, and the arches descend as one proceeds farther inward . . . one is almost terrified by the loud, ceaseless thunder of compressed air and rushing waters, the effect of which is increased by the echoed and re-echoed barking of the frightened sea-lions that plunge from the shelving niches into the water [P129].

Sheldon added to this feeling-tone when he said,

the sea lions became aware of our intrusion and then the din of barking and bellowing seemed to shake the dripping walls. Each bark had its echo that rolled and roared through the blackness, accompanied by the terrific booming caused by the suction of the receding waters as they left the mouth of the cave . . . The little boat rocked like a cradle as the barking, snorting herd plunged all about us in the blackness of earth and ocean, presenting a combination of sensations still quite vivid to memory [P146].

Apparently, visiting CUEVA PINTADA can be beautiful, frightening, and inspiring, an experience available to but the fortunate few. However, it *is* sea-lion territory; may it ever remain so!

The U. S. Coast and Geodetic Survey map found in Goodyear [C18], indicates a CAÑADA GANNADA, as does Kirk [P129, 1905], but with the spelling of CAÑADA GANADO. At about the same location on the Santa Barbara County Surveyor's map there is a place named HAZZARD'S. Here there is a spring-fed stream and a forest. A Mr. Hazard of Santa Barbara had been on Santa Cruz and had given Dr. Greene a specimen of *Lyonothamnus* in 1885 for identification purposes [J74]. There may be a possibility that the location names are interchangeable, as does so often happen.

A little over two miles east from Painted Cave is VALDEZ HARBOR, with its celebrated cave, CUEVA VALDEZ. Valdez Harbor is one of the island's three principal landing places, the other two being Prisoners' Harbor and LADY'S HARBOR [B53].

Thompson and West [B70], use the place name of CURVA DE VALDE to indicate this general area, remarking that the northern coast is volcanic with the exception of this limited section. However, Yates said that VALDEZ CAVE, itself, "is weathered out of the hard, rough, black basalt" [C19].

There are "tres bocas" or arched openings to Valdez Cave. In the center is the great arch which roofs a 400 foot cave with a thirty to forty foot high ceiling. The water is quite deep near the entrance to this cavern and here is a beautiful aquarium.

As the water becomes more shallow, one can climb from a skiff onto a pebbly beach, spacious enough to hold several hundred people. Back a little further, but still under the sheltering roof, there is warmth, dryness, and lack of draft or wind.

Leading off from this cavern are two minor arches, one to the west and one to the east. The western branch may be reached on foot through the roofed

arch. Without trees or water, it remains quite beautiful, a place where plants flourish luxuriously [U52]. The beach in front is piled high with gigantic rocks, shelly reefs, and live abalone.

The arch, or tunnel, toward the east, presents a different vista. Here, "the sea has tunneled through the rocky side of a wild mountain gorge to meet the descending stream" [P129]. Here, there is a sandy beach, cove, good harbor, but it cannot be reached in rough weather [J376].

A trail leads to the floor of the canyon and over the mountains to Main Ranch [J376]. Goodyear [C18], referred to the CAÑADA DEL VALDEZ where there is an old Indian camp at the 325 foot level in CAÑON DE LAS TASAJERAS.

Perhaps Rogers was referring to the same Indian camp when he said of Valdez Cave that there is a waterfall and here is "a small but well defined Indian camp site . . . a little back from the beach, . . . slightly above the bed of the water course" [B63].

Kinsell [P87], through *Overland Monthly,* is by far the best source for descriptive material on Cueva Valdez.

ARCH ROCK is passed before arriving at Lady's Harbor. Something like three miles east of Valdez Cave is Lady's Harbor, however it has often gone by the name of BOAT LANDING. Here at Lady's there are caves, but a negligible amount has been written about them.

Lady's Harbor has been termed "a narrow crack in the rocks with room for only two or three boats" [P179], to "a beautiful little pocket in the rocks, perfectly protected but difficult for sailboats to enter, at times, on account of the uncertain eddies of the wind and the narrow opening between a high wall of rocks on one side and dashing surf on the other" [M126].

Again, Kinsell [P87], takes the blue ribbon for her excellence in a description of this harbor; in fact she stands almost alone on its verbalization:

Rounding a wicked-looking reef, our boat plunged toward a narrow gate in the sea wall, and entering between two jawlike projections, we glided at once from the gale and rough sea into an absolutely smooth harbor. It was calm as an artificial pond, and so clear that before shoal water was reached we could see the shelly bottom. A wide strip of pebbly beach was before us, margining a little cone-shaped valley some three hundred by eighty yards in area, with a

146

small stream running through it. This apexed at the mouth of a tree-shaped cañon and was one of the prettiest spots imaginable, at once graceful and rugged, with steep, flowery bluffs on one side and a high precipice on the other.

Oak, willow, and holly, curtained the upper end of the glen; and instantly exploring this retreat we found pools of clear mountain water at the confluence of two ravines. The air was musical with the sound of cascades; each ravine, with its steep incline from highlands and over boulders, was a succession of fern beds, rushes, and lush water plants, with only the frequent flash of waterfalls to show that there was a stream.

This camping spot was our headquarters for a week . . . This was . . . ideal gipsying, the experience of a lifetime.

One cave at Lady's Harbor has a length of about 350 feet [U59].

Just to the east of POINT DIABLO is POINT DIABLO ANCHORAGE. Since Point Diablo extends out a good half mile beyond any other points, it makes for excellent shelter against the prevailing westerly winds and affords an unmistakable landmark [M126]. Davidson said that there is very deep water close under it [N34], and indicated that the Anchorage is about four miles west of Prisoners' Harbor.

Schumacher said that between the spring near the west end and Punta Diablo there reportedly was a cave filled with human bones and curious implements [N41].

As we move east along the coast, the next harbor is that of FRIAR'S, also known as FRY'S. It is three miles from PELICAN BAY [P180]. According to Waddy [P103]:

The canyon terminating in the little cove selected for our base has a perpetual rivulet of pure mountain water. The cliffs over-hang the beach from a tremendous height, and accentuate the feeling of littleness experienced amidst the awesome grandeur of these wild places.

It was here at Friar's [J66, 1905-06], that Dr. Grinnell took four *Uta stansburiana*. Ornithologists had used the area for weeks at a time [J35, 1887].

Walker of the *Los Angeles Times* [M126], says that during his memory many wealthy people from Santa Barbara came to Fry's for the summer. With them came their tents and a corps of servants, while all spent the summer months in the outdoors. The long

cañon, extending back into the hills, with its timber and its water, made for an ideal summer resort.

At this location there was both a settlement and a quarry, for stone was taken for making the Santa Barbara breakwater [J376]. Mr. A. T. Wright, who made the statement, was a relative of the More family of Santa Rosa Island and knew both Santa Rosa and Santa Cruz intimately.

There had also been an Indian settlement at Friar's, and according to H. A. Edwards [J231, 1956], *Archaeological Survey of Southern California*, it was evident that these aborigines lived almost exclusively on cockle and barnicles.

The next harbor is DICK'S, sometimes called PLATT'S. Wright informed us that the true harbor name is Dick's, although the U. S. Coast map [N34], uses the name of Platt. Dick's Harbor is about one mile east of Fry's, and three miles west of PRISONERS' HARBOR. It is a southeast lee, a good shelter, and has fresh water.

While the place names of Tinker's Cove, TWIN HARBORS, and ORIZABA are not synonomous, they tend in that direction, for these names have been used interchangeably. Wright set the tac when he explained that 'Tinker's,' as a name, had been used for 'Orizaba.' TINKER'S HARBOR, a good shelter, is indicated on the U. S. Coast map of 1889, and two hundred yards west of the cove there is a spring [N41, 1877]. TWIN HARBOR, in the same location, is shown on Bremner's map [J297].

According to Davidson, Tinker's Harbor is about two miles west of Prisoners' Harbor [N34]. We know that Twin Harbor is one and one-quarter miles west of Pelican Bay, and that Pelican Bay is one and one-eighth miles southwest of Prisoners' Harbor [N34]. The possibility for interchangeableness of the two place names, Tinker's and Twin, readily becomes apparent.

It is in the first draw, west of the west canyon of Twin Harbors, that ORIZABA PICTOGRAPH CAVE is to be found. Richard S. Finley [U59, 1965], Assistant Curator of the Santa Barbara Museum of Natural History, explained that should one stand in the mouth of the cave, the crest of ORIZABA ROCK is visible, as it is immediately offshore in a somewhat westerly direction. These are the same directions shown on Schumacher's 1875 sketch. Along the coast are ORIZABA FLATS.

The name of the pictograph cave has been changed to OLSON'S CAVE, by someone. This is probably because Ronald Olson and party, sponsored by the

Santa Barbara Museum, worked in this cave and discovered about fifty rock paintings on the walls and ceiling [U22, 1927].

They photographed such paintings and although they spent about two and one-half months on the island, the cave paintings were their biggest 'find.' Other finds took the form of utilitarian Indian artifacts. The Caires still owned the island in 1927.

Mr. R. L. Olson said that the pictographs in the cave were quite simply designed and were painted in red ochre by the Indians. These paintings included simple crosses and rake figures [U1, 1930-31].

In 1940 Gifford [U2], mentioned Orizaba as a place where Indian artifacts were to be found, and Schumacher [P114, 1876], reported that remains of an aboriginal village were to be found close by in the narrow inlet called Tinker's Cove.

PELICAN BAY next commands our attention. It is from Davidson that we learn of Pelican Bay as being the westernmost part of the Prisoners' Harbor bight. There is an anchorage in the bay, and there is a connecting trail between Pelican Bay and Prisoners' Harbor.

This trail and the curving coast line is flanked by lofty cliffs and a forest of Monterey pines, all of which add to the natural beauty of the area. The forest extends west to Orizaba, and inland toward the Cañada del Medio. According to Walker [M126], the bay of Pelican is about as large as the bay of Avalon at Santa Catalina Island, but is much better protected.

About 1904 and 1905, and somewhat thereafter, Pelican Bay had been leased to the West Coast Fishing Co. Here, they had erected a crawfish cannery [P129]. By 1923 Ira Eaton had a lease, but his lease was for the operation of a tourist camp. Yachtsmen used to enjoy the environment and the use of the camp for barbecues and cottage-housing. Here, on the *Sea Wolf,* Ira brought their loot from the wreck of the *Cuba* off San Miguel.

Rogers [B63], remarked that on a tongue of barren rock, on the southeastern side of the cove, thickly set cabins had been erected. Displayed masses of ancient [Indian] camp debris were to be found among the walks and flower beds of the then-modern camp facilities.

Originally, Prisoners' Harbor, as a location, included both Pelican Bay on its west and CHINESE HARBOR to its east. The total length of the bight was about four and one-half miles and its depth, about two miles. However, this name is now re-stricted to the center anchorage, the other two coves having anchorages of their own [N34].

This Harbor has two incidents in its history, for which it is particularly remembered. In Arthur Woodward's Introduction to *The Sea Diary of Fr. Juan Vizcaino to Alta California* [B73, 1959], he explains the explorer-fathers' visit to Santa Cruz in 1769,

. . . the padre's description of the caves along the shore at the east end of Santa Cruz Island is correct and their anchorage on the night of the 30th of March was probably in Chinese Harbor, southwest of Coche Point. This would have placed them only a trifle more than three miles from their previous anchorage at the only satisfactory landing site, on the north shore of Santa Cruz, the large Indian rancheria on the shore of Prisoners' Harbor where the watering party had landed on the 29th.

Taken from Father Palóu, here is H. H. Bancroft's [B1, 1885], recital of the watering incident and the subsequent naming of the island,

. . . At one of the islands of the channel of Santa Barbara, which is populated with heathen, they took on water. As soon as the launch approached, the natives from a village near the beach came up to welcome them with demonstrations of great joy, making them presents of fish, which they had in great abundance, and joining in to help with the water, even the women. In return the Indians were given glass beads, which they greatly prized. The missionary fathers then decided to go ashore and visit the village. They were well received by the heathen and presented with fish, in return for which the Indians were given some strings of beads. The watering finished, they returned to the ship, now late, with the determination to set sail on the following morning. In the night it was remembered that they had forgotten their staff and left it at the village. They immediately gave it up as lost, on account of the cross that it carried, for it was of iron, and it was known how the Indians coveted this metal. But they were so honest that at daybreak it was discovered that one of the little canoes of the island was coming to the ship, and that one of the heathen was carrying in his hand the staff with the holy cross. Climbing on board, he delivered it to the father, and after being rewarded, returned to the island. For this reason it was called the island of the Holy Cross (Santa Cruz), and as such it has been known ever since.

The second incident is one in which the Lower Mexican authorities ordered to be placed on Santa Cruz a number of their convicts, thus hoping to keep them isolated from the mainland population.

Bancroft [B1, 1885, Vol. III], said that a small number of convicts arrived from Mexico in 1825. This was followed by additional orders from Mexico that more prisoners would be coming, being sent from all parts of the republic "for improving the morals of the convicts and for colonizing California."

Creating a furor in Alta California, especially in Monterey and Santa Barbara, there was an exchange of letters between the Californians and the powers-that-be in Mexico. Resolutions were signed and sent to the governor, some of the signees being José Castro, Juan B. Alvarado, Abel Stearns, and William Hartnell, who had married into the de la Guerra family.

Commandante Carrillo also wrote letters to the governor in March and April of 1830, requesting that the convicts not be sent to Santa Rosa Island. This fact is worthy of note, for the sons of the Commandante, José and Carlos, were not formally promised the island of Santa Rosa until 1838.

The convicts were shipped to Santa Barbara anyway, some in March and some in April of 1830, destined for Prisoners' Harbor on Santa Cruz Island. Here is Bancroft's version of the incidents that followed:

April 23d, the María Ester, sailed for Sta Cruz Island with 31 of the number, the missions furnishing some tools, cattle, hooks, and a little grain . . . March 18th, Echeandía to commandante of Monterey from S. Luis Obispo, explaining his plan to send—apparently all—the convicts to the islands . . . Mrs. Ord . . . says the convicts were in a naked and very filthy condition on their arrival. Capt. Guerra furnished them with clothing, made a speech encouraging them to good conduct, and personally employed 8 to 10. At the islands a fire soon destroyed all they had, and after a time, getting no relief, they built rafts, and all came over to the main, landing at Carpinteria. The narrator says that as a rule they became a very good people. Nov. 2d, 13 of those sent to the island had returned and presented themselves to the commandante.

Here is Duflot de Mofras' version [B48]:

Not long after an attempt was made to colonize Santa Cruz Island, lying a short distance from the mainland, with a group of 40 galley slaves sent up from San Blas, who were equipped with live stock, agricultural implements, and seeds for planting. These men, however, left to their own resources, first ate the grain and cattle, then built crude boats with reeds and planks. In these they now traveled over to the shore near Santa Barbara and Santa Buenaventura, where the officials allowed them to scatter throughout the interior and mix with the population.

It was in November of 1830 that the situation on Santa Cruz Island had collapsed. At that time a fire destroyed the camp of the convicts. O'Neill [B53], remarked,

Doña Augustine de la Guerra de Ord recalled that the conflagaration was seen from the mainland, but because of the lack of boats, some time went by before help was sent. In the meantime [some] managed to navigate [handmade rafts across] the Channel, landing at the Rincon and at Carpinteria . . . According to Mrs. Ord, the prisoners were rounded up again, dealt with at the whipping post and distributed under supervision of officers at Santa Barbara and Monterey.

Echeandiá was governor of California between 1825 and 1831, and it was during this period of time that the convicts were brought to Alta California for distribution. This is a far-cry from Governor Arrillaga having previously agreed in 1805 to the establishment of a mission on the island.

The drama ended, no further attempt was made at this time to turn this island, or any island, into a penal colony. However, when the United States was having difficulty in 'subduing' the Apaches, General Nelson A. Miles of the U. S. Army recommended that Santa Cruz Island be made a penal colony for the Indians. This thought persisted for some time, even after 1886, but finally dwindled into nothingness [M91, 1939].

In 1896 the Caires built a sturdy wharf and landing place at Prisoners' Harbor, a windmill, and a substantial adobe house [P44]. Later, a brick warehouse for wool-storage was added. Since then, a camp has been maintained at the site for bow hunters [M171, 1969], through the Santa Cruz Island Club, under an arrangement with Dr. Carey Stanton.

Portezuelo Creek, from the central ranch, finds its way through the volcanic CAÑON DEL PUERTO, CAÑADA DEL AQUA, to Prisoners' Harbor, spreading out as it flows to the sea. Davidson described the sand beach and the surroundings at Prisoners' Harbor thusly [N34],

> [it] has small trees or shrubs (Malva), with pine trees on the western side of the harbor, and none to the eastward . . . The anchorage is an excellent refuge in northeast weather, and for moderate westerly weather, but there is no protection from the heavy swell setting in with a strong northwester; it is dangerous in a northeast wind, which, however, is rare.

When Linton and party visited Santa Cruz Island in 1908, they camped several places, one of them being at this harbor: "Here we found the Santa Cruz pines, oaks, holly, manzanita, ironwood, cherry, etc., in superabundance" [J113].

At the harbor, to the east of the harbor, and for about two and a half miles along the coast to CHINA BAY, may be found Indian village sites [P82, B63, B107]. This landing is also known as CHINESE HARBOR; three-fourths of a mile eastward from Chinese Harbor may be found fresh water [N34].

The shoreline of the harbor is quite rocky but the harbor itself is a good shelter for fishing vessels during the southeasters, according to Rogers.

McElrath [B107], and Gherini [J296], have both remarked on fish camping or fishing rights given for this area. McElrath used the name 'Campo Chino' and indicated that crawfishing was "there and about."

As one leaves the China Bay area to sail for two more miles, COCHE POINT comes into view. This is the beginning of Tract #6, established in 1923-24, the acreage once held by Aglae S. Capuccio, a Caire family member. Her holding continued east by north to include Scorpion Harbor; her total acreage was 3035.60, or seven percent of the estimated value of Santa Cruz Island. Other than to say that caves are found in the area, the author has no further insights [U59].

TYLER COVE has been paced as five and one-half miles north from Prisoners' Harbor, and is about half way between Coche Point and Cavern Point. POTATO BAY, as Tyler Cove is now called [C18], is a snug little anchorage except in northwest winds; for northeasters, McElrath remarked that Potato Bay is safer than Prisoners' Harbor. In fact, this area from Prisoners' Harbor to San Pedro Point is without safe landing places except at Potato Bay and Scorpion Bay.

In 1908 Linton [J113], wrote,

It may not be amiss to state here that twice

during the blow (nor'wester) we were nearly wrecked; once while at anchor in Potatoe Harbor, a broken anchor allowing the boat to drift within the breaker line and nearly onto the rocks.

The high rocky point known as CAVERN POINT, also called PALO PARADO [C18], is near the eastern end of the island and perhaps two and two-thirds miles west by north from San Pedro Point. Some three hundred feet above Cavern Point is a U. S. Monument, placed there by the U. S. Coast and Geodetic Survey back in the 1850s.

SCORPION HARBOR is an open roadstead, a safe landing place exposed only to the easterly winds. Located three-quarters of a mile east of Cavern Point, this harbor is used for exporting, probably sheep, for the Gherinis raised sheep on this far-eastern end of the island. The rest of the island, ninety percent of it, is being used for cattle-raising by Carey Stanton.

Here, at Scorpion Harbor, two hundred yards from the rocky little beach, may be found the old adobe ranch buildings, and a well. This was EASTERN RANCH.

When Goodyear visited the island in 1890, ". . . they were building a new house, as yet unfinished, and where there is a young plantation of fig and olive trees, and a vineyard . . ." The corners of the house were built of stone, which contained small impressions suggesting fossil leaves. This stone occupied a large area in the region south and southwest of Chinese Harbor [C18]. Obviously, there was fresh water nearby.

In 1904, when Walker visited the island [M126], the house was finished; he called it "another large stone house with a sun dial on the front of it."

Although the buildings are structurally intact, there are many signs of deterioration, including broken glass and weed-choked gardens [P167, 1964].

Back from the rocky bluffs at the rocky beach there is a narrow rocky canyon, the hills finally widening to present a valley.

SAN PEDRO POINT is the extreme eastern end of Santa Cruz Island, and lies four miles west of Anacapa. The point is a comparatively low table, with water close under. The anchorage of Scorpion Harbor is to its north, and the anchorage of SMUGGLERS' COVE lies one and one-quarter miles southwest from San Pedro Point [N34].

YELLOW BANK, with its anchorage, supposedly named for the color of the cliffs, follows Smugglers'

Cove to the south. San Pedro Point, Smugglers' Cove, and Yellow Bank all became part of the Rossi holdings, for Edmund A. Rossi, in 1923-24, was awarded Tract #7. As with Tract #6 above, it was considered seven percent of the value of the whole island. Today, tracts #6 and #7, comprising 6,253.49 acres, or ten percent of the total island acreage, belong to the Gherinis. Eventually fishing rights were granted along their whole coast by the Gherini, Rossi, Capuccio heirs.

SHAW ANCHORAGE is one mile off the southeastern point of the island [N34]. Dr. Shaw was once Superintendent for the Santa Cruz Island Co. under the English Forbes and Barron ownership—before Justinian Caire purchased the island. Dr. Shaw owned one of the finer homes in Santa Barbara. He was one of the first persons, if not the first, the Lone Woman of San Nicolas saw when she arrived at the town of Santa Barbara. It is said that she saw Dr. Shaw, "now eighty years old and yet living there, riding a horse" [P38, 1892], and displayed much amusement with the sight.

VALLEY ANCHORAGE is seven miles from Smugglers' Cove [N34], and about five and one-half miles from Shaw Anchorage. During Goodyear's time this anchorage was known as EL PUERTO DEL LA CAÑADA DEL SUR [C18]. Today it is known as BLUE BANK, where inland a short distance may be found the Sur Ranch, past which flows the stream to Blue Bank and the ocean.

Of this area Goodyear remarked that "clots of pitch or asphaltum are . . . scattered around over the rocks on the beach . . . , having been washed up by the sea from the south . . ."

Next appears three distinct places, but quite close together. SCANDAL POINT is located between ALBERT'S ANCHORAGE on its east and COCHES PRIETOS ANCHORAGE to its west. Coches Prietos means 'black pigs,' a name given for the Mexican-introduced animals, now wild, according to Sunset [P135, 1967]. Elsewhere, 'Coche' means a kind of coastal barge, with 'prietos' referring to black color.

All three places are about midway on the south shore of the island [N34]. CAÑON COCHES PRIETOS is back of the one anchorage. The Swede, Frank Hansen, had a shack at ALBERT'S COVE on a squatter-rights basis [B107]. In 1969 a skin divers' resort operated there, using six bamboo huts as shelter [M171].

Davidson had this to say about the coast line,

The northern two-thirds of the eastern end of

the island is accessible to small boats at almost any spot, except during the time of the "south-easters," when it is unapproachable. For over ten miles, the eastern end of the south side of the island presents an almost unbroken barrier of cliffs, with only two places where the most hardy fishermen sometimes make landings. The next nine miles of southern coast line offers only six anchorages, but some of these, such as Coches Prietos and Willows, are exceptionally good.

Archaeologist Schumacher indicated some of the better burying grounds as being in Cañon Coches Prietos, and ornithologist Linton [J113, 1908], further described this particular location:

Our first camp was on the southern coast at Coches Prietos. The tiny streams in the wide canyons here were lined with an abundant growth of willows and wild blackberry vines. The hills, sloping gradually to the higher range, were covered with holly, manzanita, ironwood and wild cherry, with here and there an oak, and, of course, cacti in abundance . . .

Linton and party made about a ten-day visit at this camping spot.

The next place name west of Coches Prietos is CAÑON LOS SAUCES DE LOS COLORADOS [B107]. Probably the more popular name for this locality is WILLOW HARBOR or ANCHORAGE, which should not be confused with Willow Creek farther to the west [B63].

ALAMOS ANCHORAGE lies two-thirds of the distance from the eastern point of the island, two and two-third miles west of Scandal Point, and two and one-quarter miles west from the anchorage of Coches Prietos. About a mile inland from Alamos is located the 1,200 foot high SUGAR LOAF PEAK.

In ordinary northwest weather the water at the anchorage is very smooth, with a beach at the inner side of the cove made of fine sand [N34]. Schumacher must have thought the Indian burying grounds at Alamos to be better than average for in one of his reports there is included a map of this region [N41].

On west from Cañada del Alamo is LAGUNA HARBOR and CAÑON LAGUNA. Near Laguna Canyon is a QUAIL CAÑON, where some Santa Catalina Island Quail had been released, said Carey Stanton [B107]. They appear to have flourished. Of the Catalina Island Quail, Miller [J153, 1951], had this to say,

specimens verify identification with the island race *catalinensis* as is also of those planted on

PIECES OF EIGHT

Santa Rosa. Quail were seen on Santa Cruz near the Stanton Ranch and also at Willows Anchorage, three miles southwest across a high ridge, and they were noted commonly on Santa Rosa.

PUNTA ARENA follows. Northwest of Punta Arena is the prominent crest of SIERRA BLANCA, 1486 foot high, where a few pines cling to its rocky ridges. The rhyolite series may be found in this area at CAÑADA DEL GATO near Johnston Lee, and at the peak [J297].

Almost south of Punta Arena is GULL ISLAND, to Davidson, the only real danger around the island [N34]. As he explained it, less than a mile from Gull Island there is a submarine valley about four hundred and thirty fathoms deep, but in this valley there is a fifty-fathom bank but one and a half miles south from Gull Island. Gull Island is three-quarter miles offshore. Bonnot [C2], indicated a Steller Sea Lion Rookery on this little island in 1928.

Traveling about two miles to the northwest of 'Laguna,' passing Punta Arena, is another headland known as 'Johnston's.' At times it is known as JOHNSTON LEE, and a short distance back from the shore is a fisherman's cabin, standing in the midst of Indian debris heaps of considerable depth [B63]. Indian artifacts have also been found there, as one might expect [U2].

Goodyear went to POZO HARBOR in 1890 [C18]. He explained the name 'Pozo' by saying it was "so-called because a well was once sunk to a considerable depth here in the cañon, without, however, finding any good water." Schumacher also spelled the name "Pozo" [N41].

Davidson in 1889 explained that POSA ANCHORAGE "lies . . . at the southeast entrance to the Santa Cruz Channel. It is off the mouth of a long, broad arroyo coming from the northeast" [N34].

KINTON POINT must be passed before arriving at Cañada los Sauces del Oeste. In 1929 Rogers said that there were three miles intervening between Posa and the canyon to the northwest, known as 'WILLOWS OF THE WEST' [B63]. Bremner said that it was five and a half miles from Punta Arena to Cañada los Sauces del Oeste [J297].

WILLOW-CREEK-ON-THE-WEST is WILLOW CREEK, and is about five miles long. At the mouth of the creek is a lagoon which has been formed by deposition, about 24 feet wide by 100 feet long.

Bremner offered the information that although stream terraces "are found in all the larger drainage areas, and deposits up to 30 feet in thickness were seen . . . The most important of these terraces is found in CAÑADA LOS SAUCES DEL OESTE, where large trunks of partly-carbonized Douglas fir occur in the Pleistocene sands" [J297, 1932].

According to Chaney and Mason [N3, 1934], elephant remains were found a few miles north of the creek. Rogers found two elephant teeth in an Indian burial. A third tooth was found by U.C.S.B. students in Cañada de los Sauces del Oeste [B54]. In the Carnegie Institution article they also referred to the most conspicuous of flora, *Pinus remorata,* concluding that the Willow Creek flora represented a southward extension of the northern forest of Pleistocene times [N3].

Stock [J318, 1935], said that the "southwestern end of this island has been described recently by Chaney and Mason. These beds are particularly noteworthy because of a fossil plant record which they contain."

Phil C. Orr [B54, 1968], named some of the fossil plants found in Willow Creek—Douglas fir, Gowen cypress, pine mistletoe, blue-blossom, dogwood, silk tassel bush. "Fresh water can be secured in this canyon. Forest growth is very sparse and the landing facilities leave much to be desired" [J297]. Here, there is also a small Indian site.

Goodyear said that on the crest of the ridge between Cañada de los Sauces and CAÑADA DE CERVADA [Cebada] the rock does not appear to be volcanic. Here, the pine trees and the volcanic rocks seem to end in favor of a continuation of the "red ridge" [C18].

Cañon Cervada joins with CHRISTY CAÑON [Cuesta Valley] before entering the sea. Goodyear continues,

> . . . the Western Ranch is at the mouth of the Cañon de Cervada . . . At the summit of the trail to the West Ranch (Rancho del Oueste) the altitude is not far from 1300' . . . about three quarters of a mile from the Western Ranch House there is a U. S. Coast and Geodetic Survey Station, on the edge of a bluff . . . There is a very distinct odor of petroleum along this beach [Christy Beach].

Davidson gave this bight area, which includes the mouth of Christy Canyon, a distance of two miles. Rogers [B63], further described the location,

> There is a so-called harbor at Christies, at the mouth of Cuesta Creek, but this is usually avoided by seamen. The swells which sweep in from the larger channel, concentrate upon this

place with double force, and almost insure the swamping of landing boats.

The coast line between CHRISTY BEACH and Forney's Cove, with the headland BLACK POINT on the sailing route, contains a long stretch of fairly undisturbed Indian Mounds [B107]. McElrath thought that the rocky surface, steep gullies, and profusion of cactus in the area might have had something to do with its relative lack of visitors for one purpose or another, throughout the years. In addition to these data, the only good anchorage for about ten miles along this southwestern coast is FORNEY'S COVE, several miles distant from the Indian Mounds. Furthermore, some of the Indian island residents were superstitious about disturbing these mounds, offering less than encouragement to the curious. These thoughts also came from McElrath [B107].

Both ornithologists and archaeologists have camped at Forney's, although desert camping conditions would have been on the rough side of living for those who did. Stehman Forney, of the U. S. Coast and Geodetic Survey group, worked on the island and was also helpful to both the Schumacher party and the Wheeler Expedition personnel while they were on Santa Cruz.

The projection of Frazer Point is very likely the answer for Forney's Cove being a good anchorage, as the jutting rocks of the point tend to break up the severity of the winds from the north and the swells from the channel region [B107].

From Christy Ranch to Frazer Point, the distance is about five and one-half miles. This brings us back to the point of beginning.

Geology

Some of the nicer things given to us by W. A. Goodyear is his reproduction of a U. S. Coast and Geodetic Survey map of Santa Cruz, his corrected place names for the map, and his clear location descriptions. He spent about three weeks on the island of Santa Cruz in 1890, but dealt briefly with the geology of that island [C18].

C. F. Holder appears to be the only person who has mentioned gold outcroppings on Santa Cruz, having received such information from Mr. Caire [B38].

W. W. Rand has given a brief report on the geology of Santa Cruz, after having made a five-months' geological examination of the island during the years of 1928, 1929, and 1930 [C27].

Rand's article contains worthy technical information. For the layman, one of the more important comments Rand made was that the most conspicuous structural feature of the island is the fault that divides the island lengthwise into two parts. The two parts, however, are quite unalike from a geological standpoint. Another good, but general remark, is that the volcanics of Santa Cruz are confined almost entirely to the north side of this fault.

Bradley spoke of mollusk shells [J170, 1956], and so did Bremner. Bremner furthered this discussion by remarking that "The Eocene of Santa Cruz Island contains a diagnostic fauna of both mollusca and foraminifera . . ." [J297, 1932]. And Cockerell [J319, 1938], said that there were both Eocene and Miocene sea shell fossils to be had.

It was before the Miocene period that the Santa Monica Mountains and the northern islands were folded [J297]. Then, according to Reed [B118], this island chain became a "complex, much-faulted anticlinal uplift, more or less like the eastward continuation, the Santa Monica Mountains."

The very early geologic activity laid the ground work for the late Pliocene diastrophism, which affected the entire Coast Range of California and assured the present structural features of these islands.

One of Reed's observative comments [B118, 1933], is the nearly complete absence of Pliocene rocks, thus complimenting Rand's thought on the subject— Pleistocene terrace gravels of the three upper islands offer evidence of a Pleistocene connection between these islands and the mainland.

More earth movements followed, extending into the Pleistocene. The basin between the Channel Islands and the Santa Ynez Mountains was formed, and the islands then became separated from the mainland. Although the islands were then small, they increased in size with successive upward movements [J297].

Brief as W. C. Bradley's article is [J170, 1956], he mentioned marine terraces, as did Rand, as did Bremner. Bradley referred particularly to one terrace approximately one hundred feet above sea level, from which mollusk shells were used for carbon-dating. Such dating appears to be more than 39,000 years old.

Bremner felt that the most recent geologic movement was upward, thus forming the lowest marine terraces on the shore. On the other hand, Rand had remarked about the terraces, saying that they were cut at several levels and "show that after Pliocene time the island was elevated to different heights; but drowned valley-mouths show that the latest movement was slightly downward." Evidently Bradley, too, thought that there had been a downward movement with the former shore line now lying submerged on a continental shelf.

According to Bremner, the present topography of these islands was in progress during the last glacial epoch of the Pleistocene. As a result of upward movement, some of the streams became entrenched and their present terraces were formed, while the broadened valleys became alluviated.

The most important of the stream terraces may be located in Cañada los Sauces del Oeste; here partly-carbonized Douglas fir may be found in the Pleistocene sands [J297, 1931]. But during this glacial epoch, the succeeding climatic changes were from the humid, conducive to tree growth, to the arid; thus few growths of trees remain of this past period.

Bremner's pamphlet, "Geology of Santa Cruz Island," is twenty-eight pages long. It contains maps, plates, photos and reading material organized under the headings of physiography, stratigraphy, geologic structure, and geologic history. It is a true addition to the knowledge concerning the island of Santa Cruz.

The Main Ranch

Through the mile wide east-west valley flows Portezuelo Creek. The bed of its arroyo is used as a road between Prisoners' Harbor and Main Ranch; the ranch is about three miles from the harbor. There is a high range of hills north of the valley, and a parallel range to its south.

LA PLAYA was the name of the post office at the Arroyo Principal, and with it were the cottages, old adobe house, the kitchen mess hall, warehouses, barns, and the site of the large frame house where the Caires used to live.

We are told through, "Notes from Santa Cruz Island" [J113, 1908], that there were

perhaps 40,000 sheep on the island, a few cattle, immense barley fields and grape vineyards, several ranches, a large winery, and some 100 men employed during the harvesting season.

Charles F. Holder visited with the Caires and in his book speaks of other island activities [B38, 1910],

Not far from the ranch houses is a large vegetable garden for the benefit of the men, making a most luxuriant showing, and telling the story

of the richness of the soil that produces vegetables every month in the year . . . The two ranch houses of brick covered with plaster and white-washed, with a small veranda and iron balconies wherever there was an excuse to place one, have a decidedly foreign air. In front of each is a small, old-fashioned garden, with narrow winding walks, filled with fragrant, old-fashioned plants. The dining-room is in a separate building, and at the sumptuous lunch our host informed us that everything but the champagne and flour was produced on the island ranch . . . Not far from the house is a little chapel, where services are held . . . We were shown the great bakery with its rows of Italian bread; the cook-shop, with its four or five Venetian cooks . . .

Quite full descriptions of the various buildings, and some of the changes made on them, may be found in Carey Stanton's Introduction to McElrath's book, *On Santa Cruz Island*. This same type of information may also be found in the text.

Life on the ranches of Santa Cruz was seemingly in great part the same in 1919-1921 as it was lived when Justinian Caire was in full swing with the island businesses [B107, 1967].

Carey Stanton reports that the employment records for the island go back to 1855. These records no doubt contain the names of the various superintendents for the island.

According to Thompson and West [B70, 1883], "The island is divided into six departments, each under its own administration responsible to the Governor, J. B. Joyaux." In this connection, it is noted in Goodyear's 1890 report that a Mr. Jules Moullet was at that time Superintendent of the island [C18]. Before McElrath in 1919 there was a Mr. Swain, and after McElrath in 1921, a Mr. Revel.

Charles Hillinger [M154, 1956], stated that at this much later date a Pete Olivari was serving as a general foreman; he had lived on the island since 1902. Today, and over twenty years, a Henry Duffield manages.

From the U. S. Geographical Survey's report [N45, 1876], comes Dr. Rothrock's description of the island as a sheep ranch,

. . .The island is almost wholly given up to sheep-raising. It is estimated that in the spring of 1875 there were not less than 60,000 head of them on the island. In June 15,000 were killed for the hide and tallow alone; the offal being carted down to the shore and cast into the water;

154

attracting immense numbers of fish to the spot . . . On the grounds most visited by the herds of sheep, all vegetation, save a sage-brush, *cactecs* and the *erodium* or storksbill, had been entirely swept away. The grass had gone completely, and such plants of the island flora as sheep would eat, it was with difficulty that I could get even a decent botanical specimen . . . In fact, pasture had become so thin that the sheep at the time of my visit were wandering in very small bands that they might the more readily find food. Even the sage-brush was disappearing, as year after year the sheep had eaten away its leaves and younger shoots, until there was not left sufficient of the more green, succulent tissues to elaborate the sap . . . It is impossible to conceive a more dreary waste than was here produced as the result of over-pasturage.

Thompson and West contain a description of a matanza on the island of Santa Cruz [B70, 1883],

Matanza

The island becomes at some times overstocked and may be said to be in that condition much of the time. The result is that the grasses, being cropped so close, die out, and allow the loosened soil to be removed by the wind and rain. Popular opinion is, that the amount of fertile land is thus being gradually lessened. In seasons of drouth, or when the sheep become too numerous for profitable keeping, large numbers of them are slaughtered for their pelts and tallow. A "matanza" is the designation of the huge slaughter-house where this is done. The operation consists in killing and dressing the sheep and putting the carcass in a closed boiler or steamer where the parts are subjected to such a degree of heat that everything, even the bones, is softened. The mass is then subjected to an immense pressure, forcing out all the tallow and glue, which are separated and prepared for market. The dry residuum is fed to hogs. In this way all parts are utilized. The "matanza" in this place passed 12,000 sheep through in 1875, and 25,000 had to be sacrificed in 1877, from lack of feed.

Joseph Mailliard [J102, 1899], offered a few lines about the sheep on the island,

This range [Montañon] is so steep and brushy that even with twenty experienced vaqueros only about one-half of the sheep occupying it are ever shorn and there are thousands of these animals roaming around with one, two or three years' fleece on their backs, their long tails flapping behind them as they run, in a most comical manner.

Dr. Holder also spoke of the early sheep-ranch activities [B38],

sheep-shearing . . . work requires men of this hardy stock and the finest horsemen, and probably in no other country are men seen riding over such inaccessible mountains. The sheep, of which there are thirty thousand or more, range all over the . . . acres of the island, except in the valley in the interior, devoted to the ranch and vineyard . . . the fearless Barbareños, mounted on native horses, ride over the most perilous places.

A most ingenious method of leading in the sheep is employed. The horsemen take out with them three white goats, which, when a flock of sheep is discovered, are released. The latter join them at once, and the goats turn and lead them in the direction of the corral, the sheep following blindly. When one flock of sheep is secured, the goats are taken to another, and in this way they save the herders much trouble.

Out of *Shepherd's Empire* [B125, 1945], comes perhaps the longest and best condensed description of the way Justinian Caire ran his sheep ranch. In the book, as in O'Neill's [B53], it is mentioned how the sheep were lightered to shore, while the cattle were thrown over-board to swim to shore. The authors [B125], refer to J. Caire's attention to sheep diseases and how the owners avoided many problems through their wariness. However, this was after the wool from the island had been in poor repute for sometime [B53].

In McElrath's book are several statements from Fred Caire, son, on poachers to the island, and some remarks from Edwin L. Stanton on Caire's interest in soil conservation and other efforts toward being a good environmentalist.

[Caire's] "buildings were of the best, consisting of rock, and brick that were made on the island. His plantings of trees for future generations showed a great deal of foresight" [B125].

Caire was also interested in grape-growing and wine-making, successfully trying his hand at these businesses. In the central valley, and around the ranch headquarters, Caire began and developed his vineyards about 1880; in 1896 there were capacious cellars [P44]. By the time Prohibition had arrived, the Caires had one of the largest, if not the largest, vineyards in the country [B53, 1939], with the winery storage capacity of about 200,000 gallons.

Prohibition Days of 1918-1933 must have dealt a crippling blow to the economy of the Island Company. From the *Catalina Islander* of August 19, 1931 comes a sidelight reminiscence of the 'good ol' days,' when Avalon was yet known as Timms' Landing, long before Prohibition,

The schooner 'Keywee' was 85 feet long and it made regular trips between Santa Barbara and Prisoners' Harbor at Santa Cruz Island . . . I remember one spring when we brought from Santa Cruz Island [to Catalina] about twenty 50-gallon barrels of 'Dago Red,' and we didn't leave the Island until all the wine was consumed.

The *Star of Freedom* handled much of the transportation for the Island Company in the very early days, serving others as well. It was this vessel which took Schumacher from Santa Cruz to San Nicolas [N41]. Later, the *Santa Cruz* was built as the company's own vessel, 1893. When in 1960 a 'northeaster' hit the island, the *Santa Cruz* was destroyed on the rocks at Prisoners' Harbor.

On the subject of wine, and the cruiser, and coming from the file of Stephen Bowers in the Southwest Museum, expressed is the fact that the *Free Press* of June 1, 1900, stated, "The little steamer *Santa Cruz* came into port Tuesday morning, from Santa Cruz Island, loaded with wine for L. Cerf Co. There were over ten tons of wine in the cargo."

Our best source of descriptive material on the subject of climate and its corollaries for wine-growing comes from Holder [B38],

The proprietor is French, and French and Italian laborers are employed exclusively, the original plan having been to establish here a Swiss-French colony. The little valley in the interior and its climate, so similar to that of Italy and Southern France, probably inspired the owner to reproduce a European vineyard here, and so faithfully has the idea been carried out that on entering the valley one can imagine himself in one of the wine-producing districts of France or Italy . . . Standing on the ranch house veranda, the valley was seen east and west several miles, and rising to the summit of the hills were the vines, planted in the European fashion. They were of many kinds, producing the white and the red wines which have made the Santa Cruz vintage famous. A long road lined with lofty eucalyptus trees followed the valley, passing

through acres of vines. Near at hand were two large wineries, where the wine is made and stored. It is said to have a peculiar bouquet not noticed in the mainland wines . . . the French and Italian islanders . . . pick the grapes in September and shear the sheep twice a year . . . the vintage is a season of jollification, but though in a land of wine, there is no excess in drinking. This was explained by the manager, who said that the men rarely drank water, a variety of claret being made for their special benefit. This, diluted, each man carried in a small keg when he went to the field, . . .

Most of the time the climate in the central valley, as well as the soil, was ideal for agriculture, especially vineyards. But now and then unusually bad weather would be known on the island. The unusual can happen anywhere.

Disaster came in 1878, not to the vine-growers, but to the latter-day archaeologists, and the incident was serious [B70],

Wednesday, February 19, 1878, a terrific storm at Santa Cruz Island raised the creek [Portezuelo] ten feet, so that it completely washed away the old Indian burying ground, leaving not a trace behind. Rocks weighing two or three tons were carried along the stream. The rainfall at Santa Barbara was moderate, so that the island was probably visited by a water spout or a 'cloud-burst.'

Archaeology

Schumacher's, "Some Remains of a Former People," devoted about five long paragraphs to Santa Cruz Island [P82, 1875]. Some of the material is descriptive, but he and his party found many Indian grounds, and listed them. One of the sites was 'SECRET HARBOR,' wherever that harbor is.

They spent about a month exploring the shores, gathering and digging what they could. Schumacher's list of "remains" details thirty types of artifacts; reduced through organization, such artifacts were articles for homemaking, fishing, tools and weapons, musical instruments, pipes, paints, shell-money, ornaments and carvings.

In Schumacher's, "Aboriginal Settlements of the Pacific Coast" [P114, 1876], he began with the requirements for a well-located ranchería. Then he described a typical site, choosing Tinker's Cove. Included in the article is a sketch of the cove and the section directly west of it.

This section appears to be near the location of

Orizaba Rock, and is, therefore, the pictograph cave region,

> Its location is near a narrow inlet . . . the ground upon which the station is located is of a rocky, irregular structure . . . a cove, affording an excellent boat-landing, adjoins to the westward of it; outlying rocks, of which but few appear in the sketch, are covered with edible shell-fish; a mass of kelp and seaweed grows in the adjoining waters, and is thickly stocked with fish; a spring of potable water is found in the deepest part of the cove. Sand is found only at a distance of between four and five hundred yards to the eastward, in a small hidden beach on the narrow fiord of Tinker's Cove . . .

Could this "small hidden beach" be his Secret Harbor. Schumacher appears to be the first person to have investigated this particular kitchen-midden-burying-ground.

Schumacher's "Researches in the Kjökkenmöddings of the Coast of Oregon, and of the Santa Barbara Islands and Adjacent" [N41, 1877], has about 10 paragraphs on Santa Cruz Island, and is therefore more detailed.

They made six camps, using various points around the island—Prisoners' Harbor, Tinker's Cove, Coches Prieto, Los Alamos, Smuggler's Cove, and Forney's Cove. Captain Taylor of the *Hassler* took them around at various intervals of time, as he, too, was working there by making soundings around Santa Cruz.

They last camped at Forney's Cove, where they were joined by Rothrock, Loew, and Henshaw for several days before returning to the town of Santa Barbara with 25 boxes of artifacts. There, Schumacher met Yarrow, in charge of the Wheeler Survey, before taking the *Star of Freedom* to San Nicolas.

Dr. J. T. Rothrock [#H5 of JJ of N45], offered seven paragraphs for the island of Santa Cruz, mainly descriptive in character. Among other comments, he noted "that in one or two places pepper-trees had been planted and were growing vigorously without care, and that some little grain is cultivated near Prisoners' Harbor." Rothrock served as the botanist for the Survey.

The University of California at Berkeley, Department of Anthropology, has published more invaluable information about Santa Cruz Island's ethnographic resources. There is, "The French Scientific Expedition to California, 1877-1879," [U5, 1951], and, "The Scientific Expedition of Léon de

Céssac to California, 1877-1879," [U18, 1964].

Interesting are the first-hand remarks by Céssac for his four-months' visit to the island. One of his comments [U7], was that he "was the first to discover the existence of many caverns which had served for habitation as well as graveyards."

Frenchman Céssac's entré to the island of Santa Cruz was through Frenchman Caire's ownership of the island. Céssac and Schumacher were none-too-friendly professional rivals in their collecting.

Gustav Eisen had been on the Coast in 1873 and 1897 for the California Academy of Sciences. Céssac's collecting-visit had been made during this period; nevertheless Eisen had said that he had never heard of the man, other than to recall his name [M30].

Eisen's pamphlet, "An Account of the Indians of the Santa Barbara Islands in California," published in 1904 in Prag, Czechoslovakia, is a relaxed delineation of the eight islands. Eisen personalized his remarks about each island when possible, and he managed to offer an excellent presentation. His research was done in the San Francisco area, using material from Bancroft, Powell, Salmeron's *Relaciones,* and others. The Southwest Museum has a copy of this pamphlet.

One comment in Gidney's book [B25, 1917], is that a Professor Leonard Outhwaite, anthroplogist of the University of California, was on Santa Cruz Island in 1916. Outhwaite was collaborating with Olson during this period of time. He found over one thousand Indian mounds. The one near Prisoners' Harbor was described as being one hundred fifty feet wide, three hundred feet long, and some eighteen feet in depth.

Rider [M40], remarked in 1925 that there are

> many old town sites, where the strong winds on the dunes are constantly uncovering long buried bits of [Indian] handicraft, many of them showing real artistry, such as the gracefully carved cups and flutes and pipes with mosaic inlay.

In an August 1926 *Leaflet,* Santa Barbara Museum of Natural History, is the statement that a Mr. Stuart spent several days on Santa Cruz Island, where he found an unnamed cave. So the cave was given the name, "Stuart's Cave."

This cave showed evidence of repeated occupancy and abandonment. Stuart and party dug a trench through the floor, thus revealing layers of abalone shells covered with sand, only to be reoccupied. This was, however, "after the shellfish had again grown to normal size." According to the article, there had been eight such periods of occupation.

Ronald L. Olson's article [U22], was published in 1927 in a University of California Alumni Association publication, *California Monthly.* Olson had been to Santa Cruz Island in May of that year, under the auspices of the Santa Barbara Museum of Natural History and through the courtesy of the Caires.

Olson and his party stayed on the island for two and one-half months, digging trenches, and finally removing forty-three cases of artifact-specimens. He was also on the island for six weeks the following year.

According to Olson, during this stay, they mainly experienced wind, fog, and raw cold. "It was on the west shore . . . [they] were forced to wrap the sour-dough jar, . . . in clothes taken from our own backs to keep the cold from killing the yeast."

While there, they photographed about fifty rock paintings found on the walls and ceiling of a large cave, probably Orizaba Pictograph Cave near Tinker's Cove.

In a 1929 issue of *American Archaeology and Ethnology* [U1], Julian H. Steward gave eleven lines to Dr. Olson's description of the Pictograph Cave, ending with,

> In this deposit were found mortars, pestles, asphalted pebbles, and asphalt blocks all resembling comparable objects in normal Chumash shell heaps. Many of the pictographs have been partially obscured by blackening from fires built beneath.

In the same issue, Dr. Olson had an article, "Chumash Prehistory." A. L. Kroeber and R. L. Olson were the editors of *American Archaeology and Ethnology.*

"Chumash Prehistory" included a map of the central Chumash coast, showing the four northern islands, with ten of Santa Cruz Island's more important midden sites. The largest cubic content, Site #3, at the extreme western end between Frazer Point and West Point, was where Dr. Stephen Bowers had said he spent most of his time while on the island.

Dr. Olson explained their method of workmanship, included Kroeber's statements of where the Chumash territory was, on both the mainland and the islands, and generally discussed the differences between the Early and Late periods of Indian occupation.

According to the Santa Barbara *News-Press,* David B. Rogers was on Santa Cruz Island in April

of 1927, and had thoroughly examined seven of more than one hundred village sites. The newspaper article is entitled, "Seaweed Hut is Preserved for Centuries," as Rogers reported through another the use of seaweed for hut roofs and for basket weaving [M90].

By 1929 Dr. Rogers had published his important and illucidating book, *Prehistoric Man of the Santa Barbara Coast* [B63]. His book contains considerable descriptive material, indicating more than passing acquaintance with the whole island of Santa Cruz, an invaluable aid for gaining a verbal-visual understanding of the island's topography. He was on other islands, and has maps and plates for them, as well.

Rogers regretted the human ravaging of Santa Cruz' Indian mounds and sites; about as many had been ravaged by the elements and earth movements, thus leaving only an approximate thirty-five untouched and rich in material.

He included a brief summary of previous investigations bearing on Santa Cruz and made relevant statements about the work of scientists of the Engineer Corps of the United States Army, beginning with the year 1875,

> These were under the direct supervision of First Lieutenant George M. Wheeler, and the results of their activities were later embodied in seven large volumes, under the general title of "U. S. Geographical Survey West of The Hundredth Meridian." Each volume was devoted to a special department of the survey; the results of the archaeological investigations are contained in Vol. VII, compiled and edited and largely written by Prof. Frederick W. Putnam, curator of the Peabody Museum . . .
>
> Professor Putnam, in presenting the original material at hand, did not neglect the work of others who had previously endeavored to solve a few of the ethnological problems of the region . . .

Rogers also stated his feelings of gratitude for the help of others; this included the assistance of Mr. Ralph Hoffmann of the Santa Barbara Museum, Mr. J. P. Harrington of the Southwest Museum, and the personnel of the Smithsonian Institution. Rogers was a curator of the Santa Barbara Museum; one of his assistants was Richard Van Valkenburgh. No one can fail to be rewarded for reading this nearly 500-page book by Dr. Rogers.

Richard Van Valkenburgh was on the island in 1932 [M141], as the representative of David Bank

Rogers, proposing to remain there for at least a month,

> Landing . . . near the western extremity of the island, . . . the young bone hunters discovered two shacks, built and abandoned by Chinese collectors of sea grass years ago. These [shacks] they cleaned, repaired and moved into. And therein they lived on canned grub and bottled water, . . . for a thrilling thirty days. During the thirty days . . . 132 human skeletons [were exhumed] . . . [they] uncovered the sites of forty villages . . . seventy "house rings," showing that [one] village contained seventy houses and about 800 to 1000 inhabitants . . .

Anthropological Records [U2, 1940], describes 154 types of bone artifacts, written by E. W. Gifford. There is a chart for the various locations and names of specimen-artifacts found. The chart is for the region of the Channel Islands and the adjacent towns of San Luis Obispo, Santa Barbara, Ventura, and the Los Angeles coast. This article could be helpful to many.

On McElrath's 1967 map of Santa Cruz Island, he indicated *Indian Territory* on the southern coast between Blue Bank and Yellow Bank, and remarked that the area had received its name from the number of small caves in the chalk rock hills, the walls and ceilings of which had been blackened by smoke [B107]. This particular section has not been specifically noted in the literature by archaeologists.

The most recent information this author has on Santa Cruz archaeology is, "Microblade Technology of the Channel Islands" [J212, 1974]. It is called a preliminary report and was written by three authors, Jean M. Pitzer, Thomas R. Hester, and Robert F. Heizer.

In it is stated that Rogers considered site #147 at Prisoners' Harbor to be the largest, which site was also considered to be a manufacturing area.

The authors felt that Olson's excavation and recording techniques were such that it cannot be determined at what depths the microblades were found, thus making it difficult to assess and to analyze the relationship of the microblades and the skeletal remains.

Three references have not been used: J198, 1960; J201, 1962; and J26, 1962.

Transfer of Island Title

There are two important articles written solely about Santa Cruz Island. One was published in the *Pacific Historical Review,* written by W. H. Ellison, and called, "History of the Santa Cruz Island Grant" [J239, 1937]. The article had been thoroughly researched, has a good bibliography, and is comprehensive in its purpose. It was published the same year in which Edwin L. Stanton purchased most of Santa Cruz Island.

The second article appeared in a 1964 *Westways* edition, written by Jo Ann Roe, "Slumbering Santa Cruz" [P167]. Without a bibliography, nevertheless Ms. Roe's information appears to be well-come-by, and exhibits previous research on the island. Roe is especially commendable on Justinian Caire, his ownership of the island, and his family.

Regardless of the quality of these two articles, it requires additional information and other sources for the reader to obtain a true perspective and feeling for the nuances of the island's ownership. And it is only by following, at the same time, the ownership of the Chaboya Mine near San Jose, California, that we obtain such an overview.

At one time there were at least four other men besides Castillero with an involvement in both the island and the mine:

Santa Cruz Island
Chaboya's Mine, San Jose
Captain Andrés Castillero
Alexander Forbes
James Alexander Forbes
William Forbes
Eustace Barron

———

Castillero

In a *California Historical Society* publication of 1935 may be found a thirty-eight page article, "Captain Andrés Castillero, Diplomat," written by George Tays. This account is well-recommended, especially for those interested in the man, as well as his activities [J94].

According to Marguerite Wilbur, who translated, edited, and annotated de Mofras' *Travels on the Pacific Coast* [B48, 1937], "Castillero was a Mexican captain, a prominent politician, and a friend of Governor Chico," a governor for part of the year 1836.

As a reward for his services during all those politically troublesome past years, Castillero was granted Santa Cruz Island. This came by way of an order from the president of Mexico, through a letter written by Pesado, Governor of the Department of Californias, and delivered to Governor J. B. Alvarado by Castillero.

O'Neill [B53, 1939], said that "Castillero originally had asked for Santa Catalina, but seemed to have been satisfied to accept Santa Cruz." With preliminaries accomplished, a patent to Santa Cruz Island was granted to Castillero on May 22, 1839, through Governor Alvarado.

But Castillero had not requested a confirmation to his Patent through the Land Commission, that began its functioning in 1851. It was not until the 13th of April, 1852 that such a petition was filed in the city of San Francisco. After 15 years in the courts, the final date of confirmation came on March 1, 1867. The finalities for such may be found in Book A at the Santa Barbara Courthouse.

In the meantime, Castillero had also been negligent for non-payment of taxes; by 1850 Francisco de la Guerra, then James R. Bolton, claimed a small portion of the island. Each was denied through the court. Even José Antonio Aguirre who had claimed one-half of the island in the court proceedings of 1854, 1855, and 1857, by 1858 had dismissed his claim [J239]. This is an Ellison reference, one which was obtained from the *Santa Barbara Post* of 1869.

By 1852 Castillero had transferred his rights to Santa Cruz Island to Jecker, Torre & Co. and Barron, Forbes & Co. These companies stocked the island and used the services of their Scots friend, Dr. J. B. Shaw, as Supervisor of the island.

Castillero had another interest in Alta California. The story is told in J. J. Warner, *et al, An Historical Sketch of Los Angeles County, California from the Spanish Occupancy* . . . [B76, 1876], and repeated through T. H. Hittell, *History of California* [B35, 1898]. The story is about an 1841 incident in which Castillero indirectly started an "alert" about gold in them thar' hills.

Both of these authors also included details on the Chaboya or New Almaden quicksilver mine, which Castillero had also located and leased.

The incident about finding gold happened on the mainland in Santa Clara County while Castillero was traveling from Los Angeles to Monterey. This information about the gold and quicksilver had an indirect but significant bearing on the ultimate history of California. Even the owners of Santa Cruz Island were to a degree, involved through the English-Mexican firm of Barron, Forbes & Co.

The year was 1845. In *Hutchings' California Magazine,* "The Quicksilver Mine of New Almaden"

[P26, 1856], there is an eight-page article on the subject. In part, J. M. Hutchings said,

> In 1845 a captain of cavalry in the Mexican service, named Castillero, having met a tribe of Indians near Bodega and seeing their faces painted with vermillion, obtained from them for a reward, the necessary information of its locality, when he visited it, . . . and determined the character of the metal, he registered it in accordance with the Mexican custom, about the close of the year . . . In 1846 the mine was leased out to an English and Mexican company for the term of sixteen years; . . . In 1850, the present company was formed.

Located twelve miles south of San Jose, New 'Almaden,' Spanish for 'mineral,' was the name given the mine, 1848, after first having been called Santa Clara or Chaboya's mine [B29].

Richard B. Mason, American Military-governor from 1847-1849, made a visit to both the gold country and this quicksilver mine, even before the treaty had been finalized with Mexico in 1848. His reports to Commodore Jones, then the Adjutant-general, focused Washington, D. C.'s attention on California, due to its potential through these two resources. Mason knew the future possibilities of the use of quicksilver for the mining of gold [B35].

President Polk delivered his message to Congress on the 5th of December, 1848; the message included Mason's findings, and interest in California quickened. California became a state on the 9th of September, 1850.

Mr. H. W. Halleck and Mr. William Carey Jones began collecting Land Claim papers for the United States. By 1858 Edwin McMasters Stanton was on the Coast, sent to do the same thing, as well as to collect the papers from Halleck and Jones, for organizing purposes. Papers were collected from Sacramento to San Diego.

Alexander Forbes

Alexander Forbes of the firm of Barron, Forbes & Co. was the author of the book, *History of Upper and Lower California,* 1839. Hittell [B35, 1897] said that the "chief object of the book was to call the attention of the people of Great Britain to the Californias and [to] the feasibility of their acquisition by the British Crown." The book was published in England, and was the first book to be published in English by someone who had lived on the Pacific Coast. Albeit, Alexander Forbes had not seen Alta

California until after his book had been written in 1835.

William Forbes; Eustace Barron

Both William Forbes and Eustace Barron were of the firm of Barron, Forbes & Co., a British-Mexican mercantile firm located in Tepic, Sonora, Mexico. At the same time, Eustace was the British Consul in Mexico.

During the year 1846, Barron, Forbes & Co. had been acquiring shares in Chaboya's Mine, and were bent in the direction of owning both the company and the land. They had been granted a sixteen-year lease of the mine by Castillero, which carried them to the year 1862.

By the year 1849 the Mine was in trouble. This continued to 1863. By 1858 the mine had an estimated worth of $15,000,000 and had been previously confirmed by the Land Commissioners hearing the claims. But Edwin McMasters Stanton took exception to their judgment and obtained an injunction against the further operation of the mine until real ownership could be established. The year 1858 is the same year in which the mine owners placed Santa Cruz Island on the market, "For Sale."

In the meantime, H. W. Halleck, a leading California attorney and cooperating with the Land Commission, had obtained some financial interest in the mine. He offered court testimony in behalf of the company operating New Almaden—Barron, Forbes & Co. But Stanton took an opposing view; documents in favor of the firm were disallowed, and their cause was lost.

The repossessed mine was then leased as the Quicksilver Mining Company, with many government men, it has been said, owning Quicksilver stock. In 1863 the Supreme Court, using Stanton's evidence, voided the land claim and the mining interest of Barron, Forbes & Co. See *Stanton: The Life and Times of Lincoln's Secretary of War,* 1962.

The Epilogue of this story may be found in Cleland's 1963 *The Cattle on a Thousand Hills,* Footnote #34 [obtained through Bancroft], ". . . the New Almaden grant gave rise to a futile damage claim for $16,000,000 against the United States. This claim was presented by Barron, Forbes & Co. to the British-American Claims Commission meeting at Geneva after the Civil War" [B10a].

Other incidents had occurred in 1847, for from the port of San Blas, Mexico, sailed a Robert Walkinshaw in early 1847. He was headed for Monterey, his final destination the mine, where he was to be its manager.

Information for the four following paragraphs was obtained from the *Quarterly* of the Southern California Historical Society, Vol. LVII, #4, 1975, "The Judges Colton," written by Kenneth M. Johnson [J380a].

Walkinshaw was on the *William,* owned by William Forbes of the British-Mexican company. The British schooner was seized by the United States; both the vessel and the cargo were confiscated. Although sold at auction, the successful bidder was a Barron, Forbes & Co. agent, and the *William* continued its usual functioning.

Suit for damages was filed; Judge Colton, presiding. Judge Colton would allow no appeal from his court, so Barron & Forbes filed a request for damages with the House Committee on Foreign Affairs, but without success.

The opinion rendered and upheld was that since former liability against the *William* had been previously established, a present mode of confiscation was irrelevant. Walkinshaw, and the British Vice-consul, James Alexander Forbes, who had been in Alta California since 1831, represented the firm in this court debate.

We later hear again about William Forbes, but it is in connection with the island of Santa Cruz and for the year 1869.

Dr. Barron Shaw
Superintendent, Santa Cruz Island

Dr. James Barron Shaw was a Scotsman, born in London. He came to Santa Barbara in January of 1850, then left for San Francisco in May of 1852. From there, in July of 1853 he began his trip to Mazatlan, to San Blas, and on to Tepic, Sonora, to visit his British friends, Barron and Forbes.

Barron and Forbes & Co. were bankers, operators of a general mercantile house, and were owners of a cotton spinning mill.

When Shaw returned from Mexico to Santa Barbara in May of 1853, he began his job of supervising Santa Cruz Island for his friends. This supervision continued for sixteen years, at which time Justinian Caire and his friend-investors purchased the island.

Dr. Shaw was married in 1861 in San Francisco to a Helen A. Green, also a Londoner; they had four children. Shaw was still living when Mrs. Yda Addis Storke's book was published [B69, 1891], in which she devoted about four pages to Dr. Shaw.

Dr. Shaw had been supervising Santa Cruz Island for only five years before Barron, Forbes & Co. advertised in the *Daily Alta California,* May 25, 1858, [P167, 1964].

FOR SALE: An island containing about 60,000 acres of land, well watered and abounding in small valleys of the best pasturage for sheep. There are no wild animals on it that would interfere with livestock. There is a good harbor, and safe anchorage . . .

But the sale of the island did not transpire until 1869.

Justinian Caire

In "Slumbering Santa Cruz" [P167], Roe tells of Caire coming to San Francisco from the French Alps in 1851, and there he started a business venture. Roe rehearsed something of Caire's background and spoke of his marriage to Albina in 1854.

Caire was the founder of a French Hospital and a French Savings Bank in San Francisco, but the bank did not succeed. A group of nine directors from the bank had purchased Santa Cruz Island, and Caire's final ownership and ultimate development of the island as a home and a ranch is a reflection of the bank situation, for he purchased the island from the bank directors.

Roe said that "Caire was a successful San Francisco businessman who bought the island entirely on speculation. Nevertheless, Caire's true story is equally romantic, . . ."

In Deed Book F are the names of ten men who were mortgaged to William E. Barron in the instrument dated February 16, 1869. In the Book it is stated that the price paid for Santa Cruz Island by Caire and his associates was $150,000, although Ellison was given a different view of the price, $30,000, according to an appraiser in 1937.

In Deed Book Y at Santa Barbara, for the date of March 29, 1869, the new Island owners, all from the County of San Francisco, became subject to

a mortgage bearing date the Sixteenth day of February [1869] to said William E. Barron, for the purchase money of said premises, to secure the sum of one hundred thousand dollars Gold Coin, which said mortgage the party of the second part assumes and agrees to pay.

This deed was recorded at the request of Wells Fargo & Company on May 6th A. D. 1881.

In 1897 Justinian Caire died, whereupon his wife and family became heirs to his Island estate. All seemed to go well for about fourteen years, at which time disagreement and litigation appeared to be the name of the game. The pertinent subjects appeared to be "to reincorporate or not to reincorporate," "to show tangible results or not to show."

And when the settlement finally came, it was the Montañon, both literally and figuratively, which separated the five Caire heirs from the two Caire heirs, Aglae S. Capuccio and Amelia A. Rossi. [Readers are referred to C40, C41, and Books of Deeds 81, 210, 396, and 687 at the Santa Barbara County Offices.]

Those heirs of the name 'Caire' sold their combined interests to Edwin L. Stanton; eventually the Capuccio interest went to the Rossi family, and eventually to María Rossi, aka daughter of Edmund A. and Amelia A. Rossi, aka niece of Aglae S. Capuccio, aka Mrs. Ambrose Gherini.

Readers are referred to articles J292, 1959, and J296, 1966. Both are from the Santa Barbara Museum of Natural History, fairly available, and well-recommended. Both articles are about four pages in length, offering first-hand information by two members of the Gherini family, Mrs. Ambrose Gherini for J292, and her son, Pier Gherini for J296.

Mrs. Ambrose Gherini gives personal dates and facts concerning members of her family, as well as of herself. After reading her article one cannot but feel closer to the family as real persons.

In Pier Gherini's account he speaks more of the ranch, of the personnel, and of their lovable dog-helpers, than about the immediate family. However, he does mention his father, Ambrose, a San Francisco attorney, and refers to his own and to his brother's World War II service.

With all attendant problems of novice ranchers, and sometimes absentee-ranchers, the two 'boys' managed to muddle through. While the younger Caires were running the ranches, with the help of superintendents, Clifford McElrath became an assistant superintendent in 1919. This was twenty-two years after Justinian Caire's death.

McElrath was miffed at the large numbers of Jugoslavs, Napolitanos, Austrians, and Sicilians who came to the island to fish for tuna and albacore. His complaint appeared to be primarily against this rough, lawless crowd, who did not mind rustling cattle and sheep for far more than their needs dictated. McElrath departed for Chihuahua, Mexico in 1921 [B107].

This state of affairs was in direct contrast to Justinian Caire's experiences, for it became a matter of tempers and shooting, if not killing. As the *Catalina Islander* of Jan. 11, 1921 put it, "Santa Cruz is said to be the center of a battle between poachers and sheep raisers . . . Authorities here tell of several battles that have been waged recently."

The Gherinis decided to switch to sheep-raising only, while the Caire interests maintained both sheep and cattle for many years. The change to cattle-raising only came with the transfer of title in 1937 to Edwin L. Stanton.

Of the Gherini sheep ranch, *Shepherd's Empire* [B125, 1945], remarked,

> the property is entirely fenced and divided into nine large sections, or *potreros*, which are rotated for grazing and so arranged that the flocks come out to the shearing sheds in April. After shearing, they are turned loose in the next *potrero*. Some sections are subdivided for separating rams and ewes seasonally. While the property could easily support 6,000 head, the policy has been to limit the number to 4,500.

Today, the Gherini interest is that of developing resorts at the eastern end of the island, but so far nothing really tangible has come of those ideas.

During the Depression of the 30s the island was offered to both California and the United States for the sum of $750,000, but no interest was shown for the purchase. It is ironic to realize today how much the people would like to have had Santa Cruz Island turned into a National Park. Now it is.

"Purportedly, Edwin L. Stanton of Laguna Beach purchased" from the estate the major part of the island for the sum of $1,000,000 in 1937 [M47]. Book 899 of the Santa Barbara County records indicates that the mortgage was duly paid by February 7, 1950.

The heirs of Edwin L. and Evelyn C. Stanton continued to run their part of the island as a cattle ranch, although oil and gas leases have been granted from time to time. As of July 5, 1978, however, part of the Carey Stanton holding had been sold to a conservancy. The remainder of Santa Cruz Island will go to that group in thirty years.

Under the new legislation of March, 1980 the Nature Conservancy will continue its ownership of the island, but will operate cooperatively with the National Park Service. William Ehorn is superintendent of this new park, which includes the two smallest islands, previously a national monument, and the larger Santa Cruz, Santa Rosa, and San Miguel islands.

Island Ownership

Andrés Castillero
Patent, May 22, 1839
Filed, April 13, 1852
Contested, July 3, 1855 -
March 1, 1867. Confirmed

June 23, 1857

Wm. E. Barron, Forbes & Co.
English Trading Co.
J. Caire, Mgr., 1865

Jecker, Torre & Co.
Dr. James Barron Shaw, Supt., 1857
for both companies.

February 16, 1869
Justinian Caire & Giovanni Battista Cerruti
Thomas J. Gallagher
T. Lemman Meyer
Adrien Gensoul
Alexander Weill
Camillo Martín
Nicolas Larco
Gustave Mahé
Pablo Baca
horses, sheep, cows, mules, livestock,
tools & implements

February 22, 1869
Santa Cruz Island Co. estab.
Interests of others eventually purchased by Caire

Dec. 10, 1897
Justinian Caire dies

November 30, 1911
Santa Cruz Island Co. license lost

August 28, 1913
Santa Cruz Island Co. license regained

1918-Dec. 4, 1925
Separation contested

May 23, 1932
Distribution Decree

Tract #1, Helen A. Caire
Tract #2, Fred F. Caire
Tract #3, Delphine A. Caire
Tract #4, Arthur J. Caire
Tract #5, Albina C. S. Caire

National Trading Co.
Ambrose Gherini, Mgr.

Tract #6, Aglae S. Capuccio
Tract #7, Amelia A. Rossi

April 22, 1937
Edwin L. Stanton

Mrs. Ambrose Gherini (nee Maria Rossi)
Pier Gherini
Frances Gherini
Mrs. Harold Ringrose
Mrs. Wm. McGinnes

164

Natural History

Flora

It has been said by some authors that San Clemente Island has the more interesting plant life. However, it still remains that Santa Cruz Island is the focal point for more writing on the subject than San Clemente.

Readers are referred to Greene [J258, 1886; J72, 1887], LeConte [J73, 1887], Brandegee [J61, 1888], Fewkes [J21, 1890], Yates [C21, 1890], and Cockerell [J382, 1937] for a discussion of the sea-loving *Lavatera.* All but Cockerell are 19th century botanists, and the subject is tossed about as to why *Lavatera* is found on the islands and nowhere else on the continent. A further discussion of this topic is by Brandegee [J396, 1890], "*Lavatera*—is it an Introduced Plant?" *Lavatera assurgentiflora* Kellogg, tree mallow, has also been discovered on all of the islands but San Nicolas, Hoffman having located it in 1930 on Anacapa.

Then there is the fern-leaved *Lyonothamnus,* named by Asa Gray for Mr. Lyon, for Lyon discovered it on Santa Catalina in 1884. The tree goes by two other names, "palo ferro" and Ironwood; it is deciduous and often grows to a height of 25 feet, sometimes having a trunk of five feet in diameter. Eastwood [J74, 1941], stated the position of the tree quite clearly when she said,

> The Lyonothamnus, which was brought to Dr. Greene by Mr. Hazard of Santa Barbara in 1885, differs from the species on Santa Catalina. Instead of the simple leaves of the Santa Catalina tree, this has pinnately compound leaves, each leaflet similar to the simple leaves of the Santa Catalina tree. Dr. Greene named this *Lyonothamnus asplenifolius* from the resemblance to the fronds of Asplenium. However, similar leaves are occasionally found also on the tree of Santa Catalina Island, so now it is considered as a variety only.

Carlquist [B82, 1965], also informs us on *Lyonothamnus,*

> This large tree, with unique and easily recognized leaves, is today known only as a single species, *L. floribundus,* from Santa Cruz, Santa Catalina, and San Clemente Islands.

Trask [U27, 1897], had found many groves of *Lyonothamnus* on San Clemente and by 1904 she had found it on Santa Rosa [J334]. Today, every island appears to be represented by one of the two varieties of *Lyonothamnus.*

Prunus lyoni, a large fruited cherry 'tree,' is a bush found on San Clemente, Santa Catalina, Santa Cruz, and most recently on Anacapa by Mr. Sumner. Trask, Greene, and Cornell refer to it [J334, J72, J187], with Cornell including a photo of the bush.

Another tree-like bush on Santa Cruz Island is *Ceanothus arboreus.* It is of the buckthorn family, and according to Greene and Brandegee, was new to science. This bush also may be found on Santa Rosa, and Santa Catalina Islands.

Castilleia hololeuca also falls in the "new to science" category, and is found on Santa Cruz, Santa Rosa, and San Miguel Islands.

As far back as 1890 there has been a discussion of the morning glory, *Convolvulus occidentalis macrostegius Greene* [J393]. Brandegee said that Professor Greene gathered it from Santa Cruz Island, Dr. Gray from San Clemente Island, Mr. Lyon from Santa Catalina Island, and Mr. Brandegee from Santa Rosa Island. Mr. Sumner found it on Santa Barbara Island and San Miguel Island, and Mr. Hoffmann located it on Anacapa. Only San Nicolas is left out of this distribution.

Cornell referred to a white morning glory on Santa Cruz [B83, 1938]. The reader is referred to S. B. Parish, "A Sketch of the Flora of Southern California" [U50, 1903], *Botanical Gazette* for like subject matter.

Dendromecon Harfordii, the tree poppy, was described by Kellogg for Santa Cruz, as was *Grindelia latifolia,* a succulent herb. Similar subject matter may be found in Brandegee [J61, 1888] and Greene [J72, 1887; J74, 1941]. Apparently the two plants are also on Santa Rosa Island.

Hazardia detonsa, a multi-stemmed shrub, was found on Santa Cruz and was described by Greene for Kellogg. *Saxifraga malvaefolia,* a perennial herb, now known as *Jepsonia malvaefolia,* was also described by Greene for Kellogg. Hoffmann found it "growing almost rankly" in 1930 [J376]. Apparently it is on five of the islands, but it is not on Santa Barbara, Anacapa, and San Miguel.

And, finally, *Eriogonum arborescena,* a wild buckwheat, was described by Greene for Kellogg. Trask found it on San Clemente [B38], and it is listed by Raven [B120], as being on Santa Rosa, Santa Cruz, and Anacapa islands. Should its existence on San Clemente be correct, this wild buckwheat is found on both northern and southern islands of the archipelago.

Cornell [B83], referred to two wild buckwheat species which may be found on Santa Cruz and Santa Rosa. Thus, there may be three or four species for the islands as a whole. *Eriogonum giganteum* subsp. *giganteum* is mentioned as an endemic for Santa Catalina and San Clemente [B120, J158, J334]. *Eriogonum nudum* is given for San Clemente by Trask [J334].

Toyon, *Heteromeles arbutifolia,* sometimes called California Holly, is not endemic to the islands, but when in bloom it is very impressive [J74]. Greene spoke of it for Santa Cruz [J72], Holder for Santa Catalina [B38], and Greene for San Nicolas [J252].

Evidently Alice Eastwood [J74], also found the *Comarostaphylos diversifolia,* a shrub, just as impressive. Of it, she said,

> This genus, founded on a Mexican plant, has characteristics of *Arbutus* and *Arctostaphylos* and is very different from the typical Californian manzanitas. When I was on Santa Cruz, the bushes were loaded with red berries and the color could be seen from the sea, more conspicuous than the green foliage.

Chaparral and manzanita grow profusely on Santa Cruz. Raven [B120], uses the name, *Arcotostaphylos* var. *subcordata,* for the single-island endemic manzanita found on Santa Cruz.

Arctostaphylos insularis is given as an endemic for both Santa Cruz and Santa Rosa. *Arctostaphylos catalinae* [J158], is the species on Santa Catalina. Evidently, there are about six varieties for the islands.

There are five *Malacothrix* to be found on the islands. This lava daisy goes by the name of *Malacothrix foliosa* for San Clemente and Santa Barbara islands; *Malacothrix indecora* for San Nicolas, Santa Cruz, and San Miguel islands; *Malacothrix insularis* for Santa Barbara, Anacapa, Santa Cruz, and Santa Rosa islands; *Malacothrix implicata* is named for the islands of San Nicolas, Anacapa, Santa Cruz, Santa Rosa, and San Miguel [B120]; and Trask called one *Malacothrix* "new," when she found it on San Clemente [J334]. Santa Catalina has apparently been left out for the whereabouts of this daisy, and Santa Cruz is the one island which seems to have three of the five varieties listed for it.

Pinus remorata is one of nine Willow Creek species referred to by Chaney and Mason [N3]. See also *Madroño,* 1930. The pine now lives on Santa Cruz and Santa Rosa, supposedly the only two islands where it grows.

It is known that at one time it lived at Carpinteria; Pleistocene deposits so indicate. This fact is considered another proof of a land connection between the islands and the mainland.

Alice Eastwood mentioned three groves of *Pinus remorata* on the island of Santa Cruz, "one of the largest facing the harbor." The reader is referred to page 153 of B120 for more on this pine by another author.

Not an endemic, but a native plant is *Leptosyne gigantea* [J72], now known as *Coreopsis Gigantea.* Today, it is found on Santa Cruz, but it is also found on San Nicolas [P54], Anacapa [J72], and Santa Barbara Island [N52]. Munz states that it is on all of the islands. At any rate, it appears to be a north-south, non-endemic species, even though it was first pointed out at Santa Cruz by Kellogg and Harford.

When it comes to other trees than those already mentioned for the island of Santa Cruz, Greene and/or Brandegee have more or less completely spelled them out [J72/J61]:

Author	Latin name	Popular name	Status
Greene	*Acer Macrophyllum*	large leaved maple	non-endemic
	Populus trichocarpa	black cottonwood	non-endemic
	Pinus remorata	pine	endemic
	Salix Laevigata	willow	non-endemic
	Quercus agrifolia	Calif. live oak	non-endemic
	Quercus chrysolepis	canyon oak	non-endemic
	Quercus dumosa	scrub oak	non-endemic
Greene (& Holder)	*Quercus MacDonaldii*	oak	endemic
Brandegee	*Quercus lobata*	valley oak	non-endemic
	Populus Fremonti	common cottonwood	non-endemic
Trask	*Quercus tomentella*	oak	endemic

Greene [J258], stated that there are no sycamores, *Platanus racemosa,* on Santa Cruz. McElrath remarked on the imported eucalyptus to the island; Chaney and Mason said that there are imported cypress on Santa Cruz, but on other islands the cypress is native.

Listings of island plant species have changed dramatically since first attempted. However, Santa Cruz will continue to hold its own in terms of numbers of species, endemic or otherwise. The study is an ongoing one for botanists, and the layman has difficulty in following their literature—for several reasons.

Fauna

There is something to say about the fauna of every island, sparse though it may be. In line with this thought, we find the fox and the skunk on Santa Cruz to be different from those on the mainland.

No doubt the earliest references to the fox come from the U. S. Geographical Survey approximately one hundred years ago [N45, 1876]. It was then that Dr. Loew, Dr. Rothrock and Mr. Henshaw spent about two weeks on the island of Santa Cruz, pursuing related investigations.

Dr. Loew reported [#H6 of JJ, N45]:

> . . . The most interesting animal, . . . is a fox, (*Vulpes littoralis,* Baird,) not larger than a housecat, . . . It agrees in almost every particular, except in size, with the twice-as-large *Vulpes Virginianus* of the mainland. The principal food of the small fox consists of grasshoppers, as Mr. Henshaw ascertained by dissection. There can be hardly a doubt that this animal was gradually produced by the diminishing of the size of the common fox which searched on that island in vain for a more substantial food than grasshoppers, nothing else being attainable; and thus furnishing an argument in support of the theory of transmutation of species by isolation, recently advanced by Moritz Wagner. Truly there are sea-birds whose eggs would be welcomed by this fox, but these birds are too cunning not to pick out the most secure spot for their young . . .

While Mr. Henshaw was on the islands, and particularly Santa Cruz, he made quite a large collection of zoological specimens, including birds, insects, reptiles, and fish. In discussing the Island Fox [#H12 of JJ, N45], he, too, must have found them fascinating little creatures:

> . . . In passing over the terrace-like plateaus, where the cactus-plants were tolerably thick, I had no difficulty in starting up one of these animals every few moments. No fewer than fifteen were seen in a two hours' walk. Of timidity they showed scarcely a trace, and fear of man had certainly never been inherited by the individuals I saw . . . I had no difficulty in catching one [of the litter] . . . The little fellow made no attempt to bite, but immediately began to howl most lustily, when the mother came trotting out from some retreat hard by, and, approaching to within a few feet, looked up into my face with a most earnest, pleading expression, which effectually deprived me of all desire to do injury either to her or her offspring. After a moment's silent pleading, she slowly walked off, keeping an eye on my every motion, and, having withdrawn a short distance, awaited til my departure gave her a chance to regain her progeny.

D. B. Rogers referred to the Island Fox in *Prehistoric Man* [B63, 1929], but seemingly added nothing to the discussion. However, his reference to having received aid from an authority in matters of mammalogy, Mr. Donald R. Dickey, California Institute of Technology, is reassuring.

Mr. E. Z. Rett explained to Dr. Cockerell [J382, 1937], that "the foxes on Santa Cruz about 1927, got scab from the sheep, and were almost exterminated, though they are now increasing again." Sheldon [P146, 1931], took thirty specimens of the fox to study in 1928-29.

Not only is the little fox 'cute,' it is endemic to six of the Channel Islands; no wonder it is one of the more interesting island species to study.

There is a reprint from the *Los Angeles County Museum Quarterly,* Vol. III [J178, 1943], with photo and chart material, discussing foxes and elephants of the Channel Islands. At that time Dr. Chester Stock, Curator Consultant in Science for the Museum, took about eleven paragraphs for his scientific discussion of the animals. Primarily, however, most discussion of the Dwarf Mammoth is found in the writings of Phil C. Orr.

The fox, still in existence during recent times, and the fossil elephant from the Pleistocene Epoch, is found on the three larger northern islands. Stock, too, felt that the four northern islands were once connected to the mainland at Ventura, and he gave the innovative name, "Cabrillo Peninsula," for this previous connection.

A living species, and probably an endemic, is the skunk. It, too, is found on the three northern islands. Henshaw made mention in 1879 of a Little-Striped

Skunk [H12 of N45], when he quoted,

> *Mephitis* bicolor, Gray—Though known to be a resident of California, none of this diminutive species were noted by our parties. A beautiful specimen was presented me by Captain Forney, of the Coast Survey, he having obtained it from the island of San Miguel, the outermost of the Santa Barbara group.

In 1929 Dr. Donald R. Dickey gave about four pages to the island skunk in, "The Spotted Skunk of the Channel Islands of Southern California" [J52]. Basically, he said that the skunk has been found on Santa Cruz and Santa Rosa islands.

These skunks appear to differ from each other in no essential respect, but there are enough differences in the island series to differentiate them from the mainland species; he thereby called them the Channel Islands Spotted Skunk.

Also in 1929, D. B. Rogers [B63], remarked,

> Following the retreat of the rain belt and the Monterey Pine, there also probably passed northward the little Spotted Skunk, and in its place there came a modified form more closely akin to the sub-species found in the warm, barren, near-desert region to the southeast.

Dr. Carey Stanton, as late as 1967, said that there are a few civet cats on Santa Cruz Island [B107]. He was referring to the little skunk.

Concluding remarks on the Channel Island Skunk are through R. G. Van Gelder [J226, 1965]. He theorized on how the creature got to the islands, reminding us that no fossil skunks from the islands have been found. He wondered if they arrived by raft, through man, or on their own four little feet, while there was still a peninsular mainland connection.

When it comes to the mice for the island of Santa Cruz, the Deer Mouse, *Peromyscus maniculatus*, is perhaps the most abundant, although two other species are said to exist there.

This Deer Mouse is found on all eight islands. M. B. McKusick [U40, 1959], termed it "white-faced," and a sub-species. Philbrick [U29, 1972], termed it "endemic." J. H. Lipp [J175, 1964], remarked that their bones are to be found in the middens on the three Anacapas. Grinnell, Cockerell, and Holder found this live mouse on the other three northern islands.

Bats for Santa Cruz Island are little mentioned in scientific reports. Rogers [B63], gave a slight note concerning them when he remarked that at dusk he frequently saw them flying about the mouths of canyons.

Later, years 1934, 1939, 1943, other authors referred to bats on the island. Professor von Bloeker [B120, 1967], cited the species for the island: Big-eared Myotis, California Myotis, Big Brown Bat, Lump-nosed Bat, Pallid Bat, and Free-tailed Bat.

Land Snails

Pacific Discovery [J77, 1954], contains any number of useful, enlightening photos of various forms of life on Santa Cruz. Of these U. S. Navy photographs, "Santa Cruz Island—An Island Museum," there is a close-up of the northern island endemic snail, *Helix Ayresiana*.

Probably the situation for the life and death of land snails has been about the same, whether they be *Helix Ayresiana,* or any other species. Yates was referring to *Helix Ayresiana* in "Prehistoric California" [J331, 1903], when he found the shells on the islands of San Miguel, Santa Rosa, Santa Cruz, and the Anacapas about 1878.

To Yates, the dead snails illustrated the "effects of the destruction of the vegetation upon some forms of the animal life of a region." However, there were multitudes of dead snails, left to form tree casts, long before the cattle and sheep industries became a factor in the extermination of the species.

Fewkes [J21, 1890], referred to the snail, as does Cockerell [J319, 1938], in their discussions of sheep vs. snails on the islands.

Herpetofauna

John Van Denburgh [J66, 1905-06], placed the four northern islands in the Upper Austral Zone, and the four southern islands in the San Diegan Faunal Zone.

So little is written on the herpetofauna of the islands that Van Denburgh, California Academy of Sciences, is entitled to considerable respect. Most of his material was lost in the San Francisco fire of 1906. Due to this fact, he and his assistant, Joseph R. Slevin, attempted to repeat their steps on the islands in 1914 [J68].

A *Hyla regilla,* taken by Yarrow and Cope, as reported by Mr. H. W. Henshaw, was collected there. As Van Denburgh [J66], stated it, a *Hyla* and "two species of lizards were taken from Santa Cruz."

Uta stansburiana was collected by Dr. O. Loew in 1875 [J66]. It is said that in 1889 Mr. C. H. Townsend of the *Albatross,* U. S. Fish Commission, took a series of eight *Utas* from Santa Cruz [N4], and later, Mr. Joseph Grinnell took four more [J66].

In 1875 Yarrow and Cope obtained a specimen of *Gerrhonotus scincicanda*. Townsend also reported it in 1889 [J66]. In 1910 Charles F. Holder, who had also been on the islands in those years, stated that the Alligator Lizard, *Gerrhonotus coeruleus* is to be found on Santa Cruz [B38].

Sceloporus becki was reported by Van Denburgh [J66], to have been collected on both Santa Rosa and Santa Cruz islands. By 1914 [J68], Van Denburgh and Slevin stated that three known lizard species existed for Santa Cruz. Blanche L. Trask suggested the Night Lizard, *Klauberina riversiana* [M134, 1906]. Savage [B120] named *Sceloporus occidentalis* and *Gerrhonotus multicarinatus*. Should these species named be correct, or unduplicated, the count would be seven lizard species for the island.

J. M. Savage, U. S. C., listed two salamanders, *Batrachoseps pacificus* and *Batrachoseps sp.* [B120], Van Denburgh [J66], through Beck, named *Batrachoseps attenuatus*, again leaving us uncertain.

Dr. Carey Stanton stated [B107], that although there are several species of snakes on Santa Cruz, none of them are dangerous. The *Symposium* [B120], listed three species. Both publications are of the year 1967.

Other living things on Santa Cruz, according to W. A. Goodyear [C18, 1890], are the insects,

> . . . flies, both bluebottle and domestic, are very plenty, and are a nuisance. Also the fly which exactly resembles the ordinary house fly, except in its proboscis, . . . is a constant plague to animals . . . Ladybugs were seen and gnats were encountered on the high peaks of the eastern part of the island. In some parts also there are occasional swarms of grasshoppers, which sometimes do some damage. But not a single mosquito was seen anywhere on this island . . .

In 1971 Charles F. Remington referred to the flightless pigmy grasshoppers, which the little fox includes in his diet [J251]. In 1941 Auguston found fleas on the island; he was with the Los Angeles Museum Channel Island Biological Survey.

Boars

The wild boars, imported centuries ago, have been an exciting phase of an island experience for some. The stories about them are unscientific, the creatures are not endemic, but both create reading material for those in need of respite from purely academic thoughts. One of the better boaring-accounts is found in *Southern California Historical Society Quarterly* [J369, 1945].

Although the account is mainly concerned with the life of William Staat, it also contains inside information on how the Bannings effected the change to their ownership of Santa Catalina Island. Additionally, there are a few words on Hancock Banning and friend "Billy's" visit to Santa Cruz through the invitation of a son of Justinian Caire,

> [They found] rows of grape-laden vineyards and acres of green gardens; but only forty-five regular inhabitants, all Italian and Spanish-speaking, . . . herds of sheep and cattle . . . pine and manzanita . . . fiendish cactus, out of which a furious wild hog darted suddenly to give zest to the visitors' morning ride. Only Hancock's steady aim saved disaster as their horses reared in fright; but the party sailed for home bearing a boar's head with four-inch tusk, a trophy well worth the fracas.

Kirk [P129, 1905], told of a boar encounter,

> . . . Recently a gentleman went up the canyon to sleep, that he might politely meet his boarship half way. When the meeting occurred, the boar was clad only in erect bristles and gleaming tusks and the gentleman in undress pajamas. It took four shots to silence his boarship, and the man between shots sprinted in bare feet and flying pajamas to the friendly cover of the largest rocks and trees he could find.

Lewis Barbour [P153, 1939], gets into the act with, "Boars are never Bores," when he described one boar as being six feet long, short-legged, high-shouldered with typical coarse bristles, and tusks at least five inches long.

Charles Hillinger of the *Los Angeles Times* [M154, 1956], corroberates the appearance of these wild boars and suggested that these several hundred wild things on Santa Cruz offer many inducements for being hunted, one of the reasons being the animal's ability to root up acres of land and to destroy fences in their paths.

Marine Creatures

Although Captain Kimberly had noted sea otter around Santa Cruz when he lived there as a squatter in 1855, their near extermination has not been conducive to placing the hunted species in the literature—other than to mention this fact of near-extermination.

PIECES OF EIGHT

It is the not-quite-so-near-extermination of the seals in that area that makes for a somewhat happier story, if only by degree.

Bonnot [C2, 1928], "Seals and Sea Lions of California," reported two Steller Sea Lion rookeries on Santa Cruz. The California seals were the hunted creatures, and Holder [B38], pointed to the southwest side of Santa Cruz as the location where many of them were captured for sale purposes. Boxed, hoisted, and launched, they were shipped to museums or zoological gardens all over the world.

M. J. Phillips [B56, 1927], gave another area near the island where these seals were caught, "at the precipitous upper end of the island, facing the passage between Santa Cruz and Santa Rosa, is a seal rookery where scores of the animals are bred."

> . . . Performing seals the world over come from Santa Cruz because of [their] intelligence and the docility which is also a striking characteristic.
>
> For many years Capt. George McGuire, a prominent resident of Santa Barbara, caught Santa Cruz seals for vaudeville performers and for American and foreign zoos. He retired a few years ago and the work is now carried on by Capt. Ira Eaton.

Avifauna

From available literature on birds of Santa Cruz Island, there appears to be at least eight articles containing enumerations. Usually, such enumerations indicate whether the birds were merely observed, or taken as specimens. These lists, although not mutually exclusive, could be most helpful.

1887	J35	Blake	*Auk*	28 species
1891	J398	Keller	*Zoe*	20 species
1900	N5	Oberholser	*U. S. Nat. Mus.*	25 species
1908	J113	Linton	*Condor*	4 pages
1911	J126	Howell	*Condor*	66 species not on J113
1913	J127	Wright	*Condor*	37 species
1915	J132	Dawson	*Condor*	80 species, 15 not previously reported
1951	J153	Miller	*Condor*	18 species

It remained for Alden H. Miller [J153, 1951], to offer his perception of the island's endemics, all but the jay belonging to other islands,

Orange-crowned Warbler	*Vermivora celata sordida*
Allen Hummingbird	*Selasphorus sasin sedentarius*
Loggerhead Shrike	*Lanius ludovicianus anthonyi*
Horned Lark	*Eremophila Alpestris insularis*
Song Sparrow	*Melospiza melodia clementae*
Bewick Wren	*Thryomanes bewickii nesophilus*
Santa Cruz Scrub Jay	*Aphelocoma coerulescens insularis*

About thirteen species of birds have been given more active interest than a brief listing, chief among them being the Santa Cruz Scrub Jay.

In Miller's same article, he resurrected Keller's 1891 comments about a considerable number of the northern birds being Sonoran in character. He did this by suggesting that some of the species, more particularly those of Santa Rosa Island, "indicate racial affinities toward populations on the more southern Channel Islands."

"C. B." [Linton?] mentioned in *Condor* [J101, 1899], that Mr. Rollo H. Beck "took the first recorded nests and eggs [May, 1897] of the Santa Cruz Jay on Santa Cruz Island." Beck's comments on the jay in "Nesting of the Santa Cruz Jay," is also in *Condor* [J100, 1899]. Beck was at Scorpion Harbor, 1895, and the west end, 1897.

In *Auk* [J34, 1886], there is a short article by H. W. Henshaw in which he stated that "while on a short visit to the island in June, 1875, [he] collected three specimens [of the jay] . . . Mr. Ridgway has kindly called my attention to the fact that . . . the island specimens still remain unique. I therefore hesitate no longer to describe them as representing a new species . . ."

Henshaw, in Keller, "Geographical Distribution of Land Birds in California" [J398, 1891], stated that this jay is larger in size, has deeper colors, and there is blue instead of white under tail-coverts; "being non-migratory their continued residence under new conditions has effected very considerable changes of size and coloration."

Joseph Mailliard had been on the island as early as 1898 and through *Condor* [J102], tells us,

170

Naturally enough a sight of the Santa Cruz Jay (*Aphelocoma insularis*) was eagerly desired, but it was some days before one was seen. There were no Jays within a mile or two of this harbor but some were found where the first brush commenced on the steep hillsides toward the head of Scorpion Cañon. In fact they were quite numerous among the brushy hills but were very difficult to approach more from the nature of the ground than from their wariness, though they were here comparatively shy . . . Two were taken at last in the cañon, but all the rest that fell to my lot were captured at Laplaya . . .

Among the live-oaks, . . . birds were numerous and an early morning tramp with a good deal of patience thrown in would generally be rewarded, though a dozen birds actually in one's hand by ten o'clock would be a pretty fair record, as it was not only difficult to get shots at what one wanted but also frequently more difficult to retrieve the game . . . In this locality the Santa Cruz Jay was very abundant and bold. Many were shot with the auxiliary barrel, being too close to use a larger charge.

In a 1900 issue of *Condor* [J105] Mr. Mailliard offered "Measurements of the Santa Cruz Jay," quite technical in content.

By 1915 *Condor* produced yet another article in which the jay is mentioned [J132], as W. L. Dawson said,

Through the courtesy of our distinguished fellow-member, Mr. Joseph Mailliard, and his friend, Mr. Arturo Caire, one of the present owners of Santa Cruz Island, I was permitted to spend nearly three weeks, viz., April 3rd to 22nd, with my son William, on this enchanted spot. We made camp at Prisoners' Harbor and devoted ourselves chiefly to the study of the endemic Jay, . . . of which sixteen nests were found.

Dr. Thomas R. Howell believed the jay to be a divergent, not a relict of the continental form [B120].

The Island Shrike is another species which has been followed by ornithologists as early as 1897. In Edgar A. Mearns' *Auk* article [J41, 1898], he tells us that on "Santa Cruz Island, May 6 to 11, 1897, Mr. R. H. Beck collected nine adult Shrikes and one young of the year, which were generously placed in my hands for description . . . of the Shrikes, Mr. Beck had said, 'They were the wildest land birds I ever saw by far.' "

Mr. Mailliard [J102, 1898], did not feel as Mr. Beck, Mr. Townsend or Mr. Mearns did about the Shrikes being "wild," but he did have this to say about them,

Shrikes were numerous . . . A few were lost by my not using a sufficiently heavy charge in my desire to preserve the plummage as intact as possible, but many of the specimens shot fell into the large piles of dead brush which they frequented extensively. On one of these brush piles three were bowled over at one shot and not one recovered. This pile was about six feet high and thirty feet across, the birds being in the center when fired at. While trying to find them, a nest of seven eggs was discovered and taken but the birds had slipped down irretrievably. They must have been having some sort of a row over this nest when shot. Another nest containing six eggs of this species was taken and one or two found which were not completed when I left.

This Shrike goes by the Latin name of *Lanius ludovicianus anthonyi* [J41], after Mr. A. W. Anthony of the National Museum, and was declared a new subspecies. The bird may be found on Santa Cruz, Santa Barbara, Anacapa, Santa Catalina, and Santa Rosa Islands, said Oberholser [J49, 1922].

Wright and Snyder visited Santa Barbara Island and the four northern islands in the summer of 1912. On this particular trip it was the Ashy Petrel that took the limelight [J129],

It was not until the far end of the island was reached that the "prize find" of the trip was made. We had stopped to explore the "Painted Cave" from a scenic point of view, but once there the great number of Pigeon Guillemots present invited search for their nests . . . The way was dark and as the lantern was flashed about to find secure footing it fell on a small bird crouched on the open floor of the ledge. The bird, evidently blinded by the light, was easily captured and proved to be an Ashy Petrel brooding a well incubated egg. Thus encouraged, a most careful search was made with the result that four eggs and one small young, together with the adults, were taken. The "nests" were all entirely exposed, though one was in a shallow hole in the rocky side of the cave.

Joseph Grinnell noted that *Vireo mailliardorum* is a permanent resident of Santa Cruz [J107, 1903]. In 1898 Joseph Mailliard had secured three specimens of the bird there, mentioning some of its points of difference with *Vireo huttoni* of the mainland.

PIECES OF EIGHT

Then Grinnell remarked that the species was named for Joseph and John Mailliard, "whose conscientious work with western birds deserves at least this slight token of our recognition."

In 1898, Mailliard had some experiences with the Horned Lark. He said [J102],

> The tops of the adjacent hills and some of the more rolling slopes were the abiding places at this time of numerous Island Horned Larks *(Otocoris alpestris insularis),* some thirty of which were captured . . . The birds would flush from small hollows, from the shadows of small rocks, tufts of grass, sides of trails etc., but no sign of a nest could be found . . . I came to the conclusion that their feeding and nesting grounds were not the same, and the latter remained undiscovered.

In 1899, Beck also referred to them but did not give a Latin name [J103],

> On the west end of the island there is an open, rolling stretch of land running back from the cliffs along shore. On this mesa the Horned Larks were abundant. Two nests were collected on Santa Cruz and one on San Miguel Islands. They were located by flushing the bird from the nest. In every case the nest was nearly stepped on before the bird flew and in each case it was placed in a small bunch of grass in a slight hollow and was right on the feeding ground.

Miller, 1951, listed the Horned Lark under the Latin name of *Eremophila alpestris insularis,* somewhat confusing for the amateur ornithologist.

We are not much better off with exact identification of the Spotted Towhee. Mailliard [J102, 1898], "was especially desirous of obtaining a number of specimens of the Towhee *(Pipilo maculatus _____)* of the island, but they were too wild and wary. Only one pair was taken."

Beck [J103, 1899] reported, "I found the towhee *Pipilo maculatus oregonus)* not very wild and secured without much trouble a dozen or so. Among those taken was a partial albino having many white feathers scattered among the black on the head and neck."

Keller [J398, 1891], used the Latin name of *Pipilo maculatus megalonyx* as did Miller [J153, 1951]. Confused?

There may be some surprise, but apparently no question about the Song Sparrow. While *Melospiza melodia graminea* is confined to Santa Barbara, *Melospiza melodia clementae* has been found on San Clemente, Santa Cruz, Santa Rosa, San Miguel, and

perhaps Anacapa [J398, 1891; J135, 1924].

Of the Wrens, it appears that a new subspecies exists on Santa Cruz and Santa Rosa—the *Thryomanes Bewickii Nesophilus.* This information comes from C. H. Townsend through H. C. Oberholser of the United States National Museum [N5, 1899], in "A Revision of the Wrens of the Genus *Thryomanes Sclater.*"

Willett, Senior Curator of Ornithology of Southern California Academy of Sciences [B115, 1933], gave us a lead when it came to White Pelicans. He reminded us that they visit lakes, slough, and marsh lands in fall, winter, and spring, one of their breeding places being the Salton Sea.

This makes it possible to consider another of C. F. Holder's statements when he said,

> At Santa Catalina, Anacapa, and Santa Cruz the royal tern is one of the most attractive birds in winter . . . I have (also) seen flocks of geese, ducks, and even *white pelicans* at Santa Cruz . . . I once saw a wood duck at Santa Cruz, and the American egret and the snowy heron . . . The wandering tattler is common at all the islands, and at Santa Cruz I saw a curlew . . . the great *band-tailed pigeon* . . . is seen at times at Santa Cruz and Santa Rosa . . . In winter flocks of loons and other sea birds enter the bay, and I have seen them at San Nicholas and Santa Cruz, so tame that they merely swam to the right and left as our boat moved along.

The reader recalls Holder as being the first to report the Brown Pelican at Anacapa.

Ralph Hoffmann, an ornithologist as well as a botanist, contributes to the subject of band-tailed pigeons [J148, 1932],

> Mr. Fred Caire reports a flock of about one hundred and fifty Band-tailed Pigeons (Columba fasciata) at the main ranch on Santa Cruz Island. He states that he has seen band-tails once before on the island, but there are no records for [it].

The subject of owls and woodpeckers on Santa Cruz Island came to the fore in 1898 [J102], when Mailliard commented that "No Owls or Woodpeckers . . . were seen or heard, nor had even the oldest inhabitant any knowledge of the presence of an Owl on the island, by sight or hearing."

On these two birds Ralph Hoffmann [J145, 1931], commented in *Condor.* With a paragraph on each bird, Hoffmann said that on April 15, 1931, he saw the owl *(Cryptoglaux acadica)* near Pelican Harbor,

172

where the writer studied it for considerable time.

In Miller's Miscellaneous Records [J153, 1951], he offered the information that "A Burrowing Owl was taken, substantiating the reports of the ranchers on the island that the species is established on it."

In 1930 Mr. Hoffmann noted the California Woodpecker at Scorpion Harbor, the Main Ranch, and Valdez Harbor. He felt that the woodpecker might have "invaded the island only lately." Miller noted the Acorn Woodpecker in 1951 and Pitelka noted it in 1950.

Perhaps some would like to know the classification of a bird briefly described by McElrath [B107, 1967]. He said that there was a small bird at the west end of the island they called a parrakeet, for want of a better name.

Although it was not much larger than a sparrow, it did have the sparrow's coloring, but a bill typical of a parrakeet. This 'parrakeet' seemed to remain in the area over its many acres where there was low brush and cactus. He wondered why a flock of tropical birds would settle on the island, making it a permanent home, especially on the windy and cold end of the island.

Although these few pages cannot suffice for a thorough review of the literature on Santa Cruz Island Ornithology, perhaps they will assist in opening avenues for further study. More help may come from a few additional records: *Auk,* J38, 1897; J49, 1922; *Condor,* J108, 1905; J117, 1908; J128, 1913; J134, 1923; J137, 1926; B114, 1917, *Birds of the Islands off the Coast of Southern California.*

Photos of Santa Cruz Island

Date	Code #	Author	Title	Reference
			Arches	
1897	P45	Owens	The Arch	*Land of Sunshine*
1910	B38	Holder	The Twin Arches	*Channel Islands of California*
1941	B128	Writers'	Arch Rock	*A Guide to the Channel City*
			Fauna	
1931	P146	Sheldon	A blind fox	*Westways*
1954	J77	Woodbridge	Bright-eyed fox	*Pacific Discovery*
1954	J77	Woodbridge	Endemic snail	*Pacific Discovery*
1962	M47	Hall	Native Wild Foxes	*Odyssey of the Calif. Kingdoms*
1967	M168	Linze	A fox watches the hunters	*L.A. Times*
			Flora	
1954	J77	Woodbridge	Tree poppy	*Pacific Discovery*
1954	J77	Woodbridge	Catalina Ironwood	*Pacific Discovery*
1962	M47	Hall	Almond tree in bloom	*Odyssey of the Calif. Kingdoms*
1967	B120	Axelrod	Northern population (flora)	*Symposium*
1967	B120	Axelrod	Western population (flora)	*Symposium*
			Interior	
1922	P144	McGaffey	Mount Diablo	*Touring Topics*
1929	B63	Rogers	Our Camp at Christie's	*Prehistoric Man*
1954	J77	Woodbridge	Sierra Blanca	*Pacific Discovery*
1954	J77	Woodbridge	Ornamental doorway, Christy Ranch	*Pacific Discovery*
1956	M154	Hillinger	Tiny Church, erected in 1891	*L.A. Times*
1956	M154	Hillinger	French-Mediterranean (the Apartment)	*L.A. Times*
1958	J218	Warren, Jr.	Hills hide an Idyllic Vale	*National Geographic*
1962	M47	Hall	Caire Chapel	*Odyssey of the Calif. Kingdoms*
1962	M47	Hall	Stanton Ranch (2)	*Odyssey of the Calif. Kingdoms*
1962	M47	Hall	The Caire House	*Odyssey of the Calif. Kingdoms*
1963	P166	Hillinger	Bricks fired from clay built ranch houses	*Westways*
			Lady's Harbor	
1891	P87	Kinsell	Camp at Lady Harbor	*Overland Monthly*
1897	P45	Owens	Ladies Harbor	*Land of Sunshine*
			Painted Cave	
1897	J309	Holder	Entrance to Painted Cave	*Scientific American*
1897	P45	Owens	Painted Cave	*Land of Sunshine*
1922	P144	McGaffey	Painted Cave	*Touring Topics*
1922	P144	McGaffey	Inside Painted Cave	*Touring Topics*
1967	P135		Painted Cave, Greatest Grotto on Island	*Sunset*
1969	P173	Ashkenazy	Through the Arch of Painted Cave	*Westways*
			Pelican Bay	
1904	M128	Walker	Indian skulls, Pelican Bay	*L.A. Times*
1905	P129	Kirk	Pelican Bay, safe anchorage	*Sunset*

174

Date	Code #	Author	Title	Reference
1922	P144	McGaffey	Pelican Bay	*Touring Topics*
1927	B56	Phillips	Pelican Bay	*History of Santa Barbara County*
1929	B63	Rogers	Eatons Camp, Pelican Bay	*Prehistoric Man*
1941	B128	Writers'	Pelican Bay	*A Guide to the Channel City*
1963	J376	Wright	Pelican Bay [Concession]	*So. Calif. Historical Soc.*
1967	P135		Yachts congregate at Pelican Bay	*Sunset*

People

Date	Code #	Author	Title	Reference
1964	P167	Roe	Justinian and Albina Caire	*Westways*

Prisoners' Harbor

Date	Code #	Author	Title	Reference
1896	P44	Earle	Windmill, house; Prisoners' Harbor	*Land of Sunshine*
1904	M126	Walker	Brick Residence, Prisoners' Harbor	*L.A. Times*
1904	M126	Walker	Wool Warehouse at Prisoners' Harbor	*L.A. Times*
1931	P146	Sheldon	Mouth of Portesuelo Creek, Prisoners' Harbor	*Westways*
1944	N51	Wheeler	Prisoners' Harbor	*U.S. Naval Instit. Proceedings*
1956	M154	Hillinger	Prisoners' Harbor (pier)	*L.A. Times*
1966	M112		Prisoners' Harbor	*L.A. Examiner*

Valdez Cave

Date	Code #	Author	Title	Reference
1897	P45	Owens	Cueva Valdez (2)	*Land of Sunshine*
1902	P178	Anonymous	The Cave of Valdez	*The World's Work*
1905	P129	Kirk	Looking out of Valdez Cave on Sands of Harbor	*Sunset*
1905	P129	Kirk	Valdez Cave and Harbor (excellent)	*Sunset*
1910	B38	Holder	Great Cave of Valdez	*Channel Islands of Calif.*
1917	B25	Gidney	Valdez Cave	*Hist. of S.B., S.L.O., & V. Cntys.*
1920	B123	Southworth	Valdez Cave	*Santa Barbara and Montecito*
1929	B63	Rogers	Looking out from within Valdez	*Prehistoric Man*
1954	J79	Lange	The entrance to Cueva Valdez	*Pacific Discovery*
1962	B119	Rockwell	Valdez Cave, interior (excellent)	*California's Sea Frontier*

Miscellaneous

Date	Code #	Author	Title	Reference
1922	P144	McGaffey	Fry's Harbor, at anchor	*Touring Topics*
1927	B56	Phillips	A Sheltered Cove	*History of Santa Barbara County*
1929	B63	Rogers	Coches Prietos Bay (bldgs.)	*Prehistoric Man*
1931	P146	Sheldon	Fishing fleet, Willow Cove	*Westways*
1941	B128	Writers'	Forney's Cove, habitat of Sea Lions	*A Guide to the Channel City*
1944	N51	Wheeler	Chinese Harbor	*U.S. Naval Instit. Proceedings*
1949	J270	Orr	The *Orca* and crew, Willows Anchorage	*Santa Barbara Museum Talk*
1954	J77	Woodbridge	Looking across China Bay	*Pacific Discovery*
1954	J77	Woodbridge	Diatomite at Smugglers' Cove	*Pacific Discovery*
1954	J79	Lange	Sponge Cave, a cavern	*Pacific Discovery*

Date	Code #	Author	Title	Reference
1967			Chinese Harbor	*Gateway,* to the Channel Islands
1967			Potato Bay	*Gateway,* to the Channel Islands
1967	P135		Coches Prietos anchorage	*Sunset*
1969	P173	Ashkenazy	Profile Point	*Westways*

Maps and Sketches

Date	Code #	Author	Title	Reference
1877	N41	Schumacher	Map of Los Alamos, Indian Sites	*U.S. Geolog. & Geogra. Survey*
1889	C18	Goodyear	U.S. Coast and Geodetic Survey Map (good)	*9th An. Rpt., State Mineralogist*
1896	P114	Schumacher	Sketch of Tinker's Cove; archaeol.	*Popular Science Monthly*
1905	P129	Kirk	Government Survey, many place names	*Sunset*
1929	B63	Rogers	Map, Indian sites	*Prehistoric Man*
1932	J297	Bremner	Fine map(s), topographic, geologic	*Geology of Santa Cruz Island*
1958	J218	Warren, Jr.	Map, indicating Missile Tracking Station, etc.	*National Geographic*

Santa Rosa

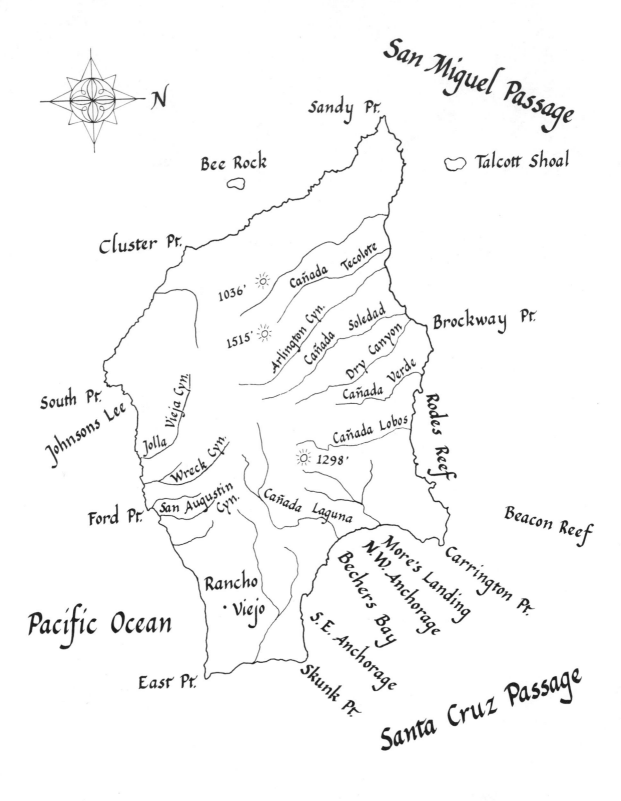

San Miguel Passage

N

Sandy Pt.

Talcott Shoal

Bee Rock

Cluster Pt.

1036′ Cañada Tecolote

1515′ Arlington Cyn. Cañada Soledad

Brockway Pt.

Dry Canyon

Cañada Verde

South Pt.

Johnsons Lee

Jolla Vieja Cyn.

Cañada Lobos

Rodes Reef

Jolla

Wreck Cyn.

1298′

Ford Pt.

San Augustin Cyn.

Cañada Laguna

Beacon Reef

More's Landing

N.W. Anchorage

Bechers Bay

Carrington Pt.

Pacific Ocean

Rancho
· Viejo

S.E. Anchorage

East Pt.

Skunk Pt.

Santa Cruz Passage

Santa Rosa

Geology and Allied Subjects

Lying five miles westward of Santa Cruz, Santa Rosa Island is said by Davidson to resemble a parallelogram, "with the direction of the longer axis almost exactly east and west, and fifteen miles in length [between East Point and Sandy Point]; and the shorter north and south, with a width of ten miles [an average of seven and one-half miles] . . . The hills are rolling, and covered with coarse grass and bushes" [N28, 1857-58].

Of the island, Reed in 1933 said that the island is largely grass-covered, and he added, "with many clear streams draining from the hills 1000-1500 feet high and with a thick section of Tertiary rocks ranging in age from Eocene to Upper Miocene . . ." [B118].

Dr. Le Conte taught geology at the University of California from about 1872 to 1892. It was during this period of time, circa 1887, that he correlated the flora of the Coast Islands with the thought that these islands had once been a part of the mainland, and, as he termed them, continental islands [J73].

A. C. Lawson followed Le Conte as a professor at the University, and became the Departmental Chairman from 1906-28. Regardless of Lawson's views, or even of Davidson's, there were sharp differences as to what happened along our Pacific Coast in geologic times.

Two of the subjects debated by others concern the lava formations and the terraces of the various islands. Lawson thought that the lava caves were formed during the molten period. Davidson concluded that the terraces were a product of ice-flows during the Pleistocene. But there appears to be evi-

179

dence of neither having been determining factors in the islands' geologic history.

Yates cannot be disregarded when it comes to theories. He felt that the weaker spots, present-day caves, in the lava were a result of wave action—and not originally formed when lava was overflowing. Then,

> After the lava flow the islands were submerged and an extensive series of strata of sand, gravel and silt were deposited, of which the greater portion have since been eroded.
>
> Some of these strata contain well-preserved fossil shells, and on Santa Rosa Island bones and teeth of the Fossil Elephant have been found by the writer and others, showing the connection of the island with the mainland during recent geologic periods [J327, 1902].

Goodyear [C18, 1890], thought there never had been a connection between the islands and the mainland; today, however, most geologists accept the land-connection theory—the fossil elephant findings on Santa Rosa being practically conclusive proof of its existence. [See also U53].

Yates offered [U52, 1890] a theory on the location of a land connection,

> It will be observed that the Anacapa Santa Cruz; Santa Rosa and San Miguel islands are on a line with point Dumas on the east and are parallel with the San Ynes mountains . . .; at this point the islands were doubtless once connected with the main land, and what is now the Santa Barbara channel was then a gulf or arm of the sea, beginning at Point Conception and running in a south-easterly direction for, say 150 miles.
>
> When these islands were thus connected with the mainland, it was easy for them to become inhabited by the larger vertebrates.

In 1929 Rogers had this to say about the Santa Rosa Island, and island Indians [B63],

> . . . Whence did this people migrate? This question, probably the most important one in connection with the study of the islanders, is also the most difficult to answer . . . That they were directly derived from Central Asian stock is strongly indicated . . . In many ways, their culture much more closely resembled that of the Aleuts than that of their nearest neighbors . . . leads me to believe that we have, in the Canalino, representatives of a race which had, for many generations, clung to the coastal is-

lands, in the long migration from northeastern Asia.

Some of the present day authorities make the land connection for the northern islands around the Ventura area; Stock gave the name "Cabrillo Peninsula" to a former land extension from that point.

Other pegs for hanging ideas come to us, mainly by geologists, as "Anacapia," "Santarosae," "Catalinia," "Guadalupia," "Inshore," "Large," "Large offshore," "Northern Channel Islands," "Southern Channel Islands." Perhaps we should also find a name for Yates' gulf or arm—equivalent to present day Baja California and its Gulf of California!

There has not been one presented theory of mainland connection, or lack of connection, which outweighs another; each has its weakness as a postulate. Yet, seemingly no one has discussed in print, the pros and cons of the Yates theory. There must be a few positive factors going for it.

Reed said that a D. B. Seymour mapped the geology of Santa Rosa Island for the Continental Oil Co. Standard Oil Co. did some study of the island's geology, and through them from William S. W. Kew [J164, 1927], it is explained that the Vaqueros, a Lower Miocene strata, is essentially a sandstone and everywhere it exists on the island it is characterized by the presence of many well-preserved fossils. And in an abstract on Kew's findings [J165, 1928], we are told that the other islands of the group differ from Santa Rosa in that they are formed mainly of volcanic rocks.

By 1949 there had been five oil wells drilled but abandoned, with a sixth in progress [J24]. Robert E. Anderson, *et al,* of Signal Oil Co., remarked that the dominant structural feature of the island is its fault with an east-west trend, which divided the island into two parts. They also said that there had been a horizontal displacement of nearly five miles along the fault.

Kew [J164], had said that the displacement was about ten miles in length, with the north block moving west in relation to the south block.

In 1812 there had been a great earthquake which struck the California coast, doing much damage. During this quake, "a large crack, 1000 yards long, more than 100 feet wide, and 50 or 60 feet deep opened up in Cañada Lobo" [Lobos] on the north coast of Santa Rosa [B54, 1968]. And it was in 1812, and shortly thereafter, that the remaining Indians of the island, perhaps in extreme fright, left the island on a permanent basis.

Dr. Lorenzo G. Yates

Rev. Stephen Bowers in 1885, in his own local publication *Pacific Science Monthly* [P113], first, but briefly, recognized Dr. Yates and his efforts.

Of the Yates' collections he had this to say, "Dr. L. G. Yates, of Santa Barbara has the largest collection of fossils, minerals and shells that is to be found on the Pacific Coast . . . His catalogue of specimens . . . will make several volumes."

And in a small footnote elsewhere, Bowers referred to assistance through Dr. Yates for the geological aspects of his, "Santa Rosa Island," in the 1877 Annual Report of the Smithsonian Institution [N12].

Ten years later, the *Land of Sunshine* [P42], written by "J. B. B." offered the readers a more comprehensive review of "The Yates Collections." Fully a whole page was given to Yates' material, in addition to saying,

Dr. Lorenzo Gordin Yates, of Santa Barbara, is one of the longest and most extensive collectors on the Coast. It is nearly half a century since he began to gather specimens; and for much more than half that time he has added the skill of the student to the amateur's zeal. Collections from him are now in Wabash College, Ind., the Smithsonian Institute, and Amherst College; but of late years he has been assembling in his own hands an enormous collection in many departments. His line of work has been that of a general educational museum rather than of the final and unswerving specialist; and his private museum would grace an important institution of learning. . .

The collection of Dr. Yates would make a good nucleus for a Southern California scientific and historical museum, if it could be obtained for that purpose. Covering so many different lines of research and outnumbering in not a few of these the largest collections of the coast, and containing many specimens not to be found anywhere else in this country, it would be a fortunate institution that secured such a store-house of treasures.

Although Dr. Yates was on San Nicolas in 1880, and had visited Santa Cruz, most of his efforts were given to the islands of Anacapa, Santa Rosa, and San Miguel. The numbers of visitors to Santa Cruz in the name of Science could have been a deterring factor for Yates;—León de Céssac [U18], Schumacher [N41], the Wheeler Expedition [N54], and the U. S. Coast and Geodetic Survey [N34].

Dr. Yates had been a member of the State Geological Survey under Professor Josiah Dwight Whitney; he had assisted Dr. James Cooper in his bird and insect collecting for Dr. Bache and/or Dr. Baird. Dr. Yates had been an honorary member of the Southern California Academy of Sciences, and an early president of the Santa Barbara Society of Natural History.

Dr. Yates was the person with Blunt and Mr. Voy when he found an elephant tusk on Santa Rosa. President of the California Academy of Sciences, Dr. Davidson [J58, 1868-72], had announced through his secretary, Mr. Blunt, a surveyor for the U. S. Coast and Geodetic Survey, that Blunt had found an elephant tooth on Santa Rosa Island. The fact that Dr. Yates had found an elephant tusk remained unannounced, other than to say that the tusk crumbled.

According to *Journal of the West* [J389, 1963], Charles L. Camp had remarked that the wonderful Yates collection, first loaned to the Los Angeles County Museum in 1912, was sold to A. J. Young in 1936 for $650. Mr. Young sold the collection to J. T. Lowry, a relative of Mrs. Yates, for $10. Young resold it in 1937 to a Frank S. Van Denbergh for $300.

Yates had died in 1909, and real recognition had not come during his lifetime, or even later. From the Court House Tower of Santa Barbara the collection was parceled out to various individuals and institutions. The remaining materials, autobiography, manuscripts, drawings, legends, were deposited in the Bancroft Library, awaiting recognition in the name of Dr. Lorenzo Gordin Yates.

Possible Inter-Island Relationships

San Miguel Island with an east-west axis, lies at the north and westerly end of the extension of the present Santa Monicas. This is in contrast to the north-westerly structural trend of the mainland north of Point Concepción. But Bremner [J298, 1933], said that San Miguel also showed a strong influence toward this latter trend.

Cortes Bank, with its Bishop Rock to the southwest of San Clemente, and San Nicolas with Cortes Shoal to its northeast, are both atop the Santa Rosa-Cortes Ridge [N34]. From Bishop Rock to the west end of San Miguel, the trend of the submarine course is north and west with a distance of 118 miles; Begg Rock being a prolongation of San Nicolas.

Eocene rock has been found on the 'shelf' just north of San Nicolas Island, as it has also been found on the three more westerly islands of the northern group. This is in contrast to the fact that no Eocene strata has been known in the Santa Monica Mountains, of which the northern group is said to be an extension [J23, 1936].

The ocean current gives San Nicolas another link with the Northern Channel Islands. Davidson was writing to Bache [N28], when he said,

> From Point Conception [the current] strikes to the southward and westward, being doubtless influenced by a current from the coast . . . Among the islands, as far as San Nicolas, the current runs to the southward, . . . On the Cortes shoal it frequently runs against the northwest wind at the rate of nearly two miles per hour. At other times it has been found to run in an opposite direction nearly as strong . . .

And Neushul, *et al* [B120, 1967], said of the current,

> The eastern edge of this current beyond Point Conception bathes San Miguel Island with cold water, some of which is deflected into the Santa Barbara Channel . . . The main stream of the California Current continues its southeasterly direction to San Nicolas Island, where some of the water from its eastern edge enters a semi-permanent counterclockwise gyre lying between San Nicolas Island and Santa Rosa and Santa Cruz islands to the north . . . Santa Barbara Island, Santa Cruz, Anacapa, and the eastern half of Santa Rosa receive both cold water from the California Current and warmer water from the south, moving up along the Southern California coast.

In apposition, the trend of San Clemente and Santa Catalina are north-westerly, with currents of warm water in their vicinity.

Blake thought the submarine range northwest of San Clemente would trend toward Santa Barbara Island and that "the soundings already made . . . show . . . a very uniform but not great depth . . . between Santa Barbara Island and Santa Catalina" [N26, 1854-55]. Blake wrote about sixteen paragraphs for the U. S. Coast and Geodetic Survey on the subject of submerged ranges in a highly intuitive, informative, and intelligent fashion.

Obviously, a discussion of the oceanic ranges by Blake is a direct, primary, and previous corollary to Davidson's thoughts on submarine valleys. In many ways, it could be more important. Yet Dr. Davidson is the one credited for recognizing the importance

of submerged valleys of the Coast of California [J65, 1898].

According to the literature, it appears that Santa Barbara Island is a southerly focal point in the direction of the California Current from the north toward San Nicolas and the warmer waters from the south. This is not surprising, considering the locations of the submarine ranges and valleys of the area.

Elephant bones purportedly found on San Nicolas Island are another feature which the island has in common with the northern group. But there is no one to say, for sure, whether some Pleistocene elephant(s) walked about 120 miles to a final resting place on San Nicolas or whether their fossil bones are merely the remains of aboriginal feast(s) obtained from the 'grocery store' on Santa Rosa or San Miguel Islands.

Three possible facets of the same story emerge. Orr has successfully pointed out [B54], that San Miguel and Santa Rosa were connected several thousands years ago, about 11,000 B. P., before their final separation.

And George Davidson has remarked that there was a shallow submarine plateau between Point Concepción and San Miguel.

Chester Stock has said [J318, 1935], that the elephant remains found on San Miguel "are among the largest types to be recorded from the island region." In contrast, the dwarfed size of the Santa Rosa elephant could have been, in part, an ongoing result of its later environmental condition, food supply, and inbreeding.

Could it possibly be that the Pleistocene elephant, migrating from the colder Bering Straits region, found a land connection between San Miguel and Point Concepción—rather than a connection much farther south, as most have indicated. Shades of Dr. Yates!

Description
Geography—Topography

J. R. Browne lived from 1831 to 1875. Coming from Ireland, he settled in California in 1855, and during that year he became Customs' Official and Inspector of Indian Affairs on the Pacific Coast. In 1861 *Harper's Monthly* published one of his articles about Indian Reservations and the corruption within the government [P23].

Among his writing efforts, his five-page article, "The Island of Santa Rosa" [P80, 1874], is one of the more interesting descriptive creations of literature that we possess about California.

J. R. Browne was invited to visit Santa Rosa Island by one of its owners, Mr. H. H. More. They left on the *Star of Freedom* through a gentle breeze, and Browne described his view of the town of Santa Barbara from the deck of the boat.

Falling in love with Santa Rosa Island, he punctuated this thought by saying,

> In my rambles about the island, I was impressed with its capabilities for many novel and interesting experiments in addition to the homely though profitable pursuit of sheep-raising . . . A suggestion casually thrown out by Mr. More was especially fascinating to my imagination. I absolve him from the responsibility of anything more than a jocular hint; but I could not help picturing to my mind what a magnificent park this would make as a preserve for the wild game of the continent!

Of the Ranch House area, Browne had these words,

> Every convenience exists for gathering up the stock, shearing, steeping, and shipping. Large and commodious store-houses, barns, and boarding-houses for the employés are situated near the place of shipment. A wharf, constructed at a cost of $15,000, extends well out into the harbor, where vessels of large capacity can receive and deliver freight.

Another article came from the *Press* of June 2, 1876. Thompson and West [B70], obtained their description of an 1876 matanza on Santa Rosa from the newspaper. By 1876 there was no longer a good wool market and besides,

> As before mentioned, a matanza has been established on this island for the wholesale slaughter of sheep when the over-stocking of the pastures, or the scarcity of feed makes it necessary. From the *Press,* of June 2, 1876 the following account of it is extracted—
> "The slaughter of sheep for their pelts and tallow on Santa Rosa Island, is still going on and will continue for some time. 25,000 sheep are to be killed which will leave from 15,000 to 20,000 on the island. The matanza works erected by the firm are said to be among the largest and most complete on the coast. The kettles are of enormous size, large enough to take in several hundred sheep at a time. The number of carcasses boiled daily averages about 1,200. The fires are kept burning from Monday morning to Saturday evening. The sheep are

skinned, the intestines taken out and the carcasses thrown into the kettles. After going through the kettles, the carcasses are thoroughly mashed up, the bones being softened so they will pulverize under the pressure of the hand. The offal is fed to hogs. In consequence of the sheep not being very fat in this year of short feed, the amount of tallow from each sheep is comparatively small, still under this systematic mode of treatment, a fair price, considering the year, can be realized per head. The skins are salted, dried and packed for market. These operations require a large force of men."

Nineteen years after Browne's article, the *Overland Monthly* favored the public with an account of the island, "Shearing Time on Santa Rosa Island" [P88, May, 1893]. Written by "K," there is reason to believe that the author is Martinette Kinsell, author of "The Santa Barbara Islands," *Overland Monthly* [P87, 1891]. Such a musical writing-style could hardly be duplicated.

The Kinsell party set sail, but they were in a calm and they had to wait for a breeze—in the meantime, sea sickness took hold. It was only after sunset that a breeze came and slowly moved the schooner to its destination. Anchorage was made about 11:30 p.m., but "landing was impossible until daylight, for the pier had been washed away, and the tide was too high to risk going through the heavy surf."

In one small section of the article are a few lines of description of the ranch buildings and surrounding area,

> Quite a little village composed of the vast storing barn and shearing room, stables, pens, and sheds, and the dining and sleeping rooms of the men, stands by itself. Across the little stream is a large natural cave in the sandstone and clay, dry and water tight, where many of the men are comfortably housed at night. A quarter of a mile away stands the ranch house, behind a group of high-shouldered Monterey cypress . . . Here the owner of the island lives when at home in his island kingdom, . . . Some trees are in cañons, and a variety of small oak covers much of the steep hillsides . . . A kind of ironwood, peculiar to the island, is found here . . . Another large plant with leaves like sweet anise, rising in a green parasol from a thick fleshy stem, was also a stranger to the visitors . . .

The party stayed at Santa Rosa Island for three weeks during a shearing season and "K" told of that process. She described the appearance of the shearers, and in nine pages vividly portrayed the "dip" activities for the sheep after their shearing, some activities of the vaqueros, the pasttimes of the Indian shearers, while it was raining and they could not work, and her party's archaeological findings.

Then, one morning the shearers sailed home and the visitors felt that "a return to civilization and the daily mail was imminent."

Dr. Perry G. M. Austin in *Noticias, Santa Barbara Bulletin of the Historical Society* [J293, 1959], offered this type of information on the life at Santa Rosa Island by saying,

> In the late nineties in Santa Barbara, I grew up in the More family, who owned Santa Rosa Island. My mother was a More and many years of her childhood were spent in the simple, New England style, white ranch house at Bechers Bay . . . Among my most cherished memories are the stories my mother would tell of her life on the island . . . In the little white school house at Bechers Bay, my mother and her brothers, with children of the sheepherders, went to school . . .
>
> Sheep shearing time was, of course, the high point of the year. To this day, I vividly remember the stream of Chinese and Mexicans who came to our back door in Santa Barbara seeking my grandfather, John M. More [sic.], to be hired for another season of sheep shearing on the island . . .
>
> For the "Spaniards", the grand finale was always a kind of fiesta, mostly dancing in the shearing barns that were swept clean, with polished floors and gay decorations . . . As a reward for work well done, there was a period of hunting, as there were on the Island many wild boar with their prized ivory tusks, the little gray foxes, and tender little deer peculiar to the Channel Islands . . . .
>
> It is a rather wild coast on Santa Rosa, . . . it is an island known for its many massive sand dunes. The almost continuous winds wrecked scores of vessels on its rocky shores and cliffs. For years we had in the family a great brass ship's bell bearing the name "The Crown of England"—a reminder of one of the many casualties in the rough seas that harrassed the Island . . .
>
> Today, there is a persistent dream that not only Santa Rosa, but all the Santa Barbara Channel Islands, may one day become a state or national park—forever the treasure of the whole American people. May this dream become a reality.

J. R. Browne [P80, 1874], gave a photo-view of Santa Rosa when he said,

> Though the general appearance of the island, looking from the ocean, is unattractive, many parts of it are conspicuous for their picturesque beauty. The views from the highest points in the interior are on a scale of grandeur rarely equaled by the best Pacific Coast scenery. Broad stretches of *mesa,* intersected by deep cañons and gorges, roll away down to the rock-bound shores, beyond which lie in full view the adjacent islands of Santa Cruz, [and] San Miguel . . .

Wright [J376], in a letter to his brother, added to the mesa idea when he described what he and his friend and teacher, Mr. Hoffmann, saw when they landed on the north shore—probably Northeast Anchorage.

> We looked west six or eight miles to the central peaks of the island. From this central massif ran long curving fingers of rounded ridges with canyons between. The higher mesa on which we were seemed to be of co-equal height with many of these ridges, as though once the island was a table land. The central hills perhaps mark a third level, but erosion is so great in their neighborhood that I can't say so for sure,—nor do I venture to say that the "higher mesa" on which we were marked a plane of table land, and that the original higher eroded plane was not somewhere high above everything . . . [it is a] region of forty square miles or so of more or less flat-topped rounded ridges, with the long lines of deep curving canyons running down to the sea and the shorter lines of smaller tributary canyons, . . .

In Mr. Holland's article [J387], reproduced for us is Mr. Voy's very rough sketch of Santa Rosa. It indicates peaks, altitudes, place names; located fossil accumulations, shale, sand dunes, canyons; and named the major points of interest along the shore. [C30 may also help the reader on Mr. Voy's material.]

Voy showed about fifteen summits, perhaps none too accurately in terms of height, but his overall effort is a decided contribution. Had this map been accepted by the Mining Bureau in 1893, it would have then been published.

There are discrepancies between some of the Yates place names and altitudes, and those of Voy. Should one feel need to consider a choice, perhaps Yates' information would be accepted.

Jones in 1901 might have had access to Voy's rough sketch, for in one place, "A," he called it "Dos Pechos," a place name found only on the Voy sketch. Since Voy gave it an altitude of 1562 feet, very likely Dos Pechos is Davidson's MT. SOLEDAD, the highest mountain on the island, 1574 feet.

Place "B" was called "Cerro Negro" by Voy, probably meaning "Sierra Negro," "Monte Negro," or "Sierra Negra," about 1298 feet. Perhaps Voy was a phonetic speller [See U5, B54, J387].

Orr stated that there were small stands of *Pinus remorata* on the sides of this mountain [B54], and Yates, gave the peak an altitude of 1325 feet, and placed it back of Bechers Bay by about five miles. "K" said there were plateaus surrounding the peak [P88].

Through *The American Geologist* [U52], Yates said that the highest points on the backbone of the island would approximate [average] 1400 feet. He referred to a group of these peaks lying within a mile circuit—BLACK MOUNTAIN, Saddle Mountain, and another, which he did not name.

Austin Tappan Wright [J376, 1963], increased our descriptive material for this same area when he said,

We were on Black Mtn. which is the northern buttress of the central massif. Here within a circle of perhaps a quarter mile in diameter were the heads of canyons running down to the north and eastern sides of the island, and within half a mile, another, perhaps the longest of all, ran southeast and opened on the sea south of the easternmost point of the Island. On the northern face of Black Mtn. there are four or five steep canyons all parallel with each other and only a hundred yards or so apart at their heads. They all run downward northerly and then the westernmost one of them curves easterly and with a higher ridge on its western and north western side gathers in, so to speak, all the others . . .

The name SADDLE MOUNTAIN does not appear on the Voy sketch, but the name SAN PABLO does. The discrepancy of Voy's 1436 feet for San Pablo and Yates' 1425 feet for Saddle Mountain is not great. And this peak is to the south of Black Mtn., as both men have indicated. There is likewise, an unnamed summit close to San Pablo, 1280 feet, slightly north, on the Voy sketch.

Yates also said, "southeasterly from Saddle Mountain and lying between Cañada de la Cruz and the ocean there is an intrusion of syenite, the extent of which has not been ascertained." On Voy's sketch, the intrusion of syenite is indicated slightly east of San Pablo. If there is but one 'intrusion of syenite' on the island, this must be it.

CAÑADA DE LA CRUZ is not shown by name on the Voy sketch and this author finds no physical features in that region to identify the canyon. However, it could be the canyon somewhat northeast of the FORD POINT area. Since the place name has appeared on the printed page only through Yates, it might be a sidelight worth noting. Should the name have no topographic significance, it could have an historic one.

MT. SOLEDAD appears to straddle the backbone near the island's center. According to Pemberton, around it large groves of the Ironwood tree, *Lyonothamnus asplenifolius*, flourished. Farther south and west is SIERRA VACA, altitude 1550 feet, another name given on the Voy sketch; the U. S. Coast and Geodetic Survey gave a more southerly unnamed peak an altitude of 1436 feet.

The interior of the island appears to be as intriguing for former Indian habitations as the coastal area. According to Yates, the rocks of the interior have so weathered by wind action that there are irregular cavities and caves in the cliffs of the canyons. This allowed the aborigines to use such as dwelling places, evidenced by bits of shell and midden debris in and around the caves [U52, 1890].

Orr [B54], has said that

more than half of the sites on Santa Rosa Island [are] located in the interior, most of them are on the highlands . . . [And] located fairly high on the island (500-1000' above sea level), the caves occur in the cliffs on the side of steep canyons [J278, 1952].

Of the many 'peaks' on the south side, Davidson noted that they were "covered with fossil shells, Indian mounds covered with mortars, pestles, arrowheads, and other ancient curiosities [were] scattered over the island . . . at present [the island] is stocked with sheep and horses" [N34].

Rogers [B63], had said that "characteristic molluscan remains of this period are to be found, even near the crest of the higher hills."

W. H. Dall, a conchologist who collected from Santa Rosa, was once employed by the U. S. National Museum. He made various types of collections, and information by him on the fossils of the Coast Range may be found in National Government publications. [C20 and J267 may help the reader].

185

PIECES OF EIGHT
Around Santa Rosa Island

WEST POINT, or SANDY POINT, is that point nearest San Miguel Island, and a Steller Lion rookery may be found there [C2,1928]. Between San Miguel and Santa Rosa is the three mile wide SAN MIGUEL PASSAGE [N34].

Close under the south side of Sandy Point small schooners of twenty or thirty tons can anchor in the summer, but Davidson warned, a thorough knowledge of the conditions is necessary in order to avoid the outlying rocks [N34].

Out from Sandy Point "the kelp stretches nearly half a mile into the San Miguel Passage to thirteen and fifteen fathoms of water, sweeping thence around the southwest face of the island for 9⅓ miles to South Point, where it is close under the shore, and thence continuing close under the shore 6½ miles toward East Point" [N34].

One and a half miles north half east (N. ½ E.) from Sandy Point is a very dangerous shoal, TALCOTT SHOAL, having as little as eleven feet of water upon it. With prevailing winds northwest, the current sets to the eastward. When this wind ceases or lightens, the current moves westwardly at about one and a half miles an hour. North of Sandy Point and around the Talcott Shoal the currents are uncertain, and frequently strong [N34].

The winds are so prevalent during the summer, says Yates, that they have earned the name, "trade winds." Both northeast and southeast windstorms have been clocked at 106 m.p.h. [B54]. Coming from San Miguel, these winds carry the sand across the passage to Santa Rosa Island. Some of the sand is deposited at the west end, and some is carried on to be eventually blown into the sea.

Orr reminded us [B120],

> that all of the sand dunes and arroyo cutting did not occur during historical times, but rather it was about 7,000 years ago and 3,000 or 4,000 years ago when the greatest of the dune building occurred.

At the west end, known as LA BOLSA [U5], the main range of mountains from the north meets the ocean. The rocks and terraces of the range are covered by the shifting sands to form white sand dunes. Reaching as high as four hundred feet in elevation, and covering one or two square miles, they are a marked feature of the point [N34].

Voy's sketch contains a summit, unnamed in this west end sand dune area, indicating a 1040 foot height. Orr had mentioned a FARREL MOUNTAIN, 1040 feet, but placed it at the head of a canyon to the northwest.

The wind-swept area did not allow for heavy woods or bush, except in the sheltered canyons [J139]. However, during the rainy seasons the various dunes produce plants, such as lupine, California poppy, and thistles [B54]. This western end of the island appears to have been more extensively occupied by the Indians than many other portions of the island.

It was Wright's understanding [J376], that the only other house built by white man, besides the ranch house, was a shack near the west end. However, Camp #9, on the eastern side, had an old site known as "the old Jack camp." Supposedly, a fence builder once made his camp here [U5].

On reaching Talcott Shoal, we have moved toward the northern side of Santa Rosa. But along this southwestern shore the island is rocky, inhospitable, and desolate before reaching GARANON CANYON [J10].

Then begins a stretch of coast, about thirteen miles in extent, with gulches and canyons containing the remains and artifacts of many of the former Indian villages. Rogers indicated Arlington, Corral, Soledad, Green, and 'Lober,' as the prominent canyons of this region.

To both the paleontologist and the geologist this northwestern area is of high interest, not only from the standpoint of the villages, but here, too, may be found the remains of the much-discussed elephant—and Arlington Man. [J166, J303, N2, J171, U60 and J305 may help the reader].

On the Voy sketch [J387], a CAÑADA SECO is about where Orr indicates SKULL GULCH; it is about halfway between Cañada Tecelote and Cañada Garanon. The spelling 'Tecelote,' is used by the U. S. Coast and Geodetic Survey.

Following the coast in a northerly direction from Voy's Cañada Seco, Voy located CAÑADA TOKOLODITO, spelled 'Tecolokito' by Orr; then comes CAÑADA TECELOTE. Between these last two locations, Voy had made a notation, "animal fossils." SURVEY POINT, along the sea cliff, is close to Cañada Tecelote, separated by a short barranca.

Orr and party camped many times in Skull Gulch in order to carry on the work of excavating. While camping there, the groups found it necessary to haul their water eighteen miles to camp, as the only drink-

186

ing water had to be obtained at the Ranch House from wells.

In Orr's article, *American Antiquity* [J10, 1951], he remarked that there were twenty-three villages and seventeen burial grounds within the Skull Gulch area. Also, at the head of Skull Gulch were found several stumps of trees four to five feet tall, measuring more than a foot in diameter. According to him, they are of inter-glacial age, as differentiated from the sand casts of San Nicolas and San Miguel, which are post-glacial.

Cañada Tecelote and ARLINGTON CANYON must be in close proximity. Roger's map [B63], indicates Arlington Canyon as being west of Brockway Point with CAÑADA CORRAL to its east. Voy's sketch shows Cañada Tecelote where Rogers placed Arlington Canyon, and agrees with Rogers as to the location of Cañada Corral.

Regardless of the above mentioned individuals, Phil C. Orr remains practically the final authority for Santa Rosa Island, at least from the archaeological and paleontological standpoints.

He has told us that in the upper reaches of Arlington Canyon are to be found nine wind-eroded caves, showing evidences of former habitation. In part, this is Orr's description of the canyon,

Arlington Canyon is the largest canyon on the Island and contains the only fresh water to reach the sea. At its mouth it is a broad, flat grassy valley with Arlington Creek cut into one side as a V-shaped arroyo about 100 feet in depth . . . About 1,300 feet from the sea cliff, a fresh water spring comes out of the bluff.

Elsewhere Orr has said that the water is but slightly brackish, runs the year around, and provides the only palatable drinking water on the entire northwest coast. He has no doubt differentiated the water from wells at the ranch house and this spring water. Furthermore, the ranch house is considered to be on the northeast coast, not on the northwest.

Orr discussed the "Arlington Springs Man" in *Science* [J305, 1962], and, of course, in his book, *Prehistory of Santa Rosa Island* [B54]. The reader is commended to a more intensive study of both Early Man remains and Pleistocene elephant remains in Arlington Canyon, and elsewhere. There has been much research and speculation on this particular subject.

Following Arlington Canyon is CAÑADA SOLEDAD. It is about ten miles from the wharf in BECHERS BAY. It was here, near the mouth of the

canyon, on a four-hundred foot high cliff that Yates and party "found an excellent exposure of strata, consisting of about 90 feet of Post Pliocene deposit, containing fossil bones of vertebrates, . . ." [U52] It seems as though Yates was trying to tell us that the first elephant remains were found at Cañada Soledad. [See also J331].

BROCKWAY POINT is high and bold, and is the rounding point on the north side of the island, lying about five and three-fourths miles from Sandy Point, and the same distance from CARRINGTON POINT. At Brockway Point and along CAÑADA CORRAL, fossils are to be found.

DRY CANYON is next indicated, then follows CAÑADA VERDE. It was probably here that W. G. W. Harford of the U. S. Coast and Geodetic Survey did some digging, although he was primarily a botanist [U5].

When Ms. "K" and party visited Santa Rosa Island for a few weeks in 1893, they found "a little river that runs through a green valley" [P88], and here they saw hundreds of wild geese. Always with an eye for nature, "K" said, "At Cañon Verdi is a room large enough for half a dozen sheep to stand and keep their fleeces dry during a sudden shower." Perhaps the Indians used the shelter, too, for Edwards [J231, 1956], made mention of the circular hut mounds with the remains of whale vertebrae painted red [at GREEN HARBOR], and the oblong houses at Cañada Verde.

Orr located Cañada Verde as reaching the ocean about the middle of the northern coast. He termed it the second largest canyon on the island, where elephant remains may be found. There are also several caves on the slopes above the valley. Cañada Verde, he said, becomes a narrow steep-sided gorge about twenty feet deep, now with but "a trickle of water in the bottom."

North of Brockway Point and southwest of Carrington Point is RODES REEF [N34]. Rogers spelled the name 'Rhodes Reef'; Voy gave it the name and spelling of 'Red Reef.'

[It is] a small rocky kelp patch seven-eights of a mile off shore, about three miles . . . from the western side of Carrington Point, one and a half miles northeast by east from Brockway Point and a third of a mile outside the range of these points. Three sunken rocks form the danger, and they lie in a northwest and southeast direction about one hundred yards apart. They break in almost all weathers [N34].

PIECES OF EIGHT

The next canyon we approach is CAÑADA LOBOS and is the site of the large fissure created by the earthquake in 1812. Then, there is Carrington Point, the northern point on Santa Rosa Island.

This point is but three-fourths of a mile from Santa Cruz' West Point, the northwestern point of that island. Both points thus form the northern entrance to the Santa Cruz Channel. By the same token, EAST POINT of Santa Rosa is the southwestern head of the south entrance to this channel.

There is a rocky bottom along the north face of Carrington Point, which point runs "for nearly a mile; it faces the sea with a bold and menacing front at least four hundred feet high" [B38, N34].

BEACON REEF, to the north of Carrington Point, has from three to four fathoms of water upon it. Davidson says that the reef rarely breaks and that there is no safe passage on the inside of it. Should one be steering eastward to enter the Santa Cruz Channel, he warns not to steer southward "until the houses at Becher Bay are open one point to the left of COYOTE POINT . . .

"[Coyote] point is one-half of a mile south-southeast from Carrington Point. Here, . . . broken patches of kelp begin and run into the FIVE MILE BIGHT or BECHERS BAY. There is good water close under the point but rocky bottom in the kelp" [N34].

Then Davidson explained his statements for he made Bechers Bay the Five Mile Bight, and the stretch of shore from the wharf northward toward Coyote Point he called the NORTHWEST ANCHORAGE. Bechers Bay according to him, includes the SOUTHEAST ANCHORAGE, which is about one and a half miles west by south (W. by S.) from CHANNEL POINT, or SKUNK POINT. There are small patches of kelp through the bight [N34].

Davidson gave Bechers Bay a broad beach "under a low table bluff that is about thirty feet high and three hundred yards wide, . . ." The Bay is semicircular, it is Santa Rosa's 'main harbor,' and, only to a certain extent offers protection from the northwest or southeast winds.

Of the Northwest Anchorage,

there is a passable anchorage in from six to ten fathoms of water, over rocky bottom, within one-third of a mile of the shore abreast of a wharf, at the end of which sixteen feet of water is reported. This wharf, constructed in 1873, . . . is marked by the ranch houses behind it on the north side of the arroyo [N34].

Of the natural conditions in this spot, Dunkle

188

[J350, 1941], remarked that a Torrey Pine grove existed about three miles south of the VAIL RANCH and the trees were abundant in that particular locality.

According to Orr, at RANCH HOUSE, or ELDER CREEK, one finds a broad flat plain, providing room for the ranch buildings, corrals, and some cultivation [J10].

Wright, too, mentioned the ranch house area,

The only settlement is three or four miles north of where we landed, and consists only of a few barns, a ranch house, and one or two other houses. The only inhabitants are men who tend the cattle . . . [there is] a long fence running straight up hill and down dale for miles, . . . with sand dunes far to the south . . .

We . . . lunched on the top of the ridge . . . At the bottom was a flat floor and very green grass, and there was a running brook . . . we reached the ranch and went through its high fenced corrals and came out near the sea . . . The canyon we were in opened upon the lower mesa behind the ranch house . . .

Both scientist and layman would profit by reading Wright's extremely interesting, seventeen-page article on Santa Cruz and Santa Rosa [J376]!

And speaking of "a long fence running straight up hill and down dale," Towne and Wentworth remark in their *Shepherd's Empire* [B125], that

No herders were required since the island was divided into quarters by fences placed at right angles and extending to the extreme boundaries. Two hundred trained goats, in lieu of sheep dogs, were used to control the flocks.

The November 19, 1883 *Morning Call,* on microfilm in Sacramento, contains this information, and more, under "An Extensive Sheep Range on Santa Rosa Island" [M72].

And as we move eastward, CAÑADA LAGUNA or WATER CANYON appears, with its mouth, too, in Bechers Bay. Should we use Voy's sketch as a guide, Cañada Laguna appears to be a long, winding canyon with its sources around DOS PECHOS. Strangely enough, although archaeologists have been in this area, we have practically no descriptive material on the canyon.

In the eastern part of Bechers Bay, even though the conditions are desert like [B63], there is a small grove of Torrey Pines on the edge of the sea cliff [J139]. Orr referred to these pine as Pleistocene relict Torrey Pine.

In the southeastern part of the Five Mile Bight, about one and one-half miles from Channel Point, there is another anchorage known as Southeast Anchorage [N34]. According to Davidson a 200-ton brig was caught there in a storm in 1873, was anchored in six fathoms of water and rode out the southeast gale. Off the north point of the anchorage may be found a small patch of kelp.

For four or five miles between this anchorage and Skunk Point there are Indian camps and refuse heaps, containing tons of abalone shells [U5]. Beyond this sandy beach there are drifts of sand for about four and one-half miles, covering the area from SKUNK POINT past East Point. In this area RANCHO VIEJO lies [U21]. It is the site of an old Indian settlement; there is also a road from Rancho Viejo to RANCH HOUSE CANYON at Elder Creek.

Orr helped a little [B54, 1968], by saying that in terms of width and length, Rancho Viejo is the largest valley on Santa Rosa Island. And in a cave "at the headwaters of the Creek is a very faint, unrecognizable painted pattern in red and black on the ceiling of an Indian shelter . . ."

EAST POINT, the eastern extremity of the island, "is moderately high, sharp and bold with very deep water on its east and south faces" [N34]. Here there are quite a number of rock-shelters [caves] which project above the general surface [P89, 1896].

About four and one-fourth miles southwestwardly from East Point, vessels have been known to anchor, especially in the summer months. One anchorage is about three and three-fourths miles northeastwardly from South Point in the FORD POINT vicinity and has five or six fathoms of water [N34].

There is about a three mile stretch of coast from Ford Point down to South Point. Up from the canyon at FORD POINT are Jones' camp sites #12, #13, and #14. At Ford Point, near the mouth of the canyon, are the remains of a mast and a donkey engine from the *S. S. Crown of England,* wrecked on the south side of the island in 1894 [B54].

There are dangers for this southeast end and Holder gave reasons for such. Nearly two-thirds of a mile from East Point and one-half mile off shore, there is a rocky cone which rises to within sixteen feet of the surface. And but two miles away from the cone there is a shoal with less than thirty feet of water over it [B38].

But there is not a writer who suggests even the possibility of using any of Santa Rosa's anchorages during stormy weather, including the Becher Bay Bight. Unfamiliarity with Channel Island currents, winds, rocks, and shoals has contributed to hundreds of ship disasters around the islands.

In Ashkenazy's *Westways* article, most of this story is crystalized in "A Graveyard of Ships," worth reading for those interested [P174].

It was early February of 1962 that the *Chickasaw,* bound from Yokohama to Wilmington, California, met its fate off Santa Rosa Island. A ten-foot swell carried the *Chickasaw* to a grinding halt while struggling on the southeast coast of the island. Two days later, with the help of the Coast Guard, the passengers and crew were taken off by breeches buoy and helicopter.

There are twelve Indian village sites from Ford Point to South Point, the largest of which is at JOHNSON'S LEE [B54]. Davidson and his men had made a study of Johnson's Lee,

> Vessels also anchor at this open roadstead, about one and a quarter miles northeastward of South Point, in from five to seven fathoms of water in the kelp, which is here nearly half a mile broad. The bight is one and a half miles long, formed by a slight retreating of the high shore and is open to southerly winds and swell, but is an excellent shelter in winds from west round by north to northeast.
>
> The South Point is a high, bold promontory and serves to mark this anchorage at a distance. When entering the bight a low, black rock, with a central peak, named SLAY ROCK, is to be observed . . . anchor in five to nine fathoms over sand . . . The bottom to the westward of Slay Rock is rocky . . . and dangerous to ground tackle . . . There is fresh water here [N34].

Holder [B38], considered Johnson's Lee a 'fair' anchorage; Rogers [B63], a 'good' anchorage, through most of the year. His complaint, should it be termed that, was that there is no beach along this shore, making a landing difficult.

According to Rogers, there is water, but containing so many mineral solutions that it is unfit for human consumption. "Only the wild hogs make use of these streams, and as a consequence that is a favorite range for them" [B63].

An Air Force radar station was placed inland from Johnson's Lee and South Point in the middle 50s. It checked on coastal craft going in and out, and was also there for defense purposes. There was a 336 acre-lease by the Air Force at this site [N52], later abandoned [B54].

PIECES OF EIGHT

SOUTH POINT, PEDRAGOSA to Jones, is a portion of a rise in altitude of the interior, and at the Point, the bluff is one hundred feet high, with the cliffs extending along the shore for half a mile. In 1925 a lighthouse was placed here.

There is kelp along the shore from South Point to WEST POINT [Sandy Point], a distance of nine and one-third miles. Close to three and one-half miles from South Point on the way to West Point, there are BEE ROCKS and reef, about seven-eighths of a mile from shore. Voyagers have been warned not to approach Bee Rocks closer than a depth of twenty to twenty-five fathoms.

Along this shore the sea cliffs are from fifty to one hundred feet in height. There is much erosion with deep, precipitous, rocky barrancas, and but scant vegetation. The sand is continually shifting, and the area is entirely uninviting.

On the south side is a valley, and on the flat lands of this valley is located an Indian village site. To Jones, this location was known as Camp #6, CAÑADA DE LA CUEVA VIEJA, or Canyon of the Cave of the Old People. The cave has since been named "Jones." To the Army, on their maps, the canyon to the valley is called CAÑADA JOLLA VIEJA—Old Cave Canyon.

In the rocks above the main creek, Jones, then Orr, found a small cave containing the only petroglyphs known on Santa Rosa Island. These petroglyphs were photographed by Jones. According to Orr, they amounted to

> a few round dots and some vertical scratches or grooves in no apparent design, although the round dots do occur in a more or less straight line or in groups and one set of grooves has a slight resemblance to a malformed four-tined fork [B54].

This description of the cave's petroglyphs offered by Orr is reminiscent of a recent publication [U21, 1972], by Heizer, "California's Oldest Historical Relic?" Heizer labors to give the "JR" stone, with similar petroglyphs [and a rude cross], some connection with Juan Rodriguez Cabrillo. This particular slab was found by Jones on a northeast site near Rancho Viejo—not to be confused with Cañada Jolla Vieja on the south coast.

Heizer spent nearly a dozen pages discussing a possible location for Cabrillo's burial, other than San Miguel Island. In briefer form, *Westways* [P177, 1974], carried some of the same material under, "A Grave Discovery."

One of the greatest stumbling blocks to another's acceptance of Heizer's thoughts concerning Cabrillo having possibly been buried on Santa Rosa Island, is the lack of harbors, as well as the kind of weather experienced by Cabrillo and his men in December, 1542 and January, 1543. See also Appendices C and H.

The junction of the creek in Canyon Jolla Vieja is about two miles from the ocean. Here Jones discovered eight caves in the canyon, three on the north fork and five on the south fork. Orr went to the site in 1950 and made his appraisal of the area.

Running up from the sea is a twenty-foot deep, steep-sided arroyo, and running down from the arroyo was found "a trickle of brackish water [B54]. When Jones saw the stream in 1901 it was continuous, and "the best I have found on the island" [U5].

There is a WRECK CANYON, whose water empties on the south side of the island, and where elephant remains may be found. According to Orr, Jones found this canyon in 1901 and named it CAÑADA LA JOLLA. It has since been renamed 'Wreck' by Orr, because it is the site of the wreck of the *S. S. Crown of England,* even though its remaining parts lie at Ford Point.

The canyon opens into a flat-bottomed valley about a mile above, and is cut by three arroyos. One of the arroyos contains good water, the other two are dry. The middle fork contains some sandstone caves, a few kitchen middens, and a little higher, several more caves [B54]. This site appears to be older than many of the others, according to Jones.

We are brought somewhat abruptly to the end of the trip around the island, for there is but little descriptive matter for most of the south and southwest sides.

CHINA CAMP is to the west of South Point. To the Vaqueros, it was known as CAÑADA ACAPULCA [B54]. "K" called it the "abalone fishers' camp" [P88, 1893], and it is found on the east side of the creek. It is also one of the island's Indian sites.

MESS CAVE, in the sandstone on the slopes of SIERRA LOPEZ, is at an elevation of 412 feet and is where some Indian deposits may be found. A CAÑADA SAN AUGUSTINE, somewhere on the southeast coast, apparently has elephant bones in its narrow gorges, also other fossil bones, which include the diving goose [B54].

A miscellaneous 'elsewhere' on the island is an OTTER POINT, fairly close to Arlington Canyon, where mammoth bones have been found. Somewhere there is an ABALONE POINT and a CLUSTER POINT. Of a STEAMBOAT POINT, "K" said,

> . . . after the natural bridge had been looked at, and the roar of the water rushing through a hole in the rocks whence it shoots into the air in vapor, making the sound of a steamer whistle that gives the locality its name, the party found they were very tired . . . They still believe that it was five miles over there and ten to return [P88, 1893].

"K" offered another cue for another natural bridge,

> . . . the last ride must be taken, and it was to be [to a] far point where the most populous Indian tumuli are found, and where another natural bridge spans a deep embrasure with caving edges that overhang the sea. The trail was rough and devious part of the way, . . .

And so the curtain falls on this tour of Santa Rosa Island.

Transfer of Title to Santa Rosa Island

The intent of this section is to trace title to the island. Sparse it would be, however, without some limited background knowledge of the family who came into possession of the island and some of the local events affecting them.

The Carlos Carrillo family

It is around two of the brothers, José and Carlos, that some of the story takes place, for they were granted the island of Santa Rosa; Rancho Sespe being another part of Carlos' holdings through his wife, María.

The two brothers were involved in the politics of Mexico and Alta California. Streeter, *California Historical Society*, "Recollections of Historical Events in California, 1842-1878" [J96], said that José Antonio Carrillo was against Governor Victoria, and favored Pío Pico as a Mexican Governor of Alta California over Echeandía. According to Streeter, José tried unsuccessfully to rule California by making his brother, Don Carlos, the governor. But Alvarado literally 'took' the job.

María Castro Carrillo's brother, José Castro, was a native of California, born in Monterey about 1810, and there attended school. He became the seventh governor of California, 1835-1836.

Then followed in the same year, Governors Gutierrez, Chico, and Juan Bautista Alvarado, nephew of Carlos Carrillo. Alvarado served for five years in

that capacity. He, too, was born in Monterey, 1809, "son of Sergeant José F. Alvarado and María Josefa Vallejo de Alvarado" [J353].

In 1839, while governor, at the age of thirty, he married Martina, daughter of Francisco María Castro of San Pablo ". . . it was a marriage by proxy" [B35]. She died in 1875 and he in 1882. Las Mariposas was one of Alvarado's ranches, purchased by Larkin for Fremont for $3000, with W. C. Jones seeing to its patent on Feb. 10, 1856, just two days after a Supreme Court decision [J380, 1974].

Followed by Micheltorena for three years, then Pío Pico for one year, it became the American Period of California's political history. From Argüello [1823], to Pío Pico [1846], there had been eleven governors of Alta California in twenty-two years.

It was against this chaotic and shifting political background that many of the land grants were made. Prior to the issuance of the Pesado Letter in 1838 and the subsequent involvement of the Carrillo's with Santa Rosa Island, Carlos Carrillo requested the grant of the Sespe tract in the Santa Clara Valley in May of 1829 [B70].

> . . . on the 29th of November following the request was acceded to the extent of two leagues (8.880 acres), and possibly to six leagues . . . The local government put him in possession of about six leagues. Whether two, or six, caused all the subsequent difficulty. This right was afterwards in 1854 purchased by T. Wallace More, who supposed that he was buying six leagues, the price that he paid, $18,000, being a full value for the larger named quantity . . . On the 18th of April 1853, the Commissioners confirmed the grant title to "six leagues and no more." . . . The United States, as the adverse party, appealed the case to the United States District Court for the Southern District of California. When the . . . grant was brought into court, it was observed for the first time that the numbers of the grant had been tampered with, and that, probably, instead of six leagues, as was confirmed by the Commissioners, two had been erased and six substituted, though when this was done, . . . it was impossible to tell . . .

In 1964 Robert Glass Cleland, *The Cattle on a Thousand Hills* [B10a], had this to say about the Sespe,

> The location of a California grant, as illustrated by the typical case of the Rancho Sespe in the Santa Clara Valley, was carried out with tolerant

191

disregard for anything remotely resembling an accurate survey. On the appointed day, the grantee, Carlos Antonio Carrillo, the magistrate in charge of the proceedings, and "the assisting witnesses," went to the "Place called Sespe," to measure and mark the boundary lines. According to the grant, the rancho lay between the lands of the Mission San Buenaventura and those of the Mission San Fernando, and between the "mountains on the north and the high hills on the south."

This set of circumstances surrounding the Sespe grant came to a horrible climax in 1877 with the murder of T. W. More (who will soon enter our story) by the settlers, who lived on the other four square leagues, the four leagues to which More thought he was entitled. Thompson and West [B70], tells the whole story in considerable detail. T. W. More had also been half owner of Santa Rosa Island until he sold his interest in 1867 to his brother, A. P. More.

"It was during the incumbency of Gov. [José de] Echeandía that the law or reglamento of 1828, relating to the granting of lands was passed by the Mexican Congress" [J353]. By 1838 the Mexican government, seeing the 'hand writing on the wall,' unable to control the smuggling and otter hunting traffic along the coast, decided to give the islands away to 'deserving' Mexican citizens.

There is a copy of an official letter from the Minister of the Interior to the Governor of California, respecting the granting of certain islands to Mexican citizens [N18]. This is the Report of William Carey Jones, Special Agent to examine the subject of land titles in California. Published in the Executive Documents as part of Jones' findings is the letter,

MOST EXCELLENT SIR: The President being desirous to protect, on the one hand, the population of the islands adjacent to this department which form a part of the national territory, and, on the other, to prevent numerous foreign adventurers from appropriating to themselves important portions of them, whereby they can do much injury to our fisheries, commerce, and interests, had determined that your excellency, in concert with the council of the department, proceed with promptness and prudence to grant and distribute lands in the said islands to citizens who desire them, his excellency recommending that (immediately) a preference be extended to citizens Antonio and Carlos Barrelo [Carrillo], for their important and patriotic services; and that such one of the said islands as they may

select be granted to them. I have the honor to give you this information for your government. For God and Liberty! Mexico, July 26, 1838.

PESADO,
Governor of the Department of Californias,
Villa de Los Angeles.

According to J. N. Bowman, "The Question of Sovereignty over California's Off-shore Islands" [J240, 1962], the original PESADO letter was personally delivered by Castillero to Governor Alvarado. See also, Appendix L.

Although José Antonio and Don Carlos could have petitioned immediately for the grant of Santa Rosa Island, they waited until September 1841 to do so, probably with good reason. In the meantime, José Castro, brother to María Carrillo, had asked for the island.

Castro had been a loyal supporter of Juan B. Alvarado, now Governor of Alta California, who desired a break from Mexico. On the other hand, Carlos Carrillo had not wanted to break with Mexico. And he had, in truth, been elected to Governorship of Alta California by the Mexican Government in Mexico, but his nephew, Alvarado, had taken over, instead [B48].

Alvarado granted the island to Castro in 1841, thus denying the Carrillos. Alvarado, himself, was grantee of several ranchos, including The Mariposa.

In 1842 Micheltorena became governor, so the Carrillos repetitioned through him for the island of Santa Rosa in 1843. Some agreement was reached between José Castro and the Carrillos, and the island finally became Carrillo property on October 4, 1843—after the Carrillos had paid some designated sum for Castro's expenses, incurred during his brief possession of the island.

Alpheus B. Thompson had married Francisca Carrillo in 1834, and John C. Jones had married Manuela Carrillo in 1838, two of Carlos Carrillo's daughters. The young ladies paid a nominal sum to their father and uncle for the island, probably Castro's expenses while owning Santa Rosa.

The following account by R. H. Dana [B15], describes an incident which included "The Sandwich Islander," [John Coffin Jones], Captain Francis Thompson, his brother, Alpheus B. Thompson, Agent Alfred Robinson, and Francisca,

The Sandwich Islander who could speak English, told us that he had been up to the town; and that we were to sail the same night. In a few minutes Captain T—, with two gentlemen and one female, came down, and we got ready to go off. They had a good deal of baggage, which we put into the bows of the boat, and then two of us took the senora in our arms, and waded with her through the water, and put her down safely in the stern. She appeared much amused with the transaction, and her husband was perfectly satisfied, thinking any arrangement good which saved his wetting his feet. I pulled the after oar, so that I heard the conversation, and learned that one of the men, who, as well as I could see in the darkness, was a young-looking man, in the European dress, and covered up in a large cloak, was the agent of the firm to which our vessel belonged; and the other, who was dressed in the Spanish dress of the country, was a brother of our captain, who had been many years a trader on the coast, and had married the lady who was in the boat. She was a delicate, dark-complexioned young woman, and of one of the best families in California.

One has to wonder who were more interested in the island of Santa Rosa, the Carrillo brothers, the two daughters, or Mr. Thompson and Mr. Jones, their husbands. By 1844 Thompson and Jones had stocked the island with cattle, horses, and sheep; Jones financed, Thompson managed. Some of Don Carlos' Rocking Horse brand cattle roamed the island [J370].

We are furnished with the information that the first house built on the island was a 15′ by 24′ structure with a 9′ height. It was constructed of wood and had a shingled roof. There was one door, one window, and a corridor, and was still standing in 1855 [J387].

Mr. Thompson later built a large ranch house in a cypress grove; its location, Ranch House Canyon. Corrals and other buildings were added; all of this taking place about 1855. The business venture was evidently prospering, and several full time vaqueros were employed to oversee the animals, which, by this time, included hogs and rabbits.

Litigation between Thompson and Jones over the proceeds from the island operation began, even as early as 1855. Jones and his family had moved to Boston in 1846, but Jones had left his business affairs in the hands of Alfred Robinson, who succeeded in his efforts for Jones. As a result of the law suit, however, the island had to be sold, and members of the More family were awaiting such an opportunity.

John C. Jones and Alpheus B. Thompson had

been in the otter hunting business as early as 1832, albeit on an illegal basis. In that year the *Crusader,* chartered by Jones, associated with Thompson, Grimes, and French, left Honolulu. They picked up Kaigani hunters from Norfolk Sound, sailed for the coast of California and Cerros Island, and returned to Honolulu after a successful voyage. During the same year the *Crusader* was for eight months again on the California coast, returning to Honolulu with a large number of otter skins.

The *Convoy,* purchased by Thompson, Eliab Grimes, Jones, and William French in 1831, equipped for sea-otter hunting, was on the California coast in 1834 from Honolulu. In 1836 they again fitted the *Convoy,* sent her to the Northwest coast, and took on a number of Indian hunters for otter hunting purposes around the Channel Islands.

Richard Henry Dana corroborates this part of the *Convoy* story when he said,

> The second morning after leaving Monterey, we were off Point Conception . . . She proved to be the brig *Convoy,* from the Sandwich Islands, engaged in otter hunting, among the islands which lie along the coast. Her armament was from her being an illegal trader. The otter are very numerous among the islands, and being of great value, the government requires a heavy sum for a license to hunt them, and lay a high duty upon every one shot or carried out of the country. This vessel had no license, and paid no duty, besides being engaged in smuggling goods on board other vessels trading on the coast, and belonging to the same owners in Oahu. Our captain told him to look out for the Mexicans, but he said they had not an armed vessel of his size in the whole Pacific. This was without doubt the same vessel that showed herself off Santa Barbara a few months before. These vessels frequently remain on the coast for years, without making port, except at the islands for wood and water, and an occasional visit to Oahu for a new outfit.

Gast, *Contentious Consul,* fills a gap in our understanding of incidents; he said of the *Convoy's* 1836 trip,

> There she became involved in an incident which stemmed from the increasing enmity between the Northwest Indian hunters employed in Hawaiian-based vessels and the resident hunters, most of whom made their homes in Santa Barbara. This was the case when, on her 1836 voyage, the Indians aboard the *Convoy* attacked a

small party of American hunters on Santa Rosa Island and were driven back with severe losses.

In Footnote #111 of Ellison [B51], it is stated that Bancroft surmised it to be the *Llama,* an English brig of 147 ton, whose Indians attacked Nidever and his men off Santa Rosa.

Nidever and Santa Rosa

In fact, Nidever, himself, might have thought so, for he remarked that a year after the fight with the Northwest Indians they ran across two of the crew of the brig who said it was they, under Captain Bancroft, who were doing the fighting.

But Gast informed us that although the *Llama* was brought into the Pacific in 1834, it was during 1837-38 that it was engaged in illicit sea otter hunting. This is the year following the 1836 attack at Santa Rosa. Eliab Grimes of Honolulu was the owner of the British brig, with Captain Bancroft in charge.

On one of George Nidever's otter hunting trips he said he met the Black Steward. Nidever continued; he

> met a Negro, an otter hunter, who had been here some time, having deserted from the "Pilgrim," a trading vessel from Boston; his proper name was Allen Light (he was very dark skinned) but he was always called "Black Steward." He was quite intelligent, well behaved and mannerly, and a good hunter. With him I made a hunt up the coast as far as Point Concepcion. We each had a boat and one Kanak. Made a very short trip and got 21 skins.

The "Pilgrim" from which Allen Light deserted was the vessel on which Richard Henry Dana had sailed from Boston to the coast of California. Dana's book, *Two Years before the Mast,* has an 1835-36 setting.

Nidever went on to say,

> After Sparks returned from the Lower Coast he and the Black Steward and I agreed to hunt together and were taken over to Santa Rosa by the "Peor es Nada" immediately after the Indians were taken off San Nicolas.

In his further accounting of the Santa Rosa incident, Nidever remarked that they had cached their supplies in a cave close to shore,

> On the northeast side of the Island and close to the present wharf there is a large cave. Its entrance is hardly larger than an ordinary doorway, but [the cave is] so large inside that a hundred persons could occupy it with ease. Here

we kept our provisions and other supplies.

The seriousness of the battle with the Indians from the brig in the Channel was not readily apparent, but many canoes and many Indians heading for the Island convinced Nidever and his men otherwise. The encounters lasted several days; with 3 Indians killed and several wounded, the brig sailed away.

Nidever and his men remained on the islands for the winter. Making Santa Rosa Island their headquarters, they also hunted off Santa Cruz and San Miguel.

From Nidever's accounting of other encounters with American vessels engaged in otter hunting, he did not seem to identify the vessel *Bolivar* with any particular personality. But it is known that the *Bolivar* was owned by John C. Jones. All the more provocative are Nidever's remarks on one of Sparks' stories. It was Sparks who wanted to capture the ship, lying off Santa Rosa Island, but it so happened that Alpheus B. Thompson was to be the leader of the group,

> They started off in the night, reached the brig, and were about to board her when, hearing a noise, Thompson was afraid that they were discovered and insisted upon giving it up, much to the disgust of Sparks and two or three others who did not believe in that way of doing things, . . .

Thompson, as a business partner of Jones, would hardly have wanted to attack a vessel of his own venture.

When the brig *Bolivar* was renamed *Oajaca* in 1843, Nidever was in the employ of Thompson and Jones, with Dye, Dawson, Sparks, and Hewitt. Sailing for Mexican waters for otter hunting, Nidever stated that they suffered not a little from hunger on their first trip to the south.

In 1846 Nidever was still in the employ of Thompson. With Fife, McCoy, and Charlie Brown, Nidever went up the coast with a few supplies. They were to obtain more supplies at Monterey on Thompson's credit—but Thompson had no credit at Monterey. So the men had to pay for their own supplies while they hunted into late 1846.

Nidever purchased a house in 1840, an adobe situated near the present railroad tracks. He married in 1841, and in 1850 he purchased his interest in San Miguel from "Bruce." In 1851 he made a few more hunts and purchased a 17-ton schooner. With his schooner Nidever did some preliminary piloting for

194

Assistant Lieutenant Commander, James Alden, of the U. S. Coast Survey.

His trip to San Nicolas Island with Charlie Brown in 1853, and their finding of the Lone Woman, is probably the climactic episode of Nidever's life. References to it are found elsewhere in this book.

The More Family

Thompson and West [B70], tell us that

The More family, . . . have been extensive purchasers of the old landed estates of the Spanish families. The Santa Rosa Island, the Patera or portion of the Hill estate, the Santa Paula y Saticoy, the Lompoc and Viejo Purissima and the Sespe came into their hands.

Even among themselves, the More family were wheelers-and-dealers; it is with difficulty that we trace the change of names to the property in which they had an interest.

Robert Glass Cleland [B10a], helped somewhat when he said that in 1860 the property of T. Wallace More, one of the large rancheros of Santa Barbara County, was assessed as follows,

Ranch or improvements	Number of Acres	Value
Rancho de San Cayetano (Sespe)	26,640 acres	$6,660
Rancho Santa Paula	17,760 acres	$4,440
½ interest, Rancho de Lompoc	24,420 acres	$6,105
¼ interest, Rancho Mission Viejo	2,200 acres	$550
¼ interest, Isla de Santa Rosa	13,440 acres	$3,125

The sad ending of the T. W. More murder case prompted Thompson and West in 1883 to conclude,

More undoubtedly bought the Sespe under the belief that he was getting six leagues, and like almost every man, wanted what he had paid for, . . . The settlers thought they were on Government land, and determined to maintain their rights . . . The wisest and best being who ever lived on earth, said: "Lead us not into temptation." The source of the temptation is in our deficient land system, which makes large landholdings and landless people possible.

T. W. More finally owned one-half interest in Santa Rosa Island in 1867. He had purchased, gradually, the Thompsons' interests. A. P. More owned one-half interest in 1865, for he had purchased the Jones' interests.

For some reason T. W. More gave up his island interest to A. P. in 1867, thus A. P. More owned the entire island. This ownership lasted until 1870 when H. H. More purchased one-half interest from A. P. More. When H. H. More passed away, his wife, Almira, owned that interest.

In the *San Francisco Morning Call*, November 19, 1883, "An Extensive Sheep Range on Santa Rosa Island," it is indicated that in 1881 A. P. More had purchased Henry H. More's widow's interest for $600,000. While the Santa Barbara Deed Book Y stated the selling price to be $100, one wonders. Perhaps there was some private transaction between the two brothers, or with the widow, before a legal record had been made.

A. P. More proceeded to lease the island, first to L. W. More, for the yearly sum of $140,000. Then John F. More took up the lease, which ran from 1891 through 1894.

Twelve years after A. P. More acquired full ownership of the island, he died intestate in Chicago, October 1893. John F. More was at that time both tenant and administrator of the A. P. More estate.

Difficulties arose between C. E. Sherman, court-appointed appraiser of Santa Rosa's assets, and John F. More. The lesseeship might reflect one of the stumbling blocks encountered by Mr. Sherman. He was not allowed on the island for appraisal purposes.

The full report on Sherman's difficulties and the state of the live stock on the island was published in the *Santa Barbara Weekly Independent,* June 15, 1895. This was one more sad finale in the More family, too long to report here, but most revealing. Part of the headline of the newspaper account read, "The Cattle, Sheep, and all Personal Effects said to be in a Very Deplorable Condition."

Deed Books 75 and 77 at the Santa Barbara Recorders Office contain much of interest about the relative value of the personal property and real estate that had belonged to A. P. More through "seizure" or acquisition. Santa Rosa Island of 53,760 acres was valued at $350,000; Rancho Los Dos Pueblos of 470.86 acres at $1,883.44; and Rancho La Goleta of 162.91 acres at $1,140.38.

In order to meet court expenses, some of the real estate had to be sold. Thomas M. Storke, first husband of Mattie More, daughter of T. W. More, purchased one piece of property for $1,695.50 and another piece for $1,026.50. C. E. Sherman, court-appraiser, purchased "Little Island" for $1,200; Helen K. Rowe, daughter of Andrew B. More, purchased other land for $4,410.

When probate was finally settled the individual shares ran from 1/27 to 1/24 to 1/8, with mathematical accuracy being the key to the division.

Two of Lawrence W. More's children conveyed their share to their brother, H. Clifford More, thus giving him a 1/8 interest. This, he sold in 1901 to Vail–Vickers for $32,500.

Two charts follow. One chart, with some detail, traces island ownership; another indicates various other land purchases by T. W. More, or by him with some other member(s) of the More family.

Closely related, although tangential, is information about others also living in the town of Santa Barbara at the same period as the Carlos Carrillo family. This information may be found in Appendix K, which includes an annotated bibliography.

Santa Rosa Island
Transfer of Title

Mexico's Pesado Letter, written July 26, 1838, favored a grant to Carrillo brothers

Governor J.B. Alvarado granted the island to José Castro, November 1, 1841

Governor Manuel Micheltorena granted the island to Carrillo brothers, October 4, 1843

	J.C. Jones dismissed as Consul 4/9/1838
	J.C. Jones baptised at Mission, 4/21/1838
Francisca Carrillo de Thompson	Manuela Carrillo de Jones
(1815- ?) married, 1834	(1820-1900) married, June 4, 1838
Had six children	Had six children

1843-1844, Captain Alpheus B. Thompson and John Coffin Jones began stocking the island. After 1844, Jones never returned to Sandwich Islands, his two amours, or his children by them

1852-1856, Halleck, Peachy and Billings helped in establishing title to island, confirmed October 3, 1871, and recorded July 20, 1874

Thompson had a home in Santa Barbara, social center for the elite	1846, Jones and family moved to Boston, disgruntled with Santa Barbara

Joint Ventures in illicit Pacific Coast trade, 1830-1843: otter hunting, hides, merchandise

1852-1860, litigation over island ownership and/or proceeds from it. Case #205, records in Salinas, California. Judgement in favor of Jones

Thompson, sued by debtors, including Estate of Stephen Reynolds, 10/6/1858	Jones, sued by debtors, incl. Parrot & Co.
Witnesses for Thompson: a brother of Manuela; brothers-in-law of J.C. Jones	Witnesses for Jones: Carlos Carrillo; Anastacio Carrillo, brother to Carlos; Nicolas A. Den; Luis Burton; Alfred Robinson
Chas. E. Huse, Attorney for T.W. More in his purchase at public auction of Thompson's ¼ island interest, 10/6/1858, $3000.00	Represented by: Chas. Fernald, Attorney; W.A. Washburn, Boston Attorney; Alfred Robinson, business agent; Abel Stearns, Receiver
The six Thompson children sold their ¼ interest in island separately for a total of $6000.00 to T.W. More, 1869-70	Manuela Jones and children sold their ½ interest to A.P. More, 2/15/1865, through Washburn, $18,000. Manuela set up trust for her five living children and second husband, George F. Kettle
Alpheus Basilio Thompson, 1797-1871. Died in Los Angeles	John Coffin Jones, 1796-1861, died in Boston

See also Manuela Carrillo de Jones, *et. al.,* vs. U.S. Case #117, U.S. District Court, (Bancroft Library), or a microfilm copy in Cabrillo National Monument Library

Santa Rosa Island
Transfer of Title

T.W. More sold to A.P. More, 1867, his ½ interest in the island

A.P. More sold to H.H. More, 1870, a ½ interest in the island

Mrs. H.H. More sold to A.P. More, 1881, her ½ interest in the island

— — — —

A.P. More rented the island to Lawrence W. More,
then
A.P. More leased the island to John F. More, 1891-1894.
A.P. More died intestate, 10/21/1893, Chicago

— — — —

First Administrator, John F. More, dismissed, died, 1899
Administratix, Eliza M. Miller, between 1895-1900

Probate handled by Miller, sister of A.P. More. After Probate, brothers and sisters and/or other heirs of deceased brothers or sisters received from 1/8 to 1/27 of the residue, $12,177.56. The island had yet to be sold

— — — —

Walter L. Vail, Edward N. Vail, Mahlon Vail, N.R. Vail, Alexander Vail (foreman), and J.V. Vickers purchased the island from the various A.P. More heirs. One 1/8 interest sold for $32,500.00, 1901

"Some of the ranch hands . . . live in a big comfortable hacienda built before the turn of the century by A.P. More family, the previous owners" [B109]

The More Family Holdings

Rancho La Goleta, 162.91 Acres. Part of Pío Pico grant to Rafaela Luisa Oliveras de Ortega, [married Daniel Hill]. Purchased by A.P. & T.W. More

Miscellaneous parcels, value of $7,132, purchased by A.P. More

"Little Island," value $1,200, purchased by A.P. More

Ortega Ranch, purchased by A.P. More

La Purisima and Mission Viejo Rancho, Lompoc, Calif., 44,000 Ac. purchased by the More family

Las Positas y Calera, Thomas Robbins, grantee, sold to the Mores

T.W. More
married Susana A. Hill
June, 1853;
murdered, 3-24-1877

A.P. More
died 10-21-1893
without heirs

Rancho Los Dos Pueblos (La Patera) 470.86 Ac. granted to Rosa [Oliveras] Hill de Den [Dr. Nicolas A. Den]; Purchased by T.W. More. Son, T.R. More, married Mary Den, lived here 1884-1889. Storke had retained 300 Ac. of the grant

Santa Paula & Saticoy Rancho, 16,000 Ac. purchased by the More family

Santa Rosa Island, Grant to Carrillos, 1843, sold to Manuela and Francisca, daughters. Passed into the hands of A.P. & T.W., & H.H. More, 1858-1870

M72, 1883, San Francisco Morning Call: "A.P. More retained an interest in Santa Cruz Island Ranch," supposedly 30%

Rancho Sespe or San Cayentano Granted 11-29-1829 to María Josefa Castro de Carrillo 2 sq. leagues; Santa Clara Valley. Sold 11-8-1854 to T.W. More by Carlos Carrillo, $18,000. Part interest sold to A.P. More, 12-18-1861. Rancho managed by C.A. Storke, attorney and son-in-law of T.W., 1875-1877. Storke retained 600 Ac.; married Yda Addis, 1890. [See B70, "The Murder of T. Wallace More," an outgrowth of bitter dispute between T.W. More and settlers over Rancho Sespe being 2 or 6 square legués, as initially represented by Carlos Carrillo]

PIECES OF EIGHT
Natural History
Flora

Dr. Kellogg and Mr. Harford were the first botanical collectors on Santa Rosa and Santa Cruz; this was in 1874. A Mr. Hazard had collected *Lyonothamnus* in 1885, and Dr. Greene made identification for all three men on their few but important plants. Greene, himself, went to Santa Cruz in July 1886, but collected only on the western side of the island [J72, J258, J259]. The following year, or perhaps 1888, Dr. Brandegee went to both Santa Cruz and Santa Rosa islands. He stayed on Santa Cruz for six weeks and collected from all parts of the island. On Santa Rosa he remained for ten days and collected on only the northern and eastern sides of the island [J61].

In 1887 during the ten collecting days on Santa Rosa, Dr. Brandegee found a total of 200 species, twenty of which were not to be found on Santa Cruz [J61]. He gave the combined known flora of Santa Cruz and Santa Rosa as close to 400, with 380 of the species being on Santa Cruz.

Dr. Greene had said that he gathered 321 species on Santa Cruz. In 1887 Dr. Le Conte, who had studied the work of Dr. Greene, thought that perhaps twenty of his species were insular in character [J73].

In 1941 Alice Eastwood used the figure 321 as the number of species for Greene's collection and remarked that Dr. Brandegee's additions to that list were eighty, thus making a total of 401 [J74]. Today, about 451 species are listed for Santa Cruz and 367 for Santa Rosa islands [B120].

Brandegee must have had some misgivings about the number of endemics for the islands [J61],

> If the insular endemic flora of these islands is supposed to number twenty species, some doubtful ones must be included; nine of these twenty endemic species inhabit also Santa Catalina and Guadalupe Islands, leaving eleven or less, peculiar to Santa Cruz, Santa Rosa and San Miguel.

Brandegee had been on Santa Catalina for collecting purposes four different times from 1884-1899.

A recent check on this "9 out of 20" relationship between Santa Catalina and the three northern islands indicates a count of "10 out of 20" for endemics in common.

Earlier, San Clemente had not been mentioned, but today the count for the two southern islands is practically identical—for this type of comparison.

As late as 1967 [B120], the count was twenty-three endemics for the mixed northern islands, mainly belonging to Santa Cruz and Santa Rosa. This is a gain of thirteen for these islands since Brandegee discussed the subject ninety years ago.

According to Raven [B120], Santa Rosa had its own three single-island endemics, two being herbs and one, a manzanita. At first it was thought that *Salvia brandegei*, a sage, belonged in that category but was later found, at least one specimen, to be growing in Baja, California. Obviously, it is not a common plant.

Erysium insulare, a wallflower, supposedly endemic for Santa Rosa, is also found on San Miguel Island; but Munz said it may be found on the mainland, too.

The closed cone pine, *Pinus remorata*, is found on Santa Cruz and Santa Rosa islands. This tree was also found in the early Pleistocene deposits on Santa Cruz by Dr. Mason, and was named by him.

In the Symposium material [B120], there are full discussions by authorities of both the *Pinus Torreyana* and the *Pinus remorata*. As a part of the discussion it is mentioned that the *remorata* seldom attains tree height, except in sheltered situations.

Generally speaking, it may be found on Santa Rosa to the north and west at an altitude of 650 feet to 980 feet, growing in scattered groups, rather than in stands. But there is one stand near Black Mountain; perhaps there are no more than 200–300 'trees' on the whole island.

Santa Rosa Island's Torrey Pine is not found on any of the other islands, but it may be found near San Diego—having a hard time in its struggle for survival. The problems seem to be drought, insects, undergrowth, and human beings. The Torrey Pine is ancient, of Ice Age vintage.

This pine may be found at the mouth of Soledad Canyon. Here, near the Vail Ranch, their stand appears to be strong. On the northeast coast in the eastern part of Bechers Bay, the grove near the sea cliff runs for about one-half mile. It is on a ridge 200 feet to 500 feet in height. Here, the trees are exposed, are wind-pruned, and none attain a height of more than thirty-five feet.

The *Eschscholtzias Californica*, California poppy, non-endemic, a sea shore plant, is found abundantly on both Santa Cruz and Santa Rosa, perhaps due to the great extent of their coast lines [J61],

> Some of the seaward slopes of Santa Rosa Island abound with *Eschscholtzias* varying in color

from red-brown to extremely glaucous. The flowers are of all shades of color between light yellow and deep orange, and vary much in size.

Both Santa Cruz and Santa Rosa grow *Ceanothus arboreus,* the island lilac, but each has a different form. No doubt there is a climatic reason back of these differences. Munz stated that the lilac also grows on Santa Catalina.

According to Brandegee, "The direct effects of an insular climate upon the vegetation, with least intervention from other forces, are best shown upon Santa Cruz and in the protected cañons of Santa Rosa."

The *Dendromecon densifolia,* tree poppy [shrub] of Santa Rosa varies with the winds; in some places it resembles the mainland variety, and in other places it resembles the insular form of Santa Cruz. Munz said that the plant needs further study.

Another of Brandegee's insights,

is the tendency that mainland shrubs and bushes show on the islands not to develop their lower limbs and branches and therefore become tree-like. The most conspicuous examples of these tree-like bushes are *Prunus ilicifolius* [Cherry], *Cercocarpus* [*betuloides*] [Mountain-mahogany], *Rhus* [Sumac], *Rhamnus* [Buckthorn], *Ceanothus* [Lilac].

There are more recent statements about Santa Rosa's plant life. Austin Wright [J376], recommended for his unusually descriptive words about the island, told of his and Hoffmann's hunt for the *Jepsonia malvifolia* of the Saxifraga family on Santa Cruz and Santa Rosa.

Actually, this bulb has been found on all of the islands except Santa Barbara, Anacapa, and San Miguel. At the time of his writing in 1930-31, however, Wright considered the Jepsonia to be very rare. Perhaps it still is,

. . . In the herbaria there are only two or three specimens of malvifolia and very few of Parryi. It was known to grow at one place near San Diego, at one place on Santa Cruz, and at one place on Santa Rosa. It was very rare and its habits little known. It was reported as flowering before leaving . . .
. . . I had the good fortune to light upon a Jepsonia malvifolia in flower. The reason we did not find it sooner was, I think, because we were too low. We found it well up the side of the canyon about 300-400 feet above sea level. It is a plant that grows out of bulb sending up a

wirey stem four to six inches long on which grows in a close cluster five or six small whitish flowers with dark dots. The leaves come up separately and lie flat on the ground . . . the bulb sends up the flower in the fall, but the leaves wait for rain . . . We found many Jepsonia and now all the great Herbariums in the United States will have specimens.

Originally, it was Greene who identified the plant and gave it the name, *Saxifraga malvaefolia,* which name has gone through a transformation.

Miscellaneous comments by various writers help in locating or naming other plants or trees on Santa Rosa. Orr said there is a very large grove of Elderberry trees [*Sambucus*] in front of Arlington Cave; however, it is not endemic to the islands. One variety has been found on Santa Cruz.

Ralph Hoffmann found a grove of Ironwoods only 200 or 300 feet above sea level [J376]. This tree, *Lyonothamnus asplenifolius,* is an island endemic, very ancient in the geneology of development, still trying to cling to life on the islands [B83]. It is also found near the center of the island in a large grove [J139].

Of canyon growth in general, Pemberton, who visited the island in 1928, said,

The deep canyons are thickly wooded with immense oaks, sycamores and willows with oak brush and other shrubs on the ridges between canyons . . . [with] the sheltered canyons of the west and south containing brush and some woods.

During Wright's and Hoffmann's canyon-exploring in 1930 they found one "canyon . . . deep, dark, and full of things . . . It was also full of boulders, blackberry vines hanging in vertical screens like old fashioned bead curtains, and dry waterfalls . . ."

The average reader is not familiar with the fact that Hoffmann knew the natural history of the northern islands very well; also that he was a teacher-friend of Wright. Neither is it common knowledge that both he and Wright met with premature deaths. Wright was in an accident in 1931; Hoffmann fell from a cliff on San Miguel Island in 1932.

Hoffmann had just published some of his material in the *Southern California Academy of Sciences Bulletin* in "Notes on the Flora of the Channel Islands off Santa Barbara, California" [J346, 1932]. Without further notes to follow, the second article under the same title [J347], would never have been given to the public. But P. A. Munz of Pomona College was able to complete this task for Ralph Hoffmann.

Since then, P. A. Munz has published a catalogue, *A Manual of Southern California Botany*, 1935. Containing over 600 pages, it offers lists of endemics for the desert, the mountain, and Cismontane regions of California, and includes separate lists for the insular flora within that region. Unfortunately, this material is thirty years old, and incompatible with another listing of island endemics through Raven in the *Symposium* material, 1967.

A more recent catalogue of over 1600 pages of *The California Flora* by Munz, with the collaboration of other authorities, is an extension of his 1935 publication; however it does not contain lists of endemics and is cumbersome to handle. A comparison of island endemics from other available sources reveals conflicting or incomplete data.

What would be worthwhile is another Alice Eastwood to coordinate and synthesize contributions from Ira W. Clokey, 1931, to the present day. What would be worthwhile is a firm, official, up-to-date, subject-to-change, listing of only island endemics and/or other species. The cumbersome task of a page-by-page catalogue search for such information is certainly no guarantee of accuracy. The author finds the islands' endemic accounting in a state of limbo.

Fauna

It is generally understood that the endemic fox, spotted skunk, and deer mouse are on Santa Rosa Island, as well as Santa Cruz. Additional comments for Santa Rosa alone are brief in nature.

Grinnell obtained twenty fox from Santa Rosa in 1927 and discussed the subject [J53]. Orr remarked that the Santa Rosa Island dwarf fox becomes seasonally semi-blinded from dirt and seeds in their eyes; this is not the same reason given for the blindness of the Santa Cruz Island fox, that being scabies from sheep. Of the Deer Mouse, Wilson said that the one of Pleistocene times is quite different from the one now living on the island [J182, 1936].

Although six species of bat are listed for Santa Cruz through Professor Von Bloeker [B120], only the *California Myotis* finds its name among Santa Rosa's living creatures.

Yates [J331, 1903], discussed land snails in his "Prehistoric California." Of Santa Rosa,

> Twenty-five years ago the writer found extensive areas . . . on Santa Rosa Island, the casts of trees were then standing, and the ground was

covered with dead snail shells in great abundance.

The *Helix Ayresiana* is found only on Santa Rosa, Santa Cruz, and San Miguel [J331].

In *American Antiquity* [J5, 1940], Arthur Woodward remarked,

> . . . the deposition of dead snail shells was a continuous process even in prehistoric times. Therefore, the discovery of these shell deposits mingled with regular midden is not surprising and I believe may safely be judged natural rather than man-made middens.

Only two references are used for the herpetofauna of Santa Rosa Island. One is John Van Denburgh's 1905, "The Reptiles and Amphibians of the islands of the Pacific Coast of North America from the Farallons to Cape San Lucas and the Revilla Gigedes" [J66]. The second, also a California Academy of Sciences reference in 1914 [J68], has the same author and Joseph R. Slevin, "Reptiles and Amphibians of the West Coast of North America."

According to Van Denburgh [J66], Dr. Eisen was on the island in 1897 and collected eight specimens of *Batrachoseps pacificus*, of the salamander family. In the later article [J68], it is said that the two authors collected *Hyla regilla*, of the frog family. Beck, on the island in 1903, found *Sceloporos becki* and *Gerrhonotus scincicanda* [J66], both of the lizard family. Other literature has mentioned *Sceloporus occidentalis* as an additional possibility for the island. Orr referred to a gopher snake on Santa Rosa.

Of insect life, "K" said [P88, 1893],

> In and out of the long lines of gray fences flitted the small, brown birds—. . . Here and there on the posts were masses of red lady bugs, like long washes of vermillion paint. Why the little creatures were there in such numbers, unless pictoral effect, the combined wisdom of the party failed to surmise.

Speaking of insects, the *Canadian Entomologist* [J98, 1897], contains an article written by H. C. Fall of Pasadena. Since the article is eleven pages long, it contains much of value for those interested in that discipline.

From the standpoint of Santa Rosa Island, on page 235 it is stated that "more than thirty species out of seventy-five taken by Dr. Gustav Eisen on Santa Rosa" must be added to the total insect record for the islands. The 1897 expedition, having collected forty-six species from the islands, included Santa Barbara, San Nicolas, and San Clemente.

In 1938 Dr. Cockerell, in his article, "San Miguel Island," *Scientific Monthly,* said that "Many years ago, the well-known zoologist Eisen collected ten species of spiders on Santa Rosa, and these were recorded in 1904 by Dr. N. Banks." Someone reported that no mosquitoes existed on Santa Rosa Island. Maybe it was the gnats on a visit from Santa Cruz that disturbed Dr. Jones' sleep.

Most everyone knows that sheep, then cattle, have been raised on Santa Rosa Island. Not everyone knows that the Mores imported elk and deer to their island, with a thought of even putting ostriches on it [B70, 1883]. No one appears to know where the wild hogs came from.

Boars

It is difficult to believe that the reverted wild hogs, or boars, were introduced on Santa Cruz by Martin Kimberly. It would be easier to accept the fact that the pigs were part of the provisions provided by the earliest explorers, in anticipation of a return trip to the islands. At any rate, there are formidable wild boars on Santa Catalina, Santa Cruz, and Santa Rosa islands. There are also mini-pigs on Santa Catalina.

Boar hunting is a sport for the huntsman, a sport presumably with some attached danger. Arthur Sanger in 1911 acquired a schooner, *The Dreamer* [P157]. And according to Mrs. Lester [B103], Sanger regularly took parties to Santa Rosa and Santa Cruz for wild boar hunting.

C. F. Holder [B38], made these comments about the wild hog,

[They] are very numerous and sometimes attack and kill the lambs. They are dangerous things for an unmounted, unarmed man to meet. Many hundreds are shot every year, but it seems difficult to exterminate them.

Then Holder repeated a description published in the East, which tells of the attempt by an Englishman to try East Indian pig-sticking on Santa Rosa:

'If my horse had stumbled I believe that pig would have ripped him [the horse] up,' he said. 'Did you see him?' 'Bristles on his back half a foot high, tusks four inches long . . .'

The hunter who had stuck pigs in India rallied first, turned his bronco, and forced it at the boar, which had stopped and stood, head up, a picture of fiendishness. It was one of the old-timers without question, combining the qualities of a

Florida razorback with the savageness of an East Indian wild boar and the staying powers of a California island wild goat.

The boar filled the air with cries and maddened squeals, then quickly charged back along the line . . . It presented a savage spectacle. Its jaws were dripping with foam, its small, black, beadlike eyes gleaming with rage and fear . . .

After they had examined the old fellow, Manuel as cleverly released the boar, and with all the fight taken out of it the animal trotted off into the brush without even looking behind.

Things Marine

The *Overland Monthly* of 1870 published "Sea-Elephant," by Captain C. M. Scammon [P78]. Scammon knew his marine mammals, and the article is authentic, and popularly written. He compared the sea-lion, sea-otter, and sea-elephant and mentioned that the elephant comes on shore, at times, for the purpose of "shedding." After this has happened they are called "slim-skin." He makes Santa Barbara Island the popular locale for sea-elephant hunting.

As early as 1870 Scammon says that "owing to the continual pursuit of the animals, they have become nearly, if not quite, extinct on the California coast, or the few remaining have fled to some unknown point for security." Treatment of the sea-elephant after it is killed is for the oil, ". . . the oil is tried out by boiling the blubber, or fat, in large pots set in a brick furnace for the purpose. The oil produced is superior to whale oil for lubricating purposes."

From O'Neill [B53], we obtain more definite facts about the hunted sea-elephant, sea-otter—and abalone:

Among marine items of the 'fifties,' we learn that the schooner *Victoria* came in with 600 gallons of elephant and seal oil on March 3, 1857, and landed another 700 gallons the following month. About the same date the *Elsie* brought twelve tons of abalone from Santa Rosa Island, and the *Ella Fisher* reported a cargo of 55 otter skins.

Of the abalone [P88, 1893], from "K," "In the crannies of the rocky shore [on Santa Rosa] are thousands of abalones, of whose dried flesh and shells the Chinese fishers ship many tons to their countrymen . . ." Even as late as 1963 the abalones appear to be plentiful as John Bugay [P180], noticed, "At low tide, the abalone are exposed on the rocks in such profusion that they look like bunches of grapes in a basket . . ."

PIECES OF EIGHT

We have an 1883 [B70] account of another marine creature. Because of the subject matter's uniqueness, and some humor, the account will also be quoted, allowing the reader to judge for himself—

July 19, 1877, a large turtle of the hawkbill species, and weighing 700 pounds, was caught near the Santa Rosa Island, by the surveying party of the *Mc Arthur*. It measured eight feet across the breast. Subsequently the *Press* estimated its weight at 1,200 pounds, but then it was to beat an Eastern turtle's weight. At another time it was reported that—

A nondescript monster of the turtle family was caught in the channel by some fisherman. Supposing it to be edible, the steward of the Morris House served it up for his guests. It was what is called a leather-back turtle. Dimensions, 5½ feet by 3½; weight, 800 pounds. No deaths recorded.

Avifauna

According to Miller [J153, 1951], Mr. C. H. Townsend of the U. S. Fish Commission collected on Santa Rosa in 1889 and obtained thirteen specimens of birds; Clark P. Streator did some collecting there for a couple of days in 1892 [N6].

J. R. Pemberton noted in his 1928 article that in 1917 A. B. Howell had listed the known species of land birds for Santa Rosa. So when Pemberton went to Santa Rosa he considered his contribution to be an additional forty for the island [J139].

The more recent record [J153, 1951], indicates that for a combination of Santa Cruz and Santa Rosa islands, there were twenty-six species in common. Miller had added six for Santa Rosa and four for Santa Cruz.

A few days later, Mr. Rett and Mr. Abbott of the Santa Barbara Museum of Natural History, were on Santa Rosa Island. Staying there for two weeks, as compared with Miller's visit of four days, "85 specimens representing 36 species of birds were collected . . ." [J275].

The main thrust of the Miller article is a comparison of the avifauna on the two islands. For instance, he found Song Sparrows on only Santa Rosa, although they had once been collected on Santa Cruz by Beck and Mailliard. He did not find Rufus-crown or Bell Sparrows on Santa Rosa. Other comparisons are made—on Loggerhead Shrikes, Bewick Wrens, House Finches, and Spotted Towhees. [See also N5, 1899 for Wren subspecies.]

Of the species taken on Santa Rosa, Miller listed the Burrowing Owl, Mountain Bluebird, Blue-gray Gnatcatcher; others were observed, but not collected. The Rett-Abbott list appears to be somewhat, probably not completely, mutually exclusive of the Miller's list.

Apparently all records had been evaluated by the Pacific Coast Avifauna [B111-116].

Indians and Archaeology

Phil C. Orr and his book, *Prehistory of Santa Rosa Island* [B54], published in 1968 is a full account of the work that has been done in the field of archaeology through the years. It contains tables, figures, bibliography, glossary, and index, all of which assist the readers in following the fairly technical subject matter.

There is a chronological listing of the previous work done on the island, and a short description of the island. A discussion of the island during Pleistocene time follows, which includes fossils and evidences of early man. Then step by step, and area by area, we are lead to Post-Pliocene man and where his sites are located.

Orr began his study of Santa Rosa and its archaeological aspects in 1947, publishing progressive results, mainly through the *Santa Barbara Museum of Natural History*, where he was Curator. He also published in *American Antiquity, Science,* and the *National Academy of Sciences*.

Some newspapers and journals followed the course of events and by April 1, 1956 the *Sacramento Union* [M80], announced in an article, "Ancient Man: Old Theories on Arrival in America Shattered." This was because Arlington Springs Man had been found.

The relatively new carbon-dating process has been used to determine the age of charred artifacts at three sites where the fossil mammoth bones existed. [M149, M189, M188, M191, and J193 offer some few further details on this subject.]

In a Department of Fish and Game Report [#118, C3, 1962], Orr remarked, "We feel confident that there are many middens much older than these on both the [Channel] Islands and the mainland, which are as yet undated." Orr named the earliest Recent Indians "Dune Dwellers," living on the island about 7,400 years ago. The middle group he termed "Highlanders," living there about 5,370 years ago. And the most recent of the recent "Canaliños," were on the island beginning about 1,860 years ago.

Other briefer, earlier comments should be included in this survey of Santa Rosa Island archaeological material. One of these is from *American Antiquity* [J5, 1940], under "Notes and News," when a report was made of Arthur Woodward's visit to San Miguel and Santa Rosa Island. Woodward said that he had found approximately forty sites on Santa Rosa,

I found two small sites where the inhabitants had apparently done nothing except manufacture olivella shell beads. I surfaced over 1700 small chert drills, a number of beads, bead blands and recent Canalino type arrowheads and knife blades.

Fifteen years earlier David Banks Rogers did some investigative work on the island and also published a book through the Santa Barbara Museum of Natural History in 1929, *Prehistoric Man of the Santa Barbara Coast* [B63]. A limited section is devoted to "Exploration of the Channel Islands," limited due to the fact that he divided his two-weeks' among the four northern islands over a period of a few successive years.

Rogers, Curator of the Santa Barbara Museum of Natural History before Phil C. Orr, worked mainly on the mainland and began at the time the Smithsonian Institution renewed a more detailed interest in the time and the locations of Pacific Coast archaeology.

Working independently, both Olson and Rogers named three distinct Indian cultures of recent geologic history. With the exception of "Canaliño," Phil C. Orr did his own naming of similar cultures for Santa Rosa Island.

Dr. Gustav Eisen, zoologist, with an old Santa Rosa Island Indian resident, named St. Iago, did a little digging and some collecting on the island for the California Academy of Sciences as early as 1897. On all of the islands for the same purpose, his pamphlet, "An Account of the Indians of the Santa Barbara Islands in California," was published in 1904 [M30].

Philip Mills Jones dug on San Nicolas Island in 1901 before going to Santa Rosa Island. In the private employ of Mrs. Phoebe Hearst, he was collecting material for the University of California at Berkeley and their new Lowie Anthropological Museum; Mrs. Hearst was a trustee of the University at the time. Fifty-five years later Jones' notes about Santa Rosa were published under the editorship of R. F. Heizer and A. B. Elsasser [U5].

Jones, too, used the services of old St. Iago, who,

it was indicated, had lived on the island from about the time of our Civil War. According to Jones, he and his helpers collected twelve cases of diggings for shipment to the Lowie Museum.

His tales of experiences with an infected wrist, sand in his eyes, running short of grub and water, a painful bruise on his left foot, being bitten by 'mosquitoes,' does not make one feel that he enjoyed his stay on the island from about the middle of February to the early part of June 1901.

It was on the 3rd of April that Jones' helpers, John and Billy, went to the Rancho Viejo area, "and returned with a load of stuff." It could have been on this trip that the "JR" stone was found. It bears the crude cross in the upper left hand corner, "JR" near the center, and a stick figure toward the bottom. Since being reviewed by Heizer [U21, 1972], the origin and meaning of this stone has created considerable discussion. A 'quien sabe' for most.

Jones and his workers spent some time in the Cañada La Jolla area, and a good discussion of it may be found in Orr's book on the *Prehistory of Santa Rosa Island*. The more recent archaeologists, including Orr, give the distinct impression that there was much to be desired in the workmanship of Philip Mills Jones.

Dr. H. C. Yarrow was a surgeon and a zoologist for the Major Powell Expedition [Wheeler Survey]. It is stated that he temporarily headed a special group in the vicinity of Santa Barbara, which included Santa Cruz Island [N45].

According to Yarrow, Mr. W. G. W. Harford belonged to the U. S. Coast and Geodetic Survey, and was on the islands of San Miguel and Santa Rosa, 1872-73. Dr. Harford "procured a small but exceedingly valuable collection of interesting objects, which came into the hands of [conchologist] Mr. William H. Dall," of the National Museum [#H13 of JJ, N45].

Word became common knowledge, and Dr. Schumacher reported the value of the Dr. Harford and Dr. Dall [1873-74] collections to the Museum. It was at this point in time that Schumacher was asked to explore the islands, as well as the mainland.

As we continue to reach back into time, there is Paul Schumacher's "Researches in the Kjökkenmöddings of the Coast of Oregon, and of the Santa Barbara Islands," in the *Bulletin* of the *U. S. Geological and Geographical Survey* of 1877 [N41].

Schumacher, in his collecting spree for the Smithsonian Institution, was on San Nicolas, San Clemente, Santa Catalina, San Miguel, and Santa Cruz, but he was not on Santa Rosa Island. Here is what he said on the subject,

I am well aware of the great deposits of kjökkenmöddings on Santa Rosa Island, as I was informed of them by the owner, who is a reliable man, and I observed some of them while passing by. I was also told that many implements are scattered over the surface, especially where the contents of a cemetery have become exposed by the winds, and the bare skeletons now bleach in the sun. Moreover, certain parties spoke of caves containing human remains, which may be authentic; but to this sort of promises I was treated on the two islands mentioned. My time and, what was more important, the amount appropriated for this work had to be taken in consideration, as well as my great desire to get all I could discover.

Nevertheless, Schumacher sent back to Washington, D. C. fifty-one boxes of ethnological specimens from the West Coast.

The Wheeler Survey party did not go to Santa Rosa either, but used the services of Rev. Stephen Bowers instead. Bowers, in turn, hired Dr. L. G. Yates to assist with the work conducted on the island.

Since there has been some confusion as to the responsibilities and the services of the survey parties, Joseph Henry's words [N10, 1875], enlighten us. As Secretary to the Smithsonian Institution, he offered an Appendix to their report and explained,

For the purpose of properly working this field, arrangements were made jointly by the Smithsonian Institution and the Indian Bureau with Mr. Paul Schumacher to proceed with a party and prosecute his explorations. The Treasury Department authorized the transportation of the party to the islands on a revenue-cutter, and the War Department furnished rations at cost-price, as well as tents, &c., while the United States Coast Survey extended the courtesy of one of its surveying vessels, under Captain Taylor. With these facilities, Mr. Schumacher gathered a large number of articles, some tons in weight, and representing a great variety of very choice specimens, such as stone mortars, pestles, ornaments of stone, shell, bone, &c.

Simultaneously with this labor of Mr. Schumacher, Lieutenant Wheeler, of the Engineer Bureau, had a party in the vicinity of Santa Barbara, in charge of Dr. H. C. Yarrow, which also made important collections. In the same field

and with satisfactory results, Rev. Stephen Bowers has also been occupied in behalf of the Centennial display . . .

The many correspondents of the Smithsonian Institution were also invited, by means of a circular, to make contributions to the same department. The returns have already been very great, amounting to many thousands of stone implements of every kind and character.

In some instances gentlemen who were not willing to present their collections permanently, have consented to lend them for the Exhibition, . . .

In addition to what has already been acknowledged, the War Department has also rendered much assistance by instructing quartermasters to receive and forward packages delivered to them for the purpose of the Centennial display [N10].

. . . An exhaustive report on the subject will be published by Major Powell, the collections themselves becoming the property of the National Museum . . . [N11].

Dr. Henshaw, and others, have referred to H. C. Taylor as being of immeasurable assistance [N45]. He belonged to the Navy Department and furthered the work of the Coast Survey in many ways, such as making soundings around the islands [N41]. His was a high degree of nautical skill, coupled with a real interest in the Cabrillo and Ferrelo routes.

For this no one could be more fully qualified than Lieut. Commander H. C. Taylor, of the Navy, whose long service on the west coast in connection with the labors of the Coast Survey has made him perfectly familiar with nearly every cape and anchorage from the Columbia River to Cape St. Lucas.

Schumacher and others were also helped by being transported on the Coast Survey steamer *Hassler* by H. C. Taylor.

Dr. Bowers' "Santa Rosa Island," was part of the 1877 Annual Report of the Smithsonian Institution [N12]. In it Bowers said that he spent a month on the island, and obtained around a ton of relics for "the Government." Professor Spencer F. Baird reported that over forty boxes of material had been supplied by Bowers. This material included arrowheads, drills, beads, bone articles, wampum, and such.

Secretary Joseph Henry remarked [N12],

The exploration by Mr. Bowers was a continuation of one undertaken in connection with Major Powell, . . . There can never be a better representation of the archaeology of the tribes of the California Coast than that now in Washington.

This comment was made over fifty years before Arthur Sanger gathered and sold collections to other museums, which perhaps rivaled the Smithsonian collection [M98, P157, J32-33, J18, J209].

For Dr. Yates' services, Dr. Bowers gave a two-sentence footnote in his report, "Dr. Lorenzo G. Yates, of Centerville, Cal., rendered me valuable assistance in the exploration of this island. The geology is principally compiled from his notes." Dr. Yates said elsewhere that the whole report was taken from his notes.

From an 1862 newspaper account, *California Farmer,* under "California Notes," Alexander S. Taylor spoke on the Indianology of California [M51]. Here is what he said on the subject of some dead Indians and their possessions on the island of Santa Rosa,

> San Buenaventura Mission Indians, Santa Rosa Island: Talking with an American resident of these parts, acting as the mayor domo for the Messrs. Moore [sic] of Saticoy Rancho, he informs us that in a recent stay on Santa Rosa island, in the summer of 1861, rodeoing cattle, he often met with the entire skeletons of Indians in the caves of that island. The signs of their rancherias or camps were very frequent, and the remains of metates, mortars, earthen pots and other vessels very common. The metates were of a dark stone, and made something after the pattern of the Mexican. Extensive caves were often met with which seemed to serve as burial places of the Indians, as entire skeletons and numerous skulls were plentifully scattered about in their recesses.

Somewhere in Taylor's notes he mentioned a "Mr. Robbins" as being Major Domo.

Father Lasuen died in 1803 and President Estevan Tapis became the leader in Mission affairs [B56]. In 1802 the Fathers of the Missions had thought that Santa Cruz and the Santa Rosa Indians might profit by having a mission established on one of the islands. But by 1805 there had been an epidemic of measles on the islands. In Tapis' March 13, 1807 report he wrote "that, as more than two hundred of the gentiles on the two islands have died of measles, correspond-

ingly fewer people exist there now . . ." [B18, J17, B26].

A. S. Taylor was also interested in Indians. In fact, he did considerable writing about them. One of his sources of information was his father-in-law, Daniel A. Hill.

Daniel A. Hill, originally from Massassachusetts, came to California from the Sandwich Islands in 1823. Captain Hill knew Father Antonio Ripoli, who was in charge of the Santa Barbara Mission from 1816 to 1827. And before Padre Ripoli left for Boston in 1828, he gave to the Captain much information about the customs of the Indians of the Santa Barbara area.

From his father-in-law, Taylor was told [M51], that although the priests had tried to Christianize the Indians, the Indians' great enemies were "the Devil and his chief earthly agent, King Alcohol."

Another of Taylor's remarks had to do with the employ by the Church Fathers of the Indians on the island for metate-making. This was being done before 1820, the metates being made "from a hard honeycomb basalt or a black rock found on the Island, and which, I am assured by several persons, is there very abundant."

No doubt there were multiple reasons for the Indians leaving this island, or any of the others. Duflot de Mofras', *Travels on the Pacific Coast* [B48, 1844], was published during Taylor's lifetime. De Mofras had this to say about their leaving, "At one time Indians inhabited these islands, but within the last few years they have been withdrawn to the mainland to avoid abuse at the hands of American sailors and other foreigners who came over to hunt sea otter and fur seals."

For whatever reason for leaving Santa Rosa, Taylor expressed the information that many of the Santa Rosa Indians were "brought over to Santa Ynez by the Priests, and they spoke entirely differently from the Santa Ynez Indians."

It was just after Taylor died that Bowers' 1877 report on Santa Rosa was published. Bowers seemed to know of a story of a famine on the island, causing the Indians to leave [N12]. But his was a query, as he also said that the only possible chance for a famine "would be in the drying up of the springs and freshwater streams, now abundant in the island . . ."

F. F. Guest, O.F.M. has an enlightening article in the first issue of Vol. LXI of the *Southern California Historical Society Quarterly.* One of his commentaries is,

PIECES OF EIGHT

In 1816 José Señán, at Mission San Buenaventura, wrote as follows: "Ignacio and certain others of our neophytes returned yesterday from a trip to the [Channel] Islands, where they had gone to look for some gentiles who wished to become converts. Our people brought back sixteen of them, and on their first trip last week they brought back twenty."

The Chumash Indians of Southern California [B41, 1963], through Leif Landberg, reported the same famine on Santa Rosa Island. Here is what Landberg, through his Southwest Museum publication, said on the subject,

. . . the only record of a "famine" among the Chumash comes from correspondence of Fr. José Señán of Mission San Buenaventura, dated June 15, 1816, about the Channel Islands. The famine occurred on Santa Rosa Island. It can be gathered from his remarks that when the mainstays of their subsistence, presumably fishing, failed there were few alternative sources of food to turn to:
"Ignacio and certain others of our neophytes returned yesterday from a trip to the Islands . . . [they] brought back 16 of them, . . . Among the crowd of yesterday there were four Russian Indians, . . . They seem to have come willingly enough because of famine conditions on Guimá

Island and because they had been told that meat is plentiful at San Buenaventura . . ."

Bowers continued in the same vein [N12],

In a large burying-place in the western portion of the island we found human bones occurring near the surface, which were broken lengthwise, as if to extract the marrow; and in the same place we found the skeletons of as many as fifty children, who would probably be the first to die in case of a famine . . . At all events, about the year 1816 the inhabitants of this island were reduced to a few individuals, and were removed by the priests of the Romish missions to the main land. They were placed in the mission of the Purissima, in the western part of what is now Santa Barbara County . . . One individual, an old man, and the last survivor of his tribe, was visited by Dr. J. L. Ord a few years since. This man's name was Omsett, and he said his tribe was called Chumas.

Dr. Ord was a brother to Major General E. O. C. Ord of the U. S. Army, and husband to María de la Guerra.

In any event, it seems evident that White Man, Time, and Tide were not good for our native brother. The Canaliños gradually slipped into the realm of the archaeologists' spade and field of interest.

Photos of Santa Rosa Island

Date	Code #	Author	Photo or Map	Reference
1903	J331	Yates	Fossil Teeth and Bones of Elephas Americanus	*So. Calif. Acad. Sci. Bulletin*
1917	B25	Gidney	Early photo of José de la Guerra home, built in the '30s at Santa Barbara	*Hist. of Santa Barbara, San Luis Obispo and Ventura Counties*
1929	B63	Rogers	Indian sites	*Prehistoric Man of the S. B. Coast*
1943	J178	Stock	Partly excavated skull of elephant	*L. A. Museum Quarterly*
1956	M154	Hillinger	Bleak Outpost (South Point)	*L. A. Times*
			Alley-oop (crane to land men and supplies)	*L. A. Times*
1958	J218	Warren, Jr.	Herefords & Angus	*National Geographic*
			Green Hills shelter Becher's Bay	*National Geographic*
			Stripped, excited ewes bound from corral	*National Geographic*
			"Borrego," a pet sheep	*National Geographic*
			Map, shows Vail & Vickers Co. Ranch; Radar Station	*National Geographic*
1962	J387	Holland	Map, from Museum of Paleontology, U.C.	*Journal of the West*
1963	P166	Hillinger	Thousands of cattle graze on the hills	*Westways*
1966	M112	————	Abandoned military installation	*L. A. Herald-Examiner*
1967	P135	————	Becher's Bay (ranch port)	*Sunset*
1968	B54	Orr	Otter Point; mammoth remains	*Prehistory of Santa Rosa Island*
			Sand cast tree (similar to those on Santa Rosa)	*Prehistory of Santa Rosa Island*
			Relict Torrey Pine, Beechers Bay	*Prehistory of Santa Rosa Island*
			Island dwarf fox, house cat size	*Prehistory of Santa Rosa Island*
			Relict pond on highlands	*Prehistory of Santa Rosa Island*
			Arlington Cave, used for living and burying	*Prehistory of Santa Rosa Island*
			Johnson's Lee, South Coast	*Prehistory of Santa Rosa Island*
			Fig. 77, Indian village site, Cañada Jolla Vieja, taken from mouth of Jones' cave	*Prehistory of Santa Rosa Island*
			Fig. 78, Interior of Cave "B," Jolla Vieja	*Prehistory of Santa Rosa Island*
			Fig. 33, Petroglyphs, or abrasion marks, Jones' Cave wall, Cañada Jolla Vieja, (Cave "A")	*Prehistory of Santa Rosa Island*

San Miguel

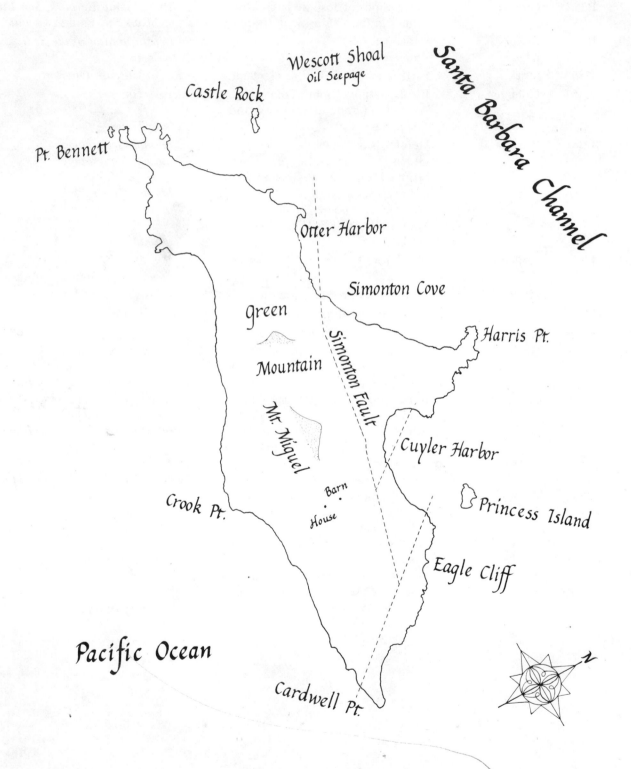

Castle Rock

Wescott Shoal
Oil Seepage

Santa Barbara Channel

Pt. Bennett

Otter Harbor

Simonton Cove

Green

Harris Pt.

Mountain

Simonton Fault

Mt. Miguel

Cuyler Harbor

Barn

Crook Pt.

House

Princess Island

Eagle Cliff

Pacific Ocean

Cardwell Pt.

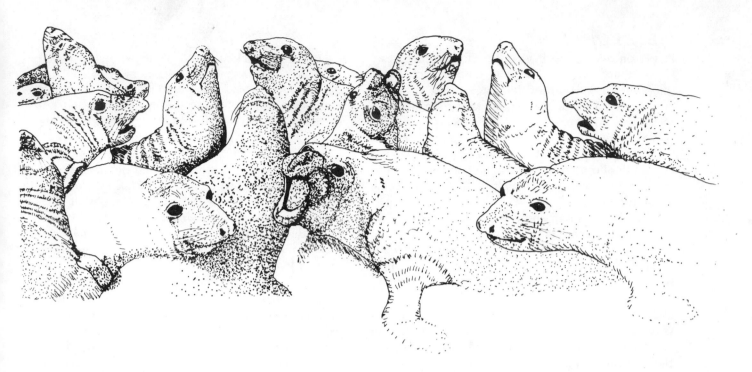

San Miguel

Environment
Physical Features
Bits of History

San Miguel is the most northern, as well as the most western island in its group. Its western point lies twenty-five miles in a southeast direction from POINT CONCEPCIÓN, the CAPE HORN OF CALIFORNIA [B15], offering the island no protection from the northwest winds that blow practically all year round.

RICHARDSON ROCK, named FARALLON DE LOS LOBOS in 1774 by Juan Perez, lies twenty-one miles in a southeast direction from Point Concepción. It is five and one-half miles from San Miguel's western point and seven and one-half miles from its northern point.

Richardson Rock is a rocky islet one hundred and sixty-five yards wide "and rises by sharp rocky cliffs to nearly fifty feet above the water" [N34]. Two smaller rocks inside of Richardson Rock toward San Miguel appear from some directions as attached to the Rock. Although there is no kelp reported around it, and even with thirty to forty fathoms to within one-third of a mile of the Rock, it was recommended that a whistling buoy be placed outside of the Rock for purposes of safer navigation.

San Miguel is the most dangerous to approach of the islands because it abounds in rocks, small islands, and shoals. Even the shores of San Miguel are bold, broken and rocky, with but few beaches along its seven and one-half by two mile [average] perimeter. The southern shore is more precipitous than the northern one, with few suggested anchorages and landings for small craft.

The current along the Santa Barbara Channel coming from the north follows the direction of the winds, but in the usual northwest weather, strong eddies run "to the westward under the lee of Point Bennett, and to the eastward under the lee of Cardwell Point in the San Miguel Passage" [N34], which is between the island and Santa Rosa Island.

These same winds that determine the direction of the currents are also playing havoc with the island's interior; some day the disappearing island will be listed as a shoal on the navigation charts!

The precipitous southern shore has a broad plateau at its eastern end, which rises to but forty to sixty feet, although the whole shore line rises from 100′ to 500′ elevations. Near the western part of this particular plateau is a projection called CROOK POINT. If one were to draw a line from CARDWELL

211

POINT on the east to POINT BENNETT on the west, Crook Point would be seen to extend about two-thirds of a mile south of that line. Crook Point appears to be a clean projection, free from outlying rocks, but with some kelp off of it [N34].

WYCKOFF LEDGE "is a sunken rock with fifteen feet of water upon it. It lies one half mile broad off the south shore, three and a half miles from the western point and four miles from the eastern point of the island" [N34].

Also on the south shore is TYLER'S BIGHT. Located one and three-quarters miles eastward of Point Bennett, it has a small indentation in its northwestern part under the high bluff. Here anchorage may be had in six and a half to eight fathoms of water [N34].

ADAMS COVE is also on the south side, and but two-thirds of a mile east of Point Bennett. Here small craft may find safe anchorage and protection from the northwest winds; however, familiarity of the approaches is important. Calcarious rock lies above the Cove.

According to Dr. Greene, who made an excursion to San Miguel in 1886 [J252], there was a

> bit of grassy headland on the southern shore well westward, a favorite camping ground with seal hunters, has been closely set about, by merry making men of that craft, with a circle of white skulls, their dark sockets looking seaward as if in contemplation of farther sunset shores, the whole array forming a lugubrious but unmistakable landmark.

Although this type of information does not give an exact location, it does allow room for conjecture as to where some sealers camped for their activities.

One home-made map shows a COMORANT ISLAND south of Adams Cove, almost opposite Point Bennett [J388].

Then comes the Point Bennett area and George Davidson remarks that it must be especially avoided! [N34]

> Point Bennett, the western point of the island, is a long, narrow, broken, and jagged bluff, rising forty feet from the water to three hundred and eighty feet within a mile. As seen from all directions, this point exhibits for two miles inland high dunes, the sand of which rises from the northwest shore and is driven by the northwesters across the island. There are three rocky islets under the south shore of the point and a number of rocks and foul ground off it.

212

One of the rocks south of Point Bennett is called SEAL ROCK [J388]. This rock, along with many of the other higher rocks, are used by the sea mammals for their basking, leaving the many lower and periodically submerged rocks to the shell fish. There is also a whistling buoy off the Point.

In 1928 [C2], Bonnot listed the Steller lion rookeries at San Miguel as being at Point Bennett, as well as at OFFSHORE ROCK, LION ROCK, Richardson Rock, WILSON ROCK and FLEA ISLAND. In 1969 Ashkenazy specified an elephant seal rookery near Point Bennett [P173]. During the Lester-tenancy, a 3,600 pound sea elephant was found on some shore of the island.

It was at Point Bennett that Ralph Hoffmann, Director of the Santa Barbara Museum of Natural History, fell to his death from an eighty-foot precipice in 1932, while hunting botanical specimens [B53]. Mrs. Lester [B103], said that the weather was foggy and although warned of the hazards under the existing conditions, Mr. Hoffmann had wandered away from his companion. What price zeal!

Point Bennett, six and one-half miles from the ranch house, has been the scene of other disasters. O'Neill states that "Off Bennett Point, . . . lie many wrecks. Among them, according to tradition, is a silver-laden Spanish galleon" [B128]. It had been recommended by Bache to Guthrie in 1854 that a light be placed on San Miguel [N26].

On one fateful day during a storm, seven U. S. destroyers crashed just north of Point Arguello and the *Cuba* ran aground on a rocky reef at Point Bennett. This was September 8th, 1923.

It was the *Reno*, speeding south as the luxury liner *Cuba* was steaming north from Panama to San Francisco, that signaled the alarm concerning the plight of the steamer. The men aboard the *Reno*, even in the thick fog, had seen an open lifeboat full of people and realized that a disaster had occurred.

The *Cuba* was sinking, with its coffee and silver bullion, but most of the passengers made it to shore [P174]—only to be met by sea lions who resented the intrusion.

A good sequel to the story, is Horace A. Sexton's "The Wreck of the Cuba," published in *Noticias, Quarterly Bulletin of the Santa Barbara Historical Society* [J295, 1959].

In slightly less than three pages, we are told how Captain Ira Eaton and his cronies headed for Point Bennett on the *Sea Wolf* to "rescue" as many of the goodies as possible from the *Cuba.* Too late to get the liquor, taken by others—these were Prohibition Days—the story tells how and what they did retrieve before the guard from San Pedro stopped them.

It was with a sigh of relief that we crossed the rip-tide between Santa Cruz and Santa Rosa, for the "Sea Wolf's" hold and cabin were crammed full and a heavy deckload lashed on, which brought her scuppers awash. We reached Pelican Bay about 11 P.M.

Pelican Bay on Santa Cruz Island is where Ira Eaton had a resort for sportsmen.

There was another wreck in the shallow waters of San Miguel Island during some heavy seas. Mabel M. Rockwell in her *California's Sea Frontier* [B119, 1962], gives no date for the incident, nor a specific location, but it is a tale about a cat's tail; a human interest story.

The *Ruth K* was a fishing vessel and when wrecked the men aboard managed to swim ashore. They must have stayed at the abandoned Lester home, built from wrecked ships, and managed to survive on a few cans of stewed tomatoes found there.

But the kitty cat on board the *Ruth K,* being true to feline nature, did not like the water, especially when the water took the form of heavy seas. So for four days and nights "pussycat" clung to the main-mast for what might have been its eighth life.

Then the *Paula* happened by, for the men were collecting abalone. The obvious was upon them; there had been a wreck, otherwise there would not be a kitty cat on a mast, with its tail dragging in the water with each dip of the vessel into the heavy sea.

Tony Ottman was the diver for the *Paula*. A photo of Tony with a dish of milk and a rescued cat sur-rounded by a warm jacket that the diver was wear-ing, all speak for the happy ending of the episode.

Dr. Greene gave some description of San Miguel's western extremity in 1886 [J252], when he remarked that it is

separated from the rest [of the island] by a long and narrow neck of sand; it is in fact a separate islet at the highest tides; and at an elevated sit-uation just above the eastern end of the sandy isthmus I found impressive relics of the species [*Lavatera assurgentiflora*] [tree mallow] as it flourished there in times past, namely a few white petrified trunks standing above the sands, the larger of which were nearly a foot in di-ameter. These monumental trunks were quite fragile and of a calcareosiliceous composition, the material which drifted upon and buried

them, it may be while they were living trees, ultimately reducing them to their present state, being a mixture of sea-shell dust and sand, the former substance predominating.

Before leaving the Point Bennett area it should be mentioned that in 1929 Rogers [B63], called the re-gion a good Indian site. Evidently more than one group of archaeologists found this to be so, for Dr. Charles Rozaire of the Los Angeles County Museum set up camp here, near where the Heye Foundation camp of 1919 had been [J234]. Rozaire had obtained a $10,000 grant from the National Park Service for an archaeological study, which was completed in 1966.

According to the *Sacramento Daily Record-Union* of July 15, 1895 [M78], under the heading of "Con-densed Coast News," we are told that Flea Island is the local name for CASTLE ROCK, off the western shore of San Miguel by about 5/8 of a mile [N34].

An indication of activity at Castle Rock is the newspaper's statement that some subterranean forces were playing havoc near the little islet with a "terrific outburst . . . deep in the bowels of the earth at the base of the rock."

Of this spot George Davidson said,

This rocky islet, two hundred and forty yards long east and west by sixty yards broad, lies one and a half miles north by east from Point Ben-nett . . . It is a three-headed islet, one hundred and forty feet in height, in the middle of the kelp-field north of Point Bennett. A depth of six and seven fathoms of water is found around it . . . One and a half miles north by east from Castle Rock the surface of the water is marked by films of petroleum supposed to arise from the springs below the surface. They are said to be also indicated by small patches of asphaltum or bitumen similar to that which is found on the coast west of Santa Barbara. The chart gives a four-fathom sounding near this spot.

Both Thompson and West [B70], and the *Museum Leaflet* of the Santa Barbara Museum Library [J282], tell of a Mr. Rogers and his brother using Flea Island to kill California Sea Lions. According to Mr. Rog-ers, when he was hunting about 1880, "The seals were so plentiful that if they had stayed quiet enough, a man could have walked over the whole island on their backs." These lions were also around Point Bennett and ISTHMUS ROCK, close by.

SIMONTON COVE, a 5 mile broad bight, is the northwest face of San Miguel. Its northeastern half is where anchorage may be had. Around its southwestern point there is very foul ground and rocks, and many shipwrecks have occurred here. George Davidson [N34, 1889] describes the bight as follows:

> The shore of this northwest bight is marked by dunes, from which the sand is driven over the highest part of the island, and over the neck into Cuyler Harbor . . . deep arroyos are cut across the island by the friction of the driving sand. The highest part of the island is channeled by these arroyos.

There is a fault line passing south of CUYLER HARBOR and extends into the sea at Simonton Cove. But this fault cannot be traced westward, since the land is covered by wind-blown sand [J298, 1933].

This sand-hidden faultline, extending westward may or may not have some relationship with the subterranean forces that were at work in 1895 off Castle Rock. There is also a Cardwell fault, with an offshoot through Cuyler Harbor.

WILSON ROCK, locally known as WEST ROCK, is only one hundred yards in extent and but fifteen feet above the water. It lies two and one-quarter miles northwest of POINT HARRIS, the north point of San Miguel. George Davidson suggested giving this area a wide berth since there is a reef stretching for about a mile northwest from the rock. Between the reef and Wilson Rock there are three sunken rocks; even another rock south of Wilson Rock. In thick or foggy weather "the deep water immediately around these dangers gives little or no warning."

George Davidson considered Point Harris to be a clean projection and basically without danger. The Point is "long, quite narrow, broken, rocky, and precipitous, and the hill behind it on the south rises to five hundred and fifty feet within a mile" [N34]. In 1886 [J252], Dr. Greene called Point Harris a promontory, a peninsula, forming the western shelter for Cuyler Harbor.

In 1875 Paul Schumacher found an especially large shell deposit on this rocky northern end, which is about a mile from the harbor [P82]. According to Mrs. Lester, Mr. Lester was buried at Harris Point "in a place of his own choosing" [B103].

Charles Frederick Holder was also familiar with San Miguel Island. And in 1910 [B38], he mentioned that at the northeastern point, which must mean Point Harris, there is an arch large enough for a yacht to pass through.

OTTER POINT is not mentioned by name in George Davidson's 1889 report [N34]. However, he refers to

the northwest point of the island; this is Otter Point. Mr. Rogers [B63, 1929], and others, refer to OTTER HARBOR, a bight on the northwest coast, suitable for small boats—and at one time suitable for otter, until they were nearly exterminated. Bremner [J298, 1933], shows Otter Harbor about one and one-quarter miles from Castle Rock. Edwards [J231, 1956] and O'Neill [B53, 1939], also use the name Otter Harbor. One author has indicated springs for the area.

Before leaving the west side of San Miguel Island, there is WESTCOTT SHOAL. Broken, rocky ground in nearly a straight line extends one and a half miles northwest three quarters west from Otter Point to a small group of sunken rocks, close together and just outside the kelp field.

From this group of rocks, the shoal extends southwest one and a half miles and then southeast for one and one-third miles. Here, visible rocks are off the western point of the island, and Castle Rock comes within these limits.

Two-thirds of a mile northeast by north half north from Westcott Shoal there is a four-fathom sounding. This sounding is near the oil well, which is one and a half miles north by east from Castle Rock [N34].

CUYLER HARBOR, on the northeast side of the island, holds more interest for most people than any other locality. The Harbor stretches out for a little more than one mile between the east and west heads. It is San Miguel's safest harbor, but it is only moderately safe at that. It has high, bold shores and approaches, with a peak at the western head at 550 feet—DEVIL'S KNOLL, below Harris Point.

Some of the safety of the Harbor is due to Point Harris to the west, serving as a wind-break. Also contributing to a safer anchorage at the harbor is Princess Island. It is one-half mile north of the eastern head of Cuyler Harbor, and aids in breaking the winds when they come from the southeast.

PRINCESS ISLAND, called PRINCE ISLAND by most, rises to 303 feet and is in extent some five hundred yards. Precipitous on its north face, it has a depth of six and seven fathoms of water on its south.

But inside the harbor, past Princess Island, there are some dangers through reefs, and at least three rocks near its middle. One reef, called MIDDLE ROCK, is but 4/5 of a mile off the west point of Princess Island.

Davidson [N34], continued his explanations by saying that in coming from around Point Harris, boats should come abreast the third high head, then move toward shore, where one finds the "first houses" next to the landing. Here it is safe from all but the more or less rare winds from the north and east.

If coming from the eastern passage, one should steer between the Islet and the eastern head of the harbor, run parallel with the southern shore, and then head for the western part of the bight.

"The Coast Survey secondary astronomical station of 1852, is on [this southwestern] part of Cuyler Harbor, about forty feet up the hillside, near the position of the house abreast the anchorage" [N34]. Water may be obtained near the small house on the hillside. These statements almost tell us where Nidever's adobe house was placed.

Holland [J388, 1963], has a 1939 photo in his *Journal of the West* article showing the remains of the adobe hut built at Cuyler Harbor by George Nidever after his occupation of the island in 1850.

And L. Sumner, Jr., Regional Wildlife Technician for the National Park Service also referred to this old adobe house. His information came to us in a 1933 publication where he mentioned that the abandoned house was washed and blown from the higher portion of the mesa at the western part of the Harbor, and eventually covered with sand. Later, then, "the walls of this historic adobe house, originally built in an erosion gulley," are now being gradually uncovered by the same forces of erosion.

Schumacher, in his 1877 article [N41], said that he and his party erected their tents and camped up this western shore of Cuyler Harbor. In his *Overland Monthly* article, 1875 [P82], he said,

Sick and scaled by the exposure to the grinding sand, and under constant fear of losing our tents in the brisk blows that lasted day and night during our stay, we were glad to be able to charter a schooner which we found in port, owned by the Stock-raising Company (who were engaged shearing their starving sheep), to take us to Santa Cruz Island.

They probably camped there because the best anchorage is in this part of the Harbor, and is close to a spring.

Of the Harbor itself, Schumacher stated [N41], that he could understand why Ferrelo "dared not to re-enter this port on account of dangerous breakers at its entrance,"

This corresponds entirely with the appearance of Cuyler Harbor during the time of rough sea, because from the eastern side of the bay to the rock-islet heavy breakers roll over the partially

exposed reef and the rocks in the bay a little to the westward of it, . . .

Rogers [B63, 1929], said of Cuyler Harbor,

. . . it suffers from a peculiarly rough and treacherous swell, due to the conflicting currents that sweep in through the eastern and northern entrances, which are separated by Princess Island.

The U. S. Coast and Geodetic Survey party was around San Miguel Island in 1852 and Cuyler Harbor was named at that time. Lieutenant Commander, R. M. Cuyler was then working in the area.

But in the 1855-56 Survey report by Bache to Guthrie it was stated that Cuyler had been relieved from the command of the hydrographic party. This command was taken over by Commander James Alden, who had previously been an assistant. One wonders whether Cuyler's 1855-56 report that "the current runs constantly during the summer to the westward and northward and westward" had anything to do with his being relieved of that command and duty.

A most interesting article was written for *San Francisco Call,* published October 11, 1895 under the title of "First Cargo of Guano." There are several comments which capture the mind and the eye—

1. The article refers to a GULL ISLAND and a Princes Island.
2. "Gull Island" gives us another place name for San Miguel.
3. Both islets are in Cuyler Harbor, from which the Schooner *Glen* from San Diego took ten tons of the fertilizer, carted to the *Glen* in sacks on the shoulders of the sailors.
4. Princess Island is spelled "Princes," from whence this change in the historical name could have originated.
5. And last but not least is their comment:

This little isle [Prince] possesses great historical interest from the decision recently reached by historians and scientists that it was somewhere along its summit that the body of Cabrillo, . . . in all probability lies.

Cuyler Harbor should not be passed without further comments. Although in 1937 Portuguese Civic groups placed their monument to Juan Rodríguez Cabrillo on a knoll overlooking the harbor as the likely place for Cabrillo's burial place [J294],

Herbie [Mr. Herbert Lester] did not share their

belief; he thought it was far more likely that Cabrillo had been placed somewhere on the monument-sized Prince Island . . . [B103, 1974].

Of Cabrillo's grave Schumacher had said [N41],

We did not spend any time in searching for [Cabrillo's] grave on San Miguel, where the best location is offered between the spring below the house and the east end of the harbor, but, to satisfy my curiosity, we dug in a place at Prisoner Harbor [Santa Cruz], which was well described to me in a letter of a southern gentleman, . . . as the grave of Cabrillo, . . .

It was Charles Hillinger [M154, 1956], who remarked that Cabrillo's monument is on DEAD MAN'S POINT overlooking Cuyler Harbor—probably a name coined to conform to the situation. This Point and Devil's Knoll are in a direct line with each other, should one look across the bay.

Thousands of California and Steller sea lions use the east coast during the mating season [B53]. And as we move southeast along the coast, a promontory called EAGLE CLIFF is seen [J298, 1933].

Next, there is a prominent Indian site opposite Point Bennett on the coast above Cardwell Point [B63, 1929].

Further on, the east end of the cliff, rising to about forty feet, is CARDWELL POINT. It is about two and one-half miles southeast from Cuyler Harbor, and Davidson recommended that this point, with foul ground and rocky bottom (NNW), be avoided. Here there is a dangerous reef that stretches one-half mile eastward into the San Miguel Passage [N34].

According to Bremner, Cuyler Harbor and Cardwell Point have something in common—a fault line which runs from the Point to the Harbor. It appears to be the most prominent fault on the island, as well as having been responsible for the development of the Harbor [J298, 1933].

Perhaps as a result of this fault, an incident in 1895 that created quite a stir and some disagreement, happened on San Miguel Island. In one of Dr. Yates' footnotes in "Prehistoric California," *Southern California Academy of Sciences, Bulletin* [J327, 1902], Dr. Yates was referring to San Miguel, and explaining about the sand slides. He is quoted as saying,

The sand accumulates on the top and down the face of the steep bluff, . . . until its weight causes it to slide down into the harbor, like a snow slide from a steep mountain side. An occurrence of this character took place several years ago which

attracted widespread notice, and the results of the sudden shifting of such an accumulation was such as to wreck a sloop anchored in the harbor, casting her ashore on the opposite side.

One of the San Francisco dailies sent a special to investigate, and printed an entire page giving a highly colored account of "The Great Earthquake on San Miguel Island."

But the *Sacramento Daily Record-Union* of March 18, 1895 [M77], also got involved, and their article appeared as, "Queer Phenomena in the Ocean." The subtitles were, "An Upheaval on the Island of San Miguel," and, "Changes Made on the Shore Line—What the Owner of the Island Has to Say About It."

Accessibility of this article being somewhat difficult, it is quoted in full.

James A. Barwick, Director of the State Weather Service in this city, yesterday received the following letter from William G. Waters, owner and occupant of San Miguel Island, one of a group of four or five islands lying off the coast of Santa Barbara. The letter is dated the 12th of this month, on the island, and says:

"*James A. Barwick*—Dear Sir: There has been quite a commotion on San Miguel Island. The land which formed the high bluff on the west side of the harbor has sunk more than sixty feet and forced itself under the beach, not only raising it, but stones which had lain at the water's edge for years are now fifteen feet above it.

"The west side of the harbor will be entirely changed, and boats cannot come so near the shore as formerly.

"The extent of this upheaval along the shore is more than 1,000 feet, and the land—or some of it—is over thirty feet above the beach. So sudden was the change that fish and crabs were left high and dry thirty feet above the water.

"I felt a shake last Thursday, the 7th of March, about 2 P. M., but as the wind was blowing hard at the time I thought but little about it. On Sunday I found out the cause. This may not be of interest to the Weather Bureau, but it may be to science.

"If you have time to spare, and would like to overlook the Island, come to Santa Barbara. Stop at the Arlington, with my old friend E. W. Gaty, who will tell you how to get here. If you have any spare rain, send me about ten inches more.

Sincerely yours,
Captain William G. Waters.

216

"LATER.—Since writing my letter the captain of my sloop has come into the harbor. He says: 'There is one fathom more water where I anchor than before.' He also says the harbor on the west side is deeper than before the upheaval.

"Have there been any shocks from earthquakes on the mainland, and was this one? I am in doubt.

W."

Some days since—but later than the date mentioned by Waters—there was a slight shock of earthquake felt on Mount Hamilton, Santa Clara County, where the Lick Observatory is located. It was short and sharp, and of the vertical kind, just such as would have caused the upheaval at San Miguel Island.

The instrument used for registering siesmic disturbances at the Observatory showed vertical displacement of about a half-inch. The disturbance was not felt elsewhere at least none was reported. It is not unlikely that the San Miguel shock had something to do with that experienced in Santa Clara.

A shock on Castle Rock the following July may not verify the earthquake theory for San Miguel in 1895, but it is in keeping with the locations of the island's two major fault lines—Simonton Cove and Cuyler Harbor, as expressed by Bremner.

Bremner's *Occasional Paper,* through the Santa Barbara Museum of Natural History, was dedicated to Mr. Ralph Hoffmann, who lost his life on the island just the year before its publication.

When it comes to other characteristics of the island, we are reminded by Dr. Greene that the island is of the nature of a tableland; this is in contrast to Santa Rosa Island containing several of them, called mesas, besides many higher peaks.

In fact, the San Miguel table-terrace has but two mound-like peaks. The one, called GREEN MOUNTAIN, attains a height of 850 feet; it has also been called WEST PEAK. SAN MIGUEL MOUNTAIN, the "EAST PEAK," is slightly higher, 861 feet, and is the location of the U. S. Coast and Geodetic Survey marker. Both peaks are near the center of the island.

A few authors have taken note of water or springs on the island. Here are Paul Schumacher's comments [N41, 1877],

On San Miguel Island are two small perennial springs; one is situated several hundred yards below the adobe building at the bay, and the other, with a little better quality of water, on the elevated northern point.

Dr. Greene [J252, 1887], *Pittonia,* seemed somewhat more expansive when he stated that "fresh water springs are all along the north and east shores."

Dr. Cockerell [J314, 1938], *Scientific Monthly,* had an eye for available water and stated that there are "several good springs where eucalyptus could grow." This water had to be carried from the springs or powered by the windmill, when possible [B103].

Bremner [J298, 1933], on the other hand, referred to streams on the island. He said that Green Mountain had two streams, one going north and one going south. Then, near the ranch house, built about 1906, there is a stream that heads for Cuyler Harbor on the north. He also referred to a WILLOW CANYON in the southeast corner of the island, which drains eastward. Obviously, water is to be had, but not in abundance.

Caves have also come under discussion in various literature, but information is quite limited and only through a miscellany of sources.

By far the earliest report on San Miguel Island caves is through the *Santa Barbara Society of Natural History* by Clark P. Streator [J263, 1887], when he wrote on "The Water Birds of San Miguel Island." Here is what he said:

One day, as I was climbing around a point of rocks, I discovered a cave, and upon entering found the bottom covered with human bones, but as it was very dark, and not having any matches, I then abandoned the search, but two or three days after, in company with Mr. Crawford, who has charge of the Island, I again visited it, and with the aid of a candle, found the roof to be covered with beautiful crystals of sulphate of lime, but the cave was not so extensive as we had at first supposed.

On coming out to the edge of a cliff we saw a great number of . . . (Pigeon Guillemots), flying in and out of a still larger cave in a position near by, but very difficult of access. Fortunately the tide was low and no waves beating against the rocks, so we ventured around the sides of the cliffs, and there being many crevices in the rocks that assisted us in climbing, we soon found our way into the cave. The birds were yet breeding, and scores of them were flying in and out when we entered, but we were lucky enough to secure half a dozen specimens of the birds and a dozen and a half of their eggs. They seemed to prefer the darkest parts of the cave for their nests, where we could not see without the aid of a candle. The examination was hurried, we fearing that the tide would rise and shut us in.

Blanche Trask might have been referring to the same cave in her *Los Angeles Times* article of Jan. 21, 1906. Phil C. Orr [B54, 1968], referred to a Hoffmann Cave, discovered and so-named about 1950, for Mr. Ralph Hoffmann. Orr commented that it "contained burials of which nothing remains today except broken and weathered bones." It is very likely that the cave Streator visited in 1877, the one mentioned by Blanche Trask, and the one Orr found, is one and the same; Streator found "the bottom covered with human bones."

Charles F. Holder [B38], explored around San Miguel Island, too. While around the northeast point [Cardwell Pt.], he not only saw an exceptionally large arch, but he discovered "a two-chambered cavern thirty feet high, . . . [and] in this cave or chamber fresh water drips from the ceiling . . ."

Orr [J272], remarked that at the west end of Prince Island he found a large sea cave. Another of his references [J276], to a cave is through *Museum Talk*, in which he referred to a FINLEY CAVE on San Miguel Island, without telling us where it is located.

Richard Finley was at one time an assistant to Phil Orr, who was Curator of the Santa Barbara Museum. In Finley Cave algae were found, a species known as *Rhodochorton*. It was Finley who had described the Orizaba Pictograph Cave on Santa Cruz—the cave mentioned by Schumacher.

Another reference, one sentence, about a cave on San Miguel, came from a 1923 *Catalina Islander*. The statement was made by Gilbert E. Bailey, "The Indians obtained ochre in the Point of Caves . . ."

There is at least one newspaper article that mentions Cardwell Point as a locality for several caves. This article came from *Los Angeles Times*, Jan. 21, 1906, written by Blanche Trask about San Miguel Island [M127].

The article illucidates on several subjects, and prepares for other discussions. Though caves are discussed only in passing, the beautifully written article is quoted here:

> . . . Prince Island is especially interesting, as it is his [Cabrillo's] reputed burial place, . . . our pilot told us of this man [Mr. Waters] who had lived here for years and was regarded as somewhat peculiar in claiming to own this island as a kingdom . . .
>
> Perhaps no other cook stove ever looked so cozy or so inviting as the one which glowed in the kitchen of the ranch-house that stormy day

in the far island of San Miguel; . . .

> The "King of San Miguel" was very busy with his shearers during our visit, . . . With his own words he confirmed the story, that he had purchased it from a Mexican to whom it had come as a Spanish grant and that it had never been formally taken possession of by the United States . . . Grover Cleveland sent a civil request [to allow official visitors] so the "King of San Miguel" . . . turned the freedom of the island over to "the boys," . . . Since the death of his wife the King spends several months of each year on the mainland . . . The prevailing northwest winds blow over it continually and fog enshrouds it half the year . . . It is separated from Santa Rosa Island by a narrow but dangerous passage about two miles in width . . . "Green Mountain" rises like an emerald in the middle of the island; . . . at its very feet the sand dunes are scattered in all directions, while its soil is dark and rich and supports a luxuriant vegetation.
>
> A flower-crowned jetty, sweet with red and pink sea verbenas, shoots out from Point Bennett windward, and along this wild shore the seals play and the strand is gay with the red abalone shell. To the east and south it is true that the little cañons are yet in existence and flowers abound, while many a green tree rears his head in old-time battlement, notwithstanding his relatives are strewn over the yellow sands on all the heights like the bones of some extinct race long since turned to ebony! These same roots burned merrily in the grates at night at the ranchhouse; so hard they are almost like coal when ignited, and give a remarkable heat.
>
> Cardwell Point rises to eastward, and from its strewn lichen-hung caves can be seen the dangerous reef which dips its golden sands into the San Miguel Passage for a half mile, and with its foul ground and rocky bottom is a menace to vessels.
>
> In one dark cave which had to be entered on the hands and knees, human bones were found deeply tinged with green. In the same cave lovely flower-like stalactites were gathered, like outspread cream-colored daisies on the walls.
>
> In under the lees of Cardwell Point live and thrive vast numbers of "blue points," shells you are always glad to find because of their beauty; besides, they appear to vary on the different islands; colors ranging from white to yellow, olive and the well-known deep blue-lipped one . . .
>
> This island was surveyed over twenty-five years ago and the beacons are yet to be seen as

well as the United States survey marks . . . San Miguel is the most dangerous of all the islands to approach, having many sunken rocks and reefs and much foul ground. Even Cuyler's Harbor is not good holding ground, nor is it sheltered, although well protected from all but north and east winds.

The rocky islets off the north and northwest coast of San Miguel are the homes of vast numbers of seals and hundreds of sea-birds rest there. In olden times there were also many others and sea lions.

Castle Rock is prominent, lying a half mile north by east from Point Bennett. It is 145 feet high and its three pinnacles were long since separated, while Richardson Rock lies five and a half miles out from the western point, its jagged edges piercing the blue.

One and one-half-miles from Castle Rock there is supposed to be an oil spring, as the water there bears the appearance of coming in contact with petroleum and patches of asphaltum are found on shore. This same indication is seen on all the Channel islands, and at times barrels of asphaltum are cast ashore on both San Clemente and San Nicolas islands, and are to be seen ever after as a stain of tar upon the rocks.

Nowhere are there days more calm nor nights more lovely than in San Miguel Island in good weather. The shadows fall from the cliffs and lie upon the sands, and the seaweeds sway to and fro and the furrows which the winds have plowed look like the tracks of some forgotten monsters. Birds sing in the little arroyos and the streamlets trickle away . . . ever in your memory San Miguel arises "phantom fair" with the gray mantle of fog falling off the bare shoulders of the cliff whose yellow hair is streaming in the seaweed.

Geology

The Santa Barbara Museum of Natural History published a 23-page pamphlet, "Geology of San Miguel Island," as an *Occasional Paper* No. 2 [J298, 1933]. Otherwise, little has been said about the island's geology to date.

Included in the pamphlet are about eight photos and a wonderfully large, folded map inside the rear cover. Charts illustrate and condense the pointed features of the article. All are worthy of review and study.

One photo entitled, "Sand cemented with calcium carbonate, preserving the forms of roots and stumps of vegetation destroyed in the past century, one mile

northwest of ranch house," is in line with the information on the generalized geologic map of San Miguel Island as shown in Mineral Information Service [C30, 1967], through Donald Lee Johnson, "Caliche on the Channel Islands."

Johnson's map indicates Eocene, Miocene, and Pleistocene marine terrace deposits, Miocene volcanics, and Dune Sands. While Point Bennett itself is of Eocene marine, the smaller area just above it, and around Adams Cove, are of sand dunes and some caliche. So is the quite large central area, which includes the section south of Cuyler Harbor, the windmill, and the ranch house.

Johnson says that caliche development is controlled by the climatic environment and the calcareous materials available. In the case of San Miguel Island the "moisture supplied by sea spray, winter rain, summer fog, and partly by the effects of dune vegetation" enabled a calcareous dune complex to develop.

Several authors refer to this phenomena, but Johnson does an excellent job with his explanation. After his study of the situation he concluded that there had been at least five episodes of caliche formation on San Miguel Island. One caliche tree log, two and one-half feet in diameter and thirty feet long, was the most unusual he had seen.

A comment which would interest most sightseers is the one which says, "It is hard to conceive of similar landscapes of equal fascination that would not have been set aside as some sort of reserve or park, were they on the mainland." His article is seven pages long.

A type of fossil is spoken of in Chester Stock's *Westways* [P150, 1936] article, "Ice Age Elephants of the Channel Islands." Though the article is not meant to be a highly scholarly one, it does offer scholarly information when it says that the California Institute of Technology has engaged in hunting and finding fossil elephants on the Channel Islands of Santa Cruz, Santa Rosa, AND San Miguel.

By 1950 the *Annual Report* of the *Santa Barbara Museum of Natural History* stated some of the business of the Sefton Expedition of 1949. Phil C. Orr was a member and was interested in finding new deposits of Dwarf Mammoths on San Miguel.

In the same year as this *Annual Report,* Orr had another opportunity to search and explore on San Miguel. The U. S. Government, it seems, gave Mr. Brooks but thirty days to remove his sheep from the island, most of them being on the western part. Mr. Orr helped Mr. Brooks round up the sheep, and by so doing was able to gain an overview of that end of the island, in terms of fossil elephants and Indian village sites. He reported that there are three localities where Pleistocene fossil elephants remained in the deposits.

If it were not for Mrs. Lester's *The Legendary King of San Miguel* [B103], we would not have become aware of Herbert Lester's part, back as far as 1932, in finding two Elphas Imperator tusks and remains on the island. According to "Herbie," "it was the greatest find of the twentieth century." With apologies and other indications of appeasement, Mr. Lester finally received the just recognition he deemed due for this initial discovery. One tusk was over six feet long, and both were nearly twenty inches in circumference. According to Cockerell [J319], these remains were found near the top of San Miguel.

Another very important fossil extraction from around the island is that of oil, tar, and gas. And historically speaking, the white man was not the first to discover its existence or usage.

Bulletin No. 118 of the *California State Mining Bureau* [C15, 1943], contains a one-page article written by Robert F. Heizer entitled, "Aboriginal Use of Bitumen by the California Indians." In a few brief sentences he mentions about six uses which the Indians made of the tar, or asphaltum, as it was called.

Perhaps the first explorer to mention the odor and the use of bitumen along the coast was the Spaniard, Fages, in 1775. In 1776 Fr. Pedro Font likewise remarked about the tar cast up on the shores.

By 1792, José Longinos Mártinez [B47] referred to the springs of bituminous petroleum in this region. The odor and sight of the "resinous substance" along the coast was discussed the following year, as well. This was by Vancouver from British Columbia. Then, in 1839 an Englishman, Sir Edward Belcher, reported experiencing the sensation as if the ship was on fire [B70],

> a scent from the shore . . . and the land breeze confirming this, it occurred to me that it might arise from naptha on the surface. The smell of this asphaltum appears to be occasionally experienced quite far from the land.

Other reports in histories indicate the same. Take de Mofras in his *Travels on the Pacific Coast* [B48, 1844]:

> Along the Santa Barbara Channel the current comes down from the north and skirts the coast. Asphalt deposits emptying into the sea spread over the surface of the water a black oily covering which is visible from afar and gives off a bituminous odor from a distance of several leagues.

Then there is Alexander S. Taylor in the *California Farmer,* Jan. 17, 1862:

> Asphaltum is found scattered in immense beds all over the county of Santa Barbara. It exists in all stages of its formation—hard as rock, brittle as resin, liquid as oil, thick as tar, plastic as dough, and in the waters of the canal, thin as water. It is all situated in the vicinity of the ocean, and is inexhaustible in quantity. It will soon form an important article of export from this part of the State.

This statement was made just about the time the oil industry began in the United States. It is also a prophetic statement, in terms of oil production off the coast of California.

In fact a Supreme Court decision not much more than a hundred years later gave to California the ownership of the waters within the three-mile limit around its islands. This spurred the California Land Commission into granting off-shore leases to various companies for oil-drilling operations.

Conservationists and environmentalists have become even more actively concerned since the Santa Barbara Channel Oil Spill of 1969. *Life* [P58], has an article by David Snell, giving the story of this Spill. It is accompanied by photos of seals and elephant seals covered with oil—dead or dying. None but those willing to steel themselves to a bit of torture in the name of the afflicted creatures should look at the photos.

Only the future holds the answer. There are about four federally granted leases in the area [P58]. Will the Santa Barbara Channel Region furnish more and more oil to hungry U. S. automobiles, or will it be adequately protected, in order to furnish future generations with the rich heritage which the whole coast and its islands have to offer. Perhaps 1980 is a poor time to feel much hope for the second option.

Transfer of Lessee-Title

If someone "owned" San Miguel Island previous to a man by the name of "Bruce," it has not been stated in literature. But we do know through George Nidever that he purchased his "rights" from this man in 1850. Nidever then placed on the island his two sons, Mark R. Nidever and George E. Nidever, to care for his stock imported to the island.

In Deed Book H of the Santa Barbara County Recorders Office, pp. 137-138, it is stated that these three grantors sold their rights to Hiram W. Mills for the sum of $5,000; such information was recorded by C. A. Thompson, Deputy, and F. A. Thompson, brother and County Recorder. The date for this transaction was May 8, 1869.

The elder Nidever was reluctant to sell, but his two sons were tired of living on San Miguel. Nidever had more to say about his use of the island in the E. F. Murray manuscript of 1878. See also Ellison [B51].

The lesseeship of the Mills brothers is befogged with detail, which may or may not be important to others. Some of the lack of clarity concerning the Mills brothers is around given names; accuracy is not guaranteed for this rendition, although the sources appear reliable.

Hiram W. Mills apparently gave up his three-fourth interest in the island and all of the personal property there to a P. F. Mohrhardt, J. M. Leuzardee, and W. H. Mills on April 6, 1870, for $1,000. This information comes from Book I, pp. 41-43. By November 1871 Hiram W. Mills for the sum of $1,000 gave up his remaining one-fourth interest in the "Island known as San Miguel," Book J, p. 31.

By April 10th of 1872 W. H. Mills had sold his undivided one-sixth part of San Miguel Island to Elmer Terry for the sum of $500, Book J, p. 416. Then the Pacific Wool Growing Co. was formed and incorporated, so that on the sixth of September, 1872, Terry, Leuzardee, and W. H. Mills transferred their interest to the Company and were given Certificates of Stock in the Company, Book J, pp. 630-631. By September 17th of the same year a John Herrington paid the sum of $100 to the Pacific Wool Growing Co. for an undivided one-sixth of the island known as San Miguel, Book J, pp. 642-643.

According to Mrs. Lester, Hiram Mills of Santa Barbara and his twin brother, Herman, of San Francisco owned San Miguel. It was Hiram who built a small two-story house for vacation stays of his son and daughter and their families [B103].

When Dr. Greene was on the island in 1886 he said [J252], that Mr. Warren H. Mills of San Francisco owned the island and that Mr. Warren F. Mills [sic.] was his, Greene's, companion and helper during his visit.

The following year, when Mr. Streator was on San Miguel Island for twenty-five days, he remarked [J263], that a Mr. Crawford was in charge of the island.

The next "lessee" was Captain William G. Waters. Captain Waters, speaking through Mrs. Trask [M127], stated that he had purchased the island from "a Mexican to whom it had come as a Spanish grant." But according to Mrs. Storke [B69, 1891], Waters and Schilling were occupying the island by possessory right, for sheep-raising.

Captain Waters had a few remarks for a *Daily News and Independent* reporter on September 25, 1916, which helps to establish the time when he took over the island,

> . . . the fact that I lived on the island for twenty-five years without anyone questioning my right, and that I built a home and other buildings there, would, I think, be accepted in Federal courts as proof of my title to the property.

Such a statement would place his "possessory right" about 1891. Evidently, the Pacific Wool Growing Co. had given up their use of the island between 1887 and 1891, a period of only four years. In the meantime, Mr. and Mrs. Waters had moved to the town of Santa Barbara from San Francisco, 1887. His wife died in Santa Barbara in the early part of 1890.

Five years after Waters acquired the island, July, 1896, he was still keeping people away from San Miguel. This included the U. S. Coast and Geodetic Survey personnel. The president of the United States, Grover Cleveland, hearing of the situation, sent a U. S. Marshall to the island to clear up the matter. This happened to be Nicolás Covarrubias, son of José María Covarrubias, who had to tell Waters that he must comply with the survey men since the island did, in fact, belong to the U. S. Government.

In February of 1897 the San Miguel Island Company filed papers of incorporation at the Santa Barbara County Recorders' office. It was Waters and a J. F. Conway who were in the corporation, along with several men from the Los Angeles area.

Waters must have had caretakers, for he did not remain on the island continuously. When, in 1910, Willett and party visited San Miguel [J122], they were met by Mr. L. A. Ward who had charge of the island. Mr. and Mrs. Ward served the men "several bountiful dinners," and extended other courtesies to them. One of the courtesies was to allow them to camp in a warehouse on the beach. "This added greatly to our bodily comfort as the heavy wind which blew during our entire stay would have made camping out decidedly unpleasant."

Before the turn of the century, Mr. Waters had

built an adobe, later abandoned. Other than the deteriorating remains of this ranch house near the windmill, and the fireplace of the newer ranch house built from some of its bricks, nothing exists of the "original."

Several reports come about the material from which the Russells built a home for Waters. Mr. O'Neill [B53, 1939], used the name *J. F. West* as the 1898 wrecked schooner from which the house received its material.

Mr. Wheeler [N51, 1944], said,

The weather-beaten ranch house and barn of this island sheep ranch were built largely from materials salvaged from shipwrecks. An important contributor was the old Pacific Mail liner *Cuba,* which crashed on the west end of San Miguel in September, 1923.

One of Mrs. Lester's visitors wrote [B103],

It is from here [Simonton Cove] that John Russell salvaged the lumber from a schooner that came to grief. With this lumber he built the new ranch house; shearing shed and ranch buildings.

An exact date for Mr. and Mrs. John Russell taking charge of the sheep for Captain Waters is unknown, but it is thought that they lived in the house that John built for about ten years. A change in caretakership occurred around 1929.

In the meantime, other events were occurring. Waters had been leasing the island from the U. S. government for five-year terms, and he had renewed his contract in 1916 for another five-year period, to end in November, 1921.

But Waters by then was seventy-eight years old. As a result of a stroke in early April of 1917, he died later that month. However, he had sold his lease, livestock, buildings, and improvements to R. L. Brooks and J. H. Moore in January, 1917.

In the Fall issue of *Noticias* of the Santa Barbara Historical Society, Vol. XXIII, No. 3, 1977, there is a comprehensive story about the Waters family [J296a]. The account is so well done that many would enjoy reading more about the legal difficulties over Waters' Will following his death. Some of the above dates during his lifetime have come from this particular source.

Robert Brooks was now in charge of the island. The Russells continued to serve; Mr. and Mrs. Brooks lived on the island, but not continuously. Then Mr. Brooks made a business arrangement with Mr. Herbert Lester, a former hospital-acquaintance.

Apparently the arrangement suited both parties; Mr. Lester found the isolation and the care of the stock to his liking. And to San Miguel he took his bride.

The house built by John Russell, and lived in from 1906, has remained a curiosity for all who saw or read about it. It was fashioned into one long leg of the letter A, the other leg being a stockade, like a corridor, sheltering the house from the northwest winds. The cross-piece of the letter A were the smaller structures—harness room, blacksmith shop, and an empty building, later made into a bar. An excellent photo of the ranch buildings and fences may be found in B103.

Mr. Lester had gone to San Miguel within Mr. Brooks' third lease-period. Although Mr. Lester had already begun to despair of an indefinite continuance of the lease, Mr. Brooks was allowed to lease many more years, before being asked to remove his sheep—1950. This was eight years after Mr. Lester's death.

Mrs. Lester has related their experience with Mr. Brooks after he had fallen on the pier and succeeded in imbedding an iron spike in his hip [B103]. The injured man found resourcefulness, imagination, courage, compassion, and intelligence in his tenants. With only a medical book and a "vanilla" bottle, Mr. Brooks was stitched with a wool-sack sewing needle, and nursed back to health before anyone on the mainland could be alerted of his plight—fourteen days later!

Mrs. Lester's book, *The Legendary King of San Miguel* is worthy of many readings. As a bride, her induction to and life on the island for twelve years unfolds through a flow of related incidents. The book leads the reader to realize that pioneering, and rising above circumstance and environment, can still be an inspiring human trait.

Her description of baking on the iron stove stoked with roots of gnarled trees, of sanitary conditions being gradually corrected, on having a revolving front door, portholes for windows, an inner garden with only two fig trees and a few vines, raising two daughters on San Miguel to ages eleven and eight, having cats, dogs, horses, mice, injured animals, and so on—all bespeak of the mettle from which both of the Lesters were cast.

The Baglins followed the Lesters and remained on the island with "Pomo," the collie, and the other animals, until Uncle Sam put an end to the sheep-raising business. San Miguel became a practice bombing range during the Korean War.

In 1956 Charles Hillinger wrote an article, "Channel Islands, California," for the *Los Angeles Times* [M154]. With photos and a review of the historical, Mr. Hillinger stated that although the ranch was supposedly abandoned,

As we prepared to make our way back to the beach at Cuyler Harbor we suddenly wondered if we actually were San Miguel's only guests.

For strung up on a sagging beam on the outside of the ranch house was a recently killed island fox, its head smashed in as though by someone who had used a rock, and then crudely ripped off its pelt . . .

As we hiked back to the beach we imagined the possibility of someone, hidden in one of San Miguel's forbidding hills, watching our movements, waiting for us to leave this haunting isle.

In *Masterkey* [J205, 1964], we are given what might be an update for San Miguel,

The National Park Service is undertaking an investigation of the scientific values of San Miguel and Prince Islands, of the Channel Group, as the result of a cooperative agreement recently signed between the Secretaries of the Interior and Navy Departments . . . [which include] rules and regulations for preserving the scientific values of the two islands which are under the jurisdiction of the Navy Department.

From a 1966 *San Francisco Daily Chronicle* article, through the Associated Press, two Los Angeles real estate men were rejected by the court on their claim of squatter's right to farm the island.

Sometime in 1969 the ranch mysteriously burned, leaving only the fireplace built by the Lesters [B103].

Natural History

Flora

It would be difficult to say whether San Miguel has been a source of little or great satisfaction to the botanist. Being the farthest north and west of the four islands, the weather has been poorer, the number of scientific-minded visitors fewer, their discoveries and insights more limited. Still, considerable progress has been made, even though the results are not as dramatic as from some of the other islands.

Take the *Mesembrianthemum crystallium,* ice plant, for instance. Not considered endemic, yet, according to Dr. Greene [J252, 1886], it grows profusely on the island and in such rank luxuriance that its excessive abundance is a source of real wonderment. There

were single specimens on the higher acres, he said, that commonly spread over a six-foot breadth of ground. Another source of wonderment for the plant is that its only other native habitat is South Africa. Greene, therefore, argued that it was not an introduced plant.

The only other type of information about the plant is from those who were in a position to know. Acting as a purgative on the sheep who ate it, they indulged themselves only when their very life was at stake. Lack of water is too difficult a decision for sheep when they are extremely thirsty.

And speaking of sheep, the bladder-pod, *Astragalus miguelensis,* was also their nemesis. Mr. Brooks of San Miguel told Dr. Cockerell [J382, 1937], that the plant was poisonous to the sheep, acting as a 'loco-weed,' and thereby avoided. As a natural corollary, the snails had the bladder-pod to themselves. The result—lots and lots of snails, thus contributing to the destruction of other islandic vegetation, even before the arrival of the sheep.

Astragalus miguelensis is found on the four northern islands. Closely related to this plant is the *Astragalus robeartisii* [J334], found by Mrs. Blanche Trask on San Clemente; *Astragalus nevinii,* as a single-island San Clemente endemic, according to Raven; and *Astragalus traskiae* on San Nicolas and Santa Barbara, according to Cockerell [J54]. This leaves only Santa Catalina Island out of the count for some form of bladder-pod.

Greene, 1886, had something to say about the California Holly, called Toyon, known botanically as *Heteromeles arbutifolia.* He found two stunted specimens, "neither of them more than ten feet high, exist in a sheltered spot near the head of a small cañon at the eastern end." As an arboreal type of vegetation, it is hardly expected on such a windswept island.

There is a variety of the plant known as *macrocarpa* on the islands; an endemic on San Miguel [J252], San Clemente, and Santa Catalina which has fruit that is red, rarely yellow, according to Munz [1935].

Another rather unusual growth was discussed by Greene, that of *Rhus integrifolia.* This tree-like shrub is not an island endemic but it has made its own history on the island of San Miguel.

To the east and to the north Greene found their petrified remains above the sands of the island. Some of the gnarled, petrified branches measure thirty feet long and about a foot from the ground [J252]. Also

223

PIECES OF EIGHT

to the east, Greene saw two or three trees yet showing feeble signs of life. To the north, on all but the higher middle portions, he found *Rhus* in a low spreading form.

Dr. Cockerell visited the Lesters in 1938. In the *Scientific Monthly* of that year [J319], he had this to say about *Rhus:*

> On the top of the island, alternating with sandy deposits, I found a caliche . . . very solid but composed of sand, and standing up on this are numerous objects which look like small trunks of trees, but are actually limy concretions formed around roots which formerly occupied the ground. Some people have thought that these objects were relicts of a former forest, but this is not the case. The roots were probably those of the Lemonadeberry, *Rhus integrifolia,* a kind of sumac which once abounded on the island, so that the wood is even now used for fuel . . . Hoffmann, of the Santa Barbara Museum, found one shrub overhanging the ocean bluff, on April 10, 1930. But on Princess Island . . . the plant still survives.

Cockerell wrote for *Nautilus, Pan-Pacific Etomologist, San Diego Society of Natural History, Scientific Monthly, Bios, Torreya,* and *Southern California Academy of Sciences,* all at about the same time.

As previously mentioned, *Lavatera assurgentiflora,* Malva Rosa, or tree mallow, was seen by Greene after Mr. Hazard had found it in 1885. About thirty small trees on the western end of the island were in an open grassy valley looking southward, and three or four more straggling bushes were growing on an open, exposed slope at the westernmost end of San Miguel.

Lavatera has been found on seven out of eight of the islands, excepting San Nicolas; Hoffmann, in the thirties, having found four or five on West Anacapa on a hillside above the sheep landing [J319]. Greene had reported that it had not been seen on Anacapa [J252, 1887]. In 1890, Brandegee [J396], had other comments about *Lavatera.*

When Dr. Greene appraised the botany of San Miguel Island in 1886, he felt that the bulk of its vegetation was made up of plants altogether insular [J252], exclusive of the grasses. As he listed about nine species, he remarked that they comprised more than two-thirds of the vegetation and that eight "in so far as we know, are endemic of San Miguel itself . . . an astonishing number of species to be confined to one small islet no farther removed than this one is from other lands . . ."

Close to one hundred years later, we continue to be confronted with the subject of endemics on San Miguel. With Raven [B120], giving the island no single-island endemic, we are left with a count through Hoffmann, Sumner, Munz, and/or others, of shared island endemics. *Astragalus miguelensis, Lavatera assurgentiflora,* and *Heteromeles arbutifolia* var. *macrocarpa* have been referred to.

Island Endemics

Plant	S.M.	S.N.	S.Cl.	S.C.	S.B.	Ana.	S.Cz.	S.R.
Erysium insulare Greene	X							X
Rhamnus crocea Nutt. var. *insularis*	X		X	X	X			
Phacelia divaricata var. *insularis*	X							X
Dedromecon densifolia	X	X	X	X	X	X	X	X
Convolvulus macrostegius Greene	X	X	X	X	X		X	X
Castilleia hololeuca Greene	X					X	X	X
Galium catalinense Grey	X		X	X			X	
Galium angustifolium Nutt. var. *Miguelense* Greene	X							X
Malacothrix saxatilis implicata	X	X				X	X	X
Malacothrix indecora Greene	X	X					X	

224

Plant	Island Endemics							
	S.M.	S.N.	S.Cl.	S.C.	S.B.	Ana.	S.Cz.	S.R.
Malacothrix Foliosa Greene	X		X		X		X	
Isocoma veneta (H.B.K.) Greene, var. *sedioides*	X						X	X
Dudleya greenei	X			X			X	X
Amsinckia spectabilis var. *nicolai*	X	X	X					
Lyonothamnus floribundus subsp. *asplenifolius*	X		X	X			X	X

Marine and Land Fauna

Abalone

Any general information about abalones obtained on any one of the islands may be considered for the other seven; specifics being another matter, of course.

Those earliest interested in the abalone were the Chinese. In 1883 Thompson and West [B70], remark that

. . . The meat is dried in large quantities by the Chinese and shipped to China. It is said to be a favorite material, when grated fine for soups. When ready for shipment it looks much like the hoofs of cattle or horses and would be without the grating process about as digestible.

One of the earlier recognitions for the total abalone product has come from Charles Lincoln Edwards of the U.S.C. Medical Department and an assistant to the California Fish and Game Commission. His eighteen-page article, "The Abalones of California," was published in *Appletons' Popular Science Monthly* in 1913 [P116].

His is an emphasis, through photos, of the Japanese camps on San Clemente and Santa Catalina, with their tents, boiling tanks, and drying racks.

Edwards' statement that "the production of culture pearls dates back to the fourteenth century in China," and his conclusion, "So abalones may be raised in the sea as easily as chickens upon the land," might have spurred some interest in the industry as a whole, for several articles followed.

The *Overland Monthly* [P101, 1914], carried a three-page article written by C. L. Edholm, "Steaks and Pearls from the Abalone." A photo shows pearl divers at work at San Miguel Island, thus including this island in the abalone industry. Edholm remarks that

the Chinese and Japanese have always regarded the mollusk itself as a great delicacy . . . [at a

depth of 40 to 60 feet] the abalones may be found in such quantities that they cover the rocks in layers five or six deep . . .

Besides the value of its shell and meat, the abalone is sought for its pearls and protruberances on the inner surfaces of the shell, known as blister pearls . . .

Edholm, too, stated that it was feared the Japanese fishermen would exterminate the abalone, so that rather stringent regulations limiting the catch were being made.

By 1925 the *Overland Monthly* through Emma Carbutt Richey presented a somewhat brighter picture in, "Abalone, A Product of our Rocky Coasts" [P105]. She remarked that the laws of California now protect the abalone. Neither the dried or raw meat, nor the shell may be shipped out of the state, whereas in 1915 even the European markets were importing as high as one hundred tons of shell per week, which they used for inlaying cabinet work, ornaments, buttons, knife and fan handles, jewelry, etc.

Each author has remarked about the value of the free abalone pearl that may be found in the shell or body of the abalone; take Edwards, for example:

They sell from fifty cents, for the smaller ones, to one hundred and twenty-five dollars for one of twenty-five grains. Occasionally pearls are so large and of such fine quality as to sell for five hundred, or even one thousand dollars.

By 1962 Keith W. Cox of The Resources Agency of California [C3], in "The California Abalones, Family Haliotidae," tells of the Department of Fish and Game transplanting some abalone from one locality at Santa Catalina to another, and to Santa Catalina from other islands.

Over one hundred pages in length, Cox has offered information on the growth periods of the pink, red, white, and black abalone. And while stating that the work involved in raising culture abalone pearls appeared not worth the effort, the fishery for red abalone continues to remain the prize, due to its high quality. San Miguel Island produces most of them. Kelp areas for the abalone is important, in terms of food—which, is also important to the sea otter, in terms of the abalone.

Seals

In 1969 Darwin Lambert went on the *Swift* with an Audubon Society group to San Miguel. It is of this island that Lambert referred to six different sea mammals congregating—the elephant seal, California sea lion, Harbor seal, Steller sea lion, Northern fur seal, and the Guadalupe seal [N52].

Some of the species from the colder waters north of Point Concepción mingle with the more southerly species, to become the sea world wildlife habitat of our Coast. This, together with the subtidal zone of both plant and animal, make San Miguel a very important island. It is a Marine-land in its own natural setting [P135].

The history for seals being in a somewhat protective environment has developed only within the last fifty years. Before, they were hunted for the oil and hides their bodies produced—and their "trimmings," which the Chinese internalized for rejuvenation purposes.

Thompson and West [B70, 1883] gave an idea of the early uses for the various parts of the seal—it was

a remunerative business on some of the islands. During the summer of 1879, Rogers & Company, of Santa Barbara, had fifteen to twenty men engaged in hunting the seal on the San Miguel and Flea Islands. The hunters follow along the beach, shooting those they find on the rocks; other parties flay off the blubber and carry it to the trying place, where it is slowly cooked to extract the oil, by an experienced person. The oil is ranked with that of the whale in value, and finds a market in San Francisco. The nose and whiskers (smellers) are sold to the Chinese for some of the customs incident to their civilization. The skins and intestines of the seals are utilized in making garments for the Alaska market . . .

A sea-lion was killed on San Miguel Island in July, 1879, that was fourteen feet long, and was estimated to weigh between 3,500 and 4,000 pounds. So says Captain Mullet who has engaged in capturing sea-lions for exhibitions, etc., for about eight years and has caught nearly 2000.

Some measure of history and an update of this situation comes through the California Fish and Game Commission and Paul Bonnot, "The Sea Lions of California" [C2, 1928]. It would appear that the sea lions were not especially the hunted species before 1860. Perhaps hunters turned to them for profit only after the near extermination of the sea otter for its fur.

There was some activity at the official level in the early years of the twentieth century for seal protection, but that did not prove to be enough—

. . . Captain H. B. Nidever, of San Pedro, has supplied me with the information that in 1907 and 1908 several men systematically hunted sea lion bulls at San Miguel Island and killed practically all the bulls of breeding age.

Since 1909 there has been no organized killing, though a small but steady drain has been acting on the herds. Several individuals add to their income by killing the breeding bulls for the penis and testicles, known in the trade as "trimmings." They are sold to the Chinese, who manufacture a medical preparation supposed to rejuvenate the aged. A number of California sea lions are taken annually to be used for exhibition purposes in zoological gardens and circuses. This species is used more exclusively, as the Steller is too large and difficult to handle.

In May of 1927 there was a legislative battle of the fishing interests vs. the conservationists. Finally the governor signed a bill continuing some protection to the California sea lion in districts 19, 20, and 20A.

But there are always those who wish to defy the law, and in June of 1927 there had been another onslaught:

. . . Bulls, cows and pups were killed indiscriminately, and only the scalps and "trimmings" removed. The carcasses were left to rot on the beaches . . . The beach at Flea Island supported a mixed rookery of nearly 400 sea lions when I visited it on June 13th. Two days later I again landed there. In the meantime, the sea lion hunter had done his work. Every pup on the rookery was dead and of the 400 animals which I counted on my first visit, a pitiful remnant of 30 or 40 was swimming timidly about in the surf. The beach was covered with dead animals and pools of stagnant blood.

Forty-six years later, 1973, the situation for the sea lion still appeared grim, but due to a different reason. Research had been conducted by the Naval Undersea Center in San Diego and the University of California at Berkeley. Reporting through the

Science Magazine, the *Los Angeles Herald-Examiner* [M119], quoted them as saying that a high concentration of DDT and other insecticide compounds are tied to the deaths of numerous sea lion pups,

> We have observed early termination of pregnancies among animals on several breeding rookeries, including those on San Miguel Island, since 1968, . . .
> In April of 1970 they counted 242 dead pups on San Miguel, . . . and the next spring the number rose to 348.

This occurrence has been repeated on San Nicolas Island, where the same types of chemicals have disrupted the sea lions' reproductive processes.

Elephant Seals, *Macrorhinus angustirostris*

Scant information has been collected concerning this sea mammal—"owing to the continual pursuit of the animals, they have become nearly, if not quite, extinct on the California coast, or the few remaining have fled to some unknown point of security" [P78, 1870]. This is what Scammon related in the *Overland Monthly.*

He offered one of the best descriptions of the mammal, called *Elefante marino* by the old Californians. He reported that one especially large sea-elephant was twenty-four feet long and with a twelve foot circumference, the average male being but eighteen feet in length. He detailed the process of killing the animal and what happened next—cutting the "horse-pieces," etc., etc.

Here are Scammon's words on the hunt:

> The mode of capturing them, is, for the sailors to get between the herd and the water; then, raising all possible noise by shouting, together with the flourishing of clubs, guns, and lances, the party advance slowly toward the rookery, when the animals will retreat, appearing in a great state of alarm. Occasionally, an overgrown male will give battle, or attempt to escape; but a ball from a musket, through his brain, dispatches him, or some one, with a lance, checks his progress by thrusting it into the roof of the animal's mouth, which causes it to settle on its haunches. Meanwhile, two men, with heavy oaken clubs, give it repeated blows about the head, until it is stunned or killed. After securing those that are disposed to show resistance, the party rush on to the main body. The onslaught creates such a panic among those harmless creatures, that, losing all control of their actions, they will climb, roll, or tumble over each other, when prevented from further retreat by the projecting cliffs. We recollect, in one instance, where sixty-five were captured, that several were found showing no signs of either being clubbed or lanced, but were smothered by numbers of their kind heaped upon them. The whole flock, when attacked, manifested alarm by their peculiar roar, the sound of which, among the largest males, is nearly as loud as the lowing of an ox, but more prolonged in one strain, accompanied by a rattling noise in the throat. The quantity of blood in this species of the seal tribe is supposed to be double that contained in a neat animal, in proportion to its size.

Evidently the sea elephant had hidden himself some place where it was fairly secure. A Mr. E. Z. Rett of the Santa Barbara Museum of Natural History reported seeing a sea elephant at San Miguel in 1926 [J272].

Woodbridge Williams' "Jumbo of the Deep," in *Natural History* [J224, 1941], is a five-page article offering more information on the sea elephant. As Williams termed it, "a tempting subject for scientific research and observation."

By 1950 Mr. Orr of the Santa Barbara Museum found fifty of the sea elephants basking on the west end of San Miguel [J272].

A six-page 1951 article written by George Lindsay, "Elephant Seals come Back," was published in the *Pacific Discovery,* a California Academy of Sciences publication [J76]. The article contains photos.

Warren's article in the *National Geographic* [J218], came out in 1958. Entitled, "Off Santa Barbara: California's Ranches in the Sea," the party visited the northern islands.

When the group came to a "wind-lashed peninsula" on San Miguel they found the huge creatures basking on the sand. Friendly enough, the sea elephants still wished to maintain their distances and showed it by hissing, exposing their savage teeth, and attempting lunging movements toward the intruders.

The *Los Angeles Times* ran an article [M171], in 1969, referring to the then recent oil slick around San Miguel. According to P. C. Orr, through Walt Anderson of the *Times,* helicopters swooping down on the island created a stampede of the sea elephants, thus trampling all seal pups in their path.

These three described elephant seal behavioral patterns are reminiscent of Scammon's remarks of 1870. Evidently, the same patterns have repeated themselves—that of self-preservation.

PIECES OF EIGHT

Sea Otter, *Enhydra lutris*

The Pacific Coast from Alaska down to Baja, California became hunters' paradise in their search for the sea otter. The story of the mass killings for the fur of the little cutie, and the otters extremely slow return to the California coast, is of universal interest.

It includes the dates from 1741, when the Alaskan sea otter was first discovered by the Vitus Bering Expedition, to about 1867, when the United States purchased Alaska. Covering a 126-year span, an extensive bibliography has developed.

This little creature played a very important part in both California's coastal mainland and island history. The Russians in Alaska under Baranov, and the American shipping interests of our East Coast, fused their commercial interests and abilities.

Captain Joseph O'Cain from Boston, with the firm of Boardman & Pope, began his successful hunting operations with the Russians in 1803. This was followed in 1806 by Captain Jonathan Winship on the *O'Cain*, and in 1811 by the *Albatross*, also under Winship. Other firms from the East Coast were involved in the hunt.

From Boston to the Sandwich Islands, then to California, came other captains and supercargoes. The names of William Heath Davis, once a 'Junior,' and in command of the *Isabella* in 1811, of Alpheus Basil Thompson and of John Coffin Jones, both of the town of Santa Barbara, of the Hawaiian Islands, and of Santa Rosa Island, are familiar.

William Goodwin Dana, originally from Boston, then from the Sandwich Islands in 1826, hired George Yount, Isaac Sparks, George Nidever, and others to hunt otter under his Mexican license. This was about 1833. These particular men were all originally overland men, not sea-faring men.

In 1826 Jedediah S. Smith, of the Rocky Mountain Fur Co., arrived with his party in California. Many remained. By land and by sea came the American fur hunters. The little town of Santa Barbara gradually emerged as the practical and/or permanent residence of many hunters, and trappers-turned-hunters.

The little Russian settlement of Ft. Ross, founded in California in 1812, independently prospered until 1841, when the Russians chose to remove themselves.

Even the missions in the area, from about 1785 to 1822, were in the business of purchasing and collecting sea otter skins. They dealt with the Russians, and even taught the Indians how to hunt sea otter. The mission interest was in being able to buy dry goods from the American ships at anchor, and to sell to the Chinese, in exchange for their quicksilver [J359].

By 1830, Russians and Americans, using Aleuts and/or Kodiaks from the North, or Kanakas from the South Seas, had already set the stage for the final extinction of the sea otter.

Though thought by many to be too little and too late for the otter, nevertheless Congress did pass a law in 1899 prohibiting the killing of the otter. Then a California law went into effect in 1913, partially insuring the preservation of the mammal.

By 1938 the effects of environmental protection through the Fish and Game Commission appeared to be taking hold, for a few sea otter in our waters were noted. Nearly ten years later, a California census figure indicated about 300 adult otters.

Pacific Discovery in 1955 [J80], published an article, "Sea Otter on San Miguel." It was less than two pages long, but as the author, Al Allanson, put it, "we had just observed two sea otters in a locality where they had not been recorded for nearly a century."

This locality was near BAT ROCK at the western end of Cuyler Harbor. Investigators of the Sefton Foundation of San Diego went in the *Orca* following this cue, but they found no sea otter on San Miguel. However, the public can be well assured that the "Little Clowns of Big Sur" are back on the California coast, not many miles south of Monterey.

J. R. Challacombe of *Westways* [P168, 1966], wrote an article and offers photos, too. In fact, for a two-page brief on a description of the sea otter and the history of it being a hunted creature, this is an ideal write-up. Challacombe then ended by saying, "Now, more than a century after the end of the great hunt, the California otters number only some six to seven hundred . . . many centuries will pass before they are as plentiful as in the pirate days of Baranof, if ever."

Fox

Lieutenant W. P. Trowbridge in 1856 was making tidal observations for the U. S. Coast and Geodetic Survey. His name appears in the *U. S. National Museum, Bulletin #62* [N8], as the individual who obtained two living specimens of San Miguel's little fox. First classified as *Vulpes littoralis*, then later as *Urocyon littoralis littoralis*, the specimens were turned over to Dr. H. C. Yarrow, a surgeon assisting with the Wheeler Survey's zoological and botanical labors.

George M. Wheeler was a 1st Lieutenant of Engineers, U. S. Army, and his name is used officially in the publication of the *U. S. Geographical and Geological Survey West of the 100th Meridian*. However, sometimes the Survey is known as the Powell Survey, Major J. W. Powell having been the Director of the Bureau of Ethnology in Washington, D. C.

This little endemic fox, about the size of a house cat, and having a shorter tail than the mainland species of fox, was found so tame that it was easily caught and killed.

As late as 1928 [J51], representatives of this diminutive Grey Fox were taken by Messrs. Chester C. Lamb and J. Elton Green for the Museum of Vertebrate Zoology in Washington, D. C. Many others have also collected the fox, even as late as 1956.

As of today, there cannot be many remaining, for besides being hunted, their decreasing population has also been the result of some form of contagious blindness, thought to have been contracted from scabied sheep. Without adequate protection, or even assistance, this endangered species could also be relegated to the group known as "extinct."

Skunk

It was a U. S. Coast and Geodetic Survey man, Captain Steham Forney, who obtained a specimen of the Spotted Skunk. In turn, he gave it to Mr. H. W. Henshaw, zoological assistant for the Wheeler Survey. The skunk was referred to as a "little-striped" skunk [N45].

Mouse

How the white-footed mouse is faring on San Miguel today is a question. Known in scientific literature as *Peromyscus maniculatus streatori*, a subspecies, it is found on all eight islands. The last noted account from San Miguel Island was from Dr. Cockerell in 1938 [J319], while visiting the Lesters.

From a housewife's point-of-view, the mouse was anything but an endangered species; it was so prolific that it became a nuisance hard to control. Realizing that it was an endemic species, Mr. Lester was adverse to eliminating them. However, at some advanced, later stage of his thinking, he decided to poison them and bury the remains in trenches.

Cats

With questionable generousness, cats were presented as 'gifts' for the mouse problem, with Mrs. Lester's mixed reactions,

The very cats I had hoped for, then abandoned hope for, began to arrive on the island disguised as "presents" and in a very short time we had something like thirty cats making their home in and around the ranch and life in the pantry became more peaceable . . .

And speaking of introduced animals, such as cats, throughout time the rest of San Miguel's menagerie has consisted of horses, cattle, sheep, and pigs. And according to Charles L. Remington [J251, 1971], of the Peabody Museum and Yale University, there was once upon a time, a burro, turned feral.

About the pigs, Nidever had remarked that he had placed pigs on the island, thus offering some credence to Max Miller's statement that he saw boars on San Miguel Island [B108].

Herpetofauna

Apparently there is no firm concensus on this subject. The main line of division appears to be between the turn of the century writers, and those since then, although they all seem to agree on the salamander.

It was John Van Denburgh of the California Academy of Sciences, serving as curator of the Department of Herpetology, who has been most helpful [J66, J68]. The San Francisco fire of 1906, having destroyed the contents of the Academy, left a poor record of what had been collected. But in an attempt to recoup some losses, Mr. Slevin and Mr. Van Denburgh revisited the island in April, 1911.

The article stated that it had been Mr. R. H. Beck who had previously collected on San Miguel for the Academy, obtaining "two species of lizards and a *Batrachoseps*" [J66]. Then in 1911 the two men "secured three species. The *Hyla* had not previously been taken on this island." Van Denburgh used the name *Batrachoseps pacificus* for the endemic salamander [J68]. Eisen found it on Santa Rosa in 1897; seemingly, it is on the four northern islands and Santa Catalina.

In the earlier article *Gerrhonotus scincicanda* was the scientific name given for one lizard, found independently on Santa Cruz, Santa Rosa, and San Miguel by Yarrow, Beck, and Townsend in 1875 and 1889. Another lizard was classified as *Sceloporus becki*, found by Grinnell and Beck on the same three islands [J66].

Mrs. Trask [M134, 1906], remarked that "San Miguel possesses a kind of lizard not found elsewhere in the known world." She mentioned the night lizard, *Klauberina riversiana*, as being on San Miguel; she also placed it on Anacapa and Santa Cruz, where others had not. As for a salamander, "new to the world [it] lives on San Miguel and Santa Rosa."

PIECES OF EIGHT

Charles F. Holder used the name *Gerrhonothus coeruleus* as a rather common species of lizard to be found on the islands [B38, U40]. J. G. Cooper [J59], called it a "Saurian" type.

One fairly recent writer stated that San Miguel had a blue-bellied lizard, an alligator lizard, and a slender salamander [J272]. Another gave the Latin names for two lizards—*Sceloporus occidentalis* and *Gerrhonothus multicarinatus*, using *Batrachoseps pacificus* for the salamander [B120].

Sumner appeared to have something of a grip on the subject when in 1939 he stated that the Blue-bellied lizard is *Sceloporus becki,* and the island salamander, *Batrachoseps pacificus,* a worm-like creature with short legs.

It is not often that fleas or gnats on the islands are mentioned as important life-forms, but Mrs. Lester called the fleas "a nuisance to be lived with."

Snails, also, have been and are abundant on San Miguel, but not as a personal nuisance.

According to Cockerell, the snails were very abundant and "have long existed on the island, as shown by their presence in the concretionary rock on the top of the island and in alluvial deposits near the shore, these surely antedating the period of human occupation . . ."—thus giving food for thought for the botanist, who is inclined to accuse the sheep for all of the vegetative destruction. [See also J331, 1903.] Dr. Yates used the scientific name *Helix Ayresiana* for this island snail, also found on the other three northern islands, where he found the sheep destructive of the species.

Cockerell found two butterflies and an endemic wasp, *"Bembex," hamata,* on San Miguel [J248]. Additionally, he collected sixteen species of bees of which "seven are new species, and five other new races of mainland species."

Avifauna

Mr. Streator was watching for the water birds that bred on San Miguel Island [J263, 1887]. However, he noticed that at breeding time they winged their way to GULL ISLAND and Flea Island, both a little less than a mile from the main island. This flight, he thought, might have had something to do with the little fox on San Miguel and his propensity for eating bird eggs.

Listing nine breeding water birds in twenty-five days, he felt that few could have escaped his notice. George Willett and party [J122], visited San Miguel in 1910 for about the same length of time and iden-

tified seventeen water birds, seven of which were already on Streator's list. Another list of water birds was made in 1939 by E. L. Sumner, who also identified seventeen birds. Since the three lists were not mutually exclusive, the total list of water birds became twenty-six.

Streator named Heremann's Gull, Double-crested Cormorant, Violet-green Cormorant, Tufted Puffin, and Surf Scoter; these were not listed by Sumner, nor did Willett list the two cormorants.

Willett and party were able to list the Royal Tern and the Western Willet, whereas Streator and Sumner did not.

Sumner offered the names of Shearwater, Common Loon, Pacific Loon, and Zantus Murrelet, which neither Streator nor Sumner had done.

Sumner probably had the best chance of identifying both the land and the water birds for San Miguel and/or Princess Island. He produced a list of sixteen land birds. Willett's list numbered eleven. Willett did not list Eared Grebe, Western Red-tailed Hawk, Barn Owl, Barn Swallow, Hermit Thrust, Western Meadowlark, Pacific Chipping Sparrow, or the White-crowned Sparrow. Sumner did not list the Sparrow Hawk, the Brewer Blackbird, nor the San Miguel Song Sparrow *(Melospiza melodia micronyz),* found to be nesting in prickly pear and wild cucumber on Princess Island. [See also J51, 1928.]

A total list of land birds numbered nineteen for San Miguel and Princess Island, which included the Bald Eagle, Burrowing Owl, and American Raven, to mention a few. None found the Osprey, a very rare species. Mrs. Lester referred to quail and plover being around the island [B103]. There may be others, to be found through additional research.

Another interesting note in the literature came from *Pacific Coast Avifauna* through George Willett [B115, 1933]. In it is stated that Captain S. Forney gave an adult specimen of Ashy Petrel from San Miguel to Mr. H. W. Henshaw, acting ornithologist for the Wheeler Survey.

The human element entered Willett's, "A Summer Trip to the Northern Santa Barbara Islands" [J122, 1910]. Their two weeks stay on the island had been an enforced one due to the weather, meaning the wind. Mr. O. W. Howard was one of the party who had gone to Princess Island. Willett continued,

We found Prince Island to be literally alive with breeding sea birds, and later obtained many interesting specimens, as well as notes and photos.
    After looking over some of the breeding col-

onies Owen and myself returned to camp leaving Howard on Prince Island with his blankets and expecting to return for him in the morning. In the morning, however, the northwester was howling again and we were unable to reach him for two days and then only with the aid of some Japanese abalone fishermen and their launch. Howard's story of how he subsisted for two days on mussels and gull's eggs, washt down with cactus juice, and how the Auklets persisted in getting in bed with him, is too harrowing to be told by an outside party . . .

We remained on San Miguel 14 days, being unable to leave as soon as we had planned on account of rough weather.

Ethnology

In the 1875 Annual Report of the Smithsonian Institution [N10], it is stated that Professor Dall of the institution was in charge of their Conchological Division. Elsewhere, we are also given the impression that Dall had some connection with the U. S. Coast and Geodetic Survey.

The following year, the *U. S. Geographical Surveys West of the 100th Meridian* published a report [N45], which included Appendix H13, written by H. C. Yarrow, U. S. Army. In the Appendix, Yarrow stated that Mr. Wm. H. Dall was a collector on San Miguel Island in 1873 and 1874, and that Harford, of the U. S. Coast and Geodetic Survey, turned over what he had collected in 1872 and 1873 to Mr. Dall. [See also J17, 1921.]

According to Mrs. M. Burton Williamson, *Southern California Academy of Sciences, Bulletin* [J333, 1904], there was in Washington, D. C., a Dr. W. H. Dall collection and a Paul Schumacher collection, Schumacher's being of both the Smithsonian Institution and the Peabody Museum.

Millspaugh and Nuttall [B105, 1923], have indicated that Dr. Dall also made a general natural history collection in the vicinity of Catalina Harbor, Santa Catalina Island, while connected with the U. S. Coast Survey under Professor B. Pierce, then Superintendent of the Survey.

There is an article, "The Lords of the Isles," in the first series of the *Overland Monthly* [1874], which was written by Dr. Dall [P79a]. The article is four pages long; some of it of no value, due to the use of generalizations. It also contains an incorrect island for the location of the abandonment of the Lone Woman.

However, after five years, a rereading of his article has indicated that some parts are worthy. Dr. Dall

had a trained mind, and as a conchologist, he must have developed powers of observation, belying the total article.

The following lengthy excerpt contains some of his personal observations of San Miguel; some relate to the Harford collection from the island; it could even be the earliest published record for this type of subject matter.

Various persons have visited these deposits, and returned more or less repaid with ethnological material—especially some of the officers of the U. S. Coast Survey, who so employed the leisure afforded by weather unfavorable for surveying work. Of these, by far the richest collection was made by Mr. Harford. It is now in the National Museum at Washington, and was obtained on the island of San Miguel. On visiting the shell-heaps on the north end of this island, the investigator is obliged to traverse about four miles of barren sandy wastes, which are intersected by sharp and broken ridges trending in an east and west direction. The shifting sands are raised in an unintermitting steady stream by the prevalent northwest tradewind, and cut the face and blind the eyes like a shower of needles. Through the sand here and there may be seen spears of a slender, dry grass; and in occasional patches the dry and dead remains of some shrubby plant, which in more favored localities raises a disproportionately small amount of tops compared with its knobby and swollen roots. Near the shell-heaps is a small grove of malva-trees, whose green leaves and penciled blossoms refresh the eyes. There are no young trees, however, as the omnipresent sheep crop every green thing within their reach close to the ground.

. . . The north point is T-shaped, forming two small coves, in one or the other of which a boat can land in almost any weather. The point is bold and rather high, with small sandy beaches in the coves. On the edge of this bank or bluff lived our ancient people. Here we see, where the sea has worn it away, a shower of pearly shells from top to bottom of the bank; . . . We find almost all the different kinds of abalone, limpets, and spiral pearly shells, which are still abundant in these waters . . . The shell-layers extend for miles along the shore . . . many springs have existed which are now dry. That these people cultivated the soil, there would seem to be little doubt. One of the most abundant relics to be found is the mortar and pestle, almost identical with those still used by the natives of New Mexico and Arizona for roughly

grinding the seeds of grasses into a kind of flour.
. . . That these were a war-like people is evident, from the number of spear and lance heads found in the shell-heaps and graves. A doubt may be thrown on the courage of at least one of them, from the fact that among the articles obtained by Mr. Harford was a pelvic bone, with a long stone lance-head driven half through from behind; attesting at once the strength of arm of the pursuer, and the fact that the defunct met his fate while running away. The majority of the weapons found are unmistakably for use in war, or in the chase; but there are certain heavy stone rings, or perforated balls, worked with a great deal of skill, and which have puzzled all the archaeologists. . .

The activity of their domestic life is attested by the presence of fish-hooks made of abalone shell, stone spindles for twisting thread, the great variety of stone mortars and pestles (often with traces of rude ornamentation), and various non-descript but very curious bone tools and implements, one whole tool-chest of which we were fortunate enough to unearth. That they were not without relaxation may be inferred from the occurrence of sundry pipes, more like a modern cigar-holder in shape than anything else; and that their aesthetic tendencies were not wholly repressed, is shown by the discovery of an actual flute—a "tibia," in a double sense— made from the bone of an albatross, and pierced with five holes. This probably had a wooden mouth-piece originally, which has perished. Personal ornaments were in use, though mostly of a rather crude description. Beads and rough *wampum* strung on twisted sinew, alternating with sections of bones cut into "bugles," or with *hyqua*-shells, are very common.

. . . Mr. Harford in one place found seventy skulls within a short distance of each other.

. . . Apart from the dead shells exposed along the edges of the bluffs, the only means by which the collector may determine where to look for ethnological material, are the portions of mortars and other implements from which the wind has cleared away the sand. These exposed portions . . . are reduced to very small dimensions, in comparison with the parts which remain imbedded and thus protected.

. . . Though they have passed away, "unwept, unhonored, and unsung," yet the rude record of the shell-heap shall keep their memory green.

It was for possible rich collections that Mr. Schumacher was asked to collect from the islands for the National Museum—under the guidance of the Rev.

Stephen Bowers, and through the auspices of the Wheeler Survey.

First working in northern California in 1875, he transferred his activity to San Miguel before sailing to Santa Cruz, San Nicolas, and Santa Catalina. His longest stay was on Santa Cruz for a month, as compared with a four day visit to San Miguel.

His map [N41, 1877], is of small value, other than to show where two springs and a large grave section were located on the west side of Cuyler Harbor. He did not get to the southwest and west sides of the island, due to weather.

León de Céssac followed Paul Schumacher on San Miguel, where he stayed for three weeks, 1878; the other islands he visited were Santa Cruz, Anacapa, and San Nicolas.

The fine and only references to de Céssac on the islands come through the Reports of the Archaeological Survey, Department of Archaeology under the editorship of Robert F. Heizer [U6, U7, 1951; U18, 1964].

In Paris in the Musee de l'homme in the Section Amerique, or in storage, are the entire de Céssac collections, perhaps 4,000 specimens; few were catalogued, according to the above reports.

Other than managing to raise the ire of Paul Schumacher for infringement of what appeared to be U.S. rights in the gathering of American Indian artifacts, de Céssac seemed to have handled himself fairly professionally. This he did by placing his collections in a store room in Santa Barbara for all to view, and by attempting to get Indian reaction to the usage of the various pieces. Then, he transported all to France.

The man seemed to have displayed a large amount of confidence when stating that from the information offered by an old Indian man and woman, he was able to reconstruct the ethnography of the Chumash. However, it is just as likely that de Céssac might have been merely displaying a bold front. His professional activities in the U.S. had not been entirely acceptable to some concerned citizenry.

Of the artifacts found on San Miguel Island, de Céssac said,

The first of these islands is unusual because of its chipped flint jasper and agate arrowpoints. I could collect there a great number of skulls, some skeletons and isolated basins as well as very beautiful ornaments, numerous bone tools and an extremely interesting series of mortars ranging from the first rough draft to the perfect achievement.

232

While on the island he made a natural history collection and a geological map; then he departed for San Nicolas Island [U7].

During the year 1886 Dr. Greene made a botanical excursion to the island of San Miguel [J252], *Pittonia.* Although a botanist, he had this to say about Indian sites, ". . . the entire coast line of four and twenty miles is an almost uninterrupted line of kitchen-midding, . . . bones . . . in a good state of preservation."

Charles G. Yale, Editor, in reporting to the Board of Examiners in the *11th Annual Report of the Journal of Mines and Geology* [C23, 1893], had this to say,

Several of the special articles prepared for this report can well be omitted altogether, since they do not relate directly to the mining interests of California, though they may be of scientific value . . . These . . . are doubtless valuable for publication through other channels . . .

He then listed an article through Dr. Bowers, one by Dr. J. G. Cooper, two by Dr. Lorenzo Yates, and the two by C. D. Voy, that were taken off the press.

What he said about Voy's forty-eight pages of manuscript, "Santa Rosa Island," he practically repeated for Voy's "San Miguel Island," quotable at this time,

"San Miguel Island," by C. D. Voy; 34 pages and eleven full-page plates. There is nothing in this chapter about minerals or mines. It gives a history of discovery, geographical location and dimensions, harbors, shape of island, soil, shells, volcanic material, Quaternary fossils, Pliocene fossils, surface of island, bluffs, ethnology of aboriginal population, shell heaps or kitchen middens, ancient stone implements, stone disks, zoology, flora, etc.

Both of these papers of Mr. Voy show research and would be useful for a geographical or ethnological society.

The lithographs for these papers mentioned have been made and printed.

And on this note, information from the 19th Century ends.

Although there is no author's name mentioned, F. W. Hodge was the Editor for the *American Anthropologist,* Washington, D. C., when the following notation was made [J2, 1907],

A series of specimens of bone, stone, and shell artifacts, obtained from ancient graves on the island of San Miguel, off the coast of Santa Bar-

bara County, California, is shown in the accompanying plates. The data and photographs were furnished by the late Horatio N. Rust of Pasadena, California.

Mr. Rust was one of the better known "pot-hunters" of his day—along with Dr. Bowers and Arthur Sanger.

By 1913 [J3], the *American Anthropologist,* n.s., made a four-page report on San Miguel Island—

. . . The San Miguel archeologica now incorporated into the Vaux Collection of the Academy of Natural Sciences of Philadelphia, include also spear and arrowheads, drills, perforators, knives, plummets, pendants, rubbing-stones, pestles and mortars, stone cups, tubes and tubular pipes, ring-stones for war-clubs and digging-sticks, and beads of stone and of shell—a typical series of about ninety specimens in all.

In 1916 the *Los Angeles Times* reported that "De Moss Bowers, son and assistant of the late Stephen Bowers, pioneer archaeologist of southern California, and Charles T. Brown of Cucamonga, [had] conducted the researches on Santa Cruz and San Miguel" [M138]. The two men later reported that San Miguel, even in 1916, was a far richer field of research than was Santa Cruz.

Mr. Ralph Glidden went to San Miguel in 1919, and stayed for almost seven months. There he made excavations for the Museum of the American Indian, Heye Foundation. Should the reader wish to read more, there is a small book entitled, *Certain Artifacts from San Miguel Island, California,* written by George G. Heye [J17, 1921].

A large part of this publication is the excellent annotated bibliography, almost twenty pages, compiled by Professor Frederick J. Teggart of the University of California, through the American Geographical Society of New York.

Photos and descriptions of the artifacts are the main contents. Skeletons exhumed by Glidden were lost when their boat capsized on the return trip. However, one small item of universal interest mentioned the finding of abalone pearls, "The largest one encountered weighs more than two ounces, . . . This specimen is 2 inches high and 1½ inches thick at the base." Arthur Sanger also supplied the Heye Indian Foundation with considerable material.

It was about ten years later that D. B. Rogers spent a little time on San Miguel, at least long enough to obtain an overview of its midden locations.

In his book, *Prehistoric Man of the Santa Barbara*

Coast [B63, 1929], he stated that the southern shore had not been very popular as a residential site by the Indians. Other remarks of Rogers, however, are entirely in keeping with Dr. Greene's statement made in 1886 that the entire coast line was covered with a practically continuous line of middens left by the Indians [J252].

Rogers' reference to Simonton Cove, as a once popular residential area, is in keeping with Barthol's statement [B103, p. 36], when he said of the Cove, "its slopes were covered with Indian mounds; its dunes the highest and its sand storms the worse."

Rogers' Indian occupation map shows Adams Cove, along Simonton Cove, the western part of Cuyler Harbor, and to the northwest from Cardwell Point on the east, to have had the greatest congestion of population.

The next publication date carries the year 1956, the *Archaeological Survey Association of Southern California's* "Newsletter." A few words written by H. Arden Edwards, "Notes on the Archaeology of the Northern Channel Islands" [J231], are the notes which were taken from Mr. Arthur Sanger, dated July, 1933.

Arthur Sanger had been traveling around the Northern Channel Islands for about thirty years. Part of his activity was escorting boar-hunting parties to Santa Cruz and Santa Rosa. He had also become acquainted with the Lesters on San Miguel Island and took recreation parties to that island on a fairly regular basis.

How Sanger also had time to amass an artifact collection, one wonders—of course, enthusiastic boar-hunters and excursionists could have been a boon to that side-line, which was a main-line with Sanger.

In these Sanger notes he refers to the WEST END, where he had found steatite beads; Otter Harbor for a bone whistle; Otter Point for a massive stone pick. In his notes there were references to the fact that whale bone ribs were used for house walls and roofs, that he had seen a peculiar mortar at the ranch house, that arrowheads had now become very scarce, that much flint had been worked on the island, with acres being covered by the chips of flint.

In 1961 Mr. Orr thought there might be about fifty very ancient village sites on the island, some perhaps 10,000 years old [J390].

Dr. Rozaire made a later study in 1966, through the Southern California Academy of Sciences.

A rehearsal of these supposed facts do not end the story of the various aspects of San Miguel's ecosystems. The Channel Islands National Monument has an active research program underway through the Museum of Santa Barbara, and there is little question that the Museum, active since 1876, has its pulse on and concerning San Miguel Island.

Photos of San Miguel Island

Date	Code #	Author	Photo or Map	Reference
1877	N41	Schumacher	Map, Indian sites	*U.S. Geolog. & Geogr. Survey*
1902, #7	J326	Yates	Cuyler's Harbor	*So. Calif. Acad. Sci., Bulletin*
1902, #9	J326	Yates	Cast of trees & Dead shells, *Helix Ayresiana*	*So. Calif. Acad. Sci., Bulletin*
1903	J331	Yates	Casts of trees	*So. Calif. Acad. Sci., Bulletin*
1907	J2	Hodge	Plates, artifacts; Horatio N. Rust	*American Anthropologist*
1913	J127	Wright & Snyder	Prince Isl., Brandt Cormorant nest	*Condor*
1912	P101	Edholm	Pearl divers at Work, San Miguel	*Overland Monthly*
1928	C2	Bonnot	Bull sea lion trimmings hung to dry Flea Island; dead animals litter Dead bull sea lion; trimmings off	*Calif. Fish and Game Quarterly*
1928	J139	Pemberton	Nest & Eggs, Bald Eagle	*Condor*
1929	B63	Rogers	Map, Indian sites	*Prehistoric Man of S.B. Coast*
1938	J319	Cockerell	Concretions, resembling trees	*Scientific Monthly*
1943	J178	Stock	Chart, adult insular foxes Map, hypothetical Cabrillo Peninsula	*Los Angeles Museum Quarterly*
1944	N51	Wheeler	Cuyler Harbor	*U.S. Naval Instit. Proceedings*
1948	J225	Walker	"Trees of Sand," 5 photos	*Natural History*
1949	_____	Coggeshall	Elephant Seals, San Miguel	*S. B. Museum of Natural History*
1955	J80	Allanson	Otter Cove in Background	*Pacific Discovery*
1956	M154	Hillinger	Cabrillo Monument Deserted wharf; Prince Island	*Los Angeles Times*
1958	J218	Warren, Jr.	Sea Elephants Cornered bull roars Glaciers of sand down Windy Cliffs A Cross on lonely San Miguel	*National Geographic Magazine*
1962	M47	Thorne Hall	The House of the King of San Miguel Windmill Barn and halters Tiny School Furnished Kitchen	*Odyssey of the California Islands*
1962	B119	M. Rockwell	Map; lights and buoys	*California's Sea Frontier*
1963	J388	Holland	Map; from U. C. Museum of Paleon.	*Journal of the West*
1963	P166	Hillinger	House built from 1898 wrecked boat	*Westways*
1963	P180	Bugay	Cuylers Harbor in background	*Yachting*
1966	P168	Challacombe	Playful sea otter Mother sea otter finds pup in kelp Otter, biting chunks of tough abalone	*Westways*
1967	B120	Bartholomew	Aerial, west end, San Miguel	*Symposium*
1969	N52	Lambert	Seals and lions relax on sands	*National Park Magazine*
1971	M173	Fradkin	Seals, Point Bennett Dwarf fox dashes across field	*Los Angeles Times*

Date	Code #	Author	Photo or Map	Reference
1974	B103	E. Lester	(over 13 photos; all excellent)	*Legendary King of San Miguel*
1977	_____	S. Rouse	(over 9 photos; all excellent)	*Noticias, S. B. Historical Society*
1979	_____	Ashkenazy	Sea lions at Adams Cove	*Westways*

Appendices

Material in the Appendices was culled
during the research for this book
and reflects information
without attention to completeness.
Subject matter in many of the
Appendices is capable
of considerable expansion.

Appendix A

Island Statistics

STATISTICS	SAN NICOLAS	SAN CLEMENTE	SANTA CATALINA	SANTA BARBARA
COUNTY	Ventura	Los Angeles	Los Angeles	Los Angeles
SQ. MI.	22	56	75	1
ACRES	14,080	35,840	48,438	640
LENGTH (MILES)	9	18½	18½	1½
WIDTH (MILES)	4	1½-4	½-7	1
LATITUDE	33° 16'	32° 9'	34° 40'	33° 30'
LONGITUDE	119° 30'	118° 30'	118° 29'	119° 32'
HIGHEST PEAK	Jackson Hill, 907' Central Peak, 850'	Mt. Thirst, 1964'	Mt. Orizaba, 2109' Black Jack Peak Ruby Peak	North Peak, 517' South Peak, 547'
NEAR ROCKS, ISLETS, BANK	Cortes Shoal, 3¾ mi. n.e. of S.N. Begg Rock, 7¾ mi., n.e. of S.N.	Castle Rock, S.W. SW end	Numerous (see text)	Sutil Island, 257' (formerly Gull Isl.) Shag Rock, 125', nw of S.B.
MILES FROM MAINLAND	61	49	20, from San Pedro	38, from L.A. ports
MILES TO AN ISLAND	28 to S.B. Island	21 to S.C. Island	23 to S.B. Island	40 to S. Cl. 25 to S.C.
OWNERSHIP	U.S. Navy, Air Missile Tracking Station	U.S. Navy, Marines, Air Force, Targets	Private, and L.A. County Conservancy	Channel Islands Nat. Park

STATISTICS	ANACAPA	SANTA CRUZ	SANTA ROSA	SAN MIGUEL
COUNTY	Ventura	Santa Barbara	Santa Barbara	Santa Barbara
SQ. MI.	1.1	91.163	84	14
ACRES	704	58,344	53,760	8,960
LENGTH (MILES)	4½	24	15	7½
WIDTH (MILES)	½	2-6½	10	2½
LATITUDE	34° 00'	34° 02'	34° 00' 05"	34° 07'
LONGITUDE	119° 22'	119° 31' 15"	120° 15' 00"	120° 25'
HIGHEST PEAK	Vela Peak, 930', W. Ana. 260', E. Ana.; 320' M. Ana.	Mt. Diablo, 2,404'	Mt. Negro, 1,285' Mt. Soledad, 1,567'	861', East Peak 850', West Peak
NEAR ROCKS, ISLETS, BANK	Arch Rock, E. Ana. Cat Rock, W. Ana.	Gull Islet, 150', south of S.Cz. Orizaba Rock, north of S.Cz.	Flea Island, west of S.R.	Princess Island, 303', ½ mi. north of Cuyler Harbor
MILES FROM MAINLAND	13	25, from town of Santa Barbara	27, from town of Santa Barbara	26
MILES TO AN ISLAND	4½ to S. Cz.	40 n.e. S.B. Island	5 to S. Cz.	4 to S.R.
OWNERSHIP	Channel Islands Nat. Park	Private, with Navy Missile Sta.; Channel Islands Nat. Park	Private, Air Force, Channel Islands Nat. Park	U.S. Navy Bombing target, Channel Islands Nat. Park

Early Voyages Along the Northwest Coast with Bibliographical Notations

ULLOA, 1539. See Burney [B7, 1806]. See Hakluyt through Davidson [N33]. See "California Voyagers, 1539-1541," translations of original documents, edited by Wagner. *California Historical Society,* Vol. III, #4, Dec., 1924, San Francisco.

ALARCON; FRANCISCO DE BOLAÑOS. See above references. Bolaños accompanied Cermeño, 1595, then Vizcaíno, 1602.

JUAN RODRÍGUEZ CABRILLO, 1542. A Portuguese navigator, with landed holdings in Guatamala, was sent by the King of Spain, through Viceroy Mendoza, to make discoveries along the coast and to discover the Straits of Anian [J374]. Bartholome Ferrer [Ferrelo, Ferrel] was chief pilot [J17].

They left Mexico on June 27, 1542 from Navidad, a small port in Xalisco. By November, 1542 Cabrillo had reached as far north as 38° before being driven back by the winds [B28], to the Isla de Posesión.

After Cabrillo's death on Jan. 3, 1543 at that island, Ferrer reached Cabo de Fortunas [Stormy Cape], about 41°; this was February 26, 1543. The cape was renamed Cape Mendocino, 40° 20', honoring the viceroy of Mexico [P33]. By March 10, 1543, having reached beyond Ulloa's limit, to 44°, it was decided they would return to Mexico, which they did, arriving April 14, 1543, after many vicissitudes of weather [B28].

It is not difficult to locate summary translations of the Cabrillo/Ferrer expedition. They may be found through the *Geographical Surveys West of the 100th Meridian* [N45]; George Davidson [N33]; H. E. Bolton [B2], *et al;* J. Burney [B7]; H. R. Wagner [B74]; and J. R. Moriarty/M. Kleistman [J391].

But one difficulty has been experienced—the identification of sources for these translations, with subsequent effects. This secondary accounting can but partially clarify what has been stated by others.

It is believed there is no extant account by Cabrillo

or Ferrer. It appears that the Archive de Indias in Seville has furnished what summary information we do possess about their voyage. From the Archive, copies of many documents were made and taken to Madrid. Some of the documents were not signed, one of them being that of the Cabrillo voyage.

Martin Fernandez de Navarrete, who copied some Seville documents, 1802, said of his Cabrillo account: "Found without the name of the author in the general archives of the Indias de Seville, in the letter of the time, among the papers brought from Simancas. File 9 of Descriptions and Populations. Examined and approved. Martin Fernandez de Navarrete." In a collection made by Muñoz, Navarrete had found a second copy of this voyage, vol. XXXVI. Navarrete inserts after his certificate of approval the words: "At the head and on the cover of this narrative occurs three times, De Juan Paez." [N45, p. 314.] Navarrete might have been trying to tell us something in addition to giving credit to Juan Paez, official chronicler of the Indies, 1555-60 [B74].

Another snag for the reader follows. From the Navarrete collection of documents, Buckingham Smith, Secretary of the United States Legation in Madrid, made his copies. It was published in Spanish in 1857. From Smith, R. S. Evans made a translation of the Cabrillo account for the United States, which translation was published by the *Geographical Survey West of the 100th Meridian* [N45, 1879].

According to Wagner, one small item emanating from the Navarrete/Smith source made for a large discrepancy, creating considerable confusion about Cabrillo's route in and among the islands and up the coast. In fact the Evans translation appears to be the basis of reasoning about the Cabrillo/Ferrer route for Davidson, Bolton, *et al.* Lasting for fifty years, those confused include ethnologist Kroeber, as he struggled with the route and place names [N16, 1925].

By 1929 Wagner, outstanding cartographer of our times, had compared Antonio de Herrera's 1615 *Historia General* account, also in Madrid, with the Navarrete/Smith account. His finding was that the Navarrete/Smith account spelled out the name "San Salvador" when discussing northern island place names. The Herrera account, instead, used the initials "S.S.," which could mean San Sebastian just as well as a place name for Santa Cruz Island; January 20th is that Saint's Day. Wagner also feels that Herrera probably had the original of the Juan Paez de Castro account when writing his history; Wagner's preference seems to be Herrera.

Wagner, as well as others, investigated the *Información, 1560-61,* found in Guatamala. This account on the cause of Cabrillo's death, etc. was based on a petition for a reward by Cabrillo's son and grandson.

Testifying, were Lazaro de Cardenas and Francisco de Vargas, both with Cabrillo on the voyage. They offer the data that the injury was a shinbone shatter [not a broken arm near the shoulder]—such type injury would require immediate personal assistance from others, rather than the reverse—help by Cabrillo for others.

Información also indicated that Cabrillo died within twelve days of the accident. The petition appears to be as much illusion or collusion as fact, and is therefore somewhat discounted by authorities.

FRANCIS DRAKE, 1578. Drake, an Englishman on the *Golden Hind,* also tried to discover the Straits of Anian [a Northwest Passage]; its existence was believed in during this century. [To King Philip of Spain, Ordaneta, 1561, had referred a rumor that the French had discovered a westward passage between Labrador and the land to its north.] See, "Drake on the Pacific Coast," *Southern California Historical Society Annual,* Vol. IX, J. M. Dixon.

The World Encompassed, 1628, tells of Drake's landing in California for ship repairing on June 17, 1579; he remained in one location for five weeks. Some historians believe the anchorage to be at Drake's Bay, where Drake planted a brass plate in the name of the Queen. Others, also experts in their fields of inquiry, believe San Francisco to be Drake's anchorage for that length of time; this subject is still under discussion. [H. E. Bolton and H. R. Wagner, authorities, were both involved in the discussion.]

FRANCISCO GALI, 1582. Forbes [B22], refers to this voyager.

SEBASTIÁN RODRÍGUEZ CERMEÑO, 1595. Accompanied by Bolaños on the *San Augustin,* Cermeño went in search of harbors and the Straits of Anian. "Cermenon" [Cermenho] was a pilot on the Manila-Acapulco route, sent on this particular mission by Governor Gómez Pérez Dasmarinas. He traveled from Manila, P. I. to Acapulco, Mexico, visited some of the Channel Islands and remained at Drake's Bay for about a month.

C. E. Chapman [B9], thought the California islands visited to be Santa Catalina and San Clemente. H. R. Wagner [J86], believed the islands to be of the northern group, which appraisal appears to be accurate.

SEBASTIAN VIZCAÍNO, 1602. King Philip III had ordered another survey of the West Coast. For this voyage Vizcaíno had two ships and a frigata. They left Acapulco, New Spain in May 1602, and entered San Diego November 10, 1602.

The *San Diego* was captained by Francisco de Bolaños, the *Tres Reyes,* with Vizcaíno aboard, was captained by Sebastian Meléndez. The frigata, *Santo Tómas,* had Gómez [B9]. According to Randolph [P33], Toribio Gómez de Corvan, an admiral, sailed in one of the ships, and ensign Martin de Aguilar in the frigata.

Fray Antonio de la Ascensión, a member of the barefoot order of Nuestra Señora del Carmen, was one of the chaplains and he kept a journal. Besides Fr. Ascensión, there was Fr. Andre de la Assumpción and Fr. Tomás de Aguino. Bolaños was pilot of the expedition. Captain Gerónimo Martín Palacios was the cosmographer. Palacios made a Derrotero [sailing directions] and a map. It is thought that he might have also drawn up a Derrotero for Bolaños. There is a Bolaños/Ascensión Derrotero, besides.

By early December the expedition had rounded Point Concepción, having gone through the canal of Santa Barbara, and had drawn the first crude maps of the eight islands and the coast [J251]. Then having reached Monterey by December 16, 1602, Vizcaíno gave the name Monterey to the Bay, thus honoring the viceroy, Count de Monterey.

Returning home, Vizcaíno recommended the establishment of colonies to prevent the occupation by other countries. And although this suggestion was favorably received in Spain, Vizcaíno died in 1608, thus ending further search for the Straits of Anian, as well as the establishment of colonies by the Spanish for about 166 years [P33].

Some have thought of Vizcaíno as being the first to discover San Francisco Bay, and he did anchor just north of it. In Hutchings' [P33], and referring to Portolá, (1769),

His latest guide was the voyage of Viscayno, who had entered the port of San Francisco on the 12th of January, 1603 and anchored under a point of land called Punta de los Reyes, namely in the bight outside the heads and north of Point Bonita.

But the Bay for almost one hundred and seventy years was left unrecognized—until Portolá "rediscovered" it while searching for Monterey, which he had unintentionally passed.

Vizcaíno's expedition was better conducted than Cabrillo's, for they left notes, plans, and sketches.

See Burney [B7], who follows Torquemada, chiefly derived from Fr. Ascensión; See Davidson [N33]; Wagner [J89, B74].

ANSON, 1742. This English Commodore cruised off the west coast of Mexico in wait for a Spanish Galleon. Successfully, he seized a chart of the coast and $1,500,000 "to boot." According to Randolph [P33], the chart was accurate from Punta de los Reyes to the south, just below which was Los Farralones—with a bay but not a name. Twenty-seven years later, San Francisco was christened.

DON GASPAR DE PORTOLÁ EXPEDITION(S), 1769. In 1768 José Gálvez, Visitador-general from Spain, arrived in Lower California. His dispatch was an order to search for San Diego, to rediscover Monterey, and to establish outposts on a colonization and missionary basis—to ward off foreign encroachment. This was but the year following Jesuit expulsion by Spain.

In this same year, Gálvez and Costansó, a layman, made a trial visit to Upper California before the real expedition started, 1769.

Captain Rivera, with Father Crespi, took the first contingent of settlers up the Peninsula on March 24, 1769 and arrived at San Diego on May 14th [B71]. Rivera then returned to Baja, California in August.

Also in May and going by land, too, was Governor Portolá, head of the enterprise, accompanied by Father Junípero Serra. Father Serra, a Franciscan originally from Spain, was slow, due to his bad leg, and did not arrive at San Diego until July 1st. There he remained to establish a mission.

The *San Carlos* and the *San Antonio* took from Mexico some of the colonists and water supplies, also heading for, but having to search for, San Diego. The *San Carlos* was under the command of Vicente Villa, a pilot of the Royal Navy, and they started from La Paz on January 9, 1769 [P56]. Lieutenant Pedro Fages, in command of military forces, and Miguel Costansó were aboard. After an exceedingly rough time at sea, the *San Carlos* arrived at San Diego about the first of May. All but the cook and

one sailor of the crew had died of scurvy while en route [P33]. The remaining were left at San Diego with Father Serra.

The *San Antonio*, under the command of Don Juan Pérez of the navigation of the Phillipines [P56], started from Cape San Lucas on February 15, 1769, with Father Gómez and Father Juan Vizcaíno on board. They arrived at San Diego about April 11, 1769. Theirs was a more fruitful journey, and even though they had also lost their way before arriving at San Diego, they had unwittingly given Santa Cruz Island its name for posterity.

By July 14, 1769 Portolá had headed up the coast from San Diego to rediscover Monterey. Along with him went a servant, Father Juan Crespi; Miguel Costansó, the engineer and political arm; Francisco Gómez; Captain Moncada; a sergeant, with twenty-six soldiers; and Lieutenant Pedro Fages with seven soldiers [P33]. Inadvertently passing Monterey by forty leagues (100 miles), they discovered San Francisco Bay!

By the time 1769-1770-1772-1776 had passed, the Franciscan Fathers and/or the military had established San Diego, Monterey Presidio, San Carlos Mission, and San Francisco. Father Serra remained in Alta California with five priests, founding fifteen missions by 1784.

Pedro Fages remained in military command after Portolá left California, July 9, 1770. With thirty soldiers he attempted to protect and carry on with the task at hand. In 1772 he traveled to San Francisco by way of Santa Clara Valley, predecessor to the Anza expedition. His command in Alta California lasted from July 9, 1770 to May 25, 1774, before Father Serra had him replaced [P33, P34, B19].

See *Land of Sunshine* for Costansó, Vol. XIV [P56], from a rare print. See "Diary of Miguel Costansó," through Teggart [U35].

See "Fray Juan Crespi," through Bolton [B13]. See Fr. Font's Diary, 1775-1776, through Bolton [B21]. With Anza, Fr. Font journeyed up the coast to San Francisco. See Father Palóu, *Historical Memoirs of New California,* through Bolton [B55].

See Fages, "Voyage en Californie," published in Spanish, 1844. See Fages, *A Historical, Political, and Natural Description of California,* translated by Priestley [B19].

See Tuthill, *The History of California,* 1866 [B71]. He used Venegas, *History of California,* Madrid, 1757.

JUAN PÉREZ, 1769, 1774. One of the passengers

aboard the *San Antonio* on the Portolá expedition of 1769 was Father Juan Vizcaíno, a Franciscan priest. Woodward [B73], offers "The Sea Diary of Father Vizcaíno," after having found the journal in 1940, buried among hundreds of unknown manuscripts in the Bibliotica de Mexico in Mexico City.

The *San Antonio* had wandered around and among the Channel Islands in the effort to reach San Diego. They cruised off San Clemente near China Point, where they were visited by canoes with Indians. Fr. Vizcaíno described the canoes and other pertinent matters of ethnological value.

Passing Santa Catalina, then San Pedro, they headed north and before they knew it they were at Prisoners' Harbor, Santa Cruz Island.

It was in the later place that Fr. Vizcaíno went ashore and got his feet wet. At this place he forgot his friar's staff which was later returned, and from which incident he gave to the island the name La Isla de la Santa Cruz.

Fr. Vizcaíno assisted Fr. Junípero Serra with the founding of Mission San Diego, July 16, 1769. But one of the Diegueño Indians had wounded Fr. Vizcaíno with an arrow. With an infected hand, he returned about a month later to Baja, California with Captain Rivera.

In 1774, on the *Santiago*, there was another Pérez Expedition. This time, Father de la Peña and Father Crespi were along as chaplains, with Fr. Crespi keeping a journal [B13]. Estevan Mártinez was the pilot and the *Santiago* sailed as far north as 54° to Cape North, British Columbia. There was no account of this voyage until 1802 when it appeared in "Introduction to the Journal of the Sutil and Mexicana" [B28]. The Fathers returned to Mexico.

JEAN-FRANCOIS GALAUP DE LA PÉROUSE, 1786. La Pérouse was a Frenchman on *A Voyage around the World*, who visited California and witnessed mission life at Carmel. See B42 for a few critical comments by La Pérouse.

MALASPINA, 1786. An Italian on a Spanish Expedition around the world; imprisoned in Spain for his political views about her colonies. States there were 6,000 Indians on the Islands. See Galbraith's "Malaspina's Voyage around the World" [J87].

JOSÉ LONGINOS MÁRTINEZ, 1792. One of the first trained observers to visit Upper California; he said that he had sent a San Gabriel Mission Indian to collect products from Santa Catalina Island. See "The Expedition of José Longinos Mártinez," translated by Simpson [B47]. See the Juan Pantoja y Arriga journal [J366]. Wagner discovered this manuscript in Mexico, which manuscript is now in the Huntington Library.

CAPTAIN GEORGE VANCOUVER, 1793. A British expedition under Vancouver on the *Discovery*, coming from Canada "had shown that there was no Northwest Passage south of the Arctic Circle," Beechey, London [1831]. [Volumes III and IV treat of California.] One of Vancouver's missions was to report on the Spanish settlements in Alta California. It was his interest, as well as Drake's, to try and establish English claim to the region.

Vancouver visited San Francisco Bay in 1792, Monterey Bay in 1793, and the town of Santa Barbara, where he met Father Miguel Miguel of the Mission [B71, B72]. Through his study of maps and charts, Vancouver practically finalized the present place names which we have for the Channel Islands and elsewhere.

G. H. LANGSDORFF, 1803-1807. In *Voyages and Travels* he observed life at the northern missions. His information was seemingly accepted by Engelhart [B18, 1912].

WILLIAM SHALER, 1804. Shaler was born in 1778. His ship was the *Lelia Byrd*, used for trading with missionaries and Indians, and he referred to the Indians and the missions of his day. His story is the first, first-hand account of California by an American. Anchoring at Avalon, Santa Catalina Island, he presents us with some ethnological material from that island [B65].

CAPTAIN FRED WILLIAM BEECHEY, R. N., 1826-27. Of English heritage; Beechey on his ship *Blossom*, gives "An Account of a Visit to California, 1826-27," 1831, London. It has been reprinted in San Francisco by the Grabhorn Press for the Book Club of California. See also, Engelhart [B18, 1912].

In the *Quarterly* for the Historical Society of Southern California, Vol. LXI, #1, 1979, Francis F. Guest, O.F.M. has an article, more or less a rebuttal on S.F. Cook's work on Forced Conversion of Indians in the California missions. In the article Guest referred several times to Beechey's voyage to California, Beechey's mention of the Indians, and their relationship with the missionaries.

Guest found Beechey to have been observant and open-minded; at the same time he felt that Beechey might have left implications that could be misinterpreted. According to Guest, some comments made by Beechey might be substantially true, but they could not be final, or even standard, without further illucidation. Perhaps one such of Beechey's comments was that a change of religion and worship for the Indians was somewhat habitual with them.

DUHAUT-CILLY, 1827-28. An account of their voyage may be found in J90.

SALUTE TO DR. KOHL. Dr. Johann G. Kohl (1808-1878) was a German geographer and was hired by A. D. Bache, Superintendent of the U. S. Coast and Geodetic Survey, to collect maps and historical accounts of North American cartographical history.

Appendix No. 64 of the Survey Annual Report, 1854-55 [N26], was written in Washington, D. C. by Kohl to Bache as an "Abstract of a complete historical account of the progress of discovery on the western coast of the United States from the earliest period; compiled, under direction of the Superintendent."

The abstract lists five areas of work done by Dr. Kohl:

1. A complete historical account of the progress of discovery.
2. A map to illustrate the historical account.
3. A collection of maps, reduced copies of originals to illustrate the history.
4. A list of place names on the western coast, settling the orthography of the names.
5. A catalogue of books, maps, manuscripts, etc. relative to discoveries on the western coast.

Kohl elucidates on these five areas, and of one he said,

> Some things relating to early Spanish expeditions of great importance, hitherto overlooked by historians, will be found in this memoir. I may mention as examples the first exploration of Fuca Strait, by the three Spanish navigators De Haro, Quimper, and Eliza, prior to Gray and Vancouver.

Kohl divided his historical accounts into interesting subdivisions which included: 3) From Drake to the Jesuits; 4) From the Jesuits to the Franciscan missionaries and their expeditions; 5) From the Franciscans to Vancouver; 6) From Vancouver to Wilkes.

Of the "printed and manuscript books and maps relating to the western coast," he listed 230 titles exclusive of those of the maps comprised in the other collection; thus there is no more complete catalogue of works on this interesting subject. Kohl was the one who substituted the name "Point Conception" as a name for "Cabo Galera," of the Spaniards.

He had wished to compile a *geographical description of the whole coast,* but was not allowed to do so; presumably, at this point Davidson began to prepare *his* "Directory of the Pacific Coast," published in 1858 [N29], as Appendix No. 44.

The Wheeler Survey, *United States Geographical Surveys West of the 100th Meridian,* 1879 [N45], contains an Appendix F, which includes some of the old maps with notes by J. G. Kohl.

Kohl's great collection is in the Library of Congress, assembled by Justin Winsor of Harvard and subsequently issued as Harvard Library Bibliographical Contribution, No. 19; Section IX relating to the northwest coast.

In the performance of Kohl's great task he was afforded the support of the libraries of the State Department, War Department, Navy Department, Topographical Bureau, and the National Observatory. "In these, and in the valuable collection of Colonel Peter Force," Dr. Kohl was able to collect his material, helping him to become the pioneer of North American cartographical history, even though that work was not allowed to come to fruition.

Channel Island Names

SAN NICOLAS. San Nicolas was first seen by Ferrer in February of 1543 [B75], Wagner. San Nicolas was named by Vizcaíno, Dec. 6, 1603, by those on the *Tres Reyes,* December 6th being the day of that saint [M30].

SAN CLEMENTE. A 1559 map shows San Clemente as "Victoria" [B8]. The Isla de Vittoria was given its name after one of Cabrillo's ships, October 7, 1542. San Clemente was named by Vizcaíno about Nov. 25, 1602, the day of that saint, [B8]. Saint Clement was martyred about 100 A.D. Miguel Costansó 'adopted' the name of "San Clement," 1769. George Vancouver saw San Clemente from a distance, 1793.

SANTA CATALINA. The "Isla de San Salvador" was given its name after another of Cabrillo's ships, October 7, 1542. Cabrillo went ashore on the east side of the Isthmus [M30]. On November 24, 1602, Vizcaíno gave the island the name of "Santa Cathalina." Vizcaíno was at the Great Depression, meaning the Isthmus, where he saw the Temple to the Sun. The Temple is well described by Vizcaíno; they set sail on December 1, 1602 [J71]. Vancouver said this island was the "easternmost of the Santa Barbara Canal" [B72].

SANTA BARBARA. This island was not visited by Cabrillo nor Vizcaíno, but Vizcaíno gave the island its name [J365], Wagner. The Saint's Day is December 4th; she was executed in 306 A.D. On Palacio's chart the island is called "Santa Barbara" [B29], and Vancouver said that the island was called "Santa Barbara" by the Spaniards [B72].

ANACAPA. This is one of two islands not receiving its name from a saint, the other being Santa Cruz. Cabrillo called the island "uninhabited," and gave it no name [B25]. When Cabrillo left the Ventura area on the 13th of October he traveled between 24 and 28 miles that day. A round trip to the Anacapas is approximately 26 miles, so Cabrillo was close enough to distinguish these islands as being uninhabited.

Costansó called West Anacapa, "Falsa Vela," [false ship], using "Las Mesitas" for the other two [J365]. In 1844 de Mofras used the name "Encapa" and/or "Santa Tomás" [J17]. [Vizcaíno's frigata was named Santo Tomás.] See J366 for Mártinez' use of Santo Tomás for East Anacapa, 1792.

The present name is a derivation of the Indian name, spelled "Enneecapah" by Vancouver [B72]; spelled "En-nee-ah-pagh" by Davidson [J71]; Costansó spelled the name "Anajup"; Gudde, spelled the name "Anyapah" [B29]; Hayes, "Anayapa." "Anacapa" is the final corruption of this Chumash Indian name.

LAS ISLAS DE SAN LUCAS. In the northward journey along the coast, Cabrillo traveled about forty miles October 14-15. How far out into the Channel they were is not stated. But it was on the 15th of October that "an island" fifteen leagues in length was cited.

But all three of the larger islands, without the intervening channels, are but twelve leagues in length; with the channels there are three additional leagues. According to Davidson, from a distance it is possible to see the three islands as one larger one, due to the visual factor of overlapping.

Within the next two days they traveled another seven leagues along the coast and by the 18th of October they were as far north as Point Concepción. Turning seaward, it became possible for the islands to be distinguished, one from the other. Two islands are mentioned, one being twice as long as the other. [San Miguel is 7½ miles long and Santa Rosa is 15 miles long.]

So, Cabrillo gave the islands the combined name of "Islas de San Lucas." For the interval of the next eight days they remained on the islands, for severe storms existed. Evidently they stayed in Cuyler Harbor of San Miguel, for even with the storm they "felt nothing while they were in the port; they called it Posesión."

By this time Cabrillo had sustained his injury, but they traveled on, even in the teeth of severe winds, but little progress was possible. And by November 23rd they found themselves south again, at the islands of San Lucas.

"While wintering on this Island of Posesión," Cabrillo "departed this life," [January 3, 1543]. But nowhere is it stated as to whether he was given a land burial or a sea burial. It could be that by changing the name of the island from "Posesión" to "Juan Rodríguez," Ferrelo was using the island itself as Cabrillo's headstone. It was also common practice to name a ship after its owner.

At this point in the Summary, the Indian names for the three islands and their villages are given, with Juan Rodríguez [San Miguel] having two villages, San Lucas [Santa Rosa], three, and San Sebastian [Santa Cruz], six, with an additional ten added to its October 15th list.

An editorial "on these islands" must have been used when stating the length of time they remained on Posesión, for the weather being what it was, there would be no reason for moving away from a safe harbor to a less desirable anchorage, without sufficient cause.

But by the 19th of January, with provisions low, they determined to set sail for the mainland in search of supplies. But once again they met with adverse weather and were forced to seek shelter, this time at San Sebastian, "another island of the San Lucas group." Such shelter they did not find for "there was no port really sheltered by the islands," and for eight days they circled the islands, finally returning to the island of Juan Rodríguez on the 27th of January.

They left Juan Rodríguez on the 29th of January for San Lucas, "which is in the center of the islands," in order to pick up some anchors and take on water. Finally they were able to reach Gaviota for wood, and other necessities, which could not be found on the islands.

Later, in March, they had to return to the islands, but that is another story. However, by this time the identification of the three northern islands is fairly crystalized—the objective of this rehearsal.

Wagner [B74], said that Lopez de Gómara, 1552, published a list of Cabrillo's place names in *Historia de las Indias*. The 1559 Homem map is also discussed by Wagner.

SANTA CRUZ. Cabrillo had named the island "San Sebastian." Vizcaíno, on the Palacio map gave the name, "Isla de Gente Barbudo" [Isle of Bearded Men]. Juan Pérez, 1769, had anchored on the north side of the island and the Fathers went ashore for awhile. From this visit, and the leaving of a staff on the island, came the name "Santa Cruz." (See Appendix B.) Also, one of the maps studied by Vancouver had the name "Santa Cruz" for a high hill on the island, so he used that name.

SANTA ROSA. Wagner's judgment was that Vizcaíno gave the name "San Ambrosio" to this island; December 7th is this saint's day [B75]. Miguel Costansó, 1769, who had not been on the islands, first called the island "Santa Cruz"; apparently realizing his mistake, he switched the name to "San Miguel" [B29].

It was Juan Pérez who, on his second trip to the islands, 1774, called the island by the name "Santa Margarita" [B8]. Vancouver, 1793, making a choice of one map over another, gave the name "Santa Rosa" to the island [J365]. In 1844 de Mofras, in using the names "San Miguel *or* Santa Rosa," must have recognized the dual set of names.

SAN MIGUEL. On the Palacios map this island is given the name "San Augustin" [J88]. [*San Augustin* is the name of the ship which Cermeño/Bolaños sailed in, 1595.] The *San Diego,* Vizcaíno's second ship on which Bolaños sailed, gave the name of "San Anicleto" to the island [B74], and Vizcaíno used the name of "Isla de Baxos" [J71]. By 1748 Commodore John Anson used the name "San Bernardo," whose Saint's Day is the 4th of December. [See Anson, Appendix B.]

By 1769 the name "San Bernardo" was still in use by Costansó [J17]. By 1774 Juan Pérez had changed the name to "Santa Rosa" [B8]. It is Wagner who seemed to think that it was previous map makers who had solidified the name "San Miguel" for the island, at least by 1790. By 1793 Vancouver took over the name "San Miguel" [B72]. The Day for Saint Michael is October 18th, an appropriate name, under the circumstances.

Chart of Alta California Governors

Spanish Rule

Gaspar de Portolá	1769-1770	....	Military Commander
Pedro Fages	1770-1774	....	Military Commander
Felipe de Neve	1774-1782	....	First Civil Governor
Pedro Fages	1782-1790		
José Antonio Romeu	1790-1792		
José J. de Arrillaga	1792-1794		
Diego de Borica	1794-1800		
José J. de Arrillaga	1800-1814		
José Arguello (ad int.)	1814-1815	....	Among 1st families of California
Pablo V. de Sola	1815-1822		

Mexican Rule

Pablo V. de Sola	1822-1823	....	Native of Spain; To Mexico prior to 1805
Luis Antonio Argüello	1823-1825	....	Born, San Francisco Presidio, June 21, 1784
José Ma. de Echeandía	1825-1831	....	Native of Mexico; returned to Mexico
Manuel Victoria	1831-1832	....	Native of Mexico
Pío Pico (ad int.)	1832	....	Born at San Gabriel Mission
José Figueroa	1832-1835	....	Died in office; native of Mexico
José Castro (ad int.)	1835-1836	....	Born at Monterey
Nicholás Gutierrez	1836	....	Native of Spain; To Mexico as a boy
Mariano Chico	1836		
Nicholás Gutierrez	1836		
Juan B. Alvarado	1836-1842	....	Born at Monterey
Manuel Micheltorena	1842-1845	....	Born at Oajaca
Pío Pico	1845-1846		

American Rule

John D. Sloat	1846	....	Military Governor
Robert Stockton	1846-1847	....	Military Governor
Stephen W. Kearny	1847	....	Military Governor
Richard B. Mason	1847-1849	....	Military Governor
Bennet Riley	1849	....	Military Governor
Peter H. Burnett	1849-1851	....	First Civil Governor

Information based on Hittell [B35, 1898], and Barrows [J353, 1900].

Geologic Time Chart for the Islands
Cenozoic Era, Age of Mammals

Epoch	Began Millions of years ago	Duration in Millions of years.	Conditions and Situations
Tertiary Period			
Paleocene	63	5	Some strata on southwestern Santa Cruz Island; sandstone, limestone, shale
Eocene	58	22	Fine-grained sediments noted on Northern Islands
Oligocene	36	11	Tropical; coarse non-marine conglomerates; gypsite, borates
Miocene	25	12	Volcanic; most of land under water
Early			————————————
Middle			Some highs above water as islands; marine sandstone, clay, siliceous shale, diatomite, source for oil through fossils
Late			Disturbances and elevations; faulting; some displacement
Pliocene	13	12	Convulsive; Preglacial; Topographic high and lows become well differentiated; emergence of Coast Ranges and Northern Channel Islands
Early			Post-Miocene Uplift; Continent subsides; Islands begin more emergence; No Pliocene strata known on islands; Scarcity of deposits and fossils; Beginnings of 3 peninsular extensions: Anacapia, Palo Verdes, and Guadalupia
Late			Elevation of islands and tilting with erosion; No southern island connected to mainland, U32; Northern islands probably connected (Orr); Hollowing out of submarine channels (Davidson); Endemism begins
Quaternary Period			
Pleistocene	1	1	Age of Ice; Sierra and Coast Range Glaciers; Fluctuations of sea level; Land bridges, submarine canyons, coral reefs, and shore-line terraces closely connected with changing sea level; Elevation on coast interrupted by general, downward depressions; marine sands, gravels, clay, decomposed granite

Quaternary Period, *continued*

Epoch	Began Millions of years ago	Duration in Millions of years.	Conditions and Situations
Pleistocene, *continued*			
Middle			Continued sea level fluctuations; [Illinoian Glacial Stage about 100,000 years duration]; Terraces or wave-cut platforms from 100′ to 300′ begin to emerge with 150′ terraces containing molluscan species; higher-than-present sea levels cover smaller islands; Northern Channel Islands still bridge-connected to mainland allow Pleistocene mammoths and land organisms to migrate; Land snails, fossil tree casts, dwarf mammoth the predominant fossils of this period (Orr)
Late	100,000 yrs. ago 20,000 yrs. ago		[Wisconsinian Glacial Age of about 70,000 years duration]; Homo Sapiens appear on earth about 35,000 years ago, arriving in New World by land bridge between Siberia and Alaska; Northern Channel Islands separated from each other by rising seas
Recent			
Holocene	18,000 yrs. ago		End of "Ice Reign"; changes in fauna and flora; Post-glacial seas rose to near present level, perhaps with a slight rise to form 5′ terraces; Physiographic features well preserved
Present Time	7,500-7,000 B.P.		Climate drying began. Period of Dune-dwellers and dune-building; Dwellers lived 1 to 1½ miles inland above present sea level
	4,000-3,000 B.P.		Climate drying continued. Period of Highlanders; Lived 300-1000′ above present sea level; Gathered seeds until about 2,500 B.P.; Forced to fish, due to forests disappearing
	2,000 B.P.		The Canaliño was firmly established as 3rd Indian culture; continued to look to sea for food
	1,200 B.P.		Great sea turtle was found
	438 B.P.		1542 A.D., Cabrillo visited the Coastal islands

Note: This chart is a compilation from many sources and contains but generalizations.

Appendix F

A Chronological List of Island Botanical Collections and/or Authorities

Dr. William Gambel

1847   Ornithologist from Philadelphia; probably 1st to collect plants on Santa Catalina; plants described by Nuttall of Harvard University.

Greene, J72, 1887: Gambel discovered *Crossosoma californicum* on Santa Catalina.

Dr. Thomas Nuttall

1848   Eastwood, J74, 1941: *Crossosoma californicum,* described by Nuttall, may also be found on San Clemente; [Dr. Nuttall was on the coast in 1836 between Monterey and San Diego, P83].

Dr. Albert Kellogg and W. G. G. Harford

1874   Kellogg published through *California Academy of Sciences, Proceedings.* Harford was of the U. S. Coast and Geodetic Survey. Kellogg described *Leptosyne gigantea* (coreopsis), *Dendromecon Harfordii, Grindelia latifolia,* found on Santa Cruz.

Greene, J72, 1887: Kellogg and Harford discovered four new species on Santa Cruz and two new ones on Santa Rosa; Greene described and classified *Saxifraga malvaefolia* (Jepsonia), *Eriogonum arborescens,* and *Hazardia detonsa.*

Mr. W. S. Lyon and Rev. Nevin

1884-85   Lyon, 2nd to have collected on Santa Catalina; three days in 1884 and three weeks in 1885; Lyons and Nevin spent four days on San Clemente, 1885; species named by Asa Gray, 1885; Lyon published in *Botanical Gazette,* included *Lyonothamnus* and *Prunus Lyoni.*

Greene, J72, 1887: Lyon collected 151 species from Santa Catalina, 81 species from San Clemente; 15 of 151 were insular.

Brandegee, J395, 1890: contains Lyon's list for Santa Catalina and San Clemente.

Eastwood, J74, 1941: Of Lyon's list, of the 81 from San Clemente, six were new to science.

Raven, J156, 1963: Of Lyon's list, 12 from Santa Catalina were endemic; 10 from San Clemente were introduced plants.

Dr. E. L. Greene

1886-89   First to collect on San Miguel, 2nd to collect plants on Santa Cruz (western half); collected on Santa Catalina after 1899. Mr. Hazard, 1885, gave to Greene from Santa Cruz, *Lyonothamnus asplenifolius* for classification.

Greene published in *California Academy of Sciences, Bulletin,* J72, 1887; *West American Scientist,* J258, 1886-87; and *Pittonia,* J252, 1887; In J72, of 321 Santa Cruz species, 48 were endemic to the islands, 28 of the 48 were peculiar to Santa Cruz; J252, Greene listed species for San Miguel and endemics; J258, Greene listed for Santa Cruz.

LeConte, J73, 1887: Discussed Greene's collections and ideas on endemism; Of Greene's 321 species collected on Santa Cruz, 28 were peculiar to Santa Cruz and 20 were insular, endemic to the islands; four species of *Lavatera assurgentiflora* Kellogg were discovered before Greene visited Santa Cruz; the *Lavateras* are "remnants of an old" species, saved by isolation.

Cockerell, J382, 1937: In 1887 Greene described 30 trees on San Miguel as *Saviniona dendroides,* 1 tree on San Clemente as *Saviniona clementina,* and 1 tree on Santa Catalina as *Saviniona reticulata*—possibly all are *Lavatera.*

Eastwood, J74, 1941: Greene found 321 species on west Santa Cruz, of which 20 were new; this is about ⅔ of what may be found on the island, but twice as much as found on the other islands; he collected 121 phanerograms, seven of which were new to science; Greene named Brandegee's list of species for the three northern islands; of this list Greene considered 36 to be insular and on Santa Cruz and San Miguel.

Dr. Lorenzo G. Yates

1890   He published "Insular Flora," in *California State Mining Bureau Annual Report*, C21; it was a 7-page tabulated list of species for the four northern islands; Yates designated which species were found by Greene, Brandegee, Prof. H. C. Ford, and Yates.

    Zoe editor, J393, was sarcastic of Yates' efforts in this regard.

Mr. T. S. Brandegee

Brandegee went to Santa Catalina in 1884, 1889, 1890, 1899, and 1916; He spent five weeks on Santa Cruz and 10 days on Santa Rosa; Brandegee was the 1st after Kellogg-Harford to collect on Santa Rosa, the 3rd to collect on Santa Cruz; he was on San Clemente in 1894.

1888   Brandegee, *California Academy of Sciences, Proceedings*, J61: He added 83 species for Santa Cruz, and 199 species for Santa Rosa; He found 20 on Santa Rosa not found on Santa Cruz; 9 of 20 endemics found are also on Santa Catalina; 11 of 20 endemics are peculiar to Santa Cruz, Santa Rosa and San Miguel.

1890   Brandegee, *Zoe*, J395: He enumerated Lyons' list of species for Santa Catalina and San Clemente; Greene's list for Santa Cruz and San Miguel, and his own list for Santa Cruz, Santa Rosa and Santa Catalina; the combined lists contained 512 species; the chart in Latin indicates where the species are; of the 512 species, 26 are not found on the mainland, as compared with Greene's 36 not to be found on the mainland; there were no species on San Miguel which did not belong to other islands; four were "doubtful" for Santa Cruz; he reduced the % of endemics for Santa Cruz to less than 1%; for the islands to less than 3%.

    Eastwood, *California Academy of Sciences, Proceedings*, J64, 1898: Brandegee found 9 species and 3 varieties for San Nicolas; he added 56 species to the Santa Catalina list, but few were endemic; he found and enumerated 199 species from eastern and northern Santa Rosa; see above, J61.

    Eastwood, J74, 1941: Brandegee's Anacapa plants were listed with her; 36 species for Santa Rosa were insular and had been named for Santa Cruz and San Miguel by Greene.

Mr. Samuel Bonsall Parish

Parish, an authority on southern California flora; lived in San Bernardino, California; he was on Santa Catalina in 1916.

1890   Parish, *Zoe*, J397; Brandegee, editor of *Zoe*.

1903   Parish, *Botanical Gazette*, U50: Parish listed his collections in a 20-page article.

Anstruther Davidson, m.d.; A. J. McClatchie [of Pasadena]

1894   Both men published in *Erythea;* see U23, U24, U25, U26; the plants were identified by Greene, Parish, Prof. Scribner, and Mr. Jepson; Davidson found *C. catalinae* and 5 of the species also found by McClatchie; McClatchie found 25 species on Santa Catalina that had not been previously reported.

Blanche Luella Trask

1897   Trask, *Erythea*, U27: Trask was the 1st to collect botanical specimens on San Nicolas.

1900   Trask, *Land of Sunshine*, P54: In 1897 Trask collected about 100 species on San Nicolas.

1903   Dr. H. E. Hasse, *Southern California Academy of Sciences, Bulletin*, J328: Trask in 1897 discovered 22 species of lichen-flora on San Nicolas.

1904   Trask, *Southern California Academy of Sciences, Bulletin*, J334, J335: In, "Flora of San Clemente Island," Trask offers about 70 plants' names and where they are found.

1910   Dr. C. F. Holder, *Channel Islands of California*, B38: Mrs. Trask was on San Clemente in 1897 and 1903 for about three months.

    Eastwood, J74, 1941: Trask listed about 80 species and varieties for San Nicolas; 12 of them were new to science; Trask describes some important species that Lyon did not list for San Clemente; fortunately, some of the Trask listings are found elsewhere than *California Academy of Sciences*, destroyed in the 1906 San Francisco fire.

1967   Raven, B120: He placed about 15 of Trask's San Clemente species in endemic categories; in J156, 1963, he refers to Dunkle, Allan Hancock Pacific Expedition, 13:247–386.

DR. C. F. MILLSPAUGH AND L. W. NUTTALL

1923   Millspaugh and Nuttall, B105: published *Flora of Santa Catalina Island*.

Eastwood, J74, 1941: Credits the book as being "the most important and latest work on the island's flora"; Millspaugh, Greene, Rose, Rydberg, Eastwood added over 30 new species, mostly endemic, to Lyons' and Brandegee's list for the island, making a total of 237.

IRA W. CLOKEY

1931   Clokey, *Southern California Academy of Sciences, Bulletin*, J345: suggested that Brandegee's 1890 *Zoe* list for Santa Cruz was the last published; Clokey lists 41 more species from the island, heretofore unpublished; Munz used Clokey for Hoffmann.

RALPH HOFFMANN (AND DR. P. A. MUNZ)

Hoffmann, ornithologist and botanist, Director of Santa Barbara Museum of Natural History.

1932   Hoffmann, *Southern California Academy of Sciences*, J346, J347: His list, chiefly of the northern islands since Brandegee, 1890; Hoffmann made about 420 additions to Greene's and Brandegee's lists; of the 420, 138 are from Santa Cruz, 200 from Santa Rosa, and 74 from San Miguel; there are 620 species on his list, with 90 of them being endemics; Hoffmann's list contains Clokey's list of 40 species; this is the 1st published list for Anacapa since Yates' list of 21 species for the northern islands, C21, 1890.

Eastwood, J74, 1941: Hoffmann knew the natural history of Santa Cruz better than anyone; he added 48 grasses and sedges, 5 fern, and 25 miscellaneous species for Santa Rosa; the pine species was mentioned; Hoffmann was on San Miguel in 1923 and found 74 species not listed by Greene, 18 of them being grasses; Hoffmann found *Lavatera* on Anacapa; he collected with Sumner on West Anacapa; Munz for Hoffmann added several species from Clokey's list for Santa Cruz.

MR J. T. HOWELL

Howell was employed by the California Academy of Sciences as Assistant Botanical Curator; he worked on the southeast end of San Nicolas.

1935   Howell, *California Academy of Sciences, Proceedings*, J69: He found 34 more species for San Nicolas, seven of them not being on Trask's list.

Eastwood, J74, 1941: Howell had been on Anacapa and furnished her with a list of plants from there; Eastwood gives her list of San Nicolas species, about 95 species and varieties.

E. LOWELL SUMNER, JR. (AND RALPH HOFFMANN)

1939   Sumner, "An Investigation of Santa Barbara, Anacapa and San Miguel Islands." Sumner was Regional Wildlife Technician for the National Park Service, Western Region.

PETER H. RAVEN

1967   Raven, B120: for vascular plants on the islands, mainly using Eastwood, Millspaugh, and Hoffmann.

	S.N.	S. Cl.	S.C.	S.B.	Ana.	S. Cz.	S.R.	S.M.
Single-island endemics	2	11 + 1	4	1	—	7	3	—
Other endemics	11	31	24	11	8	24	24	11
Native species	120	233	375	40	70	420	340	190

DR. ROBERT F. THORNE

1967   Thorne, *El Aliso*, J157: In 1967 he found 145 more species for Santa Catalina than did Millspaugh in 1923.

Thorne, *El Aliso*, J158: In 1969 he found 8 more species on Santa Catalina, one being a new genus; of Thorne's 563 species for Santa Catalina, there are 316 genera and 82 families; there are 396 indigenous plants and 17 introduced; of the 396, 43 need to be rediscovered; Thorne says there are 7 endemics on Santa Catalina, 4 of which are species, and 3 subspecies.

Raven names *Arctostaphylos insularis* for a Santa Cruz and Santa Rosa endemic.

Thorne names *Arctostaphylos catalinae* for a Santa Catalina endemic.

Raven names *Dudleya greenei* for a Santa Catalina, Santa Cruz, Santa Rosa and San Miguel endemic.

Thorne names *Dudleya hassei* for a Santa Catalina endemic.

Thorne lists 239 species for San Clemente.

RALPH N. PHILBRICK

1972   Of the Botanic Gardens, Santa Barbara, California.

Ralph N. Philbrick, Madroño, U29: "Plants of Santa Barbara Island"

Botanical Queries

While studying literature on the floristics of the islands, questions arose. Some were in terms of classification, location, or omission, but all inherent within the listing below. Code numbers lead to authors mentioning such plants; the list is alphabetized by island.

	S.N.	S.Cl.	S.C.	S.B.	Anacapa	S.Cz.	S.R.	S.M.
Castilleja ("strange")	J334-35							
Eleocharis	J74							
Suaeda (insular var.)	P54							
Astralagus robeartisii eastwood		J334-35						
Baccharis, "sp. now."		J334-35						
Dendromecon Stylophyllum albidum; Stylophyllum Virens		B38 J335						
Marrubium lyone		B38						
Oenothera ("peculiar form")		J334-35						
Salicornia Hemizonia		J334-35						
Alsine Nitens			U25					
Cornus polleyii			B38					
Dendromecon arborea			J382					
Dudleya hassei			J158					
Lupine perennis, var. of *truncatus*			B38					
Phacelia scabrella								J382
Hemizonia Streetsi, Gray		C21	C21		C21			

Indian Linguistics

Part I: Place Names

SAN NICOLAS. According to Bancroft, the Mission Indians called the island "Ghalas-at," a name seemingly accepted by Kroeber.

SAN CLEMENTE. At least two names, or their variations, are offered: Bancroft, "Haras-nga"; Hugo Reid, "Kinkipar"; the Pico-Henshaw list, which Kroeber used, "Kinki" or "Kinkipar"; Taylor, "Kinkipan"; and Gudde [B29], the Luiseño Indian name of "Kimki-harasa."

SANTA CATALINA. Hugo Reid spelled their name "Pineug-na" [B57], Bancroft also spelled it "Pineugna"; The Luiseño Indian name was "Ponga"; Kroeber used the spelling of "Pimu" or "Pipimar," from the Pico-Henshaw list. Bernice Eastman Johnston found the name "Pipimas" at the San Fernando Mission. Harrington spelled it "Pimúna."

ANACAPA. See Appendix C.

SANTA CRUZ. Ferrer spelled the name "Limum," Pinart, "Limu." Bancroft spelled it "Liniooh" [M30]; Taylor, "Limooh"; Brown [U20], gives us "Minagua"; Teggart [U35], offers "Lotolic" from Costansó; Hayes' Scrapbook, "Hujuar." The last three names must be of a later date.

Santa Cruz Villages. On October 15, 1542 Cabrillo said the names of the villages were "Niquipos," "Maxul," "Xagua," "Nitel," "Macamo," and "Nimitapal."

On Kroeber's map [N16, 1925], a new list of twelve villages are offered. Four apparently from Bancroft, "Maschal," "Nanahuani," "Lucuyumu," and "Chalosas" [M30]; and three from Tapis, "Cajatsa," "Ashuagel" [Bancroft's "Sasaguel"?] and "Liam." Others from the Pico-Henshaw list include "Nimalala" and "Shawa"; Hayes' Scrapbook repeats "Maschal."

On Brown's map [U20, 1967], a list of eleven Indian villages are given; he accepted nine of the twelve names used by Kroeber; spellings vary.

SANTA ROSA. After Cabrillo's death Ferrer furnished the name of "Nicalque" for the island. Taylor said the Mission Indian name was "Hurmal," or "Huima." Another indian name, 1816, was "Isla de Guimá"; Hayes' Scrapbook, "Mascui." [See "Maschal" above.]

Santa Rosa Indian Villages. Ferrer furnished three village names—"Nichochi," "Coycoc," and "Coloco," or "Estocoloco."

"Kichuwun" and "Kshiukshiu" are of Pico-Henshaw and placed in the Rancho Viejo area; however, Kroeber placed them in the Becher Bay area. "Etziuziu" and "Ixtemen" are placed in the Becher Bay area by Brown—an important variance; both men appear silent on the Rancho Viejo region, perhaps the largest site on the island.

SAN MIGUEL. Ferrer furnished the name "Ciquimuymu" or "Ciquimuesmu," as spelled in J255. Costansó said that the natives called the island "Thoa" [U35]. Bancroft offered the name of "Tukan" for the island, which Kroeber accepted. Kroeber, then Heizer [U21], would have liked to equate "Ciquimuymu," Indian name for San Miguel, with a Becher Bay Indian village on Santa Rosa, as per the Pico/Henshaw list. [See Santa Rosa village name of "Kshiukshiu" above.] From Hayes' Scrapbook, according to Orr [B54, pp. 107-111], Dr. James L. Ord gave the name "Wimat" for the island, obtained from Anisetto Pajilacheet [Omsett?]. See Part II of Appendix H.

San Miguel Indian Villages. Ferrer's village names were "Cico" and "Nimollollo." But Brown used "Toan" or "Tucam" for a village name—Bancroft's *island* name. Brown's other village name is "Niouiomi," which name, he said, came from La Purisima Mission.

"THE THIRD ISLAND." After naming the villages for Santa Rosa and San Miguel, Ferrer named the villages for "the third island." Considering the "15 league" island to be not just one island, but the three northern islands, a likely conclusion is that Santa Cruz was the third island, thus placing emphasis on the intent of the Summary, not the literal wording.

Santa Cruz *is* six leagues from the mainland, but less than ten leagues in length, so that the three islands are needed to complete the fifteen leagues. This would make Santa Cruz a part of "San Lucas."

The second list of village names offered for "the third island" in 1543 are: "Niquesesquela," "Poele," "Pisqueno," "Pualnacatup," "Patiquin," "Patiquilid," "Nimemu," "Muoc," "Pilidquay," and "Lilibeque."

Some have queried that these villages could belong to Santa Catalina Island. To others, this appears unlikely, for Ferrer was discussing the northern islands. In addition, Cabrillo had remained on Santa Catalina but half a day, almost too short a time interval to have learned village names. These names could have, however, been offered for Santa Catalina by Chumash Indians of the Santa Barbara region.

Part II: General Linguistic Information

In 1904 Eisen said that according to Major J. W. Powell, there were some twenty-two different Indian languages in California [M30]. Professor Kroeber [N16, 1925], accepted Powell's arrangement [N14, 1891]. Some little information by Powell may be found in the *Geological and Geographical Survey*, Vol. III, p. 439, 613.

The Shoshonee family ranges over much of the interior of the United States, as well as its southwestern corner. The Hopis are Shoshonee, and in our southern California area are the Gabrielino, with the Luiseño-Cahuilla adjacent. Dr. Loew of the Powell Survey studied their language in 1875. The four

southern islands basically belong to this language group.

The Chumash language was spoken on the mainland around Santa Barbara, and according to Céssac, each of the northern islands had its own distinct dialect of that language.

Omsett, old Indian born on Santa Rosa, said that canoes were called "toak" and "somow"; the paddles, "simihi"; the hatchets, "teho"; the small white clam, "alusha"; and the larger one, "anuckpoo" [M51].

Horatio Hale, Dr. Loew, and Father Antonio F. Jimeno studied the Santa Cruz Island dialect and obtained vocabulary samples. Dr. Loew continued his inquiry by making comparisons of many of their words—forehead, beard, arrow, sun, moon, night, leaf, water, meat, cold. Although the Santa Cruz dialect showed differences, the roots for being of the same linguistic family appeared to exist [N16, N45].

Alexander S. Taylor gave a lengthy list of words for the Santa Cruz Indians in his *Precis Indius Californicus* [M51]. These are to be found in the No. 9 issue with almost three pages of vocabulary, which vocabulary, he said, came from Father Theodoro Amat, Bishop of Monterey.

Appendix I

Museums with Channel Islands Indian Artifacts

CALIFORNIA: Bowers Memorial Museum, Santa Ana; California Academy of Sciences, San Francisco; California State Mining Bureau, San Francisco; Los Angeles County Museum, Los Angeles; San Diego Museum of Man, San Diego; Santa Barbara Museum of Natural History, Santa Barbara; Southwest Museum, Los Angeles; Southern California Academy of Sciences, Los Angeles; Stanford University, Palo Alto; University of California, Los Angeles; Anthropology Museum, Lowie Museum of Anthropology, Vertebrate Zoology Museum, University of California, Berkeley.

NEW YORK: American Indian Museum, Heye Foundation; American Museum of Natural History.

ILLINOIS: Field Museum of Natural History, Chicago.

MASSACHUSSETTS: Peabody Museum of American Archaeology and Ethnology, Cambridge.

CONNECTICUT: Peabody Museum of Natural History, New Haven.

PENNSYLVANIA: Vaux Collection of Academy of Natural Sciences of Philadelphia.

WASHINGTON, D. C.: Carnegie Institute of Washington; Rau's Archaeological Collection; Smithsonian Institution.

FOREIGN: London Museum; Museum de l'Homme, Paris; Museum d' Ethnographie, Paris; National Museum of Constantinople; Possible German, Russian Museums.

Appendix J

Precis Indius Californicus

Part I

The use of this title, one of A. S. Taylor's [M51, J92], is in honor of his memory for his interest in Indians and source material about them. Although some statements made by Taylor do not possess crystal resonance, nevertheless, there is information of "Indianological" significance obtainable through him.

It is known that as early as 1770 the Mexican government was not in favor of the mission fathers attempting to convert the islanders, and the missionaries remained agreeable to this thought. However, in the early nineteenth century, and due to changes in circumstances, the Fathers had thoughts of an island mission, to which the civil authorities were then agreeable [J239, 1937]. But decimation of the Indians by disease put an end to such thinking by Father Tapis and others.

Taylor said that "an old American resident of Santa Barbara" told him that the islands were thickly populated in the early part of the century prior to 1816, but

> They had such bloody wars among themselves, for the fishing grounds of each island, on each rancheria, that the priests had them all brought over to the mainland and placed in the Missions of Santa Barbara, San Luis Obispo, San Buenaventura, Santa Ynez, and La Purisima.

Johnston [J192], in 1955 spoke for the Gabrielinos further south when she said that they were no match for the fierce Aleuts, "Refugees from San Clemente were assigned to Mission San Luis Rey . . . [and] San Gabriel is said to have been the destination of those from Santa Catalina." Mission Registers indicate other missions, as well.

According to Bowman [J240, 1962], the first islander was baptized in 1795; thirty-seven were baptized in 1814; in 1822, according to Engelhardt [B18, 1912], a large number of the islanders became "neophytes at Missions Santa Barbara and Ventura." Fr. Antonio Ripoli, friend to Daniel A. Hill, Taylor's father-in-law, had charge of the Mission Santa Barbara between 1816 and 1827 [M51].

Alexander S. Taylor

Taylor offered many references on California Indians in terms of their language and their habits. With some apology for his bibliographical technique, his list is presented.

There is *Dictionary and Grammar of Indian Language,* compiled by Father Felipe Arroyo de la Questa [Cuesta] in Monterey County in 1815, published by Mr. John Shea, N. Y., 1861-62, in *Linguistic Series of North American Indian Languages.* Father Cuesta lived at San Juan Bautista and was an expert on the subject of Indian languages.

There is Horatio Hale's, *Philology of Wilkes' United States Exploring Expedition* of 1838-42; Railroad Survey volumes, which contain Dr. Herman's ornithological notes in the 10th volume. Emory's Mexican Boundary Survey, Bartlett's Survey of the Mexican Boundary, the bound volumes of the Spanish and Mexican Archives in the Office of the U. S. Surveyor of California in San Francisco, and Whipple's Railroad Survey are a part of Taylor's listing.

To continue, St. Mary's Catholic Library, San Francisco, and the College of San Fernando, Mexico, are quoted as locations for reviewing literature.

Additionally, the *Schoolcraft History* volumes on United States Indian tribes; Sir Francis Drake, 1579, *World Encompassed,* on the Indians of Punta de los Reyes country; Dr. Robertson's *History of America,* supposedly with a valuable bibliography; George Gibbes, on the languages of California, Oregon, and coasts north; Ludewig's bibliographical work on languages; *American Ethnology Society and Transactions,* New York; Alexander Humboldt's *Essays on New Spain;* and de Mofras, for an excellent bibliography, are offered by Taylor. Taylor especially referred to Mofras having included the Lord's prayer in the Indian languages of the twenty-one missions of California, a feat in itself, and might be most helpful.

Just as Johann G. Kohl is considered the first cartographer for the western coast, Alexander S. Taylor is a 'first' as bibliographer of California.

Robert Ernest Cowan's, "Alexander S. Taylor, 1817-1876," is a touching seven-page article on the man, his background, and his efforts [J92, 1933].

Taylor's father was a naval officer in the War of

1812, and his mother was a Londoner. The couple and family lived in Charleston, South Carolina, but in 1837 the young man, Alexander, began wandering "over the West Indies, England, India, the Red Sea, China, Singapore, and Ceylon" [J92].

Young Taylor came to California from Hongkong in 1848, living in Monterey until 1860. In that year he moved to Santa Barbara, marrying the third daughter of Daniel A. Hill, Josefa, whose dowry she probably shared with an older sister—"La Patera," a portion of "Hill's Ranch."

Taylor collected Spanish manuscripts, designated by Engelhardt [B18, 1912], as "Archbishop's Archives," now resting in the diocesan residence in San Francisco. Still extant, they may be a priceless collection, [J92].

His writing career was about a fifteen year length of time, from 1853 to 1868. A listing of his more important contributions follows.

1. *California Farmer* (see 1859 Smithsonian Report on grasshoppers).
2. *California Farmer,* "Indianology of California," four series in 150 numbers from Feb. 1860 to Oct. 1863, now extant with the University of California; some copies at the Santa Barbara Mission; some few at Southwest Museum.

In "Precis Indius Californicus," Series I, Taylor said,

A curious account in manuscript was found about 1831, giving a history of the Indians of the Mission of San Juan Capistrano, in Los Angeles County, among whom he [Boscano] had labored for twenty-five years prior to his death in 1831. A translation of his account was published in New York in 1846, in Alfred Robinson's, "Life in California."

And speaking of both Taylor and *California Farmer,* in 1861 he himself had reprinted Boscano's "Chinigchinich" in eleven weekly issues of the publication from June 28 through October 11. Taylor died in 1876, Robinson in 1895.

3. *Hesperian*
4. *Hutchings' California Magazine,* for historical and bibliographical material
5. *Sacramento Daily Union,* June 25, 1863; March, 1866, "Bibliographia California"— about 500 titles on Upper California [but with little value, said Engelhardt]
6. *San Francisco Herald,* "Discovery of California and Northwest America," chiefly a translation from Navarrete on Cabrillo.

According to the *Overland Monthly,* Vol. 13, 1874, Taylor made this translation and had it published in pamphlet form, San Francisco, 1853
7. *The Historical Summary of Lower California,* 1532-1867, 62 pages, in J. Ross Browne's *Settlement and Exploration of Lower California,* San Francisco, 1869

Dr Cowan remarked that Taylor lived "obscurely and in poverty," and like "other and greater men he was perhaps too big for the company in which he was obliged to live."

Hubert Howe Bancroft also saluted Taylor when he said, "It were well to judge a man not alone by what he has accomplished, but also by what he has conscientiously tried to perform" [J92].

In 1860 [M51], Taylor made a quaint appraisal of our gap in the history of the Indian, which bears validity, even today,

If there is any man of leisure in the world, in these volcanic and earthquake times, there is abundant material to write the history of the Monarquia Indiana Californicus; and a grand, curious, and famous work will it make, if the author has truth, liberality, and moderation for his guide, and uses the faculties of competency, patience, diligence, and the accumulated facts of history from 1540 to 1860; and his task will be no light one either.

For all of his shortcomings as a collector and a writer, Taylor is another of our unsung contributors to early West Coast history, living at a time when enthusiasm for such was sorely needed.

Part II: Other Sources; Authorities

Missions did not prove to be sufficient haven for the remaining Indians. The Indians were experiencing grave losses in their population and the missions were losing their control to the secular authorities.

Father Gonzales, who went to the Santa Barbara Mission in 1833, could find no one up or down the coast who could understand the dialect of the Lone Woman of San Nicolas in 1853. Twenty-five years later, ethnologists were fortunate to find three or four Indians who could assist with any tasks of interpretation.

Céssac and Pinart both sounded pleased when referring to their luck in obtaining in 1875 the services of Martina and Balthazar, of the San Buenaventura rancheria, for ethnological interpretations [U4, U7].

Contributions made to ethnology in this country

by Pinart are to be found in the Bancroft Library; the contributions coming from de Céssac are still in France. And should the *Los Angeles Times* of 1916 be correct,

> In the early fifties officers of a Turkish war vessel, archaeologically inclined, secured a vast treasure from the islands which is now in the National Museum at Constantinople. Strange as it may seem, it is claimed by some Scientists that to fully reconstruct the civilization of prehistoric inhabitants of the Pacific Coast islands a study of the unique collection of the Sultan of Turkey is almost imperative . . .

Evidently this point-of-view is true for France, Turkey, even Germany and Russia.

Céssac/Pinart, Henshaw/Loew/Gatschet and Schumacher/Bowers/Yates left the initial ethnological imprints.

Dr. Yates, in "Fragments of the History of a Lost Tribe" [J1, 1891], said,

> . . . statements of Justo, a Santa Barbara Indian, in answer to questions in relation to their habits and customs, which, in view of the fact that the aborigines of the region referred to are almost, if not entirely, extinct . . . at the age of about ten years he accompanied the expedition which brought the remnants of the Indian tribes from the islands off the coast of California and distributed them at the missions of Ventura, La Purisima, Santa Barbara, and other localities on the mainland . . .
>
> When Mr. H. W. Henshaw visited the region, several years ago, only one Indian remained of the Santa Rosa Island branch, and two more dialects were spoken by two or three individuals only,

It sounds as though one of the Santa Rosa Indians that Henshaw knew is the one called Omsett, reportedly born on Santa Rosa Island [J191, M51, B54]. Taylor spelled the name, if it be the same man, "Comoluatset," and Joseph "Camuluyazet," even giving his age as eighty on November 4, 1856. At another time, Taylor remarked that Joseph's age was seventy-five.

It is Taylor's thought that Omsett was baptized at the Santa Barbara Mission by Father Antonio Ripollo. (Refer to Appendix G for the spelling of "Anisetto.") Henshaw also used the services of a "Pico," for a list of Indian place names.

Using the written records by Powell [N14], from some of the investigations, A. L. Kroeber produced his *Handbook of the American Indians* [N16, 1925], through the Bureau of Ethnology, Washington, D.C.

Perhaps, spurred by Kroeber's work on the subject of Indians in 1925, a second phase of activity began through Olson [U1], and Rogers [B63, 1929-30]. While Kroeber accepted the work of others, these two men took a new tac—that of independent research, with their accompanying conclusions.

According to some reviews on the work of these gentlemen and/or on the present status of ethnology, the results do not come up to expectations [J4, J8, J230, J232]. Be that as it may, they did divide the Chumash culture into three historical catagories, thus giving later researchers opportunity for thinking in a more definitive fashion:

R. L. Olson:	Early	Intermediate	Late Islanders
D. B. Rogers:	Oak Grove	Hunting	Canaliño Cultures
(P. C. Orr:	Early	Middle	Late Canaliños, Santa Rosa Isl.)

On the subject of contributory persons and material, students should doublecheck *Land of Sunshine* and *Out West* publications. Eisen [M30], indicated that both contain translations of many original papers on the California Indians, not otherwise accessible.

F. W. Hodge, National Bulletin 30, *Handbook of American Indians*, 1907-10, is an excellent source for Indianology. Appendix B of *Pieces of Eight* should be scanned for ethnological, bibliographical sources.

W. W. Robinson, *Land in California* [B61, 1948], has several pages of fine bibliography. Harry Kelsey, "The California Indian Treaty Myth" [J378], and Francis F. Guest, O.F.M., "An Examination of the Thesis of S. F. Cook on the Forced Conversion of Indians in the California Missions" [J380b] may be found in the *Southern California Historical Society Quarterlies*.

Of broader assistance to the student is *California Indian History* [B91a], listing some 685 bibliographical references, and *The California Indians* [B32]. Under convenient headings of the latter, are references to archaeology, ethnology, and Indian history. Compiled by Heizer, Nissen and Castillo; Heizer and Whipple, there is no equal for this type of assistance, both in quality or quantity.

There were outspoken men like J. Ross Browne [P23, 1861], who scathingly rejected the attitude of the United States for its indifference and/or rejection of the Indians, but it was over a hundred years after the Mexican secularization of the mission lands, 1834, that any relief was given to the Indians of California.

It was too late for most, and too little for the remaining population, before the Indian Claims Commission began to provide some moral support and assistance.

Part III: Diagnostic Points

There appears to be at least three general diagnostic points observed in the study of Indian ethnology—their two kinds of fishhooks, their woven baskets and cordage, and their method of disposing of their dead; seemingly both inhumation and cremation have been used [B120].

The Plank Canoe belongs to the latest group of Indians, the Canaliño. Use of asphaltum for canoes, baskets, jewelry, and ornamentations were a characteristic of the Hunting Indians. Projectiles, arrowheads, metates and pestles are also of this group. But metates with manos are also characteristic of the earliest group, who collected seeds and acorns, and ate shellfish almost exclusively.

With all of the Indian artifacts available through foreign and domestic, public and private museums, plus buried written material, perhaps A. S. Taylor's wish for someone to produce a written history of the Monarquia Indiania Californicus could some day become a reality—through another's patience, diligence, and competency.

Appendix K

Residents of the town of Santa Barbara at the same period as the Carlos Carrillo family

de la Guerra Family

It was 1769 when Costansó was along the Pacific Coast. This was just ten years before Don José de la Guerra y Noriega was born in Spain, and but seven years before the American Revolution.

In 1800, when twenty-one years of age, de la Guerra was appointed as an ensign, stationed in Monterey. In 1804 he married María Antonia, the only daughter of Don Raymundo Carrillo and Tomasa [Lugo] Carrillo. From that marriage there were seven sons, five daughters, and 85 grandchildren. María Antonia was the sister of Carlos Carrillo.

By 1811 Don José was sent to San Diego, to remain for several years. In 1814 José Argüello became Spain's 7th Civil Governor of Alta California, with the military in the background, of course. But some time in 1817 de la Guerra was assigned to replace Argüello as the Captain and Commandante of the troops stationed at Santa Barbara.

History has it [B35, 1897] that the family was "miserably poor," although 326,000 acres were confirmed among some of them. And both Nidever and Wm. H. Davis independently reported seeing a chest of gold coins secreted in José's attic.

Francisca de la Guerra Dibblee

One of Francisco's daughters and one of Miguel's, it is understood, married Anglo-Americans. One of Pablo's daughters, Francisca, became Mrs. T. B. Dibblee. Available information is sketchy.

T. B. Dibblee, Albert Dibblee, and W. W. Hollister were given a franchise in 1871 to build the wharf at Santa Barbara, which was completed the following year.

Albert Dibblee, ten years previously, had been contacted by W. W. Hollister, the sheep king of the region, on the subject of buying Santa Rosa Island for sheep-raising purposes. In the letter to Albert, Mr. Hollister had said that "Mr. More" was inter-

ested in selling his share in the island for $20,000, and he thought "the other half can be bought also and for about the same sum."

Mr. Hollister went on to say that he would be willing to furnish eight thousand sheep to stock the island. He remarked that it would cost forty thousand dollars to stock, and he thought his brother, Hubbard, would manage the business.

The proposal did not materialize; at least nothing more has come to light on the subject. One reason might have been the offer itself. Another reason could have been that in 1861 neither A. P. nor T. W. More owned half of the island.

According to the Santa Barbara *Weekly Independent* of June 15, 1895, Mr. T. B. Dibblee was asked to appraise the assets of Santa Rosa Island after the death of A. P. More. But Mr. Dibblee "was confined to his bed with a severe case of pneumonia and was unable to perform any of the duties imposed upon him."

Theresa de la Guerra Hartnell

Theresa de la Guerra was the first daughter of José de la Guerra. She married Wm. E. P. Hartnell of England, and they had twenty-two children by the marriage.

The same year that Hartnell had come to California, 1822, Mexico had become politically independent of Spain. Being a linguist, Hartnell served his new country well before he passed away in 1854, for he had translated the American statutes into Spanish for the Californians.

María de la Augustias Ord

María de las Augustias de la Guerra, second daughter of José de la Guerra, married twice. By her first husband, Manuel Jimeno of Mexico, she had eleven children. Manuel Jimeno became Secretary to Governor Alvarado, and others, and was intimately connected with the land system after the missions were secularized.

María's second marriage was to Dr. J. L. Ord of the U.S. Army, with Rebecca Ord born of this marriage.

In the Bancroft Library there is an undated manuscript written by Dr. Ord. This manuscript is in Benjamin Hayes' Scrapbook of the Indians of California

261

in which Indian names of the four northern islands are furnished by the Indian, Omsett [B54].

Anna María Antonia de la Guerra Robinson

Then there was Anna María Antonia de la Guerra, the youngest, according to Richard Henry Dana. She married Alfred Robinson of Boston in 1836 and they had four boys and four girls by their marriage. A description of the wedding festivities of Anna María and Alfred may be found in Dana's *Two Years before the Mast.*

Alfred Robinson was born in 1806 and at the age of twenty-three, 1829, came to California on the *Brooklyn* as agent of Bryant and Sturgis of Boston. Theirs was the 1st American company officially entering into trade with California.

Robinson purchased hides and sold goods on the California coast. Although he traveled from port to port, exchanging the cargoes of the Boston ship for California hides, he was a resident agent continuously on the coast for twelve years.

When Captain Francis Thompson, brother to Alpheus B. Thompson, arrived at Santa Barbara in January of 1835 with the *Pilgrim,* he had a $12,000 cargo on board, plus Richard Henry Dana, and Robinson was the agent who greeted them.

No nicer compliment could be given a son-in-law than the one José de la Guerra gave to Robinson. In making Robinson executor of his Will, he said, "I have entire confidence in the honor and rectitude of my son-in-law, Señor Robinson" [B53].

In fact, others, too, believed in Robinson's honor and rectitude. It was John Coffin Jones who asked Robinson to be his business agent in California when he returned to Boston with his California wife and family, 1846.

Robinson might not have realized at that time just how much labor was ahead of him in settling the litigation between Jones and Thompson; Abel Stearns acting as receiver, 1860.

Later, Abel Stearns, too, needed help and turned to Robinson. In 1861 Abel owned 108,107 acres of land. But by 1868, through over-expansion and results of the drought, he had to mortgage all of his property. It was Alfred Robinson, a business associate, who partially succeeded in saving the Stearns estate.

Robinson left a personal narrative, "Life in California." What is just as important is the fact that in the appendix of the book was published the first translation of Fr. Geronimo Boscana's work on the Indians, "Chinigchinich." Without Robinson's pub-

lication there would have been no extant copy of the Boscana work in the United States. Dr. Hamy had taken possession of the original in 1881.

Don Raymundo Carrillo Family

Don Raymundo had married Tomasá Lugo and had a family of five children, four sons and one daughter, María Antonia, who married José de la Guerra.

Don Raymundo first held the position that José de la Guerra later held, Commandante of the Presidio of Santa Barbara and San Diego. Both gentlemen were of Spanish origin, and the two Castillians had much in common in those early days.

Carlos de Jesus Antonio Carrillo was the 1st son of Raymundo and Tomasá. Carlos was the great grandfather to Leo Carrillo, of movie fame, on the Jones' side of the family. Carlos married María Castro (1792-1853), and they had three sons and four daughters.

José Antonio Carrillo was the 4th son, 1796-1880, born in San Francisco [J96]. José Antonio married a Pico, Estefana; their daughter, María Antonia, became Luis Burton's 2nd wife, and the mother of Ben Burton.

One son of Raymundo, Domingo Carrillo, married a Pico, Concepción. María, one of their daughters, married José María Covarrubias, one time the owner of Santa Catalina Island through Thomas Robbins.

Another son, Joaquin, became a District Judge of Santa Barbara County, serving for eleven years, 1852-1863. He died Feb. 19, 1868.

William Goodwin Dana, 1797-1858, married in 1828 the eldest daughter of Don Carlos Carrillo, María Josefa. Storke [B69], gives considerable detail about the life of W. G. Dana, who at the age of eighteen went to sea under the sponsorship of his uncle, William Heath Davis, Sr.

William's mother was Eliza Davis of Boston, Massachusetts. William Dana and José Antonio Carrillo—his wife's uncle, were of nearly the same age. By 1820 Captain Dana was established in the Sandwich Islands as a merchant; by 1825 he had moved to Santa Barbara, where he remained in the sea-going trade for several years.

Dana became naturalized in 1835 and in that year petitioned for the grant of Nipomo Rancho, 37,887.71 acres (8,758.493 square leagues), which was eighty-five miles from Santa Barbara. On receiving it, he moved with his family to Nipomo, where he prospered. One son, John F. Dana, born June 22, 1838, later married Frances Caroline Thompson, daughter of Alpheus B. Thompson.

Another daughter of Carlos Carrillo was Encarnación, who married Thomas Robbins in 1834. He had come to California from Nantucket in 1827. Robbins passed away in 1857, but in the meantime he had owned Santa Catalina Island as a grantee, and the Rancho Las Positas y Calera adjoining Santa Barbara.

Streeter [J96], says,

> About 1830 he opened a store and settled in Santa Barbara, . . . In 1837-39 he commanded the schooner *California* which was in the service of Alvarado and Vallejo . . . He had the reputation for being a hospitable and good natured old fellow, whose store was a general rendezvous for traders and men of the sea.

Annotated Bibliography
For The Pioneer Residents
of Santa Barbara

C42   Santa Barbara County Recorder, Patents and Deeds, Books A, C, D, F, G, I, Y, 75, 77.

N18   1851   Executive Documents, Vol. III, Document #18 Wm. C. Jones, as Special Agent, writes to T. Ewing, Sec'y. of the Interior, about the land title situation in California. He quotes the "Pesado Letter," a very important historical document.

M72   1883   *San Francisco Morning Call,* Nov. 19, 1883, "An Extensive Sheep Range on Santa Rosa Island." Offers the information that the widow of H. H. More sold their ½ interest in Santa Rosa Island to A. P. More for $600,000. They discuss shearing of sheep, and allied topics.

B70   1883   T. H. Thompson and A. A. West, *History of Santa Barbara and Ventura Counties.* Contains biographies on the very early settlers in California, and refers to the Standard Oil Co. and their interests, especially around the Rancho Sespe region. This is the only reference giving a detailed account of the court trial for those who were supposed to have participated in the murder of T. W. More in 1877—but only one man was convicted! The account is long, with much emotional overtone.

B1   1885   H. H. Bancroft, *History of California,* Vol. III, IV. In Vol. III he refers to Castro as being the grantee of Santa Rosa Island. In Vol. IV he has some material on John C. Jones.

B69   1891   Mrs. Yda Addis Storke, *A Memorial and Biographical History of the Counties of Santa Barbara, San Luis Obispo and Ventura, California.* Mrs. Storke was the second wife of C. A. Storke. Storke, an attorney, had been married to Mattie More, daughter of T. Wallace More, and one of the heirs to A. P. More's estate. At that time her name was "Law," having remarried. Biographical information on the early settlers is similar to that of Thompson and West; perhaps both used a common source—that of the centennial history of Santa Barbara by C. E. Huse, an attorney. Very little is said about T. W. More, however, Mr. Storke was then manager of the Sespe Rancho and knew the trial situation intimately.

M88 . 1895   *Santa Barbara Weekly Independent* of June 15th gives a full report of the condition that C. E. Sherman found on the island of Santa Rosa after the death of A. P. More. John F. More had leased the island from A. P. in 1891 and was the administrator of it and the rest of the estate when A. P. More's death came. The report is not a pretty one, as Sherman was not allowed on the island, or when he was, found a complete lack of cooperation. Mr. T. B. Dibblee was appointed as a substitute, but he was ill and could not accept. This report of the poor conditions that had developed leaves the reader wondering about John F. More and his personality. The article is about 10 paragraphs and worth the reading. Eliza M. Miller, sister of John F. and A. P. More, was appointed to administer the estate after Sherman's report was made to the court.

B35   1898   Theodore H. Hittell, *History of California,* II. Hittell was an attorney and worked for J. B. Alvarado. He made a study of the early land records and had a command of knowledge concerning early settlers and the missions.

B25   1917   C. M. Gidney, *History of Santa Barbara, San Luis Obispo and Ventura Counties.* An excellent account of the early history of the three counties; it contains an early photo of the José de la Guerra home in Santa Barbara.

B53 1939   O. H. O'Neill, *History of Santa Barbara County*. Excellent; contains the story of Santa Cruz' Botany Bay, a letter from James A. Forbes to Alpheus Thompson about possibilities of sending wheat to Russia, and considerable information about the early settlers in California. O. H. O'Neill was the husband of María Antonia Hill, daughter of Daniel A. Hill who came to California in 1823.

J96 1939   William A. Streeter, "Recollections of Historical Events in California, 1843–1878," *Calif. Hist. Soc. Qtly.* Well written, there is much on the personalities of the time, including A. B. Thompson, Wm. G. Dana, Thomas Robbins, and the Carrillos.

B40a 1976   Ross H. Gast, *Contentious Consul, A Biography of John Coffin Jones, First United States Consular Agent at Hawaii,* Dawson's Book Shop, Los Angeles, Ca. Indeed fortunate are those interested in Jones and his connections with the Sandwich Island, Canton, China, and the Pacific Coast of America. It has much about Jones, for Jones was very active in both his business and private life.

We learn of William H. Davis, both senior and junior, and from whom "Jr." received his early training and knowledge about evading custom officials.

Gast fills dozens of gaps in our knowledge of Hawaiian history, trade conditions, and the relationship of Jones with Alpheus B. Thompson.

To a great extent, the information comes through the diaries of Stephen Reynolds, who worked for Jones, and that of Faxon Dean Atherton, who worked for Thompson. Whereas many accounts of this period are sketchy, *Contentious Consul* gives a feeling of satisfaction, not experienced otherwise.

Bald Eagle View, Land in Early California

The bald truth is that the land belonged to the Indians before the advent of White Man. Spain first established settlements in California, with the help of Jesuit missionaries, and therein lies the original source of conflict and plight of the Indian. The conflict was not over conversion, instruction, or 'improving the lot of the natives,' but over the wealth and power that had fallen to the Jesuits and not to the Spanish government, as a result of these activities.

After the Jesuits were driven from the Spanish domains, the Franciscan fathers furthered the establishment of additional missions and continued in essentially the same methods of management; but changes were in the offing.

Mexico established its independence from Spain in 1822. Richard Henry Dana visited the Coast the year following the 1834 Mexican Decree of Secularization of the missions. This is what he reported,

> . . . Ever since the independence of Mexico, the missions have been going down; until, at last, a law was passed, stripping them of all their possessions, and confining the priests to their spiritual duties; and at the same time declaring all the Indians free and independent *Rancheros.* The change in the condition of the Indians was, as may be supposed, only nominal: they are virtually slaves, as much as they ever were. But in the missions, the change was complete. The priests have now no power, except in their religious character, and the great possessions of the missions are given over to be preyed upon by the harpies of the civil power, who are sent there in the capacity of *administradores,* to settle up the concerns; and who usually end, in a few years, by making themselves fortunes, and leaving their stewardships worse than they found them.

Tyson's 1850 comments to George W. Crawford, Secretary of War [N17], indicated essentially the same thing,

> No property belonged to the mission, except the church, parsonage, and adjacent buildings, and a small piece of ground around them; . . . The Mexican government has resumed all the lands, and taken the missions as national property—an act, the legality of which is disputed by the missionaries. But certain portions of the land are assigned to the "mission Indians" for their support, under the administration of the priests—the former not being endowed with full civil rights.

Dana summed up his view of the entire chaotic California condition of the period when he said,

> Revolutions are matters of constant occurrence in California . . . The only object, of course, is the loaves and fishes; and instead of caucusing, paragraphing, libelling, feasting, promising, and lying, as with us, they take muskets and bayonets, and seizing upon the presidio and custom-house, divide the spoils, and declare a new dynasty. As for justice, they know no law but will and fear.

These conditions were in large part a result of the grants of land that had begun under the Spanish regime—1774, 1777, 1781, 1784, 1795, 1802, and 1814—using this method to encourage colonization, in order to protect their land from foreign encroachment [B35].

This policy was continued by the Mexican government. But there had been no regular surveys made by either the Spanish or the Mexican governments. Without surveys, grants often over-lapped and/or were not sufficiently documented. Of this situation, Hittell, who had studied land grants most carefully, said [B35],

> . . . it was the governor's duty to communicate the fact of the grant to the legislative body, where it was usually referred to a committee, which reported at a subsequent session . . . it was not infrequent for the governor to omit communicating the fact, and there was no action at all. If approved, it was customary for the secretary to deliver to the grantee, on application, a certificate of the fact; but no record or registration of approvals was kept except as contained in the written minutes of the deputation or assembly. On account of this loose method of proceeding, particularly where grantees neglected to obtain certificates, there was no evi-

dence of approval except in the journals of the legislative body; and as many of these were lost, the evidence was lost. In the early part of 1846 the departmental assembly was known to have approved many grants; but the only evidence of them were loose memoranda, apparently made for future formal entry and referring to the grants by numbers, but never in fact formally entered.

It really does not take the piercing eye of an eagle to portend future events pertaining to land grants made previous to July 7, 1846. It would be impossible to know how much land had been actually granted in California before that date, but Pío Pico in 1845, evidently seeing the trend of events in terms of the United States take-over, ordered Abel Stearns to save the archives.

The archives had supposedly all been taken to Los Angeles from Monterey, and the sub-prefect of Los Angeles, Abel Stearns, collected what he could find. When in 1846 the military-governor for California took office, he, Mason, also ordered a collection of the archives. Many persons, including Halleck, a prominent California attorney, did what they could to further this cause.

Halleck collected what he could find at Monterey; "had some translated by William E. P. Hartnell, and on March 1, 1849, presented a very full report, as the result of his examination, on the Spanish and Mexican laws and regulations respecting grants and sales of public lands, respecting mission lands, and respecting the title of lands required for fortifications, arsenals and other military structures" [B35].

This was but the beginning. By July 12th of 1849 William Carey Jones was appointed as Special Agent to examine the subject of Land Titles in California. His report went to T. Ewing, Secretary of the Interior [N18].

Included in the report was the Pesado letter, which Jones quoted in full. (See Santa Rosa Island for one version of the letter.) Purportedly the same letter as the one in J. N. Bowman [J240], "The Question of Sovereignty over California's Off-shore Islands," there are some differences.

The Bowman quotation of the letter begins with, "MEXICO, July 20, 1838"; in the Jones quotation, it begins with, "MOST EXCELLENT SIR," placing the date of July 26, 1838 on the last line of the letter. The Bowman quotation starts the letter with the words, "Desiring on the one hand to promote the settling of the uninhabited islands adjacent to that Department which are part of the national territory

266

. . ." The Jones quotation reads, "The President being desirous to protect, on the one hand, the population of the islands adjacent to this department which form a part of the national territory . . ." The Bowman quotation ends with, "God and Liberty. PESADO"; the Jones quotation is finalized by the words, "For God and Liberty! Mexico, July 26, 1838. PESADO, Governor of the Department of Californias, Villa de Los Angeles."

In other words, the Pesado letter not only recognized the islands as part of the public domain, but took into account "the population of the islands," which could only have meant the Indians. However, how many Indians were still left on the islands to be protected is unknown; probably not many.

The Pesado letter is one of Jones' greater contributions; the spelling in the report of "Carrillo" as "Barrelo," is no doubt purely a typographical error.

Jones had been commissioned to examine the archives at Monterey, San Francisco, San Diego, or elsewhere, and to procure copies of documents in Mexico City, if necessary. Jones went to San Francisco, San Jose, Monterey, Los Angeles and Mexico City, and returned to Washington, D.C. to present his report April 1850. Jones, too, reported elaborately, including copies of many documents and papers on the subject of land grants.

By March 3, 1851, Congress had passed an act intended to settle private land claims in California. The Land Commission of three opened their office in San Francisco on January 1, 1852; within two years all claimants for land under Mexican titles had to file suit against the Federal government, under penalty of forfeiting their claim to the land.

When the Commission dissolved in 1855, those whose titles had been accepted, had to again present claims to the District Court of the government for approval. In the meantime, the first case to be tried was in July 1853 by Judge Hoffman.

Some cases confirmed by the Commission were rejected by the District Court, and some cases rejected by the Commission were confirmed by the court. Perhaps it became obvious that the procedure would take too long, for some 400 cases potentially calendared for the District Court were finally dismissed.

Edwin McMasters Stanton was sent in 1858 from Washington, D.C. as special consul to further investigate the distinct possibility of fraud in the documents at hand. He was also requisitioned to furnish an orderly arrangement of all archive material.

Hittell, an attorney-specialist in land titles, offers

a clear and detailed rendition of Stanton's collecting of archives from various sources, his taking them to San Francisco, and his method of arrangement without indexes before causing such to be bound. Hittell concluded,

> The arrangement by Stanton was by no means orderly or logical . . . the volumes, substantially bound in uniform folio size and labeled . . . were deposited in the office of the United States surveyor-general for California; and there they have since remained. There are about three hundred of them, containing on an average about eight hundred pages each, mostly manuscript and in Spanish . . . As a rule, the chirography is good, sometimes excellent; but in some instances the ink is faded and in some the paper is stained, weather-worn or worm-eaten. In one or two instances, a musket-ball has gone through a number of leaves. But with all their imperfections and disarrangement, the California archives are an exceedingly interesting and valuable collection, not only as muniments of title but also as historical records, without which it would be difficult if not impossible to ascertain much about the events that occurred in the country . . .

Regardless of the inefficient method of archive arrangement by Stanton, his was a fourth and final attempt to collect the material, for the sake of preservation.

His investigations also further high-lighted the existence of a highly organized forgery ring(s), composed of influential native Californians, wealthy Americans, and British opportunists bent on deceptive practices.

A Gates article, "The Fremont-Jones Scramble for California Land Claims," *Southern California Historical Society Quarterly,* #1, 1974, focuses on John C. Fremont and William Carey Jones and their interest in acquiring land claims. Both men were well-known politicians and both were sons-in-law of Thomas Hart Benton, whose idea for settling land claims was that of merely requiring the registering of land titles and the elimination of those claims which "the proper land officers or agent of the government'" may suppose invalid.

Gates enlarged his statements by generalizing,

> The acquisitiveness of public officers during California's early days is as much a part of its history as the repulse at San Pascual or the Big Bear Flag Revolt . . . [for there was] intense concentration of 19th century politicians, professional army and navy officers and civil officials upon the accumulation of landed property.

This type of recent research and observation gives additional emphasis to much earlier primary and secondary accounts.

In 1862 Ogden Hoffman made an index of the land cases of the U. S. District Court; they may be found in that office in San Francisco and in the Bancroft Library, Berkeley, under the title *Index of California Reports.*

J. N. Bowman also researched the proceedings of the Land Commission of the U. S. District Court and made a revision, 1942, of the Hoffman Index. This *Index of California Private Land Grants* and papers may also be found in the San Francisco District Court office and the Bancroft Library [B61].

As a summary through T. H. Hittell [B35],

813 land claims had been presented
604 were finally confirmed
190 claims were rejected
19 claims had been withdrawn

The 813 claims took into account about 14,000,000 acres of land, or about 20,000 square miles, with about 85% of the claims being confirmed to the original grantees. However, very few of the old Californians were enriched by their success.

J. S. Hittell [P31], brother of T. H. Hittell, said that one in ten victorious claimants had been ruined financially by the costs of litigation. He felt that the total system and procedure had been injurious to the claimants, the country as a whole, and a chief cause of unsound business conditions in California.

According to W. W. Robinson [B61], J. N. Bowman had said that some claimants went bankrupt, some sold out to speculators and sharpers; some landowners had to wait seventeen years for their patents after filing their petitions [J240].

J. A. Graves, *My Seventy Years in California* [B27], born in 1852, said,

> With the establishment of a state government, taxes, . . . The natives were not equal to the emergencies which constantly confronted them. . .
>
> The Native Californians simply could not make headways against or in competition with American progress. One by one they faded away. Many of them died in poverty. Then children became day-laborers . . . It is a sad story of the downfall of a happy, peaceful people, passing off the earth in less than two generations . . .

267

PIECES OF EIGHT

No sadder picture could be drawn than that of the legal despoliation by the Americans, of the original grantees of these immense land holdings. . .

And finally, along with the last Curtain Call, should any pot call the kettle "black," it would probably be the truth, but it would also be a good case of projection.

Bibliography

Bibliography

JOURNALS

AMERICAN ANTHROPOLOGIST
Anthropological Society of Washington

1891   J1   Vol. IV, o.s., 373-376.
Yates, L. G. "Fragments of the History of a Lost Tribe."

1907   J2   Vol. IX, n.s., 656-657.
Rust, Horatio N. "Archaeological Collections from San Miguel Island, California." F. W. Hodge, Editor.

1913   J3   Vol. XV, n.s., 656-660.
Wardle, H. Newell. "Stone Implements of Surgery (?) from San Miguel Island, California."

1930   J4   Vol. XXXII, n.s., 693-697.
Harrington, M. R. Book Review of *Prehistoric Man of the Santa Barbara Coast*, David Banks Rogers.

AMERICAN ANTIQUITY
A Quarterly Review of American Archaeology
Society for American Archaeology
Menasha, Wisconsin

1940   J5   Vol. V, #3, 252-253.
Woodward, Arthur. "Notes and News."

1941   J6   Vol. VI, #3, 284-285.
Woodward, Arthur. "Notes and News."

        J7   Vol. VI, #4, 358.
Gifford, E. W. "Notes and News."

        J8   Vol. VI, #4, 372-375.
Heizer, Robert F. Book Review of *Prehistoric Man of the Santa Barbara Coast*, David Banks Rogers.

1949   J9   Vol. XV, #2, 89-97.
Heizer, Robert F. "Curved Single-Piece Fishhooks of Shell and Bone in California."

1951   J10   Vol. XVI, #3, 221-226.
Orr, Phil C. "Ancient Population Centers of Santa Rosa Island in California."

1953   J11   Vol. XIX, #2, 109-125.
Meighan, Clement W. and Hal Eberhart. "Archaeological Resources of San Nicolas Island, California."

1959   J12   Vol. XXIV, #4, Pt. 1, 383-405.
Meighan, Clement W. "The Little Harbor Site, Catalina Island: An Example of Ecological Interpretation in Archaeology."

1960   J13   Vol. XXV, #3, 405-407.
Swartz, B. K., Jr. "Blade Manufacture in Southern California."

AMERICAN GEOGRAPHICAL SOCIETY BULLETIN
New York

1915   J14   Vol. 47, #10, 745-761.
Sykes, Godfrey. "The Isles of California."

AMERICAN HISTORICAL REVIEW
American Historical Association

1908   J15   Vol. XIV, #1, 70-94.
"Documents, Letters of Sir George Simpson, 1841-1843."

AMERICAN INDIAN MUSEUM
Indian Notes and Monographs
Heye Foundation, N. Y.

1920   J16   Vol. VII, #2, 51-85.
Oetteking, Bruno. "Morphological and Metrical Variation in Skulls from San Miguel Island, California." Edited by F. W. Hodge.

1921   J17   Vol. VII, #4, 5-211.
Heye, George G. "Certain Artifacts from San Miguel Island, California." Edited by F. W. Hodge.

1927   J18   Vol. III-IV, #1, 64-67.
Woodward, Arthur. "Collection from the Channel Islands of California."

1930   J19   Vol. VII, #1, 52-56.
Oetteking, Bruno. "An Extreme Case of Arthritis deformans in a Skeleton from San Nicolas Island."

AMERICAN NATURALIST
An Illustrated Magazine of Natural History
A. S. Packard, Jr. & Edward D. Cope, Editors
Press of McCalla and Stavely, Philadelphia

1878   J20   Vol. XII, #9, 629.
Schumacher, Paul. "Ancient Olla Manufactory in Santa Catalina Island, California."

1890   J21   Vol. XXIV, #279, 215-224.
Fewkes, J. W. "Flora of the Santa Barbara Islands—On Certain Peculiarities in the."

AMERICAN ASSOCIATION OF PETROLEUM GEOLOGISTS
Tulsa, Oklahoma
BULLETINS

1936   J22   Vol. 20, #11, 1519.
Kemnitzer, Luis E. "The Geology of San Nicolas Island." (abstract)

       J23   Vol. 20, Pt. 2, #12, 1533-1692.
Reed, R. D. and J. S. Hollister. "Structural Evolution of Southern California."

1949   J24   Vol. 33, Pt. 2, #12, 2062.
Anderson, Robert E., Lowell Redwine and Paul McGovney. "Geology of Northern Santa Rosa Island." (abstract)

1959   J25   Vol. 43, Pt. 1, #1, 222-223.
Scholl, D. W. "Exposures of San Onofre Breccia on Anacapa Island, California."

AMERICAN PHILOSOPHICAL SOCIETY
Philadelphia

1962   J26   Vol. 106, #2, 94-105.
Heizer, Robert F. and Harper Kelley, U. of C. "Burins and Bladelets in the Céssac Collection from Santa Cruz Island, California."

AMERICAN REVIEW OF REVIEWS
New York

1909   J27   Vol. XL, #5, 615-617.
Shaw, Albert. "The Wonders of Submarine Life as seen through the Glass-Bottom Boat."

AMERICAN JOURNAL OF SCIENCE
New Haven, Connecticut

1864   J28   Vol. 38, 2nd s., 256-264.
Whitney, J. D. "Progress of the Geological Survey of California."

1887   J29   Vol. 134, 3rd s., 457-560.
Le Conte, Joseph. "The Flora of the Coast Islands of California in relation to Recent changes of Physical Geography."

1933   J30   Vol. 25, 5th s., #146, 123-136.
Smith, W. S. Tangier. "Marine Terraces on Santa Catalina Island."

1939   J31   Vol. 237, #9, 651-655.
Shepard, F. P., U. S. Grant IV and R. S. Dietz. "The Emergence of (Santa) Catalina Island." (abstract)

ART AND ARCHAEOLOGY
An Illustrated Monthly Magazine
The Archaeological Society of Washington

1930   J32   Vol. 29, #4, Pt. 1, 147-156.
Bryan, Bruce. "San Nicolas Island, Treasure House of the Ancients."

     J33   Vol. 29, #5, Pt. 2, 215-223.
Bryan, Bruce. "San Nicolas Island, Treasure House of the Ancients."

AUK
The American Ornithologists' Union
Bulletin of Nuttall Ornithological Club

1886   J34   Vol. III, n.s., Oct. 452-453.
Henshaw, H. W. "Description of a New Jay from California."

1887   J35   Vol. IV, n.s., Oct., 328-330.
Blake, Eli Whitney, Jr. "Summer Birds of Santa Cruz Island, California."

1895   J36   Vol. XII, n.s., #1, 51-52.
Anthony, A. W. "A New Species of *thryothorus* from the Pacific Coast."

1897   J37   Vol. XIV, n.s., July, 294-296.
Grinnell, Joseph. "Description of a New Towhee from California."

     J38   Vol. XIV, n.s., #3, 300-303.
Oberholser, Harry C. "Description of a new *Empidonax*, with notes on *Empidonax Difficilis*."

1898   J39   Vol. XV, n.s., #3, 233-236.
Grinnell, Joseph. "Land Birds Observed in Mid-Winter on Santa Catalina Island, California."

     J40   Vol. XV, n.s., #3, 237-239.
Grinnell, Joseph. "The San Nicolas Rock Wren."

     J41   Vol. XV, n.s., #3, 259-264.
Mearns, Edgar A. "Descriptions of Two New Birds from the Santa Barbara Islands, Southern California."

     J42   Vol. XV, n.s., #3, 230.
Ridgway, Robert. "Descriptions of Supposed New Genera, Species, and Subspecies of American Birds."

1904	J43	Vol. XXI, n.s., April, 218-223.
		Breninger, George F. "San Clemente Island and Its Birds."
1906	J44	Vol. XXIII, n.s., #3, 262-265.
		Grinnell, Joseph. "The Catalina Island Quail."
1911	J45	Vol. XXVIII, n.s., #4, 489.
		Linton, C. B. "Nests of the San Nicolas Rock Wren."
	J46	Vol. XXVIII, n.s., #4, 490.
		Mearns, Edgar A. "Notes on Two Unrecognized Forms of North American Birds."
1917	J47	Vol. XXXIV, n.s., Oct., 489.
		Stone, Wilmer, Editor. Review on A. B. Howell's *Birds of the Islands off the Coast of Southern California.*
1922	J48	Vol. XXXIX, n.s., #3, 373-380.
		Grinnell, Joseph. "The Role of the Accidental."
	J49	Vol. XXXIX, n.s., #1, 72-78.
		Oberholser, Harry C. "Notes on North American Birds."

AVIFAUNA
W. H. Hoffman, Los Angeles

| 1895 | J50 | Vol. I, #2, 24-25. |
| | | Zahn, Otto J. "The Mexican Raven on Catalina Island." |

BIOLOGICAL SOCIETY OF WASHINGTON, D.C.
PROCEEDINGS

1928	J51	Vol. 41, March, 37-38.
		Grinnell, Joseph. "The Song Sparrow of San Miguel Island, California."
1929	J52	Vol. 42, April, 157-160.
		Dickey, Donald R. "The Spotted Skunk of the Channel Islands of Southern California."
1930	J53	Vol. 43, Sep't, 153-156.
		Grinnell, Joseph. "Two New Foxes from the Southern California Islands."

BIOS
Cedar Rapids, Iowa

| 1939 | J54 | Vol. X, May, 99-106. |
| | | Cockerell, T. D. A. "Recollections of a Naturalist—The California Islands." |

BERNICE P. BISHOP MUSEUM
Honolulu, Hawaii
OCCASIONAL PAPERS

1942	J55	Vol. 17, 1-5.
		Robinson, Eugene. "Aboriginal Shell and Stone Work of the Southern California Coast."
	J56	Vol. 17, 57-64.
		Robinson, Eugene. "Shell Fishhooks of the California Coast."

CALIFORNIA ACADEMY OF SCIENCES
San Francisco
PROCEEDINGS

1868-72	J57	Vol. IV, 61-81.
		Cooper, J. G., M. D. "The Fauna of California and its Geographical Distribution."
	J58	Vol. IV, 152.
		Davidson, George, presiding. (Concerning W. G. Blunt and the fossil tooth of Santa Rosa Island.)

| | J59 | Vol. IV, 389-392. |

Cooper, J. G., M. D. "California during the Pliocene Epoch."

1873-74   J60   Vol. V, 1st s., 90-97.
Davidson, George. "The Abrasions of the Continental Shores of Northwest America, and the supposed Ancient Sea Levels."

1888   J61   Vol. I, 2nd s., 201-226.
Brandegee, T. S. "Flora of the Santa Barbara Islands."

1889   J62   Vol. II, 2nd s., 83-85.
Anthony, A. W. "Nesting Habits of the California Brown Pelican."

1898   J63   Vol. I, 3rd s., #1, 1-71.
Smith, William Sydney Tangier. "The Geology of Santa Catalina Island."

J64   Vol. I, 3rd s., #1, 89-120.
Eastwood, Alice. "Studies in the Herbarium and the Field."

J65   Vol. I, 3rd s., #2, 73-103.
Davidson, George. "The Submerged Valleys of the Coast of California, U.S.A. and of Lower California."

1905   J66   Vol. IV, 3rd s., 1-41.
Van Denburgh, John. "The Reptiles and Amphibians of the Islands of the Pacifiic Coast of North America from the Farallons to Cape San Lucas and the Revilla Gigedes."

1914   J67   Vol. IV, 4th s., 10-13.
Committee writeup on George Davidson.

J68   Vol. IV, 4th s., 131-151.
Van Denburgh, John and Joseph R. Slevin. "Reptiles and Amphibians of the West Coast of North America."

1935   J69   Vol. XXI, 4th s., #21, 277-284.
Howell, John Thomas. "The Vascular Plants from San Nicolas Island."

BULLETINS

1887   J70   Vol. II, #6, 265-268.
Davidson, George. "Submarine Valleys of the Pacific Coast of the United States."

J71   Vol. II, #6, 325-335.
Davidson, George. "Early Spanish Voyages of Discovery on the Coast of California."

J72   Vol. II, #7, 377-418.
Greene, Edward Lee. "Notes on the Botany of Santa Cruz Island."

J73   Vol. II, #8, 515-520.
Le Conte, Joseph. "The Flora of the Coast Islands of California in relation to Recent Changes of Physical Geography."

LEAFLETS OF WESTERN BOTANY

1941   J74   Vol. III, #2, 27-36.
Eastwood, Alice. "The Islands of Southern California and a list of the Recorded Plants"— I.

J75   Vol. III, #3, 54-78.
Eastwood, Alice. "The Islands of Southern California and a list of the Recorded Plants"— II.

PACIFIC DISCOVERY

1951   J76   Vol. IV, #3, 18-24.
Lindsay, George. "Elephant Seals Come Back."

1954   J77   Vol. VII, #1, 18-22.
Williams, M. Woodbridge. "Santa Cruz Island—An Island Museum."

J78   Vol. VII, #1, 22-27.
Meighan, Clement W. "The Nicoleño."

J79   Vol. VII, #3, 18-25.
Lange, Arthur. "Caves: New Science Frontier of the West."

1955   J80   Vol. VIII, #3, 24-25.
Allanson, Al. "Sea Otter on San Miguel."

1957   J81   Vol. X, #1, 11-14.
Heald, Weldon F. "Seagoing National Monument."

J82   Vol. X, #1, 24-29.
Meighan C. and K. L. Johnson. "Isle of Mines, Catalina's Ancient Indian Quarries."

1960   J83   Vol. XIII, #2, 22-25.
Taylor, E. S. "Restoring the House of the Scotch Paisano."

J84   Vol. XIII, #3, 10-13.
Norris, Robert M. "Desert San Nicolas and the Last Nicoleño."

CALIFORNIA HISTORICAL SOCIETY QUARTERLY
San Francisco

1923   J85   Vol. II, #1, 3-68.
Camp, Charles L. "The Chronicles of George C. Yount."

1924   J86   Vol. III, #1, 3-24.
Wagner, Henry R. "The Voyages to California of Sebastian Rodriguez Cermeño in 1595."

J87   Vol. III, #3, 215-237.
Galbraith, Edith C. "Malaspina's Voyage around the World."

1928   J88   Vol. VII, #1, 20-77.
Wagner, Henry R. "Spanish Voyages to the Northwest Coast."

1929   J89   Vol. VIII, #1, 26-70.
Wagner, Henry R. "Spanish Voyages to the Northwest Coast in the Sixteenth Century."

J90   Vol. VIII, #2, 131-166.
"Duhaut–Cilly's Account of California in the Years 1827-28." (translated from the French by Charles Franklin Carter)

1932   J91   Vol. XI, #4, 299-320.
Wagner, Henry R. "George Davidson, Geographer of the Northwest Coast of America."

1933   J92   Vol. XII, March, 18-24.
Cowan, Robert Ernest. "Alexander S. Taylor, 1817-1876."

J93   Vol. XII, #3, 217-239.
Ogden, Adele. "Russian Sea-Otter and Seal Hunting on the California Coast, 1803-1841."

1935   J94   Vol. XIV, #3, 230-268.
Tays, George. "Captain Andrés Castillero, Diplomat."

1938   J95   Vol. XVII, #3, 243-244.
Macdonald, Augustin S. "The Sea Otter returns to the California Coast."

1939   J96   Vol. XVIII, #2, 157-179.
Streeter, William A. "Recollections of Historical Events in California, 1843-1878."

1944   J97   Vol. XXIII, #3, 193-218.
Ogden, Adele. "Alfred Robinson, New England Merchant in Mexican California."

CANADIAN ENTOMOLOGIST
London, Ontario

1897   J98   Vol. 29, #10, 233-244.
Fall, H. C. of Pasadena, California. "A List of the Coleoptera of the Southern California Islands, with notes and descriptions of new species."

CHAMBER'S JOURNAL
W. & R. Chambers, Ltd.
London and Edinburgh

1921   J99   Vol. XI, 7th s., 814-816.
                Gordon, P. Roualeyn. "The Magic Isle."

CONDOR
A Magazine of Western Ornithology
Cooper Ornithological Club of California
Palo Alto, California

1899   J100   Vol. I, #1, 6.
                Beck, R. H. "Nesting of the Santa Cruz Jay."

        J101   Vol. I, #2, 17-18.
                Grinnell, Joseph. "The Rhinoceros Auklet at Catalina Island."

        J102   Vol. I, #3, 41-45.
                Mailliard, Joseph. "Spring Notes on the Birds of Santa Cruz Island, California."

        J103   Vol. I, #5, 85-86.
                Beck, R. H. "Additional Notes on the Birds of Santa Cruz Island, California."

        J104   Vol. I, #5, 85.
                Swarth, H. S. "Black Oystercatcher on Anacapa Island."

1900   J105   Vol. II, #2, 42.
                Mailliard, Joseph. "Measurements of the Santa Cruz Jay."

1903   J106   Vol. V, #4, 96-97.
                Robertson, Howard. "Cassin Auklet."

        J107   Vol. V, #6, 157.
                Grinnell, Joseph. "The Santa Cruz Island Vireo."

1905   J108   Vol. VII, #2, 51-52.
                Grinnell, Joseph. "The Flycatcher from the Santa Barbara Islands."

1906   J109   Vol. VIII, #3, 74.
                Grinnell, Joseph. "The *Empidonax* from Santa Catalina Island."

1908   J110   Vol. X, #2, 65-68.
                Richardson, Charles H., Jr. "Spring Notes from Santa Catalina Island."

        J111   Vol. X, #2, 82-86.
                Linton, C. B. "Notes from San Clemente Island."

        J112   Vol. X, #2, 94.
                Grinnell, Joseph. "Catalina Quail."

        J113   Vol. X, #3, 124-129.
                Linton, C. B. "Notes from Santa Cruz Island."

        J114   Vol. X, #3, 129.
                Linton, C. B. "*Salpinctes obsoletus pulverius* restricted to San Nicholas Island."

        J115   Vol. X, #3, 130.
                Grinnell, Joseph. "Some Birds of Ana Capa Island."

        J116   Vol. X, #4, 182.
                Linton, C. B. "Is not the San Clemente Shrike identical with the Island Shrike?"

        J117   Vol. X, #5, 208.
                Linton, C. B. "*Pipilo Clementae* Excluded from Santa Cruz Avifauna."

1909   J118   Vol. XI, #3, 102.
                Linton, C. B. "Ancient Murrelet at San Clemente."

        J119   Vol. XI, #4, 139.
                Grinnell, Joseph. "The Waders of Note from Santa Catalina Island."

J120   Vol. XI, #6, 193-194.
Linton, C. B. "Further Notes from San Clemente Island."

1910   J121   Vol. XII, #1, 50-51.
Robertson, Howard. "Outing Meeting."

J122   Vol. XII, #5, 170-174.
Willett, G. "A Summer Trip to the Northern Santa Barbara Islands."

1911   J123   Vol. XIII, #2, 76.
Osburn, Pingree I. "Notes on Two Birds from Santa Catalina Island."

J124   Vol. XIII, #3, 109.
Linton, C. B. "Unusual Nesting Site on the San Nicholas Rock Wren."

J125   Vol. XIII, #5, 164-167.
Burt, Homer C. "An Early Spring Trip to Anacapa Island."

J126   Vol. XIII, #6, 208-209.
Howell, Alfred B. and A. Van Rossem. "Further Notes from Santa Cruz Island."

1913   J127   Vol. XV, #2, 86-92.
Wright, Howard and G. K. Snyder. "Birds Observed in the Summer of 1912 among the Santa Barbara Islands."

J128   Vol. XV, #6, 227-228.
Wright, H. W. "The Sabine Gull in the Santa Barbara Channel."

J129   Vol. XV, #6, 229.
Wright, H. W. "Notes on the Ashy Petrel."

1914   J130   Vol. XVI, #4, 182-183.
Snyder, G. K. "Nesting of the Allen Hummingbird on Catalina Island."

J131   Vol. XVI, #5, 211-217.
Swarth, H. S. "A Study of the Status of Certain Island Forms of the *Genus Salpinctes*."

1915   J132   Vol. XVII, #6, 203-204.
Dawson, William Leon. "Supposed new Records for Santa Cruz Island."

1917   J133   Vol. XIX, #5, 172-174.
Mailliard, Joseph. Review of A. B. Howell, *Birds of the Islands off the Coast of Southern California*.

1923   J134   Vol. XXV, #4, 126-129.
Dickey, Donald R. and A. J. Van Rossem. "Additional Notes from the Coastal Islands of Southern California."

1924   J135   Vol. XXVI, #6, 217-220.
Van Rossem, A. J. "A Survey of the Song Sparrows of the Santa Barbara Islands."

1925   J136   Vol. XXVII, #4, 176-177.
Van Rossem, A. J. "The Status of the San Clemente House Finch."

1926   J137   Vol. XXVIII, #5, 240-241.
Ross, R. C. "A Spring Trip to Santa Cruz Island."

1927   J138   Vol. XXIX, #3, 165-166.
Grinnell, Joseph. "The Rock Wren of San Nicolas Island not a Recognizable Subspecies."

1928   J139   Vol. XXX, #2, 146-148.
Pemberton, J. R. "Additions to the Known Avifauna of the Santa Barbara Islands."

J140   Vol. XXX, #4, 250-251.
Meadows, Don C. "Bird Notes from Santa Catalina Island."

J141   Vol. XXX, #5, 325.
Miller, Loye. "Additions to the Faunal List of Anacapa Island."

1929   J142   Vol. XXXI, #1, 37.
Pemberton, J. R. "Some New Records for Santa Barbara Island."

J143   Vol. XXXI, #3, 129-130.
        Meadows, Don C. "Notes on the Avifauna of Santa Catalina Island."

1930   J144   Vol. XXXII, #4, 211-212.
        Meadows, Don C. "Bird Notes from Santa Catalina Island."

1931   J145   Vol. XXXIII, #4, 171.
        Hoffmann, Ralph. "Saw-whet Owl and California Woodpecker on Santa Cruz Island."

J146   Vol. XXXIII, #5, 218-219.
        Pemberton, J. R. "New Records from the Channel Islands."

1932   J147   Vol. XXXIV, #1, 46.
        Huey, Laurence M. "Some Light on the Introduction of Gambel Quail on San Clemente Island, California."

J148   Vol. XXXIV, #4, 190.
        Hoffmann, Ralph. "Bird Notes from Santa Cruz Island."

1934   J149   Vol. XXXVI, #1, 40.
        Meadows, Don C. "Additional Notes from Santa Catalina Island."

1938   J150   Vol. XL, #2, 90.
        Peters, James L. "Laysan Albatross on San Nicolas Island, California."

1947   J151   Vol. 49, #4, 165-168.
        Rett, Egmont Z. "A Report on the Birds of San Nicolas Island."

1950   J152   Vol. 52, #1, 43-46.
        Pitelka, Frank A. "Additions to the Avifaunal Record of Santa Cruz Island, California."

1951   J153   Vol. 53, #3, 117-123.
        Miller, Alden H. "A Comparison of the Avifaunas of Santa Cruz and Santa Rosa Islands, California."

1953   J154   Vol. 55, #3, 156.
        Rett, Egmont Z. "Additional Notes on the Birds of Santa Rosa Island, California."

1955   J155   Vol. 57, #6, 373.
        Miller, Alden H. "Acorn Woodpecker on Santa Catalina Island, California."

EL ALISO
Rancho Santa Ana Botanic Garden
Claremont, California

1963   J156   Vol. 5, #3, 289-347.
        Raven, Peter H. "A Flora of San Clemente Island, California."

1967   J157   Vol. 6, #3, 1-77.
        Thorne, R. F. "A Flora of Santa Catalina Island, California."

1969   J158   Vol. 7, #1, 73-83.
        Thorne, Robert F. "A Supplement to the Floras of Santa Catalina and San Clemente Islands, Los Angeles County, California."

JOURNAL OF EDUCATION
New England Publishing Co.
Boston, Mass.

1907   J159   Vol. LXV, #21, 570-572.
        Barr, James A. "Santa Catalina."

GEOLOGICAL SOCIETY OF AMERICA
New York
PROCEEDINGS

1935   J160   338-339.
        Moody, Graham B. "Geology of Santa Rosa Island." (abstract)

1937 J161 252.
        Shepard, Francis P. "San Clemente Submarine Fault." (abstract)

BULLETINS

1891 J162 Vol. II, 212-220.
        Le Conte, Joseph. "Tertiary and Post-Tertiary Changes of the Atlantic and Pacific Coasts."

1892 J163 Vol. III, 133.
        Yates, Dr. L. G. "Peculiar Geologic Processes."

1927 J164 Vol. 38, #4, 645-654.
        Kew, William S. W. "Geologic sketch of Santa Rosa Island, Santa Barbara County, California."

1928 J165 Vol. 39, #1, 267.
        Clark, B. L. and A. O. Woodford. (abstract on Wm. S. W. Kew article)

1929 J166 Vol. 40, #1, 175.
        Stock, Chester and E. L. Furlong. "Pleistocene Elephant on Santa Rosa Island, California." (abstract)

1945 J168 Vol. 56, 431-478.
        Emery, K. O. and F. P. Shepard. "Lithology of the Sea Floor off Southern California."

1953 J169 Vol. 64, Pt. 2, #12, 1513.
        Norris, Robert M. "Geological list of the San Nicolas Island Region." (abstract)

1956 J170 Vol. 67, Pt. 1, 675-678.
        Bradley, William C. "Carbon-14 Date for a Marine Terrace at Santa Cruz, California."

    J171 Vol. 67, Pt. 2, #12, 1777.
        Orr, Phil C. "Radiocarbon, Mammoths, and Man on Santa Rosa Island." (abstract)

1957 J172 Vol. 68, Pt. 2, 1840.
        Orr, Phil C. and Wallace S. Broecker. "Sea-Level Changes on Santa Rosa Island, California."

1958 J173 Vol. 69, Pt. 1, 39-59.
        Emery, K. O. "Shallow Submerged Marine Terraces of Southern California."

1960 J174 Vol. 71, 1113-1120.
        Orr, Phil C. "Late Pleistocene Marine Terraces on Santa Rosa Island, California."

1964 J175 Vol. 75, 1169-1176.
        Lipp, J. H. "Late Pleistocene History of West Anacapa Island, California."

THE HISTORICAL MAGAZINE AND NOTES AND QUERIES
concerning the Antiquities, History
and Biography of America
Charles B. Richardson, N. Y. and Trubner & Co., London

1859 J176 Vol. III, 231.
        "Letter from Rev. Mr. Bobe, A Lazarist to Monsieur De L' Isle of the Academy of Sciences, Geographer to the King, on the Quay de l'horloge, Paris."

LITTELL'S LIVING AGE
E. Littell & Co., Boston
(from Blackwood's Magazine)

1847 J177 Vol. XIV, #165, 64-71.
        Simpson, Sir George. "Narrative of an Overland Journey Round the World by Sir George Simpson, Governor-In-Chief of the Hudson's Bay Company's Territories in North America."

Los Angeles County Museum of Natural History
LEAFLET SERIES

1943   J178   Vol. III, #2-4, 6-9.
Stock, Chester. "Foxes and Elephants of the Channel Islands."

MUSEUM GRAPHIC

1926   J179   Vol. I, #4, 145-150.
Bryan, Bruce. "Collecting Indian Relics on a Desert Island."

MUSEUM ALLIANCE QUARTERLY

1968   J180   Vol. VI, #3, 4-9.
Weinstein, Robert A. "From San Pedro due South to Catalina Island."

JOURNAL OF MAMMALOGY
American Society of Mammalogists
Baltimore, Maryland

1930   J181   Vol. 11, #1, 75-76.
Fisher, Edna M. "The Early Fauna of Santa Cruz Island, California."

1936   J182   Vol. 17, #4, 408-410.
Wilson, Robert W. "A New Pleistocene Deer-Mouse from Santa Rosa Island, California."

1950   J183   Vol. 31, #2, 175-180.
Bartholomew, George A., Jr. "A Male Guadalupe Fur Seal on San Nicolas Island."

1951   J184   Vol. 32, #1, 15-21.
Bartholomew, George A., Jr. "Spring, Summer, and Fall Censuses of the Pinnipeds on San Nicolas Island, California."

MASTERKEY, for Indian Lore and History
Southwest Museum
Highland Park, California

1933   J185   Vol. VII, #2, 46-47.
M. R. H. "A Northwest Coast Warclub from Santa Catalina Island."

1936   J186   Vol. X, #4, 135.
Walker, Edwin F. "A Prehistoric California Treasure-Box."

1937   J187   Vol. XI, #4, 137-139.
Cornell, Ralph D. "The Plants of Museum Hill, The Catalina Cherry"—IV.

1938   J188   Vol. XII, #1, 28.
Walker, Edwin F. "Indians of Southern California."

1941   J189   Vol. XV, #2, 59-61.
Heizer, Robert F. "The Distribution and Name of the Chumash Plank Canoe."

1942   J190   Vol. XVI, #6, 202-209.
Robinson, Eugene. "Plank Canoes of the Chumash."

1955   J191   Vol. XXIX, #2, 62-68.
Mohr, Albert and L. L. Sample. "The Religious Importance of the Swordfish in the Santa Barbara Channel Area and Its Possible Implications."

            J192   Vol. XXIX, #6, 180-191 +.
Johnston, Bernice Eastman. "The Gabrielino Indians of Southern California."

            J193   Vol. XXIX, #6, 206.
M. R. H. "More American Elephant-Eaters."

1957   J194   Vol. XXXI, #1, 9-23.
Johnston, Bernice Eastman. "The Gabrielino Indians of Southern California."

	J195	Vol. XXXI, #5, 155-165. Johnston, Bernice Eastman. "The Gabrielino Indians of Southern California."
	J196	Vol. XXXI, #6, 176-184. Meighan, Clement and Sheldon Rootenberg. "A Prehistoric Miner's Camp."
1959	J197	Vol. XXXIII, #4, 129-152. Rozaire, Charles E. "Archaeological Investigations at Two Sites on San Nicolas Island."
1960	J198	Vol. XXXIV, #2, 62-65. Curtis, Freddie. "Some Santa Cruz Island Artifacts."
	J199	Vol. XXXIV, #2, 147-151. Rozaire, Charles E. and George Kirtzman. "A Petroglyph Cave on San Nicolas Island."
1962	J200	Vol. XXXVI, #1, 36. "Museum gets San Nicolas Petroglyph."
	J201	Vol. XXXVI, #2, 77. Rozaire, Charles E. "Underwater Finds at Dana Point."
	J202	Vol. XXXVI, #3, 85. Rozaire, Charles E. "A Burial from San Clemente Island."
	J203	Vol. XXXVI, #4, 152. Bryan, Bruce. "Museum Excavations on San Clemente Island."
1963	J204	Vol. XXXVII, #2, 45-49. Bryan, Bruce. "Southwest Museum Excavations on San Clemente Island."
1964	J205	Vol. XXXVIII, #1, 8-10. Redtfeldt, Gordon. "Excavations at the Ledge Site."
	J206	Vol. XXXVIII, #3, 98-105. Curtis, Freddie. "Microdrills in the Manufacture of Shell Beads in Southern California."
1969	J207	Vol. XLIII, #3, 84-98. Jones, Philip Mills. "San Nicolas Island Archaeology in 1901." (edited by Robert F. Heizer)
	J208	Vol. XLIII, #4, 125-131. Alliot, Hector. "Burial Methods of the Southern California Islanders." (reprinted from 1916 Southern California Academy of Sciences Bulletin)
1971	J209	Vol. XLV, #4, 156. "Arthur R. Sanger and Artifact Collecting and Death."
1973	J210	Vol. XLVII, #2, 62-67. Heizer, Robert F. "A Probable Relic of Juan Rodriguez Cabrillo."
	J211	Vol. XLVII, #3, 106-109. Hoover, Robert L. "Incised Steatite Tablets from the Catalina Museum."
1974	J212	Vol. XLVIII, #4, 125-134. Pitzer, Jean M., *et al.* "Microblade Technology of the Channel Islands."

THE MINERALOGIST
Oregon Agate and Mineral Society and
Mineralogical Society of Southern California
Portland, Oregon

1935	J213	Vol. III, #8, 7+. Randolph, G. C. "Santa Catalina Island."

NATIONAL GEOGRAPHIC MAGAZINE
Washington, D. C.

1899	J214	Vol. X, #8, 291-296. Smith, Hugh M. "Deep-Sea Exploring Expedition of the Steamer *Albatross*."

1909   J215   Vol. XX, #9, 761-778.
              Holder, Charles F. "Glass-Bottom Boat."

1942   J216   Vol. LXXXI, #1, 81-88.
              Steward, B. Anthony. "Santa Catalina—400 Years a Lure to California Travelers."

1945   J217   Vol. LXXXVII, #1, 105-128.
              Colton, F. Barrows. "Our Global Ocean—Last and Vast Frontier."

1958   J218   Vol. CXIV, #2, 256-283.
              Warren, E., Jr. "Off Santa Barbara: California's Ranches in the Sea."

NATURE MAGAZINE
American Nature Association
Baltimore, Ohio

1931   J219   Vol. XVII, #4, 241-242.
              Wyler, Lorraine. "William Wrigley, Jr.—Bird Lover."

1931   J220   Vol. XVIII, #11, 291-294.
              Ward, W. V. "Foxing the Fox by Flashlight."

1935   J221   Vol. XXV, #6, 292.
              Bryan, Bruce. "San Nicolas, the Passing Island."

1956   J222   Vol. XLIX, #10, 517-519+.
              Heald, Weldon F. "Cave of the Sea Lions."

NATURAL HISTORY
(incorporating Nature Magazine)
The Journal of the American Museum of Natural History
New York

1925   J223   Vol. XXV, July-Aug., 338-345.
              Jordan, Dr. David Starr. "Giant Game Fishes of Santa Catalina."

1941   J224   Vol. XLVIII, #3, 114-149.
              Williams, Woodbridge. "Jumbo of the Deep."

1948   J225   Vol. LVII, #1, 16-18.
              Walker, Lewis W. "Trees of Sand."

1965   J226   Vol. LXXIV, #7, 30-35.
              Van Gelder, R. G. "Channel Island Skunk; Spotted Skunk."

NAUTILUS
A Monthly devoted to the Interests of Conchologists
Boston Society of Natural History

1903   J227   Vol. 17, #6, 66-69.
              Lowe, Herbert N. "Notes on the Mollusk Fauna of San Nicholas Island."

1939   J228   Vol. 53, #1, 22-23.
              Cockerell, T. D. A. "Pleistocene Shells from San Clemente Island, California."

NEWSLETTER
Archaeological Survey Association of Southern California

1954   J229   Vol. II, #2, 7-8.
              Orr, Phil C. "Who Painted Painted Cave?"

1956   J230   Vol. III, #1, 3-4.
              Hester, Joseph A., Jr. "Channel Island Archeology."

       J231   Vol. III, #1, 5-6.
              Edwards, H. Arden. "Notes on the Archaeology of the Northern Channel Islands."

	J232	Vol. III, #1, 7-8.

J232   Vol. III, #1, 7-8.
Eberhart, Hal. "Temporal Horizons of the Santa Barbara Coast."

1962   J233   Vol. IX, #2, 2-3.
Orr, Phil C. "Arlington Spring Site, Santa Rosa Island, California."

1967   J234   Vol. XIV, #2, 5.
Rozaire, Dr. Charles. "Archaeological Work on San Miguel Island."

OOLOGIST, *Birds—Nests—Eggs*
A Monthly publication devoted to Oology, Ornithology, and Taxidermy

1909   J235   Vol. XXVI, #11, 188.
Snyder, G. K. "Dusky Warbler Haunts."

1913   J236   Vol. XXX, #5, 78.
Peyton, Sidney B. "A Collecting Trip to Anacapa Island."

OSPREY
Illustrated Monthly Magazine of Ornithology
Cooper Ornithological Club of the Pacific Coast
Galesburg, Ill.

1897   J237   Vol. I, #10, 144.
Grinnell, Joseph. "An Osprey approaching Nest."

1897   J238   Vol. II, #1, 6.
Grinnell, Joseph. "American Osprey Nest on San Clemente Island."

PACIFIC HISTORICAL REVIEW
American Historical Society
Pacific Coast Branch

1937   J239   Vol. VI, #3, 270-283.
Ellison, William Henry. "History of the Santa Cruz Island Grant."

1962   J240   Vol. XXXI, #3, 291-301.
Bowman, J. N. "The Question of Sovereignty over California's Off-shore Islands."

PACIFIC MINERALOGIST
Mineralogical Society, Los Angeles

1938   J241   Vol. V, #1, 3-5.
Knoff, E. C. "Santa Catalina Island, Minerals and Geology."

PACIFIC SCIENCE MONTHLY
San Buenaventura, California
Stephen Bowers, Editor

1885   J242   Vol. I, #4, 45-47.
Bowers, Stephen. "Relics in a Cave."

JOURNAL OF PALEONTOLOGY
Society of Economic Paleontologists and Mineralogists

1928   J243   Vol. II, #2, 142-157.
Hertlein, Lee George. "Preliminary Report on the Paleontology of the Channel Islands."

1929   J244   Vol. III, #3, 302-305.
Church, C. C. "Some Recent Shallow Water Foraminifera Dredged near Santa Catalina Island, California."

1963   J245   Vol. XXXVII, #6, 1292-1302.
Valentine, James W. and Jere H. Lipps. "Late Cenozoic Rocky-shore Assemblages from Anacapa Island, California."

PAN PACIFIC ENTOMOLOGIST
Pacific Coast Entomological Society
in cooperation with
California Academy of Sciences, San Francisco

1937   J246   Vol. XIII, #4, 148-157.
                Cockerell, T. D. A. "Bees from San Miguel Island, California."

1938   J247   Vol. XIV, #1, 31-33.
                Blaisdell, Frank E., Sr. "A New Species of Sitona from San Miguel Island."

        J248   Vol. XIV, #4, 150.
                Cockerell, T. D. A. "A New Bembecine Wasp from San Nicolas Island, California."

PASADENA ACADEMY OF SCIENCES
Pasadena, California

1897   J249   Vol. I, #1, 1-26.
                Grinnell, Joseph. "Report on the Birds recorded during a visit to the Islands of Santa Barbara, San Nicolas and San Clemente in the Spring of 1897."

PEABODY MUSEUM OF AMERICAN ARCHAEOLOGY AND ETHNOLOGY
Cambridge, Massachusetts

1878   J250   Vol. II, #2, 258-268.
                Schumacher, Paul. "The Method of Manufacture of Several Articles by the former Indians of Southern California."

PEABODY MUSEUM OF NATURAL HISTORY
New Haven, Connecticut
DISCOVERY

1971   J251   Vol. 7, #1, 3-18.
                Remington, Charles F. "Natural History and Evolutionary Genetics of the California Channel Islands."

PITTONIA
San Francisco; London; Berlin

1887-   J252   Vol. I, 74-93.
89   Greene, Edward L. "A Botanical Excursion to the Island of San Miguel."

REVIEW OF REVIEWS
An International Magazine
New York

1909   J253   Vol. XL, Nov., 615-617.
                Holder, Charles F. "The Wonders of Submarine Life as Seen Through the Glass-Bottom Boat."

ROCKS AND MINERALS
Journal of Rocks and Minerals Association
A Magazine for Mineralogists, Geologists and Collectors

1947   J254   Vol. XXII, #12, 1119-1121.
                Griesbach, John O. "Fulgurites, and Physiographical Memoranda of San Clemente Island, California."

SAN DIEGO SOCIETY OF NATURAL HISTORY
TRANSACTIONS

1911   J256   Vol. I, #3, 9-23.
                Vogdes, Anthony W. "An Address before the San Diego Academy of Natural Sciences on the Books relating to Geology, Mineral Resources and Palaeontology of California."

1938   J257   Vol. IX, #9, 37-38.
                Cockerell, T. D. A. "Bees Collected on the California Islands in the Spring."

WEST AMERICAN SCIENTIST
San Diego Society of Natural History

1886   J258   Vol. III, #20, 1-4.
                Greene, E. L. "Santa Cruz Island."

1887   J259   Vol. III, #23, 77.
                Greene, E. L. "Santa Cruz Island."

        J260   Vol. III, #25, 122.
                Bingham, Mrs. R. F. "Santa Barbara Society of Natural History."

        J261   Vol. III, #32, 243-245.
                Bowers, Stephen. "Aboriginal Fish-hooks."

1889   J262   Vol. VI, #49, 155-156.
                Yates, Lorenzo G. "Preliminary Notes on the Geology of the Anacapas."

SANTA BARBARA MUSEUM OF NATURAL HISTORY
(formerly Santa Barbara Society of Natural History)
PROCEEDINGS

1887   J263   Bulletin #1, 18-21.
                Streator, Clark P. "The Water Birds of San Miguel Island."

BULLETINS

1887   J264   Bulletin #1, 23-30.
                Yates, Dr. Lorenzo G. "Prehistoric Man in California."

1890   J265   Vol. I, #2, 8-11.
                Yates, Dr. Lorenzo G. "Notes on the Ferns of the Channel Islands off the Coast of California."

        J266   Vol. I, #2, 13-34.
                Yates, Dr. Lorenzo G. "Charm Stones, Notes on the so-called 'Plummets' or 'Sinkers'."

        J267   Vol. I, #2, 37-45.
                Yates, Dr. Lorenzo G. "The Mollusca of Santa Barbara County, California."

BULLETIN
Department of Anthropology

1956   J268   Bulletin #2, 1-10.
                Orr, Phil C. "Radiocarbon Dates from Santa Rosa Island—I."

1960   J269   Bulletin #3, 1-10.
                Orr, Phil C. "Radiocarbon Dates from Santa Rosa Island—II."

MUSEUM TALK

1949   J270   Vol. XXIV, #1, 61-68.
                Orr, Phil C. "Island Hopping."

1949-   J271   Vol. XXIV, #4, 109-113.
50   Orr, Phil C. "Third Santa Rosa Island Expedition."

1950   J272   Vol. XXV, #2, 13-18.
                Orr, Phil C. "On San Miguel Island."

1951   J273   Vol. XXVI, #1, 1-2.
                Orr, Phil C. "Cave of the Killer Whales."

        J274   Vol. XXVI, #1, 2-6.
                Orr, Phil C. "Fourth Santa Rosa Island Expedition."

        J275   Vol. XXVI, #1, 6-7.

Irwin, Margaret, Librarian. "Birds of Santa Rosa and Dall's Porpoises."

	J276	Vol. XXVI, #2, 13-19.

Orr, Phil C. "The Orca goes Underground."

| 1952 | J277 | Vol. XXVII, #1, 4-8. |

Orr, Phil C. "Fifth Santa Rosa Island Expedition."

| | J278 | Vol. II, #5, 41-43. |

Orr, Phil C. "Indian Caves of Santa Rosa Island and their Relation to Antiquity."

| | J279 | Vol. II, #10, 123-126. |

Orr, Phil C. "Discovery Series—Anacapa Island's Sea Caves."

| 1953 | J280 | Vol. XXVIII, #2, 17-20. |

Orr, Phil C. "Sixth Santa Rosa Island Expedition."

| 1956 | J281 | Vol. XXXI, #3, 40-44. |

Orr, Phil C. "Early Man on Santa Rosa Island."

MUSEUM LEAFLETS

| 1930 | J282 | Vol. V, #2, 1-3. |

"Fifty Years Ago."

| 1940 | J283 | Vol. XV, #5, 58-59. |

Orr, Phil C. "The Channel Islands Survey by the Los Angeles Museum."

| 1945 | J284 | Vol. XX, #5, 51-56. |

Irwin, M. C., Editor. "San Nicolas Island Expedition."

| | J285 | Vol. XX, #7, 75-79. |

Orr, Phil C. "Return to San Nicolas."

| 1946 | J286 | Vol. XXI, #2, 18. |

Irwin, M. C., Editor. "Canaliño Fishing Tackle."

| 1947 | J287 | Vol. XXII, #5-6, 51-52. |

Irwin, M. C., Editor. "Santa Rosa Island Field Work."

| | J288 | Vol. XXII, #8, 67-70. |

Orr, Phil C. "Santa Rosa Island Expedition."

OCCASIONAL PAPERS

| 1932 | J297 | #1, 5-33. |

Bremner, Carl St. J. "Geology of Santa Cruz Island, Santa Barbara County, California."

| 1933 | J298 | #2, 7-23. |

Bremner, Carl St. J. "Geology of San Miguel Island, Santa Barbara County, California."

| 1943 | J299 | #5, 5-61. |

Orr, Phil C. "Archaeology of Mescalitan Island and Customs of the Canalino."

SANTA BARBARA HISTORICAL SOCIETY
NOTICIAS

| 1958 | J289 | Vol. IV, #3, 8-12. |

Tompkins, Walker A. "Channel Islands Nomenclature."

| | J290 | Vol. IV, #3, 12-13. |

Gledhill, Director. (to Native Daughters on the life and home of J. M. Covarrubias)

| 1959 | J291 | Vol. V, #3, 1-17. |

Spaulding, Edward S. "Anacapa Island."

	J292	Gherini, Mrs. Ambrose. "Santa Cruz Island."
	J293	Austin, Dr. Perry G. M. "Santa Rosa Island."
	J294	Bonilla, Isaac Antonio. "The Cabrillo Monument on San Miguel Island."
	J295	Sexton, Horace A. "The Wreck of the Cuba."

1966	J296	Vol. XII, #1, 14-20.
		Gherini, Pier. "Island Rancho."
1977	J296a	Vol. XXIII, #3, 43-52.
		Rouse, Stella Haverland. "The Waters Family of San Miguel."

SCIENCE
A Weekly Journal devoted to the Advancement of Science
American Association for the Advancement of Science

1901	J300	Vol. XIV, n.s., #354, 575-577.
		Ritter, Wm. E. "Some Observations bearing on the probable subsidence during recent geological times of the island of Santa Catalina off the Coast of Southern California."
	J301	Vol. XIV, n.s., #362, 899-900.
		F. A. L. "The Work of the 'Albatross'."
1903	J302	Vol. XVI, n.s., #398, 268-269.
		Dall, Wm. H. "Dr. J. G. Cooper."
1928	J303	Vol. 68, n.s., #1754, 140-141.
		Stock, Chester and E. L. Furlong. "The Pleistocene Elephants of Santa Rosa Island, California."
1938	J304	Vol. 87, n.s., #2266, 501.
		"Channel Islands National Monument."
1962	J305	Vol. 135, n.s., #3499, 219.
		Orr, Phil C. "Arlington Springs Man."
1964	J306	Vol. 143, n.s., #3603, 243-244.
		Orr, Phil C. "Pleistocene Chipped Stone Tool on Santa Rosa Island, California."

SCIENCE NEWS LETTER
Science Service, Washington, D. C.

1957	J307	Vol. 71, 169.
		"Sea-faring Indians on Catalina in 2000 B. C."
1963	J308	Vol. 83, #14, 216.
		" 'Waterworks' indicates West Coast Indian Site."

SCIENTIFIC AMERICAN
An Illustrated Journal of Art, Science and Mechanics
New York

1897	J309	Vol. 76, Jan., 56.
		Holder, Charles F. "Some Pacific Caves."
1899	J310	Vol. 81, July, 59.
		Holder, Charles F. "A Catalina Walking Fish."
	J311	Vol. 81, Oct., 233-234.
		Holder, Charles F. "Wind-Swept Island of San Nicolas."
1902	J312	Vol. 88, May, 333.
		Holder, Charles F. "Tameness of Wild Animals."
1903	J313	Vol. 89, May, 353.
		Holder, Charles F. "Santa Catalina's Wireless Newspaper."
1904	J314	Vol. 90, Jan., 94.
		Holder, Charles F. "The Windows of the Sea."
1906	J315	Vol. 92, June, 458-459.
		Holder, Charles F. "Through a Window of the Sea."

J316   Vol. 92, July, 6+.
Holder, Charles F. "Tameness of Wild Animals."

1926   J317   Vol. 135, Aug., 122-123.
Warren, Herbert O. "A Treasure Island in the Pacific."

SCIENTIFIC MONTHLY
The Science Press Printing Co.
New York

1935   J318   Vol. 41, 205-214.
Stock, Dr. Chester. "Exiled Elephants of the Channel Islands."

1938   J319   Vol. 46, 180-187.
Cockerell, T. D. A. "San Miguel Island, California."

1939   J320   Vol. 48, 308-318.
Cockerell, T. D. A. "Natural History of Santa Catalina Island."

JOURNAL OF SEDIMENTARY PETROLOGY
Society of Economic Paleontologists and Mineralogists
Section of the American Association of Petroleum Geologists

1937   J321   Vol. VII, #2, 41-50.
Shepard, F. P. and W. F. Wrath. "Marine Sediments around Catalina Island."

1952   J322   Vol. XXII, #4, 224-228.
Norris, Robert M. "Recent History of a Sand Spit at San Nicolas Island."

1956   J323   Vol. XXVI, #2, 209.
Israelsky, Merle C. "Some Foraminifera from Rocks of Eocene Age on San Nicolas Island, Ventura County, California."

1960   J324   Vol. XXX, #1, 123-139.
Scholl, David W. "Relationship of the insular shelf sediments to the sedimentary environment and geology of Anacapa Island, California."

SOUTHERN CALIFORNIA ACADEMY OF SCIENCES
Los Angeles, California
PROCEEDINGS

1896   J325   Vol. I, #1, 1-36.
Davidson, Anstruther. "Catalogue of the Plants of Los Angeles County."

BULLETINS

1902   J326   Vol. I, #7, 82-86.
Yates, Dr. L. G. "Prehistoric California."

J327   Vol. I, #8, 97-100.
Yates, Dr. L. G. "Prehistoric California."

1902-
03   J328   Vol. II, #2, 23-26.
Hasse, Dr. H. E. "Contributions to the Lichen-flora of the Californian Coast Islands."

J329   Vol. II, #7, 84.
Cockerell, T. D. A. "New Bees from Southern California."

J330   Vol. II, #7, 87-93.
Yates, Dr. L. G. "Prehistoric Fauna of California."

J331   Vol. II, #9, 113-118.
Yates, Dr. L. G. "Prehistoric Fauna of California."

1904   J332   Vol. III, #2, 25-30.
Yates, Dr. L. G. "Prehistoric Man and his Development."

	J333	Vol. III, #3, 38-41 + .
		Williamson, Mrs. M. Burton. "Catalogue of Indian Relics found on Santa Catalina Island."
	J334	Vol. III, #5, 76-78.
		Trask, Blanche. "Flora of San Clemente Island"—I.
	J335	Vol. III, #6, 90-95.
		Trask, Blanche. "Flora of San Clemente Island"—II.
	J336	Vol. III, #8, 140.
		Trask, Blanche. "Fossil Peak, Santa Catalina Island."
1905	J337	Vol. IV, #4, 56-59.
		Baker, C. F. "Notes on the Fauna and Flora of Catalina Island."
	J338	Vol. IV, #4, 60-62.
		Wheeler, W. M. "Ants from Catalina Island."
	J339	Vol. IV, #4, 62-63.
		Ellis, J. B. and B. M. Everhart. "New Fungi from Catalina Island."
1906	J340	Vol. V, #2, 38-45.
		Hasse, H. E. "Contributions to the Lichen-flora of Southern California."
1916	J341	Vol. XV, Pt. 1, #1, 11-15.
		Alliot, S. D. Hector. "Burial Methods of the Southern California Islanders."
1917	J342	Vol. XVI, Pt. 2, #7, 41-44.
		Alliot, S. D. Hector. "Pre-historic Use of Bitumen in Southern California."
	J343	Vol. XVI, Pt. 1, 23-27.
		Ulrey, Albert B. "The Operations of the Launch *Anton Dohrn* in Southern California Waters."
1928	J344	Vol. XXVII, Pt. 1, 1-57.
		Ulrey, Albert B. and Paul O. Greeley. "A List of the Marine Fishes of Southern California with their Distribution."
1931	J345	Vol. XXX, Pt. 2, 60-61.
		Clokey, Ira W. "Notes on the Flora of Santa Cruz Island, California."
1932	J346	Vol. XXXI, Pt. 2, I, 46-60.
		Hoffmann, Ralph. "Notes on the Flora on the Channel Islands off Santa Barbara, California."
	J347	Vol. XXXI, Pt. 3, II, 101-120.
		Hoffmann, Ralph. "Notes on the Flora of the Channel Islands off Santa Barbara, California." (edited by P. A. Munz, Pomona College, after Hoffmann's death)
1936	J348	Vol. XXXV, Pt. 1, 175-180.
		Meadows, Don. "An Annotated list of the Lepidoptera of Santa Catalina Island, California."
1939	J349	Vol. XXXVIII, Pt. 3, 133-156.
		Cockerell, T. D. A. "Contributions from the Los Angeles Museum—Channel Islands Biological Survey."
1946	J350	Vol. XLV, Pt. 2, 94-107.
		Comstock, John A. "Brief Notes on the Expeditions conducted between March 16, 1940 and December 14, 1941."

SOUTHERN CALIFORNIA HISTORICAL SOCIETY
Los Angeles
ANNUAL PUBLICATIONS

1888-89	J351	Vol. I, Pt. 4, 25-29.
		Williamson, Mrs. M. Burton. "History of the Movements for the Division of the Los Angeles County."

1900   J352   Vol. V, 5-8.
King, Laura Evertsen. "The Stores of Los Angeles in 1850."

J353   Vol. V, 25-30.
Barrows, H. D. "Mexican Governors of California."

J354   Vol. V, 91-98.
Foster, Stephen C. "Biographical Sketches."

1903- J355   Vol. VI, Pt. 1, 14-31.
05   Williamson, M. B. "History of Santa Catalina Island."

J356   Vol. VI, Pt. 1, 41-47.
Guinn, J. M. "Two Decades of Local History."

1906- J357   Vol. VII, Pt. 1, 22-30.
08   Williamson, M. B. "The Haliotis or Abalone Industry of the California Coast; Preservative Laws."

J358   Vol. VII, #1, 39-46.
Guinn, J. M. "Some California Place Names."

J359   Vol. VII, #2, 103-113.
Hudson, Millard F. "The Battle of San Diego."

J360   Vol. VII, #2, 176-193.
Warner, Col. J. J. "Reminiscences of Early California from 1831 to 1846."

1912- J361   Vol. IX, Parts I-II, 43-48.
13   Guinn, J. M. "The Lost Mines of Santa Catalina." (taken from 1890, *Overland Monthly*, Vol. XVI, 2nd s., #95, 476-479, J. M. Guinn, "An Early Mining Boom on Santa Catalina")

J362   Vol. IX, Parts I-II, 75-85.
Hunt, Rockwell D. "A California Calendar of Pioneer Princes."

J363   Vol. IX, Part III, 236-243.
Baker, Charles C. "Mexican Land Grants in California."

1924   J364   Vol. XIII, #1, 5-29.
Williamson, Lillian A. "New Light on J. J. Warner."

1933   J365   Vol. XV, #4, 16-23.
Wagner, Henry R. "The Names of the Channel Islands."

QUARTERLIES

1935   J366   Vol. XVII, #4, 135-138.
Wagner, Henry R. "An Exploration of the Coast of Southern California in 1782."

1938   J367   Vol. XX, #3, 119-134.
Woodward, Arthur. "Sea Otter Hunting on the Pacific Coast."

1940   J368   Vol. XXII, #1, 33-46.
Cheetham, Francis T. "San Clemente—Fifty-two Years Ago."

1945   J369   Vol. XXVII, Pt. 2, #1, 23-45.
Wilson, Carol Green. "A Business Pioneer in Southern California."

J370   Vol. XXVII, #4, 127-149.
de Packman, Ana Begue. "California's Cattle Brands and Earmarks."

1953   J371   Vol. XXXV, #1, 3-10.
Cleland, Robert Glass. "Drought, Lawlessness and Smallpox."

J372   Vol. XXXV, #1, 41-53.
Walters, Helen B. "Confederates in Southern California."

J373   Vol. XXXV, #2, 129-152.
Newmark, Marco R. "Early California Resorts."

1958   J374   Vol. XL, #1-4, 5-372.
Hunt, Rockwell D. "Fifteen Decisive Events of California History."

1961   J375   Vol. XLIII, #2, 166-199.
Splitter, Henry Winfred. "Los Angeles Recreation, 1846-1900."

1963   J376   Vol. XLV, #1, 65-82.
Wright, Austin Tappan. "An Islandian on the Islands."

1973   J377   Vol. LV, #2, 105-140.
Jackson, Sheldon G. "Two British Plots in Alta California."

          J378   Vol. LV, #3, 225-238.
Kelsey, Harry. "The California Indian Treaty Myth."

          J379   Vol. LV, #4, 369-412.
Zavalishin, Dmitry. "California in 1824." (translated and annotated by James R. Gibson)

1974   J380   Vol. LVI, #1, 1-12.
Mawn, Geoffrey P. "Jasper O'Farrell's Surveying in Mexican California."

1975   J380a   Vol. LVII, #4, 349-359.
Johnson, Kenneth M. "The Judges Colton."

1979   J380b   Vol. LXI, #1, 1-69.
Guest, Francis F., O.F.M. "An Examination of the Theses of S. F. Cook on The Forced Conversion of Indians in the California Missions."

TORREYA
Torrey Botanical Club
New York

1890   J381   Vol. XVII, #5, 129.
Fewkes, J. W. "Flora of the Santa Barbara Islands—On Certain Peculiarities in the."

1937   J382   Vol. XXXVII, #6, 117-123.
Cockerell, T. D. A. "The Botany of the California Islands."

WARBLER
Mayflower Publishing Co.
New York

1905   J383   Vol. I, 2nd s., December.
Howard, O. W. "Nest and Eggs of Western Gull."

1906   J384   Vol. II, #1, 8-10.
Howard, O. W. "Eggs of the Dusky Warbler."

          J385   Vol. II, #2, 33.
Childs, J. L. "Eggs of Santa Barbara Flycatcher."

JOURNAL OF THE WEST
Devoted to Western History and Geography
Los Angeles

1962   J386   Vol. I, #1, 11-23.
Pourade, Richard F. "Juan Rodriguez Cabrillo: Discoverer of California." (condensed from *The Explorers*)

          J387   Vol. I, #1, 45-62.
Holland, Francis R., Jr. "Santa Rosa: An Archeological Historical Study."

1963   J388   Vol. II, #2, 145-155.
Holland, Francis R., Jr. "San Miguel Island: Its History and Archaeology."

          J389   Vol. II, #4, 377-400.
Camp, Charles L. "Old Doc Yates."

WESTERN EXPLORER
Cabrillo Historical Association
San Diego

1961 J390 Vol. I, #2, 16-24.
             Hussey, John A. "A Brief Sketch of the Archaeology of Santa Cruz Island."

1968 J391 Vol. V, #2, #3, 1-20.
             Moriarty, J. R. and M. Kleistman. "A New Translation of the Summary Log of the Cabrillo Voyage in 1542." (see San Diego Science Foundation)

ZOE
A Biological Journal
San Francisco
Townshend Stith Brandegee, Editor

1890 J392 Vol. I, #1, 27.
             Vaslit, Frank H. "Crossosoma."

      J393 Vol. I, #3, 85-86.
             Brandegee, T. S. "Convolvulus Occidentalis Gray."

      J394 Vol. I, #4, 107-115.
             Brandegee, T. S. "The Plants of Santa Catalina Island."

      J395 Vol. I, #5, 129-148.
             Brandegee, T. S. "Flora of the Californian Islands."

      J396 Vol. I, #6, 188-190.
             Brandegee, T. S. "Lavatera—Is it an Introduced Plant?"

      J397 Vol. I, #10, 300-303.
             Parish, S. B. "Notes on the Naturalized Plants of Southern California."

1891 J398 Vol. I, #11, 337-343.
             Keeler, Charles A. "Geographical Distribution of Land Birds in California." (IV, "The Island Fauna")

1892 J399 Vol. III, July, 135-140.
             Bryant, Walter E. "A Check-list of the Water Birds of California."

      J400 Vol. III, #3, 262-263.
             Seavey, F. A. "Insects of Catalina Island."

1893 J401 Vol. IV, #2, 160-167.
             Parish, S. B. "Additions to the Flora of Southern California."

PERIODICALS

ARENA
The Arena Publishing Co.
Boston

1897 P1   Vol. 17, #86, 215-216.
            Clark, James G. "Santa Catalina." (a poem)

ARROWHEAD
A Monthly Magazine of Western Travel and Development
Los Angeles and Salt Lake Railroad
Editor, Douglas White

1906 P2   Vol. II, #5, 8-13+.
            Fleming, David P. "Catalina, The Magic Isle."

1907 P3   Vol. III, #3, 14.
            "An Island Wonderland."

1908   P4   Vol. V, #3, 17.
"Catalina, the 'Isle of Summer'."

BETTER HOMES AND GARDENS
E. T. Meredith, Des Moines

1959   P5   Vol. XXXVII, Mar., 154 + .
Waite, Elmont. "Catalina: California's Hawaii."

BUSINESS WEEK
McGraw-Hill Publishing Co.
New York

1930   P6   May 21, 28. "Selling Catalina by the Ton."

CALIFORNIAN
A Western Monthly Magazine

1881   P7   Vol. III, #17, 432-434.
Hittell, John S. "California under the Friars."

CALIFORNIAN ILLUSTRATED MAGAZINE
California Publishing Co.
C. F. Holder, Editor, San Francisco

1892   P8   Vol. I, #2, 100-108.
Evans, Richard S. "The Voyage of Cabrillo." (translator of Buckingham Smith text)

            P9   Vol. I, #3, 215-220.
Evans, Richard S. "The Voyage of Cabrillo." (translator of Buckingham Smith text)

1891- P10   Vol. I, #4, 254.
92   Mathis, Juliette Estelle. "The Channel of Santa Barbara." (a poem)

1892   P11   Vol. II, #1, 129-134.
Holder, Charles F. "The Haunts of the Pacific Jew Fish."

          P12   Vol. III, #1, 64-73.
Holder, Charles F. "An Isle of Summer, Catalina Island."

1893   P13   Vol. III, #2, 229-244.
Holder, C. F. "The California Academy of Sciences."

          P14   Vol. IV, #1, 3-9.
Mayhew, Walter. "Yachting in Southern California."

          P15   Vol. IV, #5, 661-667.
Gibbons, James M. "The Wild Woman of San Nicolas Island."

COMMONWEAL
Calvert Publishing Corp.
New York

1930   P16   Vol. XI, Jan., 363-364.
Frant-Walsh, Joseph. "St. Catherine's Isle."

COUNTRY CALENDAR
Review of Reviews Book Co.
New York

1905   P17   Vol. I, July, 240-243.
Holder, Charles F. "Capturing the Leaping Tuna of Avalon."

COUNTRY LIFE
Doubleday, Page & Co.
New York

1905   P18   Vol. VIII, June, 176-177.
Holder, Charles F. "Fishing for Tuna—A California Vacation."

CURRENT LITERATURE
A Magazine of Contemporary Record
Current Literature Publishing Co.
New York

1901   P19   Vol. XXX, #6, 686-687.
Chicago Record. "The Home of a Vanished People."

DESERT MAGAZINE
Palm Desert, California
Randall Henderson, Editor

1952   P20   Vol. 15, Jan., 5-8.
Van Valkenburgh, Richard. "We Found the Lost Indian Cave of the San Martins."

FORBES
New York

1970   P21   Vol. 106, Nov., 22-33.
"Island Kingdom of P. K. Wrigley."

1971   P22   Vol. 109, April, 11.
Renton, J. J. "Development of Santa Catalina Island."

GRIZZLY BEAR MAGAZINE

1947   P22a   Vol. 80, 4-5.
Murbarger, Nell. "California's Vanished Islanders."

HARPER'S NEW MONTHLY MAGAZINE
Harper & Bros., N. Y.

1861   P23   Vol. 23, Aug., 306-316.
Browne, J. R. "The Coast Rangers."

1891   P24   Vol. 82, Mar., 515-525.
Ralph, Julian. "The Chinese Leak."

HOLIDAY
The Curtis Publishing Co.
Philadelphia

1950   P25   Vol. VII, April, 80 + .
"Catalina Island."

HUTCHINGS' CALIFORNIA MAGAZINE
Hutchings & Rosenfield, San Francisco

1856   P26   Vol. I, #3, Sep't, 97-105.
Hutchings, J. M. "The Quicksilver Mine of New Almaden."

P27   Vol. I, #5, 209-211.
Russell, C. J. W. "Narrative of a Woman who was Eighteen Years Alone upon the Island of San Nicolas, Coast of California."

1857   P28   Vol. I, #7, 293-296.
"The Hair Seal of the Pacific."

P29   Vol. I, #8, 347-348.
"The Indian Woman of San Nicolas."

P30   Vol. I, #10, 478-479.
Editor's Table. (on Captain Russell)

1858   P31   Vol. II, #10, 442-448.
Hittell, John S. "Mexican Land-Claims in California."

1860   P32   Vol. IV, #12, 545-549.
T. H. S. "Fragmentary Memorials of Father Kino."

1861   P33   Vol. V, #6, 263-270.
Randolph, Edmund. "Historical California."

         P34   Vol. V, #7, 308-314.
Randolph, Edmund. "Historical California."

         P35   Vol. V, #12, frontpiece.
"Stand by the Union." (a poem)

         P36   Vol. V, #12, 550-551.
Pollock, Edward. "Disunion." (a poem)

1962   P37   Hutchings, J. M. (*California Magazine*, 1856-1861). *Scenes of Wonder and Curiosity.* Edited
by R. R. Olmsted. Howell-North: Berkeley, California.

ILLUSTRATED AMERICAN
New York

1892   P38   Vol. X, April, 365.
"The Isle of Skulls."

LAMP
Standard Oil Co., New Jersey

1971   P39   Vol. 53, #3, 26-29.
Hutter, Richard. "Oil from the Deep Sea."

LAND OF SUNSHINE
An Illustrated Monthly Descriptive of Southern California
Published by F. A. Pattee & Co., Los Angeles
Edited by Charles F. Lummis

1894   P40   Vol. I-II, Nov., 110-111.
Holder, Charles F. "Famous Fish of Southern California."

1895   P41   Vol. II, #2, 36.
"Some Big Things." (photo of Elderberry "Bush" on Santa Catalina Island)

         P42   Vol. II, #6, 98.
J. B. B. "The Yates Collections."

1896   P43   Vols. V & VI, #1, 25.
Wayne, Arthur Wellington. "Catalina." (a poem)

         P44   Vols. V & VI, #6, 227-230.
Earle, Homer P. "The Santa Barbara Islands."

1897   P45   Vol. VII, #2, 54-58.
Owens, Robert C. "Caves of Santa Cruz Island."

         P46   Vol. VII, #4, 153-160.
Trask, Blanche. "The Heart of Santa Catalina."

         P47   Vol. VII, #5, 192-197.
Britton, J. R. "Our Summer Isles."

1898   P48   Vol. VIII, #6, 260-266.
Lummis, Charles F. "The New League for Literature and the West."

         P49   Vol. IX, #2, 100-103.
H. E. S. "Yachting on the Pacific."

         P50   Vol. IX, #2, 153.
Trask, Blanche. "Avalon, Santa Catalina Island." (a song)

1899   P51   Vol. X, #2, 65-72.
Smith, Ruth Tangier. "One of California's Desert Islands."

         P52   Vol. XI, #2, 77-84.
Holder, Charles F. "A California Aquarium and Zoological Station."

P53 Vol. XI, #6, 336-346.
"Pioneers of the Far West."

1900 P54 Vol. XIII, #2, 95-100.
Trask, Blanche. "Dying San Nicolas."

P55 Vol. XIII, #6, 406-415.
"Royal Sport."

1901 P56 Vol. XIV, #6, 486-496.
"Early California History, The Expeditions of 1769." (a Costansó translation)

LIFE
Time, Inc., Chicago

1941 P57 Vol. X, June 9, 134-137.
"Life visits Catalina with two Movie Girls."

1969 P58 Vol. 66, #23, 22-27.
Snell, David. "Iridescent Gift of Death."

McCLURE'S MAGAZINE
S. S. McClure, Ltd., New York

1901 P59 Vol. XVI, Feb., 369-374.
Holder, Charles F. "Adventures with the Leaping Tuna."

MOTOR BOATING
(formerly Motor Boating and Sailing)
The Yachtsman's Magazine
The Hearst Corp., N. Y.

1967 P60 Vol. 119, May, 28-29 + .
Kelton, Richard. "Cruising to the Garden of the Hesperides."

1969 P61 Vol. 123, Jan., 242-248.
Kingett, Robert P. "Avalon Looks Up."

MUNSEY'S MAGAZINE
New York

1901 P62 Vol. XXIV, #5, 655-665.
Foster, Maximilian. "The Greatest Game Fishing."

NATION
A Weekly Journal
New York

1889 P63 Vol. XLIX, Oct. 17, 307-327.
Finck, H. T. "Santa Catalina Island."

NATION'S BUSINESS
J. H. Richards & Co.
New York

1938 P64 Vol. XXIV, Sep't, 26-29 + .
Haig, John Angus. "A Business Version of the Fuller Life."

NEW ENGLAND MAGAZINE
J. N. McClintock & Co.
Boston

1904 P65 Vol. XXXI, Nov., 283-289.
Quincy, E. S. "Catalina—The Wondrous Isle."

NEWSWEEK
Weekly Publications, Inc.
New York

1958	P66	Vol. LII, Dec. 29, 22. "Preview of Power."
1965	P67	Vol. 66, July 5, 50. "Long Island West?"

OUTING
Sport, Adventure, Travel
New York

1917	P68	Vol. 70, Sep't, 775-87. McCoy, William M. "San Nicolas Island, Time's Hour Glass."

OUT WEST
A Magazine of the Old Pacific and the New
(formerly *Land of Sunshine*)
Western Publishing Co., Los Angeles

1903	P69	Vol. XIX, n.s., #1, 115-127. Wells, A. J. "California Summer Resorts."
1904	P70	Vol. XX, n.s., #2, 161. Trask, Blanche. "Catalina Fog." (a poem)
	P71	Vol. XX, n.s., #5, 471. Lewis, Eleanore F. "At Catalina." (a poem)
	P72	Vol. XX, n.s., #6, 524-528. Wood, Williard. "Gathering Sea Shells in California."
1909	P73	Vol. XXX, n.s., #5, 423-465. Edholm, Charlton, Lawrence. "The Seaward Suburbs of Los Angeles."
1912	P74	Vol. III, n.s., #5, 337-341. Rosamond, Roy Reuben. "Camping on Anacapa."
1914	P75	Vol. VIII, n.s., #5, 282-287. White, Mowbray. "Santa Catalina Island." (a poem)

OVERLAND MONTHLY
San Francisco
First Series

1870	P76	Vol. IV, #1, 24-25. Stoddard, Charles Warren. "Avalon." (a poem)
	P77	Vol. IV, #1, 25-30. Scammon, Captain C. M. "Sea Otters."
	P78	Vol. IV, #2, 112-117. Scammon, Captain C. M. "Sea-Elephant Hunting."
1872	P79	Vol. IX, #1, 173-175. Walcott, Josephine. "Hona Maria."
1874	P79a	Vol. XII, #6, 522-26. Dall, W.H. "The Lords of The Isles."
	P80	Vol. XIII, 209-213. Browne, J. R. "The Island of Santa Rosa."
	P81	Vol. XIII, #4, 297-302. Schumacher, Paul. "Some Kjökkenmöddings and Ancient Graves of California."
1875	P82	Vol. XV, #4, 374-379. Schumacher, Paul. "Some Remains of a Former People."

Second Series

1883   P83   Vol. II, #10, 409-416.
               Parry, C. C. "Early Botanical Explorers of the Pacific Coast."

1889   P84   Vol. XIV, #84, 625-630.
               O'Meara, James. "A Chapter of California History."

1890   P85   Vol. XVI, Aug., 186-195.
               Eames, Ninetta. "The Mystery of Catalina."

        P86   Vol. XVI, #95, 476-479.
               Guinn, J. M. "An Early Mining Boom on Santa Catalina."

1891   P87   Vol. XVIII, Dec., 617-631.
               Kinsell, M. "The Santa Barbara Islands."

1893   P88   Vol. XXI, May, 492-501.
               "K." "Shearing Time on Santa Rosa Island."

1896   P89   Vol. XXVII, #159, 337-342.
               Yates, Dr. L. G. "Aboriginal Weapons of California."

        P90   Vol. XXVII, #161, 538-544.
               Yates, Dr. L. G. "The Deserted Homes of a Lost People."

        P91   Vol. XXVII, #162, 625.
               Covey, Sylvia Lawson. "The Paths of Catalina." (a poem)

1896   P92   Vol. XXIX, Jan.-June, 642.
               Pruyn, Marion. "Santa Catalina." (a poem)

1897   P93   Vol. XXX, #177, 275.
               Covey, Sylvia Lawson. "A Catalina Island Cañon." (a poem)

        P94   Vol. XXX, #177, 276-282.
               Driscoll, N. W. "The Idol Cup." (fiction)

1898   P95   Vol. XXXII, July-Dec., 420.
               Macnab, Leavenworth. "The Birth of Catalina." (a poem)

1901   P96   Vol. XXXVIII, #4, 306.
               Field, Benjamin Franklin. "The Banyan Tree at Avalon." (a poem)

1903   P97   Vol. 41, #4, 253-259.
               Vore, Elizabeth. "The Men who make our Books."

1910   P98   Vol. LVI, July-Dec., 96.
               Wilson, Neill C. "Santa Catalina." (a poem)

1911   P99   Vol. LVIII, July-Dec., 208-212.
               Paul, O. M. "A Female Robinson Crusoe."

1912   P100   Vol. LIX, #5, 472.
               Koch, Felix J. "The Pet of Avalon Beach."

1913   P101   Vol. LXII, #4, 383-386.
               Edholm, C. L. "Steaks and Pearls from the Abalone."

1915   P102   Vol. LXV, April, 314.
               Shepard, Odell. "Avalon, Catalina Island." (a poem)

1920   P103   Vol. 75, #1, 8-12.
               Waddy, F. V. "The California Islands."

1921   P104   Vol. 78, #5, 11-13.
               Clifford, Josephine. "San Nicolas Island, Hona Maria."

1925   P105   Vol. 83, #2, 61+.
               Richey, Emma Carbutt. "Abalone, A Product of our Rocky Coasts."

1931	P106	Vol. 89, #11, 21.
		Phillips, Mabel Whitman. "Moonlight at Avalon." (a poem)
1934	P107	Vol. 92, Aug., 137+.
		Overholt, Alma. "Wild Life at Catalina."

PACIFIC MONTHLY
Published by Gardner & Mary E. Hart
Portland, Oregon

1890	P108	Vol. II, #4, 111-114.
		Gardner, Charles. "Catalina—The Island of the Blest." (fiction)
	P109	Vol. II, #7, 160-161.
		Gardner, Charles. "The Belle of Avalon." (a poem)
1889-91	P110	Vols. I-III, #6 and #7, 242-245.
		Morley, Duane. "The Hermit of Santa Catalina." (a poem)
1907	P111	Vol. XVIII, #1, 1-12.
		Holder, Charles F. "The Rod on the Pacific Coast."
	P112	Vol. XVIII, #1, 23-30.
		Tenney, W. A. "The Hermit of San Nicholas."

PACIFIC SCIENCE MONTHLY
Stephen Bowers, Editor
Ventura, California

| 1885 | P113 | Vol. I, #3, 38. |
| | | Bowers, Stephen. "Cave in the San Martin Mountains." |

POPULAR SCIENCE MONTHLY
Science Press, New York

1876-77	P114	Vol. X, Jan., 353-356.
		Schumacher, Paul. "Aboriginal Settlements of the Pacific Coast."
1896	P115	Vol. XLVIII, Mar., 659-662.
		Holder, Charles F. "The Ancient Islanders of California."
1913	P116	Vol. LXXXII, June, 532-550.
		Edwards, Charles Lincoln. "The Abalones of California."
1932	P117	Vol. CXX, Jan., 29.
		"Stone Map Guides to Buried Relics."

ROCK PRODUCTS
Maclean-Hunter Publishing Co.
Chicago

1950	P118	Vol. LIII, #8, 184-186.
		Lenhart, Walter B. "Catalina Island Stone Quarry."
1957	P119	Vol. LX, Aug., 155-156+.
		Meschter, Elwood. "As Traffic Problems Mounted, this Stone Company took to the Water."

ST. NICHOLAS
Century Co., New York

1895	P120	Vol. XXII, Part 2, 891-897.
		Lockwood, Dewitt C. "Carrier-Pigeons."
1916	P121	Vol. XLIII, Sep't, 1035-1039.
		Holder, Charles F. "The Tameness of Wild Animals."

SATURDAY REVIEW
New York

1961   P122   Vol. XLIV, Aug. 19, 26-28.
Sutton, Horace. "Bargain Bali H'ai."

SCRIBNER'S MONTHLY
Illustrated Magazine for the People
(reprinted by Schauer Printing Studio, Santa Barbara)

1880   P123   Vol. 20, #5, 657-664.
Hardacre, Emma C. "Eighteen Years Alone."

SOUTHERN CALIFORNIA PRACTIONER
Stoll and Thayer, Los Angeles

1887   P124   Vol. II, #11, 405-407.
McCarty, T. J. "Mineral Springs of Catalina Island."

SOUTHERN CALIFORNIA RANCHER
San Diego, California

1947   P125   Vol. XII, #10, 12.
Gunn, Guard D. "Ranches of the Sea."

SOUTHERN WORKMAN
(Hampton Institute), Virginia

1930   P126   Vol. LIX, April, 193-194.
Momyer, George R. "Aboriginals make the Frog Dance; Catalina Islanders."

SPORTS ILLUSTRATED
Time, Inc., Chicago

1961   P127   Vol. XV, July 10, 30-35.
Williams, Roger. "A Local South Sea Isle."

SUNSET
(formerly of Southern Pacific Railroad)
The Magazine of Western Living
Lane Magazine & Book Co.
Menlo Park, California

1901   P128   Vol. 6, #3, 73-83.
Holder, Charles F. "Rod, Reel and Gaff in Southern California."

1905   P129   Vol. 14, #3, 235-240.
Kirk, Heatherwick. "Another Treasure Island."

1911   P130   Vol. 26, Feb., 205-209.
Saunders, Charles F. "Winter on the Isle of Summer."

1928   P131   Vol. 60, Apr., 37+.
Hemphill, Josephine. "Catalina, Isle of Magic Beauty."

1930   P132   Vol. 64, Mar., 18-20.
Overholt, Alma. "Catalina Aviaries."

1962   P133   Vol. 129, Sept., 56-65.
"Catalina Holiday."

1963   P134   Vol. 130, June, 34.
"By U-Drive Boat along Catalina."

1967   P135   Vol. 138, April, 78-85.
"Following the Santa Monicas as They March out to Sea."

| 1973 | P136 | Vol. 151, May, 56. |
| | | "Across the Sea to Lovely Santa Barbara Island." |

TIME
Time Inc., New York

| 1942 | P137 | Vol. XL, Dec. 28, 16. |
| | | "Catalina Converts." |

TRAVEL
The Magazine that Roams the Globe
Travel Magazine Co., New York

1909	P138	Vol. XV, Oct., 31-32.
		Saunders, Charles F. "Santa Catalina Island."
1912	P139	Vol. XX, #1, 8-10.
		Saunders, Charles F. "Unexplored Catalina."
1944	P140	Vol. XXCII, #6, 12-14+.
		Zahn, Curtis. "California's Lost Islands."
1958	P141	Vol. CX, #2, 25-28.
		Monroe, Keith. "Catalina."
1964	P142	Vol. CXXI, #6, 24-29.
		Winchester, James H. "Catalina, California's Sunny Isle is Ideal for Offshore Idling."

WESTERN SPORTING GOODS REVIEW
Newell Publishing Co., Los Angeles

| 1957 | P143 | Vol. 37, #2, 4-5+. |
| | | Bryan, Bruce. "Prehistoric California Fishermen." |

WESTWAYS
Automobile Club of Southern California
(before 1934 as *Touring Topics*)

1922	P144	Vol. 14, #8, 16-20+.
		McGaffey, Ernest. "Cruizing with the Caprice."
1928	P145	Vol. 20, #5, 11.
		Egan, Carrie W. "Santa Barbara Island." (a poem)
1931	P146	Vol. 23, #10, 12-15+.
		Sheldon, H. H. "Saints in the Sea."
1932	P147	Vol. 24, #7, 46.
		Hanna, Phil Townsend. "Notes about the Channel Islands."
1933	P148	Vol. 25, #2, 16-18+.
		Lawrence, Eleanor. "Fortunes in Otter."
1935	P149	Vol. 27, #1, 16-17+.
		Crouch, Charles Willard. "Capri with A Coney Touch."
1936	P150	Vol. 28, June, 14-15.
		Stock, Chester. "Ice Age Elephants of the Channel Islands."
1938	P151	Vol. 30, #6, 34.
		Hanna, Phil Townsend. "Island Monument."
	P152	Vol. 30, #9, 14-15.
		"Return of the Sea Otters."
1939	P153	Vol. 31, #10, 20-21.
		Barbour, Lewis. "Boars are never Bores."

1941	P154	Vol. 33, #1, 22-23. Stock, Chester. "Ancient Sea Lizards of California."
1944	P155	Vol. 36, #1, 18-19. Laudermilk, J. D. "The Case of the Vanishing Island."
	P156	Vol. 36, #7, 6-7. Langley, Nancy. "Maritime Catalina."
	P157	Vol. 36, #11, 10-11 Clark, Robert. "The Thrills of Relic Hunting."
1946	P158	Vol. 38, #3, 38. Hyatt, Robert. "Catalina Gold Strike."
1947	P159	Vol. 39, #8, 10-11 + . Ferry, Philip. "Return of the Great Race."
1952	P160	Vol. 44, #5, 4-5. "Catalina Past."
1956	P161	Vol. 48, #6, 6-7. Miller, Max. "The Strange Legacy of San Nicolas."
	P162	Vol. 48, #7, 10-11. Thornburgh, Margaret. "Rugged Anacapa."
	P163	Vol. 48, #11, 6-7. Miller, Max. "Are our Sea Serpents Sea Elephants."
1962	P164	Vol. 54, #5, 28-29. "Discover Anacapa."
1963	P165	Vol. 55, #4, 31-33. "Unknown Catalina."
	P166	Vol. 55, #6, 24-26 + . Hillinger, Charles. "Mystery Islands Offshore."
1964	P167	Vol. 56, #10, 18-20. Roe, Jo Ann. "Slumbering Santa Cruz."
1966	P168	Vol. 58, #7, 42-44. Challacombe, J. R. "The Little Clowns of Big Sur."
1967	P169	Vol. 59, #11, 37-38. Ainsworth, Ed. "Digging the Southwest."
1968	P170	Vol. 60, #2, 2-5. Cass, W. W. "A Catalina Safari."
	P171	Vol. 60, #5, 10-15 + . Powell, Lawrence Clark. "California Classics Reread."
	P172	Vol. 60, #10, 37-39 + . Ashkenazy, Irvin. "Catalina's Pigeon Express."
1969	P173	Vol. 61, #14, 29-32 + . Ashkenazy, Irvin. "Island Voyage Aboard the 'Swift'."
1971	P174	Vol. 63, #3, 30-39 + . Ashkenazy, Irvin. "A Graveyard of Ships."
1972	P175	Vol. 64, #5, 55-59. Powell, Lawrence Clark. "Massacre and Vengence in Apacheria."
1973	P176	Vol. 65, #10, 43-47. V. C. "Under the Sea Life."

| 1974 | P177 | Vol. 66, #4, 25-27. |
| | | McGinty, Brian. "A Grave Discovery." |

WORLD'S WORK
Doubleday, Page & Co., N. Y.

| 1902 | P178 | Vol. IV, Aug., 2424-2426. |
| | | Stevens, R. "Picturesque Island off the Pacific Shore." |

YACHTING
Yachting Publishing Co.
New York

1954	P179	Vol. 95, #4, 70-72 + .
		Robertson, Stewart. "California Cruise."
1963	P180	Vol. 113, #5, 40-42 + .
		Dugay, John. "Cruising the Santa Barbara Channel."
1965	P181	Vol. 117, Jan., 106-107 + .
		Crowe, William P. "Off Shore California: The Channel Islands."

BOOKS
with Interest Prior to 20th Century

1885   B1   Bancroft, H. H. *History of California*, II, III, IV. San Francisco: A. L. Bancroft & Co.

1916   B2   Bolton, Herbert Eugene, Editor. *Spanish Explorations in the Southwest, 1542-1706*. New York: Charles Scribner's Sons.

1932   B3   Bolton, Herbert Eugene, Donee. *New Spain and the Anglo-American West*, II. Los Angeles: privately printed.

(1855)   B4   Browne, J. Ross. *Confidential Agent in Old California*. By Richard H. Dillon. Univ. of Ok : 1965.

1855   B5   Browne, J. Ross. *The Indians of California*. San Francisco: Colt Press, Series of California Classics.

1970   B6   Bryan, Bruce. *Archaeological Explorations on San Nicolas Island*. Southwest Museum, Los Angeles, Ca: Southland Press.

1806   B7   Burney, James. *A Chronological History of the Voyages and Discoveries in the South Sea or Pacific Ocean*, Part 2. London: Luke Hansard.

(1542)   B8   Cabrillo, Juan Rodriguez. *Juan Rodriguez Cabrillo, Discoverer of the Coast of California*. San Francisco: Ca. Hist. Soc. Special Pub. #17, 1941.

1921   B9   Chapman, C. E. *A History of California—The Spanish Period*. New York: The Macmillan Co.

1922   B10   Cleland, Robert Glass. *A History of California—The American Period*. New York: The Macmillan Co.

1963   B10a   Cleland, Robert Glass. *Cattle on a Thousand Hills*. San Marino, Ca : Huntington Lby.

1842   B11   Cleveland, J. P. *Voyages, Maritime Adventures, and Commercial Enterprises*. London: N. Bruce, Peterborough Court.

1956   B12   Cowan, Robert G. *Ranchos of California, a list of Spanish Concessions, 1775-1822 and Mexican Grants, 1822-1846*. Fresno, Ca: Academy Library Guild.

(1769)   B13   Crespi, Fray Juan. *Missionary Explorer on the Pacific Coast, 1769-1774*. H. E. Bolton, ed. Univ. of Ca: 1927.

1868   B14   Cronise, Titus Fey. *The Natural Wealth of California*. San Francisco: H. H. Bancroft & Co.

(1835)   B15   Dana, Richard Henry. *Two Years before the Mast*. Boston and New York: Houghton Mifflin Co., 1911.

(1846) B16 Davis, William Heath. *An American in California, The Biography of William Heath Davis, 1822-1909.* By Andrew F. Rolle. Henry E. Huntington Lby: 1956.

1841 B17 Dawson, N. *California in '41, Texas in '51, Memoirs of N. Dawson.* Privately printed.

1912 B18 Engelhardt, Zephyrin, Fr. *The Missions and Missionaries of California,* I, II, IV. San Francisco: James H. Barry Co.

(1769) B19 Fages, Pedro. *A Historical, Political, and Natural Description of California.* Trans. by H. I. Priestley. Univ. of Ca : 1937.

1850 B20 Farnham, T. J. *Life, Adventures and Travels in California.* N. Y: Cornish, Lamport and Co.

(1775) B21 Font, Pedro, Fr. *Font's Complete Diary, A Chronicle of the Founding of San Francisco, 1775-1776.* Trans. from the original Spanish manuscript and ed. by H. E. Bolton. Univ. of Ca : 1933.

1839 B22 Forbes, Alexander. *California: A History of Upper and Lower California.* London: Smith, Elder & Co.

1935 B23 Garrison, Myrtle. *Romance and History of California Ranchos.* San Francisco: Harr Wagner Pub. Co.

1965 B24 Geiger, Maynard, O.F.M. *Mission Santa Barbara, 1782-1965.* Santa Barbara, Ca : Franciscan Fathers.

1917 B25 Gidney, C. M. *History of Santa Barbara, San Luis Obispo and Ventura Counties,* Vol. I. Chicago: Lewis Pub. Co.

1965 B26 Grant, Campbell. *The Rock Paintings of the Chumash, A Study of a California Indian Culture.* Berkeley: Univ. of Ca. Press.

(1857) B27 Graves, J. A. *My Seventy Years in California, 1857-1927.* Los Angeles: Times-Mirror Press, 1928.

1844 B28 Greenhow, Robert. *The History of Oregon and California and the other Territories on the Northwest Coast of North America.* Boston: Charles C. Little and James Brown.

1960 B29 Gudde, Erwin G. *California Place Names.* Berkeley: Univ. of Ca. Press.

1902 B30 Guinn, J. M. *Historical and Biographical Record of Southern California.* Chicago: Chapman Pub. Co.

(1846) B31 Hawley, Walter A. *The Early Days of Santa Barbara, California, from the First Discoveries by Europeans to December, 1846.* First pntg.; Santa Barbara: Schauer Pntg. Studio, 1910. Reprinted at Santa Barbara, 1920.

1951 B32 Heizer, R. F. and M. A. Whipple, eds. and comps. *The California Indians, A Source Book.* Berkeley: Univ. of Ca. Press.

1963 B33 Heizer, Robert. *Aboriginal California.* Berkeley: Univ. of Ca. Press.

1971 B34 Heizer, Robert F. and Alan F. Almquist. *The Other Californians, Prejudice and Discrimination under Spain, Mexico, and the United States to 1920.* Berkeley: Univ. of Ca. Press.

1898 B35 Hittell, Theodore H. *History of California,* II. San Francisco: N. J. Stone & Co.

1905 B36 Hodge, F. W. *Handbook of the American Indians North of Mexico.* Bulletin #20, Bur. of Amer. Ethn., Smithsonian Inst. Wash., D. C.

1901 B37 Holder, Charles F. *An Isle of Summer, Santa Catalina; its History, Climate, Sports, and Antiquities.* Los Angeles: R. Y. McBride & Co.

1910 B38 Holder, Charles F. *The Channel Islands of California.* Los Angeles: R. Y. McBride & Co.

1891 B39 Johnsson, Arthur T. *California, An Englishman's Impression of the Golden State.* New York: Duffield and Co.

1962 B40 Johnston, B. E. *California's Gabrielino Indians.* Los Angeles: Southwest Mus., VIII.

1976 B40a Jones, John C. *Contentious Consul: A Biography of John Coffin Jones.* By Ross H. Gast. Los Angeles: Dawson's Book Shop.

(1816) B41   Landberg, Leif C. W. *The Chumash Indians of Southern California.* Los Angeles: South-land Press, 1965.

(1786) B42   Lapérouse, Jean Francis De Galaup. *The First French Expedition to California, Lapérouse in 1786.* Trans. and Intro. by Charles N. Rudkin. Los Angeles: Glen Dawson, 1959.

1896   B43   Lauer, Solon. *Life and Light from Above.* San Diego: Life and Light Pub. Co.

(1856) B44   Lecouvreur, Frank. *From East Prussia to the Golden Gate.* Trans. and comp. by Julius C. Behnke, Occidental College. Ed. by Mrs. Josephine Rosana Lecouvreur. Leipzig, Los Angeles, New York: Angelina Book Concern, 1906.

1889   B45   Lewis Publishing Co., comp. *An Illustrated History of Los Angeles County, California.* Chicago, Il.

1890   B46   Lunt, Howard Leslie. *Catalina, the Bride of the Pacific.* (a poem) Los Angeles: W. A. Vandercook Co., Engravers and Printers.

(1792) B47   Mártinez, José Longinos. *California in 1792, The Expedition of José Longinos Mártinez.* Trans. by Lesley Byrd Simpson. Henry E. Huntington Lby., Univ. of Ca. Press, 1938.

(1844) B48   de Mofras, Duflot. *Travels on the Pacific Coast,* I. Trans., ed., annot. by Marguerite Eyer Wilbur. Ed. by Fred Webb Hodge, Southwest Museum. Santa Ana, Ca : The Fine Arts Press, 1937. The original printed in Paris, *Explorations of the Oregon and California Territories,* 1844.

1900   B49   Moorehead, Warren King. *Prehistoric Implements,* Section VII. Cincinnati, Ohio: The Robert Clarke Co.

1930   B50   Newmark, Harris. *Sixty Years in Southern California, 1853-1913.* Boston: Houghton Mifflin Co.

1937   B51   Nidever, George. *The Life and Adventures of, 1802-1883.* Ed. by William Henry Ellison. Berkeley: Univ. of Ca. Press.

1959   B52   Olmsted, R. R., ed. *History of Los Angeles County, California.* Berkeley: Howell-North, pubs.

1939   B53   O'Neill, O. H. *History of Santa Barbara County.* Santa Barbara, Ca : Harold McLean Meier. Pacific Coast Odyssey Pub. Co.

1968   B54   Orr, Phil C. *Prehistory of Santa Rosa Island.* Santa Barbara: Santa Barbara Museum of Natural History.

(1769) B55   Paloú, Fray Francisco. *Historical Memoirs of New California.* Ed. by H. E. Bolton. Berkeley: Univ. of Ca. Press, 1926.

1927   B56   Phillips, M. J. *History of Santa Barbara County, California from its Earliest Settlement to the Present Time,* I. Los Angeles: Clarke Pub. Co.

(1840) B57   Reid, Hugo. *The Indians of Los Angeles County.* From the *Los Angeles Star.* Bancroft Lby : Univ. of Ca., 1926.

(1852) B58   Reid, Hugo. *A Scotch Paisano, Hugo Reid's Life in California, 1832-1852.* By Susanna Bryant Dakin. Univ. of Ca., 1939.

1911   B59   Richman, Irving Berdine. *California under Spain and Mexico, 1535-1847.* Boston: Houghton Mifflin Co.

(1828) B60   Robinson, Alfred. *Life in California.* (also translations of Boscana's work, from the original Spanish manuscript.) New York: Wiley and Putnam, 1846. Oakland: Biobooks.

1948   B61   Robinson, W. W. *Land in California.* Berkeley: Univ. of Ca. Press.

1957   B62   Robinson, W. W., editor. *The Pacific Northwesterner.* Los Angeles Corral: The Westerners Brand Book #7. (Arthur Woodward, "Juana Maria; sidelights on the Indian occupation of San Nicolas Island.")

1929   B63   Rogers, David Banks. *Prehistoric Man of the Santa Barbara Coast.* Santa Barbara: Santa Barbara Mus. of Nat. Hist.

(1874) B64 Scammon, Charles M. *Marine Mammals of the Northwest Coast of North America*. San Francisco: Carmany. Riverside: Manessier Publishing Co., 1969.

(1804) B65 Shaler, William. *Journal of a Voyage between China and the North-Western Coast of America, made in 1804 by William Shaler*. Intro. by Lindley Bynum. Claremont, Ca : Saunders Studio Press, 1935.

(1841) B66 Simpson, Sir George. *Narrative of a Voyage to California Ports in 1841-42*. San Francisco: Thomas C. Russell, private press, n.d.

(1879) B67 Snow, H. J. *In Forbidden Seas, Recollections of Sea-Otter Hunting in the Kurils*. London: Edward Arnold, pubs. to the India Office, 1910.

(1860) B68 Spence, Clark C. *British Investments and the American Mining Frontier, 1860-1901*. New York: Amer. Hist. Assoc., 1958.

1891 B69 Storke, Mrs. Yda Addis. *A Memorial and Biographical History of the Counties of Santa Barbara, San Luis Obispo and Ventura, California*. Chicago: Lewis Pub. Co.

1883 B70 Thompson and West, Publishers. *History of Santa Barbara and Ventura Counties*. Oakland, Ca.

1866 B71 Tuthill, Franklin. *The History of California*. San Francisco: H. H. Bancroft & Co.

1798 B72 Vancouver, George. *A Voyage of Discovery to the North Pacific Ocean, and Round the World*, I-III. London: printed for G. G. and J. Robinson.

(1769) B73 Vizcaíno, Fr. Juan. *The Sea Diary of Fr. Juan Vizcaíno to Alta California*. Intro. and trans. by Arthur Woodward. Los Angeles: Glen Dawson, 1959.

1929 B74 Wagner, Henry Raup. *Spanish Voyages to the Northwest Coast of America in the Sixteenth Century*. San Francisco: Ca. Hist. Soc. Spec. Pub. #4.

1937 B75 Wagner, Henry Raup. *The Cartography of the Northwest Coast of America to the Year 1800*, Vol. II. Berkeley: Univ. of Ca. Press.

1876 B76 Warner, J. J. *et al*. *An Historical Sketch of Los Angeles County, California from the Spanish Occupancy by the founding of the mission San Gabriel Archangel, September 8, 1771, to July 4, 1876*. Los Angeles: Louis Lewin & Co., 1876. Los Angeles: O. W. Smith (for Dr. J. P. Widney), 1936.

1972 B77 Weber, Rev. Francis J. *A Select Bibliographical Guide to California History 1863-1972*. Los Angeles: Dawson's Book Store.

1901 B78 Willard, C. D. *History of Los Angeles City*. Los Angeles: Kingsley-Barnes and Neuner Co.

1891 B79 Wood, Stanley. *Over the Range to the Golden Gate*. Chicago: R. R. Donnelley & Sons, 1891.

BOOKS
with Emphasis on 20th Century

1924 B80 Bailey, Gilbert Ellis. *California, A Geologic Wonderland*. Los Angeles: Times-Mirror Press.

1928 B81 Breeden, Marshall. *The Romantic Southland of California*. Los Angeles: Kenmore Pub. Co.

1965 B82 Carlquist, Sherwin. *Island Life, A Natural History of the Islands of the World*. American Museum of Natural History. Garden City, N. Y: Nat. Hist. Press.

1938 B83 Cornell, Ralph D. *Conspicuous California Plants*. Pasadena, Ca : San Pasqual Press.

1963 B84 Doran, Adelaide. *The Ranch that was Robbins'—Santa Catalina Island*. Glendale, Ca : Clark Co.

1923 B85 Dawson, William Leon. *Birds of California*, Vol. I. San Diego, Los Angeles, San Francisco: South Moulton Co.

1935	B86	Drury, Aubrey. *California, An Intimate Guide*. N. Y: Harper & Bros.
1941	B87	Emery, K. O. and Francis P. Shepard. *Submarine Topography off the California Coast*. Geological Soc. of Amer. Spec. Paper #31.
1960	B88	Emery, K. O. *The Sea off Southern California*. N. Y: Wiley.
1950	B89	Gleason, Joe Duncan. *Islands of California, their History, Romance and Physical Characteristics*. Los Angeles: Sea Pub. Co.
1958	B90	Gleason, Joe Duncan. *The Islands and Ports of California, a Guide to Coastal California*. N. Y: The Devin-Adair Co.
1926	B91	Hasse, Leo G. *Little Geological Studies*. Long Beach, Ca : privately printed.
1975	B91a	Heizer, Robert F.; Nissen, Karen M., and Castillo, Edward D. *California Indian History*. Ramona, Ca : Ballena Press.
1951	B91b	Heizer, Robert F. and Whipple, M. A. *The California Indian*. Berkeley: Univ. of Ca. Press.
1921	B92	Herr, Charlotte. *Their Mariposa Legend, A Romance of Santa Catalina*. Pasadena: Post Pntg. and Binding Co.
1902	B93	Holder, Charles F. *The Adventures of Torqua*. Boston: Little, Brown & Co.
1906	B94	Holder, Charles F. *The Log of a Sea Angler*. Boston: Houghton Mifflin Co.
1908	B95	Holder, Charles F. *Big Game at Sea*. N. Y: The Outing Pub. Co.
1909	B96	Holder, Charles F. and David Starr Jordan. *Fish Stories*. N. Y: Henry Holt & Co.
1910	B97	Holder, Charles F. *Recreation of a Sportsman*. N. Y.: G. P. Putnam's Sons.
1911	B98	Holder, Charles F. *Life in the Open*. N. Y: G. P. Putnam's Sons.
1912	B99	Holder, Charles F. *The Fishes of the Pacific Coast*. N. Y: Dodge Publishing Co.
1913	B100	Holder, Charles F. *Game Fishes of the World*. N. Y: Hodder and Stoughton.
1924	B101	Holder, Charles F. *The Big Game Fishes of the United States*. N. Y: The McMillan Co.
1948	B102	Hoover, M. B., H. E. Rensch and E. G. Rensch. Rev. by Ruth Teiser, Intro. by Dr. Robert Glass Cleland. *Historic Spots in California*. Stanford, Ca : Stanford Univ. Press.
1974	B103	Lester, Elizabeth Sherman. *The Legendary King of San Miguel, The Lesters at Rancho Rambouillet*. Goleta, Ca : Kimberly Press.
1921	B104	McGroarty, John Steven. *Los Angeles from the Mountains to the Sea*. Chicago: Amer. Hist. Soc.
1923	B105	Millspaugh, Charles Frederick and Lawrence William Nuttall. *Flora of Santa Catalina Island*. Chicago: Field Mus. of Nat. Hist., Pub. 212, Botanical Ser., V.
1914	B106	Markham, Edwin. *California the Wonderful*. New Jersey: Quinn and Boden Co.
1967	B107	McElrath, Clifford. *The Ranching Recollections of Clifford McElrath*. Santa Barbara Hist. Soc. Los Angeles: Dawson's Book Shop.
1959	B108	Miller, Max. *And Bring All Your Folks*. Garden City, N. Y: Doubleday & Co., Inc.
1963	B109	Monroe, Keith. *California*. N. Y: E. P. Dutton & Co.
1960	B110	O'Dell, Scott. *Island of the Blue Dolphins*. Boston: Houghton, Mifflin.

PACIFIC COAST AVIFAUNA
Cooper Ornithological Club

1909	B111	#5. Grinnell, Joseph. *A Bibliography of California Ornithology*, 1st installment covering between 1797-1907.
1912	B112	#7. Willett, G. *Birds of the Islands off the Coast of Southern California*.
1915	B113	#11. Grinnell, Joseph. *A Distributional List of the Birds of California*.
1917	B114	#12. Howell, A. B. *Birds of the Islands off the Coast of Southern California*. Ed. by Joseph Grinnell and Harry S. Swarth. Hollywood, Ca : Univ. of Ca.

1933	B115	#21. Willett, George. *A Revised List of the Birds of Southwestern California.* (material by species, not author)
1944	B116	#27. Grinnell, Joseph and Alden H. Miller. *The Distribution of the Birds of California.* (material by species, not author)
1939	B117	Parks, Marian. *History of Santa Barbara County, Its People and Its Resources.* O. H. O'Neill, Editor-in-Chief, State of California. Santa Barbara, Ca : Harold McLean Meier.
1933	B118	Reed, Ralph D. *Geology of California.* Tulsa, Ok.: Amer. Assoc. of Petroleum Geologists.
1962	B119	Rockwell, Mabel M. *California's Sea Frontier.* Santa Barbara, Ca : McNally and Loftin.
1967	B120	Santa Barbara Botanic Garden. *Proceedings of the Symposium on the Biology of the California Islands.* Ralph N. Philbrick, ed. Santa Barbara, Ca : Rapid Blue Print Co.
1913	B121	Saunders, Charles Francis. *Under the Sky in California.* N. Y: McBride, Nast & Co.
1923	B122	Saunders, Charles Francis. *Finding the Worth While in California.* N. Y: Robert M. McBride & Co.
1920	B123	Southworth, John R. *Santa Barbara and Montecito, Past and Present.* Santa Barbara, Ca : Schauer Printing Studio.
1911	B124	Sterling, George. *House of Orchids.* San Francisco: A. M. Robertson.
1945	B125	Towne, C. W. and N. Wentworth. *Shepherds' Empire.* Univ. of Okla. Press. ("Sheep Against the Sea," 204-212)
1956	B126	Vaughn, Ruben V. *Doc's Catalina Diary.* Los Angeles: Limb Pub. Co.
1931	B127	Windle, Ernest. *History of Santa Catalina Island.* Avalon: Catalina Islander Press.
1941	B128	Writers', Southern California. *Santa Barbara, A Guide to the Channel City and its Environs.* American Guide Series, Calif. State Dept. of Ed. Sponsor, Santa Barbara State Coll., Wm. H. Ellison. N. Y: Hasting House.

NATIONAL PUBLICATIONS

NATIONAL ACADEMY OF SCIENCES
National Research Council
Washington, D. C.

Proceedings

1966	N1	Vol. 56, #5, 1409-1416. Orr, Phil C. and Rainer Berger. "The Fire Areas on Santa Rosa Island, California."

CARNEGIE INSTITUTE OF WASHINGTON

1927	N2	Pub. 322B, 42-43. Hay, Oliver P. "The Pleistocene of the Western Region of North America and its Vertebrated Animals."
1934	N3	Pub. #415, 3-25. Chaney, Ralph W. and Herbert L. Mason. "A Pleistocene Flora from Santa Cruz Island, California."

NATIONAL MUSEUM
Proceedings

1890	N4	Vol. XIII, 131-142. Townsend, Charles H. "Scientific Results of Explorations by the U. S. Fish Commission steamer *Albatross.*"
1899	N5	Vol. XXI, Nov., 421-449. Oberholser, H. C. "A Revision of the Wrens of the Genus *Thryomanes Sclater.*"

| 1900 | N6 | Vol. XXII, #1196, 229-234. |
| | | Oberholser, H. C. "Notes on Some Birds from Santa Barbara Islands, California." |

Bulletins

1907	N7	Bulletin #56, Pt. 1
		Mearns, E. A., M. D. *Mammals of the Mexican Boundary of the United States.*
1909	N8	Bulletin #62, 212.
		Lyon, Marcus Ward, Jr. *Catalogue of the Type-Specimens of Mammals in the United States National Museum, including the Biological Survey Collection.*

SMITHSONIAN INSTITUTION
Annual Reports

1874	N9	335-350.
		Schumacher, Paul. "Ancient Graves and Shell-Heaps of California."
1875	N10	7-48.
		Henry, Joseph. Secretary Report
1877	N11	7-91.
		Henry, Joseph. Secretary Report
1878	N12	316-320.
		Bowers, Stephen, Rev. "Santa Rosa Island."
1886	N13	Pt. 1, 296-305.
		Yates, Dr. L. G. "Charm Stones."
1891	N14	Vol. VII, 68.
		Powell, J. W., Director. "Indian Linguistic Families of America."
1902	N15	161-188.
		Holmes, William Henry. "Anthropological Studies in California."

BUREAU OF AMERICAN ETHNOLOGY

| 1925 | N16 | Bulletin #78. |
| | | Kroeber, A. L. *Handbook of the Indians of California.* |

EXECUTIVE DOCUMENTS

1850	N17	99-103.
		Philip T. Tyson to George W. Crawford, Secretary of War, 1850-53. "Information in relation to the geology and topography of California."
1851	N18	Vol. III, Document #18, 1-95.
		Jones, William C., Special Agent to examine the subject of Land Titles in California, to T. Ewing, Secretary of the Interior. 1st Session of the Senate, 31st Congress, 2nd Session of the Senate Documents publication.
1852	N19	Document #87, 1-3.
		Stuart, Alexander H. H., Secretary of the Interior. 32nd Congress, 1st Session.
1862	N20	Vol. 50, Series I, Pt. 1, 804.
		Lamont, D. S. *The War of the Rebellion.*

DEPARTMENT OF COMMERCE AND LABOR
Bureau of Fisheries

1908	N21	Vol. XXVIII, Pt. 1, 199-207.
		Holder, Charles F. "Sport Fishing in California and Florida."
	N22	Vol. XXVIII, Pt. 2, 1139-1141.
		Holder, Charles F. "A Method of Studying the Life History of Fishes."
	N23	Vol. XXVIII, Pt. 2, 1309-1314.
		Holder, Charles F. "A Plan for an Educational Exhibit of Fishes."

Fish Commissioner Report
George M. Bowers, Commissioner

1898   N24   Pt. 24, 24-29.
Gilbert, Charles H. "Report on Fishes obtained by the Steamer *Albatross* in the Vicinity of Santa Catalina Island and Monterey Bay."

COAST AND GEODETIC SURVEY OF THE U. S.
Annual Reports

1853   N25   1-104.
-54   Superintendent A. D. Bache to Hon. James Guthrie, Sec'y of Treasury.

Appendix #66, 218-219.
T. H. Stevens to A. D. Bache.
A. D. Bache to Hon. P. G. Washington, Acting Sec'y of Treasury.

1854   N26   Appendix #6, 117.
-55   A. D. Bache.

Appendix #26, 176-185.
George Davidson, in charge of Sub-office in San Francisco to A. D. Bache.

Appendix #28, 186-188.
Wm. M. Johnson to A. D. Bache.

Appendix #30, 193-200.
A. D. Bache.

Appendix #64, 374-375.
J. G. Kohl to A. D. Bache.

Appendix #65, 377-398.
Wm. P. Blake to A. D. Bache.

Appendix #76, 410.
A. D. Bache to Hon. James Guthrie.

Appendix #83, 415-416.
A. D. Bache to James Guthrie.

Appendix #84, 417.
A. D. Bache to James Guthrie.

1855   N27   Section X, 1-91.
-56   A. D. Bache to James Guthrie. "Coast of California, from the Southern Boundary to the Forty-second Parallel, North Latitude."

Appendix #86, 355-356.
Lieut. Comd. MacRae to A. D. Bache.
A. D. Bache to James Guthrie.

1856   N28   Section X, 108-114.
-57   A. D. Bache to Hon. Howell Cobb, Sec'y of Treasury.

Appendix #44, 392-395.
W. E. Greenwell to A. D. Bache.

1857   N29   Appendix #44, 297-320.
-58   George Davidson to A. D. Bache to Howell Cobb.
"The Islands of the Santa Barbara Channel." (1st edition)

Appendix #44, 297-348.
Directory for the Pacific Coast of the United States.
Report of the Superintendent of the Coast Survey. (also issued separately)

1859   N30   Section X, 93-97.
-60   Wm. M. Johnson to W. E. Greenwell.
A. D. Bache to Hon. Philip F. Thomas, Sec'y of Treasury.

311

1861	N31	Section X, 59-60.
-62		A. D. Bache to Hon. S. P. Chase, Sec'y of Treasury.
		Appendix #39, 269-292.
		George Davidson to A. D. Bache to S. P. Chase.
		"The Islands of the Santa Barbara Channel." (2nd edition)
1864	N32	227ff.
		Report of the Superintendent of the Coast Survey showing the Progress of the Survey during the year 1863.
1885	N33	Appendix #7, 155-245.
-86		Davidson, George. "An Examination of some of the Early Voyages of Discovery and Exploration on the Northwest Coast of America, from 1539-1603."
1889	N34	68-99.
		Coast Pilot of California, Oregon, and Washington. Davidson, George. "The Islands of the Santa Barbara Channel." (4th edition)
1907	N35	459-496.
		Tittmann, O. H., Superintendent. "Tables of Depths for Channel and Harbors."
1909	N36	Tittmann, O. H. *United States Coast Pilot—Pacific Coast—California, Oregon and Washington.*

DEPARTMENT OF COMMERCE
Bureau of Mines
Information Circular

| 1932 | N37 | July, 3-15. |
| | | Roalfe, George Adams. "Quarrying and Crushing Methods and Costs at the Santa Catalina Island Quarry of Graham Bros., Inc., Santa Catalina Island, California." |

DEPARTMENT OF THE INTERIOR
Bureau of Land Management

| 1850- | N38 | Private Land Claims, #547 *et al.* |

Annual Reports

1896	N39	Pt. I, 46.
-97		Charles D. Walcott, Director. 18th U. S. Geological Survey Report.
	N40	Pt. II, 459-496.
		Smith, W. S. T. "A Geological Sketch of San Clemente Island."

U. S. GEOLOGICAL AND GEOGRAPHICAL SURVEY
F. V. Hayden, U. S. Geologist-In-Charge
Bulletins

1877	N41	Vol. III, #1, 37-56.
		Schumacher, Paul. "Researches in the Kjökkenmöddings of the Coast of Oregon, and of the Santa Barbara Islands and Adjacent Mainland."
1888	N42	Nos. 1-25.
-92		Davidson, George. "The Islands of the Santa Barbara Channel." (3rd edition)

U. S. GEOGRAPHICAL SURVEY WEST OF 100TH MERIDIAN
Published by Authority of War Department
George M. Wheeler, 1st Lieut. of Engineers

| 1879 | N45 | Vol. VII, Pt. 1, 1-314. |
| | | Putnam, F. W. "The Southern Californians." |

Appendix. "Translation from the Spanish of the Account by the Pilot Ferrel of the Voyage of Cabrillo along the West Coast of North America in 1542."

Appendix #H5 of Appendix JJ, 202-213.
Rothrock, J. T.

Appendix #H6 of Appendix JJ, 214-222.
Loew, Oscar.

Appendix #H8 of Appendix JJ, 224-278.
H. W. Henshaw.

Appendix #H12 of Appendix JJ, 306-307.
H. W. Henshaw.

Appendix #H13 of Appendix JJ, 312-321.
H. C. Yarrow.

Appendix #H16 of Appendix JJ, 330-343.
A. S. Gatschet.

DEPARTMENT OF THE NAVY
Geological Survey *Circulars*

1956	N46	Open-file

Vedder, J. G., *et al.* "Preliminary Report on the Geology of San Nicolas Island, California."

Geological Survey *Bulletins*

1958	N47	#1071-B, 55-68.

Olmsted, F. H. "Geologic Reconnaissance of San Clemente Island, California."

Geological Survey *Professional Papers*

1963	N48	Paper #369.

Vedder, J. G. and Robert M. Norris. "Geology of San Nicolas Island, California."

Water-Supply Papers

1963	N49	Paper #1539-0, 1-43.

Burnham, W. L., *et al.* "Hydrogeologic Reconnaissance of San Nicolas Island, California."

U. S. Naval Institute
Annapolis
Proceedings
Menasha, Wisconsin

1942	N50	Vol. 68, Pt. II, 1417-1426.

Flynn, S. E., Lieut. Commander. "The History of San Clemente Island."

1944	N51	Vol. 70, #3, 257-267.

Wheeler, Stanley A. "California's Little Known Channel Islands."

NATIONAL PARKS MAGAZINE
National Parks Association

1969	N52	Vol. 43, April, 4-7.

Lambert, Darwin. "Escape to the Channel Islands."

NATIONAL WILD LIFE
National Wildlife Federation

1973	N53	Vol. 11, Aug., 40-47.

Scott, Vance H. "Twentieth Century 'progress' threatens to disenchant California's idyllic Channel Islands."

STATE OF CALIFORNIA RECORDS

DEPARTMENT OF FISH AND GAME

Bulletins

1913   C1   Bulletin #1, 5-15.
Edwards, C. L. "The Abalone Industry in California."

1928   C2   Bulletin #14, 7-61.
Bonnot, Paul. "Report on the Seals and Sea Lions of California."

1962   C3   Bulletin #118.
Cox, Keith W. "California Abalones, Family Haliotidae."

Quarterlies

1914   C4   Vol. I, #1, 9-19.
Holder, Charles F. "Attempts to Protect the Sea Fisheries of Southern California."

       C5   Vol. II, #1, 14-19.
French, Dwight G. "Fishing at Santa Catalina Island—Its Development and Methods."

       C6   Vol. II, #1, 29-30.
Newkirk, Garrett. "Dr. Charles Frederick Holder."

       C7   Vol. II, #1, 182-185.
Oliver, J. H. "Abalone Pearl Formation."

1918   C8   Vol. IV, #1, 1-15.
Starks, E. C. "The Skates and Rays of California with an account of the Rat Fish."

       C9   Vol. IV, #3, 105-107.
Crandall, W. C. "A Review of the Kelp Industry."

       C10   Vol. IV, #4, 182-183.
Thompson, W. F. "Rare Fish appear off Southern California."

1920   C11   Vol. VI, #1, 32-33.
Thompson, W. F. "Notes from the State Fisheries Laboratory."

1951   C12   Vol. XXXVII, #1, 65-68.
Bartholomew, George A. and Robert D. Collyer. "The Sea Lion Population of Santa Barbara Island, California, in the 1950 Breeding Season."

DEPARTMENT OF NATURAL RESOURCES

California Division of Mines

1865   C13   Vol. I, Chapter VI, Section 5, 182-186.
Whitney, J. D. *Second California Geological Survey.* "Report of Progress and Synopsis of the Field-work, from 1860-1864 of the Islands off the Coast of Southern California."

1904   C14   *Bibliography relating to the Geology, Paleontology, and Mineral Resources of California.*

Bulletins

1943   C15   Bulletin #118, 74.
Heizer, Robert F. "Aboriginal Use of Bitumen by the California Indians."

1954   C16   Bulletin #170.
Johns, R. E., editor. *Geology of Southern California.*
     Emery, K. O. "General Geology of the Offshore Area, southern California," Pt. 7, Chapter II, 107-111.
     Putnam, W. C. "Marine Terraces of the Ventura Region and the Santa Monica Mountains, California," Pt. 7, Chapter V, 45-48.
     Corey, William H. "Tertiary Basins of Southern California." Chapter III, #8, 73-83.

California Division of Mines and Geology
State Mining Bureau;
Annual Reports

1890	C17	Vol. IX, 57-61.
		Bowers, Dr. Stephen. "San Nicolas Island."
	C18	Vol. IX, 155-170.
		Goodyear, W. A. "Santa Cruz Island."
	C19	Vol. IX, 171-174.
		Yates, Dr. Lorenzo G. "Stray Notes on the Geology of the Channel Islands of California."
	C20	Vol. IX, 175-178.
		Yates, Dr. Lorenzo G. "The Mollusca of the Channel Islands of California."
	C21	Vol. IX, 179-188.
		Yates, Dr. Lorenzo G. "Insular Flora."
1891	C22	Vol. X, 277-298.
		Preston, E. B. "Santa Catalina Island, Los Angeles County."
1893	C23	Vol. XI, 3-7.
		Yale, Charles G., editor. "Editor's Report to the Board of Examiners."
1893 -94	C24	Vol. XII.
		Crawford, J. J. "Mines and Mining Products of California."
1915 -16	C25	Vol. XV, 465-514.
		Hamilton, F. "Mines and Mineral Resources of Portions of California."
1927	C26	Vol. XIII, 32-39.
		Tucker, W. Burling. "Mineral Resources of Santa Catalina Island."
1931	C27	Vol. XXVII, #2, 214-219.
		Rand, W. W. "Preliminary Report of the Geology of Santa Cruz Island, Santa Barbara County, California."

California Journal of Mines and Geology

1944	C28	Vol. XL, 291-360.
		Heizer, Robert F. and Adan E. Treganza. "Mines and Quarries of the Indians of California."
1954	C29	Vol. L, #3 & #4, 467-709.
		Gay, Thomas E., Jr. and Samuel R. Hoffman. "Mines and Mineral Deposits of Los Angeles County, California."

Mineral Information Service

1967	C30	Vol. 20, #12, 151-158.
		Johnson, Donald Lee. "Caliche on the Channel Islands."

ARCHIVES
State Land Office

(1850)	C31	Vol. XIX, 41ff.
		Records of Encience.

Los Angeles County Recorder

(1903)	C32	*Miscellaneous Records.* Map showing Small Hill Mining Claim.
(1880)	C33	U. S. Survey Assessment Map showing Santa Catalina Island subdivided.
	C34	*Miscellaneous Records.* Books 1, 2, 3.
	C35	*Book of Patents.* Book 1.
	C36	*Books of Deeds.* Book 1, 6, 7, 8, 9, 279, 561, 769, 819.

315

Los Angeles County Engineer

C37   *Miscellaneous Records.* Book 34, 67-72.

Los Angeles County Clerk

C38   Files #48, #1826, #30501, and #176694.

Santa Barbara County

C39   *Miscellaneous Maps.* Book 3, 25.

C40   *Surveyors Office.* Book 17, 178-181.

C41   *Notices of Action.* Book F, 56.

Santa Barbara County Recorder
Patents and Deeds

C42   Book A   Pages 34-44; 202-204.

       Book B   Pages 527-528.

       Book C   Pages 288-289.

       Book D   Pages 581-584.

       Book F   Pages 355-356; 357-359; 724; 792-800.

       Book G   Pages 670;710.

       Book H   Pages 137-138; 300-301; 684.

       Book I   Pages 61; 87; 156.

       Book J   Pages 31; 416; 630-631; 642-643; 681-683; 802-803.

       Book K   Pages 234-236; 240-241.

       Book Y   Pages 134-135; 170-179.

       Book 17   Pages 177-181.

       Book 75   Pages 33-43.

       Book 77   Pages 345-357; 508.

       Book 81   Page 376.

       Book 210 Pages 311-312.

       Book 396 Page 36.

       Book 687 Page 131.

Lease Book

       Book L   Page 253.

Ventura County
Lease Books

C43   Book 5   Pages 278-379.

       Book 6   Pages 179-180.

UNIVERSITIES

UNIVERSITY OF CALIFORNIA
Berkeley

AMERICAN ARCHAEOLOGY AND ETHNOLOGY

1930   U1   Vol. 28, 1-21.
-31   Olson, R. L. "Chumash Prehistory."

ANTHROPOLOGICAL RECORDS

1940   U2   Vol. 3, #2, 153-237.
             Gifford, E. W. "Californian Bone Artifacts."

1950   U3   Vol. 9, #4, 303.
             Bennyhoff, J. A. "Californian Fish Spears and Harpoons."

1952   U4   Vol. 15, #1, 1-84.

Pinart, Alphonse. "California Indian Linguistic Records." Robert F. Heizer, editor.

1956   U5   Vol. 17, #2, 201-280.
Jones, Philip Mills. "Archaeological Investigations on Santa Rosa Island in 1901." Robert F. Heizer and A. B. Elsasser, editors.

REPORTS OF THE ARCHAEOLOGICAL SURVEY
Department of Anthropology

1951   U6   Report #12, Paper #13, 13.
de Céssac, Leon. "Observations on Sculptured Stone Fetishes in Animal Form Discovered on San Nicolas Island."

        U7   Report #12, Paper #14, 6-13.
Hamy, E. T. "The Pinart-de Céssac Expedition."

1957   U8   Report #15, Paper #17, 1-12.
Heizer, R. F. "A Survey of Cave Archaeology in California."

        U9   Report #38, Paper #53, 10.
Heizer, R. F. "A Steatite Whale Figurine from San Nicolas Island."

1960   U10   Report #50, Paper #76, 1.
Heizer, R. F. "A San Nicolas Island Twined Basketry Water Bottle."

       U11   Report #50, Paper #77, 4.
Heizer, R. F. "Some Prehistoric Wooden Objects from San Nicolas Island."

       U12   Report #50, Paper #83, 24.
Schumacher, Paul. "The Manufacture of Shell Fish-Hooks by the Early Inhabitants of the Santa Barbara Channel Islands."

1961   U13   Report #55, 121-181.
Heizer, Robert F. and Albert B. Elsasser. "Original Accounts of the Lone Woman of San Nicolas Island."

1963   U14   Report #59, 1-60.
Elsasser, Albert B. and Robert F. Heizer. "The Archaeology of Bowers' Cave."

       U15   Report #59, Paper #2, 61-64.
Hamy, E. "The Fishhook Industry of the Ancient Inhabitants of the Archipelago of California."

       U16   Report #59, 73-74.
Bowers, Stephen. "Aboriginal Fish-Hooks."

       U17   Report #59, 77-79.
Schumacher, Paul. "The Method of Manufacture of Several Articles by the Former Indians of Southern California."

1964   U18   Report #61, 1-24.
Reichlen, Henry and Robert F. Heizer. "The Scientific Expedition of Leon de Céssac to California, 1877-1879."

       U19   Report #61, 25-74.
Anderson, E. N., Jr., compiler. "A Bibliography of the Chumash and Their Predecessors."

1967   U20   Report #69, 1-100.
Brown, Alan E. "The Aboriginal Population of the Santa Barbara Channel."

Lowie Museum of Anthropology

1972   U21   Heizer, Robert F. "California's Oldest Historical Relic?" (pamphlet)

CALIFORNIA MONTHLY

1927   U22   Vol. 21, #3, 166+.
Olson, Ronald. "On the Island of the Dead."

ERYTHEA
A Journal of Botany, West American and General
Department of Botany

1894   U23   Vol. II, #1, 1-2 (I).
Davidson, Anstruther. "California Field Notes."

         U24   Vol. II, #2, 27-30 (II).
Davidson, Anstruther. "California Field Notes."

         U25   Vol. II, #5, 76-80 (I).
McClatchie, Alfred James. "Additions to the Flora of Los Angeles County and Catalina Island."

         U26   Vol. II, #7, 122-125 (II).
McClatchie, Alfred James. "Additions to the Flora of Los Angeles County and Catalina Island."

1897   U27   Vol. V, #2, 30.
Trask, Mrs. Blanche. "San Clemente Island."

1899   U28   Vol. VII, Nov., 135-146.
Trask, Mrs. Blanche. "Field Notes from Santa Catalina Island."

MADROÑO
A West American Journal of Botany
California Botanical Society
Department of Botany

1972   U29   Vol. 21, #5, Pt. 2, 329-353.
Philbrick, Ralph N. "The Plants of Santa Barbara Island, California."

HILGARDIA
Division of Agricultural Sciences

1967   U30   Vol. 38, #16, 579-606.
Goeden, Richard D., Charles A. Fleschner and Donald W. Ricker. "Biological Control of Prickly Pear Cacti on Santa Cruz Island, California."

Department of Geology

1893   U31   Vol. I, #4, 115-160.
Lawson, A. C., editor. "The Post-Pliocene Diastrophism of the Coast of Southern California."

1900   U32   Vol. II, #7, 179-230.
Smith, W. S. Tangier. "A Topographic Study of the Islands of Southern California."

1924   U33   Vol. XV, #3, 49-68.
-26   Woodford, Alfred O. "The Catalina Metamorphic Facies of the Franciscan Series."

Academy of Pacific Coast History

1911   U34   Vol. II, #1, 5-119.
Rose, Robert Selden, editor. "The Portolá Expedition of 1769-1770, Diary of Vicente Villa."

         U35   Vol. II, #4, 164-327.
Teggart, Frederick J. "Diary of Miguel Costansó."

SIXTH PACIFIC SCIENCE CONGRESS *PROCEEDINGS*

1940   U36   Vol. III, 501-504.
Cockerell, T. D. A. "The Marine Invertebrate Fauna of the California Islands."

Publications in Zoology

1933   U37   Vol. 40, 71-234.
Grinnell, Joseph. *Review of the Recent Mammal Fauna of California.*

BIBLIOGRAPHY

REPORTS OF THE ARCHAEOLOGICAL SURVEY, U.C.L.A.
Department of Anthropology and Sociology

1958   U38   McKusick, M. B. and F. J. Clune, Jr. "Archaeological Reconnaissance on Anacapa Island, California." (pamphlet)

      U39   Swartz, B. K. and C. J. Sutton, III. "Archaeological Reconnaissance on Santa Barbara Island." (pamphlet)

1959   U41   107-183.
McKusick, M. B. and C. N. Warren. "Introduction to San Clemente Island Archaeology."

1960   U42   1-134.
Reinman, Fred M. and S. J. Townsend. "Six Burial Sites on San Nicolas Island, California."

1962   U43   11-22.
Reinman, Fred M. "New Sites on San Nicolas Island, California."

1964   U44   47-80.
Reinman, Fred M. "Maritime Adaptation on San Nicolas Island, California."

ANNUAL REPORTS

1959   U40   71-104.
McKusick, M. B. "Introduction to Anacapa Island Archaeology.

      U45   Meighan, Clement W. "Activities of the Archaeological Survey, Los Angeles, 1958-1959."

UNIVERSITY OF SOUTHERN CALIFORNIA
Allan Hancock Foundations

1949   U46   Vol. VIII, 1-56.
Dawson, E. Y. "Contributions toward a Marine Flora of the Channel Islands."

INSTITUTE OF OCEANOGRAPHY
La Jolla

1951   U47   Vol. 6, #1, 1-26.
Arthur, Robert S. "The Effect of Islands on Surface Waves."

INSTITUTE OF ARIZONA
THE KIVA
A Journal of the Archaeological and Historical Society

1960   U48   Vol. 26, #1, 7-9.
Swartz, B. K., Jr. "Evidence for the Indian Occupation of Santa Barbara Island."

UNIVERSITY OF CHICAGO
JOURNAL OF GEOLOGY

1944   U49   Vol. 52, #5, 351-354.
Clemente, Thomas and Stephen W. Dana. "Geologic Significance of a Coarse Marine Sediment from near Santa Catalina Island, California."

BOTANICAL GAZETTE

1903   U50   Vol. XXXVI, July-Dec., 259-279.
Parish, S. B. "A Sketch of the Flora of Southern California."

UNIVERSITY OF MINNESOTA
AMERICAN GEOLOGIST

1888   U51   Vol. I, Jan.-June, 76-81.
Le Conte, Joseph. "The Flora of the Coast Islands of California in relation to Recent Changes of Physical Geography."

1890 U52   Vol. XIV, Jan.-June, 43-52.
Yates, L. G. "Notes on the Geology and Scenery of the Islands forming the Southern Line of the Santa Barbara Channel."

1897 U53   Vol. XX, July-Dec., 213-245.
Fairbanks, Harold W. "Oscillations of the Coast of California during the Pliocene and Pleistocene."

UNIVERSITY OF NEW MEXICO
SOUTHWESTERN JOURNAL OF ANTHROPOLOGY

1952 U54   Vol. VIII, #2, 211-225.
Orr, Phil C. "Review of Santa Barbara Channel Archeology."

1955 U55   Vol. XI, #2, 214-230.
Wallace, William J. "A Suggested Chronology for Southern California Coastal Archaeology."

1960 U56   Vol. XVI, #2, 160-173.
Sellards, E. H. "Some Early Stone Artifact Developments in North America."

STANFORD UNIVERSITY
STANFORD GROTTO MONTHLY REPORT
School of Mineral Sciences

1950 U57   Vol. I, #2, #3, #4, #5, #7, #9, #10, #12.
Danehy, Edward. "Bibliography of California Speleology." (5) Vol. II, #1, #3, #5, #10— bibliographical additions.

1965 U58   Vol. I, #10, 1-2.
"J. W. Sefton Foundation Channel Islands Sea Cave Expedition."

     U59   Vol. I, #10, 2-3.
Finley, Richard S. "Notes on the Orizaba Pictograph (Olson's) Cave, Santa Cruz Island, Santa Barbara County, California."

UNIVERSITY OF UTAH
ANTHROPOLOGICAL PAPERS

1956 U60   Paper #26, 74-81.
Orr, Phil C. "Dwarf Mammoths and Man on Santa Rosa Island."

MISCELLANEA

EPHEMERA
Atchison, Topeka, and Santa Fe Railroad

1893 M1   Higgins, C. A. *To California and Back.*

1895 M2   "Summer in Southern California."

Burlington Route Railroad

1905 M3   Steele, James W. "California, brief Glimpses of her Valleys, Mountains, Lakes and Famous Places."

1908 M4   Bolser, M. O. "Submarine Gardens, Catalina Island."

Southern Pacific Railroad

1883 M5   Nordhoff, Charles. "A Guide to California, The Golden State."

1896 M6   "California Game 'Marked Down'."

Rock Island Lines

1907 M7   Sebastian, John. "California, the Golden State."

1893 M8   Hollenbecks. "Vistas in Southern California." San Francisco: A. C. Bilicke & Co.

1902   M9   Knights of Pythias. "Santa Catalina Island."

1904   M10   Martin, R. C. *Souvenir, Los Angeles.* Locomotive Engineers. Los Angeles: Kingsley, Moles, and Collins Co.

1906   M11   Pierce, Norman. "Southern California, The Hotels and Resorts." Los Angeles.

MANUSCRIPTS

1861   M12   Hollister, Col. W. W. Letter to A. Dibblee, Esq.

1869   M13   Thompson, Albert F. Letter to John F. Dana, Esq.

1877   M14   Bowers, Stephen. Report on Aboriginal Man in Santa Barbara County, California. Sent to F. V. Hayden, U. S. Geologist.

1878   M15   Murray, E. F. "The Indian Woman of San Nicolas Island."

1895   M16   Bowers, Stephen. "The Recent Origin of Man."

1896   M17   Sheridan, Edwin M. Information from *The Evening Post* of San Francisco. Donated by Ventura County Free Library, 1925.

1897   M18   Bowers, Stephen. "The Santa Barbara Indians."

1897   M19   Kelley, John L. "Description of a Trip to San Nicolas Island in the Year 1897."

1901   M20   Jones, Philip Mills. Letter to Charles Lummis concerning San Nicolas Island.

1902   M21   Bowers, Stephen. "The Geology of California."

1915   M22   Bowers, Stephen. "Concerning George Nidever's son on Santa Cruz Island."

1916   M23   Bowers, DeMoss. Letter to Dr. Alliot.

1941   M24   Bailey, E. H. "Mineralogy, Petrology, and Geology of Santa Catalina Island." Stanford University, Doctoral dissertation.

PAMPHLETS AND BOOKLETS

1866   M26   Lovett, W. E. To Austin Wiley, Superintendent of Indian Affairs in California.

1892   M27   Bowers, Stephen. "The Lone Woman of San Nicolas Island."

1897   M28   Rust, Horatio N. "Catalogue of Pre-historic Relics from San Nicolas Island."

1903   M29   Newman. Tract Directory of Los Angeles County.

1904   M30   Eisen, Gustav. "An Account of the Indians of the Santa Barbara Islands in California."

1905   M31   Reider, M. "Santa Catalina Island." Los Angeles.

1905   M32   Williams, Iza. "Santa Catalina Island."

1914   M33   Benton. "Semi-Tropic California, The Garden of the World." Los Angeles.

1914   M34   Holder, Charles F. *Angling and Netting: the Conservation of Marine Fishes of Southern California.*

1915   M35   Pacific Novelty Co. "The Land of Living Color." (from *Sunset*)

1919   M36   Grey, Zane. "Great Game Fishing at Catalina." (from *Tale of Fishes*)

1924   M37   Dashiell, N. E. *Catalina.* Washington.

1926   M38   Stuart, J. N. *Catalina's Yesterdays.* Los Angeles: Mayers Co.

1926   M39   "A Cruise among the Channel Islands."

1927   M40   Rider, Arthur Fremont. *Rider's California, A Guide-book for Travelers.* New York: The Macmillan Co.

1939   M41   Bandini, Ralph. "Veiled Horizons, Stories of Big Game Fish of the Sea." New York: The Derrydale Press, Inc.

1940   M42   National Park Service. "Report on the California Channel Islands."

1941   M43   Robinson, W. W. *The Island of Santa Catalina.* Los Angeles: Title Guarantee and Trust Co.

1956   M44   Hillinger, Charles. "Channel Islands, California." *Los Angeles Times.*

1958	M45		Hillinger, Charles. *The California Islands*. Hawthorne, Ca: Academy Press.
1958	M46		Overholt, Alma. *The Catalina Story*. Philip K. Wrigley Fund.
1962	M47		Hall, Thorne. "Odyssey of The California Kingdoms." Santa Barbara: Pacific Coast Odyssey Pub. Co.
1965	M48		Coulter, Harry. "Catalina, The Beguiling Isle." Southern California Automobile Club *News*.
1970	M49		Dutton, Davis. "A California Portfolio, The Golden State in Words and Pictures." *Westways*.
1970	M50		National Park Service. *Channel Islands National Monument, California*.

NEWSPAPERS

CALIFORNIA FARMER AND JOURNAL OF USEFUL SCIENCES

| 1860 -63 | M51 | | Taylor, Alexander S. "The Indianology of California." |

DAILY ALTA CALIFORNIA
San Francisco

1853	M52	June 13	"Santa Catalina and Its Goats."
	M53	June 16	"Shoal off San Clemente and San Nicolas."
	M54	July 15	"The Goat Trade."
1857	M55	Apr. 27	(about Santa Cruz Island)
	M56	Nov. 13	(about Santa Cruz Island; San Nicolas Island)
1864	M57	June 12	"Letter from Santa Catalina."
	M58	Sept. 25	"Letter from Santa Catalina."
1895	M59	Oct. 11	"First Cargo of Guano."

SAN FRANCISCO CHRONICLE

1898	M60	May 29	"Strategic Value of the Channel Islands."
1902	M61	Nov. 13	"Marooned Men likely to Starve."
	M62	Nov. 17	"Marooned Fishermen Rescued."
	M63	Dec. 20	"Hail, Thunder and Lightning at Catalina."
1904	M64	Nov. 2	"Clubhouse at Catalina Island."
	M65	Dec. 12	"Will Organize Exclusive Club."
1942	M66	Sept. 20	(about proposed change of name to the Cabrillo Isles)
1965	M67	July 28	(about descendents of Justinian Caire)
1966	M68	Aug. 22	"A Victory for the Sea Lions."

SAN FRANCISCO DAILY EVENING BULLETIN

| 1856 | M69 | Nov. 25 | "A California Crusoe." |
| | M70 | Dec. 27 | "Further Particulars of the California Crusoe." |

EVENING POST
San Francisco

| 1896 | M71 | July 27 | "The Lost Woman of San Nicolas." |

MORNING CALL
San Francisco

| 1883 | M72 | Nov. 19 | "An Extensive Sheep Range on Santa Rosa Island." |

SAN FRANCISCO CALL

| 1898 | M72a | Oct. 11 | "First Cargo of Guano" |

OAKLAND TRIBUNE

| 1965 | M73 | Apr. 4 | "Channel Islands up for Park Survey." |

SACRAMENTO DAILY RECORD-UNION

1889	M74	Apr. 16	"Catalina Island."
1892	M75	Jan. 20	"The Catalina Island."
1893	M76	Nov. 29	"Pacific Coast Items."
1895	M77	Mar. 18	"Queer Phenomena in the Ocean."
	M78	July 15	"Condensed Coast News."
1903	M79	Feb. 3	"Catalina Landing."
1956	M80	Apr. 1	"Ancient Man: Old Theories on Arrival in America Shattered."

SACRAMENTO DAILY UNION

1856	M81	Dec. 29	"Further Particulars of the California Crusoe."
1860	M82	June 2	(about Andres Castillero)
1870	M83	Jan. 1	(about Santa Cruz Island Incorporation)

PIONEER
San Jose

| 1879 | M84 | Feb. 15 | "Left Alone on a Desert Island for Eighteen Years; California's Feminine Crusoe." |

SAN LUIS OBISPO COUNTY TELEGRAM-TRIBUNE

| 1962 | M85 | Jan. 4 | "A Human Skeleton discovered on the Santa Barbara Channel Islands was 10,000 years old, according to carbon dating tests revealed." |

SANTA BARBARA PRESS

| 1889 | M85a | Aug. 17 | A rewrite of "A Party of Scientists." |

SANTA BARBARA DAILY INDEPENDENT

| 1889 | M86 | Aug. 16 | "A Party of Scientists at Sea." |
| | M87 | Oct. 10 | "Preliminary Notes on the Anacapas." |

SANTA BARBARA WEEKLY INDEPENDENT

| 1895 | M88 | June 15 | (about A. P. More) |
| | M89 | Sept. 5 | "Innumerable Caves." |

SANTA BARBARA NEWS PRESS

1927	M90	Apr. 30	"Seawood Hut is preserved for Centuries."
1939	M91	Jan.	"Scheme to 'Jail' Apaches on Channel Isle Recalled."
1942	M92	June 22	"Lester 'King' of San Miguel Island, found Shot to Death."
1944	M93	Feb. 20	"Woman of San Nicolas not Myth."
1945	M94	Apr. 15	"New Material on Nicoleños."

VENTURA WEEKLY OBSERVER

| 1892 | M95 | Dec. 20 | "Lone Woman of San Nicolas Island." |

LOS ANGELES STAR

| 1856 | M96 | Dec. 13 | "Interesting Narrative." |

LOS ANGELES DAILY NEWS

| 1870 | M97 | | "Boundaries of the School Districts of Los Angeles County" |
| 1954 | M98 | Apr. 2 | "Collector irked by ban on digging Indian Relics." |

LOS ANGELES EVENING HERALD AND EXPRESS

| 1940 | M99 | Dec. 13 | "Find Big Cache of Ancient Curios." |

LOS ANGELES EXAMINER

| 1951 | M100 | Aug. 26 | "150 Caves mapped on Anacapa." |

LOS ANGELES HERALD-EXAMINER

1962	M101	Dec. 4	"Fatal Sea Descent."
	M102	Dec. 6	"Skindiver Death Puzzles."
	M103	Dec. 9	"Experts to Seek Fatal Dive Cause."
	M104	Dec. 19	"Films of Divers' Death Plunge Viewed Here."
	M105	Dec. 30	"Probe Clears Scientist in Diver Deaths."
1963	M106	Feb. 12	"Diving Bell Victim's Widow Found Dead."
	M107	Mar. 16	"New Catalina Radar to Aid Weatherman."
1965	M108	July 18	"Catalina Drinks from the Sea Now."
	M109	Oct. 14	"Island Causeways Seen."
1966	M110	Jan. 17	"Catalina Beaches Mop Up."
	M111	Mar. 7	"7 Killed as Planes Crash on Fog-Shrouded Island."
	M112	Aug. 7	"Our Channel Islands—an Adventure right off our Coastline."
1967	M113	June 7	"Ocean Bottom Map Completed."
	M114	Dec. 7	"Tidelands Riches Fight in Court."
1971	M115	May 18	"Opening San Clemente Island to Public Urged."
	M116	Sept. 21	"New Channel Drilling Ban."
	M117	Oct. 5	"Torrey Pines now Face Trampling."
1973	M118	Oct. 9	"USC Gets Marine Study Aid."
	M119	Oct. 9	"Deaths of Sea Lions Tied to Pesticides."
1975	M120	Feb. 24	"Catalina Territory Donated."

LOS ANGELES TIMES

1898	M121	Oct. 23	"The Interior of Catalina."
1899	M122	Jan. 8	"The Lone Woman of San Nicolas."
1901	M123	Aug. 4	"Twenty Years Alone."
1904	M124	July 24	"California's Islands."
	M125	July 31	"Shells upon the Shore."
	M126	Sept. 4	"The Channel Islands."
1906	M127	Jan. 21	"San Miguel Island."
	M128	May 13	"The Great Depression."
	M129	June 17	"Indian Workshop."
	M130	July 22	"Old Days at Catalina."
	M131	Oct. 14	"Invasion of Catalina."
	M132	Oct. 14	"Marine Curiosities."
	M133	Oct. 21	"Our Island Fauna." (snakes)
	M134	Nov. 11	"Land Animals Inhabiting the Channel Islands."

	M135	Dec. 2	"Our Island Fauna." (goats)
1909	M136	Aug. 15	"Cruising in a Sailboat."
1914	M137	Feb. 14	"The Story of Santa Catalina."
1916	M138	Jan. 30	"New Evidences of Early Race."
1918	M139	May 12	"Early Days in California."
1930	M140		"Desert Island Holds Repute."
1932	M141	Dec. 11	"The Saddest Little Island on California Coast."
1936	M142	Aug. 9	"Mrs. Robinson Crusoe."
1937	M143	Dec. 5	"San Miguel Island."
1939	M144	April 2	"Explorers leave for Isle's Study."
1941	M145	Jan. 21	"Lee Side o' L.A."
1946	M146	July 29	"Islands sought by Mexico rich in Historic Interest."
1949	M147	April 25	"Sea Lion Herds Bask on Island."
1951	M148	July 9	"Indians once lived on Channel Islands."
	M149	Dec. 24	"New Discoveries found on Santa Rosa Island."
1953	M150	Aug. 10	"Thriving Indian Colony seen in Indian Relics."
1954	M151	July 5	"Island Pot-Hunters."
	M152	Sept. 21	"Artist Whistler Etching part of 1854 Island Paper."
1955	M153	Jan. 9	"Beginning of Cities."
1956	M154	Mar. 11-19	"Channel Islands, California."
1957	M155	Dec. 15	"Indian Origin Clues found in Twining."
1961	M156	May 8	"Indian Culture found on San Nicolas Island."
1963	M157	Mar. 20	"Prehistoric Waterworks found on Offshore Isle."
1964	M158	Jan. 13	"Ancient Southlanders used Catalina Wares."
	M159	June 1	"Avalon, Judge work together 57 Years."
	M160	July 13	"Grant Aids Survey of Island's Archeology."
1965	M161	Feb. 7	"Santa Catalina: Major Transformation Due."
	M162	Mar. 21	"Conversion Plant Assures Santa Catalina of Water."
	M163	Mar. 22	"Santa Catalina Water Supply Assured."
1966	M164	Jan. 7	"Channel Islands Park Plan to go to Congress."
	M165	Jan. 14	"Santa Cruz Island Resort Supported."
	M166	Jan. 14	"Catalina Face-lifting to Raze Old Landmarks."
	M167	Apr. 4	"Santa Cruz Island Hunters' Paradise."
1967	M168	Apr. 9	"Happy Hunting Ground."
	M169	June 25	"New Catalina Era."
1968	M170	Dec. 13	"Judge Windle, Sage of Avalon, Succumbs."
1969	M171	Aug. 3	"The Channel Islands."
1970	M172	Dec. 20	"Channel Isle Key to Early Tribe."
1971	M173	May 23	"A National Park? Channel Islands: Step into History."
	M174	Sept. 7	"San Clemente Island: Navy Preserve or Public Domain?"
	M175	Sept. 7	"Battle Lines forming over use of Island."
	M176	Sept. 26	"Avalon's Problem: How to end its Stagnation."
1972	M177	Mar. 12	"Los Angeles once was Cool, Wet, Tar Pit Fossil Wood Shows."
	M178	Apr. 18	"Catalina for Credit."

PIECES OF EIGHT

	M179	Aug. 31	"Santa Catalina—Up Tight Island over 'Invasion'."
	M180	Dec. 21	"Gravestone believed to be Cabrillo's Displayed at UC."
1973	M181	Apr. 13	"Coastal Area—'Off Limits' to Marine Activities."
1974	M182	Feb. 1	"Plan to Boost Public Use of Catalina OK'd."

SANTA CATALINA ISLAND PUBLICATIONS

1888	M183	*CATALINA JEWFISH*
1893	M184	*AVALON CRUSOE*
(1903)	M185	*CATALINA WIRELESS*
1908	M185a	*CATALINA DAILY MIRROR*
(1913)	M186	*THE ISLANDER*
(1914)	M187	*CATALINA ISLANDER* [Sea Serpent Story] 1918

LONG BEACH PRESS-TELEGRAM

| 1957 | M188 | Dec. 27 | "Bones, 30,000 years old, found on Island." |

SAN DIEGO UNION

| 1957 | M189 | Dec. 26 | "Isle Yields Bones 29,000 Years Old." |

NEW YORK TIMES

| 1953 | M190 | Aug. 7 | "Indian Village Sites found on Pacific Isle." |
| 1958 | M191 | Jan. 3 | "Santa Rosa Isle Yields Rich Find." |

NEW YORK HERALD-TRIBUNE

| 1963 | M192 | June 23 | "Mexico's Old Soldiers Lay Claim to California Isles." |

Author Index

Ainsworth, Ed. P169, 1967

Allanson, Al. J80, 1955

Alliot, S. D. Hector. J341, 1961; J342, 1917; J208, 1969

Anderson, E. N., Jr. U19, 1964

Anderson, Robert E., Lowell Redwine and Paul McGovney. J24, 1949

Anthony, A. W. J62, 1889; J36, 1895

Arthur, Robert S. U47, 1951

Ashkenazy, Irvin. P172, 1968; P173, 1969; P174, 1971

Austin, Dr. Perry G. M. J293, 1959

Bache, Sup't A. D. N25, 1853; N32, 1864

Barbour, Lewis. P153, 1939

Barr, James A. J159, 1907

Bartholomew, George A., Jr. J183, 1950; J184, 1951; C12, 1951

Bailey, E. H. M24, 1941

Bailey, Gilbert Ellis. B80, 1924

Bancroft, H. H. B1, 1885

Bandini, Ralph. M41, 1939

Baker, C. F. J337, 1905

Baker, Charles C. J363, 1912-14

Barrows, H. D. J353, 1900

Beck, R. H. J100, 1899; J103, 1899

Bennyhoff, J. A. U3, 1950

Benton. M33, 1914

Bingham, Mrs. R. F. J260, 1887

Blaisdell, Frank E., Sr. J247, 1938

Blake, Eli Whitney, Jr. J35, 1887

Blake, Wm. P. N26, 1854-55

Bobe, Rev. J176, 1859

Bolton, Herbert Eugene. B2, 1916; B3, 1932; B55 (ed.), 1926; B13, 1927

Bonilla, Isaac Antonio. J294, 1959

Bonnot, Paul. C2, 1928

Bowers, Rev. Stephen. M14, 1877; N12, 1878; P113, 1885; J242, 1885; J261, 1887; C17, 1890; M27, 1892; M16, 1895

Bowers, DeMoss. M23, 1916

Bowman, J. N. J240, 1962

Bradley, William C. J170, 1956

Brandegee, T. S. J61, 1888; J393, 1890; J394, 1890; J395, 1890; J396, 1890

Breeden, Marshall. B81, 1928

Bremner, Carl St. J. J297, 1932; J298, 1933

Breninger, George F. J43, 1904

Britton, J. R. P47, 1897

Brown, Alan E. U20, 1967

Browne, J. Ross. B4, 1855; B5, 1855; P23, 1861; P80, 1874

Bryan, Bruce. J179, 1926; J32, 1930; J33, 1930; J221, 1935; P143, 1957; J203, 1962; J204, 1963; B6, 1970

Bryant, Walter E. J399, 1892

Burnham, W. L., et al. N49, 1963

Burney, James. B7, 1806

Burt, Homer C. J125, 1911

Camp, Charles L. J85, 1923; J389, 1963

Carlquist, Sherwin. B82, 1965

Cass, W. W. P170, 1968

Céssac, León de. U6, 1951

Challacombe, J. R. P168, 1966

Chaney, Ralph W. and Herbert L. Mason. N3, 1934

Chapman, C. E. B9, 1921

Cheetham, Francis T. J368, 1940

Childs, J. L. J385, 1906

Church, C. C. J244, 1929

Clark, B. L. and A. O. Woodford. J165, 1928

Clark, James G. P1, 1897

Clark, Robert. P157, 1944

Cleland, Robert Glass. B10, 1922; J371, 1953; B10a, 1963

Clements, Thomas and Stephen W. Dana. U49, 1944

Cleveland, J. P. B11, 1842

Clifford, Josephine. P104, 1921

Clokey, Ira W. J345, 1931

Cockerell, T. D. A. J329, 1902-03; J246, 1937; J382, 1937; J257, 1938; J248, 1938; J319, 1938; J54, 1939; J228, 1939; J320, 1939; J349, 1939; U36, 1940

Colton, F. Barrows. J217, 1945

Comstock, John A. J350, 1946

Cooper, J. G., M.D. J57, 1868; J59, 1868

Corey, William H. C16, 1954

Cornell, Ralph D. B83, 1938; J187, 1937

Coulter, Harry. M48, 1965

Covey, Sylvia Lawson. P91, 1896; P93, 1897

Cowan, Robert Ernest. J92, 1933

Cowan, Robert G. B12, 1956

Cox, Keith W. C3, 1962

Crandall, W. C. C9, 1918

Crawford, J. J. C24, 1893-94

Crespi, Fray Juan (H. E. Bolton). B13, (1769)

Cronise, Titus Fey. B14, 1868

Crouch, Charles Willard. P149, 1935

Crowe, William P. P181, 1965

Curtis, Freddie. J198, 1960; J206, 1964

Dakin, Susanna B. B58, 1939

Dall, Wm. H. J302, 1903; P79a, 1874

Dana, Richard Henry. B15, (1835)

Danehy, Edward. U57, 1950

Dashiell, N. E. M37, 1924

Davidson, Anstruther. U23-24, 1894; J325, 1896

Davidson, George. N26, 1854-55; N29, 1857-58; N31, 1861-62; J58, 1868-72; J60, 1873-74; N33, 1885-86; J70, 1887; J71, 1887; N42, 1888-92; N34, 1889; J65, 1898

Davis, William Heath (Andrew F. Rolle). B16, (1846)

Dawson, E. Y. U46, 1949

Dawson, N. B17, 1841

Dawson, William Leon. J132, 1915; B85, 1923

Dickey, Donald R. J52, 1929

Dickey, Donald R. and A. J. van Rossem. J134, 1923

Dillon, Richard H. B4, 1965

Doran, Adelaide. B84, 1963

Driscoll, N. W. P94, 1897

Drury, Aubrey. B86, 1935

Dugay, John. P180, 1963

Duhaut-Cilly (Charles Franklin Carter). J90, 1929

Dutton, Davis. M49, 1970

Eames, Ninetta. P85, 1890

Earle, Homer P. P44, 1896

Eastwood, Alice. J64, 1898; J74-75, 1941

Eberhart, Hal. J232, 1956

Edholm, Charlton Lawrence. P73, 1909; P101, 1913

Edwards, Charles Lincoln. P116, 1913; C1, 1913

Edwards, H. Arden. J231, 1956

Egan, Carrie W. P145, 1928

Eisen, Gustav. M30, 1904

Ellis, J. B. and B. M. Everhart. J339, 1905

Ellison, William Henry. J239, 1937; B51, 1937; B128, 1941

Elsasser, Albert B. and Robert F. Heizer. U14, 1963

Emery, K. O. C16, 1954; J173, 1958; B88, 1960

Emery, K. O. and Francis P. Shepard. B87, 1941; J168, 1945

Engelhardt, Zephyrin, Fr. B18, 1912

Evans, Richard S. P8-9, 1892; N45, 1879

Fages, Pedro (trans., H. I. Priestley). B19, 1937

Fairbanks, Harold W. U53, 1897

Fall, H. C. J98, 1897

Farnham, T. J. B20, 1850

Ferry, Philip. P159, 1947

Fewkes, J. W. J381, 1890; J21, 1890

Field, Benjamin Franklin. P96, 1901

Finck, H. T. P63, 1889

Finley, Richard S. U59, 1965

Fisher, Edna M. J181, 1930

Fleming, David P. P2, 1906

Flynn, S. E., Lieut. Commander. N50, 1942

Font, Pedro, Fr. (by H. E. Bolton). B21, 1933

Forbes, Alexander. B22, 1839

Foster, Stephen C. J354, 1900

Foster, Maximilian. P62, 1901

Frant-Walsh, Joseph. P16, 1930

French, Dwight G. C5, 1914

Galbraith, Edith C. J87, 1924

Gardner, Charles. P108-09, 1890

Garrison, Myrtle. B23, 1935

Gast, Ross H. B40a, 1976

Gatschet, A. S. N45, 1879

Gay, Thomas E., Jr. and Samuel R. Hoffman. C29, 1954

Geiger, Maynard, O.F.M. B24, 1965

Gherini, Mrs. Ambrose. J292, 1959

Gherini, Pier. J296, 1966

Gibbons, James M. P15, 1893

Gidney, C. M. B25, 1917

Gifford, E. W. U2, 1940; J7, 1941

Gilbert, Charles H. N24, 1898

Gleason, Joe Duncan. B89, 1950; B90, 1958

Gledhill. J290, 1958

Goeden, Richard D., Charles A. Fleschner and Donald W. Ricker. U30, 1967

Goodyear, W. C18, 1890

Gordon, P. Roualeyn. J99, 1921

Grant, Campbell. B26, 1965

Graves, J. A. B27, 1928

Greene, E. L. J258, 1886; J72, 1887; J259, 1887; J252, 1887-89

Greenhow, Robert. B28, 1844

Greenwell, W. E. N28, 1856-57

Grey, Zane. M36, 1919

Griesbach, John C. J254, 1947

Grinnell, Joseph. J237-38; 1897; J249, 1897; J37-40, 1897-98; J101, 1899; J107, 1902; J108, 1905; J44, 1906; J109, 1906; J112, 1908; J115, 1908; J119, 1909; B111, 1909; B113, 1915; J48, 1922; J138, 1927; J51, 1928; J53, 1930; U37, 1933; B116, 1944

Gudde, Erwin G. B29, 1960

Guest, Francis F., O.F.M. J380b, 1979

Guinn, J. M. P86, 1890; B30, 1902; J356, 1903-05; J358, 1906-08; J361, 1912-14

Gunn, Guard D. P125, 1947

Haig, John Angus. P64, 1938

Hall, Thorne. M47, 1962

Hamilton, F. C25, 1915-16

Hamy, E. T. U7, 1951; U15, 1963

Hanna, Phil Townsend. P147, 1932; P151, 1938

Hardacre, Emma C. P123, 1880

Harrington. M. R. J4, 1930

Hasse, Dr. H. E. J328, 1902-03; J340, 1906

Hasse, Leo G. B91, 1926

Hawley, Walter A. B31, 1910

Hay, Oliver P. N2, 1927

Heald, Weldon F. J222, 1956; J81, 1957

Heizer, Robert F. J189, 1941; J8, 1941; C15, 1943; C28, 1944; J9, 1949; U8-13, 1957-61; B33, 1963; U21, 1972; J210, 1973

Heizer, Robert F. and Alan F. Almquist. B34, 1971

Heizer, Robert F. and Harper Kelley. J26, 1962

Heizer, Robert F., Karen M. Nissen, and Edward D. Castillo. B91a, 1975

Heizer, Robert F. and M. A. Whipple. B32, 1951

Hemphill, Josephine. P131, 1928

Henry, Joseph. N10-11, 1875-77

Henshaw, H. W. J34, 1886; N45, 1879

Herr, Charlotte. B92, 1921

Hertlein, Lee George. J243, 1928

Hester, Joseph A., Jr. J230, 1956

Heye, George G. J17, 1921

Hillinger, Charles. M44-45, 1956-58; P166, 1963

Hittell, John S. P31, 1858; P7, 1881

Hittell, Theodore H. B35, 1898

Hodge, F. W. B36, 1905

Hoffmann, Ralph. J145, 1931; J346-47, 1932; J148, 1932

Holder, Charles F. P11-13, 1892-93; P40, 1894; P115, 1896; J309, 1897; J311, 1899; P52, 1899; N22-23, 1908; P59, 1901; P128, 1901; B33, 1901; J312, 1902; B93, 1902; J313-14, 1903-04; P17-18, 1905; J315-16, 1906; B94, 1906; P111, 1907; N21, 1908; B95, 1908; J215, 1909; J253, 1909; B96, 1909; B97, 1910; B38, 1910; B98, 1911; B99, 1912; B100, 1913; M34, 1914; C4, 1914; P121, 1916; B101, 1924

Holland, Francis R. J387-88, 1962-63

Hollister, Col. W. W. M12, 1861

Holmes, William Henry. N15, 1902

Hoover, M. B., H. E. and E. G. Rensch. B102, 1948

Hoover, Robert L. J211, 1973

Howard, O. W. J383-84, 1905-06

Howell, Alfred B. B114, 1917

Howell, Alfred B. and A. van Rossem. J126, 1911

Howell, John Thomas. J69, 1935

Hudson, Millard F. J359, 1906-08

Huey, Laurence M. J147, 1932

Hunt, Rockwell D. J362, 1912-14; J374, 1958

Hussey, John A. J390, 1961

Hutchings, J. M. P26, 1856; P30, 1857

Hutchings, J. M. (R. R. Olmsted, editor). P37, 1962

Hutter, Richard. P39, 1971

Hyatt, Robert. P158, 1946

Irwin, M. C. J284, 1945; J286, 1946; J287, 1947; J275, 1951

Israelsky, Merle C. J323, 1956

Jackson, Sheldon G. J377, 1973

Johnson, Kenneth M. J380a, 1975

Jones, Philip Mills. M20, 1901; J207, 1969

Jones, Philip Mills (Robert F. Heizer, editor). U5, 1956

Jones, William C. N18, 1851

Johnson, Donald Lee. C30, 1967

Johnson, Wm. M. N26, 1854-55; N30, 1859-60

Johnsson, Arthur T. B39, 1891

Johnston, Bernice Eastman. J192-195, 1955-57; B40, 1962

Jordan, Dr. David Starr. J223, 1925

Keller, Charles. J398, 1891

Kelley, John L. M19, 1897

Kelsey, Harry. J378, 1973

Kelton, Richard. P60, 1967

Kemnitzer, Luis E. J22, 1936

Kew, William S. W. J164, 1927

King, Laura Evertsen. J352, 1900

Kingett, Robert P. P61, 1969

Kinsell, M. P87, 1891; P88, 1893

Kirk, Heatherwick. P129, 1905

Knoff, E. C. J241, 1938

Koch, Felix J. P100, 1912

Kohl, J. G. N26, 1854-55

Kroeber, A. L. N16, 1925

Lambert, Darwin. N52, 1969

Lamont, D. S. N20, 1862

Landberg, Leif C. W. B41, 1965

Lange, Arthur. J79, 1954

Langley, Nancy. P156, 1944

Laperouse, Jean Francis de Galaup (Charles N. Rudkin, trans.). B42, 1959

Laudermilk, J. D. P155, 1944

Lauer, Solon. B43, 1896

Lawrence, Eleanor. P148, 1933

Lawson, A. C. U31, 1893

LeConte, Joseph. J29, 1887; J73, 1887; U51, 1888; J162, 1891

Lecouvreur, Frank (Julius C. Behnke, trans.). B44, 1906

Lenhart, Walter B. P118, 1950

Lester, Elizabeth Sherman. B103, 1974

Lewis, Eleanore F. P71, 1904

Lewis Publishing Co. B45, (1889)

Lindsay, George. J76, 1951

Linton, C. B. J111, 1908; J113, 1908; J117, 1908; J114, 1908; J116, 1908; J118, 1909; J120, 1909; J45, 1911; J124, 1911

Lipp, J. H. J175, 1964

Lockwood, Dewitt C. P120, 1895

Loew, Oscar. N45, 1879

Lovett, W. E. M26, 1866

Lowe, Herbert N. J227, 1903

Lummis, Charles F. P48, 1898

Lunt, Howard Leslie. B46, 1890
Lyon, Marcus Ward, Jr. N8, 1909

Macdonald, Augustin S. J95, 1938
Macnab, Leavenworth. P95, 1898
MacRae, Lieut. Comd. N27, 1855-56
Mailliard, Joseph. J102, 1899; J105, 1900; J133, 1917
Markham, Edwin. B106, 1914
Martinez, Jose Longinos (Leslie Byrd Simpson, trans.). B47, 1938
Mathis, Juliette Estelle. P10, 1891-92
Mawn, Geoffrey P. J380, 1974
Mayhew, Walter. P14, 1893
McCarty, T. J. P124, 1887
McClatchie, Alfred James. U25-26, 1894
McCoy, William M. P68, 1917
McElrath, Clifford. B107, 1967
McGaffey, Ernest. P144, 1922
McGinty, Brian. P177, 1974
McGroarty, John Steven. B104, 1921
McKusick, M. B. U40, 1959
McKusick, M. B. and F. J. Clune, Jr. U38, 1958
McKusick, M. B. and C. N. Warren. U41, 1959
Meadows, Don C. J140, 1928; J143-44, 1929-30; J149, 1934; J348, 1936
Mearns, Edgar A. J41, 1898; N7, 1907; J46, 1911
Meighan, Clement W. J78, 1954; U45, 1959; J12, 1959
Meighan, Clement W. and Hal Eberhart. J11, 1953
Meighan, Clement W. and K. L. Johnson. J82, 1957
Meschter, Elwood. P119, 1957
Miller, Alden H. J153, 1951; J155, 1955
Miller, Loye. J141, 1928
Miller, Max. P161, 1956; P163, 1956; B108, 1959
Millspaugh, Charles Frederick and Lawrence W. Nuttall. B105, 1923
de Mofras, Duflot (M. E. Wilbur, trans.). B48, 1937
Mohr, Albert and L. L. Sample. J191, 1955
Momyer, George R. P126, 1930
Monroe, Keith. P141, 1958; B109, 1963
Moody, Graham B. J160, 1935
Moorehead, Warren King. B49, 1900
Moriarty, J. R. and M. Kleistman. J391, 1968
Morley, Duane. P110, 1889-91
Murbarger, Nell. P22a, 1947
Murray, E. F. M15, 1878

Newkirk, Garrett. C6, 1914
Newmark, Harris. B50, 1930
Newmark, Marco R. J373, 1953
Newman (Tract Directory). M29, 1903
Norris, Robert M. J322, 1952; J169, 1953; J84, 1960

Oberholser, Harry C. J38, 1897; N5-6, 1899-1900; J49, 1922
O'Dell, Scott. B110, 1960
Oetteking, Bruno. J16, 1920; J19, 1930
Ogden, Adele. J93, 1933; J97, 1944
Oliver, J. H. C7, 1914
Olmsted, F. H. N47, 1958
Olmsted, R. R. B52, 1959
Olson, Ronald L. U22, 1927; U1, 1930-31
O'Neill, O. H. B53, 1939
O'Meara, James. P84, 1889
Orr, Phil C. J283, 1940; J299, 1943; J285, 1945; J288, 1947; J270-80, 1949-53; J10, 1951; J54, 1952; J229, 1954; J171, 1956; J281, 1956; J268, 1956; U60, 1956; J172, 1957; J174, 1960; J269, 1960; J305, 1962; J233, 1962; J306, 1964; N1, 1966; B54, 1968
Osburn, Pingree I. J123, 1911
Overholt, Alma. P132, 1930; P107, 1934; M46, 1958
Owens, Robert C. P45, 1897

de Packman, Ana Begue. J370, 1945
Paloú, Fray Francisco (H. E. Bolton, ed.). B55, (1769)
Parish, S. B. J397, 1890; J401, 1893; U50, 1903
Parks, Marian. B117, 1939
Parry, C. C. P83, 1883
Paul, O. M. P99, 1911
Pemberton, J. R. J139, 1928; J142, 1929; J146, 1931
Peters, James L. J150, 1938
Peyton, Sidney B. J236, 1913
Philbrick, Ralph N., ed. B120, 1967; U29, 1972
Phillips, M. J. B56, 1927
Phillips, Mabel Whitman. P106, 1931
Pinart, Alphonse (Robert F. Heizer, ed.). U4, 1952
Pitelka, Frank A. J152, 1950
Pitzer, Jean M., *et al.* J212, 1974
Pollock, Edward. P36, 1861
Pourade, Richard F. J386, 1962
Powell, Lawrence Clark. P171, 1968; P175, 1972
Powell, J. W. N14, 1891
Preston, E. B. C22, 1891
Priestley, H. I. B19, 1937
Pruyn, Marion. P92, 1896
Putnam, F. W. N45, 1879
Putnam, W. C. C16, 1954

Quincy, E. S. P65, 1904

Ralph, Julian. P24, 1891
Rand, W. W. C27, 1931
Randolph, Edmund. P33-34, 1861
Randolph, G. C. J213, 1935
Raven, Peter H. J156, 1963
Redtfeldt, Gordon. J205, 1964

Reed, Ralph D. B118, 1933
Reed, R. D. and J. S. Hollister. J23, 1936
Reichlen, Henry and Robert F. Heizer. U18, 1964
Reid, Hugo. B57, (1840); B58, (1852)
Reider, M. M31, 1905
Reinman, Fred M. U42-44, 1960-64
Remington, Charles F. J251, 1971
Renton, J. J. P22, 1971
Rett, Egmont Z. J151, 1947; J154, 1953
Richardson, Charles H., Jr. J110, 1908
Richey, Emma Carbutt. P105, 1925
Richman, Irving Berdine. B59, 1911
Rider, Arthur Fremont. M40, 1927
Ridgway, Robert. J42, 1898
Ritter, Wm. E. J300, 1901
Roalfe, George Adams. N37, 1932
Robertson, Howard. J106, 1903; J121, 1910
Robertson, Stewart. P179, 1954
Robinson, Alfred. B60, 1846
Robinson, Eugene. J55-56, 1942; J190, 1942
Robinson, W. W. M43, 1941; B61, 1948; B62, 1957
Rockwell, Mabel M. B119, 1962
Roe, Jo Ann. P167, 1964
Rogers, David Banks. B63, 1929
Rolle, Andrew F. B16, 1956
Rosamond, Roy Reuben. P74, 1912
Rose, Robert Selden, ed. U34, 1911
Ross, R. C. J137, 1926
Rothrock, J. T. N45, 1879
Rouse, S. H. J296a, 1977
Rozaire, Charles E. J197, 1959; J199, 1960; J201, 1962; J202, 1962; J234, 1967
Rudkin, Charles N. B42, 1959
Russell, C. J. W. P27, 1856
Rust, Horatio N. M28, 1897
Rust, Horatio N. (F. W. Hodge, ed.). J2, 1907

Saunders, Charles F. P138, 1909; P130, 1911; P139, 1912; B121, 1913; B122, 1923
Scammon, Capt. C. M. P77, 1870; P78, 1870; B64, (1874)
Scholl, D. W. J25, 1959; J324, 1960
Schumacher, Paul. N9, 1874; P81, 1874; P82, 1875; P114, 1876; N41, 1877; J20, 1878; J250, 1878; U12, (1878); U17, (1878)
Scott, Vance H. N53, 1973
Seavey, F. A. J400, 1892
Sellards, E. H. U56, 1960
Sexton, Horace A. J295, 1959
Shaler, William. B65, (1804)
Shaw, Albert. J27, 1909
Sheldon, H. H. P146, 1931
Shepard, F. P. J161, 1937
Shepard, F. P., U. S. Grant IV and R. S. Dietz. J31, 1939
Shepard, F. P. and W. F. Wrath. J321, 1937
Shepard, Odell. P102, 1915

Sheridan, Edwin M. M17, 1896
Simpson, Sir George. B66, (1841); J177, 1847
Smith, Hugh M. J214, 1899
Smith, Ruth Tangier. P51, 1899
Smith, William Sidney Tangier. N40, 1896; J63, 1898; U32, 1900; J30, 1933
Snell, David. P58, 1969
Snow, H. J. B67, (1879)
Snyder, G. K. J235, 1909; J130, 1914
Southworth, John R. B123, 1920
Spaulding, Edward S. J291, 1959
Spence, Clark C. B68, (1860)
Splitter, Henry Winfred. J375, 1961
Starks, E. C. C8, 1918
Sterling, George. B124, 1911
Stevens, R. P178, 1902
Stevens, T. H. N25, 1853-54
Steward, B. Anthony. J216, 1942
Stock, Dr. Chester. J318, 1935; P150; 1936; P154, 1941; J178, 1943
Stock, Chester and E. L. Furlong. J303, 1928; J166, 1929
Stoddard, Charles Warren. P76, 1870
Stone, Wilmer, ed. J47, 1917
Storke, Mrs. Yda Addis. B69, 1891
Streator, Clark P. J263, 1887
Streeter, William A. J96, 1939
Stuart, Alexander H. H. N19, 1852
Stuart, J. N. M38, 1926
Sutton, Horace. P122, 1961
Swarth. H. S. J104, 1899; J131, 1914
Swartz, B. K. J13, 1960; U48, 1960
Swartz, B. K. and C. J. Sutton, III. U39, 1948
Sykes, Godfrey. J14, 1915

Taylor, E. S. J83, 1960
Tays, George. J94, 1935
Teggart, Frederick J. U35, 1911
Tenney, W. A. P112, 1907
Thompson, Albert F. M13, 1869
Thompson and West (Pubs.). B70, (1883)
Thompson, W. F. C10-11, 1918-20
Thornburgh, Margaret. P162, 1956
Thorne, R. F. J157-58, 1967-69
Tittmann, O. H. N35, 1907; N36, 1909
Tompkins, Walker A. J289, 1958

Towne, C. W. and N. Wentworth. B125, 1945
Townsend, Charles H. N4, 1890
Trask, Blanche. P46, 1897; U27, 1897; P50, 1898; U28, 1899; P54, 1900; P70, 1904; J334, 1904; J335, 1904; J336, 1904
Tucker, W. Burling. C26, 1927
Tuthill, Franklin. B71, 1866
Tyson, Philip T. N17, 1850

Ulrey, Albert B. J343, 1917
Ulrey, Albert B. and Paul O. Greeley. J344, 1928

Valentine, James W. and Jere H. Lipps. J245, 1963
Vancouver, George. B72, 1798
Van Denburgh, John. J66, 1905
Van Denburgh, John and Joseph R. Slevin. J68, 1914
Van Gelder, R. G. J226, 1965
Van Rossem, A. J. J135, 1924; J136, 1925
Van Valkenburgh, Richard. P20, 1952
Vaslit, Frank H. J392, 1890
Vaughn, Ruben V. B126, 1956
Vedder, J. G., et al. N46, 1956
Vedder, J. G. and Robert M. Norris. N48, 1963
Viscaíno, Fr. Juan (Arthur Woodward, trans.). B73, 1959
Vogdes, Anthony W. J256, 1911
Vore, Elizabeth. P97, 1903

Waddy, F. V. P103, 1920
Wagner, Henry Raup. J86, 1924; J88, 1928; J89, 1929; B74, 1929; J91, 1932; J365, 1933; J366, 1935; B75, 1937
Waite, Elmont. P5, 1959
Walcott, Charles D., Director. N39, 1896-97
Walcott, Josephine. P79, 1872
Walker, Edwin F. J186, 1936; J188, 1938
Walker, Lewis W. J225, 1948
Wallace, William J. U55, 1955
Walters, Helen B. J372, 1953
Ward, W. V. J220, 1931
Wardle, H. Newell. J3, 1913
Warner, J. J. J360, 1906-08
Warner, J. J., et al. B76, 1876

Warren, E., Jr. J218, 1958
Warren, Herbert O. J317, 1926
Wayne, Arthur Wellington. P43, 1896
Weber, Rev. Francis J. B77, 1972
Weinstein, Robert A. J180, 1968
Wheeler, Stanley A. N51, 1944
Wheeler, W. M. J338, 1905
Wells, A. J. P69, 1903
White, Mowbray. P75, 1914
Whitney, J. D. J28, 1864; C13, 1865
Wilbur, Marguerite E. B48, 1937
Willard, C. D. B78, 1901
Willett, George. J122, 1910; B112, 1912; B115, 1933
Williams, Iza. M32, 1905
Williams, Woodbridge. J224, 1941; J77, 1954
Williams, Roger. P127, 1961
Williamson, Lillian A. J364, 1924
Williamson, Mrs. M. Burton. J351, 1888; J333, 1904; J357, 1906
Wilson, Carol Green. J369, 1945
Wilson, Neill C. P98, 1910
Wilson, Robert W. J182, 1936
Winchester, James H. P142, 1964
Windle, Ernest. B127, 1931
Wood, Stanley. B79, 1891
Wood, Williard. P72, 1904
Woodford, Alfred O. U33, 1924
Woodward, Arthur. J18, 1927; J367, 1938; J5, 1940; J6, 1941; B73, 1959
Wright, Austin Tappan. J376, 1963
Wright, Howard W. J129, 1913; J128, 1913
Wright, Howard and G. K. Snyder. J127, 1913
Wyler, Lorraine. J219, 1931

Yale, Charles G. C23, 1893
Yates, Dr. Lorenzo G. N13, 1886; J264, 1887; J262, 1889; J265, 1890; J266, 1890; J267, 1890; C19, 1890; C20, 1890; C21, 1890; U52, 1890; J1, 1891; J163, 1892; P89, 1896; P90, 1896; J326, 1902; J327, 1902; J330, 1902; J331, 1902; J332, 1904
Yarrow, H. C. N45, 1879

Zahn, Curtis. P140, 1944
Zahn, Otto J. J50, 1895
Zavalishin, Dmitry. J379, 1973

General Index

Compiled by Anna Marie and Everett Gordon Hager

Abalone: 48, 52, 57, 66, 98, 125, 203, 225; artifacts of, 14, 17
Abalone Cave (Ana.): 136
Abalone Point (S.R.): 191
Abbott, ——: 204
Abbott, Clinton G: 54
Active (ves.): 21
Ada Hancock (ves.): 75
Adams Cove (S.M.): 212, 219
Agee, Frances: 23
Agee, Roy: 23
Agee, Mrs. Roy E: 19
Agee Ranch (S.N.): 25
Aguirre, José Antonio: 160
Alamos Anchorage (S.Cz.): 151
Albatross (ves.): 58, 116, 168, 228
Albert's Anchorage (S.Cz.): 151
Albion (mine): 71, 92
Alden, James: 21, 195, 215
Alert (ves.): 36, 81
Aleuts: 60, 117, 228
Algae Cave (S.Cz.): 144
Allan Hancock Foundation, U.S.C: 29
Allen, Harry (of U.C.L.A.): 18
Allin, T. D: 75
Alliot, Hector: 29, 33
Alvarado, Juan Bautista: 91-93 *passim;* 149, 160, 191, 192, 197
Alvarado, Martina Castro: 191
American Indian Museum: 60
ANACAPA ISLANDS: caves, 55; map, 122; 123-138; archaeology, 129-130; avifauna, 126-129 *passim;* caves, 123-124, 134-136; fauna, 126; flora, 126; geology, 123-124; Indians, 129-130; National Park status (1938) 119-120, (1980) officially a Park, 120; photographs listed, 137-138; seals, 124; volcanic evidences, 123, 124, 133
Anacapa West: 132-134 *passim*
Anchorage (S.N.): 23
Anderson, Robert E: 180
Anderson, Walt: 227
Anthony, A. W: 58
Apache Indians: 88
Aquaje (Escondido) (S.Cz.): 143
Aquarium, Avalon (S.C.): 85
Arabian Horse farm (S.C.): 77
Arch Point (S.B.): 114
Arch Rock: Ana., 130; S.Cz., 146
Archaeology: Anacapas, 129-130; S.Cle., 60-61; S.N., 26-30 *passim;* S.B., 119; S. Cz., 156-159

Argentine (mine) (S.C.): 70, 92
Arlington Canyon (S.R.): 187, 190
Arlington Springs Man (S.R.): 187, 204
Army Beach Camp (S.N.): 19, 21
Arrow Point (S.C.): 66
Arroyo Principal (S.Cz.): 143
Asphaltum: 18, 27, 151, 213, 219, 220
Auk (pubn.): 58, 60
Austin, Perry G. M: 184
Avalon (S.C.): 45, 73
Avifauna: Ana., 126-129 *passim;* S.Cl., 58-60; S.M., 230-231; S.N., 26; S.B., 118-119; S.C., 84-85; S.Cz., 170-173; S.R., 204
Avon (ves.): 34, 35, 42, 74

Baby's Cave (S.Cz.): 144
Baca, Pablo: 164
Bache, Alexander Dallas: 54-57 *passim;* 112, 118, 124, letter to, 130-131
Baglins, ——: 222
Bailey, Gilbert E: 218
Baird, Spencer F: 206
Ballast Point (S.C.): 68
Banks, N: 203
Banning, Anna O: 96
Banning, Hancock: 75, 95, 99, 169
Banning, Joseph Brent: 94, 99
Banning, Katherine S: 96
Banning, Phineas: 75, 98-99
Banning, William: 76, 94, 95, 99
Banning Company: 95, 106
Barnard, Cyrus: 27
Barron, Eustace: 161
Barron, William E., *et al:* 49
Barron, Forbes & Company: 160, 161, 162, 164
Bartholomew, George A., Jr: 26
Barwick, James A: 216-217
Basques: 15, 22
Bat Ray Cove (Ana.): 132
Bat Rock (S.M.): 228
Beacon Reef (S.R.): 188
Bechers Bay (S.R.): 184-189 *passim;* 200
Beck, Rollo H: 144, 170-172 *passim;* 229
Bee Rocks (S.R.): 190
Beechey, Fred. William: 243-245
Begg (or Begg's) Rock (S.N.): 17, 21
Beghn, Johann: *see* Behn, John
Behn, John: 68, 75
Behn's Place (S.C.): 68
Belcher, Edward: 220

Ben Weston Cove (S.Cl.): 52, 53
Ben Weston Point (S.C.): 76
"Big Ben" (seal): at S.C., 66, 97-98
Big Dog Dave (S.Cl.): 48, 60
Big Springs Cañon (S.C.): 72, 76
Binnacle Rocks (S.C.): 66
Bird Rock (S.C.): 65, 66
Bishop (ves.): 21
Bishop Rock (S.N.): 21, 181
Black Hawk (Indian): 38
Black Jack Mine (S.C.): 96
Black Jack Peak (S.C.): 77, 80, 88
Black Mountain (S.R.): 185
Black Point (S.Cz.): 153
Black Rock (S.Cz.): 144
"Black Steward": *see* Light, Allen
Blair, E. G: 53, 54
Blair, Pauline: 53
Blake, William P: 21, 182
Blake's Caves (S.C.): 71
Blue Bank (S.Cz.): 143, 151, 159
Blue Cavern (S.C.): 71-72
Blunt, ——: 181
Boars (S.Cz.): 169; S.R., 203
Boat Landing (S.Cz.): 146
Bolivar (ves.): 42, 43, 194; *see also Oajaca* (ves.)
Bolton, James R: 160
Bonnot, Paul: 50, 226
Boobry Morfki (Russian for sea otter): *see* Sea Otters
Boolottian, ——: S.N. rept., 26
Botanical Gazette (pubn.): 56, 81
Bouchette (Boushey, Bouchet), Louis: 67
Bouchette, Stephen: 67, 94
Boushey: *see* Bouchette
Boushey's (S.C.): 66
Bowers, DeMoss: 28, 33, 233
Bowers, Stephen: 13-14, 28, 33, 156, 158, 181, 206-208 *passim;* 232, 233
Bowers Memorial Museum (Santa Ana, Calif.): 61
Box Canyon (S.Cl.): 50
Bradley, W. C: 153, 154
Bradshaw's Fort (S.C.): 74
Brandegee, Townshend Stith: 56, 82, 200, 201
Bremner, Carl St. J: 152-154 *passim;* 216, 217
Breninger, George F: 53, 58, 59
Brinkerhoff, S.B: 37, biog. sketch 42
Brinkley, John ("Chicken John"): 76, 84

Brisk (ves.): 132
Britton, J. R: 14, 60, 113, 114
Brockway Point (S.R.): 187
Brooks, R. L: 219, 222, 223
Brooks, Robert: 22, 23
Brown, Charlie: 194, 195, 233; *see* Dittmann, Carl
Browne, J. Ross: 182-183, 184
Bryan, Bruce: named Snug Harbor, 19; 21, 22; S.N. map, 23; 29, 30, 61
Buena Vista (S.Cz.): 143
Buena Vista Park (S.C.): 100
Buffalo Springs Reservoir (S.C.): 76
Burgert, Louis: 125
Burnham, W. L: 20
Burt, Homer C: 125, 127-128
Burton, Luis T: 33; biog. sketch, 42; 197
"Burton Mound": 42, 43
Button Shell Beach (S.C.): 73, 97

Cabrillo, Juan Rodríguez: 190; stone on S.R., 205; monument on S.M., 215-216; 240
Cabrillo Harbor (S.C.): 72
Cactus Peak (S.C.): 77
Caire, Albina C.S: 164
Caire, Arthur J: 164, 171
Caire, Delphine A: 164
Caire, Fred F: 155, 164, 172
Caire, Helen A: 164
Caire, Justinian: 26, owner S.Cz., 49; 142; family and activities, 143-144, 148-159 *passim*, 161, 162-164 *passim*
California Academy of Sciences: 38, 55, 94, 157
California Land Commission: 220
California (ves.): 36, 43
California Illustrated (pubn.): 53
Camp, Charles L: 181
Camps, var. locations on S.C: list of, 77
Cañada Acapulca (S.R.): 190
Cañada del Agua (S.Cz.): 143, 149
Cañada del Alamo (S.Cz.): 151
Cañada de Cervada (Cebada) (S.Cz.): 152
Cañon Coches Prietos (S.Cz.): 151
Cañada Corral (S.R.): 187
Cañada de la Cruz (S.R.): 185
Cañada de la Cueva Vieja (Cave of the Old People) (S.R.): 190; *see also* Jones Cave
Cañada Ganada (Grannada) (S.Cz.): 146
Cañada del Gato (S.Cz.): 152
Cañada Jolla Vieja (Old Cave Canyon) (S.R.): 190
Cañada La Jolla: *see* Wreck Canyon
Cañon Laguna: S.Cz., 151; S.R., 188
Cañada Lobo (S.R.): 180, 188
Cañada del Medio (S.Cz.): 142, 143, 148
Cañada Pomona (S.Cz.): 142, 143
Cañada del Portezuelo (S.Cz.): 143
Cañada del Puerto (S.Cz.): 143, 144, 149
Cañada San Augustine (S.R.): 190

Cañada los Sauces del Oeste (S.Cz.): 152, 154
Cañon los Sauces de los Colorados (S.Cz.): 151; *see* Willow Harbor
Cañada Seco (S.R.): 186
Cañada Soledad (S.R.): 187
Cañon de las Tasajeras (S.Cz.): 146
Cañada Tecelote (S.R.): 186, 187
Cañada Tokolodito: *see* Cañada Tecelote
Cañada del Valdez (S.Cz.): 146
Cañada Verde (S.R.): 187
Canaliño Indians (S.R.): 180
Cape Canyon Reservoir (S.C.): 76
Cape Horn (S.Cl.): 52
Cape Paez (S.Cl.): 51
Cape Pinchot (S.Cl.): 47
Caplan, R. I: 26
Capuccio, Aglae S. (Caire): of S.Cz., 150, 151, 162, 164
Cardwell Point (S.M.): 211, 216, 218
Carlquist, Sherwin: 81
Carlson, J. J: 84
Carrillo, Anastacio: 197
Carrillo, Carlos Antonio: 33, otter hunter, 36, 42; 92; owner S.R., 191, 192, 197, 199
Carrillo, Concepción Pico: 92
Carrillo, Domingo: 92
Carrillo, José: 92
Carrillo, José Antonio: part owner S.R., 191, 192
Carrillo, María Castro: 191, 192
Carrillo, Raymundo: 92, 262-263
Carrington Point (S.R.): 187, 188
Carter, President Jimmy: (1980) estab. Five Islands' status to National Park, 120
Casa del Monte (P. K. Wrigley's home) (S.C.): 100
Casino Point (S.C.): 66
Castillero, Andrés: 159-160, 161
Castle Rock: S.Cl., 50; S.M., 213, 214, 217, 219
Castro de Carrillo, María Josefa: 199
Castro, José (1825-36): 149, 191, 192, 197
Cat Canyon (S.B.): 114
Cat Rock (Ana.): 127, 134
Catalina: *see* Santa Catalina Island
Catalina Airport (S.C.): 81
Catalina Harbor (S.C.): 65, 68
Catalina Head (S.C.): 68
Catalina Islander (newsp.): 23, 29, 49-50, 51, 56, 65, 66, 76, 86, 88, 96, 98; issues listed 106-108, 218
Catalina Peak (S.C.): *see* Black Jack Peak
Catalina Weather Bureau (S.C.): 77
Catalina Yacht Club, Avalon (S.C.): 99
Cathedral Cave and Cove (Ana.): 130; *see* Painted Cave, Ana.; S.Cz., 144
Cave Canyon (S.Cl.): 51; S.B., 114
Cave of the Killer Whales (S.N.): 19
Cavern Point (S.Cz.): 150; aka "Palo Parado"

Caves: *see* individual islands
Celery Creek (S.N.): 20
Cemeteries (S.N.): 14
Centennial Exposition, Phila., (1876): 26
Center Mountain (S.Cz.): 142
Central Peak (S.N.): 19
Central Valley, (S.Cz.): 142
Cerf, L: 156
Cermeño, Sebastián Rodríguez: 241
Cerruti, Giovanni Battista: 164
Céssac, León de: 26, 27, 28, 129, 157, 232-233
Chaboya Mine (San Jose, Calif.): 159-160, 161
Chalk Cliff Canon (S.Cl.): 52-53
Channel Islands National Monument: 234
"The Channel of Santa Barbara": poem by Juliette Estelle Mathis, 121
Channel Point (S.R.): 189; *see* Skunk Point
Charleston (ves.): 51
Chase Anchorage (S.Cz.): 145
Cheetham, Francis T: 45, 49
Cherry Cove (S.C.): 68
Chickasaw (ves.): 189
"Chicken John": *see* Brinkley, John
China Bay (S.Cz.): 143, 150
China Camp (S.R.): 190
China Canyon (S.Cl.): 50, 51
China Point: S.C., 76; S.Cl., 47, 50, 51, 60
Chinese: abalone hunters, 14, 48, 125, 225, 226
Chinese Camp (S.N.): 22
Chinese Harbor: S.N., 19, 20, 27; S.Cz., 150
Chinetti, ——(died in Red Canyon): *see* Ramirez, Salvador
Chinetti Canyon (S.Cl.): 51
Christy Beach (S.Cz.): 153
Christy Canyon (S.Cz.): 142, 152
Christy Ranch (S.Cz.): 142, 143, 153
Chumash Indians: 28
Church Rock (S.C.): 66, 76
Clemente Anchorage (S.Cl.): 48, 50
Cleveland, Grover: *re* S.M., 218, 221
Cleveland, R. J: 73
Cliff Canyon (S.B.): 114
Clokey, Ira W: 202
Cluster Point (S.R.): 191
Coast Guard Beach (S.N.): 19
Coche Point (S.Cz.): 148, 150
Coches Prietos (Black pigs) (S.Cz.): 143, 144, 151, 157
Cockerell, T.D.A: 18, 23, 25, 79, 118, 224, 230
Comorant Island (S.M.): 212
Condor (pubn.): 54, 119
Conejo Volcanics (West Ana.): 133
Convoy (ves.): 42, 193, 194
Conway, J. F: 221
Cook, I. N: 132
Cooper, J. G: 17, 54, 57, 77, 111, 112, 114, 118

Cooper, James: 181
Cornell, Ralph D: 83, 165, 166
Corral Harbor (S.N.): 14, 19, 20, 29
Cortes (ves.): 21
Cortes Bank: 21, 181
Cottonwood Canyon (S.C.): 76, 77
Courier (ves.): 74
Covarrubias, José María: 91, 92-93 *passim;* 221
Covarrubias, Nicolás: 92, 221
Cox, Keith W: 66, 225-226
Coyote Point (S.R.): 188
Crab, James: 22
Craig Beach (S.C.): *see* Mills Landing
Crawford, ——: of S.M., 217
Creal, Dr. ——: (1850), 69
Crocker, Charles: 94, 95
Crockett, ——(1866): 93
Crook Point (S.M.): 211, 212
Cropper, Captain, ——: 21
Crown of England (ves.): 189, 190
Crusader (ves.): 42, 193
Cuba (ves.): 148, 212, 222
Cuesta Creek (S.Cz.): 143, 152-153
Cuesta Valley (S.Cz.): 143
Cueva Pintada (S.Cz.): 146
Cueva de Valde (S.Cz.): 146
Cueva Valdez (S.Cz.): 146
Cunningham, William H: 74, 75
Curtis, James F: 88
Cushing, C: 91
Cuyler, R. M: 215
Cuyler Harbor (S.M.): 214-219 *passim;* 228

Daily Alta California (newsp.): 37, 39, 162
Dakin's Cove: *see* Avalon
Dall, William H: 88, 185, 205, 231
Dana, Richard Henry: 36, 81
Dana, William G: 22, 34, 35, 36; biog. sketch, 42; 74
Dark Cave (Ana.): 136
Darwin, Charles: 25
Darwin, Francis: 25
Davidson, Anstruther: 82
Davidson, George: quoted, 19; S.Cl., 47-55 *passim;* S.B., 112-115 *passim;* Ana., 123; S.Cz., 147-152 *passim;* S.R., 179-189 *passim;* S.M., 212-214 *passim*
Davis, William Heath, Jr: 21-22
Davis, William Heath, Sr: 33
Dawson, N: 22
Dawson, W. L: 171
Daytona Beach (S.N.): 19
Dead Man's Point (S.M.): 216
Deep Tank Reservoir (S.C.): 76
Den, Nicolas A: 197, 199
Den, Rosa Oliveras Hill de: 199
Dentzel, Carl S: 30
Devil's Knoll (S.M.): 214, 216
Diatomaceous soil: S.Cl., 51; S.C., 80
Dibblee, Albert: 262

Dibblee, Francisca de la: 261
Dibblee, T. B: 262
Dickey, Donald R: 167, 168
Dick's Harbor (S.Cz.): 147
Diltz, D. B: 68
Dimmick, L. N: biog. sketch, 42
Dittmann, Carl: quoted 20; 32, 34, 35, 40; biog. sketch, 42; aka "Charlie Brown" "Don Alonzo": 49
Don Quixote (ves.): 22
Doran, E. L: 89
Don Pechos (S.R.): *see* Mt. Soledad
Dover, William: 125
Downey, John G: 93
Drake, A. M: 84
Drake, Francis: 241
Drake, Waldo: 56
Dreamer (ves.): 14, 29, 203
Drigg's Cove (S.Cl.): 49; *see* West Cove, S.Cl.
Dry Canyon (S.R.): 187
Duffield, Henry: 154
Duflot de Mofras, Eugene: 49, 55, 149
Dunn, Harry H: 124-125
Dunn, John Dunning: 90
Dutch Harbor (S.N.): 19, 30
Dye, Francis D: 35

Eagle Cliff (S.M.): 216
Eagle Nest (S.C.): 76
Eagle Ranch (S.Cl.): 47, 50; aka "Half Way House"; "Hay Ranch"
Eagle Rock (S.C.): 65
Eagles (Bald Eagle): 127-128
Earle, Homer P: 14, 49, 85
Earthquake (1812): S.R., 180, 188; (1895), S.M., 216-217
East Anacapa Island: 130-131
East Fish Camp (Ana.): 129, 132
East Peak: *see* San Miguel Mountain
East Point (S.R.): 188, 189
Eastern Ranch (S.Cz.): 150
Eastwood, Alice: 19, 24, 25, 82-84 *passim;* 166, 200, 202
Eaton, Ira: 170, 212-213
Echeandía, José María: 74, 149, 192
Echo Lake (Crater Lake) (S.C.): 77
Edholm, Charlton Lawrence: 225
Edwards, Charles Lincoln: 57-58, 225
Edwards, H. A: 147
Eel Cove (S.Cl.): 50
Eel Point (S.Cl.): 50
Egan, Carrie W: "Santa Barbara Islands" poem, 121
Ehorn, William: 163
Eisen, Gustav: 26, 27, quoted, 84; 88, 119, 157, 202-205 *passim*
El Aliso (pubn.): 83
Elder Creek (S.R.): 188, 189
Elephant fossils: S.M., 219-220; S.Cz., 152; S.R., 180-190 *passim*

Elephant Seal Rookery (S.M.): 212
Elephant Seals (S.M.): 227; *see also* Sea Lions
Eleventh Naval District (S.Cl.): 54
Elizabeth (ves.): 91
Ella Fisher (ves.): 203
Elliot, Captain ——: on Ana., 125, 132, 134
Elliot, L. P: 23
Elsie (ves.): 203
Emerald Bay (S.C.): 68
Empire Landing (S.C.): 72, 80
Empress (ves.): 86
Ethnology (S.M.): 231
Euphemia (ves.): 21, 35
Ewing (ves.): 21, 130

Fair, James G: 88
Fall, H. C: 84, 118, 202
Famer (La Fama?) (ves.): 43
Farnell, S. B: 91
Farrel Mountains (S.R.): 186
Fauna: Ana., 126; S.Cl., 57-58; S.M., 225-230 *passim;* S.N., 15-16, 25-26; S.B., 118; S.C., 84; S.Cz., 167-169; S.R., 202-203
Fernald, Charles, 197
Ferrelo's Point (S.N.): *see* Coast Guard Beach
Ferrer, Bartholome: 240
Figueroa, José: 74
Finley, Richard S: 147, 218
Finley Cave (S.M.): 218
Fisherman's Bay or Cove (S.C.): 25, 68
Five Mile Bight: *see* Bechers Bay, S.R.
Flea Island (S.M.): 212, 213, 226, 230
Fleming, David P: 84, 100
Flora: Ana., 126; S.Cl., 56-57; S.M., 223-225; S.N., 15-16, 24-25; S.B., 115-116; S.C., 81-84; S.Cz., 165-167; S.R., 200-202
Flynn, S.E: 46-53 *passim*, 57
Forbes, Alexander: 160-161
Forbes, James Alexander: 36, 161
Forbes, William E: 161, 162, 164
Ford, H. C: 132
Ford, William: 132
Ford Point (S.R.): 189
Forney, Stehman: 153, 229, 230
Forney's Cove (S.Cz.): 144, 153, 157
Forster, John: 93
Fort Ross (Calif.): 228
Fossils (S.C.): 78
Fourth of July Cove (S.C.): 68
Foxen, Julien: 43
Foxes, on S.N: 15
Franklin (ves.): 74
Frazer Point (S.Cz.): 144, 153, 158
Free Press (pubn.): 156
French, William: 193
Frenchy's Cove (Ana.): 125, 133
Freshwater Cave (Ana.): 129, 135-136

Friar's Harbor (S.Cz.): 147
Frog Rock (S.C.): 66
Fry's Harbor: *see* Friar's Harbor

Galena (mineral) (S.C.): 70-71, 80, 81, 87
Gallagher, Thomas J. (Tom): 46, 49, 50, 53, 73, 164
Gallagher Beach (S.C.): 73
Gallagher's Cove (S.Cl.): 45, 47, 49, 50
Gallagher's Landing (S.Cl.): 54
Gambel, William: 81
Garanon Canyon (S.R.): 186
Garnet Peak (S.C.): 81
Garnets: on S.C., 81
Gaty, E. W: 216
Gaylord, H. A: 119
Geiger, Maynard: 40
Gem of the Ocean (mine) (S.C.): 71
Gensoul, Adrien: 164
Geology: Ana., 123-124; S.Cl., 54-56; S.M., 219-220; S.N., 17; S.B., 114, 115; S.C., 77-80; S.Cz., 153-154; S.R., 180
Gherini, Ambrose: 163, 164
Gherini, Mrs. Ambrose: 162, 163, 164
Gherini, Frances: 164
Gherini, Pier: 162, 163, 164
Gherinis: Sheep raisers on S.Cz., 150, 151, 164
Gibbons, James M: 32-33
Gifford, E. W: 159
Glass bottomed boats (S.C.): 85-86
Glen (ves.): 215
Glen Haven (S.C.): *see* Fourth of July Cove
Glidden, Ralph: 29, 60, 90, 233
Goat Harbor (S.C.): 72, 82
Goats: on S.Cl., 49, 69, 90, 188; on S.Cz., 153
Golisch, William Herman: 29
Goller, ——: 75
Gomez, Joaquin: 35
González, José María de Jesús: 40
Goodyear, W. A: 150-154 *passim*, 169, 180
Graham Bros., Long Beach: 96
Grand Arch (Ana.): *see* Arch Rock
Grand Canyon: S.Cl., 46, 47, 49, 52; S.C., 76
Grant, U.S: 18
Graveyard Canyon (S.B.): 114
Gray, Asa: 56, 81
Greeley, George: 76
Green, J. Elton: 229
Green Mountain (S.M.): 217
Greene, Edward Lee: 82, 141, 146, 200, 201, 212-217 *passim;* 221, 223-224
Grey, Zane: 52
Griesbach, John C: 48, 55
Griffon (ves.): 42
Grimes, Eliab: 21, 193, 194
Grinnell, Joseph: 26, 52, 57-59 *passim;* 60, 85, 114, 115, 118, 126-129 *passim;* 147, 171-172

Grizzley Bear (pubn.): 61
Guano (Ana., S.M.): 130, 215
Guerra, Francisco de la: 160
Guerra, Pablo de la: 91
Guerra family: 261-262
Guerra y Noriega, José de la: 261
Guerrero, Francisco: 71
Gull Island: S.M., 215, 230; S.B., 114; S.Cz., 152

Halleck, H. W: 91, 160, 161
Halleck, Peachy and Billings: 197
Halsey, Abraham: 22
Hamilton, Agnes M: 22
Hamilton, William: 22
Hamlin, Homer: 18, 23, 28
Hansen, Frank: 151
Hardacre, Emma Chamberlain: 34, 42
Harding, Warren G: 100
Hardy, I. B: 132
Harford, W. G. W: 88, 187, 200, 205, 231, 232
Harlow, Marcus: 35
Harriet Blanchard (ves.): 42
Harrington, J. P: 158
Harris, ——: squatter on S.C., 53, 94
Harris Point (S.M.): 214
Hartnell, Theresa de la Guerra: 261
Hartnell, William: 149
Hassler (ves.): 157, 206
Hawxhurst, Walter: 93
Hayes, Benjamin: 34
Haypress Reservoir (S.C.): 76
Hazard, ——: 165, 224
Hazeltine, William: 68
Hazzard's (S.Cz.): 146
Heald, Weldon F: 130, 145
Hearst, Phoebe: 205
Heizer, Robert F: 27, 39, 159; Cabrillo gravesite search, 190, 205
Hen Rock (S.C.): 66
Henshaw, H. W: 167, 168, 170, 229, 230
Hermosa (ves.): 95
Herrington, John: 221
Hester, Thomas R: 159
Heye, George E: 60
Hides: salting of, 91
Hijar-Padre Colony: 92
Hill, Daniel A: 199, 207
Hill, Mrs. Daniel (Rafaela L. Olivares de Hill): 199
Hill, W. L: 67
Hillinger, Charles: 20, 24, 25, 169
Hinchman, A. F: 42
Hitchcock, ——: 93, 94
Hodge, Frederick Webb: 33, 233
Hoffmann, Ralph: 158, 172, 173, 184, 201, 217, 218, death 212
Holder, Charles Frederick: 14, 23, 32-33, 47, 48, 57, 59, 60, 72, 82, 85-86 *passim;* soapstone quarry, 89, 90, Aquarium, 97; 114, 115, 129, 134, 142, 144, 153, 154, 156, 172, 203, 214, 230

Holland, George: *see* Howland: Howland's Ranch, Bay
Hollister, W. W: 262
Holmes, William Henry: 28, 72, 89, 90
Hoover, Robert L: 90
Horse Beach (S.Cl.): 47, 51
Horse Canyon (S.Cl.): 50
Howard, O.H: 59
Howard, O. W: 24, 84, 119, 230, 231
Howell, A. B: 204
Howell, John Thomas: 25
Howell, Thomas R: 171
Howland, Charles: 49, 53, 54, 57, 60; *see also* Howland's Bay, Ranch
Howland, George (Holland): 48, 51, 53
Howland, Percy H: 66, 75-76
Howland, Robert: 53
Howland, William S: 22, 53, 68, 69, 71, 94
Howland's Bay (S.Cl.): 49
Howland's Landing (S.C.): 68
Howland's Ranch (S.Cl.): 49
Hubbard, Charles: 35
Huey, Lawrence M: 54
Huse, Chas. E: 197
Hyder, Alvin: 115
Hyder, Captain ——: 23
Hyla (ves.): 229

Indian Cave (Ana.): 135
Indian mounds (S.Cz.): 153
Indian Reservation: proposed for S.C., 88
Indian Rock (S.C.): 65
Indians: Ana., 129-130; S.Cl., 60-61; S.M., 218, 220, artifacts, 232-234; S.B., 114, 119; S.C., burial grounds 73, middens, 76-77, 87-90; S.Cz., 143, 147, 148, 150, 151, 152, 156-159 *passim;* S.N., 18, 20; S.R., 180, 185, 189, 194, 204-208; *see also* Aleuts, Chumash, Juana María, Kodiak, Turei
International Mining Syndicate, Ltd., of England: 94, 96
Iron Bound Cave (S.C.): 66
Irwin, M. C: 30
Isabella (ves.): 116, 228
Israelsky, Merle C: 18
Isthmus (S.C.): 68, 69
Isthmus Cove (S.C.): 65, 67, 68, 69-70
Isthmus Rock (S.M.): 213
Italian Gardens (S.C.): 72
Itata (ves.): 51

J. F. West (ves.): 222
Jackson Hill (S.N.): 19
Japanese: abalone hunters, 21, 52, 57, 225, 231
Jasper: on S.C., 76
Jecker, Torre and Company: 160, 164
Jehemy Beach (S.N.): 30
Jenkins, Harry: 132
Jensen, Peter: 49

Jewfish Point (S.C.): 76
John Begg (ves.): 21
Johnson, Donald Lee: 219
Johnson, Mrs. Floyd: 70
Johnson, James Charles: 66, 71, 85, 93
Johnson, Jim: 67
Johnson, John L: 66, 71
Johnson, W. M: 124
Johnson's Harbor (S.C.): 71
Johnson's Landing (S.C.): 66, 67
Johnson's Lee (S.R.): 152, 189
Johnston, Bernice Eastman: 60
Jones, John Coffin: 22, 33, 35, biog. sketch 42; 74, 192-197 *passim;* 228
Jones, Manuela Carrillo: 192, 193, 197, 199
Jones, Philip Mills: 23, 28, 39, 190; discovers Cabrillo slab, 205
Jones, William Carey: 160, 191, 192
Jones Cave (S.R.): 190
Joyaux, J. B: 154
Juana María: stories about, on S.N., 14, 29, biog., 32-43; bibliography *re,* 41-43

"K": *see* Kinsell
Keen, Richard: 132
Kelly, John L: 13-14
Kemnitzer, Luis A: 18
Kettle, George F: 197
Kew, William S: 180
Keyhold Cave (Ana.): 136
Keywee (ves.): 156
Kimberly, Jane Merritt (Mrs. Martin M. Kimberly): 22, story of the *Winfield Scott,* 132; 142
Kimberly, Martin M: 22, 39, 68, 132, 142, 169, 203
King, Edward A: 91
"King of San Miguel": *see* Waters, William G.
Kinsell, Martinette ("K"): quoted, 132, 141-147 *passim;* 183-184, 187, 190, 191, 202
Kinton Point (S.Cz.): 152
Kirk, Heatherwick: 144, 145, 146, *re* Painted Cave
Knopf, E. C: 83
Koch, Felix J: 98
Kodiak Indians: 38, 228
Kohl, Johann G: 244

La Bolsa (S.R.): 186
Lady's Harbor (S.Cz.): 146, 147
La Fama (ves.): 42
Laguna Harbor (S.Cz): 151
Lamar, Lucius Cincinnatus: 88
Lamb, Chester C: 229
Lambert, Darwin: 115, 226
Lambert, Reggie H: 23
Lambert, Mr. and Mrs. R. H: 25
Land claims in Calif: 265-268
Landing Cove (S.B.): 114

Land of Sunshine (pubn.): 45, 46
Lands End (S.N.): 24, 26; *see* Vizcaíno Point
La Paloma (ves.): 95, 99
La Playa (S.Cz.): 154
Larco, Nicolas: 164
"Larsen Swayne": 73
Las Positas y Calera, S.B. County: 199
Lasuén, Fermín de: 207
Lawson, Andrew C: 54, 55, 179
Lawson, Swain: 71
Laysan albatross: Killed on S.N., 23
LeConte, Joseph: 54, 55, 57, 179, 200
Lecouvreur, Frank: 75
LeDreau, Raymond "Frenchy": 125, 126
LeDreau Cove (Ana.): 129, 133
Lelia Byrd (ves.): 73
Lester, Herbert (Herbie): on S.M., 214-216 *passim;* 220, 222, 229
Lester, Mrs. Herbert (Elizabeth Sherman): 212, 214, 220-224 *passim;* 229, 230
Leuzardee, J. M: 221
Lick, James: evicts squatters from S.C., 53; mentioned, 55, 67, 72, 76, 93-95 *passim*
Lick Observatory: 94, 217
Light, Allen ("Black Steward"): 194
Light (Ana.): 130-131
Lighthouse, Arch Point (S.B.): 114
Linton, C. B: 23-24, 53, 57-58, 119, 144, 150, 151
Linton, C. B., Sr: 24
Lion Rock (S.M.): 212
Lipps, Jere H: 79
Little Gem of the Ocean (mine) (S.C.): 92
Little Gibralter Point (S.C.): 72
Little Harbor (S.C.): 66, 76
Little Springs Canyon (S.C.): 76, 89
Lizards: on S.M., 229-230
Llama (ves.): 194
Lobster Bay (S.C.): 66
Lobsters: on Ana., 125-126
Long Point (S.C.): 72
Lorenzo Tank (S.Cl.): 47
Loriot (ves.): 35, 42, 43
Los Alamos (S.Cz.): 157
Los Angeles County Museum: 29, 53
Los Angeles County Santa Catalina Nature Conservancy: 98, 100
Los Angeles Star (newsp.): 37, 38
Los Angeles Times (newsp.): 14, 18, 23, 25, 30, 56, 125
Louisa (ves.): 42
Lowe, Oscar: 18, 167, 168
Lowe, F. F: 88
Lowe, Frank H: 95, 96
Lower Buffalo Corral (S.C.): 76
Lowry, J. T: 181
Lowry, W. H: 93
Lummis, Charles Fletcher: 28, 39
Lyon, William S: 56, 57, 81

McArthur (ves.); 204
MacClain, Alma: 23
McClatchie, A. J: 82
McCoy, William M: 14-15
McElrath, Clifford: 143, 150, 153-155 *passim;* 159, 162; map of S.Cz., 159
McEwen, George F: 55
McGimpsey, W. J: 23
McGinnis, Mrs. William: 164
McGuire, George: 170
McKusick, M. B: 30, 50, 60, 134, 168
McMurtrie, ——: 131
MacRae, ——: 21
Madroño (pubn.): 115
Mahé, Gustave: 164
Mailliard, Joseph: 155, 170-171
Main Ranch (S.Cz.): 142, 143, 154-156 *passim*
Manna, Frank: 23
Margarita (ves.): 42
María Ester (ves.): 149
Marin (ves.): 116
Marine Fauna (S.M.): 225-230 *passim*
Marine gardens (Ana.): 135; S.C., 85-87
Marine Mammals (S.R.): 203-204
Martin, Camillo: 164
Martin, Clarence M: 23
Mártinez, José Longinos: 87, 220
Mason, Richard B: 160
Masterkey (pubn.): 28, 29, 39, 61, 83, 90
Matanza: on S. Cruz, 155; on S.R., 183
Mathis, Juliette Estelle: "The Channel of Santa Barbara" (poem), 121
Mayhew, Walter: 53
Meadows, Don: 84
Mearns, Edgar A: 58, 59, 118, 171
Meighan, Clement W: 30, 90
Mercury (ves.): 116
Merritt, Charles: 39
Mesnager, Louis le: 125, 133
Mess Cave (S.R.): 190
Metropole Hotel (Avalon, S.C.): 45, 95, sale 96
"Mexican Joe": *see* Presciado, José
Meyer, T. Lemman: 164
Michaelis, ——: 52
Micheltorena, Manuel: 92, 197
Middle Anacapa: 131-133 *passim*
Middle Canyon: S.B., 114; S.C., 77
Middle Point (S.Cl.): 50
Middle Ranch Canyon (S.Cl.): 50, 53
Middle Rock (S.M.): 214
Middleton, D. W: 92
Miles, Nelson A: 149
Miller, Alden H: 85
Miller, Eliza M: 198
Miller, L: 119
Miller, Max: 18
Mills, Herman: 221
Mills, Hiram W: 36, 125, 221
Mills, Warren H: 125, 221

Mills Landing (S.C.): 76
Millspaugh, Charles F: 83
Minas de los Indios (S.Cz.): 142
Mineral Hill: *see* Small Hill, S.C.
Mines and mining (S.C.): 70, 80-81, 90-97 *passim*
Minnie (ves.): 51
Missile Island: *see* San Nicolas
Missions: Santa Barbara, 40; San Buenaventura, 208; San Gabriel, 74
Mofras: *see* Duflot de Mofras
Mohrhardt, P. F: 221
Monster Consolidated Company: 71
Monster Mining Company: 92
Montañon (S.Cz.): 143, 155
Moonstone Beach (S.C.): *see* Button Shell Beach
Moore, J. H: 222
More, Almira: 195
More, Andrew P: 192-199 *passim*
More, H. Clifford: 196
More, Henry H: 183, 184, 195, 198, 199
More, John F: 184, 195, 198
More, L. W: 195, 196, 198
More, Mattie: *see* Storke, Mrs. Thomas M.
More, T. R: 199
More, T. Wallace: 191-199 *passim*
Morning Call (newsp.): 53, 188
Mosquito Harbor (S.Cl.): 46, 49, 52
Motor, Helen K: 65-66
Moullet, Jules: 154
Mt. Ada, S.C: 77, 100
Mt. Banning (S.C.): 77; *see* Black Jack Peak
Mt. Cortez (S.Cl.): *see* Mt. Thirst
Mt. Diablo (S.Cz.): *see* Picacho del Diablo
Mt. Hamilton, Santa Clara County: 217
Mt. Martha (S.C.): 77
Mt. Orizaba (S.C.): 77, 79, 80
Mt. Shatto (S.C.): 77
Mt. Soledad (S.R.): 185
Mount Thirst (S.Cl.): 46, 51
Mt. Torquemada (S.C.): 66
Mt. Vizcaíno (S.C.): *see* Cactus Peak
Mt. Washington (S.C.): 77
Mt. Wilson (S.C.): 77
Munz, Phillip A: 200, 201, 202
Murbarger, Nell: 61
Murbarger, Wilbur B: 61
Murphy, Mr. and Mrs. Theo: 53
Murphy, E. F: 32, 33, 34, 35, 221
Museum of the American Indian, Heye Foundation: 29, 233

National Marine Fisheries Service: 129
National Museum, Washington, D.C: 231
National Park Status (1938) (S.B.): 119-120
National Trading Company: 164
Navarrete, Martin Fernandez: 240
Ned Beale (ves.): 75
Nelson, Captain ———: 19, 21, 22

Nevin, J. C: 56, 81
New Almaden Quicksilver Mine: 160, 161
New England (mine) (S.C.): 92
Nidever, George: 27, 32-40 *passim;* biog. sketch 43; 119, 194, 215, 220, 221, 228
Nidever, George E: 39, 220
Nidever, H. B: 226
Nidever, Mark R: 220
Nobel, William: 132
Norris, ———: 19
North Peak (S.B.): 114,115
Northwest Anchorage: S.Cl., 47; S.R., 188
Northwest Harbor: S.Cl., 47-49 *passim;* 54, 60, 61; S.N., 19, 24; S.Cz., 144
Northwest Point (S.Cl.): 47-48
Nuttall, L. W: 83
Nuttall, Thomas: 81

Oajaca (ves.): 194
Oberholser, H. C: 58-60 *passim;* 85, 172
O'Cain, Joseph: 228
O'Cain (ves.): 116, 228
Oetteking, Bruno: 29
Offshore Rock (S.M.): 212
O'Leary, Aleck: 46, 52
Olivari, Pete: 154
Olmsted, R. R: 55
Olson, Ronald L: 147, 148, 158, 159
Olson's Cave (S.Cz.): 147
Omsett (S.R. Indian): 208
Oölogist (pubn.): 125
Orca (ves.): 98, 144, 228
Ord, Augustine de la Guerra: 149
Ord, J. L: 208
Ord, María de la Augustias: 261-262
Orizaba (S.Cz.): 147, 148
Orizaba Flats (S.Cz.): 147
Orizaba Pictograph Cave (S.Cz.): 218
Orizaba Rocks (S.Cz.): 147
Ornithology: *see* Avifauna
Orr, Phil C: 26, 29-30, renames Painted Cave, Ana., 135, 136; 144, 167, 185-189 *passim,* 204, 205, 219, 227
Ortega, Rafaela Luisa Oliveras de: *see* Hill, Mrs. Daniel
Osburn, P. I: 85
Osprey (pubn.): 59
Otter Harbor (S.M.): 214, 234
Otter hunting: 32, 35, 36, 37, 73, 74, 75, 169
Otter Point: S.M., 214, 234; S.R., 190
Ottman, Tony: 213
Outhwaite, Leonard, 157
Overland Monthly (pubn.): 27
Owens, Rob C: 145
Oystercatchers (Black) (Ana.): 127

Pacific Mail Steamship Company: 132
Pacific Wool Growing Company: 22, 125, 221
Packard, Albert: 68, 91, 92

Painted Cave: Ana., 134-135; S.Cz., 142, 144; list of articles about, 145, 146
Paloú, Fr. Francisco: 148
Paragon (ves.): 33
Parish, S.B: 81-82
Parker, D. O: 30
Parrot and Company: 197
Parsons, Captain ———: 17, 23, 68
Parsons, "Uncle Thof": 66
Parson's Landing (S.C.): 66
Patrick, J. H: 100
Patrick Reservoir (S.C.): 76
Paul, O. M: 39
Paula (ves.): 213
Pearls: described, 57-58
Pebble Beach (S.C.): 76, 96
Pelican Bay (S.Cz.): 147, 148, 213
Pelican Harbor (S.Cz.): 172-173
Pelicans: on Ana., 129, 130
Pemberton, J. R: 119, 204
Penwell, ———: 53
Peor es Nada (Better-than-Nothing) (ves.): 32, 35, 194
Perdition Cave (S.C.): 71, 72
Pérouse, Jean-François de la Galaup: 243
Pesado Letter (1838): 191, 192, 197
Peterson, Captain ———: 45
Petroleum: *see* Asphaltum
Peyton, Sidney B: 125, 128
Phillbrick, Ralph N: 115, 118
Phillips, M. J: 132
Picacho del Diablo (S.Cz.): 142, 143
Picacho de los Encinos (S.Cz.): 142
Pico, Concepción: 92; *see also* Carrillo
Pico, Pío: 91, 92, 191, 199
Pictograph Cave (S.Cz.): 147, 158; *see also* Olson's Cave
Pierce, B: 231
Pilgrim (ves.): 81, 194
Pin Rock (S.C.): 65
Pinchot, Gifford: 57
Pinnacle Rocks (S.C.): *see* Twin Rocks
Pioneer (ves.): 75
Pitzer, Jean M: 159
Platt's Harbor (S.Cz.): 147
Point Argüello (Calif.): 212
Point Bennett (S.M.): 211-216 *passim;* 219
Point Concepción (Calif.): 131, 181, 182
Point Diablo (S.Cz.): 147
Point Diablo Anchorage (S.Cz.): 147
Point Harris (S.M.): 214
Polley, Harry: 82
Port Los Angeles: *see* Santa Monica
Port Roussillon (S.C.): 73; *see also* Avalon
Portezuelo Creek (S.Cz.): 143, 154
Portolá, Gaspar de: 242
Pot Hole Harbor: *see* Pots Valley, S.C.
Potato Bay (S.Cz.): 150
Potato Harbor (S.Cz.): 143
Pots Valley: S.Cl., 52; Valley of Ollas, S.C., 72, 89, 90

Potstone (S.C.): 89
Powell, J. W: 229
Pozo (Poso) Harbor (S.Cz.): 152
Prentice, Milton: killed Semerenko on S.N., 23
Prentiss (Prentice), Samuel: 67
Presciado, José ("Mexican Joe"): 68, 69, 81
Primero Canyon (S.B.): 114
Princess (Prince) Island (S.M.): 214, 215, 218, 223, 230-231
Prisoner's Harbor (S.Cz.): 142-150 *passim;* 154-159 *passim;* 171, 216, 243
Profile Point (S.Cz.): 145
Prohibition (1918-1933): 155-156
Puerto de la Cañada del Sur (S.Cz.): *see* Blue Bank
Puerto de Santa Catalina: *see* Isthmus Cove
Punta Arena (S.Cz.): 142, 152
Putnam, Frederick W: 28, 158
Pyramid Cove (S.Cl.): 51
Pyramid Head (S.Cl.): 50, 51, 52

Quail: 85
Quail Cañon (S.Cz.): 151-152
Quarries (rock) (S.C.): 72
Queen City (Wilson's Valley) (S.C.): 71
Quicksilver Mining Company: 160, 161

Ragged Mountain (S.Cz.): 142
Ram Point (S.C.): *see* Stony Point
Ramirez, Salvador (Chinetti): 51
Rand, W. W: 153
Ranch House (S.R.): 183, *see* Elder Creek
Ranch House Canyon (S.R.): 189, 193
Ranch House Landing (S.N.): 19
Rancho Agua Caliente (Calif.): 38
Rancho Castaic (Calif.): 92
Rancho Chino (Calif.): 43
Rancho Los Alamitos (Calif.): 75
Rancho La Goleta (Calif.): 195, 199
Rancho Huasma (Calif.): 43
Rancho de Lompoc (Calif.): 195, 199
Rancho Major (S.Cz.): 143
Rancho Mission Viejo (Calif.): 199
Rancho Viejo (S.R.): 189
Rancho Nipomo (Calif.): 42
Rancho Pismo (Calif.): 43
Rancho Las Positas y Calera (Calif.): 43
Rancho los dos Pueblos (La Patera) (Calif.): 195, 199
Rancho La Purísima: 199
Rancho San Cayetano (Sespe), (Calif.): 195, 199
Rancho Santa Paula (Calif.): 195, 199
Rancho Saticoy (Calif.): 199
Rancho Sespe (Calif.): 191, 192, 195, 199
Rasselas (ves.): 42
Raven, Peter H: 79, 83, 84, 115
Ray, J. H: 75, 92, 93
Red Canyon (S.Cl.): 51

Red Hill (S.Cz.): 142
Reid, Hugo: biog. sketch, 38
Reinman, ——: 20, 21
Remington, Charles F: 169
Reno (ves.): 212
Renton, M. J: 96
Renton Vein (S.C.): 76
Reservoirs (S.C.): 76
Rett, E. Z: 26, 167, 204, 227
Revel, ——: 154
Rhoads, Harvey: 68
Rhodes, ——: 54
Ribbon Rock (S.C.): 65
Richardson, Charles H., Jr: 85
Richardson Rock (S.M.): 211, 212, 219
Richey, Emma Carbutt: 225
Rider, ——: 47
Ringrose, Mrs. Harold: 164
Ripoli, Fr. Antonio: 207
Rippers Cove (S.C.): 72
Ritter, ——: 78
Rivers, J. J: 84
Robbins, Encarnación Carrillo (Mrs. Thomas Robbins): 92
Robbins, Thomas M: 36, biog. sketch 43; 74, 90-94 *passim;* 199, 207, 263
Robearts, Johnny: 49
Robearts' Gorge (S.Cl.): 49
Robert (ves.): 51
Robertson, ——: 24
Robertson, H: 118, 119
Robinson, Anna María de la Guerra: 262
Robinson, Alfred: 192, 193, 197, 262
Rocking Horse Brand (S.R.): 193
Rodes Reef (S.R.): 187
Roe, E. P: 132
Roe, Jo Ann: 159
Rogers, David Banks: 158, 159, 167, 168, 180, 186, 187, 205, 233, 234
Roosevelt, Franklin Delano: est. 1938 National Monuments, 119-120
Rossi, Amelia A. (Caire): 162, 164
Rossi, Edmund A: 151, 162
Rossi, María: *see* Gherini, Mrs. Ambrose
Rossita (ves.): 75
Rothrock, J. T: 154-155, 157, 167
Rowe, Helen K: 196
Rozaire, Charles: 61, 213, 234
Rubio, González: 40
Ruby Peak (S.C.): 80
Russell, C.J. W: 27, 32, 36, 37, 38, 39
Russell, John: 222
Russian traders: 14, 38, 228
Rust, Horatio N: 28, 233
Ruth K. (ves.): 213

Sacramento Daily Record-Union (newsp.): 216
Saddle Mountain (S.R.): 185
St. Iago (S.R. Indian, 1897): 205
Salte Verde Point (S.C.): 76

San Antonio (ves.): 242, 243
Sanchez, Sinforosa: *see* Nidever, Mrs. George
Sanchez, T. A: 93
SAN CLEMENTE ISLAND: map, 44; 45-62, list of visitors (1863-1917), 56; avifauna, 58-60; fauna, 57-58; flora, 56-57; geology, 54-56; Indians, 60-61; lessee titles, 53-54; natural history, 56-60; photographs listed, 62; silver, 53; volcanic evidences, 47, 51, 55; wire-drag survey (1936), 56
San Clemente Sheep and Wool Company: 52, 53, 54, 59
San Diego: 73
San Diego (ves.): 45
Sandstone tree casts (S.N.): 18
Sandy Point (S.R.): 186, 187, 190; *see also* West Point
San Francisco (mine) (S.C.): 92
Sanger, Arthur: 14, 29, 203, 207, 233, 234
SAN MIGUEL ISLAND: 92, 181, map, 210; 211-235; avifauna, 230-231; caves, 217-219; ethnology, 231; fauna, 225-230 *passim;* flora, 223-225; geology, 219-220; herpetofauna, 229-230; Indians, 212, 218, 220, 231-234; lessee-titles, 220-223; marine fauna, 225-230 *passim;* National Park, 120; photographs listed, 235
San Miguel Island Company, Inc: 221
San Miguel Mountain (S.M.): 217
San Miguel Passage: 186, 211, 218
SAN NICOLAS ISLAND: desc., 13-43; archaeology, 26-30 *passim;* avifauna, 26; fauna, 25-26; flora, 15, 16, 24-25; geology, 16-19 *passim;* Indians, 18, 20; land snails, 18; Missile Testing Range, U.S.N., 24; photographs listed, 31; Templeton Crocker Expedition, 25; volcanic evidences, 19, 21; weather station, 24
San Nicolas Development Company: 23
San Pedro (Calif.): 34, 43, 67, 72, 74-75, 95
San Pedro Point (S.Cz.): 144, 150, 151
Santa Barbara (ves.): 34, 42
SANTA BARBARA ISLAND: 111-121; archaeology, 119; avifauna, 118-119; fauna, 118; flora, 115-116; geology, 114-115; Indians, 114, 119; maps, 114; National Park status, 119-120; natural history, 115-116; otters, 116-118; photographs listed, 120; seals, 116-118; volcanic evidence, 111, 112
Santa Barbara (Calif.): 32
Santa Barbara Channel Oil Spill (1969): 220
"Santa Barbara Islands": poem by Carrie W. Egan, 121
Santa Barbara Mission: 33
Santa Barbara Museum of Natural History: 30, 147, 204, 205, 217, 219, 227, 234
Santa Barbara News Press (newsp): 40
Santa Barbara Post (newsp.): 160
Santa Catalina (mine) (S.C.): 92

SANTA CATALINA ISLAND: map, 64; 65-108; avifauna, 84-85; fauna, 84; flora, 81-84; geology, 77-80; Indians, 76-77, 87-90 *passim;* marine gardens, 85-87; minerals, 80-81, 92, 93; motion pictures at, 108; photographs listed, 103-108; poems about, 102; Quail, 151-152; under Bannings, 106; under Wrigleys, 106-108; volcanic evidence, 76, 80; wireless station, 66

Santa Catalina Development Company: 95; Banning,96: Wrigley, 96, 97, 98

Santa Cruz (ves.): 156

SANTA CRUZ ISLAND: map, 140; 141-176; archaeology, 156-159; avifauna, 170-173; caves, 144-148 *passim;* convicts on, 75; fauna, 167-169; flora, 165-167; geology, 153-154; herpetofauna, 168-169; Indians, 152, 156-159 *passim;* National Park, 120, 163; otters and seals, 169-170; Painted Cave, material on, 145; photographs, listed, 174-176; sale of, 49; volcanic evidence, 143, 144

Santa Cruz Island Club: 149

Santa Cruz Island Company: 151, 164

Santa Monica (Calif.): 112, 153

SANTA ROSA ISLAND: 42, map 178; 179-209; avifauna, 204; caves, 187, 189; fauna, 202-203; flora, 200-202; geography, 182-185 *passim;* geology, 179-185 *passim;* Indians, 180, 185, 189, 194, 204-208; National Park, 120; photographs listed, 209; titles, 197-199; volcanic evidence, 180

Santa Ynez Mountains (Calif.): 153

Savage, J. H: 84, 169

Scammon, Charles M: 116, 227

Scandal Point (S.Cz.): 151

Schumacher, Paul (1875): 26, 27-28; map, 68; 72, 84, 88-89, 147, 156, 157, 205-206, 214, 215, 216, 232

Schumacher, Paul J. (1959): 119

Scorpion Canyon (S.Cz.): 170, 171, 173

Scorpion Harbor (S.Cz.): 150

Scorpion Ranch (S.Cz.): 143, 144, 150

Scripps Institute of Oceanography: 19

Sea Elephant Beach: S.N., 19; at S.C., 68; S.R., 203

Sea Lion Beach (S.N.): 18

Sea Lion Cave (Ana.): 136

Sea Lions: S.B., 111, 112, 113, 116-118 *passim;* S.Cz., 144-145, 146, 170

Sea Otters: Ana., 124; S.M., 228; S.B., 116-118 *passim;* 119; S.Cz., 169-170; S.R., 193, 194; *see also* otters

Sea Otter Island: *see* San Nicolas Island

Seal Harbor Point (S.Cl.): 50

Seal Rock: S.Cl., 46; S.M., 212; S.C., 66, 76

Seals: Ana., 124, 130; S.Cl., 46; S.M., 213, 216, 226-227; S.B., 116-118 *passim;* 119; S.Cz., 170

Sea Serpents (S.C.): 86-87

Seavey, F. A: 84

Sea Wolf (ves.): 148, 212, 213

Secret Harbor (S.Cz.): 156

Sefton Foundation: 134, 228

Sellers, Frank H: 66, 67

Semerenko, Steve: poacher, 23

Señan, Fr. José: 208

Sentinel Rock (S.C.): 66, 76

Sexton, Horace A: 212-213

Seymour, D. B: 180

Shade, Al: 52

Shag Rock (S.B.): 114

Shaler, William: 73

Shatto, Clara: 94

Shatto, George R: 45, 72, 76, 94-95, 96

Shatto (S.C.): *see* Avalon

Shaw, James Barron: biog. sketch 43; 151, 160, 161-162, 164

Shaw, L. M: 23

Shaw Anchorage (S.Cz.): 151

Sheep: on Ana., 125; S.Cl., 49, 53; S.M., 215, 219, 221-223 *passim;* S.N., 16, 19, 22; S.B., 112, 113; S.C., 66, 70, 72, 75-76, 97; S.Cz., 150, 154-156, 163; S.R., 183, 188, 195

Sheldon, H. H: 24, 142, 145-146

Shepard, F. P: 18, 56, 79

Sherman, C. E: 195, 196

Ship Rock (S.C.): 65

Shipley, R. I: 68

Sierra Blanca Peak (S.Cz.): 142, 152

Sierra Lopez (S.R.): 190

Sierra Vaca (S.R.): 185

Signal Peak (S.B.): 114, 115

Silver Canyon (S.C.): 77

Silver Creek (S.C.): 77

Silver Hill (S.C.): 66

Silver Peak (S.C.): 66

Simonton Cove (S.M.): 213, 214, 217, 222, 234

Skull Gulch (S.R.): 186, 187

Skunk Point (S.R.): 188, 189

Slay Rock (S.R.): 189

Slevin, Joseph R: 57, 84, 126, 168, 169, 202, 229

Small Hill Mining Claim (S.C.): 66, 67, 94

Smith, Jedediah S: 73-74, 228

Smith, Ruth Tangier: 46, 50, 51

Smith, W. S. T: 54, 55, 77-78, 79

Smith, William Tangier: 46

Smithsonian Institution: 28

Smuggler's Cove (S.Cl.): 46, 47, 48, 51, 52, 58; S.Cz., 143, 144, 150-151, 157

Smuggling: S.N., 21; S.C., 65, 74, 75

Snails *(Helix facta):* 18, 25, 112, 118, 168, 230

Snell, David: 220

Snyder, G. K: 85, 127

Snyder Camp (S.Cl.): 52

Snow, H. J: 119

Snow Cañon (S.N.): 23

Soledad Canyon (S.R.): 200

Soapstone Quarry (S.C.): 89-90; *see also* Steatite

Sophia (ves.): 33

South Bay (S.Cl.): 52, 53

South Point (S.R.): 189, 190

Southeast Anchorage (S.R.): 188, 189

Southern California Academy of Sciences: 26

Southern California Edison Company: 76

Southern Point (S.Cl.): 50

Southwest Museum (Los Angeles): 19, 28, 29, 30, 33, 61, 156, 157, 158, 208

Sou'west's Arrowhead Point (S.Cl.): 50

Southworth, John: 123

Sparks, Isaac J: 32, biog. sketch 43; 194, 228

Spear, Nathan: 22

Sponge Cave (S.Cz.): 144

Spouting Cave (S.C.): 71, 72

Squatters (S.C.): 53, 67

Staats, William: 95, 169

Stanton, Carey: on S.Cz., 149, 150, 151, 154, 168, 169

Stanton, Edwin L: of S.Cz., 142, 143, 155, 159, 162, 163, 164

Stanton, Edwin McMasters: 160, 161

Stanton, Evelyn C: 163

Stanton Ranch (S.Cz.): 152

Star of Freedom (ves.): 156, 157, 183

Stearns, Abel: 21, 74-75, 98, 149, 197

Steamboat Point (S.R.): 191

Steatite: 66, 80, 90

Steller Sea Lion Rookery (S.M.): 212, 226; S.Cz., 144, 152

Stevens, T. H: 21; ltr. to Bache, 130-131, 132

Stingaree Bay (Ana.): 132

Stock, Chester: 167

Stony Point (S.C.): 66

Storke, C. A: 199

Storke, Thomas M: 195

Storke, Mrs. Thomas M. (Mattie More): 195

Stout, E. S: 23

Streator, Clark P: 204, 221, 230

Strobel, Max: 93-94

Stuart, ——: 157-158

Stuart's Cave (S.Cz.): 157

Sugar Loaf Peak (S.Cz.): 151

Sugar Loaf Rock (S.C.): 66

Sullivan, Eugene: 92

Sullivan, John: 67, 90

Sumner, Charles A: 94-95

Sumner, E. Lowell: 125, 126, 128, 230

Sumner, Lowell: 115, 118, 119, 215

Sur Ranch (S.Cz.): 142, 143, 151

Sutil (ves.): 114

Sutil Island (S.B.): 114

Swain's Canyon (S.C.): 73, 77, 82

Swain's Landing (S.C.): *see* Willow Cove

Swarth, H. S: 26, 126-127
Swift (ves.): 226

Talcott Shoal (S.R.): 186
Tapis, Fr. Estevan: 207
Taschenberger, Arthur: 29
Taylor, Alexander S: 207, 220, 257-258
Taylor, H. C: 206
Tays, George: 159
Teggart, Frederick J: 233
Temple, F. P. F: 94
Temple to the Sun (S.C.): 61, 88
Templeton Crocker Expedition: 25
Terry, Elmer: 221
Terry, J: 33
Thompson, Alpheus Basil: 33-36 *passim;*
    biog. sketch 43; 75, 192, 193, 194, 197,
    228
Thompson, Dixie (Dixey) Wildes: 32, 33,
    43
Thompson, Francisca Carrillo: 192, 193,
    197, 199
Thompson Dam (S.C.): 76
Thorne, R. F: 83
Thousand Springs (S.N.): 18, 19, 20
Timms, Augustus W: 75
Timms' Landing (S.C.): 75, 76; *see also*
    Avalon
Tinker's Cove (S.Cz.): 142, 147, 148, 156-
    157, 158
Torqua Springs (S.C.): 77
Touring Topics: see Westways
Townsend, Charles H: 57, 58, 59, 118, 168-
    172 *passim;* 204
Townsend, E. D: 88
Toyon Bay (S.C.): 73
Trask, Blanche Luella: 13, 15, 20-25 *pas-
    sim;* 49, 53-57 *passim;* 67, 68, 78, 82, 84,
    89, 90, 169, 217, 229
Trask, John B: 54
Trowbridge, W. P: 228
Trusil, ——: 39
Tule Creek (S.N.): 19, 20
Turei, Indian Chief (S.C.): 67
Twin Harbor (S.Cz.): 147
Twin Rocks (S.C.): 66
Tyler, J., Jr.: 91
Tyler Harbor (S.Cz.): 143, 150; *see also*
    Potato Bay
Tyler's Bight (S.M.): 212

United States Bureau of Fisheries: 58
United States Coast and Geodetic Survey:
    21, 54, 55, 153, 205, 215, 221
United States Fish Commission: 204
United States Geological Survey: 50
United States National Herbarium: 15
United States Navy: on S.N., 24
University of Southern California Marine
    Science Laboratory (S.C.): 97, 98
Upper Buffalo Springs (S.C.): 76

Vail, Alexander: 198
Vail, Edward N: 198
Vail, Mahlon: 198
Vail, N. R: 198
Vail, Walter L: 198
Vail Brothers: 22, 53
Vail Ranch (S.R.): 188, 200
Vail-Vickers (S.R.): 196
Valdez Cave (S.Cz.): 146
Valdez Harbor (S.Cz.): 144, 146
Valentine, James W: 79
Valley Anchorage (S.Cz.): 151
Valley of Ollas (S.C.): *see* Pots Valley
Vancouver, George: 243
Van Denbergh, Frank S: 181, 202
Van Denburgh, John: 57, 84, 118, 126, 168,
    169, 229
Van Valkenburgh, Richard: 129, 158-159
Van Rossem, A. J: 58, 119
Vaslit, Frank: 81
Vedder/Norris Geologic Survey: 18, 19, 20
Vela Peak (Ana.): 133
Vellim, Cal: 126
Vickers, J. V: 198
Victoria (ves.): 203
Vineyards (S.Cz.): 155-156
Vizcaíno, Fr. Juan: 243
Vizcaíno, Sebastián: 241-242
Vizcaíno Point (S.N.): 18, 19
Volcanic evidences: *see* individual islands
Volunteer (ves.): 42
von Bloeker, Jack C., Jr: 84
Voy, C. D: 181, 184-185, 186, 233

Wagner, Henry Raup: 55, 240-241
Wagner, Moritz: 167
Walkenshaw, Robert: 161
Walker, ——: 147
Wall Rock Canyon (S.Cl.): 50
Ward, L. A: 221
Warner, Juan José: 34, 37-38, 91
Warren, Earl, Jr: 142, 227
Washburn, W. A: 197
Washington (ves.): 43
Water Canyon (S.R.): 188
Waters, William G: 92, 216-217, 218, 221-
    222; death of "King of San Miguel," 222
Waverly (ves.): 42, 74
Way, Daniel E: 68
Weber, Charles H: 100
Webster, Ray: 125, 127, 128
Webster Bay (Ana.): 125; *see also* "Fren-
    chy's Cove"
Webster Point (S.B.): 114
Weill, Alexander: 164
West, Captain ——: 68
West Anacapa Island: 132-134 *passim*
West Coast Fishing Company: 148
Westcott Shoal (S.M.): 214
West Cove (S.Cl.): 50
West End: S.Cl., 49, *see also* Drigg's Cove;
    S.M., 234

West Fish Camp (Ana.) 134
West Peak (S.M.): *see* Green Mountain
West Point: S.Cz., 144, 145; S.R., 186, 190
West Ranch (Rancho del Oeste) (S.Cz.):
    152
West Rock (S.M.): 214
Western (ves.): 23
Western Ranch (S.Cz.): *see* Christy Ranch
Weston, Ben: 76
Weston, E. J: 94
Westways (pubn.): 98, 131, 159, 189, 190
Whale Rock (S.C.): 65
Wheeler, George M: 52, 54, 57, 158, 228-
    229
Wheeler Survey: 157
Whistler, James Abbot McNeil: 131
White Point (San Pedro): 66
White Rock: *see* Bird Rock (S.C.)
White's Cove (Landing) (S.C.): 73
White's Landing (S.C.): 66; 267, Indian
    skeletons unearthed, 90
Whitney, Edwin J: 76
Whitney, Etta M: names Avalon, 76
Whitney, Josiah D: 17, 111, 181
Whittemore, ——: 38
Whittley, Frank: 53, 66, 69, 94
Whittley, Thomas: 68, 69
Whittley Peak (S.C.): 77
Whittley's Cove: *see* White's Cove or Land-
    ing (S.C.)
Wilbur, Marguerite Eyer: 159
Wildes, Dixie: 43
Willett, George: 26, 53, 127, 129, 172, 230
William (ves.): 161
Williams, Isaac: 35; biog. sketch 43
Williamson, Mrs. Burton: 90
Willow Canyon (S.M.): 217
Willow Cove (S.C.): 73
Willow Creek (S.Cz.): 151, 152
Willow Harbor (S.Cz.): 142, 151, 152
Willows of the West: *see* Cañada los Sauces
    del Oeste
Wilmington Transportation Company: 95
Wilson, Joseph S: 93
Wilson, Spencer H: 68, 71
Wilson Cove: S.Cl., 45, 46, 50, 54; S.C.,
    68
Wilson Rock (S.M.): 212, 214
Wilson's Harbor (S.C.): 68
Wilson's Valley (S.C.): 67
Windle, Ernest: 18, 23, 65, 67, 75, 90
Winfield Scott (ves.): 126, 130-131 *passim;*
    132
Winship, Jonathan; 228
Wire-drag surveys: 56
Wireless Telegraph Station (S.C.): 73
Wood, Benjamin: 93
Woodford, Alfred Oswald: 78, 80
Woods, H. O: 18
Woodward, Arthur: 19, 23, 29, 33, 40, 48,
    52, 129, 148, 205

Wreck Canyon (S.R.): 190

Wright, ——(1864): 87-88

Wright, Austin Tappan: 147, 185, 201

Wright, H: 127

Wrigley, P. K: 100

Wrigley, William (son of P.K.): 100

Wrigley, William, Jr: 77, 90, 96; biog. sketch, 100

Wrigley Memorial and Botanical Garden (S.C.): 100

Wrigley Reservoir (S.C.): 76

Wrigleys: 106-108

Wyckoff Ledge (S.M.): 212

Yarrow, H. C: 84, 89, 157, 205, 206, 228, 231

Yates, Lorenzo Gordin: 55, 123-124, 132-133, 146, 168, 180-186 *passim;* 206, 207

Yates Cave (Ana.): *see* Painted Cave

Yellow Bank (S.Cz.): 150, 151, 159

Young, A. J: 181

Yount, George C: 36, 38, 52, 66-67, 117, 228

Zahn, Otto J: 84, 119

Zinc (S.C.): 96, 97

Zoe (pubn.): 56, 81, 82

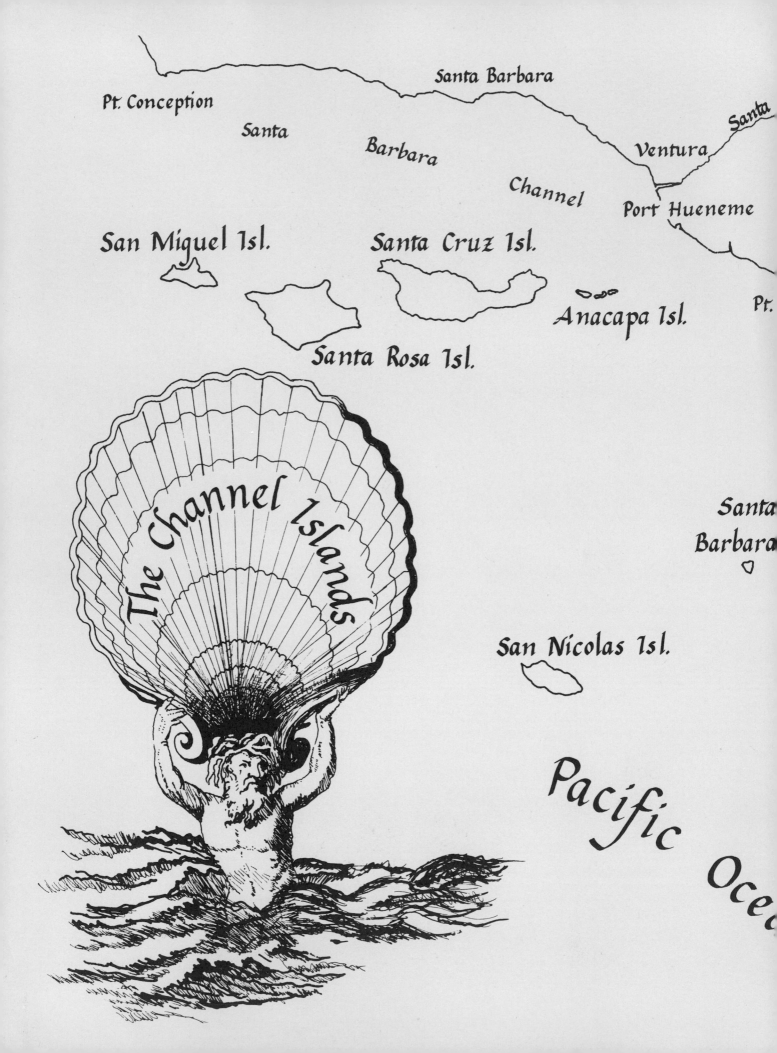

Pt. Conception

Santa Barbara

Santa

Barbara

Ventura

Santa

Channel

Port Hueneme

San Miguel Isl.

Santa Cruz Isl.

Anacapa Isl.

Pt.

Santa Rosa Isl.

The Channel Islands

Santa
Barbara

San Nicolas Isl.

Pacific Ocea